ESSENTIALS OF MARKETING MANAGEMENT

ESSENTIALS OF MARKETING MANAGEMENT

Published by McGraw-Hill/Irwin, a business unit of The McGraw-Hill Companies, Inc., 1221 Avenue of the Americas, New York, NY, 10020.

Some ancillaries, including electronic and print components, may not be available to customers outside the United States.

This book is printed on acid-free paper.

1 2 3 4 5 6 7 8 9 0 DOW/DOW 1 0 9 8 7 6 5 4 3 2 1 0

ISBN 978-0-07-802878-6
MHID 0-07-802878-7

Vice president and editor-in-chief: *Brent Gordon*
Publisher: *Paul Ducham*
Executive editor: *Doug Hughes*
Director of development: *Ann Torbert*
Editorial coordinator: *Gabriela Gonzalez*
Vice president and director of marketing: *Robin J. Zwettler*
Marketing manager: *Katie Mergen*
Vice president of editing, design and production: *Sesha Bolisetty*
Project manager: *Dana M. Pauley*
Lead production supervisor: *Carol A. Bielski*
Senior designer: *Mary Kazak Sander*
Senior photo research coordinator: *Lori Kramer*
Photo researcher: *Allison Grimes*
Senior media project manager: *Greg Bates*
Typeface: *10/12 Palatino*
Compositor: *Laserwords Private Limited*
Printer: *R. R. Donnelley*

Library of Congress Cataloging-in-Publication Data

Marshall, Greg W.
   Essentials of marketing management / Greg W. Marshall, Mark W. Johnston.—1st ed.
     p. cm.
   Includes index.
   ISBN-13: 978-0-07-802878-6 (alk. paper)
   ISBN-10: 0-07-802878-7 (alk. paper)
   1. Marketing—Management. I. Johnston, Mark W. II. Title.
  HF5415.13.M3634 2011
  658.8—dc22

                             2009049181

www.mhhe.com

ESSENTIALS OF MARKETING MANAGEMENT

Greg W. Marshall
ROLLINS COLLEGE

Mark W. Johnston
ROLLINS COLLEGE

McGraw-Hill Irwin

To Patti and Justin

-Greg

To Susan, my love, and Grace, my joy, thank you

-Mark

ABOUT THE AUTHORS

Greg W. Marshall

Greg W. Marshall is the Charles Harwood Professor of Marketing and Strategy in the Roy E. Crummer Graduate School of Business at Rollins College in Winter Park, Florida. He earned his Ph.D. in Business Administration from Oklahoma State University, taking a marketing major and management minor, and holds a BSBA in marketing and MBA from the University of Tulsa. Before joining Rollins, Greg was on the faculty at the University of South Florida, Texas Christian University, and Oklahoma State University.

Prior to returning to school for his doctorate, Greg's managerial industry experience included 13 years in consumer packaged goods and retailing with companies such as Warner Lambert, Mennen, and Target Corporation. He also has considerable experience as a consultant and trainer for a variety of organizations in industries such as hospitality, financial services/insurance, defense contracting, consumer products, information technology, government, and not-for-profit. Greg has been heavily involved in teaching Marketing Management at multiple universities to both MBA and undergraduate students and has been the recipient of several teaching awards both within his schools and within the marketing discipline.

He is editor of the *Journal of Marketing Theory and Practice* and from 2002–2005 was editor of the *Journal of Personal Selling & Sales Management.* Greg serves on the editorial review boards of the *Journal of the Academy of Marketing Science, Industrial Marketing Management,* and *Journal of Business Research,* among others. Greg's published research focuses on the areas of decision making by marketing managers, intraorganizational relationships, and sales force performance.

Greg is past president of the American Marketing Association Academic Division and also was a founder and served for five years on its Strategic Planning Group. He is a Fellow and past-president of the Society for Marketing Advances, presently serves as president-elect for the Academy of Marketing Science, and is a member of the board of directors of the Direct Selling Education Foundation.

ESSENTIALS OF MARKETING MANAGEMENT

Greg W. Marshall
ROLLINS COLLEGE

Mark W. Johnston
ROLLINS COLLEGE

McGraw-Hill Irwin

ESSENTIALS OF MARKETING MANAGEMENT
Published by McGraw-Hill/Irwin, a business unit of The McGraw-Hill Companies, Inc., 1221 Avenue of the Americas, New York, NY, 10020. Copyright © 2011 by The McGraw-Hill Companies, Inc. All rights reserved. No part of this publication may be reproduced or distributed in any form or by any means, or stored in a database or retrieval system, without the prior written consent of The McGraw-Hill Companies, Inc., including, but not limited to, in any network or other electronic storage or transmission, or broadcast for distance learning.

Some ancillaries, including electronic and print components, may not be available to customers outside the United States.

This book is printed on acid-free paper.

1 2 3 4 5 6 7 8 9 0 DOW/DOW 1 0 9 8 7 6 5 4 3 2 1 0

ISBN 978-0-07-802878-6
MHID 0-07-802878-7

Vice president and editor-in-chief: *Brent Gordon*
Publisher: *Paul Ducham*
Executive editor: *Doug Hughes*
Director of development: *Ann Torbert*
Editorial coordinator: *Gabriela Gonzalez*
Vice president and director of marketing: *Robin J. Zwettler*
Marketing manager: *Katie Mergen*
Vice president of editing, design and production: *Sesha Bolisetty*
Project manager: *Dana M. Pauley*
Lead production supervisor: *Carol A. Bielski*
Senior designer: *Mary Kazak Sander*
Senior photo research coordinator: *Lori Kramer*
Photo researcher: *Allison Grimes*
Senior media project manager: *Greg Bates*
Typeface: *10/12 Palatino*
Compositor: *Laserwords Private Limited*
Printer: *R. R. Donnelley*

Library of Congress Cataloging-in-Publication Data

Marshall, Greg W.
    Essentials of marketing management / Greg W. Marshall, Mark W. Johnston.—1st ed.
       p. cm.
    Includes index.
    ISBN-13: 978-0-07-802878-6 (alk. paper)
    ISBN-10: 0-07-802878-7 (alk. paper)
    1. Marketing—Management. I. Johnston, Mark W. II. Title.
    HF5415.13.M3634 2011
    658.8—dc22

                                                           2009049181

www.mhhe.com

Mark W. Johnston

Mark W. Johnston is the Alan and Sandra Gerry Professor of Marketing and Ethics in the Roy E. Crummer Graduate School of Business at Rollins College in Winter Park, Florida. He earned his Ph.D. in Marketing in 1986 from Texas A&M University. Before receiving his doctorate, he worked in industry as a sales representative for a leading distributor of photographic equipment. His research has been published in a number of professional journals including *Journal of Marketing Research, Journal of Applied Psychology, Journal of Business Ethics, Journal of Marketing Education, Journal of Personal Selling & Sales Management,* and many others. Mark is also an active member in the American Marketing Association and Academy of Marketing Science.

Mark has been retained as a consultant for firms in a number of industries including personal health care, chemical, transportation, hospitality, and telecommunications. He has consulted on a wide range of issues involving strategic business development, sales force structure and performance, international market opportunities, and ethical decision making. Mark also works with MBA students on consulting projects around the world for companies such as Tupperware, Disney, and Johnson & Johnson.

He has conducted seminars globally on a range of topics including the strategic role of selling in the organization, developing an ethical framework for decision making, improving business unit performance, and structuring an effective international marketing department. Mark continues to provide specialized seminars to top managers on strategic marketing issues.

For more than two decades Mark has taught Marketing Management working with thousands of students. His hands-on, real-world approach to marketing management has earned him a number of teaching awards.

In addition to working together on *Essentials of Marketing Management,* Greg and Mark are the co-authors of three other McGraw-Hill/Irwin titles: *Marketing Management,* 1st edition, *Relationship Selling,* 3rd edition, and *Churchill/Ford/Walker's Sales Force Management,* 10th edition.

INTRODUCTION

No doubt about it, the field of marketing is *really changing*—so much so that the American Marketing Association recently unveiled a change in the "official definition" of marketing:

> Marketing is the activity, set of institutions, and processes for creating, communicating, delivering, and exchanging offerings that have value for customers, clients, partners, and society at large.

Recent changes in the practice of marketing management are dramatic and important, and call attention to a number of organizational issues in today's business milieu that differ from the past. In general, marketing management today is:

- Very strategic—customer centricity is now a core *organizational* value.
- Focused on facilitating value for the customer.
- Concerned with internal alignment of people, processes, systems, and strategies to effectively compete through a customer focus.
- Accountable to top management through diligent attention to metrics and measurement.
- Oriented toward service as the driver of product.
- Long-term customer relationship-centered understanding of the need to develop deep commitments from current profitable customers while also cultivating new ones.
- "Owned" by everybody in the firm, to one degree or another.
- Critically committed to exhibiting the utmost ethical behavior in all dealings.

In contrast, marketing management in the past has been:

- Much less strategic in nature.
- Very 4Ps oriented—more tactical.
- Less relationship-centered, thus focused on shorter time horizon decision making.
- Less focused on the ability to facilitate value for the customer.
- Oriented toward product as the core deliverable.
- Done by marketing *departments.*
- Much less accountable to upper management in terms of measurement of marketing success.

WHY WE WROTE THIS BOOK

Given the dramatic changes in the field of marketing, it is a sure bet that the job of leading and managing marketing's contributions to (quoting from the last line of the AMA definition) "customers, clients, partners, and society at large" has changed at a concurrent level. Yet, no marketing management book on the market today fully and effectively captures and communicates to students how marketing management is really practiced in the 21st-century world of business. Clearly, it was time for an updated approach to teaching and learning within the field. This book is designed to fulfill this need.

We hear it from colleagues all the time—the complaint that the book they are using in their marketing management course "doesn't say what I believe the students need to hear" or that it "doesn't match what my MBAs actually do on the job" or that it "reads like an encyclopedia of marketing" or that it "has too much about everything and not enough focus on anything." During the development process for this book we've heard comments like these and others from hundreds of colleagues in focus groups, in written reviewer comments, and in numerous casual conversations about the course. We've become convinced that such comments truly are pervasive among instructors who teach marketing management, whether as the introductory MBA course, capstone undergraduate course, or first focal course after the undergraduate marketing principles course. Many marketing management instructors are looking for a book that is:

- Written for today's students in an up-to-date, user-friendly, yet professional and thorough, style.
- Able to strike an effective balance between presenting the new world order of marketing at the strategic, operational, and tactical levels.
- A step up from the previous norm in terms of support materials for the classroom.

Marshall/Johnston's *Essentials of Marketing Management* has taken great effort to represent marketing management the way it is actually practiced in successful organizations today. In our view, leading and managing the aspects of marketing to improve individual, unit, and organizational performance—**marketing management**—is a *core business activity*. Its relevance is not limited to just marketing departments or marketing majors. And business students of all backgrounds should appreciate the impact of effective marketing management on their own professional careers as well on as the overall success of their organizations. Bottom line, the ability to do great marketing management is relevant to *everyone in a firm*.

The content of the book reflects the major trends in the managerial practice of marketing, and the pedagogy is crafted around *learning and teaching preferences in today's classroom*. Above all, it is written in a style that is appealing for both students and instructors so that students will actually enjoy reading the material and instructors will be proud to teach from it and confident about presenting its up-to-date, professional, and thorough approach to their courses.

STRUCTURE OF THE BOOK

Marshall/Johnston's *Essentials of Marketing Management* has four major parts, reflective of the logical sequence of building blocks for the course.

- **Part One: Introduction to Marketing Management.** In this part, students gain an understanding of the dynamics of the field. Significant attention is paid to framing the importance of studying marketing to future success as a manager. Global marketplace issues are presented early in the book based on the idea that today, truly *all marketing is global.* And to kick off the marketing planning theme early in the course, comprehensive coverage of this aspect along with an example marketing plan appears in Part One.

- **Part Two: Information Drives Marketing Decision Making.** It has often been said that information is the fuel that fires the engine of marketing management decision making. With this in mind, Part Two begins with a unique and highly useful treatment of customer relationship management (CRM), presented in the context of connecting CRM capabilities with other relevant competencies and capabilities of successful marketers. It also includes a substantive discussion of how managers select and execute marketing metrics for decision making. The remainder of this part focuses on effective management of information to better understand competitors and customers, both in the consumer and business marketplaces.

- **Part Three: Developing the Value Offering.** Effective segmentation, target marketing, and positioning are at the core of successful marketing and this part provides a modern managerial treatment of these critical topics, followed by a comprehensive drill-down into today's world of product strategy, branding, and new-product development. Reflecting the notion that service is a key driver of product success, the book makes important links between service and the overall offering. Part Three concludes with a fresh, managerially relevant treatment of pricing decision making.

- **Part Four: Communicating and Delivering the Value Offering.** This part takes an integrative approach to the multitude of modes at a manager's disposal today by which an offering can be made available to customers as well as the array of new-age and traditional marketing communication vehicles.

ETHICAL DIMENSION

Reflective of the centrality of ethical practices to marketing management, each chapter includes a real-world example of business ethics related to chapter material. These lively boxed features highlight how ethical issues permeate every marketing decision.

POP-OUT EXAMPLES

Each chapter contains numerous pop-out examples so that students can immediately connect chapter content to real-world application.

translate that information into specific strategies. Tracking public statements is certainly one way of identifying what a competitor is considering.

Twitter, the free social messaging utility, has an added value that makes it extremely appealing to giants Google and Facebook. Twitter has a rich stream of data that it could sell as a service to marketers that want reports about products and topics that are discussed on the site. This information lets companies pinpoint people interested in their business and provides detailed analyses of individuals that follow particular companies.⁴⁴

Additional information can be learned from a company's annual report as well as mandatory documents filed with the Securities and Exchange Commission (SEC)

MARKETING PLAN EXERCISE

Each chapter connects the key content to a semester-long marketing plan project activity, integrated by Marketing Plan Pro software. Marshall/Johnston's *Essentials of Marketing Management* effectively threads a marketing planning focus throughout the textbook itself. Whether or not a semester marketing plan project is used by the instructor, the marketing plan exercise feature does a great job of tying together important planning concepts for students.

MARKETING PLAN EXERCISES

ACTIVITY 2.1: Elements of a Marketing Plan

In the chapter, you learned that marketing planning drives the activities of the marketing manager and you were provided a framework for marketing planning. Before you move further through this course, it is important to be sure that you understand the flow and content of a typical marketing plan.

1. Read the annotated marketing plan example presented on this book's Web site (www.mhhe.com/marshalless1e).
2. Make notes about any questions you may have about the example plan, and be prepared to bring those questions to class for clarification.
3. If you are going to be using Marketing Plan Pro Software to develop your marketing plan, take this opportunity to open your copy of the software and familiarize yourself with its functionality. An electronic template for your marketing plan that follows Exhibit 2.2 in the chapter (which is the same format used in the CloudCab Small Jet Taxi Service example located on our Web site) can be accessed at www.mhhe.com/marshalless1e.

If you are using Marketing Plan Pro, a template for this assignment can be accessed at www.mhhe.com/marshalless1e.

GLOSSARY OF TERMS

A complete glossary of key terms and definitions is provided at the end of the book. The glossary serves as an important reference as well as a handy study aid for students preparing for exams.

OTHER FEATURES IN EACH CHAPTER

- *Learning objectives:* set the stage for what students will achieve by reading and studying the chapter.
- *Summary:* at the end of each chapter, reminds students of the highlighted topics.

- *Application questions:* These engaging questions at the end of each chapter are designed to direct students' thinking about the topics to the next level of application. Throughout the book all of these questions have been specially designed to simulate managerial decision making.

Assurance of Learning Ready

Assurance of learning is an important element of many accreditation standards. Marshall/Johnston's *Essentials of Marketing Management* is designed specifically to support your assurance of learning initiatives. Each chapter in the book begins with a list of learning objectives, which are then addressed throughout the chapter, as well as in the end-of-chapter problems and exercises. Every test bank question is also linked to one of these objectives, in addition to level of difficulty, topic area, Bloom's Taxonomy level, and AACSB skill area. EZ Test, McGraw-Hill's easy-to-use test bank software, can search the test bank by these and other categories, providing an engine for targeted Assurance of Learning analysis and assessment.

AACSB Statement

The McGraw-Hill Companies is a proud corporate member of AACSB International. Understanding the importance and value of AACSB accreditation, Marshall/Johnston's *Essentials of Marketing Management* has sought to recognize the curricula guidelines detailed in the AACSB standards for business accreditation by connecting selected questions in the test bank to the general knowledge and skill guidelines found in the AACSB standards.

The statements contained in Marshall/Johnston's *Essentials of Marketing Management* are provided only as a guide for the users of this text. The AACSB leaves content coverage and assessment within the purview of individual schools, the mission of the school, and the faculty. While Marshall/Johnston's *Essentials of Marketing Management* and the teaching package make no claim of any specific AACSB qualification or evaluation, we have labeled selected questions according to the six general knowledge and skills areas.

SUPPLEMENT PACKAGE

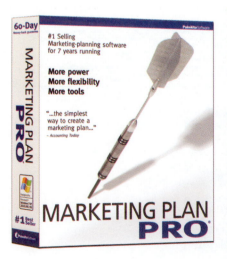

Marshall/Johnston's *Essentials of Marketing Management* is committed to having the best supplement package in the marketing management textbook arena.

MARKETING PLAN PRO

Marketing Plan Pro is the most widely used marketing plan software program in the industry, and it includes everything students need to create professional, complete, and accurate marketing plans. Marketing Plan Pro can be packaged with Marshall/Johnston's *Essentials of Marketing Management* for a nominal fee (approximately $20). In addition, Marshall/Johnston's *Essentials of Marketing Management* will have a Correlation Guide provided at no extra cost linking the Marketing Plan Exercises at the end of each chapter to the Marketing Plan Pro software. This eliminates the need for instructors to spend time in office hours and in class showing how to use this program.

BUSINESSWEEK VIDEO NEWSLETTER

Bi-monthly you will receive an electronic newsletter from the authors including synopses of current *BusinessWeek* videos as well as discussion questions that correlate to relevant topics in the textbook.

INSTRUCTOR'S RESOURCE CD

The Instructor's Resource CD contains instructor supplements including the Instructor's Manual, PowerPoint slides, and Test Bank. These supplements are also available on the password-protected Instructor Online Learning Center.

- The Instructor's Manual contains a chapter outline for each of the 14 chapters in the text as well as PowerPoint thumbnail references, sample syllabi, and end-of-chapter text solutions.
- The PowerPoint slides include examples from the text and additional lecture support.
- The Test Bank contains true/false, multiple-choice, short answer, and essay questions that are tagged to the appropriate Learning Objective within each chapter as well as applicable AACSB Learning Outcomes.

ONLINE LEARNING CENTER

Students using Marshall/Johnston's *Essentials of Marketing Management* will have access to resources located on the Online Learning Center, including Chapter Quizzes and a Marketing Plan Guide. The Marketing Plan Guide is a correlation guide linking the Marketing Plan Exercises at the end of each chapter to the Marketing Plan Pro software. This guide walks students through the Marketing Plan Pro software, providing direct correlations to show how to complete the marketing plan exercises using the online software.

CONCLUSION

Our overarching goal is to introduce the first really new marketing management book in over a decade—one that truly captures the managerial practice of marketing in a way that is fully relevant to today's business students, professors, and managers. As stated earlier, we strongly believe that leading and managing the aspects of marketing to improve individual, unit, and organizational performance—**marketing management**—is a core business activity that is relevant to any MBA or undergraduate business student, regardless of their functional area of focus. At the end of the course, we want this book to allow marketing management instructors to have accomplished these key objectives:

- Clearly bring knowledge leadership in managerial aspects of marketing into the classroom, especially focusing on marketing management decision making in this new era of marketing.
- At the same time, cover the core areas of day-to-day management of marketing functions, but with a focus always on application and managerial decision making.
- Integrate the following themes as systematic focal areas of the course experience: marketing planning, leadership, metrics, value, customer centricity, globalization, ethics, technology and data-driven marketing, and marketing's interface with other business functions.
- Speak to today's students in an up-to-date, user-friendly, yet professional and thorough writing style with vivid examples of actual marketing managers and leaders doing their jobs and making decisions about marketing problems and opportunities.
- Provide a state-of-the-art supplement package that enhances instructional effectiveness and the student's learning experience.
- Ultimately, provide a book today's instructor's will be proud to teach from, secure in the knowledge that students will *want* to read it and that it represents the field of marketing management the way it is practiced in today's business milieu.

Acknowledgments

Writing a textbook requires the talents of many dedicated people. First and foremost, we want to thank the McGraw-Hill/Irwin team for sharing the vision of this project with us from the very beginning. Particularly given the dynamic nature of marketing management both as a professional field and as a course of study, it was critically important that throughout the development process the authors and the editorial, production, and marketing team remain steadfast in believing in the vision of the project. The high level of mutual enthusiasm never waned, and we commend McGraw-Hill/Irwin for this.

In particular, we want to recognize and thank the following individuals at McGraw-Hill/Irwin who played a significant part in the successful development of Marshall/Johnston's *Essentials of Marketing Management.* Key contributors on the publisher's side include Paul Ducham, Doug Hughes, Katie Mergen, Gabriela Gonzalez, and Andy Winston. We would also like to thank Carol Bielski, Mary Sander, Greg Bates, and Dana Pauley for their substantial contributions. All of these great professionals made our job as authors much more enjoyable, and we are indebted to them for their significant contributions to the project.

In addition, we appreciate the contributions of Paul Borges and Hannah Walsh of the Rollins College Crummer Graduate School of Business family. Both worked diligently with us on this edition. Leroy Robinson, Jr., at the University of Houston—Clear Lake did a masterful job in creating and managing the supplements program for the book. Leroy, you have our utmost thanks for a job exceptionally well done! Likewise, Jill Solomon at the University of South Florida developed an outstanding set of testing materials to accompany the book, and without your exceptional contribution the value of the overall course package would not be what it is. Thank you so much.

Many colleagues participated in the developmental process of Marshall/ Johnston *Essentials of Marketing Management* through focus groups and chapter reviews. Thanks go to each of the following people for their guidance and suggestions through this process:

Kalthom Abdullah, *INTERNATIONAL ISLAMIC UNIVERSITY OF MALAYSIA*

Denise Ammirato, *WESTFIELD STATE COLLEGE*

David Amponsah, *TROY UNIVERSITY MONTGOMERY*

David Andrus, *KANSAS STATE UNIVERSITY*

Paul Arsenault, *WEST CHESTER UNIVERSITY OF PENNSYLVANIA*

Semih Arslanoglu, *BOSTON UNIVERSITY*

Parimal Baghat, *INDIANA UNIVERSITY OF PENNSYLVANIA*

William Baker, *SAN DIEGO STATE UNIVERSITY–SAN DIEGO*

Roger Baran, *DEPAUL UNIVERSITY*

Danny Bellenger, *GEORGIA STATE UNIVERSITY*

John Bellenoit, *WESTFIELD STATE COLLEGE*

Parimal Bhagat, *INDIANA UNIVERSITY OF PENNSYLVANIA*

Subodh Bhat, *SAN FRANCISCO STATE UNIVERSITY*

Carol Bienstock, *RADFORD UNIVERSITY*

Diedre Bird, *PROVIDENCE COLLEGE*

Douglas Boyd, *JAMES MADISON UNIVERSITY*

Steve Brokaw, *UNIVERSITY OF WISCONSIN–LACROSSE*

Laura Buckner, *MIDDLE TENNESSEE STATE UNIVERSITY*

Tim Calkins, *NORTHWESTERN UNIVERSITY*

Barb Casey, *DOWLING COLLEGE*

Bob Cline, *UNIVERSITY OF IOWA*

Cathy Cole, *UNIVERSITY OF IOWA*

Mark Collins, *UNIVERSITY OF TENNESSEE–KNOXVILLE*

David Conrad, *AUGSBURG COLLEGE*

Bob Cutler, *CLEVELAND STATE UNIVERSITY*

Geoffrey Da Silva, *TEMASEK POLYTECHNIC*

Lorie Darche, *SOUTHWEST FLORIDA COLLEGE*

F. Robert Dwyer, *UNIVERSITY OF CINCINNATI*

Michael Edwards, *UNIVERSITY OF ST. THOMAS*

Ken Fairweather, *LETOURNEAU UNIVERSITY*

Bagher Fardanesh, *JOHNS HOPKINS UNIVERSITY*

Andrew Forman, *HOFSTRA UNIVERSITY*

Fred Fusting, *LOYOLA COLLEGE OF MARYLAND*

Mahesh Gopinath, *OLD DOMINION UNIVERSITY*

Shiv Gupta, *UNIVERSITY OF FINDLAY*

Deborah Gray, *CENTRAL MICHIGAN UNIVERSITY*

Liz Hafer, *UNIVERSITY OF COLORADO–BOULDER*

Mahmod Sabri Haron, *UNIVERSITI SAINS MALAYSIA*

Angela Hausman, *UNIVERSITY OF NORTH CAROLINA AT PEMBROKE*

Chuck Hermans, *MISSOURI STATE UNIVERSITY*

Asep Hermawan, *UNIVERSITAS TRISAKTI*

Mahmood Hussain, *SAN FRANCISCO STATE UNIVERSITY*

Donna Rue Jenkins, *WARREN NATIONAL UNIVERSITY*

Johny Johansson, *GEORGETOWN UNIVERSITY*

Amit Joshi, *UNIVERSITY OF CENTRAL FLORIDA*

Mahmood A. Kahn, *VIRGINIA TECH UNIVERSITY*

Fred Katz, *JOHNS HOPKINS UNIVERSITY*

Craig Kelley, *CALIFORNIA STATE UNIVERSITY–SACRAMENTO*

Elias Konwufine, *KEISER UNIVERSITY*

Robert Kopp, *BABSON COLLEGE*

Michael Levens, *WALSH COLLEGE*

Cesar Maloles, *CALIFORNIA STATE UNIVERSITY–EAST BAY*

Avinash Malshe, *UNIVERSITY OF ST. THOMAS*

Susan Mantel, *INDIANA UNIVERSITY–PURDUE UNIVERSITY–INDIANAPOLIS*

Norton Marks, *CALIFORNIA STATE UNIVERSITY–SAN BERNARDINO*

Thomas Maronick, *TOWSON UNIVERSITY*

H. Lee Mathews, *OHIO STATE UNIVERSITY*

Melvin Mattson, *RADFORD UNIVERSITY*

Denny McCorkle, *UNIVERSITY OF NORTHERN COLORADO*

Michael Menasco, *CALIFORNIA STATE UNIVERSITY–SAN BERNADINO*

Morgan Miles, *GEORGIA SOUTHERN UNIVERSITY*

Chad Milewicz, *UNIVERSITY OF CENTRAL FLORIDA*

Herb Miller, *UNIVERSITY OF TEXAS*

Mark Mitchell, *COASTAL CAROLINA UNIVERSITY*

Jean Murray, *BRYANT UNIVERSITY*

Thomas Noordewier, *UNIVERSITY OF VERMONT*

Nicholas Nugent, *SOUTHERN NEW HAMPSHIRE UNIVERSITY*

Carl Obermiller, *SEATTLE UNIVERSITY*

Azizah Omar, *UNIVERSITI SAINS MALAYSIA*

Barnett Parker, *PFEIFFER UNIVERSITY*

Vanessa Patrick, *UNIVERSITY OF GEORGIA*

Dennis Pitta, *UNIVERSITY OF BALTIMORE*

Salim Qureshi, *BLOOMSBURG UNIVERSITY*

Pushkala Raman, *TEXAS WOMANS UNIVERSITY–DENTON*

K. Ramakrishna Rao, *MULTIMEDIA UNIVERSITY*

Molly Rapert, *UNIVERSITY OF ARKANSAS–FAYETTEVILLE*

Richard Rexeisen, *UNIVERSITY OF SAINT THOMAS*

Subom Rhee, *SANTA CLARA UNIVERSITY*

Robert Richey, *UNIVERSITY OF ALABAMA–TUSCALOOSA*

Torsten Ringberg, *UNIVERSITY OF WISCONSIN–MILWAUKEE*

Ann Root, *FLORIDA ATLANTIC UNIVERSITY–BOCA RATON*

David Rylander, *TEXAS WOMAN'S UNIVERSITY–DENTON*

Ritesh Saini, *GEORGE MASON UNIVERSITY*

Dennis Sandler, *PACE UNIVERSITY*

Matt Sarkees, *PENNSYLVANIA STATE UNIVERSITY*

Linda Saytes, *UNIVERSITY OF SAN FRANCISCO*

Shahid Sheikh, *AMERICAN INTERCONTINENTAL UNIVERSITY*

Susan Sieloff, *NORTHEASTERN UNIVERSITY*

Karen Smith, *COLUMBIA SOUTHERN UNIVERSITY*

Sharon Smith, *DEPAUL UNIVERSITY*

Jill Solomon, *UNIVERSITY OF SOUTH FLORIDA*

Ashish Sood, *EMORY UNIVERSITY*

Robert Spekman, *UNIVERSITY OF VIRGINIA*

James Spiers, *ARIZONA STATE UNIVERSITY–TEMPE*

Samuel Spralls, *CENTRAL MICHIGAN UNIVERSITY*

Thomas Steenburgh, *HARVARD BUSINESS SCHOOL*

Geoffrey Stewart, *UNIVERSITY OF LOUISIANA–LAFAYETTE*

John Stovall, *GEORGIA SOUTHWESTERN STATE UNIVERSITY*

Ziad Swaidan, *UNIVERSITY OF HOUSTON AT VICTORIA*

Michael Swenson, *BRIGHAM YOUNG UNIVERSITY*

Leona Tam, *OLD DOMINION UNIVERSITY*

Blodwen Tarter, *GOLDEN GATE UNIVERSITY*

Niwet Thamma, *RAMKHAMHEANG UNIVERSITY*

Meg Thams, *REGIS UNIVERSITY*

Rungting Tu, *PEKING UNIVERSITY*

Bronislaw Verhage, *GEORGIA STATE UNIVERSITY*

Guangping Wang, *PENNSYLVANIA STATE UNIVERSITY*

Cathy Waters, *BOSTON COLLEGE*

Art Weinstein, *NOVA SOUTHEASTERN UNIVERSITY*

Darin White, *UNION UNIVERSITY–JACKSON*

Ken Williamson, *JAMES MADISON UNIVERSITY*

Dale Wilson, *MICHIGAN STATE UNIVERSITY*

Walter Wochos, *CARDINAL STRITCH UNIVERSITY*

Khanchitpol Yousapronpaiboon, *KHONKHEN UNIVERSITY*

Yong Zhang, *HOFSTRA UNIVERSITY*

Shaoming Zou, *UNIVERSITY OF MISSOURI–COLUMBIA*

And finally, we want to offer a very special and heart-felt note of appreciation to our families and friends. Their encouragement and good humor throughout this process were integral to the end result.

Greg W. Marshall, *ROLLINS COLLEGE*

Mark W. Johnston, *ROLLINS COLLEGE*

January 2010

BRIEF TABLE OF CONTENTS

TABLE OF CONTENTS

part ONE

Introduction to Marketing Management

CHAPTER 01

Marketing in Today's Global Business Milieu

LEARNING OBJECTIVES

- Identify typical misconceptions about marketing, why they persist, and the resulting challenges for marketing management.

- Define what marketing and marketing management really are and how they contribute to a firm's success.

- Appreciate how marketing has evolved from its early roots to be practiced as it is today.

- Recognize the impact of key change drivers on the future of marketing.

- Explain the global experience learning curve.

WELCOME TO MARKETING MANAGEMENT

Welcome to the world of marketing management! In late 2007, the American Marketing Association announced a new "official" definition of marketing as follows: **marketing** is the activity, set of institutions, and processes for creating, communicating, delivering, and exchanging offerings that have value for customers, clients, partners, and society at large.[1]

An exciting aspect of modern marketing is that it is an inherently global enterprise. Later in this chapter we will present strong evidence that marketing and global marketing are basically synonymous today.

Now is a great time to be studying about marketing. In fact, marketing as a field of study has much to offer everyone, regardless of whether or not the word *marketing* appears in a job title. Whether your interest and training is in engineering, accounting, finance, information technology, or fields outside business, marketing is relevant to you. You can be confident that, when finished with this course about marketing management, you will emerge with a set of knowledge and skills that will not only enhance your personal effectiveness as a leader and manager regardless of your area of responsibility or job title, but will also positively impact the performance of your work group and firm. Mastering great marketing is useful for anyone!

Despite the strong case for the value of learning about marketing, marketing is often misunderstood for a variety of reasons. Let's start by clearing the air. Before you learn about great marketing and how to successfully manage it, it is important to address some misconceptions and stereotypes about marketing. Getting these out in the open will give you the opportunity to challenge your own perceptions of the field. After this section, attention will quickly turn from marketing misconceptions to *marketing realities* in today's global business milieu.

MARKETING MISCONCEPTIONS

When you think of *marketing,* what sorts of ideas and images initially come to mind? Close your eyes and think about the essence of the word. What images flow in? The images will vary depending on your age, professional background, and whether you have worked in some aspect of the marketing field. Here is a short list of perceptions commonly conjured up about marketing:

- Catchy and entertaining advertisements—or perhaps the opposite, incessant and boring advertisements.
- Pushy salespeople trying to persuade someone to *buy it right now.*
- Famous brands and their celebrity spokespeople, such as Nike's athlete endorsers.
- Product claims that turn out to be overstated or just plain false, causing doubt about the trustworthiness of a company.
- Marketing departments "own" an organization's marketing initiative.
- Marketing is just another cost of doing business.

Exhibit 1.1 expands on these examples of common stereotypes and misconceptions about marketing.

Behind the Misconceptions

Several important factors have contributed to the development of these misconceptions: marketing's inherent visibility and its tendency toward buzzwords and "spin."

EXHIBIT 1.1 | **Marketing Misconceptions: What Marketing Is *Not***

MISCONCEPTION NO. 1: Marketing is all about advertising.

THE REALITY: Advertising is just one way that marketing is communicated to potential customers. Advertising is highly visible to the general public, so many people naturally think of advertising when they think of marketing. A famous axiom: *Good advertising makes a bad product fail faster.*

MISCONCEPTION NO. 2: Marketing is all about selling.

THE REALITY: The general public also experiences a lot of selling. Much of this day-to-day selling is in retail store environments. Selling, or more correctly "personal selling," is simply another method of marketing communication. Marketers have to decide on a mix of marketing communication approaches that (in addition to advertising and personal selling) might also include public relations/publicity, sales promotion, and direct marketing. Later chapters discuss how and when each might be most effective in communicating the message.

MISCONCEPTION NO. 3: Marketing is all about the *sizzle.*

THE REALITY: Yes, some aspects of marketing are inherently fun and glitzy. Hiring Tiger Woods as a celebrity spokesperson had to be a real thrill for everybody at Nike, not to mention the pleasure and fun it gave Nike fans. But marketing also has aspects that involve sophisticated research, detailed analysis, careful decision making, and thoughtful development of strategies and plans. For many organizations, marketing represents a major investment and firms are naturally reluctant to invest major resources without a reasonable level of assurance of a satisfactory payback.

MISCONCEPTION NO. 4: Marketing is inherently unethical and harmful to society.

THE REALITY: Marketing is no more inherently unethical than other business areas. The accounting scandals at Enron, WorldCom, and other firms in the early 2000s show that to be true. However, when some element of marketing proves to be unethical (or even illegal), it tends to be visible to the general public. Untrue advertising claims, arm-twisting sales tactics, and nonenvironmentally friendly product packaging are a few very visible examples of marketing not behaving at its best.

MISCONCEPTION NO. 5: Only marketers market.

THE REALITY: Everybody does marketing. Everybody has a stake in the success of marketing. Regardless of your position in a firm or job title, learning how to do great marketing is a key professional asset. People with strong marketing skills achieve greater success—both on the job and off. If you've never thought of yourself in the context of being a "personal brand" that needs to be effectively communicated, just consider how useful such an approach could be in job seeking or positioning yourself for a promotion.

MISCONCEPTION NO. 6: Marketing is just another cost center in a firm.

THE REALITY: The mind-set that marketing is a cost, rather than an investment, is deadly in a firm because costs are inherently to be reduced or avoided. When management doesn't view marketing as earning its keep—that is, marketing being able to pay back its investment over the long term—it becomes very easy for firms to suboptimize their success in the long run by avoiding investment in brand and product development in favor of cutting costs. This is the classic argument that successful firms must simultaneously monitor costs to ensure short-term financial performance while also investing in marketing to ensure long-term competitive strength.

Marketing Is Highly Visible by Nature

Unlike most other key areas of business, marketing as a field is highly public and readily visible outside the confines of the internal business operation. Think of it this way: Most aspects of financial management, accounting, information technology, production, operations management, and human resource management take place behind the curtain of an organization, out of the general public's sight. But marketing is very different. A good portion of marketing is very public. Marketing is seen through the Web page that stimulates interest in seeking more product information, the (hopefully) good service received from the salesperson representing a firm's products, the enjoyment and interest generated from a clever advertisement on Super Bowl Sunday, or the well-stocked shelves at the neighborhood Target Store.

Of all the business fields, marketing is almost certainly the most visible to people outside the organization. While the other fields also have negative stereotypical images (think accountants with green eyeshades or IT computer geeks), you'd be hard pressed to identify another business field about which nearly everyone has formed a deeply held set of images and opinions or about which nearly everybody thinks they know enough to confidently offer advice! Think about how many times casual conversation in a social setting turns to something marketing related. Have you ever had similar social exchanges about the ins and outs of financial management or the complexities of computerized production systems? Of course not, but it seems almost anybody is comfortable talking about elements of marketing—from the week's advertised specials at the supermarket to this year's fashion for kids heading back to school to the service received at a favorite vacation hotel—marketing is a topic everyone can discuss!

> Whole Foods captures customers by the stories it tells about products. Large signs, such as "Why Buy Organic," above food products are meant to make customers feel good about the food they are purchasing. Whole Foods is clever at finding creative ways to get customers to abandon their usual products in favor of new and more exotic food offerings. For example, at some stores a small sign stuck into a pile of Russian banana potatoes reads, "How cute are these?" Of course, Russian banana potatoes are considerably more expensive than your basic Idaho spud.[2]

Why is the notion that marketing is visible and accessible to nearly everyone so important to students of marketing management? Despite the fact that much of marketing is easily observable to almost anyone, marketing as a professional field worthy of serious study doesn't always get the respect it deserves, maybe in part because of its overexposure. The business functions of financial management, operations, IT, and the rest seem to be viewed by many MBA and undergraduate students (and also unfortunately by managers in many firms) as the more "serious" parts of an enterprise—topics that are perceived as more concrete, more scientific, and more analytical than marketing, thus implying they are topics worthy of more substantial investment in time, money, and other resources.[3] In the past, marketing has had few useful metrics or measures to gauge the performance impact of a firm's marketing investment, while other areas of the firm have historically been much more driven by measurement of results. The old adage "if it can't be measured, it can't be managed" has plagued marketing for years. This is changing, and today measurement of marketing's performance and contribution is a focal point in many firms.[4] In fact, so many great marketing metrics are available that we've included a whole chapter on the topic at the end of the book.

Marketing Is More Than Buzzwords

Given the inherently transparent nature of marketing and the prior lack of ways to effectively measure its impact on a firm's success, it should be no surprise that some managers consider marketing to be little more than a necessary evil—a *cost* they reluctantly have to incur.[5] They're not sure *how* marketing works, or even *if* marketing really does work, but for competitive reasons—or maybe just because it's always been done—they continue to invest large sums of money in its many facets including market research, brand development, advertising, salespeople, public relations, and so forth. With so much ambiguity historically surrounding the management and control of marketing, a "flavor of the month" club mentality

No good deed goes unmapped.

It's all part of the growing **Be Hospitable Index**. Simply go to **behospitable.com** to share any good deed you see. Recognize acts of kindness from your friends, relatives and neighbors as well as acknowledging perfect strangers. Tell us your story, get on the map and watch the hospitality spread.

The Hilton Family. Nine distinct hotels, one simple philosophy...be hospitable.

The Hilton Family
be hospitable®

Hilton communicates its image as a customer-friendly company by its "Be Hospitable Index."

has developed around the field of marketing, often promoted by consultants and authors looking to make a quick buck by selling their latest and greatest ideas complete with their own catchy buzzwords for the program.

Anyone who doubts the pervasiveness of quick-fix approaches to marketing should visit a bookstore or online bookseller. Go to the business section and look at the marketing titles. Among the buzzwords right in the book titles are such gems as *guerilla marketing, permission marketing, holistic marketing, marketing warfare, marketing rainmaking, buzz marketing, integrated marketing* . . . the list goes on and on. Although there may be some degree of usefulness in each of these approaches, the circus-like atmosphere surrounding the field has detracted from its position as a respectable business function.

Beyond the Misconceptions and Toward the *Reality* of Modern Marketing

Of course, buzzwords are just window dressing, and most popular press prescription approaches to marketing don't do much to improve the *long-term* performance of an organization. Effective marketing management isn't about buzzwords or quick fixes. Nor is the essence of marketing really about the kinds of stereotypical viewpoints identified earlier in this section. In today's global business milieu, marketing is a central function and set of processes essential to any enterprise.[6] Moreover, leading and managing the facets of marketing to improve individual, unit, and organizational performance—**marketing management**—is a *core business activity,* worthy of any student's study and mastery.

Luxury fashion accessory maker Coach effectively serves different customers through different price points. With styles such as the Francine bag at $798 and the Bonnie Signature bag at $248, Coach sells to customers at various price levels yet maintains its trendy brand image. To reach an even larger audience, Coach has introduced a new line of smaller and more affordable purses that start at $150. Coach's highly effective marketing management practices helped propel it to No. 1 in *BusinessWeek's* ranking of top 50 performers in 2008.[7]

The chapters that follow lay the groundwork for developing the knowledge and skills around marketing that will allow you to build a more successful career as a leader and manager, regardless of department, area of specialization, level in the organization, or job title. Is marketing relevant to *you?* You bet it is, because *everyone* in an organization does marketing in some way and must share ownership of its success or failure.

Learning about marketing management is not just about reading a book or taking a course, although dedication to these activities is a great starting point. Instead, great marketing is a lifelong journey that requires dedication to continuous learning and improvement of your knowledge and skills as a leader and manager. It is in this spirit that we enthusiastically invite you to begin your journey into the field of marketing management!

DEFINING MARKETING

Over 50 years ago, the late management guru Peter Drucker, often referred to as the father of modern management, set the stage for defining contemporary marketing and conceiving of its potential power. Consider this quote from Drucker, circa 1954 (emphasis added):

> If we want to know what a business is we have to start with its *purpose*. There is only one valid definition of business purpose: *to create a customer*. It is the customer who determines what a business is. For it is the customer, and he alone, who through being willing to pay for a good or service, converts economic resources into wealth, things into goods. What the business thinks it produces is not of first importance—especially not to the future of the business and its success. What the customer thinks he is buying, what he considers "value" is decisive. . . . Because it is the [purpose of a business] to create a customer, [the] business enterprise has two—and only two—business functions: *marketing* and *innovation*.[8]

Consider the power of these ideas: a business built around the customer with resources and processes aligned to maximize customer value. Within this context, Drucker is not talking just about "marketing departments," but rather marketing in much broader terms. More on that distinction later. For now, consider this subsequent quote from Drucker circa 1973:

> Marketing is so basic that it cannot be considered a separate function (i.e., a separate skill or work) within the business . . . it is, first, a central dimension of the entire business. It is the *whole business* . . . seen from the *customer's* point of view. Concern and responsibility for marketing must, therefore, permeate all areas of the enterprise.[9]

Clearly, Peter Drucker was a man whose business philosophy was way ahead of his time. Now fast forward to this decade. Today, the American Marketing Association defines marketing as the activity, set of institutions, and processes for creating, communicating, delivering, and exchanging offerings that have value for customers, clients, partners, and society at large. Note three key areas of focus within this definition:

- The more *strategic* aspects of marketing, which positions marketing as a core contributor to overall firm success.
- Marketing as an *activity*, *set of institutions*, and *processes*—that is, marketing is not just a "department" in an organization.
- The concept of *value*—creating, communicating, delivering, and exchanging offerings of value to various stakeholders.

Just who are the relevant stakeholders of marketing? **Marketing's stakeholders** include any person or entity inside or outside a firm with whom marketing interacts, impacts, and is impacted by. For example, internal stakeholders—those inside a firm—include other organizational units that marketing interacts with in the course of business. Strong, productive relationships between marketing and finance, accounting, production, quality control, engineering, human resources, and many other areas in a firm are necessary for a firm to do business successfully.[10] The range of external stakeholders—those outside a firm—is even broader and includes

Green marketing isn't a theme one might expect to see Waste Management, Inc., conveying, yet the company has a powerful environmental message.

ETHICAL DIMENSION 1

The Green Product Challenge

Environmental awareness coupled with a sense of social responsibility is leading many companies to assess their environmental policies and business practices. Companies such as General Electric are developing environmentally sensitive products while others, including Starbucks, have adopted tough recycling programs that minimize environmental waste. Companies worldwide acknowledge a concern for the environment, seek to minimize environmental damage, and commit resources to their environmental programs.

One challenge for manufacturers around the world is to transform environmentally harmful products into environmentally friendly products. In some industries, making products more environmentally safe has been relatively straightforward. For instance, air conditioner manufacturers moved from the refrigerant known by the brand name Freon to a more environmentally friendly product, Puron, that reduced chlorine emissions and depletion of the ozone layer.

In other situations, it is more difficult to create environmentally sensitive products. Consider Nike, a company that built its running shoe business through outstanding products and creative marketing communications. A key product feature for Nike has been a small pocket of air in its Nike Air shoes. The extra cushion was a significant product innovation when it was introduced and proved to be a major market differentiator for the company. However, the pocket of "air" was not just air; it also contained a small amount of sulfur hexafluoride, or SF6, a gas that damages the ozone layer.

In 1992, questions about Nike's use of SF6 gas became public. While the Nike air cushion was a key factor in the company's success, Nike realized that continued use of SF6 posed an environmental problem. Unfortunately, replacing SF6 with a solution that minimized environmental damage while providing the same product benefits (long-lasting cushion and support) proved challenging.

After millions of dollars and 14 years, a team of 60 Nike engineers replaced the old product with a new, greener solution using sophisticated manufacturing techniques to replace the SF6 with nitrogen. The AirMax 360 was the first shoe to incorporate the new technology. Interestingly, the new shoe actually increases comfort and weighs less than older models, making the environmentally sensitive solution the best business solution as well. Nike's focus on product performance and technical innovation created a better, environmentally friendly product that is successful in the marketplace.

As part of the product development process, Nike kept environmental groups informed of the progress. While there were tensions as the process took longer than anyone planned (14 years), the communication between Nike and stakeholders helped minimize long-term negative publicity. The challenge for marketers is finding the right balance between consumer demand and environmental stewardship.[11]

Ethical Perspective

1. **Nike:** How would you prioritize what are often two conflicting demands: consumer product performance expectations and the demand for eco-friendly products?

2. **Consumers:** Would you choose a Nike shoe that provided less comfort but was more environmentally friendly? Would you pay a premium for an environmentally friendly Nike shoe?

3. **Environmental groups:** Nike took 14 years to create a new sole for its air cushion; would you allow a company that much time to deal with an environmentally damaging product?

---

customers, vendors, governmental bodies, labor unions, and many others. One important challenge in marketing management is deciding how to prioritize these internal and external stakeholders in terms of their relevance and importance to the firm.[12] Most firms place the customer first, but a key question is: how do you decide which of the others deserve the most attention?

At the broadest conceptual level, members of society at large can be viewed as a stakeholder for marketing, a concept called **societal marketing.** As one example, the concept of environmentally friendly marketing, or *green marketing,* has been a growing trend in socially responsible companies. Today the movement has evolved into a part of the philosophical and strategic core of many firms under the label **sustainability,** which refers to business practices that meet humanity's needs without harming future generations.[13] Sustainability practices have helped socially responsible organizations incorporate *doing well* *by doing good* into their overarching business models so that both the success of the firm and the success of society at large are sustained over the long term. Ethical Dimension 1 looks at environmentally friendly marketing at several firms.

Value and Exchange Are Core Marketing Concepts

Throughout the various topics encompassed within this book, the idea of value as a core concept in marketing will be a central theme. From a customer's perspective, we define **value** as a ratio of the bundle of benefits a customer receives from an offering compared to the costs incurred by the customer in acquiring that bundle of benefits.[14] Another central tenet of marketing is the concept of **exchange,** in which people give up something of value to them for something else they desire to have.[15] Usually an exchange is facilitated by money, but not always. Sometimes people trade or barter nonmonetary resources such as time, skill, expertise, intellectual capital, and other things of value for something else they want. For any exchange to take place, the following five conditions must be present:

1. There must be at least two parties.
2. Each party has something that might be of value to the other party.
3. Each party is capable of communication and delivery.
4. Each party is free to accept or reject the exchange offer.
5. Each party believes it is appropriate or desirable to deal with the other party.

Just because these conditions exist does not guarantee that an exchange will take place. The parties must come to an agreement that results in both being better off, hence the phrase in the AMA definition of marketing "... exchanging offerings that *have value* ... (emphasis added)." Value implies that both parties win from the exchange.

Since Tata Motors Limited, India's largest automobile company, introduced its first prototype of the Nano in 2008, some 350,000 individuals across India have put down an $80 deposit to enter a lottery to purchase one of the 100,000 available Nanos. Tata's Nano, the world's cheapest car, is spacious, stylish, and gets nearly 50 miles per gallon. Tata communicates such strong value to customers that it has a "problem" most companies could only dream of—*too many customers.* The company priced the car at $2,000, well below competitor Suzuki's $3,300 Maruti 800.[16]

The AMA definition of marketing highlights marketing's central role in creating, communicating, delivering, and exchanging offerings that have value. But marketing's central focus hasn't always been on value and customer relationships, and the truth is that even today some firms lag in these areas. The next section offers perspectives on marketing's roots and evolution, and explains why some firms today are frozen in past approaches to marketing.

MARKETING'S ROOTS AND EVOLUTION

In the spirit of the old adage that he who ignores history is doomed to repeat its mistakes, here's a short marketing history lesson. Exhibit 1.2 illustrates the flow of marketing's evolution as a field.

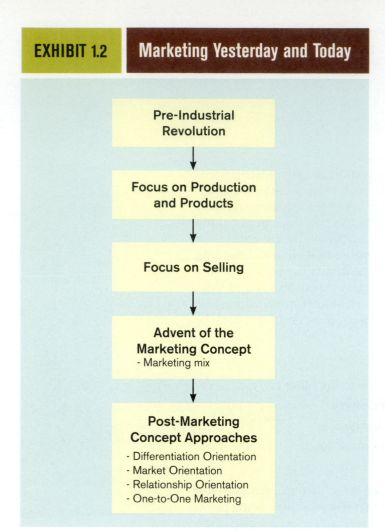

EXHIBIT 1.2 | **Marketing Yesterday and Today**

Pre-Industrial Revolution

↓

Focus on Production and Products

↓

Focus on Selling

↓

Advent of the Marketing Concept
- Marketing mix

↓

Post-Marketing Concept Approaches
- Differentiation Orientation
- Market Orientation
- Relationship Orientation
- One-to-One Marketing

Pre-Industrial Revolution

Before Henry Ford and his contemporaries created assembly lines and mass production, marketing was done very much on a one-to-one basis between firms and customers, although the word *marketing* wasn't really used. Consider what happened when a person needed a new pair of shoes, pre-industrial revolution. One would likely visit the village cobbler, who would take precise measurements and then send the customer away with instructions to return in a week or so to pick up the new shoes. Materials, styles, and colors would be limited, but customers likely would get a great fit since the cobbler created a customized pair of shoes for each person. And if they didn't fit just right, the cobbler would adjust the shoes to a customer's liking—right on the spot.

Focus on Production and Products

The industrial revolution changed nearly everything in business by shifting the focus from meeting demand one item at a time to mass production via assembly line. Maximizing production capacity utilization became a predominant concern. For the early part of the 20th century, the focus was on this **production orientation** of improving products and production efficiency without much regard for what was going on in the marketplace. In fact, consumers snapped up this new pipeline of reasonably priced goods, even if the products didn't give much choice in style or function. Having a Ford Model T was great, but as Henry Ford himself said, "People can have the Model T in any color—so long that it's black."[17]

A production orientation assumes that customers will beat a path to your door just because you have a great product that functions nicely; build a better mousetrap and they will come. You will learn throughout your study of marketing management that great products alone do not assure success. Unfortunately, firms that are stuck in a production orientation mentality likely will have great difficulty competing successfully for customers.

Focus on Selling

Around the end of World War I, production capacity utilization began to decline for several reasons. First, capacity had been increased greatly for the war. Second, a number of firms that had dominated their respective industries before the war now found themselves with stiff competition for sales because many new competitors had flooded into the marketplace. And third, financial markets were becoming more sophisticated and were placing more pressure on firms to continually increase sales volume and profits.

These factors resulted in the rise of many of the great sales organizations of today. A **sales orientation** suggests that, to increase sales and consequently production capacity utilization, professional salespeople need to "push" products into the hands of customers, both businesses and end users. For years, the most vivid image of a salesperson in the public eye was that of the peddler, the classic outside salesperson pushing product on customers with a smile, promise, and handshake. Gradually, customers of all kinds grew wary of high-pressure selling, sparking laws at all levels to protect consumers from unscrupulous salespeople. For many customers, the image of marketing became permanently frozen as that of the pushy salesperson. And just as with the production orientation, to this day some firms still practice mainly a sales-oriented approach to their business.

Advent of the Marketing Concept

After World War II, business began to change in many long-lasting ways. Business historians point to a number of reasons for this shift, including:

- Pent-up demand for consumer goods and services after the war.
- Euphoric focus on family and a desperate need to regain a normalcy of day-to-day life after years of war (which produced the baby boomer generation).
- Opening up of production capacity dominated for years by war production.
- Advent of readily available mainframe computing capability, and especially the associated statistical analytic techniques that allowed for more sophisticated market research.

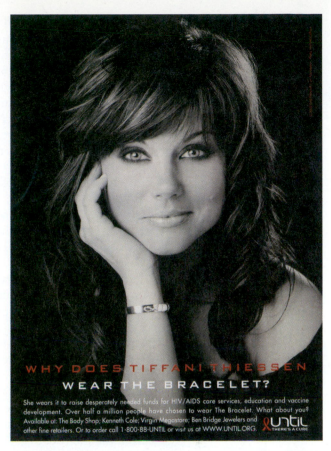

Charitable organizations like AIDS awareness group UNTIL.org often use celebrities and sophisticated imagery in their approach to gaining loyal donors.

In the 1950s, these forces, combined with growing frustration with high-pressure selling, sparked a shift in the focus of American business. The resulting business philosophy has been labeled the **marketing concept,** which is an organization-wide customer orientation with the objective of achieving long-run profits.[18] General Electric's *1952 Annual Report* is often cited as the first time the marketing concept was articulated in writing by a major corporation. Clearly delighted to herald its new-age management philosophy, GE wrote the following to stockholders in its *1952 Annual Report* (in this historical period, the assumption was that business professionals would be male):

> [The marketing concept] . . . introduces the marketing man at the beginning rather than at the end of the production cycle and integrates marketing into each phase of the business. Thus, marketing, through its studies and research, will establish for the engineer, the design and manufacturing man, what the customer wants in a given product, what price he is willing to pay, and where and when it will be wanted. Marketing will have authority in product planning, production scheduling, and inventory control, as well as in sales distribution and servicing of the product.[19]

The articulation of the marketing concept was a major breakthrough in business, and in the 1960s and 70s it spread like wildfire throughout companies of all kinds. Soon firms everywhere were adopting the practice of letting the market decide what products to offer. Such an approach required substantial investment in ongoing market and consumer research and also necessitated an organization-wide commitment to marketing planning. As a result, the idea of the marketing plan became codified in most organizations' business processes. We'll come back to the idea of marketing planning in Chapter 2.

The Marketing Mix

The articulation of the marketing concept and its quick adoption across a gamut of industries quickly led to a major focus on teaching marketing courses in colleges and universities. In the mid-1960s, a convenient way of teaching the key components was developed with the advent of the **marketing mix,** or **4Ps of marketing,** originally for *product, price, place,* and *promotion.*[20] The idea was that these fundamental elements comprise the marketer's "tool kit" to be applied in carrying out the job. It is referred to as a "mix" because, by developing unique combinations of these elements, marketers set their product or brand apart from the competition. Also, an important rubric in marketing is the following: making a change in any one of the marketing mix elements tends to result in a domino effect on the others.

Today, the basic concept of the marketing mix persists but with considerably greater sophistication than in the 1960s. The *product* is now regarded broadly in the context of an overall *offering,* which could include a bundle of goods, services, ideas (for example, intellectual property), and other components, often represented by strong overarching branding. Many marketers today are more focused on *solutions* than products—the characterization of an offering as a solution is nice because of the implication that a solution has been developed in conjunction with specific, well-understood customer wants and needs.[21] *Price* today is largely regarded in relationship to the concept of value. *Place* has undergone tremendous change. Rather than just connoting the process of getting goods from Point A to Point B, firms now understand that sophisticated, integrated supply chain approaches are a crucial component of business success.[22] And finally, to grasp the magnitude of changes in *promotion* since the 1960s one need only consider the proliferation of high-tech media options available to marketers today, from the Internet to cell phones and beyond.

Marketers have long dreamed of tracking shoppers' behaviors and hitting them with specially targeted ads or coupons. A team of analysts at Sense Networks can track the movements of nearly 4 million cell phone users over the course of the year. This information can provide incredibly rich information to every company that wants to advertise, sell a product, or provide a service.[23]

Over the years some authors have proposed various additions to the original marketing mix—that is, adding "more Ps." Especially outside the setting of marketing physical goods, as in the context of marketing services or ideas, the case is frequently made for the need to add more elements to the marketer's tool kit.[24] This issue has been hotly debated for years. You will find as you progress in your reading of this book that we follow the basic topical flow of creating, communicating, delivering, and exchanging offerings that have value. The core elements of the original 4Ps of marketing are there, but presented within the context of the terminology and work processes used by *today's* marketing managers.

Beyond the Marketing Concept

Close perusal of the definition of the marketing concept reveals several issues that still resonate widely in today's business milieu. The decision to place the customer at the core of the enterprise (often referred to as a **customer-centric** approach to business), focus on investment in customers over the *long term,* and marketing as an *organization-wide* issue (that is, not just relegated to a "marketing department") are all relevant and important topics in business classes and boardrooms today, and each will be discussed further in later chapters.[25] Referring again to Exhibit 1.2, the four evolutionary steps beyond the original marketing concept warrant further discussion now: differentiation orientation, market orientation, relationship orientation, and one-to-one marketing.

Differentiation Orientation

More sophisticated research and analytical approaches have made it possible to do increasingly precise refinement of market segmentation, target marketing, and positioning of products to serve very specific customer groups, processes you will learn more about in Chapter 7. The idea is to create and communicate **differentiation,** or what clearly distinguishes your products from those of competitors in the minds of customers.[26] The ability for marketers to tailor and deliver different product messages to different groups also has been greatly enhanced by the proliferation of multiple types of media that can be used with great precision to communicate to very specifically defined customer groups.

Many companies are experimenting with building brand loyalty through online social networking. The use of social networks worldwide has been growing at a pace of about 40 percent per year. Nike's creation of Nike+, a technology that tracks data on runners, contributed to a rise in Nike's share of total running shoe sales in the United States from 48 percent in 2006 to 61 percent by 2008. More than an attempt to increase sales, the company has used Nikeplus.com as a gathering place to promote healthy living—the community of runners there has logged over 130 million miles so far.[27]

Market Orientation

A great deal of research has been devoted to learning how a firm can successfully put the marketing concept into practice. Think of **market orientation** as the implementation of the marketing concept. The notion of market orientation, one component of which is **customer orientation**—placing the customer at the core of all aspects of the enterprise—takes the guiding business philosophy of the marketing concept and works to more usefully define just how to implement it within a firm.[28] A central purpose of this book is to aid managers (and future managers) in adopting and implementing a market orientation in their firms.

Relationship Orientation

Marketing managers today recognize the power of securing, building, and maintaining long-term relationships with profitable customers.[29] The original marketing concept clearly recognized the need for an orientation toward the longer term in marketing—that is, not just making the next quarter's financial projections but rather cultivating customers for the long haul. The move toward a **relationship orientation** by firms has been driven by the realization that it is far more efficient and effective to invest in keeping and cultivating profitable current customers instead of constantly having to invest in gaining new customers that come with unknown return on investment.[30] Certainly most firms simultaneously focus on both current and new customers, but no company wants to be in a position of losing great customers and having to scramble to replace the associated lost revenue.

Companies are investing more on very loyal customers. Zappos.com, the online shoe retailer, routinely provides free standard shipping on both orders and returns to all customers. Now, Zappos also has created a VIP service for its most loyal customers, providing upgrades to next-day delivery. Companies such as Zappos maintain loyalty by consistently investing in their very best customers.[31]

A relationship orientation draws its power from the firm's capability to effectively collect and use ongoing, real-time information on customers in marketing management decision making. Implementation of a relationship orientation is discussed in Chapter 3 in the context of customer relationship management (CRM).

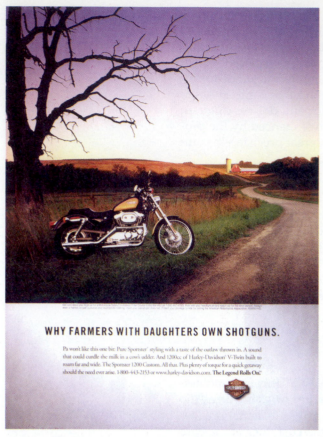

WHY FARMERS WITH DAUGHTERS OWN SHOTGUNS.

Pa won't like this one bit: Pure Sportster® styling with a taste of the outlaw thrown in. A sound that could curdle the milk in a cow's udder. And 1200cc of Harley-Davidson® V-Twin built to roam far and wide. The Sportster 1200 Custom. All that. Plus plenty of torque for a quick getaway should the need ever arise. 1-800-443-2153 or www.harley-davidson.com. **The Legend Rolls On.**®

Harley markets itself as much more than just the physical motorcycle it sells—instead, it's all about the experience and the community of those owning one.

Much of CRM is designed to facilitate higher levels of customer satisfaction and loyalty, as well as to provide a means for identifying the most profitable customers—those worthy of the most marketing investment.[32]

One-to-One Marketing

Remember the earlier example of the pre-industrial revolution cobbler who would customize a pair of shoes for each customer? In many ways marketing's evolution has come full circle back to a focus on creating capabilities for such customization. In their books and articles, Don Peppers and Martha Rogers have popularized the term **one-to-one marketing,** which advocates that firms should direct energy and resources into establishing a learning relationship with each customer and then connect that knowledge with the firm's production and service capabilities to fulfill that customer's needs in as custom a manner as possible.[33]

Some firms come close to one-to-one marketing by employing **mass customization,** in which they combine flexible manufacturing with flexible marketing to greatly enhance customer choices.[34] The most famous example is Dell's Web site, which allows the customer to build a seemingly endless variety of combinations of features into a laptop or desktop to create a computer that, if not perfectly customized, certainly gives the buyer the strong impression of creating his or her very own machine.[35]

So far in this chapter we have explored common misconceptions about marketing and then moved well past the stereotypes to begin to gain a solid foundation for understanding what marketing management really is about today. Given the increasingly rapid pace of changes in today's business environment, it's highly likely that marketing's role will evolve even more rapidly than in the past. Let's look to the future to identify important change drivers that are sure to impact marketing over the next decade and beyond.

CHANGE DRIVERS IMPACTING THE FUTURE OF MARKETING

A great way to systematically explore the future of marketing is by considering several well-documented broad trends that are likely to impact the future of the field. These trends are well under way, but their ultimate impact on marketing and on business in general is not yet fully known. Five areas of shift are:

- Shift to product glut and customer shortage.
- Shift in information power from marketer to customer.
- Shift in generational values and preferences.
- Shift to demanding return on marketing investment.
- Shift to distinguishing Marketing ("Big M") from marketing ("little m").

Shift to Product Glut and Customer Shortage

Fred Wiersema, in his book *The New Market Leaders,* builds a powerful case that the balance of power is shifting between marketers and their customers, both in business-to-consumer (B2C/end user) markets and business-to-business (B2B)

EXHIBIT 1.3 **Fred Wiersema's New Market Realities**

Fred Wiersema has identified several factors, which he calls "new market realities," contributing to the shift to product glut and customer shortage.

COMPETITORS PROLIFERATE

Most companies are facing ever accelerating competition—sometimes referred to as *hypercompetition* because of the speed at which competitors and their products enter and leave markets. And this competition often comes from unexpected sources. For example, Boeing now lends money to customers to buy its planes, thus making Boeing a competitor of banks. And McDonald's famously missed for several years the trend of full-service restaurants such as Outback Steakhouse and TGI Friday's offering call-ahead drive-up food pickup, which in essence made this genre of restaurant faster and more convenient than the supposedly "fast-food" outlets like McDonald's.

ALL SECRETS ARE OPEN SECRETS

Today no company can expect its best practices to remain proprietary very long. Firms are becoming more adept at learning competitors' secrets and adapting them for their own purposes. Everybody seems to be imitating everybody else. The acceleration of technology and proliferation of information only exacerbate this process.

INNOVATION IS UNIVERSAL

Product life cycles keep getting shorter and continuous innovation is now *expected* and even common. It has gotten so frantic that customers are inundated with products (over 25,000 new packaged goods in a typical year) and suppliers are dizzy from pursuit of "the next best thing." Today, innovation is not optional; firms either innovate or perish.

INFORMATION OVERWHELMS AND DEPRECIATES

Everyone is swamped with information. Quoting Wiersema: "Junk mail fills mailboxes; magazines stuffed with ads run as long as 500 pages . . . advertisers stamp their logos on every conceivable surface, from cruising blimps and ski-lift towers to e-mail screens and bus roofs. Some television markets offer 200 cable channels. An Internet surfer discovers a Milky Way of random data, much of it conflicting and some of it stupefying." Our problem as managers today isn't how to generate and disseminate information, it's how to screen and prioritize it, digest the relevant portions, and make sense of how to apply it to our business challenges.

EASY GROWTH MAKES HARD TIMES

Growth as the overarching mantra of business has its drawbacks. U.S. carmakers routinely produce 30 to 40 percent more cars than can be readily sold. Airlines keep squeezing costs to pack more and more passengers into fewer and fewer planes and routes. The cellular phone industry continues to condense the number of providers to take advantage of network infrastructure and increased bandwidths. In industry after industry, technology and other factors make it possible to make more things faster. Yes, in business, growth *is* sacred but it can also lead to overcapacity, a shortage of customers, fewer sales, lowering prices, and ultimately falling margins and profits, especially when a focus on cost cutting for profit growth diminishes new-product development.

CUSTOMERS HAVE LESS TIME THAN EVER

For a host of cultural and workplace-related reasons, many people today simply have very little time left in their daily lives for watching an ad or even shopping for a product! A company's biggest threat might not be its competitive rival, but rather the escalating demands on customers' time. Pressed for time and overstimulated by too many choices, people cope by tuning out. Brands and their messages have to catch people's attention in a nanosecond because that's all the time they will give. They are not paying attention; they are scanning. And this is going to keep getting much worse!

markets. He identifies "six new market realities" in support of this trend: Competitors proliferate, all secrets are open secrets, innovation is universal, information overwhelms and depreciates, easy growth makes hard times, and customers have less time than ever.[36] Wiersema's ideas are expanded in Exhibit 1.3 above.

Wiersema's central point is that not only is a customer orientation desirable, but in today's market it is also a *necessity for survival*. Coming to grips with the impact of his six market realities greatly heightens the role of marketing in the firm as the nexus of an organization's customer-focused strategies.

Amazon makes distinctions between customer experience and customer service. Founder Jeff Bezos explains, "Customer experience includes having the lowest price, having the fastest delivery, having it reliable enough so that you don't need to contact anyone. Then you save customer service for the truly unusual situations (for example, I got my book and pages 47 through 58 are missing)." One customer, Lisa Dias, ordered a book that was supposed to be "like new." However, the worksheets were already filled in. Amazon immediately gave her a refund and let her keep the book. Now *that's* customer service![37]

Shift in Information Power from Marketer to Customer

Nowadays, customers of all kinds have nearly limitless access to information about companies, products, competitors, other customers, and even detailed elements of marketing plans and strategies. This is analogous to Wiersema's "All Secrets Are Open Secrets," but here we're talking about the customer's perspective. For decades, marketers held a degree of information power over their customers because firms had access to detailed and sophisticated information about their products and services that customers couldn't get without the help of somebody in the firm (usually a salesperson). Now, customers are empowered to access boundless information about all kinds of products and services on the Internet.[38]

For competitive reasons, firms have no choice but to be more open about their businesses and products. Even if they wanted to, firms can't stop chat rooms, independent Web sites, Web logs or blogs, and other customer-generated modes of communication from filling Web page after Web page with information, disinformation, and opinions about a company's products, services, and even company dirty laundry. Consider Walmart, one of the world's most successful companies. In recent years Walmart has been caught off guard by the number and voracity of uncontrollable information sources about it and its activities. Another example of this shift in information power is the physician/patient relationship. Between open direct-to-consumer advertising by pharmaceutical companies and innumerable Web sites devoted to every medical malady, more and more patients arrive at the doctor's office self-diagnosed and ready to self-prescribe![39]

The trend toward more information in the hands of the customer is not going to diminish. Marketing approaches must be altered to reflect and respond to this important change.

Shift in Generational Values and Preferences

Aspects of generational marketing will be discussed in more detail in Chapter 7. For now, the inexorable shift in values and preferences from generation to generation deserves mention as one of the key trends affecting the future of marketing. One clear impact is on the firm's message and the method by which that message is communicated. For example, GenY consumers tend to be much more receptive to electronic commerce as a primary mode of receiving marketing communication and ultimately purchasing than are prior generations.[40] Yet, many of the big insurance firms continue to rely on face-to-face selling as their primary business model. State Farm, Allstate, and Farmers Insurance Group all have been affected by upstarts such as Progressive and GEICO, which appeal to a younger customer who is disinterested in being sold in person by an agent and more inclined to engage in a quick in-and-out transaction online or by phone—and often at a lower price. This preference has clear implications for how marketing carries out its management of customer relationships across generations and also calls into question how much *value* younger customers derive from the different approaches to relationships. That is, do members of the younger generation appreciate, or even need, the kinds of close personal relationships companies like State Farm provide through their agents, or are they perfectly happy to interact with firms exclusively through electronic means?

Generational shifts also impact marketing in terms of human resources. Consider how generational differences in attitudes toward work life versus family life, expectations about job satisfaction and rewards, and preferred modes of learning and working (e.g., electronic versus face-to-face) affect the ability of firms to hire people into various marketing-related positions. For example, firms often wish to differentiate themselves by offering great service to their customers. Yet, nearly all organizations are severely challenged today in hiring and keeping high-quality customer service personnel because of a severe shortage of capable, qualified customer care personnel.[41]

Generational changes are nothing new. Both in the context of customers and organization members, understanding the generational differences and how to work to appeal to different generations' values and preferences is a critical part of marketing management. Today, the importance of this issue is accentuated and accelerated in marketing due to propensities among generational groups to differentially use technology and the impact of generational differences on workplace design and management practice.

Shift to Distinguishing Marketing (Big M) from marketing (little m)

Earlier it was established that the marketing concept is intended to be an overarching business philosophy in which firms place the customer at the core of the enterprise. Also, you have learned through reading some of the stereotypical impressions of what marketing is (and is not) that marketing—at least the *image* of marketing—can be fairly fragmented and often quite tactical in nature. How can marketing as a discipline that is both strategic and tactical be rectified?

Begin by thinking of marketing as occurring on two dimensions within an organization. These dimensions exist in tandem, and even intersect on occasion, but still hold fundamental differences in goals and properties. For convenience, we can distinguish these dimensions by capitalizing the word for one ("Marketing"—"Big M") and leaving the word in lower case for the other ("marketing"—"little m"). Exhibit 1.4 portrays this relationship. Let's investigate these concepts further.

EXHIBIT 1.4 **Strategic and Tactical Marketing**

Marketing (Big M)
Strategic Marketing

Customer at the Core

marketing (little m)
tactical marketing

Marketing (Big M)

Marketing (Big M) serves as a core driver of business strategy. That is, an understanding of markets, competitors, and other external forces, coupled with attention to internal capabilities, allows a firm to successfully develop strategies for the future. This approach is often referred to as **strategic marketing,** which means a long-term, firm-level commitment to investing in marketing—supported at the highest organization level—for the purpose of enhancing organizational performance.

Going back to the AMA definition, marketing's focus as ". . . the activity, set of institutions, and processes for creating, communicating, delivering, and exchanging offerings that have value for customers, clients, partners, and society at large," contains substantial elements of Marketing (Big M): The core concepts of customer value, exchange, customer relationships, and benefit to the organization and its stakeholders are all very strategic in nature and help form the core business philosophy of a firm. Earlier we saw that the marketing concept includes a strong Marketing (Big M) thrust: ". . . an organization-wide customer orientation with the objective of achieving long-run profits." Certainly the core marketing concept characteristics of an organization-wide customer orientation and long-run profits are very strategic. Both the AMA definition of marketing and the long-standing marketing concept provide evidence of the centrality of Marketing (Big M) to the firm as a core business philosophy.

The concept of Marketing (Big M) necessitates several important actions on the part of the organization to maximize marketing's impact. Consider these action elements required for successful Marketing (Big M):

- Make sure *everyone* in an organization, regardless of their position or title, understands the concept of customer orientation, which places the customer at the core of all aspects of the enterprise. It doesn't matter whether or not the organization member directly interfaces with customers outside the firm. The point is that everybody has customers within the organization, and through the process of effectively serving those internal customers, the firm can better serve its external customers. In this way, everyone in the firm has a stake in the success of Marketing (Big M).

- Align all internal organizational processes and systems around the customer. Don't let the IT system, telecommunications system, billing system, or any other internal process or system become an impediment to a customer orientation. If the people inside a firm understand the power of a customer-centric business approach, but the internal systems don't support it, Marketing (Big M) won't be successful.

- Find somebody at the top of the firm to consistently champion this Marketing (Big M) business philosophy. The CEO is the most appropriate person for this role, perhaps manifest through the CMO (chief marketing officer). Like anything else of importance in a business organization, Marketing (Big M) takes resources, patience, and time to acculturate and implement, and it won't happen unless someone at the top is consistently supportive, both with resources and leadership.

- Forget the concept that the marketing department is where Marketing (Big M) takes place. Marketing (Big M) is not about what one department does or does not do. Marketing (Big M) is the basis on which an organization approaches its whole enterprise–remember Peter Drucker's words: "[Marketing] is the *whole business* . . . seen from the *customer's* point of view. Concern and responsibility for marketing must, therefore, permeate all areas of the enterprise." Drucker was right!

- Create *market-driving*, not just *market-driven*, strategies. It is imperative to study the market and competition as part of the marketing planning process. Firms today must break out of linear thinking when developing new products and markets. Certainly research on markets and customers can uncover unmet needs and offer guidance on designing products to fulfill those needs. But the process contributes little toward **market creation**–approaches that drive the market toward fulfilling a whole new set of needs that customers did not realize was possible or feasible before. Classic examples of market creation include Microsoft's revolution of the information field, Disney's creation of the modern theme park industry, and Apple's revolution in integrated telecommunications via the iPhone. These were all market-driving strategies that created really new markets.

marketing (little m)

In contrast, **marketing (little m)** serves the firm and its stakeholders at a functional or operational level; hence, marketing (little m) is often thought of as **tactical marketing.** In fact, marketing (little m) almost always takes place at the functional or operational level of a firm. Specific programs and tactics aimed at customers and other stakeholder groups tend to emanate from marketing (little m).[42] But marketing (little m) always needs to be couched within the philosophy, culture, and strategies of the firm's Marketing (Big M). In this way, Marketing (Big M) and marketing (little m) should be quite naturally connected within a firm, as the latter tends to represent the day-to-day operationalization and implementation of the former. Everything from brand image, to the message salespeople and advertisements deliver, to customer service, to packaging and product features, to the chosen distribution channel—in fact, all elements of the marketing mix and beyond—exemplify marketing (little m).

Understanding these two dimensions of marketing helps clarify much of the confusion surrounding the field today. It certainly helps explain much of the confusion surrounding what marketing management is supposed to be, and how and why the field tends to have a bit of an identity crisis both inside firms and with the public at large. Occasionally throughout this book, the Marketing (Big M), marketing (little m) notion will be brought up to add explanatory power to important points. But for the most part, we'll just use one version of the word, assuming we all understand it contains both levels.

Shift to Justifying the Relevance and Payback of the Marketing Investment

The final change driver affecting the future of marketing is a topic on the minds of many CEOs and CMOs today. The issue is how management can effectively measure and assess the level of success a firm's investment in various aspects of marketing has had. Appropriate and effective **marketing metrics** must be designed to identify, track, evaluate, and provide key benchmarks for improvement just as various financial metrics guide the financial management of the firm.[43] The Marketing Science Institute (MSI) has commissioned research for the marketing field funded by a number of large companies. Every two years, MSI publishes a list of research priorities that top organizations are willing to fund with large sums of money to further the practice of marketing management. In recent years, the topic of marketing metrics has been one of the highest priorities for most MSI member companies, especially connecting appropriate metrics to marketing management decision making.[44]

Why the intense focus on metrics? Here are several important reasons:

- *Marketing is a fuzzy field.* Marketing has often historically viewed itself as working within gray area comfort zones of a business. That is, if what marketing contributed was mostly creative in nature, how can the impact of such activities effectively be measured? For the marketer, this can be a somewhat attractive position to be in, and historically many marketers probably took advantage of the idea that their activities were above measurement. Those days are over.

- *If it can't be measured, it can't be managed.* As with all aspects of business, effective management of the various aspects of marketing requires quantification of objectives and results. The marketing plan is one of the

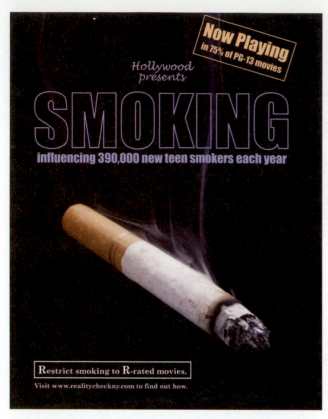

Marketing is a powerful tool in gaining regulatory changes.

Courtesy Tobacco Control Program, New York State Department of Health.

most important elements of a business plan. Effective planning requires metrics.

- *Is marketing an expense or an investment?* Practicing marketers tend to pitch marketing internally as an investment in the future success of the organization. As an investment, it is not unreasonable that expected returns be identified and measured.

- *CEOs and stockholders expect marketing accountability.* A few years ago, MSI published a report with the provocative title "Can Marketing Regain Its Seat at the Table?" The report centered on the fragmentation of marketing and ways marketing can recover its relevance in firms where it has become underutilized and undervalued, and has therefore lost its seat on the executive committee. One of the major conclusions of the report is that marketers need to create tools for ongoing, meaningful measurement of marketing productivity. More and more, CMOs are being held accountable for marketing performance in the same manner as are CFOs and leaders of other functional aspects of the business.[45]

This section has identified and examined several core change drivers that are sure to impact the future of marketing. Clearly, many other trends in the macrolevel environment of business also affect marketing, including the obvious examples of globalization, ethnic diversification, and the growth and proliferation of technology. The next section develops the concept of global marketing a bit further.

MARKETING IS NOT LIMITED BY BORDERS

From large multinationals to small start-up companies, business is no longer confined to a company's local market. Worldwide distribution networks, sophisticated communication tools, greater product standardization, and the Internet have opened world markets. Large companies such as Nestlé, Procter & Gamble, IBM, and General Electric leverage their considerable assets to build global companies that do business anywhere in the world (see Exhibit 1.5). At the same time, with relatively minimal investment, small companies access international markets with only a Web site and an international shipping company.[46]

While the opportunities have never been greater, the risks have also never been higher. Global marketing mistakes are expensive. The international competitive landscape includes sophisticated global companies as well as successful local organizations. The operating environment varies dramatically around the world creating real challenges for companies moving into new markets. Global customers demand different products, which means that successful products in a company's local market frequently have to be adapted to new markets.[47] All these factors establish global marketing as one of the most demanding but rewarding areas in marketing.

As you study topics such as marketing communications, product development, or consumer decision making, consider how each is affected by global markets. Our goal is to identify very early in your study of marketing management the challenges marketers face in global markets today. While it is certainly true that the global marketing manager for Huggies has different challenges than the marketing manager for a small software company, it is equally true that both need

EXHIBIT 1.5 **World's Largest International Companies in 2009**

Company	Revenue ($ Millions)
ExxonMobil	$442,851
Walmart	405,607
Chevron	263,159
Conoco Phillips	230,764
General Electric	183,207
General Motors	148,979
Ford Motor	146,277
AT&T	124,028
Hewlett-Packard	118,364
Valero Energy	118,298

Source: From *Fortune Global 500*, May 4, 2009. Copyright © 2009 *Time*, Inc. All rights reserved.

to know how marketing internationally is similar and different to marketing in their home market. Because marketing has no borders we put this discussion at the beginning of the book.

Procter & Gamble is the world's largest producer of household and personal products by revenue. It owns multiple popular brands including Crest, Charmin, Gillette, and Tide. Even though only 15 to 20 percent of new products succeed, P&G's success rate exceeds 50 percent. P&G's priority is global branding; in this industry its products are exposed to more than half of the world's 6.7 billion consumers. Much of P&G's future growth will be through emerging global markets, with the majority of future manufacturing facilities being built there.[48]

THE GLOBAL EXPERIENCE LEARNING CURVE

An understanding of marketing beyond home markets develops over time as a company gets more international business experience. This process is referred to as the **global experience learning curve**. In some cases this happens quickly. General Motors moved into Canada in 1918, only two years after being incorporated, and eBay opened in the United Kingdom during its first year of operation. However, other companies take much longer to push into global markets. Walmart opened its first international store in Mexico City in 1991; nearly 30 years after Sam Walton opened the first store in

Bennetton takes a global perspective targeting the United States and other countries around the world with many different products.

Bentonville, Arkansas. Exhibit 1.6 lists the global expansion histories of a number of companies.

The global experience learning curve moves a company through four distinct stages: no foreign marketing, foreign marketing, international marketing, and global marketing. The process is not always linear; companies may, for example, move directly from no foreign marketing to international marketing without necessarily engaging in foreign marketing. In addition, the amount of time spent in any stage can vary; some companies remain in a stage for many years.

Companies with Indirect Foreign Marketing

Many companies with **indirect foreign marketing** do business with international customers through intermediaries or limited direct contact. In these cases, however, there is no formal international channel relationship or global marketing strategy targeted at international customers. Of course, any company with a Web site is now a global company as someone can visit the site from anywhere in the world, but companies with no foreign marketing consider any sales to an international customer as incidental.

The typical company with no foreign marketing is usually small with a limited range of products. Increasingly though, small companies move into international

EXHIBIT 1.6	Examples of Expansion into Global Markets	
Years to Expansion	**U. S. Company**	**First Expansion**
29	Walmart (est. 1962)	1991: Walmart opens two units in Mexico City.
20	Hewlett-Packard (est. 1939)	1959: HP sets up a European marketing organization in Geneva, Switzerland, and a manufacturing plant in Germany.
26	Tyson Foods (est. 1963)	1989: Tyson establishes a partnership with a Mexican poultry company to create an international partnership.
25	Caterpillar (est. 1925)	1950: Caterpillar Tractor Co. Ltd. in Great Britain is founded.
19	Home Depot (est. 1979)	1998: Home Depot enters the Puerto Rican market followed by entry into Argentina.
18	Gap (est. 1969)	1987: The first Gap store outside the United States opens in London on George Street.
12	Goodyear (est. 1898)	1910: Goodyear's Canadian plant opens.
10	FedEx (est. 1971)	1981: International delivery begins with service to Canada.
1	PepsiCo (est. 1965)	1966: Pepsi enters Japan and Eastern Europe.

markets much faster than even a decade ago. This is due, in part, to domestic distributor relationships, local customers with global operations, and effective Web sites, which have all created international opportunities for many small companies with limited resources.

Companies with Direct Foreign Marketing

Companies often develop a more formal international strategy by following their existing customers into foreign markets. Domestic customers with global operations may demand more service or place additional orders that require the company to work with their foreign subsidiaries. This stage of the global experience learning curve is called **direct foreign marketing** and involves developing local distribution and service representation in a foreign market in one of two ways. One method is to identify local intermediaries in appropriate international markets and create a formal relationship. The second approach is for the company to establish its own direct sales force in major markets, thereby expanding the company's direct market reach.

In either scenario, key activities (product planning and development, production) are still done in the company's home market, but products are modified to fit international requirements. Global markets are important enough for management to build international sales forecasts, and manufacturing allocates time specifically to international production. At this point, international markets are no longer an afterthought but, rather, an integral, albeit small, part of the company's growth model.[49]

International Marketing

When a firm makes the commitment to produce products outside its domestic market it is engaged in **international marketing.** While companies can be heavily involved in international markets with extensive selling organizations and distribution networks, the decision to produce outside its home market marks a significant shift toward an integrated international market strategy. Global markets become an essential component of the company's growth strategy, and resources are allocated to expand the business into those markets. The company incorporates an international division or business unit that has responsibility for growing the business in targeted foreign markets.

International marketing aligns the company's assets and resources with global markets, but, in the vast majority of companies, management still takes a "domestic first" approach to the business. As a result, the corporate structure still divides international and domestic markets.

Global Marketing

A **global marketing** company realizes that all world markets (including the company's own domestic market) are, in reality, a single market with many different segments. This frequently happens when a company generates more than half its revenue in international markets. Exhibit 1.7 highlights companies considered traditional American companies but that generate more than half their revenue outside the United States.

The most significant difference between international and global marketing organizations is management philosophy and corporate planning. Global marketers treat the world as a single, unified market with many different segments that may or may not fall along country political boundaries. International marketers, on the other hand, define markets along traditional political boundaries and, most often, assign unique status to their domestic market.

Company	Percent of Sales from International Markets
Coca-Cola	71%
McDonald's	66
Hewlett-Packard	65
Dow Chemical	62
Nike	62
3M	61
Motorola	54
Caterpillar	52
Chevron	52

YOUR MARKETING MANAGEMENT JOURNEY BEGINS

Some students take the marketing management course because they "have to," not necessarily because they see inherent value in marketing for their career as a leader and manager. It is our hope that if you initially fell into this category, you can now see that gaining the knowledge and skills required for marketing management will increase your worth as an asset to any firm, regardless of your position or job title.

As you progress through this course, keep in mind that marketing management is not so much a position or a job title as it is a process and a way of approaching decision making about important business opportunities and challenges. Our presumption throughout this book is that you are seeking knowledge and skills that will enable you to use marketing to its fullest potential to positively impact organizational performance. Be assured from the outset that a high level of personal and career value can be derived by investing time and energy now in mastering the leadership and management of marketing.

SUMMARY

Marketing as an activity, set of institutions, and processes adds value to a firm and its internal and external stakeholders in many ways. For a marketing manager to be successful, he or she must approach the job with a strong understanding of what it takes to do great marketing *today,* which because of a variety of change drivers is very different from doing marketing in the past. Leading and managing the facets of marketing in order to improve individual, unit, and organizational performance—marketing management—is a core business activity in today's business milieu, worthy of study and mastery by any student of business regardless of job title or professional or educational background.

Global marketing has become synonymous with marketing. Companies cannot rely solely on their domestic markets for long-term growth. Technology and sophisticated distribution systems make it easy for a company anywhere in the world to become an international marketer. However, companies generally go through a global experience learning curve as their international business expands.

APPLICATION QUESTIONS

1. Put yourself in the role of a marketing manager. From this perspective, do you agree with the concepts of societal marketing and sustainability? Why or why not? How does a focus on sustainability affect the marketing manager's role and activities? Identify two organizations that you believe do a great job of paying attention to sustainability and present the evidence that leads you to this conclusion.

2. Review the section on change drivers, including Fred Wiersema's list of new market realities. Select any two of the key change drivers (these can include any from Wiersema's list or any of the others) within the section. Pick an organization of your choice and answer the following questions:

   a. In what ways do each of the change drivers impact the firm's ability to successfully do marketing?

   b. How is the firm responding to the change drivers in the way it approaches its business? What should it be doing that it is not doing at present?

   c. What role do you believe the marketing manager has in proactively preparing for these and future change drivers?

3. You are the marketing manager for a small company located in the United States that manufactures specialized parts for high-end ink-jet printers. The company's largest customer (Hewlett-Packard) has asked your company to supply parts to 10 of its distribution and repair sites around the world. The company has never sold products outside the United States so this represents a significant step for the company. What stage in the global experience learning curve is the company likely entering and why? Identify the activities the company should undertake at this stage.

CHAPTER 02

Elements of Marketing Strategy and Planning

LEARNING OBJECTIVES

- Examine the concept of value and the elements and role of the value chain.

- Understand the conditions required for successful marketing planning: Marketing planning is focused on the value proposition and is a dynamic process.

- Identify various types of organizational strategies.

- Conduct a situation analysis.

- Use the framework provided for marketing planning, along with the content in future chapters, to build a marketing plan.

VALUE IS AT THE CORE OF MARKETING

In Chapter 1, the concept of value was introduced as a core element of marketing. Value was defined from a customer's perspective as a ratio of the bundle of benefits a customer receives from an offering compared to the costs incurred by the customer in acquiring that bundle of benefits. From the late management guru Peter Drucker's early writings in the 1950s to the recently updated American Marketing Association official definition of marketing, it is clear that marketing plays a central role in creating, communicating, delivering, and exchanging offerings that have value.

Let's examine the idea of value a bit more carefully now. One can think of value as a ratio of benefits to costs, as viewed from the eyes of the beholder (the customer). That is, customers incur a variety of costs in doing business with any firm, be those financial costs, time, opportunity costs, or others. For the investment of these costs, the customer has a right to expect a certain bundle of benefits in return. A **benefit** is some type of utility that a company and its products (and services) provide its customers. **Utility** is the want-satisfying power of a good or service.[1] Four major kinds of utility exist: form, time, place, and ownership. *Form utility* is created when the firm converts raw materials into finished products that are desired by the market. The other three utilities—*time, place,* and *ownership*—are created by marketing. They are created when products

America's milk producers continue to market their product through strong personal appeals.

are available to customers at a convenient location when they want to purchase them, and facilities of *exchange* are available that allow for transfer of the product ownership from seller to buyer. Chapter 1 mentioned that facilitating exchange between buyers and sellers is another core element of marketing.

Since value is a ratio of benefits to costs, a firm can impact the customer's perceptions of value by altering the benefits, the costs, or both. Assume that a person is faced with the decision of buying one of two automobiles. One should expect that a purchase decision will be greatly influenced by the ratio of costs (not just monetary) versus benefits for each model. That is, it is not just pure price that drives the decision. It is price compared with all the various benefits (or utilities) that Car 1 brings versus Car 2.[2] These benefits could relate to availability, style, prestige, features—all sorts of factors beyond mere price.

South Korean automaker Hyundai understands that price is not the only influence on purchase decisions. Hyundai became the first automaker in the United States to offer a full vehicle return policy that allows an owner to walk away from a loan or lease without any negative equity. "Hyundai Assurance" lets buyers who lose their jobs in the first year of ownership return their car with no harm to their credit. The program builds confidence in the purchase and reflects very favorably on the value of Hyundai to customers. It resulted in an immediately favorable impact on sales.[3]

Recall that marketing is charged not just with *creating* offerings that have value, but also with *communicating, delivering,* and *exchanging* those offerings. When a firm communicates the **value proposition** of its products to customers, the value message may include the whole bundle of benefits the company promises to deliver, not just the benefits of the product itself.[4] For example, when South Korean-based Samsung first brought its brand to the United States, it communicated a message centered primarily on functionality at a moderate price—a strategy designed to provide an advantage over pricier Japanese brands. But over time, Samsung's value proposition has expanded to include innovativeness, style, and dependability—the latter of which was helped significantly by high ratings of many of the company's products by sources such as *Consumer Reports*.[5]

For years, firms have been preoccupied with measuring **customer satisfaction,** which at its most fundamental level means how much the customer likes the product. However, for firms interested in building long-term customer relationships, having satisfied customers is not enough to ensure the relationship is going to last. A firm's value proposition must be strong enough to move customers past mere satisfaction and into a commitment to a company and its products and brands for the long run. Such a commitment reflects a high level of **customer loyalty,** which increases **customer retention** and reduces **customer switching.**[6]

Customer loyalty almost always is directly related to the various sources of value the customer is presently deriving from the relationship with the company and its brands. Except in situations of monopoly (which creates forced loyalty), loyal customers by definition tend to also experience a high level of satisfaction.[7] However, not all satisfied customers are loyal. If a competitor comes along with a better value proposition, or if a value proposition begins to slip or is not effectively communicated, customers who are presently satisfied become good candidates for switching to another company's products.[8]

To retain customers longer, some companies are selling products through storytelling. Jeff Gomez, founder of Starlight Runner, creates narratives to help companies such as Disney, Coca-Cola, and Mattel expand their franchises. Starlight Runner conceived a backstory for Coca-Cola by creating the "Happiness Factory," a television commercial featuring an Oz-like world where flying fish and furry creatures toil inside vending machines. Such backstories are intended to get customers hooked on an existing idea—whether a movie, toy, soda, or other offering.[9]

The Value Chain

A highly useful approach to bringing together and understanding the concepts of customer value, satisfaction, and loyalty is the **value chain.** Created by Michael Porter in his classic book *Competitive Advantage,* the value chain serves as a means for firms to identify ways to create, communicate, and deliver more customer value within a firm.[10] Exhibit 2.1 portrays Porter's value chain concept.

Basically, the value chain concept holds that every organization represents a synthesis of activities involved in designing, producing, marketing, delivering, and supporting its products. The value chain identifies nine relevant strategic activities the organization can engage in that create/impact both sides of the value equation: benefits and costs. Porter's nine **value-creating activities** include five primary activities and four support activities.[11]

The five *primary activities* in the value chain are:

1. *Inbound logistics*—how the firm goes about sourcing raw materials for production.
2. *Operations*—how the firm converts the raw materials into final products.
3. *Outbound logistics*—how the firm transports and distributes the final products to the marketplace.

EXHIBIT 2.1 | **Porter's Value Chain**

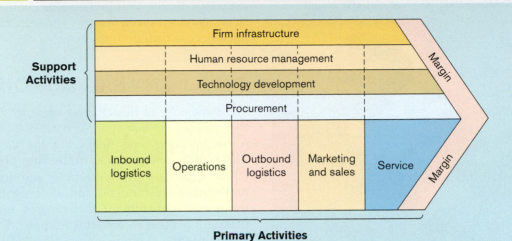

4. *Marketing and sales*—how the firm communicates the value proposition to the marketplace.

5. *Service*—how the firm supports customers during and after the sale.

The four *support activities* in the value chain are:

1. *Firm infrastructure*—how the firm is set up for doing business; are the internal processes aligned and efficient?

2. *Human resource management*—how the firm ensures it has the right people in place, trains them, and keeps them.

3. *Technology development*—how the firm embraces technology usage for the benefit of customers.

4. *Procurement*—how the firm deals with vendors and quality issues.

The value chain concept is highly useful in understanding the major activities through which a firm creates, communicates, and delivers value for its customers. CEOs in recent years have been concentrating on *aligning* the various elements of the value chain, meaning that all facets of the company are working together to ensure that no snags will negatively impact the firm's value proposition.[12] From a customer's perspective, when the supplier's value chain is working well, all the customer tends to see are the *results* of a well-aligned value chain: quality products, good salespeople, on-time delivery, prompt service after the sale, and so on. However, it takes only one weak link in the value chain and the whole process of cultivating satisfied and loyal customers can be circumvented.

Consider, for example, what happens if a glitch in the value chain of one of Walmart's vendors delays delivery of products at the peak selling season, resulting in stock-outs in Walmart stores. If this happens repeatedly, it can damage the overall relationship Walmart enjoys with its customers as well as the relationship between Walmart and that supplier. To minimize the potential for this happening, Walmart, as well as a growing list of other firms, requires all vendors to link with its IT system so that the whole process of order fulfillment and inventory management is as seamless as possible.[13]

THE MOST IMPORTANT DECISIONS START WITH THE MOST IMPORTANT PEOPLE.

There's strong. And then there's Army Strong. You taught them right from wrong. You told them they could do anything. Now they want the discipline, leadership training and college benefits that come from being in the U.S. Army. If your son or daughter wants to talk about joining, listen. You just might be proud of what they have to say. Find out more at goarmy.com/for_parents.

U.S.ARMY
ARMY STRONG.

Private Matthew Bryan

Governmental entities such as the U.S. Army often do sophisticated marketing planning, as evidenced by this ad.

One final element depicted at the end of the value chain is margin, which refers to profit made by the firm. Intelligent investment in the primary and support activities within the value chain should positively enhance profit margin through more efficient and effective firm performance.[14]

Planning for the Value Offering

The remainder of this chapter presents the approach that marketing managers use to plan for creating, communicating, and delivering the value offering. This is often referred to as **marketing planning**—the ongoing process of developing and implementing market-driven strategies for an organization—and the resulting document that records the marketing planning process in a useful framework is the **marketing plan.**[15]

MARKETING PLANNING IS BOTH STRATEGIC AND TACTICAL

Recall that one key trend identified in Chapter 1 was the practice of marketing on two dimensions or levels within an organization. Although these dimensions exist in tandem and even intersect on occasion, each holds fundamental differences in goals and properties. At the strategic level, Marketing (Big M) serves as a core driver of business strategy. That is, an understanding of markets, competitors, and other external forces, coupled with attention to internal capabilities, allows a firm to successfully develop strategies for the future. At the functional or operational level, marketing (little m) represents the specific programs and tactics aimed at customers and other stakeholder groups and includes everything from brand image, to the message salespeople and advertisements deliver, to customer service, to packaging and product features—in fact, all elements of operationalizing the marketing mix and beyond.[16]

Vodafone, the telecommunications company, aims to outdo competitors in the mobile phone applications business with marketing planning that is both strategic and tactical. The company works hard to stay ahead of competitors in products and markets, and it will soon offer a product with the capability to pinpoint the location of customers when they're using applications on their phone. This offering could open up a wide range of innovative new wireless Internet capabilities and support geo-targeting. In addition, Vodafone will offer applications that will work across a variety of handset software environments—something that Apple and Nokia do not yet offer.[17]

Although these two levels of marketing are distinctly different in scope and activities, the common link is in the process of marketing planning. Marketing managers must be able to grasp both the big picture of strategy formulation and the details of tactical implementation. In fact, many a marketing plan has failed because either the formulation of the strategies was flawed or their implementation was poorly executed. A well-written marketing plan must fully address both

Marketing (Big M) and marketing (little m) elements. Ultimately, the following must be in place for effective marketing planning to occur:

- *Everyone* in an organization, regardless of their position or title, must understand and support the concept of customer orientation, which places the customer at the core of all aspects of the enterprise. Firms that promote and practice a high level of customer focus are often referred to as *customer-centric* organizations.[18]
- To operationalize a customer-centric approach, all internal organizational processes and systems must be aligned around the customer. A firm's internal structure and systems cannot be allowed to become an impediment to a customer orientation.[19] Anyone who has ever placed a phone call for service and been driven through a maze of phone transfers with a string of people (or machines) unable to help knows how poor structure and systems can impact customer satisfaction and loyalty!

Success often results from marketing an *experience* rather than just a physical product. Customer-centric companies such as Starbucks, McDonald's, and Cold Stone Creamery set out to make a deep emotional connection with customers, while defining and guiding customers' experiences. Former Cold Stone Creamery CEO Doug Ducey wanted the brand to be known as the "ultimate ice cream experience." Cold Stone separates itself from other ice cream stores by the experience it provides: employees who will sing for tips, free ice cream on your birthday, and the creative names "like it" "love it" "gotta have it" for small, medium, and large portions.[20]

- The CEO and others at the top of the organization must consistently set the tone for market-driven strategic planning through the customer-centric business philosophy. As with a firm's internal structure and systems, its culture must be supportive of such an approach for a marketing plan to be successful. Upper management must also support the process through consistent investment of resources necessary to make it work. Marketing planning is not a "sometimes" process; rather, it should be a driving force in the firm day in and day out.[21]

At this point in the learning process about marketing management, you may begin to feel concerned that you are getting a lot of structure for marketing planning but not enough specific content to fill in the elements of the marketing plan template. That reaction is quite natural, as by design the depth of content for most of the various sections of a marketing plan is covered later in the book. Your next task is to familiarize yourself with the overall process and framework for marketing planning so that as the content pieces unfold chapter by chapter, it will be very clear how those pieces fit together into a complete marketing plan. Beginning with this one, each chapter ends with an activity called "Marketing Plan Exercises." These are designed to help you make the connections between the content in each chapter and the requirements of your marketing plan template.

ELEMENTS OF MARKETING PLANNING

To get you started, we'll first walk through the process and content involved in marketing planning. A condensed framework for this process is presented in Exhibit 2.2. Then at the end of this chapter you'll find a URL to an abbreviated marketing plan example for the fictitious company CloudCab Small Jet Taxi Service. You'll want to access that URL to see what the key elements of a marketing plan look like in practice.

EXHIBIT 2.2 | **Condensed Framework for Marketing Planning**

- Ensure the marketing plan is connected to the firm's business plan including organizational-level mission, vision, goals, objectives, and strategies.
- Conduct a situation analysis.
  - Macro-level external environment
  - Competitive environment
  - Internal environment
- Perform any needed market research.
- Establish marketing goals and objectives.
- Develop marketing strategies.
  - Product-market combinations
  - Market segmentation, target marketing, positioning

- Marketing mix strategies:
  - Product/branding strategies
  - Service strategies
  - Pricing strategies
  - Supply chain strategies
  - Integrated marketing communication strategies
- Develop implementation plans.
  - Programs/action plans for each strategy including timetable, assignment of responsibilities, and resources required
  - Forecasting and budgets
  - Metrics for marketing control
  - Provide for contingency planning

Connecting the Marketing Plan to the Firm's Business Plan

How does a marketing plan fit into a firm's overall business planning process? As we have learned, marketing is somewhat unique among the functional areas of business in that it has the properties of being both a core business philosophy (Marketing, Big M) and a functional/operational part of the business (marketing, little m). As such, all business-level strategy must be market-driven to be successful. Hence, the term **market-driven strategic planning** is often used to describe the process at the corporate or strategic business unit (SBU) level of marshaling the various resource and functional areas of the firm toward a central purpose around the customer.[22]

A great example of how these levels of planning fit together is General Electric. GE contains numerous SBUs that compete in very different markets, from lighting to jet engines to financial services. CEO Jeff Immelt oversees a **corporate-level strategic plan** to serve as an umbrella plan for the overall direction of the corporation, but the real action in marketing planning at GE is at the individual SBU level. Each GE business has its own **SBU-level strategic plan,** and part of GE's historical leadership culture has been to turn SBU management loose to run their own businesses under their own plans, so long as they meet their performance requirements and contribute satisfactorily to the overall corporate plan.

Portfolio Analysis

Portfolio analysis, which views SBUs and sometimes even product lines as a series of investments from which it expects maximization of returns, is one tool that can contribute to strategic planning in a multi-business corporation. Two of the most popular approaches are the **Boston Consulting Group (BCG) Growth-Share Matrix** and the **GE Business Screen.** These are portrayed in Exhibits 2.3 and 2.4.

The concept of the BCG approach to portfolio analysis is to position each SBU within a firm on the two-dimensional matrix shown in Exhibit 2.3. The competitive market-share dimension is the ratio of share to that of the largest competitor.

EXHIBIT 2.3 **Boston Consulting Group Growth-Share Matrix**

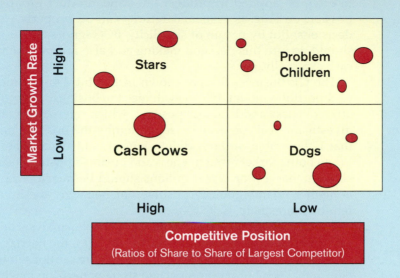

EXHIBIT 2.4 **GE Business Screen**

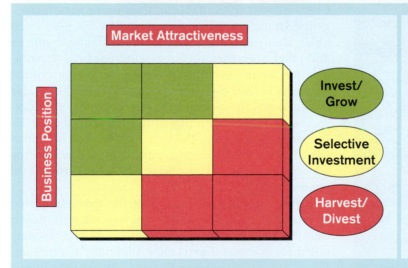

Business Position (high, medium, and low): Assess the firm's ability to compete. Factors include organization, growth, market share by segment, customer loyalty, margins, distribution, technology skills, patents, marketing, and flexibility, among others.

Market Attractiveness (high, medium, and low): For the market, assess size, growth, customer satisfaction levels, competition (quantity, types, effectiveness, commitment), price levels, profitability, technology, governmental regulations, sensitivity to economic trends, among others.

Source: "GE Business Screen," *Business Resource Software Online*, www.brs-inc.com/pwxcharts.asp?32, accessed May 16, 2008.

The growth dimension is intended as a strong indicator of overall market attractiveness. Within the BCG matrix you find four cells, each representing strategy recommendations:

- *Stars* (high share, high growth): important to building the future of the business and deserving any needed investment.
- *Cash Cows* (high share, low growth): key sources of internal cash generation for the firm.
- *Dogs* (low share, low growth): potential high cash users and prime candidates for liquidation.
- *Problem Children,* or Question Marks (low share, high growth): high cash needs that, if properly nurtured, can convert into stars.[23]

For purposes of strategy development, the BCG matrix approach is seductively simple and has contributed to decision making about internal cash generation and usage across SBUs. It has also morphed in application downward to often be applied to product lines and product groups, which is nominally possible so long as costs and returns can be properly isolated for investment decisions. But by nature of simplicity, BCG ignores other important factors that should go into this decision making and also ignores the viability of generating cash externally.

The GE Business Screen, shown in Exhibit 2.4, is a more realistic and complex portfolio model. It also evaluates the business on two dimensions—market attractiveness and business position, which refers to its ability to compete. The investment decision is again suggested by the position on a matrix. A business that is favorable on both dimensions should usually be a candidate to grow. When both market attractiveness and business position evaluations are unfavorable, the harvest or divest options should be raised. When the matrix position is neither unambiguously positive nor negative, the investment decision will require more analysis.

For now, it is important to note that portfolio analysis does not offer a panacea for corporate strategy formulation. In fact, since the heyday of the use of portfolio analysis in the 1970s and 1980s, firms are more cautious in its application and recognize that it is but one approach to strategy decision making.[24]

Functional Level Plans

Each of a firm's SBU plans incorporates **functional-level plans** from operations, marketing, finance, and the other operational areas. Just as the individual SBU CEOs are held accountable for their unit's performance to Jeff Immelt within the context of GE's plan, each SBUs chief marketing officer, chief financial officer, and other operational-level executive is held accountable for the performance of his or her portion of the SBU plan to their own business unit CEO.[25] While GE's system certainly may be larger in scope and complexity than many business planning situations, the logic is the same regardless of the type or size of an organization. Hence, the marketing plan is nested within the context of an overall corporate and/or business-level strategic plan.

Before each of the sections of the marketing plan is identified and described, you are referred to Jet-Blue Airways as an example of a firm that has become noted for successful marketing planning. Clearly, Jet-Blue's not perfect, and in the turbulent airline industry it's really tough to do great marketing planning. In Chapter 1 we discussed Fred Wiersema's "new market realities," one of which is "all secrets are open secrets." During his tenure as chairman and CEO, Jet-Blue founder David Neeleman was quite transparent about his strategies and plans for the company, not only discussing them openly with the business press but also placing a substantial amount of organizational information on the company Web site. This approach has continued in the post-Neeleman era of the firm. And when JetBlue has made missteps, the company has been forthright in recognizing and addressing the errors. As each of the elements of the marketing planning process is described below, JetBlue will be used as a thematic example of each piece in practice.

Marketing planning and strategy, while analytical in nature, often yield very funny marketing communication programs.

Organizational Mission, Vision, Goals, and Objectives

Marketing planning does not occur in a vacuum; it must connect with the firm's overall mission and vision. A **mission statement** articulates an organization's purpose, or reason for existence. A well-conceived mission statement defines the fundamental, unique purpose that sets a company apart from other firms of its type and identifies the scope of a company's operations, products, and markets.[26]

Most mission statements also include a discussion of what the company would like to become in the future—its **strategic vision.** According to ex-GE CEO Jack Welch, "Good business leaders create a vision, articulate the vision, passionately own the vision, and relentlessly drive it to completion."[27] The vision of what the firm is capable of in the future and where it *wants* to go, as championed by its top leadership, sets the tone for everything that follows in the planning process. **Goals,** general statements of what the firm wishes to accomplish in support of the mission and vision, eventually become refined into specific, measurable, and (hopefully) attainable **objectives** for the firm.[28] Objectives at the corporate and SBU level provide the benchmarks by which organizational performance is assessed. Unfortunately, despite a formal mission, vision, goals, and objectives, it is all too easy for senior management and even the board of directors to become distracted and stray off course. Such action can create major problems both inside and outside the company, as demonstrated by the HP scandal featured in Ethical Dimension 2.

JetBlue Airways took to the air February 11, 2000, flying from John F. Kennedy International Airport in New York to Fort Lauderdale in Florida. Today, the upstart airline is rapidly becoming a major player, serving more than 50 cities (including several Caribbean locations) with well over 100 aircraft, and it has ambitious plans for continued growth. The company's vision is to offer great service with low fares—and make a profit—even when other air carriers are struggling to survive. Several important goals back up this vision:

- Start and remain well-capitalized.
- Fly new planes.
- Hire the best people.
- Focus on service.
- Practice responsible financial management.

JetBlue has mostly stayed true to course. While most of the major carriers continuously bleed red ink, JetBlue, though not perfect in bringing in every quarter's sales and profit goals, appears to be much more stable financially than the majority of other airlines. Much of the airline's success can be attributed to great market-driven strategic planning.

In terms of specific and measurable objectives, Neeleman established high performance expectations for financial results, operational processes, and customer satisfaction and loyalty. As mentioned earlier, JetBlue's Web site is very transparent in laying out company leaders' plans for the firm—Neeleman was always quite confident that the company had created a unique value offering that few (if any) competitors could readily duplicate. In the winter of 2007, JetBlue suffered a highly publicized operational meltdown at its JFK airport home base due to a massive snow and ice storm, and Neeleman was right there on the Web site and in the public media. In addition to offering an apology, he also provided full refunds, free replacement tickets, and travel vouchers to stranded passengers and established the first passengers' bill of rights in the industry.

In developing a marketing plan, the marketing manager must proceed in the process with a strong understanding of and commitment to the firm's mission, vision, goals, and objectives. JetBlue's well-conceived and executed marketing plan is an integral element in its success.

HP's Ethical Scandal Impacts Marketing Strategy

Developing a strategic marketing focus in an organization requires a commitment from senior management. As Jack Welch mentioned, good managers create, articulate, become passionate about, and focus the company on a vision. That requires a clear focus on what *is* and, critically, what *is not* important to the firm.

Many issues confront senior managers and it is easy to lose focus. For example, senior management is rightfully concerned about competitors or even the general public gaining access to sensitive company information (for example, financial data, cost figures, future marketing strategies, product plans, and pricing programs). To help protect sensitive data from getting into the wrong hands, companies implement sophisticated security measures. At the same time, the Sarbanes-Oxley Act of 2002 (commonly referred to as SOX) established specific procedures and processes to ensure ethical conduct at the highest levels of a company including the board of directors and senior management.

In the vast majority of companies the conflicting demands of securing sensitive information and open disclosure of business procedures exist relatively harmoniously. However, occasionally the system fails and the result is scandal and even criminal activity. Hewlett-Packard (HP), one of the leading global technology companies, found itself involved in a scandal that led to the dismissal of two members of its Board of Directors and the firing of several employees. The scandal was initiated when *The Wall Street Journal* reported sensitive information about future business plans that were meant to be communicated only inside the company and in internal discussions among the Board of Directors. Former HP Chairman Patricia Dunn was determined to find out who was leaking the information and started an investigation into the personal and business communications (phone calls, e-mail, etc.) of several board members without their knowledge.

Were the people involved in this mess simply unethical by nature? Evidence about some of the players' career tracks suggests just the opposite. Indeed, one of the fired HP officers was the ethics chief for the company and also a well-respected attorney. While stopping the leak of sensitive information was a valid goal, poor, even illegal, decisions were made about how to accomplish that goal. At critical decision moments, no one stepped back to reflect and ask important questions like: Does this make sense? Is this activity appropriate or ethical?

HP CEO Mike Hurd, while involved in the scandal, was not directly connected to the illegal activity. He admitted that mistakes were made during the process and the company subsequently instituted a number of changes to its ethics policies and business practices. While HP's market performance remained strong, employees reported considerable conflict as the company dealt with changes to ethics procedures and policies. Hurd has admitted the scandal has been a distraction for him and the company, and of course negative publicity about a company is never a good thing for customer confidence in its brands. When management gets distracted by ethics scandals, the company loses strategic focus and the company's brands could lose market share to competitors who take advantage of the scandalized firm's weakened state in the marketplace.[29]

Ethical Perspective

1. **Senior management:** How should senior management incorporate ethical standards at all stages of the marketing planning process?

2. **Marketing managers:** A company's brands can be quickly impacted by negative publicity surrounding ethical scandals. How might they be impacted and what might a marketing manager do to reestablish a brand damaged in this way?

3. **The public:** Company image and trust can be regained by a CEO's quick public acknowledgment of an ethics problem accompanied by plans for changes in practice. What could HP's CEO have done better?

Organizational Strategies

At the firm level, a **strategy** is a comprehensive plan stating how the organization will achieve its mission and objectives. Put another way, strategy is like a road map to get the organization where it wants to go, based on good information gathered in advance. The choice of which direction a firm should go ultimately boils down to a *decision* by a firm and its managers. Strategy has two key phases: formulation (or development) and execution. And it occurs at multiple levels in the firm: corporate level, SBU (or business) level, and functional level (marketing, finance, operations, etc.). As we have discussed, the strategies developed and executed at each of these levels must be aligned and directed toward the overall organizational mission and goals.

A firm's **generic strategy** is its overall directional strategy at the business level.[30] Fundamentally, all firms must decide whether they wish to (or are able to) *grow,* and if not, how they can survive through *stability* or *retrenchment.* Exhibit 2.5 provides options for generic strategies for each of these three directions. The choice of generic strategy is usually driven by resource capabilities of the firm, as well as the competitive landscape. In the growth-oriented business culture in the United States, stockholders and financial analysts are constantly interested in knowing a firm's next growth strategy and can become quickly disenchanted, even with firms that are growing but at a slower than predicted rate. Yet, sometimes for reasons related to the competitive landscape or resource constraints, the best generic strategy for a firm may not actually be growth but stability or retrenchment instead. Interestingly, the pressure to constantly achieve accelerated growth is much less intense in many business cultures outside the United States.

Competitor analysis is discussed in greater detail later in this chapter. For now, it is worth noting that Michael Porter identifies three primary categories of **competitive strategy:** low cost, differentiation, and focus (or niche). Exhibit 2.6 describes each of these, and Exhibit 2.7 illustrates them further within a matrix format. Porter's overarching premise is that firms must first identify their **core competencies,** or the activities the firm can do exceedingly well. When these core competencies are superior to those of competitors, they are called **distinctive competencies.** Firms should invest in distinctive competencies, as they offer opportunity for **sustainable competitive advantage** in the marketplace, especially if the competencies cannot be easily duplicated or usurped by competitors. Sources of differential advantage will be developed further in Chapter 7.

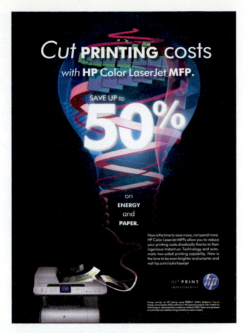

HP does a great job of communicating the value proposition of its color LaserJet printers through strong environmental and cost-saving advertising.

EXHIBIT 2.5	Generic Business Strategies

Growth

- Organizations that do business in dynamic competitive environments generally experience pressure to grow in order to survive. Growth may be in the form of sales, market share, assets, profits, or some combination of these and other factors. Categories of growth strategies include:

Concentration–via vertical or horizontal integration.
Diversification–via concentric or conglomerate means.

Stability

- The strategy to continue current activities with little significant change in direction may be

appropriate for a successful organization operating in a reasonably predictable environment. It can be useful in the short term but potentially dangerous in the long term, especially if the competitive landscape changes.

Retrenchment

- An organization in a weak competitive position in some or all of its product lines, resulting in poor performance and pressure on management to quickly improve, may pursue retrenchment.

- Essentially, retrenchment involves pulling assets out of underperforming parts of the business and reinvesting in aspects of the business with greater future performance potential.

Source: J. David Hunger and Thomas H. Wheelen, *Essentials of Strategic Management,* 4th ed. (Upper Saddle River, NJ: Prentice Hall, 2007).

COST LEADERSHIP

The organization strives to have the lowest costs in its industry and produces goods or services for a broad customer base. Note the emphasis on *costs* not *prices*.

DIFFERENTIATION

The organization competes on the basis of providing unique goods or services with features that custom-ers value, perceive as different, and for which they are willing to pay a premium.

FOCUS (OR NICHE)

The organization pursues either a cost or differen-tiation advantage, but in a limited (narrow) customer group. A focus strategy concentrates on serving a specific market niche.

EXHIBIT 2.7	Competitive Strategy Matrix

Competitive Advantage

		Lower Cost	Differentiation
Competitive Scope	**Broad Target**	Cost Leadership	Differentiation
	Narrow Target	Cost Focus	Focused Differentiation

As illustrated in Exhibit 2.8, Miles and Snow propose several categories of firms within any given industry based on **strategic type.** Firms of a particular strategic type have a common strategic orientation and a similar combination of structure, culture, and processes consistent with that strategy. Four strategic types are pros-pectors, analyzers, defenders, and reactors—depending on a firm's approach to the competitive marketplace.

JetBlue has historically followed an internal growth strategy. As some of its rivals continue to falter, it will be interesting to see how aggressive JetBlue might become in terms of growth through concentration via acquisitions. Like its much larger competitor Southwest Airlines, JetBlue executes a low-cost strategy in the competi-tive marketplace. Because it has no unions, hedges on fuel prices, and standardizes the types of planes flown, JetBlue enjoys numerous cost advantages over the com-petition. However, JetBlue differs from Southwest in that its strategy (in the context of Exhibit 2.8) is cost focus, while Southwest's is cost leadership. The difference is

EXHIBIT 2.8 | **Miles and Snow's Strategy Types**

- **Prospector:** Firm exhibits continual innovation by finding and exploiting new product and market opportunities.
- **Analyzer:** Firm heavily relies on analysis and imitation of the successes of other organizations, especially prospectors.
- **Defender:** Firm searches for market stability and production of only a limited product line directed at a narrow market segment, focusing on protecting established turf.
- **Reactor:** Firm lacks any coherent strategic plan or apparent means of effectively competing; reactors do well to merely survive in the competitive marketplace.

Source: Adapted from Raymond E. Miles and Charles C. Snow, *Organizational Strategy, Structure, and Process* (New York: McGraw-Hill, 1978). Reprinted with permission of the authors.

that Southwest has defined the scope of its competitive marketplace much more broadly then has JetBlue; for instance, Southwest is basically a nationwide carrier, while JetBlue focuses on some specific geographic markets. In terms of strategic type, JetBlue can be labeled a prospector. It has enjoyed strong **first-mover advantages** by providing television, movies, and games in every seat along with comfy leather accoutrements and plenty of legroom—all at bargain prices! Exhibit 2.8 provides typical characteristics of firms that fall into each of the strategy types.

To summarize, for purposes of marketing planning, it is necessary to be mindful of the organizational strategies in play when developing marketing strategies. One could reasonably argue that a fine line exists between organization-level strategies and marketing strategies, and, in many firms, the market-driven strategies developed within the context of the marketing plan ultimately rise to the organizational level.[31] Fortunately, the distinction is moot so long as the strategies developed and implemented are fully supportive of the organization's mission, vision, and goals.

Situation Analysis

The marketing manager must perform a complete **situation analysis** of the environment within which the marketing plan is being developed. The situation includes elements of the macro-level external environment within which the firm operates, its industry or competitive environment, and its internal environment.[32] Think of external environmental factors as those a firm must be mindful of and plan for, yet has little or no direct ability to impact or change. On the other hand, internal environmental factors include the firm's structure and systems, culture, leadership, and various resources, all of which are under the firm's control. Ironically, when undertaking a situation analysis, managers often have more difficulty assessing the internal environmental components than the external, perhaps because it is much more difficult to self-assess and potentially criticize that for which the managers are responsible.[33]

Macro-Level External Environmental Factors

Major categories for analysis within the external environment include:

- *Political, legal, and ethical.* All firms operate within certain rules, laws, and norms of operating behavior. For example, JetBlue has myriad regulations administered by the Federal Aviation Administration, the National Transportation Safety Board, and the Transportation Security Administration. In the airline industry, the regulatory environment is a particularly strong external influence on firms' marketing planning.

- *Sociocultural/demographic.* Trends among consumers and in society as a whole impact marketing planning greatly. Many such trends are demographic in nature, including changing generational preferences and the rising buying power of minority groups domestically and consumers in developing nations in the global marketplace.[34] Speaking of generational preferences, JetBlue jumped on the video game trend among children and teens by providing in-seat games, much to the delight of parents who no longer have to entertain the kids for the duration of the flight.

Many companies such as Procter & Gamble, Johnson & Johnson, Verizon, and General Mills are investing substantial advertising dollars on marketing aimed at Hispanics. According to a consumer survey conducted for the Hispanic television and radio company Univision Communications, Hispanic consumers like to buy brands that are advertised on TV. When General Mills began purchasing more ads in Spanish-language media, it saw sales of Progresso and Honey Nut Cheerios soar among Hispanic consumers.[35]

- *Technological.* Constantly emerging and evolving technologies impact business in many ways. The goal is to try to understand the future impact of technological change so a firm's products will continue to be fresh and viable. JetBlue ordered a number of new downsized "regional jets," planes that carry about 50 passengers and allow for entry into smaller, underserved markets. The airline is banking on these attractive, comfortable new aircraft to provide a market edge over the competition.

- *Economic.* The economy plays a role in all marketing planning. Part of a marketing plan is a forecast and accompanying budget, and forecasts are impacted by the degree to which predicted economic conditions actually materialize.[36] Fuel prices are a major economic cost element for any airline. JetBlue was a pioneer in hedging against rising fuel prices—that is, making speculative long-term purchase commitments betting on fuel prices going up.

- *Natural.* The natural environment also frequently affects marketing planning.[37] JetBlue's highly publicized winter weather fiasco at JFK airport in 2007 prompted immediate changes in the way the company communicates with its customers. And on a broader scope, the concept of environmentally friendly marketing, or *green marketing*, has been a growing trend in socially responsible companies. *Sustainability*, which refers to business practices that meet humanity's needs without harming future generations, has evolved into a part of the philosophical and strategic core of many firms.

Competitive Environmental Factors

The competitive environment is a particularly complex aspect of the external environment. Later in the chapter we provide a more complete grounding in competitor analysis. For now, let's identify several factors, or forces, that comprise a basis for assessing the level and strength of competition within an industry. The forces are portrayed in Exhibit 2.9 and summarized below:

- *Threat of new entrants.* How strong are entry barriers based on capital requirements or other factors? A cornerstone of JetBlue's initial market entry success was the fact that it was exceptionally well-capitalized. Not many new airlines are.

Pepsi executes a strong differentiation strategy by making connections with young, hip, urban consumers.

- *Rivalry among existing firms.* How much direct competition is there? How much indirect competition? How strong are the firms in both categories? JetBlue's industry contains a number of firms that are much larger, but based on JetBlue's unique value proposition few of them can deliver the same customer experience that JetBlue can.

- *Threat of substitute products.* Substitutes appear to be different but actually can satisfy much or all of the same customer need as another product. Will teleconferencing PC-to-PC (using products such as Skype) reach a point in the near future such that business travel is seriously threatened, thus impacting JetBlue and other airlines?

- *Bargaining power of buyers.* To what degree can customers affect prices or product offerings? So far, JetBlue has not been in much head-to-head competition with Southwest, AirTran Airways, Frontier Airlines, or other low-fare carriers in its primary markets. Should this change, passengers will have more power to demand even lower fares and/or additional services from JetBlue.

- *Bargaining power of suppliers.* Suppliers impact the competitive nature of an industry through their ability to raise prices or affect the quality of inbound goods and services. Jet fuel literally fires the airline industry's economic engine. Also, few manufacturers of commercial aircraft still exist. Both of these factors point to a competitive environment with strong supplier power.

One other competitive force not directly addressed by Porter is the *relative power of other stakeholders*. This force is becoming more and more relevant in assessing

EXHIBIT 2.9	Forces Driving Industry Competition

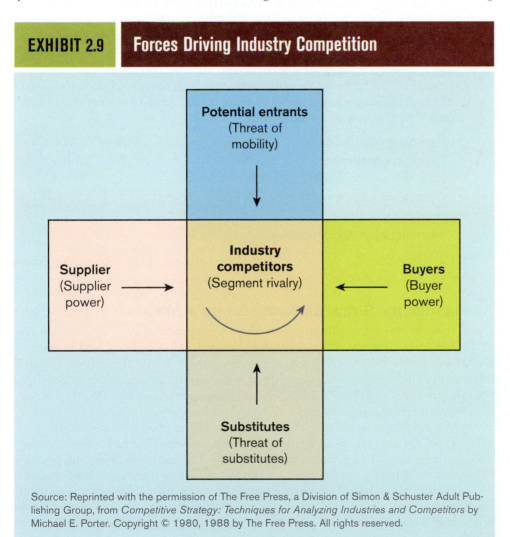

industry competitiveness. The level of activity by unions, trade associations, local communities, citizen's groups, and all sorts of other special-interest groups can strongly impact industry attractiveness.[38] Founder David Neeleman established JetBlue as a non-union shop with the goal of keeping it that way by hiring the very best people and treating the people right. The union environment in the airline industry adds multiple complexities to the ability to stay competitive.[39]

Internal Environmental Factors

Major categories for analysis in the internal environment include:

- *Firm structure and systems.* To what degree does the present organizational structure facilitate or impede successful market-driven strategic planning? Are the firm's internal systems set up and properly aligned to effectively serve customers? David Neeleman had his organizational chart right on the company Web site and talked openly about being a lean and mean operation. It's hard to find much evidence that JetBlue's structure and systems offer impediments to its marketing planning.

- *Firm culture.* As discussed previously, successful marketing planning requires a culture that includes customer orientation as a core value. If a firm's culture does not value and support a customer orientation and customer-centric approach to the overall business, marketing planning will likely disappoint.[40] A close review of the communication with customers on JetBlue's Web site provides evidence that customer orientation is a core value at the company.

- *Firm leadership.* Of course, the CEO must believe in and continuously support (financially and otherwise) the structure, systems, and culture necessary for market-driven strategic planning.[41] JetBlue's employee-friendly—and customer-friendly—approach epitomizes such leadership and commitment.

- *Firm resources.* Finally, internal analysis involves taking an honest look at all aspects of a firm's functional/operational-level resources and capabilities and how they play into the ability to develop and execute market-driven strategies.[42] Key resources for study are:
  - Marketing capabilities.
  - Financial capabilities.
  - R&D and technological capabilities.
  - Operations and production capabilities.
  - Human capabilities.
  - Information system capabilities.

JetBlue historically has performed better than almost all the competition on all these resource dimensions.

Summarize the Situation Analysis into a SWOT

Upon completion of the situation analysis, a convenient way to summarize key findings is into a matrix of strengths, weaknesses, opportunities, and threats—a **SWOT analysis.** Exhibit 2.10 provides a template for a SWOT analysis. Internal analysis reveals strengths and weaknesses, while external analysis points to potential opportunities and threats. Based on the situation analysis and SWOT, it is now possible to begin making decisions about the remainder of the marketing plan.

Besides helping a marketing manager organize the results of a situation analysis, the SWOT analysis template is also useful in beginning to brainstorm marketing strategies that might be appropriate depending on which of four possible combination scenarios predominate in a firm's situation: internal strengths/external opportunities, internal strengths/external threats, internal weaknesses/external opportunities, or internal weaknesses/external threats. During the situation analysis it is essential to begin to critically and realistically examine the degree to which a firm's external and internal environment will impact its ability to develop

EXHIBIT 2.10 | SWOT Analysis Template

INTERNAL FACTORS / EXTERNAL FACTORS	Strengths (S) List 5–10 *internal* strengths here	Weaknesses (W) List 5–10 *internal* weaknesses here
Opportunities (O) List 5–10 *external* opportunities here	**S/O Based Strategies** Generate strategies here that use **strengths** to take **advantage** of **opportunities**	**W/O Based Strategies** Generate strategies here that take **advantage** of **opportunities** by **overcoming weaknesses**
Threats (T) List 5–10 *external* threats here	**S/T Based Strategies** Generate strategies here that use **strengths** to **avoid threats**	**W/T Based Strategies** Generate strategies here that **minimize weaknesses** and **avoid threats**

Source: J. David Hunger and Thomas H. Wheelen, *Essentials of Strategic Management*, 4th ed. (Upper Saddle River, NJ: Prentice Hall, 2007). Reprinted from *Long Range Planning* 15, no.2 (1982), Weihrich "The TOWS Matrix–A Tool for Situational Analysis," p.60. Copyright 1982 with permission of Elsevier and Hans Weihrich.

marketing strategy. The more honest and accurate the portrayal provided by the SWOT analysis, the more useful the remainder of the marketing planning process will be.

Analyzing Competitors

Identifying competitors, while crucial, is only the first step in understanding the competition. It is important to remember the goal in this process is to deal more effectively with competitive threats. As a result, a company must not only identify but also assess each competitor and then develop an action plan for competitive success.

Competitor analysis yields two primary benefits. First, companies can evaluate their own strategies against competitors and make adjustments. For example, many retailers have adjusted their pricing strategies to accommodate Walmart's low-cost strategy. It is also valuable to evaluate new strategies against the competition to assess their reaction. **Competitive scenario analysis** enables companies to test competitors' reactions to possible strategic scenarios such as product modifications or new advertising campaigns. Second, competitor analysis can identify new opportunities and/or threats. It is always possible to learn from competitors. While automobile manufacturers already had hybrid technology in development, the success of Toyota's Prius spurred Ford, General Motors, and others to accelerate the introduction of their own hybrid vehicles. There are more than 19 hybrid models available in the United States, up from 11 in 2006 and at least 10 new models were scheduled to be introduced by 2010. The five specific areas of focus in a competitor analysis are: strategies, resources, culture, objectives, and finally strengths/weaknesses.[43]

Strategies

Companies, even industries, frequently follow an established strategic model. Product introductions (new car models frequently debut in the fall), price increases (price changes in the theme park industry are often announced in the spring), and new advertising campaigns (soft drink companies introduce new campaigns at the beginning of the year) often track historical patterns. Studying these trends, particularly with respect to specific competitors, can be a source of insight into their future behavior. Mistakes can sometimes be avoided by learning from the competition. David Neeleman, founder of JetBlue, studied the major airlines and learned from their mistakes. As a result, JetBlue implemented a strategy that differed dramatically from that of the major airlines and included such changes as in-flight multimedia entertainment and extra-spacious seats and legroom. JetBlue created a new category of airline—a low-cost carrier with amenities.

Resources

The ability to access financial resources and a quality workforce represents a significant advantage for a competitor. The competitive landscape can change dramatically very quickly as a result of resource constraints or an infusion of money from an outside source. It is important to know the competitor's resources in order to plan accordingly. To evaluate a competitor's financial resources consider the following questions:

- What is the company's bond rating? Bond rating is an indicator of the cost of capital.
- What are the company's operating costs (does it have a cost advantage)?
- What is the company's investment in plant and equipment (future commitments)?
- How easily can it access the equity market (stock)? What has been the company's stock performance over the past 12 months?
- Does the company have a lot of cash on hand?

Employees are another critical resource that should be evaluated.

- How many employees currently work at the company?
- Is the company actively recruiting for certain positions (recruiting for new engineers or product development employees may indicate a strategy focused on new products)?
- What are the salary ranges of major job positions at the company?
- What is the ratio of employees to sales (for example, how many employees does it take to generate a million dollars in sales)? Compare that with other companies in the industry.
- What is the hiring policy of the company? Does it hire experienced people from other companies in the industry or younger, less-experienced individuals and train them internally?
- Does the company pay below, equal to, or above the industry average at key positions?

Through most of its history, JetBlue has received positive financial evaluations from Wall Street analysts. Also, it is a non-union company with a very successful track record of hiring and retaining high-quality people.

Culture

A company's culture is a critical element in competitor analysis. A good place to begin evaluating a competitor's culture is the senior management team. Senior management sets the tone in an organization, and studying the backgrounds of key senior people (particularly the CEO) can offer insights into a company's tolerance for risk and overall corporate focus. Larry Ellison, CEO of Oracle, has a reputation as an aggressive executive. One of his favorite books, *The Art of War* written by Sun Tzu in the sixth century, inspires his overall approach to Oracle's business strategy.

When there is a change at the top, a new CEO will often seek to put his or her "stamp" on the organization. By studying the individual's background, it is possible to understand the strategies they have used in the past. Mark Hurd, HP's CEO, was brought in from NCR to help turn around Hewlett-Packard, and his experience in turning around NCR was cited as a reason for his selection. At NCR, Hurd had aggressively cut costs and redirected the company to focus on core businesses; he has followed a similar strategy at HP with successful results.

It is also helpful to know the overall reputation of the company. Over time, most companies develop a reputation. The reputation is affected by and, in turn, influences the company culture. For example, 3M has a history of innovation. The company's success is based, in part, on a culture that encourages research and development leading to new products. Knowing the company's corporate culture is an indicator of potential future strategy. Of course, companies do go "outside the box" and make significant and dramatic strategic shifts, but, even in those situations, the company will rely on the existing culture to implement the strategy.

JetBlue's culture is one that embraces teamwork, innovation, fun, company loyalty, and putting the customer first.

Corporate Objectives and Goals

When you know the goals and objectives of a competitor, you have a pretty good idea of the company's strategy. One benefit of search engines such as Google or Lexis/Nexis is the ability to examine a vast amount of information—if it is in the public domain a good search engine can find it. But internal management discussions at a competitor firm about things such as goals and strategies obviously won't be overtly posted online (at least by most firms). But if you find a company newsletter that states: "Our goal is to improve customer satisfaction," or "We expect to see significant growth in this market," you can usually translate that information into specific strategies. Tracking public statements is certainly one way of identifying what a competitor is considering.

Twitter, the free social messaging utility, has an added value that makes it extremely appealing to giants Google and Facebook. Twitter has a rich stream of data that it could sell as a service to marketers that want reports about products and topics that are discussed on the site. This information lets companies pinpoint people interested in their business and provides detailed analyses of individuals that follow particular companies.[44]

Additional information can be learned from a company's annual report as well as mandatory documents filed with the Securities and Exchange Commission (SEC) such as the 10-K. Available at the SEC government Web site, 10-K reports present a great deal of information about the company's operations and strategies. In particular, Part 1, Item 1–Business, and Part 2, Item 7 and 7a–Management Discussion on Operations and Market Risk, include specific discussions of current business activities and ongoing operations. Although these data may be available from other sources such as trade publications, the 10-K offers unique insights on management's current view of business operations. When coupled with a company's annual report, the 10-K provides significant insights about a competitor.

JetBlue's founder David Neeleman believed in transparency and full disclosure to customers and other stakeholders through JetBlue's Web site. Even though he has moved on to other ventures, this philosophy still holds true in the firm today and you will find all sorts of interesting "insider strategy" information on JetBlue online.

Starbucks provides data about itself in a variety of ways. Visit a Starbucks and you can find information on the company's products, business philosophy, and social responsibility initiatives. Each store also has a bulletin board that posts local community events.

Strengths and Weaknesses

A competitor analysis also includes a summary of each competitor's strengths and weaknesses. A competitor's strength is regarded as a threat while a competitor's weakness is an opportunity to attack. Depending on their magnitude, threats (competitor strength) and opportunities (competitor weakness) can lead a company to develop specific strategies that effectively minimize or neutralize strengths while exploiting weaknesses.

JetBlue looks especially closely at the strengths and weaknesses of other sizable low-fare carriers, especially Southwest and AirTran.

Benchmarking

An important management tool called benchmarking enables a company to evaluate its business processes against other companies to determine what it does well and what it can improve. After assessing the company's business processes, managers look for industries and, more specifically, companies with similar characteristics. Companies targeted as leaders in critical areas are identified, and the company learns through interviews or research as much as possible about that "best practice," or benchmarks, with the express purpose of incorporating the benchmark company's success into its own business practices. This process is particularly useful in competitor analysis because the company can evaluate competitor business processes in an effort to learn how to do things better or to exploit competitor weakness if the company identifies areas where it outperforms the competitor.[45]

Because JetBlue is uniquely positioned as a low-priced airline that also offers comfort, great service, and entertainment amenities, few good benchmark firms exist in this industry. Thus, JetBlue must seek out best practices along these lines from firms outside the airline space.

Additional Aspects of Marketing Planning

Additional elements of marketing planning are identified below. As they derive their content primarily from future chapter topics, reference is made where relevant to the chapters from which the content can be derived.

Perform Any Needed Market Research

Chapter 3 provides ideas on how a CRM (customer relationship management) system enhances marketing planning and decision making and introduces some important marketing metrics. Chapter 4 discusses collecting and analyzing market information. And Chapters 5 and 6 outline key aspects of understanding customers in consumer and business markets, respectively. JetBlue has an effective CRM system through its TrueBlue rewards program. It also engages in ongoing market and consumer research to pinpoint trends and opportunities.

To solidify its position as market leader, McDonald's is putting more emphasis on creating and marketing lower-priced products, such as specialty salads. It is implementing computerized systems to allow restaurants to adjust prices due to changes in consumer demand. In China, some restaurants have cut the price of some combo meals at lunch by one-third. Through these systems, McDonald's also is examining customer behavior—everything from whether customers are ordering smaller value meals to how much customers are willing to pay for a Big Mac.[46]

Establish Marketing Goals and Objectives

What is expected to be accomplished by the marketing plan? Based on what is learned from the situation analysis, competitor analysis, and market research,

EXHIBIT 2.11 | Product-Market Combinations

Product Emphasis

		Existing Products	New Products
Market Emphasis	**Existing Markets**	**Strategy = Market penetration** — Seek to increase sales of existing products to existing markets	**Strategy = Product development** — Create growth by selling new products in existing markets
	New Markets	**Strategy = Market development** — Introduce existing products to new markets	**Strategy = Diversification** — Emphasize both new products and new markets to achieve growth

Source: From H. Igor Ansoff, *The New Corporate Strategy* (New York: John Wiley & Sons, 1988). Reprinted with permission of John Wiley & Sons, Inc.

goals and objectives can now be developed related to what the marketing manager intends to accomplish with the marketing plan. JetBlue's marketing goals focus on enhancing the safety, comfort, and fun of customers' travel experience, building high satisfaction and loyalty among JetBlue users, and attracting new users to the brand.

Develop Marketing Strategies

As we mentioned earlier, marketing strategies provide the road map for creating, communicating, and delivering value to customers. An overarching decision that must be made is determining which combinations of products and markets to invest in. A product-market combination may fall into one of four primary categories, as illustrated by Exhibit 2.11, Igor Ansoff's Product-Market Matrix:

- **Market penetration strategies** involve investing in existing customers to gain additional usage of existing products.
- **Product development strategies** recognize the opportunity to invest in new products that will increase usage from the current customer base.
- **Market development strategies** allow for expansion of the firm's product line into heretofore untapped markets, often internationally.
- **Diversification strategies** seize on opportunities to serve new markets with new products.

JetBlue began business with a primary focus on product development. The clean new planes, comfy leather seats, full spectrum entertainment console, and friendly staff were all welcomed by fliers as a long overdue change from other airlines' cattle-call mentality. However, more recently the company focused on taking its winning formula into a number of new geographic markets. This market development strategy dramatically increased the number of cities on JetBlue's route system and especially increased opportunities for customers from underserved smaller cities such as Sarasota, Florida; White Plains, New York; and Rutland, Vermont, to experience the airline. JetBlue has also added international destinations into the travel mix such as Cancun, Aruba, and Nassau.

Once the product-market combinations have been established, it is time to develop the value offering, which is the topic of Part 3. This involves market segmentation, target marketing, and positioning strategies. In addition, strategies for branding, service, and pricing must be worked out.

Finally, supply chain and integrated marketing communication strategies must be put in place to successfully communicate and deliver the value offering to customers. Chapters 11 to 14 in Part 4 provide the background necessary to complete this section of the marketing plan.

Evidence of JetBlue's success in creating, communicating, and delivering its value offering can be found on the airline's Web site. There one can view current television ads, take a virtual tour of the aircraft, peruse the list of available in-flight entertainment, and even send a virtual JetBlue postcard to a friend.

Create an Implementation Plan Including Forecast, Budget, and Appropriate Marketing Metrics

As pointed out earlier, strategy *development* is only part of marketing planning. The other part is strategy *implementation*, including measuring results. The process of measuring marketing results and adjusting the marketing plan as needed is called **marketing control.**

It takes money to make money is a relevant phrase to reflect an approach by Hyundai's U.S. marketing boss, Joel Ewanick. To increase consumer confidence, the carmaker has been getting more creative in its marketing. It is spending millions of dollars for Super Bowl spots and TV time during high-profile shows, such as the Academy Awards telecast. To stimulate immediate purchase, Hyundai has also increased its discounts. Incentives on its Santa Fe SUV and other models averaged $2,611 per vehicle in 2009, which is triple the prior year's figure. The result—Hyundai has improved its brand reputation to rank close to Honda and Toyota.[47]

In a marketing plan, every strategy must include an implementation element. Sometimes these are called action plans or programs. Each must discuss timing, assign persons responsible for various aspects of implementation, and assign resources necessary to make the strategy happen. Forecasts and their accompanying budgets must be provided. Then, appropriate metrics must be identified to assess along the way to what degree the plan is on track and the strategies are contributing to achievement of the stated marketing objectives. Chapter 3 provides the background necessary for selecting marketing metrics appropriate for various marketing objectives and strategies. Detailed instructions on preparing action plans for implementation, developing forecasts and budgets, establishing controls and contingency plans, and conducting a marketing audit are located on our Web site at www.mhhe.com/marshalless1e.

On the JetBlue Web site, the Investor Relations and Press Room sections provide compelling evidence that the company is highly oriented toward measurement of marketing results. Although the airline industry as a whole has suffered in recent years due to increased costs, JetBlue has generally received better reviews than most other airlines from Wall Street analysts in part because of the clarity of JetBlue's goals, metrics, and controls.

Develop Contingency Plans

A final step marketing managers should take is to develop contingency plans that can be implemented should something happen that negates the viability of the marketing plan.[48] As you've learned, in marketing planning, flexibility and adaptability by managers is critical because unexpected events and drastic changes in various aspects of the external environment are the norm rather than an exception. To address this eventuality, a firm should incorporate contingency plans into the process.

Contingency plans are often described in terms of a separate plan for a worst-case, best-case, and expected-case performance against the forecast. That is, the implementation of the marketing strategies would be different depending on how performance against the forecast actually materializes. If better, the firm could quickly shift to a best-case implementation scenario. If worse, then the shift would be to a worst-case scenario. Having these contingency plans in place avoids scrambling to decide how to adjust marketing strategies when performance against a forecast is higher or lower than expected.

When developing contingency plans, the firm should be realistic about the possibilities and creative in developing options for minimizing any disruption to the firm's operations should it become necessary to implement them. Some firms use contingency planning to reduce the chances they would make a public relations blunder when confronted with an unexpected challenge that generates negative publicity in the media such as product tampering or failure, ethical or legal misconduct of an officer, or some other aspect of their operation that garners bad press.[49] More information on contingency planning can be found on our Web site at www.mhhe.com/marshalless1e.

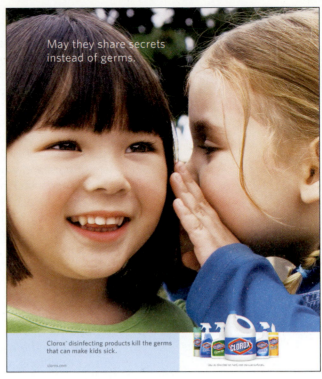

May they share secrets instead of germs.

Clorox disinfecting products kill the germs that can make kids sick.

clorox.com

Well-executed marketing strategy can result in very powerful messages and branding.

CLOROX ® is a registered trademark of The Clorox Company. Used with permission. Clorox ® advertisement. © 2010 The Clorox Company. Reprinted with permission. Image © Sven Wiederholt.

With changes in consumer preferences, economic conditions, and the competitive landscape, even Starbucks has had to do contingency planning to adjust and become more flexible. CEO Howard Schultz introduced a loyalty card program and breakfast combos to entice customers reluctant to splurge on premium-priced coffee. This move is quite a contrast to Starbucks' original marketing strategy, which had little or no price-based promotion.[50]

Recently, JetBlue has had to invoke a contingency plan for growth due to general economic conditions and volatile jet fuel costs (the entire industry has felt the impact). For all airlines, fuel costs have raised ticket prices and squeezed profit margins, drastically affecting achievement of forecasts. In reaction to a worst-case scenario, JetBlue has cut orders for new planes and postponed entry into some new market areas that it would like to develop. At best, in this environment JetBlue hopes to achieve stability in the short run at its current size and would also obviously benefit if other competitive carriers decide to stop operating.

TIPS FOR SUCCESSFUL MARKETING PLANNING

Developing a marketing plan is an essential process for firm success. In addition to its direct impact on a firm's ability to compete, ongoing marketing planning also has a strong internal organizational benefit of providing a rallying point for developing creative ideas and for gaining input from important stakeholders throughout the various areas within an organization.[51] Who should be involved in marketing planning? The answer is anyone from any unit at any level whose contribution and participation in the process will enhance the likelihood of a successful outcome. Marketing planning provides a unique opportunity for organization members to contribute to the success of a firm in a very concrete and visible way.

Here are a few final tips for achieving a successful marketing planning experience.

1. *Stay flexible.* Marketing plans are not set in stone. Markets and customers change, competitors do unexpected things, and the external environment has a nasty habit of creating unexpected surprises. Great marketing managers understand when to adjust a plan. Nimble organizations tend to be much more successful in their marketing strategies.

   In his provocative book, *The Rise and Fall of Strategic Planning,* strategy expert Henry Mintzberg builds the case that organizations sometimes spend so much time focused on planning for the long term that they miss the opportunities presented by the next customer who walks through the door.[52] Mintzberg's concern is valid and points to the need for viewing planning as an ongoing, organic process in which managers exhibit flexibility and adaptability to changing market conditions. After a plan is prepared, myriad changes in the firm's external and internal environment may create a need for marketing managers to quickly alter their strategies in the marketplace.[53] The more nimble a company is in changing course to address new conditions as they arise, the more successful its marketing strategies will be.

2. *Utilize input, but don't become paralyzed by information and analysis.* Great marketing managers value research and analytics, but also know when to move forward with action.

3. *Don't underestimate the implementation part of the plan.* This is such a common mistake it is nearly synonymous with poor marketing planning. The quality of the action plans and metrics often make or break the success of the plan. Put another way, a good plan on paper is useless without effective implementation.

4. *Stay strategic, but also stay on top of the tactical.* Remember that marketing has these two levels of interrelated issues, and both the strategic and tactical elements have to be right for the plan to be successful.

5. *Give yourself and your people room to fail and try again.* Marketing planning is by no means a predictable science. It is more realistic to think of it as both science and art, and creativity and risk-taking are to be rewarded. All great marketing managers have experienced both success and failures in marketing planning. As in baseball, it's not one or two times at bat but rather the long-term batting average that separates the great from the average performer.

VISIT OUR WEB SITE FOR A MARKETING PLAN EXAMPLE

Often the best way to learn is through example, so on our Web site we have provided an abbreviated example marketing plan for the fictitious company Cloud-Cab Small Jet Taxi Service (www.mhhe.com/marshalless1e). Take this opportunity early in the course to familiarize yourself with the flow and content, albeit abbreviated, of a typical marketing plan.

In addition, at the end of each chapter you will find Marketing Plan Exercises designed to highlight aspects of that chapter as they pertain to a manager's ability to build an effective marketing plan. Use these activities to build your own knowledge and skill in the marketing planning process.

SUMMARY

Marketing planning is an ongoing process of developing and implementing market-driven strategies for an organization. Great marketing planning is essential for success in the marketplace. Once established, marketing plans are not set in stone. Instead, marketing managers must be flexible enough to constantly assess changes in the external and internal environment and adjust strategies and tactics accordingly. The chapter introduces the essential elements of marketing planning. The content elements for completing the various aspects of the template are covered in the chapters throughout the remaining three parts of the book.

APPLICATION QUESTIONS

1. What is a value proposition? For each of these brands, articulate your perception of their key value proposition:
   a. Caterpillar earth mover
   b. Apple iPod
   c. Wii home gaming system
   d. McDonald's hamburgers
   e. FedEx overnight delivery service

2. Consider the concept of the value chain. Identify a firm that you believe does an especially good job of investing in elements in the value chain to gain higher profit margins versus competition. Which two or three elements in the value chain does that firm handle especially well? For each of those elements, what do they do that is better than their competition?

3. Historically, the theme park industry in Orlando is heavily affected by a large number of macro-level external environmental factors. From each of the five major categories of macro-level external factors, identify a specific example of how some element within that category might impact a theme park's marketing planning for the next couple of years. Be sure to explain *why* you believe each of your examples will be important for marketing managers to consider as they develop their marketing plans.

MARKETING PLAN EXERCISES

ACTIVITY 2.1: Elements of a Marketing Plan

In the chapter, you learned that marketing planning drives the activities of the marketing manager and you were provided a framework for marketing planning. Before you move further through this course, it is important to be sure that you understand the flow and content of a typical marketing plan.

1. Read the annotated marketing plan example presented on this book's Web site (www.mhhe.com/marshalless1e).

2. Make notes about any questions you may have about the example plan, and be prepared to bring those questions to class for clarification.

3. If you are going to be using Marketing Plan Pro Software to develop your marketing plan, take this opportunity to open your copy of the software and familiarize yourself with its functionality. An electronic template for your marketing plan that follows Exhibit 2.2 in the chapter (which is the same format used in the CloudCab Small Jet Taxi Service example located on our Web site) can be accessed at www.mhhe.com/marshalless1e.

If you are using Marketing Plan Pro, a template for this assignment can be accessed at www.mhhe.com/marshalless1e.

ACTIVITY 2.2: Situation Analysis

In the chapter you also learned about the key situation analysis areas of external macro-level environmental factors, competitive forces, and internal environmental factors that marketing managers must consider in marketing planning. You also saw how this information can be conveniently summarized and portrayed in a SWOT analysis.

1. Using the chapter discussion on situation analysis along with Exhibit 2.10 as a guide, develop a short list of internal strengths and weaknesses and external opportunities and threats. Focus on issues that you believe will be most important to your marketing planning over the next year or so.

2. Exhibit 2.10 suggests that you consider the four different scenario combinations of the SWOT analysis to begin to brainstorm possible strategies. Based on what you know at present, develop one idea for a marketing strategy that might be appropriate for each of the four situational scenario combinations represented in the exhibit—that is, one strategy that uses internal strengths to take advantage of external opportunities you have identified; one strategy that uses internal strengths to avoid external threats you have identified; one strategy that takes advantage of opportunities by overcoming internal weaknesses you have identified; and one strategy that minimizes internal weaknesses and avoids external threats.

If you are using Marketing Plan Pro, a template for this assignment can be accessed at www.mhhe.com/marshalless1e.

ACTIVITY 2.3: Thinking Globally; Marketing Plan Tasks

For any company doing business in a global market it is essential to consider the unique elements of that market in developing the marketing plan. Consider the discussion of global marketing in Chapter 1 as you:

- Identify possible global markets for a new product.
- Determine essential information needed to assess the market opportunity.

Keep in mind that specific marketing strategies will be presented throughout the book. However, it will be important to keep the global marketing discussion in mind as you develop your marketing plan.

If you are using Marketing Plan Pro, a template for this assignment can be accessed at www.mhhe.com/marshalless1e.

part TWO

Information Drives Marketing Decision Making

CHAPTER 03

Perspectives on CRM and Marketing Metrics

LEARNING OBJECTIVES

- Define CRM and articulate its objectives and capabilities.

- Describe the CRM process cycle.

- Understand the concept of customer touchpoints and why touchpoints are critical in CRM.

- Distinguish customer marketing from consumer marketing, and understand why the distinction is important.

- Discuss what happens when CRM fails and how to avoid potential failure.

- Understand the concept of a marketing dashboard and how it improves marketing planning for a firm.

- Explain return on marketing investment (ROMI), including cautions about its use.

- Identify other relevant marketing metrics and how they are applied.

WHAT IS CRM?

Defining CRM (customer relationship management) is a great place to begin. CustomerThink.com, formerly CRMGuru.com, bills itself as "the global thought leader in customer-centric business strategy." CRMGuru.com founder Bob Thompson has offered the following definition of CRM:

> CRM is a business strategy to select and manage the most valuable customer relationships. CRM requires a customer-centric business philosophy and culture to support effective marketing, sales, and service processes. CRM applications can enable effective customer relationship management, provided that an enterprise has the right leadership, strategy, and culture.[1]

You should quickly recognize that the above concept is consistent with much of the learning from Chapter 1, which emphasized that value and customer relationships are two of the core concepts in marketing. Chapter 2 discussed marketing planning as the means by which firms create, communicate, and deliver value to customers. You have seen how concepts of customer orientation and a customer-centric philosophy of business are essential ingredients of organizational success. CRM enables and supports the implementation of a customer orientation.[2]

Up front, it is important to state that some people have already (mistakenly) dismissed CRM as just another business fad that has passed its prime. Remember the various marketing buzzwords introduced in Chapter 1? Some might say that CRM is just another consultant-hyped repackaging of business principles everyone already knows. However, thoughtful managers understand and view CRM differently. Let's consider other definitions of CRM offered by several highly regarded sources:

From Professor George Day of the Wharton Business School:

> CRM is a cross-functional process for achieving a continuing dialogue with customers, across all of their contact and access points, with personalized treatment of the most valuable customers, to increase customer retention and the effectiveness of marketing initiatives.[3]

Customer-centered leadership is at the core of Chick-fil-A's service. Chick-fil-A understands the concept that "nobody can sell your business better than your customers." When Chick-fil-A opens a new restaurant, it seeks out Chick-fil-A aficionados already in the area. Regulars at other Chick-fil-A locations get a special free dinner the night before the official opening. This builds customer advocates that are happy to spread the word and willing to go the extra mile to support Chick-fil-A.[4]

From Ron Swift, author of *Accelerating Customer Relationships* and vice president at leading CRM firm Teradata, a division of NCR:

> CRM is an enterprise approach to understanding and influencing customer behavior through meaningful communications in order to improve customer acquisition, customer retention, customer loyalty, and customer profitability.[5]

From Don Peppers and Martha Rogers, founding partners of the Peppers and Rogers group and coauthors of several books on one-to-one customer relationships:

> CRM is an enterprisewide business strategy for achieving customer-specific objectives by taking customer-specific actions.[6]

CRM enables great marketing in part because of its ability to facilitate two-way interactions with customers through smart phones and other convenient communication modes.

The core message of how CRM contributes to firm success provides compelling evidence that CRM is not merely a fad. Careful perusal across these definitions yields strong commonalities, synthesized within the following key points. CRM:

- Cuts across the whole business enterprise.
- Is a business strategy, set of operational processes, and analytic tools.
- Is enabled by technology but is not just "the software."
- Has the ultimate goal of maximizing performance of the customer side of the enterprise.
- To be successful requires a customer-centric philosophy and culture, as well as leadership and commitment to CRM from the top.

Why a strong focus on CRM in a marketing management textbook? Two simple reasons: (1) CRM is a timely and relevant topic that ties together a number of important concepts of modern marketing management; and (2) CRM is an important *enabler* of great marketing. From a managerial perspective, gaining an understanding of CRM *now* will set the stage for much of what follows in this book. Any competent marketing manager must understand CRM. The goal of this chapter is not to transform you into an instant CRM guru. Rather, it is to provide perspectives on CRM that will assist you as a current or future manager in developing and implementing a customer-centric approach to your business, an activity that is central to maximizing firm success and far from a fad.[7]

In fact, you will find that the overview of CRM in this chapter builds directly on what you learned in Part 1 about value and customer relationships at the core of marketing and then later connects directly to many of the elements of marketing management to be developed in future chapters, including market research, marketing communication, and marketing metrics. Let's begin by connecting CRM to what we've learned so far.

OBJECTIVES AND CAPABILITIES OF CRM

To begin, we can now offer our own preferred definition of **CRM (customer relationship management):** a comprehensive business model for increasing revenues and profits by focusing on customers. Significantly, this definition does not speak to who should "own CRM" within the organization. In the mid-1990s, the introductory days of CRM systems by Siebel and others, CEOs tended to relegate the operation of a firm's CRM system to the information technology group. After all, CRM is technology-based, isn't it? But legendary horror stories abound about CEOs who purchased multimillion-dollar CRM installations purely on the recommendation of the IT department, without any significant consultation with those in the firm who would be the system's primary *users,* such as salespeople, marketing managers, and customer service representatives. In the end, through the school of hard knocks, firms learned that no one group should have "ownership" of the CRM system. Positioning CRM as a comprehensive business model provides the impetus for top management to properly support it over the long run and for various internal stakeholder groups to have the opportunity to both use it and impact how it is used.[8]

Fortunately, with many of the initial CRM adoption misfires relegated to the past, most companies are now adopting CRM as a mission-critical business strategy. It is considered mission-critical largely because of competitive pressures in the marketplace; nobody can afford to be the lone wolf that does not have a handle on the customer side of an enterprise in a competitive space.

To optimize CRM's potential for contribution to the bottom line, companies are redesigning internal structures, as well as internal and external business processes and systems, to make it easier for customers to do business with them. Although marketing does not "own" CRM, because of CRM's focus on aligning the organization's internal and external processes and systems to be more customer-centric, marketing managers are a core contributor to the success of CRM by virtue of their expertise on customers and relationships.[9] And in particular, as Chapter 14 will discuss in detail, the sales force in CRM-driven organizations has taken center stage in executing a firm's customer management strategies, complete with new titles befitting the new sales roles such as "client manager," "relationship manager," and "business solution consultant."

Ultimately, CRM has three major objectives:

1. *Customer acquisition*—acquire the *right* customers based on known or learned characteristics that will drive growth and increase margins.

2. *Customer retention*—retain satisfied and loyal customers and channels that are profitable over the long run.

3. *Customer profitability*—increase individual customer margins, while offering the right products at the right time.[10]

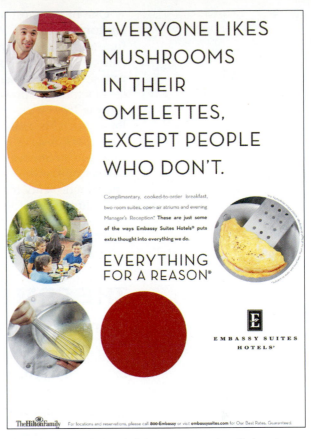

Hoteliers such as Embassy Suites can customize offerings to loyal users by maintaining customer preference profiles.

Accomplishing these objectives requires a clear focus on the product and service attributes that represent value to the customer and that create customer satisfaction and loyalty. **Customer satisfaction** means the level of liking an individual harbors for an offering—that is, to what level is the offering meeting or exceeding the customer's expectations? **Customer loyalty** means the degree to which an individual will resist switching, or defecting, from one offering to another. Loyalty is usually based on high satisfaction coupled with a high level of perceived value derived from the offering and a strong relationship with the provider and its brand(s). Customer satisfaction and loyalty are two extremely popular metrics used by marketing managers to gauge the health of their business and brands.[11]

BMW's Mini has become an international success with high levels of customer satisfaction and loyalty. The Mini was originally launched in 1959 and since has gone through multiple corporate owners until eventually becoming one of the most successful relaunches in brand history. The car has a multitude of hard-core loyalists that are thoroughly enthralled by the brand, publish blogs and monthly magazines in its honor, and operate numerous groups on Facebook.[12]

All of this implies strong integration of CRM into the overall marketing planning process of a firm. Perusal of the elements of marketing planning presented in Chapter 2 reveals numerous points at which information derived from a CRM system can assist in the strategy development and execution process. Key parts of a marketing plan that rely on CRM-generated information include the situation analysis, market research, strategy development, implementation, and measurement phases of marketing planning. In fact, many of the metrics that marketing managers use to assess their success are derived directly from the firm's CRM system.[13]

One of the most important metrics in CRM is that of the **lifetime value of a customer.** Fredrick Reichheld in his books on customer loyalty has demonstrated time and again that investment in CRM yields more successful long-term relationships with customers, and that these relationships pay handsomely in terms of cost savings, revenue growth, profits, referrals, and other important business success factors. It is possible to actually calculate an estimate of the projected financial returns from a customer, or **return on customer investment (ROCI),** over the long run. This analysis provides a very useful strategic tool for deciding which customers deserve what levels of investment of various resources (money, people, time, information, etc.). Later in this chapter we will introduce a sampling of other marketing metrics. Many of the most useful marketing metrics derive their power and functionality from CRM.

Proliferation of ROCI analysis has raised the prospects of **firing a customer** who exhibits a low predicted lifetime value, and instead investing resources in other more profitable customers. Of course, such action assumes other more attractive customers exist.[14]

THE CRM PROCESS CYCLE

The process cycle for CRM may be divided into the following four elements: (1) knowledge discovery, (2) market planning, (3) customer interaction, and (4) analysis and refinement. Elements of the process cycle are portrayed in Exhibit 3.1 and discussed below.

Knowledge Discovery

Knowledge discovery is the process of analyzing the customer information acquired through various customer touchpoints, or customer "contact and access points" in the terminology of George Day's definition of CRM.[15] At their essence,

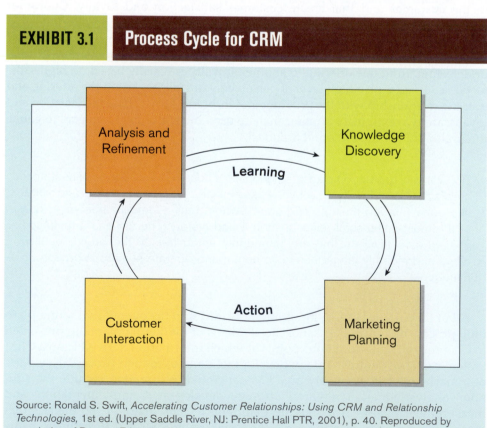

EXHIBIT 3.1 **Process Cycle for CRM**

Source: Ronald S. Swift, *Accelerating Customer Relationships: Using CRM and Relationship Technologies*, 1st ed. (Upper Saddle River, NJ: Prentice Hall PTR, 2001), p. 40. Reproduced by permission of Pearson Education, Inc., Upper Saddle River, New Jersey.

touchpoints are where the selling firm touches the customer in some way, thus allowing for information about him or her to be collected. These might include point-of-sale systems, call-center files, Internet accesses, records from direct selling or customer service encounters, or any other customer contact experiences. Touchpoints occur at the intersection of a business event that takes place via a channel using some media, such as online inquiry from a prospect, telephone follow-up with a purchaser on a service issue, face-to-face encounter with a salesperson, and so on.[16]

A **data warehouse** environment is the optimal approach to handling all the customer data generated through the touchpoints and transforming it into useful information for marketing management decision making and marketing planning. A data warehouse affords the opportunity to combine large amounts of information and then use data mining techniques to learn more about current and potential customers.[17]

Data mining is a sophisticated analytical approach to using the massive amounts of data accumulated through the CRM system to develop segments and micro-segments of customers either for purposes of market research or development of market segmentation strategies. It is important to remember the concepts of a data warehouse and data mining as you read in Chapter 4 on market research about internal sources of data for marketing decision making.[18]

The knowledge discovery phase of the CRM process cycle becomes the focal point for many direct marketers. Direct marketing involves utilizing the data generated through this phase to develop "hit lists" of customer prospects, who are then contacted individually by various means of marketing communication. This activity is often referred to as **database marketing.**[19]

Marketing Planning

The next phase in the CRM process cycle is marketing planning, which represents a key use of the *output* from the knowledge discovery phase. That is, the information enables the capability to develop marketing and customer strategies and programs. CRM input into the marketing planning process is particularly useful in developing elements of the marketing mix strategies, including employing the marketing communication mix in integrated ways to customize approaches to different customer groups (this concept of integrated marketing communication will be discussed in Chapters 13 and 14).[20]

Customer Interaction

The customer interaction phase represents the actual implementation of the customer strategies and programs. This includes the personal selling effort, as well as all other customer-directed interactions. These must be aimed at all the customer touchpoints, or channels of customer contact, both in person and electronically.[21]

Analysis and Refinement

Finally, the analysis and refinement phase of the CRM process is where **organizational learning** occurs based on customer response to the implemented strategies and programs. Think of it as market research in the form of a continuous dialogue with customers, facilitated by effective use of CRM tools. With such

Even a manufacturer like Campbell's Soup can utilize touchpoints to communicate highly usable information to customers, in this case via a recipe for a new meal idea using soup and risotto.

an ongoing commitment and capability related to customer research, continuous adjustments made to the firm's overall customer initiatives should result in more efficient investment of resources and increasing ROCI.[22]

MORE ON CUSTOMER TOUCHPOINTS

You have read that CRM initiatives depend heavily on interactions with customers, suppliers, or prospects via one or more touchpoints—such as a call center, salesperson, distributor, store, branch office, Web site, or e-mail. CRM entails both acquiring knowledge about customers and (where feasible) deploying information to customers at the touchpoint. Some touchpoints are *interactive* and allow for such two-way information exchange. That is, they involve *direct interface* between a customer and a firm's customer contact person in the form of a salesperson, telemarketer, customer service representative, interactive Web site, and so on. Other touchpoints are *noninteractive*; that is, the customer may simply provide information on a static Web site's data entry form or by mail, without the capability of simultaneous direct interface with a company representative. To maximize a firm's ability to successfully use touchpoints, an ongoing concerted effort must be undertaken to: (1) identify *all* potential touchpoints, (2) develop specific objectives for what kind of information can be collected at each touchpoint, (3) determine how that information will be collected and ultimately integrated into the firm's overall customer database, and (4) develop policies on how the information will be accessed and used.

For decades, companies have tried relentlessly to get into the mind of the customer. Dunnhumby, a firm that specializes in identifying customers' purchasing behavior, has assisted many companies, including the British supermarket chain Tesco, Kroger, Home Depot, and most recently Macy's, in boosting sales. Rather than helping companies find new shoppers, Dunnhumby reveals hidden facts about clients' *current customers* through interactive and noninteractive touchpoints. Insights from Dunnhumby helped Kroger boost sales by 5 percent.[23]

The aspect of CRM involving customer information collected through touchpoints raises substantial ethical and legal issues for the firm regarding privacy, particularly in the consumer marketplace. Clearly, a key component of a strong customer relationship with a firm is a high level of *trust*.[24] Customers must be absolutely certain that the information a firm collects and stores about them will not be used for unintended purposes. Often referred to as the "dark side of CRM," this issue has become so prominent in some industries that firms are beginning to publicly promote guarantees of nonabuse of stored customer information as a means of attracting customers.[25] It is a feature that resonates well with customers and likely provides a strong point of differentiation over competitors. Ethical Dimension 3a looks at customer trust and what can happen when that trust is violated by theft of personal information.

Touchpoints: The USAA Experience

For an example of how information collected through touchpoints works to the benefit of both a firm and its customers, consider the case of USAA Insurance, based in San Antonio, Texas. USAA's core market began with military officers and their families; the firm was established because many years ago officers had difficulty getting insurance at reasonable rates due to the extreme mobility associated with their career paths. USAA has grown to become a broad-based insurance and financial services provider with a bank, virtual retail store, and one of the largest volume credit-card operations worldwide. Ninety-nine percent of USAA's

ETHICAL DIMENSION 3a

CRM's Dark Side: The Cost of Protecting Customer Data

A critical success factor of CRM is the ability to collect, analyze, and act on customer data. This often means gathering *confidential* customer data. An inherent problem with collecting this information, making it available to individuals inside the organization, and then empowering them to deal with the customer is the resulting opportunity for theft of confidential customer records.

One industry particularly vulnerable to data theft is financial services, which collects and uses sensitive customer information, such as specific purchase patterns (what, where, when, and how much customers spend), then links the information to account numbers and other private information. Securing information and making it available only to those who really need to know it is a vital part of keeping customers' trust.

Both customers and firms are increasingly concerned about securing critical customer data. The size of the company and level of security doesn't always protect against theft, as security breaches have occurred at Bank of America, Wachovia Bank, FedEx, Blue Cross, and TJ Maxx, for example. Any company is vulnerable either from external hackers who gain access to data or internal sources (employees) who violate company policies to steal sensitive data from the inside.

The costs of data theft are high and extend well beyond the direct cost/value of the data itself. Checkpoint, a leader in identification and verification services, was hacked by thieves who stole confidential data for 145,000 customers. The result was the identity theft of more than 700 individuals, resulting in over $26 million in legal fees and fines and a major public relations meltdown for the company. A firm's company image, reputation, and brands can be severely damaged when customer trust is breached in this way, and once customer trust is lost it is difficult—maybe impossible—to regain. One study suggests that companies can expect 20 percent of their customers to defect after such an event and another 40 percent to take steps toward defecting, including checking out alternative vendors.

For firms, the cost of data protection is high with encryption, back-up data files, and other security measures running in the millions of dollars. As a result, companies often take a wait-and-see attitude on investing in such measures, as noted in a recent study where only one-third of financial service companies reported encrypting data in storage. Of course, the cost of customer defection based on lost trust is also very high. The challenge for many companies is finding the right balance between securing customer data and incurring unnecessary levels of data security costs. Unfortunately, many companies end up copping an attitude of "it won't happen to us."[26]

Ethical Perspective

1. **Companies:** What priority would you place on securing customer data? For example, would you invest $10 million in greater security for customer data or an upgrade for a four-year-old network?

2. **Customers:** How would you respond if your bank told you that your data had been compromised? Would you consider changing banks?

---

business is conducted over the phone or online. The company also has one of the most sophisticated and best-managed CRM systems in the world. USAA was rated the No. 1 customer service champ in *BusinessWeek*'s first-ever ranking of companies where the customer is king.[27]

USAA takes great care to protect the information stored about its customers, who are called members. The company is very transparent in asking members for permission before information is shared even between USAA's own internal divisions (insurance, bank, retail, credit card, etc.), let alone with any outside companies. Whenever a member makes contact with USAA, the level of security becomes very apparent through access codes and verifications of identity. USAA is diligent about collecting and continually updating information on members yet is not obtrusive either in how it collects the information or in how it uses the information for outbound communication.

Firms typically use customer information collected for purposes of up-selling and cross-selling current customers on other available products and services they might want and need—and USAA is no different. One way CRM facilitates customer relationships is through a firm's capability to better customize its product line to individual customers, a process known as one-to-one marketing. However, unlike some other firms, USAA has very strict policies on the voracity with which such selling can be executed. USAA will not risk damaging a long-term member relationship through overly aggressive selling approaches.

Even though a USAA member is likely to never meet a USAA employee face-to-face, USAA continually scores among the highest of any financial services firm on customer satisfaction and loyalty; USAA members simply do not leave. One of the key results of USAA's commitment to CRM is the capability for any one of the thousands of USAA customer representatives a member may reach on a given call to pull up that member's record and carry on a conversation as though they have been doing business for years. Customer representatives undergo extensive training not just on the technical aspects of the CRM system, but also on the strategic aspects of using CRM to operationalize a customer-centric culture and build long-term relationships with members. Ask USAA members how they like doing business with the company, and they are likely to respond very favorably and with conviction. USAA executives, and USAA members, attribute much of the success of the firm to its customer-centric culture, operationalized through well-executed CRM.[28]

CUSTOMER MARKETING VERSUS CONSUMER MARKETING

An important distinction in organizational philosophy and focus can be spotted by observing whether a firm's marketing managers tend to talk about customers or consumers. The following description of consumers is only partially facetious. In marketing, consumers tend to be thought of in the role of faceless reactors to a firm's marketing strategies to the masses. In fact, the term **mass marketing** was coined to connote this classic style of consumer marketing. In this context, consumers are the perennial subjects of sophisticated marketing research in the form of surveys, focus groups, and purchase diaries. But to actually get to know a consumer individually—to make a concerted effort to respond to his or her unique needs and wants—is a very different way of thinking from that of traditional mass marketing approaches.[29]

Mass marketing is still alive and well today, but many firms are evolving away from it as their primary approach to marketing. In the 1960s, many firms began to apply principles of segmentation, target marketing, and positioning to mass markets to create different strategies and marketing programs for different consumer groups within those markets. A major change in mind-set precipitates a shift from targeted **consumer marketing** (i.e., marketing to big groups of like-minded buyers) to **customer marketing,** or a focus on developing relationships with individuals. Ultimately, it is the sophistication and multiplicity of available technology today—and especially CRM—that enables the shift to mass customization and one-to-one marketing as introduced in Chapter 1.[30] Firms that choose to make the investment are now able to better customize offerings to the wants and needs of individual users. Exhibit 3.2 shows the phases of this evolutionary process in marketing, with characteristics and technology attributes of each.

Visa does a great job of customer marketing by identifying and customizing their offering to the wants and needs of individual users. Visiting the URL in this ad opens the door to an array of discounts offered from a diverse selection of companies for customers from all walks of life.

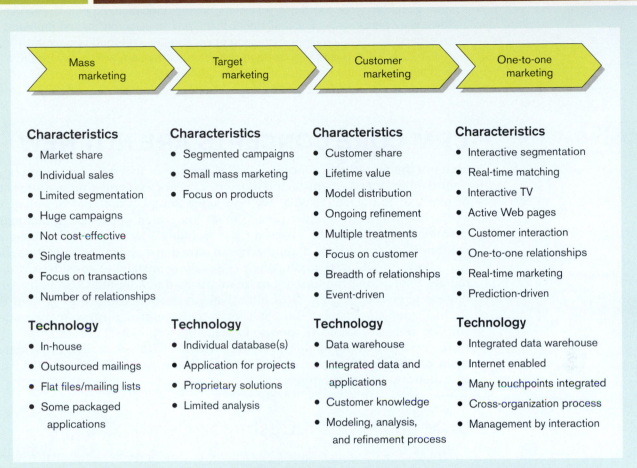

Mass marketing	Target marketing	Customer marketing	One-to-one marketing

Characteristics

- Market share
- Individual sales
- Limited segmentation
- Huge campaigns
- Not cost-effective
- Single treatments
- Focus on transactions
- Number of relationships

Characteristics

- Segmented campaigns
- Small mass marketing
- Focus on products

Characteristics

- Customer share
- Lifetime value
- Model distribution
- Ongoing refinement
- Multiple treatments
- Focus on customer
- Breadth of relationships
- Event-driven

Characteristics

- Interactive segmentation
- Real-time matching
- Interactive TV
- Active Web pages
- Customer interaction
- One-to-one relationships
- Real-time marketing
- Prediction-driven

Technology

- In-house
- Outsourced mailings
- Flat files/mailing lists
- Some packaged applications

Technology

- Individual database(s)
- Application for projects
- Proprietary solutions
- Limited analysis

Technology

- Data warehouse
- Integrated data and applications
- Customer knowledge
- Modeling, analysis, and refinement process

Technology

- Integrated data warehouse
- Internet enabled
- Many touchpoints integrated
- Cross-organization process
- Management by interaction

Source: Ronald S. Swift, *Accelerating Customer Relationships: Using CRM and Relationship Technologies,* 1st ed. (Upper Saddle River, NJ: Prentice Hall PTR, 2001), p. 38. Reproduced by permission of Pearson Education, Inc., Upper Saddle River, New Jersey.

Advantages of Customer Marketing

CRM-driven one-to-one marketing has several advantages over traditional mass marketing including the following:

- Reduced promotional costs due to decreased reliance on expensive mass media and redirection of promotional investment to more targeted promotional vehicles such as targeted advertising and direct marketing.
- Improved targeting of specific customers by focusing on their needs and wants.
- Improved capability to track the effectiveness of a given promotional campaign.
- Increased effectiveness in competing on value-adding properties such as customization and service, thus reducing reliance on price competition.
- Increased sensitivity to the differing levels of potential across customers, thus reducing overspending on low-ROI customers or underspending on high-ROI customers.
- Increased speed in the time it takes to develop and market a product (product development cycle).
- Improved use of the customer channel, enabling customers to interact more directly and efficiently with the firm, thus making the most of each contact with a customer.[31]

CRM CORE CONCEPTS ARE NOT NEW

Many of the underlying concepts of CRM are not all that new. You could open a marketing management textbook from 25 years ago and find a discussion of many of the tenets of what we now refer to as CRM. What has changed in the environment to allow for the more integrated approach to managing customers represented by modern CRM is today's technology; the development of more sophisticated approaches to data management became the spark that allowed CRM to flourish. Yet, it is a serious mistake to consider CRM as merely a software program. In fact, many firms that adopted CRM in its early days struggled with their CRM initiatives precisely because they bought the sophisticated software but did not have the culture, structure, systems, leadership, or internal technical expertise to make the initiative successful.[33]

The next sections highlight two characteristics of CRM—its ability to facilitate a customer-centric culture and its ability to enable the transformation of a firm into a relationship-based enterprise.

CRM Facilitates a Customer-Centric Culture

A firm that is customer-centric places the customer at the core of the enterprise including everything that happens, both inside and outside the firm. Customers are the lifeblood of any business—without them a firm has no sales, no profits, and ultimately no business. As such, marketing managers must approach their role with the attitude that customers are worth investing considerable resources against so long as an acceptable return on that investment can be anticipated.

At the strategic marketing level, a customer-centric culture includes, but is not limited to, the following major components:

1. Adopting a relationship or partnership business model overall, with mutually shared rewards and risk management.
2. Redefining the selling role within the firm to focus on customer business consultation and solutions.
3. Increasing formalization of customer analysis processes.
4. Taking a proactive leadership role in educating customers about value chain opportunities available by developing a business relationship.
5. Focusing on continuous improvement principles stressing customer satisfaction and loyalty.[34]

The effort a firm makes toward cultivating a customer-centric culture requires a high degree of formalization within the firm. **Formalization** means that structure, processes and tools, and managerial knowledge and commitment are formally established in support of the culture. With these elements in place, strategies and programs can be successfully developed and executed toward the goals related to customers, accompanied by a high degree of confidence they will yield the desired results. Today, the most prevalent formalization mechanism of a customer-centric culture is CRM.

As mentioned in Chapter 1, firms that are customer-centric have a high level of customer orientation. Organizations practicing a customer orientation place the customer at the core of all aspects of the enterprise and:

1. Instill an organization-wide focus on understanding the requirements of customers.

2. Generate an understanding of the customer marketplace and disseminate that knowledge to everyone in the firm.

3. Align system capabilities internally so that the organization responds effectively to customers with innovative, competitively differentiated, satisfaction-generating products and services.[35]

How do the concepts of customer centricity and customer orientation connect to the actions required by individual members of a firm? One way to think about how an organization member might exhibit a customer orientation is through a **customer mind-set,** which is a person's belief that understanding and satisfying customers, whether internal or external to the organization, is central to the proper execution of his or her job.[36] It is through organization members' customer mind-set that a customer orientation "comes alive" within a firm. Exhibit 3.3 provides example descriptors of customer mind-set both in the context of customers outside the firm as well as people inside the firm with whom one must interact to get the job done (internal customers).

Walmart has been working hard to solidify its community connectedness, organizational culture, and business model to allow the "world's largest retailer" to become an enabler of customer relationships.

The travel Web site Kayak.com has an unusual business model. Founder Paul English truly believes that understanding and satisfying customers is a central element of all employees' jobs. Thus, Kayak.com does not have a dedicated customer-service staff. Instead, each employee (including English) spends about 20 minutes of each workday responding to online queries and complaints. The more than 200 customer feedback forms filled out each day are divided among the 58 employees. Clearly, Kayak.com employees have a strong customer mind-set and understand that they and the firm will perform better when they better understand their customers.[37]

CRM Enables Transformation into a Relationship-Based Enterprise

As we surmised from the various experts' definitions of CRM earlier in the chapter, CRM represents a business strategy, a set of operational processes, and analytic tools to enable or facilitate a truly customer-driven enterprise. Facilitating long-term, win-win relationships between buyer and seller firms—a **relationship-based enterprise**—is a central goal of CRM. To move toward being such a firm, and to improve the effectiveness of CRM's role in this process, several critical questions must be answered by marketing managers.[38]

EXHIBIT 3.3   Do You Have a Customer Mind-Set?

External Customer Mind-Set

I believe that …

- I must understand the needs of my company's customers.
- It is critical to provide value to my company's customers.
- I am primarily interested in satisfying my company's customers.
- I must understand who buys my company's products/services.
- I can perform my job better if I understand the needs of my company's customers.
- Understanding my company's customers will help me do my job better.

Internal Customer Mind-Set

I believe that …

- Employees who receive my work are my customers.
- Meeting the needs of employees who receive my work is critical to doing a good job.
- It is important to receive feedback from employees who receive my work.
- I focus on the requirements of the person who receives my work.

Score yourself from 1–6 on each item such that 1 = strongly disagree and 6 = strongly agree. Total your score; a higher score equates to more of a customer mind-set.

Source: Karen Norman Kennedy, Felicia G. Lassk, and Jerry R. Goolsby. Reprinted with kind permission from Springer Science + Business Media: *Journal of the Academy of Marketing Science*, "Customer Mind-Set of Employees Throughout the Organization," Vol. 30, 2002, pp.159–171, by Koren Norman Kennedy, et al. Copyright©2002.

These questions are grouped by categories: customers, the relationship, and managerial decision making.

Customers

1. Who are our customers?
2. What do our customers want and expect?
3. What is the value proposition of our customers?

The Relationship

4. What kind of relationship do we want to build with our customers?
5. How do we foster exchange of value between us and our customers?
6. How do we work together and *share* control?

Managerial Decision Making

7. Who are we and what is our value proposition?
8. What do our products and brands represent to customers?
9. How do we organize to move value closer to our customers?
10. How do we measure and manage our performance?
11. How do we increase our capacity for change?

Clearly, these questions are not trivial. The amount of time and other resources invested toward gaining satisfactory answers to these questions is directly related to the capability of CRM to enable a relationship-based enterprise. The answers guide (1) the evolution of the firm's relationships with customers, (2) the creation of a companywide relationship management strategy, and (3) the selection of CRM solutions with the most appropriate combination and application of supporting technologies.[39]

Oracle CRM On Demand has been successful providing subscription-based CRM applications that allow salespeople, marketers, service personnel, and customer contact people to access customer data easily. Moreover, its customizable applications encourage users to easily input customer data into the company's customer information system. Reprinted courtesy of Oracle Corporation.

WHAT HAPPENS WHEN CRM FAILS?

Not surprisingly, when CRM fails it is usually not because of the *software* part of CRM. Rather, CRM failures are usually attributable to something related to the *people* part—a firm's culture, structure, and strategy. Specifically, issues related to leadership and management are the most commonly cited reasons CRM does not live up to its potential in a firm.

Consider the following problems that are not at all uncommon in firms adopting CRM. Each problem is coupled with an appropriate "fix."

- *Flavor of the month club*—Trying one CRM software package after another, usually through upgrading, occurs under the pretense that no system has been a good fit. To correct this, the process must be reversed. Involve *every user* in determining *in advance* what the key desired deliverables are from the CRM system, then purchase the system that meets those goals.

- *No allowances for organizational change*—Successful adoption of CRM can't be a "technology first, change later" process. Instead, organization-wide discussions and formal plans for organizational change must be in place *before* implementing the CRM program. This includes changes in culture, structure, processes, systems, and leadership and management.

- *Low level of employee buy-in*—Because CRM is an enterprisewide initiative, it will touch nearly everyone in a firm in some way over time. The time spent up front in involving everyone in the organization with the CRM selection/design process will pay dividends later through better utilization and results. It is particularly important that the firm realign its performance management system, such as incentives and rewards, to motivate utilization of CRM by organization members.

- *Business units silos*—CRM needs cross-functional integration of information gathering, analysis, and dissemination inside a firm to work. Lack of cross-functional planning and poor communication among departments within a firm cause difficulties in CRM. The biggest mistake is thinking CRM is "owned" by the IT people in a firm simply because the process is technology-driven. No one functional group should control CRM. Instead, with strong leadership support from the top, cross-disciplinary teams should be established from the very initiation of the planning stages for CRM that require IT, marketing, operations, and the other functional areas to work together to maximize the opportunity CRM affords.

- *Poor training*—CRM doesn't work on autopilot, and even the best CRM system in the hands of a poorly trained user will add little value to a firm's customer initiatives. When a firm makes a commitment to invest in CRM, it is also making an implicit commitment to make initial and ongoing training *priority one* in implementing CRM. Firms should develop a system for employee feedback to management on CRM successes and failures and should foster a climate for employee input on ideas for system improvements. The best firms institutionalize these processes through reward systems with payoffs to employees whose ideas help increase the effectiveness of the CRM initiative.[40]

When Harley-Davidson experienced a drift in product quality some years back, it had to figure out ways to get customers back once the quality issues were corrected. Part of recapturing customers was through an aggressive advertising campaign and the other part was better understanding of what customers want. How did Harley-Davidson do this? President and Chief Operating Officer Jim McCaslin stated, "Basically, management started going to events to reconnect with the customers ... riding with our customers, hanging out with our customers, talking with our customers, learning and listening and then coming back and making changes based on what we had heard. That's probably one of the key things that we did as a company early on: Management went out with the customers. And we still do that today." Harley-Davidson's success in reconnecting with its customers has created the foundation for one of the strongest relationship-based enterprises in all of business.[41]

Implementing a CRM system and then having it disappoint or fail is much worse for a firm than if it had never attempted CRM. It is much harder to go back after the fact and correct fundamental mistakes in CRM implementation. Not only can a CRM failure represent a substantial financial hit for the company, but it also is demoralizing to the organizational culture, particularly when competitive firms may be visibly successful in using a similar system. When considering CRM, the likelihood of a successful implementation increases dramatically when the firm can demonstrate the following characteristics:

- Strong internal partnerships exist throughout the firm around the CRM strategy.

- Organization members at all levels and in all areas are actively involved in collecting information using the CRM system.

- CRM tools are employee- and customer-friendly.

- Reporting consists only of data the firm can actually use.

- The CRM system is only as high-tech as necessary; if a lower tech solution is sufficient, it should be used.

In the end, the software part of CRM will work, and can probably do far more for any firm than expected. CRM's real strengths, as well as its fragilities, rest with how the organization chooses to use CRM as a means of enabling a customer-centric culture and operationalizing a customer orientation as an ongoing driver of the enterprise. CRM across all dimensions—as a business strategy, set of processes, and analytic tools—has amazing potential to facilitate great marketing planning and management.

THE MARKETING DASHBOARD

Consider how a dashboard of a car, airplane, or even a video game provides you with a lot of crucial information in real time and in a convenient format. So it should be with a **marketing dashboard,** which is a comprehensive system providing managers with up-to-the-minute information necessary to run their operation including data on actual sales versus forecast, progress on marketing plan objectives, distribution channel effectiveness, sales force productivity, brand equity evolution, and whatever metrics and information are uniquely relevant to the role of the marketing manager in a particular organization.[42] Clearly, a dashboard metaphor for this process of capturing, shaping, and improving marketing effectiveness and efficiency is a good one.[43]

Marketing touches many aspects of a company's operations. For example, Oracle uses its customer experience program to drive customer improvement and growth. After obtaining results from its CRM program, Oracle regularly links its customer feedback data to its operational and financial data, including turnaround time, wait time, license revenue, and maintenance revenue. In linking the data analyses, the firm can manage its customer relationships by applying appropriate metrics and determine the ROI on investments to improve the customer experience.[44]

How does a marketing dashboard manifest itself? It could appear in your inbox weekly or monthly in the form of a color printout, be beamed through cyberspace as e-mail updates, or be accessible on a password-protected Web site on your company intranet. Its physical form and layout should be developed within your organization *by* managers *for* managers. Search the Internet for "Marketing Dashboards" and you will be amazed at how many consulting firms come up, each working hard to convince you that its proprietary approach to a marketing dashboard is the right one for you. To successfully compete in today's market, firms must focus on marketing planning so that managers and executives have the core information about progress toward relevant goals and metrics at their fingertips *at all times.* This is what a dashboard approach delivers.

A marketing dashboard approach to enhance marketing planning delivers five key benefits summarized in Exhibit 3.4.

Goals and Elements of a Marketing Dashboard

An effective dashboard is organic, not static. The dashboard must adapt and change with the organization as objectives are clarified and redefined, as causal relationships are established between metrics and results, and as confidence in predictive measures grows. About the only thing you know for certain about your first version of a marketing dashboard is that it will likely look very different in a year or two.

Two primary goals of any dashboard are diagnostic insight and predictive foresight—with a special emphasis on the latter. Some dashboard metrics are diagnostic, looking at what has happened and trying to discern why. Probably the most important metrics you'll come to rely on, however, are predictive, using

---

[42]A number of concepts in this section are derived from the following outstanding book, which is the best single source for understanding marketing dashboards. It is highly recommended as a guidebook on the topic for marketing managers: Patrick LaPointe, *Marketing by the Dashboard Light: How to Get More Insight, Foresight, and Accountability from Your Marketing Investments,* New York: ANA, 2005.

EXHIBIT 3.4   Benefits of a Marketing Dashboard

1. **Alignment of Marketing with the Firm**
   A marketing dashboard aligns marketing objectives with the company's financial objectives and corporate strategy through the selection of critical metrics and sharing of results.

2. **Development of Internal Relationships with Marketing**
   The marketing dashboard not only creates organizational alignment *within* marketing by linking all expenditures back to a smaller set of focused objectives, but it also clarifies the relationships *between* marketing and other organizational areas. It crystallizes roles and responsibilities to ensure everyone understands the inherent interdependencies. The result of all this alignment fosters greater job satisfaction within a culture of performance and success.

3. **Establishment of Direct Links between Marketing Spending and Profits**
   A dashboard uses graphical representations of crucial metrics in ways that begin to show, often for the first time, the causal relationships between marketing initiatives and financial results. It portrays historical data in a fashion that makes it easier for any manager to grasp and understand the implications. The result is a greater ability to make smart resource allocations and increase both the efficiency and effectiveness of marketing spending.

4. **Facilitation of Smoother Decision Making**
   A marketing dashboard fosters a learning organization whose members make decisions based on hard facts, creativity, and experiential intuition, rather than as a result of battles based on pure subjectivity. The real benefit of this evolution to a culture of "everyone has the information" is a dramatic reduction in time spent in highly politicized arguments, which greatly speeds decision making in organizations.

5. **Enhancement of Marketing's Ability to Contribute**
   A dashboard creates transparency in marketing's goals, operations, and performance, creating stronger alliances between marketing and the rest of the firm. This elevates marketing's perceived accountability, earning greater trust and confidence from the CEO, CFO, board, and other key decision makers and influencers.

Source: Patrick LaPointe, *Marketing by the Dashboard Light: How to Get More Insight, Foresight, and Accountability from Your Marketing Investments* (New York: ANA, 2005). Courtesy of Marketing NPV LLC © 2003–2008. All rights reserved.

the diagnostic experience to better forecast results under various assumptions of circumstances and resource allocations.[45]

A great marketing dashboard is comprised of the nine elements described in Exhibit 3.5.

Potential Pitfalls in Marketing Dashboards

Although taking a dashboard approach to marketing metrics goes a long way toward enabling successful marketing planning, several potential pitfalls exist in its execution, including the following:

- *Overreliance on "inside-out" measurement.* Having too many internal measures puts the focus on what you already know instead of on the unpredictably dynamic external marketplace. A focus on monitoring external factors likely to cause significant changes to the marketing plan is what makes a dashboard especially valuable.

- *Too many tactical metrics; not enough strategic insight.* Because of the focus over the past decade on holding marketing accountable for financial results, tactical, or "intermediary," metrics have proliferated. Numerous books and articles provide list after list of calculations and ratios to assess all sorts of marketing programmatic results (brand awareness, customer trial, lead conversion, etc.). Although these are valuable and having the right set of intermediary metrics on the dashboard is important, it is critical that they do not overshadow measures of strategic importance to the firm.

- *Forgetting to market the dashboard internally.* One measure of the success of a marketing dashboard is the level at which it is embraced and *used* by managers and executives throughout the firm. As we've emphasized consistently, marketing is not just a department, but rather a part of the strategic and cultural fabric of the enterprise. As such, it is important to market the dashboard internally to key stakeholders, not just to marketers. You want the percentage of senior executives who both believe in and understand what the dashboard is presenting to be very high. Obviously, the CEO should be a target for internal marketing, but just as important is your CFO. The greater the affinity a CFO has for marketing and especially for marketing as a contributor to the firm's long-term success the better.[46]

RETURN ON MARKETING INVESTMENT (ROMI)

CEOs today expect to know exactly what impact an investment in marketing has on a firm's success, especially financially. Hence, it has become critical to consider **return on marketing investment (ROMI)**.[47] Throughout this book we focus on marketing as an *investment*, not as an expense, because a goal-driven investment approach to marketing maximizes the opportunity for a firm's offerings to reach their full potential in the marketplace. The alternative view-point—approaching marketing as an expense tied to a percentage of historical or forecasted sales—both limits market opportunities and thwarts the ability to meaningfully plan for and measure marketing results.[48]

Similar to other investment decisions, investment decisions in marketing must consider four basic elements:

- Level of investment.
- Returns.
- Risks.
- Hurdle rates.

As with any investment, the projected results (returns minus costs) must exceed a certain investment hurdle rate for a given level of risk (both defined by the firm). Hence, ROMI represents either the revenue or the margin generated by a marketing program divided by the cost of that program at a given risk level. The ROMI hurdle rate is defined as the minimum acceptable, expected return on a program at a given level of risk. Consider an example of a relatively low-risk marketing program with costs of $1 million and new revenue generated of $5 million. This program has a ROMI of 5.0. If the company has a marketing budget of $5 million and needs to generate $20 million in revenue, then the ROMI hurdle rate for any low-risk marketing program is 4.0. This means that any marketing program must generate at a minimum $4.00 in revenue for every $1.00 in marketing expenditure. The example ROMI of 5.0 above surpasses the ROMI hurdle rate and is therefore an acceptable marketing program.[49]

Companies have to set their own hurdle rates based on differing levels of potential risk across marketing programs. Risk also tends to vary quite a bit by industry and by whether the marketing plan involves a start-up or an established product line. At its core, ROMI is a tool to help yield more out of marketing. This tool and the way of thinking promoted by the use of the tool within an organization will help marketing managers better conceptualize and execute marketing plans and programs. It puts them in a much better position to connect their planning, measurement, and results to the firm's goals and expectations and, when successful, provides gravitas for the CMO to go back to the CEO for more investment money for marketing.

Cautions about Overreliance on ROMI

Given the above, it's no wonder that ROMI is the *metric du jour* for many firms' marketing bottom line. Several offshoots of ROMI have been developed that apply the same principles to customers (ROCI), brands (ROBI), and promotion (ROPI).[50] Overall, the trend in boardrooms and executive suites of expecting more quantification of marketing's contributions has been a positive one. But remember that within the marketing dashboard concept, what organizations should be reviewing is an *array of relevant metrics*, selected for inclusion on the dashboard because together they paint a picture of firm performance. Managers should always temper the interpretation of ROMI results with review of other appropriate metrics.

In addition, it is important to remember that ROMI was originally designed for comparing capital projects, where investments are made once and the returns flow in during the periods that follow. In marketing, capital projects are analogous to discrete marketing programs or campaigns that have well-defined goals and

---

[47]The single best source for understanding ROMI is the following book, which is highly recommended for marketing managers: Guy R. Powell, *Return on Marketing Investment: Demand More from Your Marketing and Sales Investments*, Albuquerque, NM: RPI Press, 2002. The ideas in this section are drawn from this source.

clear points of beginning and end. However, in practice, ROMI is often applied in situations that have no clear beginning or end. Here are six other commonly expressed objections about an overreliance on ROMI:

1. While a firm may "talk the talk" of marketing as an investment, not an expense, typically marketing expenditures are not treated as an investment in a company's accounting system.

2. ROMI requires the profit to be divided by expenditure, yet all other bottom-line performance measures consider profit or cash flow *after* deducting expenditures.

3. The truth is, ROMI is maximized during the period when profits are still growing. Pursuit of ROMI during flat periods can be viewed as "causing" under-performance and suboptimal levels of activity, thus firms tend to reduce marketing reinvestment at that time in an attempt to maximize profits and cash flow. The result is a self-fulfilling prophecy of downward performance.

4. Calculating ROMI requires knowing what would have happened if the incremental expenditure hadn't occurred. Few marketers have those figures or can conjure up something meaningful to replace them.

5. ROMI has become a fashionable surrogate for "marketing productivity" in executive suites and boardrooms, yet there is mounting evidence that firms interpret the appropriate calculation of ROMI quite differently. When executives discuss ROMI with different metrics in mind, confusion results and the value of the metric degrades.

6. ROMI by nature ignores the effect of the marketing assets of the firm (for example, its brands) and tends to lead managers toward a more short-term decision perspective. That is, it typically considers only short-term incremental profits and expenditures without looking at longer-term effects or any change in brand equity.[51]

Proceed with Caution

The expectation is that ROMI and other metrics of marketing performance will continue to proliferate, as firms home in on attempting to better quantify marketing's contribution to various dimensions of organizational success. Marketing managers should embrace the opportunity to quantify their contributions, and by taking a more holistic dashboard approach to goal-driven measurement, the potential downsides to focusing on one or a few metrics are largely mitigated.

In the end, marketing management is both a science and an art. The scientific side craves quantification and relishes the ability to provide numeric evidence of success to superiors in a firm and to stockholders. But the artistic side understands that sometimes the difference between an average new-product introduction and a world-class one rests largely on creativity, insight, and the good fortune to have a great idea that is hitting the market at just the right time.

An interesting question, given the current focus in business toward sustainability and socially responsible business practices, is how would metrics related to such aspects (say for example, ROSI, or return on social investment) operate in tandem with other more traditional performance measures? Ethical Dimension 3b provides some insights into this important issue.

Sainsbury's Supermarkets are famous for combining a successful bottom line with a strong sense of social responsibility. The company even has a tagline "Make the Difference Today."

When the Bottom Line Is Profit *and* Social Responsibility

A new kind of company is emerging that encompasses both profitability and social responsibility in its business model, creating not just one bottom line but two. These hybrid companies, founded by entrepreneurs who are focused as much on doing the right thing as on making a profit, are redefining traditional metrics for success. On the surface, the "do the right thing" and "maximize profit" models might seem to be incompatible, which can create challenges for entrepreneurs looking for funding.

Socially responsible companies today operate in a wide variety of industries and can include environmentally sensitive consumer products companies, organic grocers, fair trade coffee producers, and many others. These firms are often started after the founder is already committed to a social agenda. That is, the company is the tool by which the founder achieves a targeted social objective (better environment, better working conditions for the poor, etc.). Applying a socially responsible agenda frequently increases costs and suggests companies that want to follow a two bottom-line business model need to do business at the premium end of their market or else be relegated to lower expected margins. Melinda Olson, founder of Earth Mama Angel Baby, a manufacturer of premium natural products for young mothers and babies, believes that her gross margins are 12 to 15 percent lower than her competitors' (if she priced at parity).

In addition, if a company is really going to be socially responsible it must "walk the talk." This includes using energy-friendly products and paying living wage rates to employees. While all the choices may be the right thing to do, collectively they add to the cost of running the business.

A significant challenge for entrepreneurs desiring to develop a two bottom-line business model is finding investors who understand and are willing to support such a goal. Most investors are looking for the ROI not the ROSI (return on social investment). As a result, many of these organizations are underfunded and fail. Another challenge is how to measure success. Investors and managers all understand traditional success metrics such as profitability, ROI, and market share. However, when the bottom line also includes a company's social responsibility, the relevant success metrics become more difficult to determine.[52]

Ethical Perspective

1. **Investors:** Should investors be concerned only with a company's profitability? What metrics might an investor use to measure the social responsibility success of a company?

2. **Entrepreneurs:** Is a two bottom-line business model realistic in the long term? Is it sustainable?

3. **You:** Would you invest in a company with a two bottom-line strategy (profitability and social responsibility)?

A SAMPLING OF OTHER MARKETING METRICS

This section provides a mix of metrics for your consideration. Because a variety of excellent books exist that provide hundreds of potential metrics for assessing the gamut of marketing planning activities, we provide only a sampling here. Throughout the following section these symbols are used: $ = a monetary figure; % = a percentage figure; # = a figure in units; I = an index figure, such as a comparative or average, often interpreted as a percentage.[53]

Market Share

Definition: The percentage of a market (defined in terms of units or revenue) accounted for by a specific product, product line, or brand.

---

[53]In this section, the example formulas and descriptions are selected from the following outstanding treatise on marketing metrics, which is a must-have book for marketing managers: Paul W. Farris, Neil T. Bendle, Philip E. Pfeifer, and David J. Reibstein, *Marketing Metrics: 50+ Metrics Every Executive Should Master,* Upper Saddle River, NJ: Wharton School Publishing, 2006.

- Unit Market Share (%) = Unit Sales (#) ÷ Estimated Total Market Unit Sales (#)
- Revenue Market Share (%) = Sales Revenue ($) ÷ Estimated Total Market Revenue ($)

Marketers need to be able to translate sales forecasts into the context of market share, which will provide evidence if forecasts are to be attained by growing with the market or by capturing share from competitors. The latter will almost always be more difficult to achieve. Market share is closely monitored for signs of change in the competitive landscape, and it frequently influences strategic or tactical marketing planning. Importantly, market share is highly dependent on how the manager defines his or her market.[54] For example, Diet Coke would report varying market share numbers depending on whether it is comparing itself to all beverages, all carbonated beverages, or diet sodas.

Penetration

Definition: A measure of brand or category popularity. It is defined as the number of people who buy a specific brand or category of goods at least once in a given time period, divided by the size of the relevant market population.

- Market Penetration (%) = Customers Who Have Purchased a Product in the Category (#) ÷ Total Population (#)
- Brand Penetration (%) = Customers Who Have Purchased the Brand (#) ÷ Total Population (#)
- Penetration Share Formula 1 (%) = Brand Penetration (%) ÷ Market Penetration (%)
- Penetration Share Formula 2 (%) = Customers Who Have Purchased the Brand (#) ÷ Customers Who Have Purchased a Product in the Category (#)

Often, marketing managers must decide whether to seek sales growth by acquiring existing category users from their competitors or by expanding the total population of category users, attracting new customers to the market. Penetration metrics help indicate which of these strategies would be most appropriate and also help monitor the success of the strategy.[55]

Margin on Sales

Definition: The difference between selling price and cost. This difference is typically expressed either as a percentage of selling price or on a per-unit basis.

- Unit Margin ($) = Selling Price per Unit ($) − Cost per Unit ($)
- Margin (%) = Unit Margin ($) ÷ Selling Price per Unit ($)

Marketing managers need to know margins for almost all decisions. Margins represent a key factor in pricing, ROMI, earnings forecasts, and analyses of customer profitability.[56]

Cannibalization Rate

Definition: Cannibalization is the reduction in sales (units or dollars) of a firm's existing products due to the introduction of a new product. The cannibalization rate is generally calculated as the percentage of a new product's sales that represents a loss of sales (attributable to the introduction of the new entrant) by a specific existing product or products.

- Cannibalization Rate (%) = Sales Lost from Existing Products (# or $) ÷ Sales of New Product (# or $)

Cannibalization rates represent an important factor in the assessment of new-product strategies, since how robbing some of the sales of Brand X by introducing Brand Y impacts overall sales must be considered in the financial projections for the introduction.[57]

Customer Lifetime Value (CLV)

Definition: The dollar value of a customer relationship based on the present value of the projected future cash flows from the customer relationship. When margins and retention rates are constant, the following formula can be used to calculate CLV:

- CLV ($) = Margin ($) X (Retention Rate [%] ÷ 1 + Discount Rate [%] − Retention Rate [%])

Present value is the discounted sum of future cash flows. The discount rate is usually set at a corporate level, with the goal of compensating for the time value of money and the inherent risk of the particular activity. Generally, the riskier the project, the greater the discount rate to use. Techniques for setting discount rates are beyond the scope of this chapter. Suffice it to say that separate discount rates are appropriate on a by-project basis because the risk varies. A government contract might be a fairly certain project compared to a handshake agreement with a private client.[58]

Overall, CLV is an important concept in that it encourages firms to shift their focus from quarterly profits to the long-term health of their customer relationships. CLV is an important number because it represents an upper limit on spending to acquire new customers.[59]

Sales Force Effectiveness

Definition: By analyzing sales force performance, marketing managers can make changes to optimize sales going forward. Toward that end, there are a number of ways (beyond just sales volume) to gauge the performance of individual salespeople and of the sales force as a whole.[60] Among the sales force effectiveness (SFE) ratios are the following:

- SFE = Sales ($) ÷ Contacts with Clients (Number of Calls) (#)
- SFE = Sales ($) ÷ Potential Accounts (#)
- SFE = Sales ($) ÷ Active Accounts (#)
- SFE = Sales ($) ÷ Customer Buying Power ($)
- SFE = Selling Expenses ($) ÷ Sales ($)

Supply Chain Metrics

Definition: Measures of important indicators of a firm's success in its supply chain.

- Stock-Outs (%) = Outlets Where Brand or Product is Listed but Unavailable (#) ÷ Total Outlets Where Brand or Product is Listed (#)
- Service Level Re: On-Time Delivery (%) = Deliveries Achieved in Time Frame Promised (#) ÷ All Deliveries Initiated in the Period (#)
- Inventory Turns (I) = Product Revenues ($) ÷ Average Inventory (#)

Supply chain tracking helps ensure that companies are meeting demand efficiently and effectively.[61]

Promotions and Pass-Through

Definition: Of the promotional value provided by a manufacturer to its distributors and retailers (often referred to as "the trade"), the pass-through percentage represents the portion that ultimately reaches the end-user consumer.

- Percentage of Sales on Deal (%) = Sales with Any Temporary Discount ($ or #) ÷ Total Sales ($ or #)
- Pass-Through (%) = Value of Temporary Promotional Discounts Provided to End-User Consumers by the Trade ($) ÷ Value of Temporary Discounts Provided to the Trade by the Manufacturer ($)

Manufacturers offer many discounts to the trade with the objective of encouraging them to offer their own promotions, in turn, to their customers. If trade customers or end-user consumers do not find promotions attractive, this will be indicated by a decline in the percentage of sales on a deal. Likewise, low pass-through percentages can indicate that too many deals, or the wrong kinds of deals, are being offered.[62]

Cost per Thousand Impressions (CPM) Rates

Definition: The cost per thousand advertising impressions. This metric is calculated by dividing the cost of an advertising placement by the number of impressions (expressed in thousands) that it generates.

- CPM = Cost of Advertising ($) ÷ Impressions Generated (# in thousands)

CPM is useful in comparing the relative efficiency of different advertising opportunities or media and in evaluating the costs of overall campaigns.[63]

Share of Voice

Definition: Quantifies the advertising "presence" that a specific product or brand enjoys. It is calculated by dividing the brand's advertising by total market advertising, and it is expressed as a percentage.

- Share of Voice (%) = Brand Advertising ($ or #) ÷ Total Market Advertising ($ or #)

For purposes of share of voice, there are at least two ways to measure "advertising": (1) in terms of dollar spending, or (2) in unit terms, through impressions or gross rating points (GRPs). By any of these measures, share of voice represents an estimate of a company's advertising as compared to that of its competitors.[64]

Click-Through Rates

Definition: The percentage of impressions that leads a user to click on an online ad. It describes the fraction of impressions that motivate users to click on a link, causing a redirect to another Web location.

- Click-Through Rate (%) = Click-Throughs (#) ÷ Impressions (#)

Most Internet-based businesses use click-through metrics. Although these metrics are useful, they should not dominate all online marketing analysis. Unless a user clicks on a "Buy Now" button, click-throughs measure only one step along the path toward a final sale.[65]

Microsoft "relaunched" its search engine, Bing (also known as Kumo), in Spring 2009 with the goal of creating loyal fans that will routinely use it for certain types of queries rather than turning to Google. Unfortunately for Microsoft, from Spring 2008 to Spring 2009, Google's share of the search market rose from 61.6 percent 64.2 percent, while Microsoft's market share dropped from 9.1 to 8.2. Bing's relaunch–highly publicized directly by Microsoft CEO Steve Balmer–is hoped to regain market share by offering valuable services for Google and Yahoo!, and Balmer is spending an astounding $100 million on advertising Bing to make that happen.[66]

SUMMARY

Customer relationship management (CRM) is a comprehensive business model for increasing revenues and profits by focusing on customers. CRM works effectively by focusing on acquisition and retention of profitable customers, thus enhancing customer satisfaction and loyalty. Successful CRM runs on information acquired through various customer touchpoints such as a salesperson, customer care representative, or Web site. After this information is collected it must be protected to avoid breaching customer trust and privacy. CRM enables *customer marketing*—a focus on developing relationships with *individuals*—instead of consumer or mass marketing, which is marketing to big groups of like-minded buyers.

Successful marketing planning requires the application of a variety of marketing metrics for assessing performance against the plan's goals. Marketing dashboards provide a comprehensive approach to ensure managers have relevant, timely, and accurate information in a convenient format for use in decision making.

APPLICATION QUESTIONS

1. Consider each of the brands below. Assuming that a strong CRM system is in place in each brand's parent firm, what specific actions can marketing managers take in each case to ensure high satisfaction and loyalty among the most profitable customers?

   a. Chick-fil-A

   b. State Farm Insurance

   c. Amazon.com

   d. Dell computer

   e. GE home appliances

2. Pick a firm that interests you and for which you have some knowledge of its offerings.

   a. How would this firm benefit from a marketing dashboard approach?

   b. What elements would you recommend it put onto its dashboard? Why do you recommend the ones you do?

   c. How could the firm avoid some of the pitfalls potentially associated with marketing dashboards?

3. Pick any two of the marketing metrics presented in the chapter. For each, pick any brand or product and discuss how each of those brands or products would benefit from the application of each of the marketing metrics you selected. That is, what will the information reveal that will be useful in marketing planning?

MARKETING PLAN EXERCISES

ACTIVITY 3.1: Plan for a CRM System

In this chapter, you learned about the value of CRM in fostering a customer-centric culture and establishing a relationship-based enterprise. At this point in the development of your marketing plan, the following steps are needed:

1. Establish the objectives of your CRM system with regard to customer acquisition, customer retention, and customer profitability. Pay particular attention to driving high customer satisfaction and loyalty among profitable customers.

2. Map out the CRM process cycle you will employ in your business. Identify all the relevant touchpoints you plan to utilize—both interactive and noninteractive.

3. Prepare a set of guidelines on the ethical handling of customer data, with a focus on avoiding misuse and theft.

4. Consider the reasons for CRM failure identified in the chapter. Develop an approach to ensure that each can be avoided in your firm.

If you are using Marketing Plan Pro, a template for this assignment can be accessed at www.mhhe.com/marshalless1e

ACTIVITY 3.2: Metrics

1. Select appropriate metrics for use in your marketing plan.

2. Prepare action plans in support of your marketing plan. For each action plan be sure to list budget items, and then aggregate these into an overall budget for your marketing plan. Also, be sure to specify relevant controls.

3. Select and justify the forecasting approaches you will employ in your marketing plan.

4. Develop expected-case, best-case, and worst-case scenarios for your marketing plan.

If you are using Marketing Plan Pro, a template for this assignment can be accessed at www.mhhe.com/marshalless1e.

part FOUR

CHAPTER 04

Managing Marketing Information

LEARNING OBJECTIVES

- Describe the difference between market information systems and market research systems.

- Identify how critical internal (inside the firm) information is collected and used in making marketing decisions.

- Explain essential external (outside the firm) information collection methods.

- Recognize the value of market research and its role in marketing.

- Define the market research process.

- Illustrate current research technologies and how they are used in market research.

- Examine the primary sources of competitive information.

MAKING GOOD MARKETING DECISIONS—THE NEED TO KNOW

Information is power speaks to the importance of good information in decision making. Companies realize the right information at the right time and in the right format (a critical but often neglected part of the process) is essential for decision makers. Marketers are usually the ones entrusted with scanning the environment for changes that might affect the organization. As a result, creating procedures that collect, analyze, and access relevant information is a critical part of marketing management.[1]

A significant problem for most managers today is not having too little information but having too much. They frequently see interesting information that has no relevance to the immediate problem. As a result, companies need information systems that can collect and analyze huge amounts of information and then keep it for the right time and circumstance. Pulte Homes is one of the largest home builders in the United States. The company conducts research to learn how people move around in a home (the design flow), what features consumers want (for example large master bedrooms and bathrooms), and what extras they want (upgraded countertops and wood trim). Also, Pulte studies demographic changes. For example, a large segment of the population, baby boomers (ages 45–60), is moving toward retirement; this may lead the company to design and build smaller homes with more special features. Also, the downturns in the real estate market has led the federal government to adopt changes in real estate financing, and many states have followed suit with additional legislation. Finally, Pulte also needs to study changes in federal and state laws that affect home construction, such as the modifications to home building codes in Louisiana after Hurricane Katrina. These changes affect the homes people buy and, as a result, Pulte needs to be knowledgeable in all these areas.[2]

In addition to storing large amounts of data, marketing managers need a system to design and execute research that generates precise information. Consider the Apple iPhone. Before introducing the product, Apple conducted tests with actual users to be sure the product fit their needs and performed as promised. The company also studied a wide range of other issues including which markets offered the greatest growth potential, competitors such as Research In Motion, and long-term technology trends to identify key technologies for iPhone now and in the future such as the touch-screen interface. Marketing managers needed this information to make critical decisions as iPhone was being developed and the

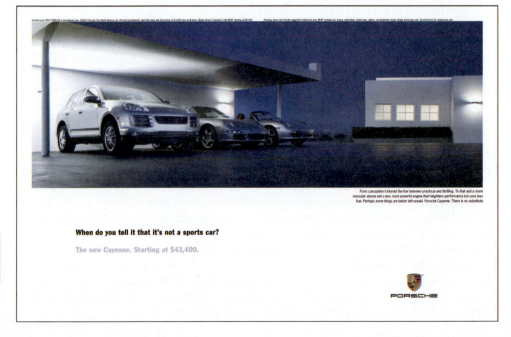

When do you tell it that it's not a sports car?

The new Cayenne. Starting at $43,400.

PORSCHE

Porsche studied SUV buyers to develop an SUV that embodied what SUV and Porsche buyers want in an SUV. The result was the Cayenne, which reflected the core elements of Porsche and the practicality of an SUV.

The PORSCHE CREST, PORSCHE, BOXSTER, CARRERA, CAYENNE, and the distinctive shape of the PORSCHE 911 and BOXSTER automobiles are registered trademarks in the United States of Dr. Ing. h. c. F. Porsche AG and Porsche Cars north america, Inc. Copyrighted by Dr. Ing. h.c. F. Porsche AG. Porsche Cayenne print ad published Spring 2007 in the United States.

marketing plan put together. With the success of iPhone, competitors study it to learn how key features can be duplicated in their own products.[3]

These examples highlight the two fundamental types of market information decision makers need today. The first is data related to broad areas of interest such as demographic and economic trends, or the customer order fulfillment process inside the company. These data are used in strategic planning to help forecast potential new opportunities for company investment or deal with possible problems before they become a major issue for the company.[4] The second type of information needed addresses a specific question, for example, what is the best kitchen design for a retired baby boomer couple? Or, what features would a young urban professional want on an iPhone? Questions like this require unique research designed to answer specific questions.[5] This chapter will examine both types of information needs. We'll start by discussing the market information system that is designed to bring together many different kinds information useful to the marketing decision maker. Then we'll look at marketing research, which is the process marketers use to conduct research on specific market questions.

> As more and more cities and states passed laws that mandate the use of hands-free cell-phone devices while driving, Bluetooth headset products flooded the marketplace. As this market has become saturated, companies such as Aliph and BlueAnt have focused on developing headsets with enhanced performance, such as longer battery life and better sound quality.[6]

MARKET INFORMATION SYSTEM
The Nature of a Market Information System

As noted earlier, marketing decision makers need limited amounts of the right data at any given time. Put simply, managers need what they need when they need it. When there is too much information, managers tend to either spend an excessive amount of time analyzing or get overwhelmed and ignore all the data. If they have too little information, managers are more likely to make poor decisions because they don't have all the facts. In either case, incorrect decisions are often the result. Exhibit 4.1 summarizes the various ways marketing research is used in making marketing decisions. As you can tell from Exhibit 4.1, market research takes many forms both inside and outside an organization.

A **market information system (MIS)** is not a software package but a continuing process of identifying, collecting, analyzing, accumulating, and dispensing critical information to marketing decision makers. The MIS is really an "information bank" where data relevant to the company's marketing efforts are collected and stored until such time as management needs to "withdraw" it. Generally, this information is not specific to a particular problem or question; rather, it is important information that the marketing decision maker will need at the appropriate time.[7] A company needs to consider three factors in creating an MIS.

First, what information should the system collect? In evaluating internal and external information sources, companies need to consider not only what information is important but also the source of the data. Think about all the ways a company gets competitor data—salespeople and customers in the field, competitor materials and Web sites, business-related Web sites such as Hoover's, and many others. Because there are so many sources of information, decisions must be made about what information will be collected and where it will come from.

Second, what are the information needs of each decision maker? Not all managers need the same information. The CEO probably doesn't want or need daily sales figures across individual product lines, but the local sales manager does. A good MIS is flexible enough for managers to customize the information they receive and, in some cases, the format they receive it in.

EXHIBIT 4.1 — Marketing Research Is Critical to Marketing Decisions

Stages or Processes within Marketing Planning	Appropriate Marketing Research
Situation Analysis • Identification of competitive strengths and weaknesses • Identification of trends (opportunities and threats)	• Competitive barrier analysis • Analysis of sources of competitive advantage • Trend analysis • Positioning analysis • Identification of public and key issues concerns • Measure of market share
Selection of a Target Market • Analysis of the market • Selection of a target market	• Identification of segmentation bases • Market segmentation study • Needs assessment • Determination of purchase criteria • Buyer behavior analysis • Market demand estimation
Plan of the Marketing Mix • Product	• Product design assessment • Competitive product analysis • Competitive packaging assessment • Packaging trends assessment • Definition of brand image descriptors • Identification of brand name/symbol • New-product ideation (concept development) • Package development or redesign
• Price	• Measure of price elasticity • Industry pricing patterns • Price-value perception analysis • Analysis of the effects of various price incentives
• Distribution	• Merchandising display assessment • Inventory management assessment • Location analysis (site analysis) • Market exposure assessment
• Promotion	• Message assessment • Content analysis • Copy testing • Media assessment • Media buy assessment
Marketing Control • Marketing audit	• Promotion effectiveness study • Assessment of effectiveness of marketing mix

Source: Reprinted from Donald R. Cooper and Pamela S. Schindler, *Marketing Research*, 2006. Copyright © 2006 The McGraw-Hill Companies, Inc.

Third, how does the system maintain the privacy and confidentiality of sensitive information? Company databases hold a great deal of confidential data on customers, suppliers, and employees. By limiting access to the data to those with a need to know, companies protect relationships and build trust.

Internal Sources—Collecting Information inside the Company

At the heart of marketing is the relationship among the company, its products, and customers. Critical to that relationship is a clear understanding of what is,

Salesforce.com has been successful in providing CRM applications via the cloud computing model that allow salespeople to access customer data easily. The usability of its customizable applications encourage salespeople to input customer data into the system.

and is not, working in the customer interface. Think about the senior manager at Microsoft who is concerned about rising dissatisfaction with customer support among its Office suite users. While there could be a number of reasons for this increase, the manager will first want to look at internal customer service metrics that include call wait times, ability of customer service representatives to handle the problems efficiently and effectively, number of customers who call back to address a problem, and a host of other metrics. These are all internal sources of data. By looking at such critical internal metrics collected as part of the market information system, management is able to do two things. First, in our example, management might see that an increase in call wait times has led to higher customer dissatisfaction. Here information is used to identify the problem. A second and more effective use of market information systems is to proactively address issues before they become a problem.[8] For example, management can set a benchmark stating that call wait times will not exceed two minutes. In this way, management can deal with a problem before it becomes a significant concern for the company. Of course, the investment in time and money needed to create and monitor such a system is significant.

A market information system can be as complicated as the company wants or can afford. It is expensive to collect and analyze data, and most companies don't maximize their existing information. Often, simply checking secondary sources such as legitimate Web sites will provide sufficient information for the marketing manager to make a decision in a particular situation. More formal information systems, however, provide a great deal more information that can help guide strategic decisions (changes in demographics can lead to new market opportunities) or address critical tactical issues (shorten call wait times for customer service).[9] Exhibit 4.2 identifies five common internal sources of data collected as a regular part of doing business. Unfortunately, managers are often not aware of all the information in their own company.

Marketing research projects can vary in scope depending on how specific a firm wants to be in selecting a sample population. Marketing managers must consider this when using research data for promotional planning. Chevrolet learned this lesson the hard way when the automaker decided, based on data from a highly specialized research project, to become the headlining sponsor of a 16-concert Christian music tour. As a result, many non-Christian consumers were offended by Chevy's apparent religious affiliation.[10]

External Sources—Collecting Information Outside the Company

Staying connected to the business environment is no longer optional. Success is based, in part, on both the quality and quantity of information available to management. As a result, most companies engage in collecting, analyzing, and storing data from the macro environment on a continuous basis known as

EXHIBIT 4.2 Internal Information Sources

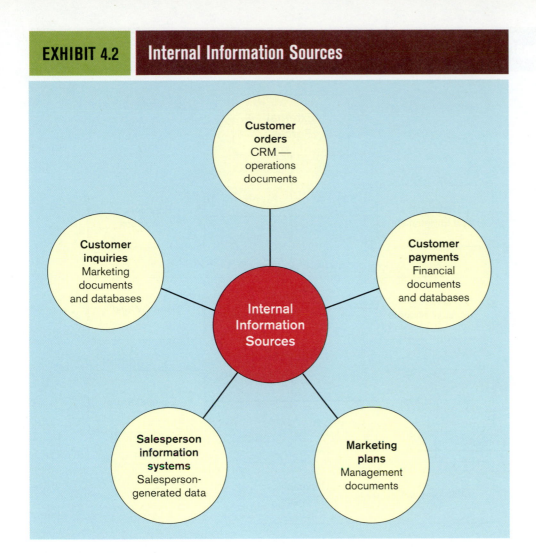

marketing intelligence. The ability to do this well is a competitive advantage; successful companies accurately analyze and interpret environmental information then develop strategies to take advantage of opportunities and deal with threats before they become a problem (see Exhibit 4.3).

Demographics

Populations change over time, and companies must be aware of those changes. Not tracking and responding to demographic changes is a management failure because the data are easy to obtain and major changes occur slowly. Surprisingly, many companies do not do a good job of either learning about demographic trends or responding to them.

Demographics can be defined as the statistical characteristics of human populations, such as age or income, used to identify markets. They provide a statistical description of a group of people and are extremely useful in marketing for two reasons. First, *demographics help define a market.* How old is a typical customer? How educated? What is the typical customer's income? These are all demographic characteristics that help describe a market. For example, a typical Mercedes-Benz automobile owner in the United States is a male, successful, and over 50 years old. By analyzing demographics, a company can define not only the "typical" customer but also its market at large. Second, *studying demographics helps identify new opportunities.* As baby boomers age, they will need, among other things, retirement communities. This represents an opportunity for companies to build unique retirement properties specifically for baby boomers.

EXHIBIT 4.3 **External Forces Affect Marketing Decisions**

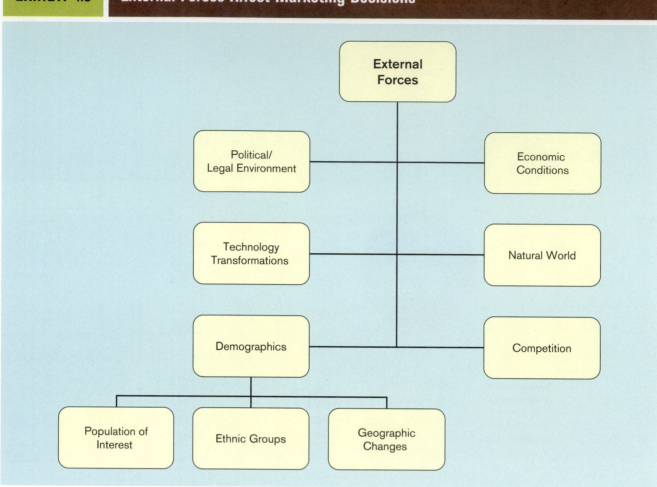

Companies that deal directly with consumers develop customer profiles based on demographic information and compare their profiles against those of competitors. For example, the typical Mercedes-Benz owner tends to be older than a BMW owner. Companies even create pictures of their "average" customer, highlighting key demographic data (age, gender, and ethnicity).

Populations of Interest Marketers are not interested in all groups, only populations of interest. The difficult part for many marketers is separating relevant demographic data from irrelevant. For example, does cell phone maker Nokia need to know that world population growth is faster in less developed countries (among less developed countries the population is growing at 2 percent per year while developed countries are growing at less than 1 percent)? Your first response might be no as Nokia is likely interested in more developed countries with established cellular networks and people who can afford the technology. However, while less developed countries do not need the new, expensive Nokia phones, they could use older, less expensive technology to encourage economic development and build a communication network. Targeting less developed countries may offer Nokia an opportunity to establish a market presence in these countries even as they develop economically.

Ethnic Groups Many countries are becoming more ethnically diverse as individuals increase their mobility. While some countries, such as the United Arab Emirates in the Middle East, have populations composed of a single ethnic group, others like the United States are much more ethnically diverse.

Nearly three-quarters of the U.S. population is white, but trends project that whites will be less than 50 percent of the population in less than 30 years. Hispanics have shown the greatest increase among ethnic groups in the United States over the past 10 years. They are currently the second-largest minority group (recently passing African Americans) and are expected to continue growing as a percentage of the U.S. population.

The European Union has made it possible for individuals to move freely around member countries. While many of the member countries are still dominated by local ethnic groups, the European continent is becoming more ethnically diverse. For the most part, this leads to greater opportunities; however, some countries such as France find it difficult to assimilate certain groups into their culture. The market challenge then becomes developing effective marketing strategies across different ethnicities living in the same area.

Geographic Changes People are moving not only in the United States but around the world. As we just noted, the opening of borders in the European Union has increased the mobility of those living in the EU. A decades-old trend—people moving from the countryside to the city—continues around the globe, and some cities, such as Mexico City, Sao Paulo, and others, find it difficult to cope with the influx of people that stretches their ability to provide social services (see Exhibit 4.4).

The Hispanic market represents one of the fastest growing demographic groups in the United States. Extended Hispanic families can be comprised of several generations.

The changes present opportunities but also challenges. The growth of Asian cultures means many companies must adjust their marketing strategies to fit the unique needs of Asian consumers. Appliance companies such as Whirlpool have redesigned their products to fit in smaller Asian kitchens. Coincidentally, downsizing products is a strategy consistent with the migration of people to urban centers. Mr. Coffee, Braun, and others have created coffeemakers designed for single households in the smaller living environments often found in large cities.

Economic Conditions

Companies are keenly interested in the ability of their customers to purchase products and services. It is not surprising then that a good understanding of current and future economic trends is important in an effective market information system. There are two principal types of economic knowledge. The study of individual economic activity (firm, household, or prices) is known as **microeconomics.** At the other end of the spectrum, **macroeconomics** refers to the study of economic activity in terms of broad measures of output (gross national product or GNP) and input as well as the interaction among various sectors of an entire economy. Both are important for marketing managers. Microeconomics helps marketing managers understand how individuals set priorities and make buying decisions. Macroeconomics, on the other hand, gives a "big picture" perspective for an economy and can be helpful at looking for broad economic trends.

Indicators such as the GNP measure the health of an economy and are helpful in spotting trends. For example, if the GNP goes up, it is generally viewed as a sign the economy is doing well. As an economy slows, the GNP will slow. Exhibit 4.5 defines key economic terms used by marketing managers to assess the economic conditions of a market.

EXHIBIT 4.4

Top 10 Cities in Population with Projected Growth Rates

Agglomeration	Country	Population (millions)			% of Average Annual Change	
		1975	2007	2025	1975–2007	2007–2025
Tokyo	Japan	26.6	35.7	36.4	0.92	0.11
New York-Newark	USA	15.9	19.0	20.6	0.57	0.44
Ciudad de México (Mexico City)	Mexico	10.7	19.0	21.0	1.80	0.55
Mumbai (Bombay)	India	7.1	19.0	26.4	3.08	1.83
São Paulo	Brazil	9.6	18.8	21.4	2.10	0.71
Delhi	India	4.4	15.9	22.5	4.00	1.92
Shanghai	China	7.3	15.0	19.4	2.24	1.44
Kolkata (Calcutta)	India	7.9	14.8	20.6	1.96	1.83
Dhaka	Bangladesh	2.2	13.5	22.0	5.64	2.72
Buenos Aires	Argentina	8.7	12.8	13.8	1.19	0.41
Los Angeles-Long Beach-Santa Ana	USA	8.9	12.5	13.7	1.05	0.50
Karachi	Pakistan	4.0	12.1	19.1	3.48	2.52
Al-Qahirah (Cairo)	Egypt	6.4	11.9	15.6	1.91	1.49
Rio de Janeiro	Brazil	7.6	11.7	13.4	1.38	0.74
Osaka-Kobe	Japan	9.8	11.3	11.4	0.43	0.04
Beijing	China	6.0	11.1	14.5	1.91	1.50
Manila	Philippines	5.0	11.1	14.8	2.49	1.60
Moskva (Moscow)	Russian Federation	7.6	10.5	10.5	0.99	0.04
Istanbul	Turkey	3.6	10.1	12.1	3.21	1.03

Source: *United Nations World Urbanization Prospects, The 2007 Revision* (New York: United Nations, 2007).

Technology Transformations

Few areas in business have been more affected by technology than marketing. Technology has been one of the major catalysts for change in the marketplace. Faster, smaller, and easier-to-use computers and powerful software facilitate sophisticated analyses right on the desks of front-line managers from anywhere in the world. Complex supply chain and manufacturing processes coupled with Internet connectivity allow customers real-time access to the entire manufacturing process. Consider the online order process for Hewlett-Packard. A consumer places the order online, gets a final price and expected delivery date, then follows it from the assembly plant literally to the front door with a tracking number from the shipping company.

Consumer Price Index (CPI)

A measure of the average amount (price) paid for a market basket of goods and services by a typical U.S. consumer in comparison to the average paid for the same basket in an earlier base year.

Gross National Product (GNP)

Value of all the goods and services produced in an economy, plus the value of the goods and services imported, less the goods and services exported.

Inflation

Increase in the overall level of prices over an extended time period.

Interest

The annual earnings that are sacrificed when wealth is invested in a given asset or business. The interest sacrificed is often called the cost of capital.

Source: FACSNET, www.facsnet.org/tools/ref_tutor/econo_term/glossary.html), accessed May 2009.

Sometimes technology companies have a hard time convincing manufacturers to embrace new technological breakthroughs. Such was the case when Synaptics developed "projective capacitive" sensor technology, which greatly improved on the sensitivity and durability of previous touch-screen technologies. Synaptics pushed the technology for years, but there was little interest among electronics manufacturers until the Apple iPhone was released in 2007. Suddenly, manufacturers realized what Synaptics had been trying to tell them all along.[11]

Marketing managers need to know the role of technology in their business today and also, perhaps even more importantly, its role in the future. Successfully assimilating technology into a business takes time and money. Almost every organization has had at least one negative experience with technology. Hershey Foods, for example, tried to bring a new CRM system online at the busiest selling season of the year for candy, Halloween, only to find problems implementing the system. The company estimated it was unable to fill $100 million worth of candy orders as a result of issues related to integrating the new software.[12] Read Ethical Dimension 4 to see a growing concern in collecting accurate information over the Internet.

Natural World

Everyone lives on planet Earth, and business operates within the constraints of available natural resources. Two key issues drive marketers' need to know about the natural world. First, individuals, governments, and business all recognize the need to manage the available resources well. It took the world roughly 150 years to use 1 trillion barrels of oil; however, it is predicted the world will use the next trillion barrels by 2030 and, while there may be a lot of oil left, it will be harder to get and more expensive. Governments and businesses are concerned about the effect of increasing energy costs on economic growth. Other resources such as water are also becoming increasingly scarce in parts of the world. In the Western United States, for example, growth in communities such as Phoenix is considered in the context of water access, which limits future development as water becomes scarcer.

A second concern regarding the natural world is pollution. In some parts of the world, pollution takes a significant toll on the quality of life and economic growth in a community. In Mexico City, driving is limited for everyone to certain days during the week as congestion and smog create huge clouds of pollution that hang over the city. Concern about water pollution has led Chinese government officials

The Source of the Click

Internet ad spending is projected to double in five years to more than $30 billion. The pay structure has evolved along two distinct lines. About half of all Internet ads are priced based on the number of people viewing the ad, similar to traditional television advertising. The other model for Internet advertising charges by the click. If someone views an ad and then chooses to click on the ad through to the advertiser, the advertiser pays a fee ranging from a few pennies to $20. A critical assumption is the click's legitimacy; it is supposed to represent someone actively seeking information from the advertiser's site.

Two companies control the vast majority of Internet ad placements—Yahoo and Google. While Google and Yahoo generate most of their revenue on legitimate Web sites, they also send ads to affiliated sites, known as "domain parking Web sites," which are basically advertising sites with very little content. Publicly they state these sites provide a useful service by directing Internet surfers to relevant information. However, companies are starting to express concern that some of these sites may actually be generating illegitimate clicks, clicks by individuals (or other computers) who are not legitimate potential customers.

Click fraud, estimated at $1 billion, has become a big issue for many Internet advertisers. Web sites with names such as "insurance1472.com" are dummy sites located primarily in Asia and Eastern Europe that generate false clicks. The process works like this. First, ABC Company contracts with Google or Yahoo to advertise on the Internet and negotiates the fee ABC will pay for each click from an ABC ad to the company Web site. Second, Google or Yahoo displays the ad on legitimate Web sites but also sends the ad to domain parking Web sites. Third, these sites distribute the ads to parked Web sites that are often just lists of ads. Fourth, the owner of the parked Web site sends out a list of sites to individuals known collectively as "paid-to-read groups." These individuals' role is to click on ads for which they receive a small payment. Finally, Google or Yahoo charges ABC Company for the click, then shares part of the revenue with the domain parking Web site, which shares it with the other participants in the fraud.

Adding to the challenge for advertisers is the difficult position of Google and Yahoo, which make more money when click fraud occurs. Both companies strongly deny any wrongdoing and actively police their ad placements. However, both have settled click fraud class action suits with advertisers and instituted a number of changes to their business model to curb the problem.[13]

Ethical Perspective

1. **Advertisers:** How would your view of Internet advertising change if the statistics related to the number of people who "click through" an ad were not accurate?

2. **Google and Yahoo:** While you are concerned with click fraud, the process actually generates significant revenue. What do you do?

to declare "more than 70 percent of the rivers and lakes have been polluted to some extent" and count losses in the billions of dollars. These concerns influence marketers as they make decisions about how and where products are manufactured. For example, energy companies such as Chevron are investing billions to identify and develop more environmentally safe energy.

Political/Legal Environment

Political judgments and, more broadly, the legal environment significantly affect company decisions and sometimes an entire industry. In 2003, the National Do Not Call Registry was created to minimize intrusive telemarketing calls. By registering, individuals protect themselves from telemarketing calls. Telemarketing companies are subject to significant fines if they call someone listed on the register. Millions of people signed up, and many companies were forced to reconfigure their marketing communications strategy.[14]

Local, state, and federal legislatures pass more business-related legislation than ever before. In addition, government agencies are more active in monitoring business activity. During the 1990s the Securities and Exchange Commission actively pursued several antitrust actions, the largest against Microsoft for illegal monopoly activity. As a result, Microsoft made changes to Windows Vista that opened it up to outside software vendors.

Successful social networking Web sites such as Facebook have benefited greatly from gathering and analyzing their users' information. The use of social networks as a marketing channel is a core component of Facebook's marketing activities. Unfortunately, cyber-criminals also recognize social networks as a powerful tool for obtaining users' personal information. As a result, social networking sites must constantly improve their security systems and ease any reservations their customers may have any time they are asked to surrender personal information.[15]

Competition

One of the most important external environmental factors to consider is the competition. Companies want to know as much as possible about competitors' products and strategies. In highly competitive markets, companies are constantly adjusting their strategies to the competition. Airlines, for example, track competitor pricing and adjust their pricing almost immediately to changes in the marketplace. When one airline offers a sale in a specific market, competitors will soon follow with sales in the same market.

MARKETING RESEARCH SYSTEMS

Marketing managers are confronted with an unlimited number of problems, opportunities, and issues that require specific answers. Sometimes the information needed is not available from other sources or even from the company's own market information system. To get specific answers to important management questions, marketing research is necessary.

The Importance of Market Research to Managers

Consider the following:

- You are a marketing manager for Harley-Davidson, and 90 percent of your motorcycles are sold to men. You believe women are a great potential target market but have had little success selling Harleys to them. What do you do?
- You are the director of advertising for McDonald's, and the company is getting ready to roll out a new advertising campaign designed to increase sales of a new sandwich. However, senior management wants to know if it will work. What do you do?

The answers to situations like these lie in market research. **Market research** is the methodical identification, collection, analysis, and distribution of data related to discovering then solving marketing problems or opportunities and enhancing good decision making. Several things come out of this definition. Good marketing research:

- **Follows a well-defined set of activities and does not happen by accident.** Rather, it comes as a result of the methodical identification, collection, analysis, and distribution of data.
- **Enhances the validity of the information.** Anyone can "Google" a topic and come up with a lot of information. However, following the market research process enhances the confidence that the research will discover then solve marketing problems and opportunities.
- **Is impartial and objective.** It does not prejudge the information or develop answers to fit an already decided outcome; rather, it enhances good decision making.

EXHIBIT 4.6

Top Five Market Research Companies in the United States

Organization	Headquarters	Total Revenue ($U.S.)
The Nielsen Company	New York, NY	2.231 billion
Kantar Group	London, UK	918.5 million
IMS Health Inc.	Norwalk, CT	842.0 million
Westat Inc.	Rockville, MD	469.5 million
IRI	Chicago, IL	454.0 million

Marketing research is also big business. In 2008, nearly $8.1 billion was spent on marketing research in the United States and even more was spent in the rest of the world. This does not include the research conducted in-house by internal market research departments.[16] Some of these departments, such as McDonald's internal research group, are larger than many research companies and spend hundreds of millions of dollars a year conducting market research for their own organizations. Exhibit 4.6 lists the top market research companies in the United States.

The Marketing Research Process

At the heart of the marketing research process is a search for understanding. Sometimes management seeks answers to a particular problem. In other situations, an opportunity needs to be evaluated before committing resources. By following the marketing research process, marketing managers can have greater confidence in the information they are receiving and, hopefully, make better informed decisions. As shown in Exhibit 4.7 the process consists of six steps.

Define the Research Problem

One of the biggest challenges facing a marketing researcher is accurately defining the problem. What exactly is the issue/opportunity/problem? Often managers are not clear about the problem and need help defining it. It is not uncommon for a market research professional to get a call that starts something like this, "I have a problem. Sales have been falling for six months and I am losing business to my competitors." The researcher knows that the real problem is not the company's declining sales; falling sales are the result, a symptom, of the real issue. Market research can be a useful tool helping senior managers identify and deal with the real issue.[17]

EXHIBIT 4.7 The Marketing Research Process

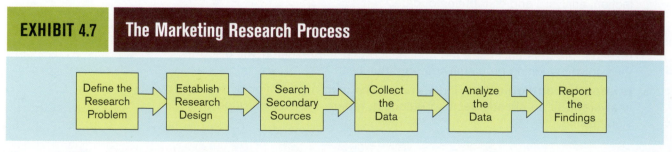

Define the Research Problem → Establish Research Design → Search Secondary Sources → Collect the Data → Analyze the Data → Report the Findings

Given that management often does not have a clear understanding of the problem, defining the research problem involves two distinct steps. First, management, working with researchers and marketing decision makers, defines the **management research deliverable.** Exactly what does management want to do with this research? Keep in mind that decision makers are looking for information to help them make better, more informed decisions. For example, if you are the director of advertising for McDonald's, you want to increase sales of a new sandwich, and a new advertising campaign can help accomplish that goal. However, before you decide to spend a lot of money on the campaign, you want to know if it is going to be successful.

Once the management research deliverable has been identified, the next step is to define the **research problem.** Exactly what information is needed to help management in this situation? In our example that means assessing the target market's response to the new advertising campaign.

In the McDonald's example, the research problem is fairly straightforward. However, there are often multiple research problems and researchers will have to prioritize which problems to study first. Consider the example of Harley-Davidson motorcycles and targeting more female riders. Management may want to know: (1) How many women would be in the market for a motorcycle and, more specifically, how many women would be in the market for a large bike like a Harley? (2) What kind of motorcycle would they want to buy? (3) If Harley-Davidson were to create a new bike, how would loyal, dedicated Harley-Davidson owners react to it? You can begin to see why it is necessary for management and researchers to prioritize the problems and identify which research issues to address first.[18]

Establish the Research Design

Following problem definition, companies must establish a research design, or a plan of action for attacking the research problem. Research designs consist of five activities, each of which is designed to address a specific question about the research process as shown in Exhibit 4.8. It is critical that researchers develop and execute a research design so that decision makers can have confidence in the research findings. Effective market research is dependent upon creating a research design and then executing it.[19] Conversely, and this is a problem for decision makers, bad market research cannot yield good information. When this happens, it severely limits management's confidence in the results.

While multiple designs often could work in any research situation, it is important to specify one design and follow it throughout the research. Decisions made at the research design stage affect the rest of the project, and it is not appropriate to start over once a project has begun. Let's examine each of these activities.

EXHIBIT 4.8	Research Design Activities

Activity	Question to Be Answered
Type of research	What kind of research needs to be done?
Nature of data	What kind of data do we need?
Nature of data collection	How should we collect the data?
Information content	What do we need to know?
Sampling plan	Who should be included in the research?

Type of Research: What Kind of Research Needs to Be Done? Not all marketing research involves complex, costly studies. People do marketing research all the time and don't think of it that way. For example, a salesperson who visits a Web site to learn more about a customer before a sales call is engaged in marketing research. The key is to fit the research to the unique requirements of the situation.

There are three basic types of research: exploratory, descriptive, and causal. While the complexity and methodology changes for each type of research it is not necessarily true that causal research is better than exploratory. Let's look at each research type more closely.

As the name implies, **exploratory research** is really about discovery. Reasons for conducting exploratory research include:

- Clarify the research problem.
- Develop hypotheses for testing in descriptive or causal research.
- Gain additional insight to help in survey development or to identify other research variables for study.
- Answer the research question.

Many times conducting exploratory research will provide sufficient information to answer the research question. Even if more sophisticated research is needed, exploratory research is usually the first step.

Descriptive research seeks to describe or explain some phenomenon. Often this involves something going on in the marketplace and can include issues such as:

- Identify the characteristics of our target market.
- Assess competitor actions in the marketplace.
- Determine how customers use our product.
- Discover differences across demographic characteristics (age, education, income) with respect to the use of our product or our competitors.

Descriptive research uses many different methods including secondary data, surveys, and observation. Some of these methods are also used in exploratory research. The difference is how you use the information. Descriptive research uses a different, more restrictive and rigorous methodology than exploratory research.

Descriptive research identifies associations between variables; for example, the customers for Harley-Davidson motorcycles tend to be middle-aged, successful men.

Causal research tries to discover the cause and effect between variables.

For example, in our Harley-Davidson example, does an increase in Harley-Davidson advertising directed toward men lead to increased sales of Harley-Davidson motorcycles? This can be particularly useful in making important marketing decisions. Consider a critical decision faced by

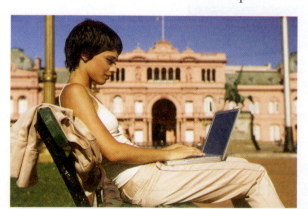

Exploratory research is often good enough. With wireless access it is possible to do research almost anywhere.

all marketing managers: What effect will a price increase have on sales? Causal research can determine the change in the number of sales for different price levels.

The types of research vary a great deal, so the question becomes what kind of research is appropriate in a given circumstance? The following factors help make that determination.

Benefit versus cost: Before making any other decisions about the type of marketing research to use, it is essential to assess the benefits versus the costs. Put simply, if the benefits of doing the research do not exceed the cost, don't do the research.

Time until decision: Decision makers sometimes have very little time between realizing a need for additional information and making the decision. When time is very short (a matter of days) it is simply not possible to conduct in-depth marketing research. The Internet can cut the time needed for a study from months to weeks, but when time is short researchers may have to rely on more exploratory research and the use of secondary data.

Nature of the decision: The more strategic the decision the more important the information and the greater the need for primary data. Conversely, if the decision is primarily tactical (for example, decisions about where to place advertising) secondary data, like reviewing a media's demographics and rate card, will likely be sufficient to make the decision.

Availability of data: As we saw in Chapter 3, companies already have a lot of data as a result of CRM and other internal information systems. Consequently, it may not always be necessary to collect primary data when existing or secondary data will provide the necessary answers to the research problems.

Nature of Data: What Kind of Data Do We Need? Once the type of research has been determined, the next step is to evaluate what kind of data is needed for the research. The nature of the data will determine how the data are collected and is driven by the kind of research the company is undertaking.[21] The basic question is, does the research require **primary data**—data collected specifically for this research question—or will **secondary data**—data collected for some other purpose than the problem currently being considered—be sufficient? Even if primary data are collected, almost all research involves some secondary data collection, which we will talk about in the next section.

Primary data are collected using one of two approaches: qualitative and quantitative. **Qualitative research** is less structured and can employ methods such as surveys and interviews to collect the data; qualitative research employs small samples and is not meant to be used for statistical analyses. **Quantitative research** is used to develop a more measured understanding using statistical analysis to assess and quantify the results.[22] Now let's look at the nature of data collection.

Nature of Data Collection: How Should the Data Be Collected? No one technique is better than another, but it is important to use the right technique based on an assessment of the research problem and research type. Let's evaluate the various approaches to collecting primary data. Exploratory research techniques include focus groups and in-depth interviews.

Without question, the most widely used qualitative research technique is focus groups. Perhaps for this reason, it is also one of the most misused.[23] A **focus group** is a meeting (either in person or increasingly online) of 6 to 10 people that is moderated by a professional who carefully moves the conversation through a defined agenda in an unstructured, open format. Generally, the participants are selected on the basis of some criteria.[24] For example, they may be current customers or possess certain demographic characteristics (age, income, education) but they will all have at least one shared attribute.

The value of focus groups lies in the richness of the discussion. A good moderator can draw out a lot of information from the participants. For example, the marketing manager for Harley-Davidson might use focus groups to learn how women

Harley-Davidson does market research to learn more about developing products that appeal to women.

relate to motorcycles. The trade-off is a deeper understanding of each participant versus a more superficial knowledge of additional people. Herein lies the mistake many people make with focus groups. They assume that the results of a focus group are generalizable to a population of interest. This is not the case. Focus groups are not a representative sample, and care should be taken to interpret the results properly. However, focus groups do provide insights on an issue that are useful to researchers as they develop quantitative research techniques. Focus group data provide a good starting point from which researchers can develop specific questions used in survey instruments.[25]

Another common qualitative technique is the in-depth interview. An **in-depth interview** is an unstructured (or loosely structured) interview with an individual who has been chosen based on some characteristic of interest, often a demographic attribute. This technique differs from focus groups in that the interview is done one on one rather than in a small group. The same advantages and disadvantages are present here as with focus groups so researchers most often use this technique to help formulate other types of research (surveys, observational research).

Descriptive research techniques include surveys, behavioral data, and observational data.

Of the quantitative research techniques used to collect primary data, surveys, in their various forms, are the most prevalent. While they can be used informally in exploratory research, their most common purpose is in descriptive research. **Surveys** are structured questionnaires given to a sample group of individuals representing the population of interest and are intended to solicit specific responses to explicit questions.[26]

There are a number of survey methods. Historically, mail and telephone surveys were most common. Today, electronic surveys have become widely adopted for their speed, ease of use, and relatively low cost. E-surveys can easily be done over the Internet using services such as Zoomerang or Survey Monkey.[27]

Behavioral data include information about when, what, and how often customers purchase products and services as well as other customer "touches" (for example, when they contact the organization with a complaint or question). When companies match this kind of information with demographic and psychographic information they can see differences in purchase patterns. Behavior is usually more reliable than surveys because it is based on what the respondents actually do rather than what they say they are going to do.

Although more commonly used for gaining insights about their customers, data mining techniques are also utilized by firms to develop sophisticated models of their employees. Cataphora in Redwood City, California, uses data mining techniques to create employee models based on factors such as productivity and accident record. Companies use these models to predict the future performance of their employees and consider this information when making decisions regarding employee promotions or terminations.[28]

It is possible to get a lot of insight about people by simply watching what they do in various situations. **Observational data** are the behavioral patterns among the population of interest. One of the most common uses of this type of research is in retailing. Retailers' watch how people move through a store, noting what aisles they go down and where they spend their time. In recent years a more intrusive approach to observational data has been used to actually examine people in a personal setting (for example, their homes). In this approach the observer enters into the world of the individual rather than standing back and simply watching activities. Researchers see people in a very personal environment to better understand how people use and interact with products.

A variation of observational data is mechanical observation. **Mechanical observation** uses a device to chronicle activity. Some forms of mechanical observations are benign and not intrusive on the individual. Turnstiles, for example, record people coming or going out of an area. Traffic counters record the number of cars on a given street for a set time period.

There are, however, mechanical devices that are more invasive. *Mechanical devices* can be very useful for researchers but are often used sparingly because of the cost and also the bias associated with the respondent's awareness of the device. Eye cameras can track the movement of an eye as the individual watches an ad. From this researchers can determine what the person sees first, what he is focusing on in the ad and how his eyes move around the ad. Another device, the galvanometer, is attached to the skin and measures subtle changes in skin temperature. Researchers can then determine if the respondent found the ad interesting.

Information Content: What Do We Need to Know? A critical part of research design involves determining exactly what information is needed and how to frame the questions to get that information. From the questions used in focus groups to long questionnaires, it is important to consider the structure and wording as well as the response choices. Most often this issue comes up in designing questionnaires. As the most commonly used primary research technique, the survey questionnaire allows a lot of variability in its design and structure. Some surveys, such as the comment cards, are short and ask only a few questions. Others, such as new car satisfaction surveys, can be much longer and ask dozens of questions. No matter what the situation, careful attention must be paid to the design, structure, and format of each question. For years marketers have been interested in building and measuring customer loyalty.

Today, researchers must also consider the method of survey delivery. For example, mail surveys differ significantly from telephone surveys because respondents interact with the questions differently. Electronic surveys present a different challenge, although their structure is more easily adapted from a mail questionnaire.

Researchers must consider which of the many types of question formats is most appropriate for the situation. One of the most basic decisions is whether to use open-ended or closed-ended questions. **Open-ended questions** encourage respondents to be expressive and offer the opportunity to provide more detailed, qualitative responses. As a result, these kinds of questions are often used in exploratory research. **Closed-ended questions,** on the other hand, are more precise and provide specific responses. As a result, they allow for more quantitative analysis and are most often used in descriptive research. Frequently, questionnaires will contain a mix of open-ended and closed-ended questions to get both qualitative and quantitative information in a single survey.

Sampling Plan: Who Should Be Included in the Research? Once the other elements of the research design have been developed, it is time to consider who will be selected for the research. The most basic decision is whether to conduct a census or to sample a group of individuals from the population. A **census** is a comprehensive record of each individual in the population of interest, while a **sample** is a subgroup of the population selected for participation in the research. A census may seem like the better approach because everyone in the population is included in the study. Unfortunately, most of the time the number and diversity of the population is so large that it is simply not physically or financially possible to communicate with everyone. As a result, sampling is by far the preferred method of selecting people for marketing research.[29]

There are two basic approaches to sampling: probability and nonprobability sampling. One is not necessarily better than the other; rather, the key to making the right choice is to match the sampling approach with the research. Budgetary constraints will also likely influence the decision. **Probability sampling** uses a specific set of procedures to identify individuals from the population to be included in the research. From here, a specific protocol is identified to select a number of individuals for the research. As an example, suppose Bank of America is interested in finding out more about a group of its customers holding a certain kind of credit card. Let's assume there are 10 million customers holding this particular card. The bank wants to randomly choose 5,000 individuals for the survey. That means that everyone has a $5,000/10,000,000 = .0005$ chance of being selected. Next, Bank of America will create an algorithm to randomly identify 5,000 individuals from the list of 10 million. The algorithm ensures that, while everyone has a .0005 chance of being selected, only 5,000 will be sampled from the entire group.

A second approach is called **nonprobability sampling** and, as the name implies, the probability of everyone in the population being included in the sample is not identified. The chance of selection may be zero or not known. This type of sampling is often done when time and/or financial constraints limit the opportunity to conduct probability sampling. The most significant problem with nonprobability sampling is that it significantly limits the ability to perform statistical analyses and generalize conclusions beyond the sample itself.

Search Secondary Sources

Secondary data are almost always part of marketing research. Searching a wide variety of sources and compiling additional information provide greater insight to the research problem and supplement the primary data collected for a specific study. We have already discussed the availability of information inside the company, so let's turn our attention to external sources of secondary data.

Government Sources Federal, state, and local governments are an important resource in collecting information on a variety of topics. For example, the U.S. Census Bureau publishes a library full of reports on business and consumer demographic trends. In 2007, the Economic Census, released by the Census Bureau, provides an in-depth analysis of business activity in the United States. Often, data are available by zip code, which can be useful for marketers in targeting specific groups of people. States also publish additional data on economic activity. Finally, local governments publish records such as business licenses as well as general economic activity in that area. Governments provide a great deal of information on a variety of activities. From here marketers can identify areas, even down to specific streets, and get detailed demographic information, which is very useful in a number of ways including targeted marketing communications campaigns.

Market Research Organizations A number of market research organizations publish data helpful to marketers. One resource many people are familiar with is Nielsen Media Research's TV ratings. The ratings are the basis for establishing national, cable, and local advertising rates. Another service well known to automobile enthusiasts is the J. D. Power automobile quality and customer satisfaction rankings. While automobile manufacturers pay a fee for more detailed information, the public has access to the overall rankings.

Other organizations publish data that can be useful to marketers in particular industries. For example, Ypartnership advertising agency, in partnership with the Yankelovich research firm, publishes the National Travel Monitor for both leisure and business markets every year. The monitor profiles travel patterns and market segments in the travel industry. This research is very useful for any business connected to the travel industry such as airlines, hotels, and cruise lines.

There are also information data services such as Information Resources, InfoScan, and Nielsen's ScanTrack that track scanner data from thousands of retailers. These organizations match sales data with demographic records to give a detailed picture of how well a product is doing in a particular area or within a certain target market. This information is useful for consumer products companies that want to assess the success of specific marketing activities (for example, how well is an advertising campaign working with a target market).

Luxury Cruise Line

Yankelovich®
Insights Integration℠

Luxury Cruise Line Identifies Next Generation of Cruisers

BUSINESS OBJECTIVE

A luxury cruise line was searching for new list rental sources of prospective cruisers. The cruise line understood its current passengers mainly from a demographic perspective, limiting the company's prospecting capabilities.

CLIENT NEEDS

- Find new sources of targeted prospect names
- Find tools to help prioritize marketing efforts more effectively

PUTTING ATTITUDES TO WORK

The passenger database was profiled using attitudinal data elements from Yankelovich's MindBase® and Lists with Attitude℠. The proportions of cruise line passengers for each of these attitudinal data elements were compared to the total population, identifying groups most apt to be passengers. The attitudinal data helped the cruise line understand their passengers—what interests them, and what their travel style is—creating a more robust profile than demographics alone. New list rentals by attitudinal data were recommended to expand the customer acquisition universe.

ANALYSIS RESULTS

- The cruise line identified the best current passengers using MindBase. By both sheer numbers and when compared to the rest of the US population, best passengers comprised between 35%-70% of the customer base depending on product category.

- Based on the new customer profile, the business was able to identify potential future passengers through MindBase and Lists with Attitude for targeted prospect list rentals.

The Internet It is now possible to access a huge amount of information using search engines to identify hundreds, even thousands, of information sources. Care should be taken, however, to evaluate the validity of the data and the reliability of the source. Generally two kinds of data sources can be found on the Internet. The first are market research organizations (such as the ones we just discussed) willing to share or sell market data. A second source is "general knowledge" sites such as business publications, academic research sites, or other independent sources that have data applicable to the research problem.[30]

Advantages and Disadvantages of Secondary Data Sources As we discussed earlier, secondary data are almost always the first place to go in conducting a market research project. Even if primary data are collected, it is a good idea to see what has been done already that may be applicable now. Secondary data come with two primary advantages. First, it's a fast way to get information. Just a few minutes on a search engine can yield a lot of information. Of course, it takes much longer than that to look through it all. A second, and related advantage, is cost. Secondary data are relatively less expensive. Even if a company chooses to subscribe to organizations such as J. D. Power and Associates, thereby getting access to more detailed data, it is still more cost effective than conducting a primary research study.

Of course, there are very distinct disadvantages. First and most important, secondary data will, almost by definition, not fit the research problem exactly. As a result, a specific answer to the research problem will not be possible using secondary data alone. Second, secondary data are not current. Sometimes the information may be only a few weeks or months old or it may be dated to the point where it is no longer useful for the current project. Third, without a clear understanding of the methodology used to collect and interpret the secondary data one should be a little skeptical about its validity.[31]

Collect the Data

Now, it is time to find and engage the respondent to collect the data. **Data collection** involves access and distribution of the survey to the respondent then recording the respondent's responses and making the data available for analysis. A company can choose to collect the data using its own resources or hire a market research firm to administer the data collection. The choice often depends on the company's internal expertise in market research as well as the resources required to complete the job.

This stage in the market research process presents several unique challenges. First, data collection is often the most costly element in the market research process. Second, the greatest potential for error exists as data are collected.[32] For example, respondents may not respond to certain questions or fill out the survey incorrectly. Finally, the people collecting the survey may be biased or make mistakes.

Technology, in the form of online surveys, can help to mitigate some of the issues with data collection. For example, electronic survey methods are often more cost effective than other survey methodologies. In addition, there is less chance of transcription error as no one has to input the data into a computer. Unfortunately, not everyone has access to a computer. As a result, certain target markets may be underrepresented if a survey requires completion of an online survey. Additionally, people may still input inaccurate responses.[33] We will talk about online research tools in the next section.

Analyze the Data

Once the data are collected, coded, and verified, the next step is to analyze the information. The appropriate analysis is performed based on the research questions developed at the beginning of the research. A common mistake is using unsuitable analyses that are not supported by the data.

Analysis of the data will lead to findings that address the research questions. These findings are, in a sense, the "product" of the research. In most cases, researchers will also interpret the findings for decision makers.

Report the Findings

The best research projects are only as good as the final report and presentation. If the research is done well but the report is poorly written and presented, managers will not benefit from the research. Exhibit 4.9 provides a basic framework for a research report. For managers,

Photodex ProShow Gold is one of many software packages designed to enhance presentations. The presentation of a research report often includes sophisticated software designed to clearly present research findings and recommendations.

EXHIBIT 4.9 — Outline of a Research Report

Report Modules	Short Report		Long Report	
	Memo or Letter	Short Technical	Management	Technical
Prefatory Information		1	1	1
Letter of transmittal		✓	✓	✓
Title page		✓	✓	✓
Authorization statement		✓	✓	✓
Executive summary		✓	✓	✓
Table of contents			✓	✓
Introduction	1	2	2	2
Problem statement	✓	✓	✓	✓
Research objectives	✓	✓	✓	✓
Background	✓	✓	✓	✓
Methodology		✓ (briefly)	✓ (briefly)	3
Sampling design				✓
Research design				✓
Data collection				✓
Data analysis				✓
Limitations		✓	✓	✓
Findings		3	4	4
Conclusions	2	4	3	5
Summary and conclusions	✓	✓	✓	✓
Recommendations	✓	✓	✓	✓
Appendices		5	5	6
Bibliography				7

Source: Reprinted from Donald R. Cooper and Pamela S. Schindler, *Marketing Research, 2006.* Copyright © 2006 The McGraw-Hill Companies, Inc.

the key section of the report is the Executive Summary as it presents a summation of the analysis and essential findings. Keep in mind that managers are not really interested in the number of secondary data sources, questionnaire design, or sampling plan; rather, they want to see the findings.

Market Research Technology

Market research has benefited from better, more cost-effective technology. The use of powerful software tools and online technologies brings research to any level in the organization. Sales managers can survey customers, analyze the results, and make decisions without costly, time-consuming external studies. Sophisticated software incorporating CRM and marketing decision support systems can do in-depth analyses that offer unique insights about customers or market trends not possible just a few years ago. In most respects, making market research tools available throughout the company has been a big success. Unfortunately, as the access to market research technology has increased, so has the misapplication of the technology. Without implementing the market research process presented earlier, no amount of technology can create worthwhile results.

Online Research Tools

Online research tools fall into three categories: databases, focus groups, and sampling. Each of these three categories offers unique opportunities to expand the reach and usefulness of market research. Let's examine each more closely.

Online Databases An **online database** is data stored on a server that is accessed remotely over the Internet or some other telecommunications network. Many, if not most, companies now have databases available to employees, suppliers, even customers. Information on orders, shipments, pricing, and other relevant information is available to salespeople and customer service personnel who need to access it.[34]

Independent online databases available from government and other sources are extremely useful tools in market research. Organizations such as the World Bank offer a wide range of databases with country-specific economic data, most of which is free. Fee-based services, while expensive, offer access to a wide range of information. Lexis/Nexis, for example, enables market researchers to access thousands of business and trade publications and market studies. These services make it possible to review market research reports, industry and company analyses, even market share information.[35]

Online Focus Groups The virtual focus group is becoming a viable alternative to the traditional focus group format (6 to 10 people in a room). Offering distinct advantages in terms of convenience and cost-efficiency, online focus groups provide data quickly and in a format that is usually easier to read and analyze. Traditional focus groups require someone to transcribe the spoken words into a transcript. With online focus groups, everything is already recorded by computer.

The primary disadvantage of online focus groups is that participants are limited to those with access to a computer or workstation. In addition, as people often participate remotely, it is not possible to verify who is actually responding to the questions. Measures can be employed to verify participation (for example, passwords), but the reality is that, in most cases, you must rely on the individual to be honest. One final problem is the lack of control over the environment. Traditional focus groups create an environment where participants are required to focus on the questions. Online focus groups enable participants to be at home, work, or even a remote location with wireless access. As a result, participants can become distracted and environmental factors can affect their concentration and responses.

SAS offers powerful analysis tools to help managers more clearly understand market data.

Online Sampling If someone has access to a computer with an Internet connection, that person can complete a questionnaire. Online sampling has become increasingly popular as a data collection methodology. As with online focus groups, the primary advantages are convenience and cost-efficiency. Respondents are free to complete the survey when it is best for them, and sending a survey online is essentially free. Online survey companies such as QuestionPro offer a complete service from survey design and a variety of delivery methods (traditional e-mail, pop-up surveys, company newsletter integration, and others) to data analysis and presentation of findings.[36]

Statistical Software

One of the real benefits of market research technology today is the ability to put powerful statistical software in the hands of front-line managers. With the proper training and data, it is now possible for managers to conduct analyses that were not possible even five years ago. Two software packages dominate desktop statistical analysis—SPSS and SAS. SPSS offers a range of marketing analytical tools. Its statistical software combines an easy-to-use interface with powerful statistical tools in a format that managers at all levels can use. The other widely used package is called SAS and it offers many of the same features. One of the real advantages of these packages is their ability to take the findings of the data analysis and create tables and reports.[37]

Demand Media, a social media technology company in California, analyzes data from thousands of online sources including Web analytics and search engines. This information is factored into complex algorithms that guide freelance writers in their creation of Web content that is of interest to specific audiences. Advertisers can then pay to have certain ads tacked on to specific Web content so they can be confident that the right ads are showing up in front of the right consumers.[38]

Interestingly, while dedicated statistical packages offer powerful analytical tools and outstanding reporting capabilities, probably the most widely used tool for analyzing business data is one almost everyone already has on their computer—Excel spreadsheets. Part of the Microsoft Office suite of products, Excel offers the ability to analyze data using formulas created by the user or statistical functions already embedded in the software. In addition, there exist many add-on programs, applications, and plug-ins for Microsoft Excel that give it more advanced statistical abilities, such as StatTools for Excel. While not a dedicated statistical package, it is certainly a useful tool in basic data analysis.

COLLECTING COMPETITIVE INTELLIGENCE

Today the primary issue in collecting competitive information is not too little but too much. The Internet provides an almost unlimited number of resources. As a result, it is important to discern which sources provide the most reliable, current, and cost-effective information. Let's examine the primary sources of competitive information.

Company Web Site

The single best source for competitive information is the company's own Web site. Publicly traded companies will post their annual report and other data, often in the "investor relations" area. Many companies have press kits available online that include current company news and biographies of senior management. For example, the ExxonMobil Web site posts streaming video of senior executives talking about various issues related to the company.

New-product introductions, detailed explanations of existing products, changes in personnel, even new programs and strategies are frequently located on the company Web site. Accordingly, it is a good idea to visit competitors' Web sites on a regular basis. While competitors are not likely to divulge company secrets on their Web sites, these sites should be among the first places to go in conducting a competitor analysis.

Government Sources

As we mentioned, the Securities and Exchange Commission is a great source for company information, but other government sites also provide helpful information. The United States Trademark and Patent Office provides details about patent applications and is an excellent source of information about competitor's new-product developments. Detailed descriptions of product ideas as well as developments in basic research as filed in a patent application are posted to the agency's Web site. This kind of information is valuable to large companies and small entrepreneurs that want to keep track of competitors or check the viability of a product idea. New-product developers spend a great deal of time investigating possible patents that may conflict with a new product or seeking product opportunities.

Local governments are a good source of information about competitor operations in that area. For example, if a competitor is seeking to expand manufacturing capacity, any legal notices will be filed with the appropriate local or state agencies. Keeping track of all these information sources becomes a real challenge when the competitor is a large company. This is one reason an established information system is so important.

Business Publications

There is no shortage of business publications and Web sites. *The Wall Street Journal, BusinessWeek, Fortune, Forbes,* and many others feature articles in every issue on industry trends as well as analyses of individual companies. In addition, online sites such as Hoover's provide detailed information on thousands of companies, much of it at little or no cost. While the Internet is a great tool offering incredible access to information about competitors, it is important to evaluate all information. All sources of competitive data should be reviewed with a critical eye to the reliability of the information.

The Innovation section of *BusinessWeek's* Web site offers articles related to new, innovative companies, products, and ideas. One article examined how business leaders could learn valuable lessons from the scientific community. The article looks at the collaborative management style at the Large Hadron Collider particle accelerator at CERN, a research facility composed of more than 7,000 scientists from 85 countries. Project leaders at CERN promote collective ownership and the creation of mutual trust among the facility's vast workforce of scientists to ensure the project's success—tactics that can be just as effective in the corporate world.[39]

Search Engines

Popular search engines tap an unlimited supply of information. In a matter of minutes it is possible to get hundreds, even thousands, of links. As we mentioned previously, the problem then is sorting through all the available data to find the most relevant information. One way to sort is to use fee-based search engines such as ProQuest and Lexis/Nexis. These search engines can access more data with sophisticated filters that will target specific information more easily.[40]

Salespeople

In the business-to-business environment, salespeople are frequently the most important link between the company and external marketing information. Their access to customers and suppliers is a vital source of competitor information. At trade conferences, at supplier meetings, and in customer offices, salespeople often hear information about competitor strategies including new-product launches and marketing communication campaigns. Unfortunately, many companies fail to capitalize on this valuable information source. Formal systems for collecting data from salespeople frequently do not exist and, when information is collected, it is not made available to everyone.

Customers

Another underutilized source of competitor information is the company's own customers. Through appropriate market research, it is possible to get a great deal of information about the competition by simply asking customers specific and relevant questions. In retailing, for example, consumers are frequently asked about their shopping habits. Where do you purchase this product? Which company has the best customer service? Who has the lowest price? This information is all part of the competitive analysis.

SUMMARY

Marketers know that accurate, relevant, and timely information is an essential element in marketing management. There are two sources of information: that which comes from outside the company and that which can be found internally. Being aware of environmental forces such as demographic profiles and changes, economic conditions, emerging technologies, changes in the natural world, and the political and legal environment enables marketers to create more effective short- and long-term marketing strategies.

Critical to assessing marketing information is a thorough understanding of the market research process. The process involves six specific steps: define the problem, establish the research design, search secondary sources, collect the data, analyze the data, and present the research findings. Researchers must follow the market research process to ensure the data are valid and useful for decision makers.

APPLICATION QUESTIONS

1. Imagine you are the vice president of sales for a large security company and you have been asked to put together a sales information system that collects, analyzes, interprets, and distributes information from the sales force. How would you do it? What information would you ask salespeople to collect?

2. As a market manager at Lenovo, what key information from outside the company would be important to help in the design of a new laptop for small- and medium-sized businesses?

3. The marketing manager for Disney Cruise Line wants to know what demographic trends will affect the cruise line business over the next five years. What kind of research is needed to address this question? Conduct some secondary research and try to identify two or three important demographic trends that might affect the cruise line business.

MARKETING PLAN EXERCISE

ACTIVITY 4.1: Identify Critical Information

This exercise asks you to identify the critical information needed to create the marketing plan. In that regard it is important to evaluate existing information (internal inside and secondary data) as well as new information gathered through primary research. This assignment includes:

1. Catalog internal sources of information available to you inside the organization and what information you will receive from each source.

2. Identify secondary data sources and the specific information you need from each source.
   a. List sources.
   b. Date.
   c. Assess the relevance of the data to the project.

3. List primary data needs to create the marketing plan. Then develop the specific instruments (focus group questions, surveys) that you will use later in the marketing plan.

If you are using Marketing Plan Pro, a template for this assignment can be accessed at www.mhhe.com/marshalless1e.

CHAPTER 05

Understanding Customers: Business-to-Consumer Markets

LEARNING OBJECTIVES

- Understand the value of knowing the consumer.

- Recognize how internal factors affect consumer choices.

- Consider the role of personal and psychological factors in consumer decision making.

- Identify significant factors outside the consumer that have an effect on consumer choices.

- Appreciate the critical and complex role of cultural, situational, and social factors in a consumer purchase decision.

- Understand the consumer decision-making process.

THE POWER OF THE CONSUMER

It's a Friday night and a group of people are considering how to spend the evening. A consensus forms around watching a movie. The discussion focuses on two choices: Visit the local multiplex theater to see a first-run showing of the latest hit movie, or go to a friend's house and watch a classic on the 50-inch plasma television with surround sound. Ultimately, they decide to watch *Iron Man* at the friend's house. This interaction is repeated thousands of times each weekend and represents just one example of consumer decision making.

Regal Cinemas is investing millions of dollars to attract movie-goers to its theaters.

Marketers are fundamentally interested in learning about the process people use to make purchase decisions. In our example, the implications of the seemingly innocuous decision to watch a movie at home are very significant. Movie theater owners are concerned because attendance has been falling for a decade while sales of video discs and video on demand have been growing at double-digit rates and internet video continues to gain popularity. Theater owners are investing millions of dollars to get people to choose a night out at the movies instead of going home. At the same time, movie studios such as Paramount, Sony, Time Warner, and Disney are paying attention. Because they want to maximize revenue, they have shortened the time between theatrical release and home video sales, in addition to making first-run movies available via video on demand.[1] Finally, theme parks such as Universal Orlando Resort are interested because they invest millions to combine successful movies with live-action shows and rides to extend the movie's experience.

Delivering value to the customer is the core of marketing, and a company can only do that with a thorough, accurate and timely understanding of the customer. Complex forces influence consumer choices, and these forces change over time, which adds to the challenges marketers face. Exhibit 5.1 displays a model of the consumer decision process, which is a complex interaction of internal (personal and psychological characteristics) and external (cultural, situational, and social stimuli) forces that, joined with a company's marketing activities and environmental forces, affect the purchase decision process. This chapter will identify the internal and external forces affecting the process, then focus on the consumer decision process itself.

INTERNAL FORCES AFFECT CONSUMER CHOICES

Among the most difficult factors to understand are those internal to the consumer. Often, consumers themselves are not fully aware of the role these important traits play in their decision making. Compounding the challenge is the fact that these characteristics vary by individual, change over time, and affect decisions in complex ways that are difficult to know. Exhibit 5.2 identifies examples of internal forces.

Personal Characteristics

Personal attributes are frequently used to define an individual. Age, education, occupation, income, lifestyle, and gender are all ways to identify and classify someone. The *American Heritage Online Dictionary* defines **demographics** as, "The characteristics of human populations and population segments, especially when used to identify consumer markets." It is helpful to understand the demographics of a target market for two reasons. First, knowing the personal characteristics of a

EXHIBIT 5.1

Model of the Consumer Decision Process

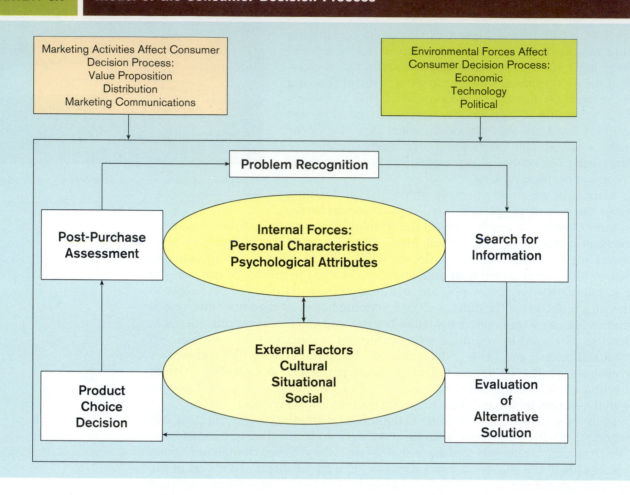

Marketing Activities Affect Consumer Decision Process:
Value Proposition
Distribution
Marketing Communications

Environmental Forces Affect Consumer Decision Process:
Economic
Technology
Political

Problem Recognition

Post-Purchase Assessment

Internal Forces:
Personal Characteristics
Psychological Attributes

Search for Information

External Factors
Cultural
Situational
Social

Product Choice Decision

Evaluation of Alternative Solution

target market enables marketers to evaluate relevant statistics against competitors and the overall population using broad demographic studies like the U.S. Census reports. Comparing demographic data such as age and income to competitor data enables you to assess how your target markets match up with competitors. Second, personal characteristics like age, income, and education play a critical role in consumer decision making, affecting information search, possible product

EXHIBIT 5.2 **Internal Forces Affecting Consumer Choices**

Personal Characteristics	Psychological Attributes
Age	Motivation
Education	Attitude
Occupation	Perception
Income	Learning
Lifestyle	Personality
Gender	

choices, and the product decision itself.[2] Demographics are also an important tool in market segmentation, and Chapter 7 will explore how demographics are used to make decisions about targeting customer groups.

The Internet has become an integral part of many people's social lives and continually more user-defined. Internet marketers have used the creation of personas that put these "Web-empowered consumers" into groups based on their interests, attitudes, and personalities. The next step in personas marketing is called "personas 2.0.," which considers consumers portray themselves socially on the Web, aiding marketers in the understanding of consumers' relationship with the Web community and company brands.[3]

Life Cycle Stage (Age)

As individuals age, their lives change dramatically, and as a result, so do their purchase patterns. From childhood to retirement, purchase behavior is shaped by a person's stage of life, and while specific aspects of the marketing mix change from one generation to the next, children still want to play, families still need homes and everything that goes in them, and seniors still focus on retirement. Marketers realize that changes in life stage (for example, graduating from college, getting married, or having a child) transform an individual's buying habits and are referred to as the **family life cycle.** These life changes mirror the individual's family environment and include the number, age, and gender of the people in the immediate family.

Facebook has been successful in becoming one of the core ways for younger people to connect with one another. As these consumers move on to the next stage of their lives, will they bring their Facebook account along with them? Facebook executives are grappling with how to enable the social networking site to grow up with its loyal users while not alienating the next generation of potential customers.[4]

Historically, age has been a primary construct for identifying a person's life cycle. A new trend is emerging, however, as people move beyond traditional roles. Young adults are marrying and having kids later in life, altering the traditional view of 30-somethings as family builders. Concurrently, American couples are having children far into their 40s, significantly changing the buying behavior of individuals who might normally be planning retirement. Consider U.S. population trends by age (see Exhibit 5.3). One important marketing insight from examining these population trends is that while the population is growing, it is also getting older.

Occupation

People are influenced by their work environment. From the executive suite to the plant floor, people who work together tend to buy and wear similar clothes, shop at the same stores, and vacation at the same places.[5] As a result, marketers identify target groups based on an individual's position in an organization.

In addition to broad occupational categories (union worker, management) marketers also target specific occupations. Given the amount of time spent working, it is not surprising that individuals develop similar interests and purchase behaviors.

Lifestyle

Even though people share the same life cycle stage or occupation, their lifestyles may be dramatically different. **Lifestyle** references an individual's perspective on

EXHIBIT 5.3 | **U.S. Population Trends by Age**

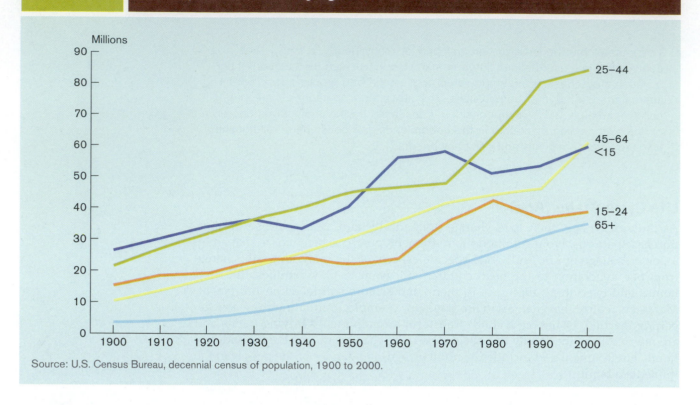

Millions

- 25–44
- 45–64
- <15
- 15–24
- 65+

Source: U.S. Census Bureau, decennial census of population, 1900 to 2000.

life and manifests itself in that person's activities, interests, and opinions (AIO). By learning what the person likes to do, his or her hobbies, and views about the world, marketing managers develop a holistic view of the individual. As the name implies, lifestyle is how people choose to live and how a person lives dictates what she or he buys. By choosing particular activities, developing unique interests, and holding on to specific opinions, an individual identifies what is really important. Marketers seek to match their products and services with the consumer's lifestyle.[6] New technologies enable marketers to not only know a great deal about their customers but also to direct targeted marketing messages. However, privacy issues and the intrusive nature of these technologies can increase ethical concerns (see Ethical Dimension 5). Exhibit 5.4 summarizes important lifestyle trends in the United States.

Gender roles are behaviors regarded as proper for men and women in a particular society. These roles change over time and across cultures. In general, women have been adding new roles as they move into the workforce and positions of political power. In the United States, this means that men and women are more likely to share responsibilities than live in a traditional household where the men work and women stay at home to raise the children.

Differences in women's roles have created vastly different market segments. At one end are traditional homemakers who derive satisfaction primarily from maintaining the household and nurturing the family. At the other extreme is the career woman who is either single or married and who makes a conscious choice

Acura links its products to specific target markets using lifestyle activities like instant messaging.

Hello, Who Are You?

You probably thought your cell phone was just for phone conversations, right? Well, not anymore. Meet the new "sell phone," which combines Internet tracking data with your location to target very personal, specific ads right to your cell phone. Marketers are now testing technology tools that will deliver a message right to you about a store or promotion just as you pass that store. You will be able to see a Starbucks coupon pop up on your cell phone with a note that tells you the nearest Starbucks is one block away on your right.

Presently, the limiting factor is not the technology but the cellular service providers, which are not sure how best to move forward. Many advertisers are also taking a wait-and-see approach as everyone works through Federal Communications Commission (FCC) rules regarding use of private customer data such as location information. At this point, the FCC is requiring mobile advertisers to get an individual's permission to release sensitive customer data before the cellular service can release the information to the advertiser. Similar rules apply to e-mail but spammers do not get the necessary permission before filling your mailbox.

Medio Systems and other companies are moving ahead and delivering targeted advertising to phones serviced by Verizon, T-Mobile, and others. Sprint Nextel is also implementing location-based targeted advertising. Advertisers see the potential to bypass much of the communications clutter that people disregard every day. By some estimates, people are exposed to as many as 3,000 ads each day, with the vast majority of the messages being ignored.

Cellular companies can locate a user within 50 to 300 meters and offer advertisers a captive audience. The marketing company collects Internet tracking data then matches where the consumer has been on the Internet with his or her actual location. If someone has visited the Barnes & Noble Web site recently and her location shows her close to a Barnes & Noble, a specific message that could include a coupon or other promotion can be sent directly to the cell phone. In 2008 advertisers spent in excess of $3 billion on mobile advertising, a minuscule sum compared to traditional advertising channels, but that number is expected to grow dramatically to $19 billion in 2011.

A number of individuals and advocacy groups, however, are concerned about the potential invasion of consumer privacy. At minimum, advertisers will learn customer cell numbers, and many cell phone users are not happy about that prospect.[7]

Ethical Perspective

1. **Advertisers:** The ability to reach targeted customers at the right moment has been the goal of advertising for decades. This new technology enables "just-in-time" advertising. As an advertiser, would you consider mobile advertising? How would you address customer concerns about privacy?

2. **Cellular service providers:** A potential source of revenue, the ability to target cell phone users, is available today and represents very little incremental cost to the service provider. Just because it is possible, should marketing companies be allowed to send mobile ads? How do you safeguard the privacy of your customer?

3. **Consumers:** Ensuring customer confidentiality is an essential element of the contract between cell service provider and consumers. Would you want to receive mobile ads?

---

to work and derives personal satisfaction from her employment. Other segments include trapped housewives that are married but prefer to work and trapped working women who would prefer to be at home but must work because of financial necessity or family pressure.

Marketing managers understand that men and women vary not only in the products they require but also in the marketing communications they are receptive to. For example, women constitute the majority of Internet users in the United States and have for several years.[8] In addition, women and men both read magazines but the kinds of magazines they read vary greatly so marketers place ads in different magazines to reach both groups.

Psychological Attributes

The consumer decision process involves a number of psychological forces that profoundly affect the consumer choice process. These forces drive the need, shape

EXHIBIT 5.4 | **Lifestyle Trends in the United States**

	Trend	Marketing Example
Health-conscious eating	Americans are turning to healthier eating styles, which can be seen in most restaurants with new low-calorie and low-carbohydrate menus.	Season's 52, Darden Restaurants' new restaurant chain, features a changing menu of healthy foods.
Single-parent homes	Although the majority of families in the United States consist of two-parent homes, single-parent homes are increasing steadily.	Target, Walmart, and other retailers offer a wide range of books, DVDs, and other products targeted at single parents.
Online era	There has been a steady increase in online shopping and information gathering. This is only expected to increase as technology increases.	Amazon, one of the first and largest online shopping Web sites, continues to experience double-digit growth every year.
Women in the workforce	In 2009, 46% of the workforce was made up of women and is continuously growing. As more and more women begin their careers, we have seen more and more men help in raising the kids.	Companies are including on-premise day care centers as part of their benefits packages; in addition, private centers continue to see significant growth.

the content and format of information stored in memory, and have an effect on point of view about products and brands.

Motivation

At any given time people experience many different needs. Most are not acted upon; however, when need reaches a particular strength or intensity, it becomes a motive that drives behavior. People prioritize needs, making sure that stronger, more urgent needs get met first. **Motivation** is the stimulating power that induces and then directs behavior. It is the force by which powerful unmet needs, or motives, prompt someone to action. Many theories have been developed over the years to explain human motivation. Exhibit 5.5 summarizes four popular theories of motivation and how they are used in marketing.

Note that any theory on motivation provides a good summary of human needs but should not be considered a comprehensive model. Marketing managers find motivational theory beneficial in identifying where products fit into an individual's overall needs. Products are often targeted at more than one set of needs. For example, dining at an upscale restaurant is certainly designed to satisfy the basic physiological need for food. However, the atmosphere and interior design encourages conversation with friends and a sense of belonging, thus meeting customers' social needs. Finally, if the restaurant is popular it may address an individual's need for status, respect, and prestige, thus fulfilling a self-esteem need.

When Nike released its limited edition Lobster Dunk sneakers, parents waited in line up to three days to be sure their kids would show up at school with a pair. Some marketers believe that the success of emotional marketing to motivate kids to pester their parents until they get the cool new thing can be translated to adults. While many would say that the kind of deep emotional yearning for a new product that children often express is a result of their age, it is argued that adult consumers acted similarly when Apple first released the iPhone.[9]

EXHIBIT 5.5   **Contemporary Theories of Motivation**

	Theory	Key Elements	Marketing Implications
Maslow's Hierarchy of Needs Theory	Humans have wants and needs that influence their behavior. People advance only to the next level if the lower needs are meet.	1. Physiological 2. Safety 3. Love/Social 4. Self-Esteem 5. Self-Actualization	Individuals are not interested in luxuries until they have had basic needs (food, shelter) met.
Herzberg's Two-Factor Theory	Certain factors in the workplace result in job satisfaction.	1. Motivators: challenging work, recognition, and responsibility 2. Hygiene factors: status, job security, salary, and benefits	Satisfying hygiene factors does not create a loyal employee or customer. For a company to really create satisfied employees it is important to focus on motivators.
Aldelfer's ERG Theory	Expansion on Maslow's hierarchy placing needs in three categories.	1. Existence 2. Relatedness 3. Growth	People need a sense of belonging and social interaction. Creating a relationship with the customers extends the customers' satisfaction with the product.
McClelland's Achievement Motivation Theory	There are three categories of needs and people differ in the degree in which the various needs influence their behavior.	1. Need for Achievement 2. Need for Power 3. Need for Affiliation	Companies can be successful targeting one of three basic needs.

Attitude

From religion to politics, sports to tomorrow's weather, people have an attitude about everything. An **attitude** is defined as a "learned predisposition to respond to an object or class of objects in a consistently favorable or unfavorable way."[10] Several key points come from this definition. First, attitudes are learned or at least influenced by new information. This is important for marketers because they seek to affect a person's attitude about a product. Second, attitudes are favorable or unfavorable, positive or negative. In other words, attitudes are seldom, if ever, neutral. As a result, marketers pay close attention to people's attitudes about their products because they play an important role in shaping a person's purchase decision.

Initially, a person's attitudes are formed by their values and beliefs. There are two categories of values. The first refers to cultural values based on national conscience. Americans, for example, value hard work and freedom among other things. In Japan, national values include reciprocity, loyalty, and obedience. The second category is personal values held by the individual. Products possessing characteristics consistent with a person's value system are viewed more favorably.

While values may be based, in part, on fact, beliefs are a subjective opinion about something. Since they are subjective (emotional and not necessarily based on fact) marketers become concerned that a negative product belief will create a negative attitude about that product, making the attitude more difficult to

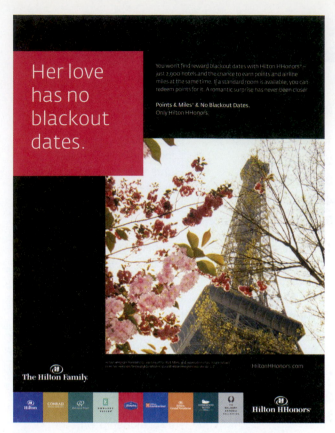

Her love
has no
blackout
dates.

You won't find reward blackout dates with Hilton HHonors® — just 2,900 hotels and the chance to earn points and airline miles at the same time. If a standard room is available, you can redeem points for it. A romantic surprise has never been closer.

Points & Miles® & No Blackout Dates.
Only Hilton HHonors.

The Hilton Family.

HiltonHHonors.com

Hilton HHonors®

There is a common belief among many in loyalty reward programs that they will not be able to use their points for rewards. Hilton attempts to deal with that belief by delivering a message about the availability of rooms using points without blackout dates.

overcome.[11] It is also important to note that beliefs, once formed, are resistant to change. Personal experiences, marketing communication, and information from trusted sources, such as family members or friends, all shape a person's belief system.

Values and beliefs come together to shape attitudes about an object whether it is Coke, the environment, or your favorite sports team. This overall predisposition is the result, generally, of an individual's assessment of that object on several attributes.

Because people's beliefs/values impact their purchase decisions, marketing managers try to learn about those beliefs/values. They do that by having customers check off rating scales that evaluate a product's performance on a list of attributes. This is important information because most attitudes result from an individual's assessment of an object using a **multiattribute model** that evaluates the object on several important attributes. Learning which attributes are used and how individuals rank those attributes is particularly helpful to marketers in creating specific marketing messages as well as the overall value proposition.[12] For instance, individuals who value the environment and ecology will place a higher priority on fuel economy and other environmentally friendly characteristics in the purchase of a car.

Perception

People are inundated with information. Indeed, there is so much information that it is not possible to make sense of everything so people use a process called perception to help manage the flow of environmental stimuli. **Perception** is a system to select, organize, and interpret information to create a useful, informed picture of the world.

In marketing, perception of a product is even more important than the reality of that product because, in a very real sense, an individual's perception is his or her reality. Perception drives attitudes, beliefs, motivation, and, eventually, behavior. Since each individual's perception is unique, everyone's perceptual response to the same reality will vary.

Perception is shaped by three psychological tools: selective awareness, selective distortion, and selective retention.

Selective Awareness An individual is exposed, on average, to between 2,000 and 5,000 messages daily.[13] People cannot process, let alone retain, all those messages, so they employ a psychological tool known as **selective awareness** to help them focus on what is relevant and eliminate what is not. The challenge for marketers is breaking through people's decision rules, which are designed to reject the vast majority of stimuli they see every day.

Research provides several insights about these decision rules. First, not surprisingly, people are more likely to be aware of information that relates to a current unmet need. Someone looking to change cellular providers will pay more attention to ads from cellular companies than someone who is happy with her current service. Second, people are more receptive to marketing stimuli when they expect them. Customers entering a Best Buy anticipate seeing audio equipment and, as a result, pay more attention to it. Finally, people are also more likely to become aware of marketing stimuli when it deviates widely from what is expected. For several years, GEICO used a caveman as its primary "spokesperson." In addition to the creativity behind this approach, one of the reasons the campaign did well was because it deviated from normal insurance ads. People didn't expect to see a caveman talking about insurance.[14]

Selective Distortion Breaking through the customer's selective awareness is an important first step. However, even if a stimulus is noticed, there is no guarantee it will be interpreted accurately. Information can be misunderstood or made to fit existing beliefs, a process known as **selective distortion.**

The issue for marketers is that selective distortion can work for or against a product. If an individual has a positive belief about a powerful brand or product, information that is ambiguous or neutral will likely be interpreted positively. Even negative data can be adjusted to align with an individual's existing beliefs. For example, despite the negative implications of the information, a recall of Toyota Prius cars did not slow sales, in part, because people's perception of Toyota's overall quality offset the negatives associated with a product recall.

Selective Retention Even if a stimulus is noticed and interpreted correctly, there is no guarantee it will be remembered. While selective awareness significantly controls the amount of information available to the individual's consciousness, selective retention acts as an additional filter. **Selective retention** is the process of placing in one's memory only those stimuli that support existing beliefs and attitudes about a product or brand. Selective retention creates a real challenge for marketers trying to overcome negative beliefs and attitudes since people are less likely to be aware of or retain information to the contrary. **Memory** is where people store all past learning events; in essence it is the "bank" where people keep their knowledge, attitudes, feelings, and beliefs.[15] There are two types of memory— short and long term. **Short-term memory** is what is being recalled at the present time and is sometimes referred to as working memory, while **long-term memory** is enduring storage, which can remain with the individual for years and years. Marketing managers are particularly interested in understanding an individual's long-term memory recall about their brand.

In an effort to better inform consumers who suffer from coronary disease or diabetes, the Food and Drug Administration requires that all nutrition facts panels on food product packaging list the trans fat content. However, studies have indicated including this information on the packaging has little impact on consumers' perceptions of how unhealthy the foods are. Most consumers do not understand how trans fats are measured; for example, is 4 grams of trans fat a lot or a little?[16]

One last point about perception regards a controversial issue—the effect of subliminal stimuli on perception. While people are aware of most stimuli around them, a number of other stimuli go unnoticed. In most cases, the stimuli are either presented so fast they are not recognized or they overload the individual and are "lost" in the person's consciousness. These stimuli are termed subliminal, and many critics of advertising suggest the stimuli can affect consumer behavior. Despite many claims to the contrary, however, research has uncovered no evidence that a subliminal message, whether sent deliberately or accidentally, has any effect on product attitudes or choice behavior.

Given the psychological processes people use to limit their awareness of marketing stimuli and control retention of any remaining information, it is easy to see why marketers must deliver a message over and over. Without repetition, the message is not likely to break through selective awareness and even less likely to be retained by the individual.[17]

Learning

How does an individual become a consumer of a particular product? Most consumer behavior is learned through a person's life experiences, personal characteristics, and relationships.

Learning is any change in the content or organization of long-term memory or behavior. Learning occurs when information is processed and added to long-term memory. Marketers can therefore affect learning by providing information using a message, format, and delivery that will encourage customers to retain the information in memory.

There are two fundamental approaches to learning. The first, conditioning, involves creating an association between two stimuli. There are two types of conditioning: classical and operant. **Classical conditioning** seeks to have people learn by associating a stimulus (marketing information, brand experience) and response (attitude, feeling, behavior).[18] Recently, many companies have started using popular songs from the 1960s and 1970s in their advertising. When individuals, particularly baby boomers, hear that music it connects them with positive memories and, not coincidentally, the product and brand being advertised. This is conditioned learning, by connecting the stimulus such as music with a response such as a positive association with a particular brand.

The other type of conditioning, **operant conditioning,** entails rewarding a desirable behavior, for example a product trial or purchase, with a positive outcome that reinforces that behavior.[19] For example, many different types of food retailers offer product samples in their stores. Frito-Lay, for instance, offers free in-store samples of Doritos for the express purpose of getting people to try the product, enjoy the product, and finally purchase a bag of Doritos. Enjoying the Doritos reinforces the positive attributes of the product and increases the probability of a purchase. Since the consumer must choose to try the product for operant conditioning to occur, Frito-Lay wants to make the trial as easy as possible.

While conditioning requires very little effort on the part of the learner, **cognitive learning** is more active and involves mental processes that acquire information to work through problems and manage life situations.[20] Someone suffering from the flu and seeking information from friends, doctors, or medical Web sites about the best over-the-counter remedy for specific symptoms is engaged in cognitive learning. That person is looking for information to help solve a problem. Marketers must understand consumers sometimes engage in this type of activity and be proactive in providing the information sought by the consumer.

Personality

When people are asked to describe someone, most of us do not talk about the person's age or education. Rather, our response generally reflects the individual's personality and is based on our interactions with that person in different situations. Our descriptions usually include various personality dimensions such as kind, outgoing, or gentle. **Personality** is a set of unique personal qualities that produce distinctive responses across similar situations.

Many theories of personality have been developed, but marketers tend to focus on personality trait theories because they offer the greatest insights on consumers. Personality trait theories all have two basic assumptions: (1) each person has a set of consistent, enduring personal characteristics, and (2) those characteristics can be measured to identify differences between individuals. Most believe personality characteristics are formed at a relatively early age and can be defined in terms of traits such as extroversion, instability, agreeableness, openness to new experiences, and conscientiousness. These core traits then lead to outward characteristics, which are what people notice.

Verizon Wireless wants small business owners to consider it the best option in dealing with mobile e-mail solutions.

Courtesy Verizon Wireless

Pom Wonderful understands the importance of creating a certain personality around its brand of pomegranate juice, with a retail price of $4.99 per 16-ounce bottle. The distinctive curvy bottle design is eye-catching and has even been featured in ads with a pearl necklace around its neck. Also, Pom Wonderful strives to create an elegant brand personality by sponsoring events such as Fashion Week in New York City and the Aspen Food & Wine Classic festival.[21]

EXTERNAL FACTORS SHAPE CONSUMER CHOICES

While internal factors are fundamental in consumer decision making, forces external to the consumer also have a direct and profound effect on the consumer decision process. These factors shape individual wants and behavior, define the products under consideration, target the selection of information sources, and shape the purchase decision. Three wide-ranging external factors that have the most significant impact on consumer choices are: cultural, situational, and social.

Cultural Factors

Culture is a primary driver of consumer behavior because it teaches values and product preferences and, in turn, affects perceptions and attitudes. Beginning in childhood and continuing on throughout life, people respond to the culture in which they live. In recent years, despite the globalization of communications and universal nature of the Internet, people have developed a heightened awareness of their own culture and subculture.

Marketers need to be aware of culture for two reasons. First, learning a target market's culture is essential to an effective marketing strategy. Creating a value proposition that incorporates cultural cues is a prerequisite to success. Second, failing to understand cultural norms has a significant negative effect on product acceptance.

Culture

Culture assimilates shared artifacts such as values, morals, beliefs, art, law, and customs into an organized system that enables people to function as members of society. In school, children learn basic cultural values through interaction with classmates and formal classroom learning. At a very early age, young people learn values and concepts about their culture. Among the values shared by Americans, for example, are achievement, hard work, and freedom while Japanese value social harmony, hierarchy, and devotion.

While culture affects people in many ways, three factors are particularly relevant in consumer behavior: language, values, and nonverbal communications. **Language** is an essential cultural building block and the primary communication tool in society. At the most basic level it is important to understand the language, making sure that words are understood correctly.[22] However, language conveys much more about a society and its values. In addition, language is such an important cultural element that frequently a culture will seek to protect its language. France, for example, has passed a number of laws to prohibit English words from being used in advertising, banning terms such as *crossover* and *showroom*.[23]

Cultural values are principles shared by a society that assert positive ideals. These principles are often viewed on a continuum. Consider the value of limited versus extended family. In the United States, the obligation and commitment to family is often limited to an individual's immediate family, including their parents, children, and siblings. Most Latin American cultures, on the other hand, have a more wide-ranging definition of family that includes extended family members such as cousins and grandparents and also more inclusive with extended family members living together.

The last cultural factor is **nonverbal communication.** One important element of nonverbal communication is time. The perception of time varies across cultures. Americans and Western Europeans place a high value on time and view it in discrete blocks of hours, days, and weeks. As a result, they focus on scheduling and getting as much done in a given period as possible. Latin Americans and Asians, on the other hand, view time as much more flexible and less discrete. They are not as concerned with the amount of work that gets done in a given time block. How does this affect marketing? Salespeople who have been trained in an American sales environment are often frustrated to find their Asian and Latin American customers less concerned about specific meeting times and more concerned about spending time building a personal relationship.

Subculture

As consumer behavior research has discovered more about the role of culture in consumer choices, it has become evident that beyond culture, people are influenced even more significantly by membership in various subcultures. A **subculture** is a group within the culture that shares similar cultural artifacts created by differences in ethnicity, religion, race, or geography. While part of the larger culture, subcultures are also different from each other. The United States is perhaps the best example of a country with a strong national culture that also has a number of distinct subcultures (see Exhibit 5.6).

Situational Factors

At various points in the consumer decision process, situational factors play a significant part. Situational factors are time-sensitive and interact with both internal and external factors to affect change in the consumer. Because they are situational, they are difficult, if not impossible, for the marketer to control. However, it is possible to mitigate their effects with a good marketing strategy.

Physical Surroundings

People are profoundly affected by their physical surroundings. An individual viewing an ad on *American Idol* will react differently whether watching the show alone or at a party with friends. Same show, same ad, but a different reaction as

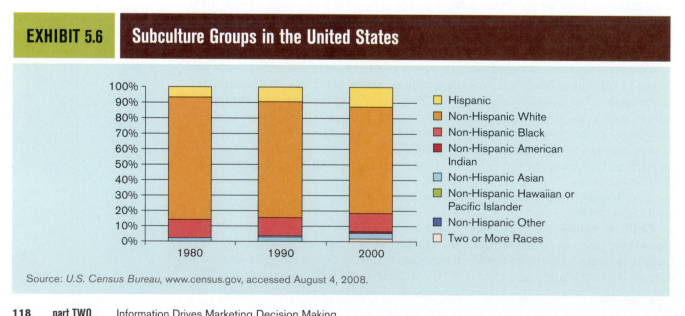

EXHIBIT 5.6 **Subculture Groups in the United States**

Source: *U.S. Census Bureau*, www.census.gov, accessed August 4, 2008.

a result of the physical surroundings at the time the marketing message is being delivered. As we will see in Chapter 12, retailers devote a lot of time and resources to creating the right physical surrounding to maximize the customer's shopping experience. They know people respond differently to changes in color, lighting, location of the product within the store; indeed, almost every element of the customer's experience is considered important in the consumer choice process.

Air travel is not generally known to be a pleasant or enjoyable experience. Even if a traveler's experience is free of unexpected inconveniences such as flight delays or lost luggage, dealing with routine activities such as check-in and security screenings is enough to test one's patience and comfort level. However, some airports have invested heavily in promoting the happiness of their travelers. Dallas-Fort Worth International Airport has done so by speeding up the security screening process, integrating more technological amenities, and creating a food court that features local food options rather than the usual fast food.[24]

Personal Circumstances

An individual's behavior is always filtered through his or her immediate personal circumstances. Parents with crying children shop differently than parents with small kids enjoying the experience, and parents without the kids along shop differently than parents with their children present. At the point of consumer choice, many things can influence the final purchase. If the line at the checkout is too long, people may eliminate certain discretionary items or forgo the entire purchase. While it is not possible for marketers to control personal circumstances, it is important to understand how personal situations influence the choice process.

Time

Time is a critical situational factor that affects individuals throughout the consumer choice process. An emerging consumer trend in many industrialized countries is the willingness to trade time for money. This is evidenced in a study that reported a majority of Americans would like to have more time for family and are seeking ways to simplify their lives.[25] For many people, time is a resource to be used, spent, or wasted and, for these people the issue is not always the best price but, rather, the best service. Increasingly, customers are asking if the purchase of this product will give them more time or be less of a hassle than another product. Automobile manufacturers and dealers have responded by creating more "hassle-free" shopping experiences. Instead of going through a difficult negotiation process to get the lowest price, dealers are offering low, fixed prices that reduce some of the hassle.

Social Factors

Humans are social beings. Everyone seeks social interaction and acceptance on some level. As people move through life, they affect and, in turn, are affected by various social factors. These factors include groups like their family, social class, reference groups, as well as individual opinion leaders.

Family

The first group any individual belongs to is the family. Families are the single most important buying group and they influence the consumer choice process in two ways. First, the family unit is the most influential teacher of cultural values. Children are socialized into a community and its values primarily through the family unit as they interact with parents, siblings, and extended family members. Second, children learn consumer behavior from their parents. As adults and later parents, they model the behavior first learned as a child.

The most basic definition of a **family** is a group of two or more people living together and related by birth, marriage, or adoption. Historically, in the United States and much of the world, the traditional family included a married couple with children of their own or adopted children. However, the last 40 years have witnessed changes in the family structure. In the 1970s the traditional family comprised 70 percent of all households. Today that number has dropped to a little over half of all households (53 percent).

New family structures are now much more prevalent. These emerging family structures create a number of challenges for marketers.[26] Single-parent households, for example, often report discretionary time is in short supply. Grocery stores have seized on this opportunity by creating deli bars that cater to working fathers and mothers who pick up dinner on their way home from work.

The **household life cycle (HLC)** is fundamental to understanding the role of family in the consumer choice process (see Exhibit 5.7). The traditional family life cycle consists of a fairly structured set of activities that begins when single people get married (20s), start a family (30s), raise kids (40s to 50s), watch as the kids grow up and leave home (50s to 60s), and finally enter into retirement (60s and beyond). However, while this model is still relevant in many cases, several new models have emerged to reflect changes in the household life cycle. People are marrying later and putting off the start of a family. Women are having children later in life for a variety of reasons (marry later, focus on career). Couples raise kids then divorce and remarry, creating blended families, or they start new families of their own.

Each group in Exhibit 5.7 offers opportunities and challenges for marketing managers. From basic needs that motivate individuals to engage in the process

EXHIBIT 5.7	Stages in the Household Life Cycle

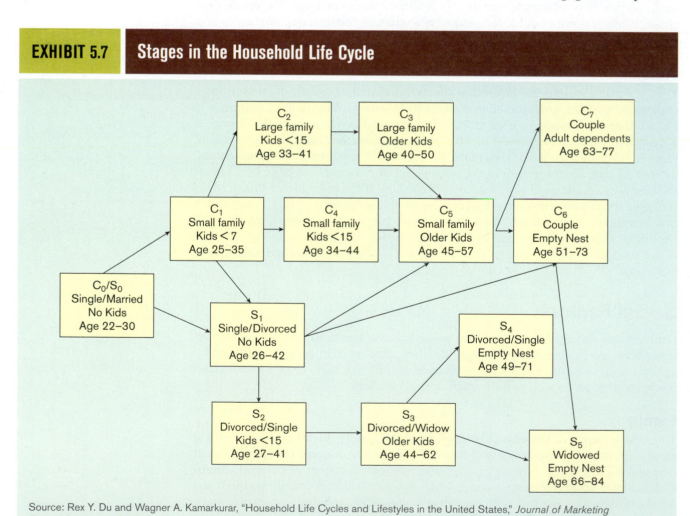

Source: Rex Y. Du and Wagner A. Kamarkurar, "Household Life Cycles and Lifestyles in the United States," *Journal of Marketing Research*, 43, no.1 (2006).

through information search and then on to final purchase decision, each group thinks and behaves differently. It is essential to identify and understand the HLC group for each target market. Each group makes different choices based on their stage in the life cycle.[27] For example, two couples (35 years old, married, professionals)—one with two children the other without—have very different lifestyles, values, and purchase priorities.

Individual responsibility in family decision making references the way individuals inside the family make decisions. There has been a great deal of research on the roles of various family members in the decision-making process. Across all the purchases in a household, research suggests, not surprisingly, that husbands and wives each dominate decision making in certain categories and jointly participate in others. For example, husbands tend to dominate insurance purchase decisions while wives are primary decision makers in grocery shopping.[28] Children, even at an early age, exert influence and dominate decisions for products such as cereal and indirectly influence decisions on things like vacations. However, traditional family responsibilities are changing as family units change. Single-parent households have shifted traditional purchase decisions. For example, single fathers must take on the responsibility for selecting their child's school.

Social Class

In every society, people are aware of their social status; however, explaining the social class system to someone from outside the culture is often a challenge. People learn about social class and their social status at a very early age from their parents, school, friends, and the media. **Social class** is a ranking of individuals into harmonized groups based on demographic characteristics such as age, education, income, and occupation.

Most Western cultures have no formal social class system; however, there is an informal social ranking. These informal systems exert influence over an individual's attitudes and behavior. Two factors drive social status. Success-driven factors have the greatest effect on social status and include education, income, and occupation. Innate factors, the second category, do not result from anything the individual has done but, rather, are characteristics the individual has inherited from birth. Gender, race, and parents are the primary innate factors determining social status.

Social class is not the result of a single factor, such as income, but rather a complex interaction among many characteristics. While some social class drivers are not in the individual's control, people do make choices about their education and occupation. Therefore, it is possible for people, particularly in societies providing educational opportunities, to move into new social classes based on their achievements. In addition, the availability of easy credit, creative pricing, and new financing arrangements enable and even encourage people to engage in aspirational purchases. **Aspirational purchases** are products bought outside the individual's social standing. Over 50 percent of the luxury cars sold in the United States are leased. By offering special financing terms, individuals with lower income levels now drive a BMW, Mercedes-Benz, or Lexus. This enables people to drive a car they normally could not afford, an aspirational purchase.

From a marketing perspective, the impact of social status on consumption behavior is profound, affecting everything from the media people choose to view (lower classes watch more TV while upper classes tend to read more) to the products they buy (lower classes tend to buy more generics while the upper classes select more branded products).

Retail stores create different product mixes based on the social status of the shoppers at that store. Target, for example, maintains the same basic product mix across all its stores. However, it does add higher-priced brand names in stores serving primarily upper-class neighborhoods while stores with a middle-class demographic get a slightly different product mix.

Burberry has historically targeted wealthy individuals with their expensive clothes and accessories. However, more recently the company has introduced less expensive items to appeal to a broader target audience.

Opinion Leaders

The previous discussion on external factors focused primarily on group influences such as social and cultural factors; however, external factors also include personal influences. **Opinion leaders** fulfill an important role by classifying, explaining, and then bestowing information, most often to family and friends but occasionally to a broader audience. People seek out opinion leaders for a variety of reasons, including unfamiliarity with a product, reassurance about a product selection before purchasing, and anxiety resulting from high involvement with the purchase of a particular product. Anyone whose opinions are valued by the individual can be an opinion leader. For instance, the friend who enjoys cars could be an opinion leader about automobiles; the relative with a background in information technology might be the expert on technology.

While opinion leaders are often defined by product class, another influential group has emerged. This new group, whose members are called **market mavens,** has information about many kinds of products, places to shop, and other facets of markets, and the members initiate discussions with consumers and respond to requests from consumers for market information.[29] The key difference between opinion leaders and market mavens is the focus on their market knowledge. Market mavens have a broader understanding and expertise that goes beyond product to include other elements of the purchase decision such as shopping experience and price.

In their role as information gatekeepers, opinion leaders and market mavens exert influence over an individual's product and brand choice. As a result, marketers seek to understand the roles of these two groups so they can identify the members and, in turn, encourage them to try a particular product. Marketers encourage these individuals using these activities:

- Market research. As a primary source of information for interested individuals, it is critical that opinion leaders and market mavens are familiar with a product and understand its advertising so they can convey the information accurately. Many market researchers focus on the way these individuals interpret messages to ensure the marketing mix is working correctly.

- Product sampling. Testing a product is an essential part of any gatekeeper's acceptance. As a result, the leaders are prime targets for product sampling.

- Advertising. Companies use opinion leaders and market mavens to influence decision makers whether it is a business leader or an individual consumer. Accenture Consulting hired Tiger Woods as its spokesperson because he is an opinion leader. The company hopes Tiger's qualities—successful, focused, and a winner—influence business leaders looking for a consulting firm.

References Groups

Everyone identifies with and is influenced by groups. In most cases, the individual may belong to the group or seek membership, while in other situations the group is perceived negatively and the individual works to disassociate himself. A **reference group** is group of individuals whose beliefs, attitudes, and behavior influence (positively or negatively) the beliefs, attitudes, and behavior of an individual.[30] Three characteristics are used to categorize reference groups: association, desirability, and degree of affiliation.

A key characteristic impacting the degree a group affects the individual is the extent to which an individual desires to be associated with the group. **Desirability** is the extent and direction of the emotional connection an individual wishes to have with a particular group. Individuals can really want to belong to a group or not, and the linkage can be either positive or negative. For example, sports teams encourage participation at many levels.

The **degree of affiliation** indicates the amount of interpersonal contact an individual has with the reference group. **Primary groups** are marked by frequent contact, while less frequent or limited dealings are known as **secondary groups.** Individuals come in frequent contact with co-workers, close friends, and other groups such as religious, special-interest, or hobby groups that may be primary or secondary depending on the level of contact. Over time, the degree of affiliation will likely change; for example, when someone changes jobs the primary group of co-workers will also change.

THE LEVEL OF INVOLVEMENT INFLUENCES THE PROCESS

One significant outcome of motivation, discussed earlier, is **involvement** with the product because it mediates the product choice decision. Involvement is activated by three elements: the individual's background and psychological profile, the aspirational focus, and the environment at the time of the purchase decision. As we noted, motivation is unique to each individual and drives purchase decisions. Aspirational focus is anything of interest to the buyer and is not limited to the product itself. It is possible to be involved with a brand, advertising, or activities that occur as a result of product use. The environment changes the level of involvement. Time, for example, can limit involvement if there is pressure to make a decision quickly but can enhance involvement if there is sufficient time to fully engage in the decision process. Involvement influences every step in the choice decision process, and as a result, marketers create strategies based on high and low levels of involvement.

Decision Making with High Involvement

Greater motivation that leads to greater involvement results in a more active and committed choice decision process. When someone is concerned with the outcome of the process, they will spend more time learning about product options and become more emotionally connected to the process and the decision. Someone stimulated to acquire new information is engaged in **high-involvement learning.** A high level of involvement usually means the entire process takes longer. High-involvement consumers report high levels of satisfaction in their purchase decision. This is not surprising since these consumers spend more time engaged in the decision process and, therefore, are more comfortable in their decision.

Many companies look to high-involvement customers for insights on product development and strategy. In an effort to improve on generally poor reception of Windows Vista, Microsoft decided its next operating system, Windows 7, needed to be far more user-defined. Microsoft released a limited number of fully functional copies of the proposed new operating system to users who agreed to take it for a spin on a separate, dedicated computer. Microsoft software engineers then used the testers' feedback to create the foundation on which they built the final version of Windows 7.[31]

Decision Making with Limited Involvement

While high-involvement purchases are more significant to the consumer, the vast majority of purchases involve limited or low involvement. From the purchase of gasoline to the choice of restaurants, decisions are often made almost automatically, often out of habit, with little involvement in the purchase decision. The reality is that consumers tend to focus their time and energy on high-involvement purchases while making many purchases with little or no thought at all.

Low-involvement learning happens when people are not prompted to value new information. This is more prevalent than high-involvement learning because the vast majority of marketing stimuli occur when there is little or no interest in the information. People do not watch TV for the commercials, they watch for the programming; advertising is just part of the viewing experience. Likewise, print advertising exists alongside articles and is often ignored. While people are not actively seeking the information, they are exposed to advertising and this, in turn, affects their attitudes about a brand. Research suggests that people shown ads in a low-involvement setting are more likely to include those brands in the choice decision process. Low-involvement consumers spend little time comparing product attributes and frequently identify very few differences across brands. Because the decision is relatively unimportant, they will often purchase the product with the best shelf position or lowest price with no evaluation of salient product characteristics.[32]

Marketers consider several strategies in targeting low-involvement consumers. The objective of these strategies is to raise consumer involvement with the product. Generally, time is the defining characteristic for these strategies. Short-term strategies involve using sales promotions such as coupons, rebates, or discounts to encourage trying the product and then hoping the consumers will raise their product involvement. Long-term strategies are more difficult to implement. Marketers seek to focus on the product's value proposition, creating products with additional features, better reliability, or more responsive service to increase customer satisfaction. Additionally, strong marketing communications campaigns that speak to consumer issues or concerns can raise involvement with the product. A classic example of this tactic is Michelin's highly effective and long-running advertising campaign that links a relatively low-involvement product, tires, with a significant consumer concern, family safety. Tires are not typically a high-involvement product, however, when the voiceover on the commercial says, "Because so much is riding on your tires" while showing a baby riding in the car, consumer involvement in the product and more specifically the brand increases.

While low-involvement consumers demonstrate little or no brand loyalty, they are also, by definition, open to brand switching. As a result, brands can experience significant gains in consumer acceptance with an effective, comprehensive marketing strategy.

THE CONSUMER DECISION-MAKING PROCESS

Every day, people make a number of consumer decisions. From breakfast through the last television show watched before going to bed, people are choosing products as a result of a decision-making process. Learning about that process is a vital step for marketers trying to create an effective marketing strategy.

Years of consumer research have resulted in a five-stage model of consumer decision making. While not everyone passes through all five stages for every purchase, all consumers apply the same fundamental sequence beginning with problem recognition, followed by search for information, evaluation of alternatives, product choice decision, and finally post-purchase evaluation. Each time a purchase decision is made, the individual begins to evaluate the product in preparation for the next decision (see Exhibit 5.8).

EXHIBIT 5.8 **Consumer Decision-Making Process**

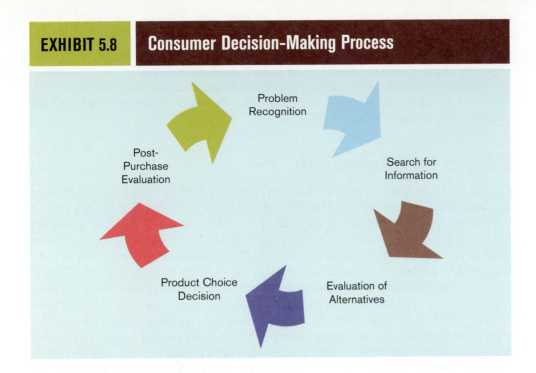

However, as noted earlier, someone driving home from work does not go through an extensive search for information or evaluate a number of alternatives in purchasing gasoline for the car. In all likelihood, the consumer buys from a station he or she knows well and shops at regularly. Nevertheless, this model is helpful because it illustrates what can be called the "complete decision-making process," which occurs when people are fully involved in the purchase.

Problem Recognition

Every purchase decision made by an individual is initiated by a problem or need that drives the consumer decision-making process. Problems or needs are the result of differences between a person's real and preferred state.

People live in the perceived reality of present time or **real state.** At the same time, people also have desires that reflect how they would like to feel or live in the present time and this is known as a **preferred state.** When the two states are in balance, the individual does not require anything and no purchase occurs. However, where there is a discrepancy in the two states, a problem is created and the consumer decision-making process begins.

The discrepancy, or gap, can be created by internal or external drivers. Internal drivers are basic human needs such as hunger and security. Someone is hungry (real state) and wants to eat (preferred state). This will lead to a number of choices: eat at home, dine out, or go to the grocery store. It may even trigger other options such as calling a friend, which addresses a need for social interaction. External drivers happen as people interact with the world. Some of these triggers result from a company's marketing efforts but most arise when an individual experiences something that creates a desire, like seeing a friend driving a new car or hearing about a good new restaurant.

Despite internal or external stimuli, people do not respond to every gap between a real and preferred state. Sometimes the disparity is not sufficient to drive the person to action. A person may want a new car but does not act on that feeling because he or she lacks the financial resources or simply cannot justify the purchase. When the conflict between real and preferred states reaches a certain level, the decision-making process begins.

Marketers need to understand problem recognition for several reasons. First, it is essential to learn about the problems and needs of the target market to create value-added products. Second, key elements of an effective marketing strategy, particularly communication, are predicated on a good knowledge of problem recognition triggers. For example, the classic advertising campaign by the California Milk Processor Board, "Got Milk?," spoke directly to the recognition of the problem—do you have milk in your refrigerator? The success of the campaign has been credited with reinvigorating the sale of cow's milk since the ads started running in the early 1990s.

Search for Information

Once a problem is recognized and action is required, people seek information to facilitate the best decision. The search for information is not categorical; rather, it operates on a continuum from limited to extensive. Consider the following examples. A couple notices the low-fuel light comes on as they are driving home from a party. The driver recalls their "local" station is on the way home and, without any additional information, stops at the station and fills up the car. This is an example of **minimal information search.** The same couple now finds out they are going to have a baby and realize their Infiniti G37 coupe has to be replaced with a more practical vehicle. They engage in a thorough information search reviewing car magazines, soliciting opinions from friends and family, conducting online research, reading *Consumer Reports,* and test-driving a number of new cars and SUVs before making a final purchase decision. This is an example of **extensive information search.** Between these two extremes is **limited information search,** which, as the name implies, involves some, albeit restricted, search for information.

Tylenol Cold provides a great deal of information on the package to help consumers make a decision in the store at the point of purchase.

Information Sources

There are two basic sources of information: internal and external. **Internal information search,** as the name implies, is all information stored in memory and accessed by the individual. This is always the first place people consider for information. Past experiences, conversations, research, preexisting beliefs and attitudes create an extensive internal database that is tapped by the individual once the problem is recognized. In our example of the car low on gas, the driver searched internal information and found past experiences provided sufficient information to make a decision.

Even when additional information is needed, internal information is used to frame the external search. Price limits and key performance metrics, criteria often used in the evaluation of alternatives, are frequently derived from information stored in memory. People gather and process information even if they are not actively involved in the purchase decision process. Consequently, an individual's internal information is changing all the time. As people get older, gain more experience with a product or brand, and gather more information, they often rely more on internal information and conduct a less external information search.

The second fundamental source of information is external. Once people have determined internal information is not sufficient to make the purchase decision, they seek information from outside sources. **External information sources** include independent groups (sources), personal associations (friend and family), marketer-created information (sales brochures, advertising), and experiences (product trial and demonstrations).

An organization's marketing communications represent only one source, albeit an important one, among several external information source options. However, company marketing communications can play an important role in influencing other sources of information such as personal contacts. Exhibit 5.9 summarizes external information sources and highlights the diversity of available information resources.

Defining the Set of Alternatives

At some point in the search for information, often during the internal information search, people begin to limit the number of alternatives under consideration. From a practical perspective, it is simply not possible to gather and process information on many different options. This is known as bounded rationality and defines people's limited capacity to process information.

People begin with a very large set of possible alternatives known as the **complete set.** This set includes a variety of options across different brands and perhaps even products. Based on the individual's choice criteria, however, this large set of possible options will be reduced. Keep in mind that the complete set is not *all* options available to the buyer; rather, the set is the options that the buyer is aware of when the search process begins. The extent of the buyer's knowledge about the problem and available options determines the set of possible alternatives in the complete set.

As consumers move through the search for information, certain products may be eliminated in favor of others and brands will be evaluated and discarded. The **awareness set** reduces the number of options. At a minimum, the number of different product categories, if considered, will be reduced and some brands discarded. Interestingly, the awareness set can include choices across product

EXHIBIT 5.9	Sources of External Information

External Information Sources	Example	Marketing Implications
Independent groups	*Consumer Reports* *Consumer's Union*	Favorable reviews from independent sources are an important source of external information. Marketers need a strategy to reach independent sources with relevant information.
Personal associations	Family Friends	These associations can be an important external source of information in certain decisions. Marketers seek to influence reference groups and opinion leaders through favorable product reviews and effective marketing communications.
Marketer information	Advertising	Effective marketing communications reinforce messages to other external information sources such as independent groups.
Experiential	Product trials	Product samples for certain categories such as food are easy to provide. Encourage people to seek out product trials and demonstrations when a sample is not appropriate (electronics, automobiles).

categories. From the awareness set, individuals conduct an additional information search. Based on additional information and evaluation, a **consideration (evoked) set** is created, which encompasses the strongest options. It is from the consideration set that the product decision is made.

Marketing managers are vitally interested in learning about the information search process for two reasons. First, marketers must identify important external information sources so they can direct their resources to the most effective external sources. Second, they must learn how consumers choose products for inclusion in their awareness and consideration sets to create marketing strategies that increase the probability of being in the consideration set.

Evaluation of Alternatives

Concurrent with the search for information are the analysis and evaluation of possible product choices. As we discussed previously, consumers move, sometimes quickly, from many options to a more restricted awareness set and from there to a final consideration set from which a decision is made. During this process, the individual is constantly evaluating the alternatives based on internal and external information.

The consumer choice process is complex and ever changing. Environmental and personal factors at the moment of decision dramatically affect the purchase decision. As a result, it is impossible to develop a consumer choice model for every purchase. However, years of research suggest consumers make product choices primarily from three perspectives: emotional, attitude based, and attribute based.

Emotional Choice

Not all purchases are made strictly for rational reasons. Indeed, product choices can be **emotional choices,** based on attitudes about a product, or based on attributes of the product depending on the situation. Frequently, the product choice encompasses a mix of all three. An individual goes to Starbucks for the personal pleasure of enjoying a cappuccino (emotional). That same person also considers Starbucks the best choice for getting together with friends after evaluating other choices (attitude based). Finally, the individual finds Starbucks' cappuccinos simply taste better than other competitors (attribute based).

While emotions have been considered an important factor in decision making for many years, it is only recently that marketers began to develop specific marketing strategies targeting emotion-based decisions. Product design and execution even focus on creating an emotional response to the product. From there, marketing communications connect the product to the target audience using images and words that convey an emotional connection. Exhibit 5.10 shows an ad that communicates emotion to the reader.

| EXHIBIT 5.10 | Ketel One Offers an Emotional Choice |

Ketel One is connecting to customers on an emotional level reinforcing the old adage "One picture is worth a thousand words."

Attitude-Based Choice

Early in the evaluation of alternatives, people regularly use beliefs and values to direct their assessment. As consumers create the awareness set, they discard or include products and brands using existing attitudes. **Attitude-based choices** tend to be more holistic, using summary impressions rather than specific attributes to evaluate the options and affect even important purchases such as a car or house. It is not uncommon for beliefs to affect the actual product decision. For example, "it is important to buy cars made in America" or the opposite, "foreign cars are better than American products." When two brands are judged to be relatively the same, people frequently look to existing attitudes to guide their decision. When someone responds to a question about why he bought a particular product with, "I always buy . . ." or "this is the only brand I use . . ." they are likely making an attitude-based choice decision.

Attribute-Based Choice

By far the most prevalent approach to product decisions is **attribute-based choice** based on the premise that product choices are made by comparing brands across a defined set of attributes. These evaluative attributes are the product features or benefits considered relevant to the specific problem addressed in the purchase decision. Antilock brakes are a product feature that translates into a consumer benefit—better control in a hazardous situation. Most consumers could not describe how antilock brakes actually work but are quite aware of the benefits and would eliminate a car from the choice process if it failed to have that product feature. Not all evaluative attributes are tangible. Brand image, prestige, attitudes about a brand or product can also be used as evaluative criteria.

"Organic" has become one of the most prominent product attributes over the past few years. As a result, companies such as Procter & Gamble have released organic versions of their cleaners and detergents. While many consumers will pay a premium for a product that they feel is better for them and the environment, it is different when it comes to cleaning products. Market analysts have found that very few consumers are willing to pay a premium for an organic cleaning product that does not perform as well as its nonorganic counterpart.[33]

Product Choice Decision

The end result of evaluating product alternatives is an intended purchase option. Until the actual purchase, it is still only an "intended" option because any number of events or interactions can happen to dissuade or alter the final purchase decision. Four purchase event characteristics affect the actual choice decision:

Physical surroundings—the environment for the purchase. From store colors to the employees, consumers respond to their physical environment. For example, while the color red creates awareness and interest, it also creates feelings of anxiety and negativity. Blue is calmer and considered the most conducive in creating positive feeling with the customer. Crowding can have a negative effect on purchase decisions because, if the store becomes too crowded, people will forgo the purchase, perhaps going somewhere else.

Social circumstances—the social interaction at the time of purchase. Shopping is a social activity and people are influenced by the social interaction at the time of purchase. Trying on an outfit alone may lead to the purchase; however, when putting on the outfit while shopping with a friend, it is unlikely the clothing will be purchased if the friend does not like it.

Time—the amount of time an individual has to make the purchase. The product choice decision can be affected by time pressure. The consumer will be less willing to wait for the best solution and more likely to purchase an acceptable alternative.

State of mind—individual's state of mind at time of purchase. An individual's mood influences the purchase decision. People in a positive state of mind are more likely to browse. Negative mood states are less tolerant and lead to increased impulse and compulsive purchases.

As a result of these purchase event characteristics, the intended purchase can be altered despite the information search and evaluation process. Some of these characteristics are at least nominally in the marketer's control. Other characteristics, such as an individual's state of mind, are uncontrollable and must be dealt with at the moment of purchase by employees who, it is hoped, have the skills and training needed to handle difficult situations.[34]

The final purchase decision is not a single decision, but rather, the consumer confronts five important decisions:

What: Select the product and, more specifically, the brand. Included as part of the product choice are decisions about product features, service options, and other characteristics of the product experience.

Where: Select the point of purchase. Select the retailer and, increasingly, the channel—retail store (bricks) or online (clicks)—through which the product is to be purchased.

How much: Choose the specific quantity to be purchased. For example, warehouse clubs, such as Sam's Club and Costco, offer consumer options on purchase quantity. If you have the ability to store products, it is possible to save money by purchasing in larger quantities.

When: Select the timing of the purchase. The timing of the purchase can make a difference in the final purchase price. Car dealers traditionally offer better deals at the end of the month as they try to meet monthly sales quotas. Through sales and other marketing communications, marketers encourage consumers to purchase sooner rather than later.

Payment: Choose the method of payment. The selection of a payment method makes a big difference to the consumer and marketer. Marketers want to make it easy for the consumer to purchase; however, not all payment methods are equal. Credit cards charge the retailer a fee that, in turn, is passed back to the consumer. One payment method, the debit card, is becoming popular with younger adults and combines the convenience of a credit card with the fiscal responsibility of using cash. Indeed, the consumer can often choose to not purchase the product at all, as other choices are available besides purchase. They can rent or lease products such as automobiles, making it possible to use products they could not normally afford.

Consumers make a number of decisions at the point of purchase. Often, the selection of where the product will be purchased is done in conjunction with the product evaluation.

Post-Purchase Assessment

Once the purchase is complete, consumers begin to evaluate their decision. Attitudes change as they experience and interact with the product. These attitudinal changes include the way the consumer looks at competitors as well as the product itself. At the same time, marketers want to foster and encourage the relationship and, as we discussed in Chapter 3, increasingly focus resources to build the customer relationship. Most of a CRM program is built around the customer's experience after the purchase. The four critical characteristics of post-purchase assessment are: dissonance, use/nonuse, disposition, and satisfaction/dissatisfaction.

Dissonance

High-involvement, large purchases often lead to a level of doubt or anxiety known as **post-purchase dissonance.** Most purchases occur with little or no dissonance.[35] The likelihood of dissonance increases if one or more of the following purchase decision attributes are present: (1) a high degree of commitment that is not easily revoked; (2) a high degree of importance for the customer; (3) alternatives are rated equally and the purchase decision is not clear. Also, the individual's own predisposition for anxiety can create additional dissonance. Big-ticket purchases frequently include several of those characteristics.

How do consumers reduce dissonance? The single most effective method is a thorough information search and evaluation of alternatives. When consumers are confident that due diligence has been done, they have less anxiety after the purchase. If dissonance remains a problem, additional information can be sought to reduce anxiety and reinforce the decision. Marketers can direct marketing communications to reduce dissonance particularly with large purchases such as automobiles. As part of a CRM program, many companies follow up with customers after the purchase to assess their satisfaction.

Use/Nonuse

Consumers buy a product to use. Marketers are acutely interested in learning how customers use the product for several reasons. First, it is important the customer knows how to use the product correctly. Buying a new television can quickly become a negative experience if it is not set up properly. As a result, marketers want to be sure the customer understands how the product is to be used and any setup procedures that may be needed to ensure proper function. Second, a satisfied customer means a greater likelihood of additional purchases. Buying and riding a bicycle means the consumer is more likely to buy a helmet, light, bike rack, and other accessories.

Many products are purchased but not used or at least not consumed immediately. Some products are returned because the consumer has a negative experience such as a defective product. Marketers, of course, work to avoid a negative experience. Building customer relationships and making sure the customer understands the product and how it is to be used reduce the probability of consumers returning the product. Another potential post-purchase problem can be that the product is purchased and not used. In these situations, marketers seek to stimulate product usage. Many packaged foods include expiration dates encouraging consumers to use the product quickly and repurchase.

Disposal

Increasingly, marketers are concerned about how products are disposed of once they are no longer in use. Environmental concerns consistently rank as a major issue for consumers in many parts of the world. People living in the United States, for example, produce nearly 2,000 pounds (1 ton) of garbage per person every year. Once a product is consumed, in most cases, a physical object remains and needs to be disposed of. New technologies such as computer CPUs and monitors are particularly difficult to discard because they contain dangerous chemicals.

Timberland is one of many companies that uses recycled materials in its packaging.

Satisfaction/Dissatisfaction

Consumers evaluate every aspect of the product. As previously noted, this includes any dissonance present at the time of purchase, use or nonuse of the product, the product disposition, the purchase experience, and even the value equation. This results in the consumer's satisfaction or dissatisfaction with the product and purchase decision. In addition, various dimensions of the overall experience will be satisfactory or unsatisfactory. A customer may love the product, but dislike the dealer or retailer.

Most products are evaluated on two dimensions—instrumental performance and symbolic performance. **Instrumental performance** relates to the actual performance features of the product and answers the question: Did the product do what it was supposed to do? **Symbolic performance** refers to the image-building aspects of the product and answers the question: Did the product make me feel better about myself? A product that performs poorly on instrumental dimensions will ultimately lead to dissatisfaction. However, for a consumer to be fully satisfied with the product, it must perform well both instrumentally and symbolically. A new Hyundai automobile may have scored high on instrumental performance but low on symbolic performance. Is the customer dissatisfied? No, but it is not certain that person will purchase another Hyundai.

There are two primary outcomes of consumer dissatisfaction with a product: a customer will either change his or her behavior or do nothing. When a customer has an unfavorable experience at the bank, she may not leave but her opinion of the bank diminishes. Over time, this will erode the consumer's evaluation of the bank. The second result of consumer dissatisfaction is a change in behavior. The consumer may simply choose to stop shopping at that store or purchasing a particular product. Another option is to complain to management. Marketers are aware that for every complaint, there are eight "quiet" but dissatisfied consumers who chose to walk away. An even greater concern is consumers telling friends about a bad experience or complaining to government agencies. Finally, dissatisfied consumers who believe their legal rights have been violated may take legal action for damages related to the purchase experience.

SUMMARY

A thorough knowledge and understanding of customers is an essential element in developing an effective value proposition. For business-to-consumer companies this means learning about how and why consumers buy products and services. This chapter talks about the consumer buying decision process. We discuss the two complex, critical forces (internal and external) that shape the consumer decision-making process. We offer an in-depth analysis of the process a consumer uses in making a purchase decision. The distinction is made between high- and low-involvement decisions, which dramatically affects the degree to which the consumer engages in the entire buying decision process.

APPLICATION QUESTIONS

1. Understanding the consumers in a target market is critical to creating an effective value proposition. Assume you are the vice president of marketing for Regal Cinemas. What do you think is the demographic profile (including the age, income, and life cycle stage) of your largest target market? As part of a mini-market research project, visit a movie theater on a weekend and track the people entering. How old are they? Are they families or people meeting friends?

2. You are the marketing manager for the Bowflex Series 7 treadmills. You believe the product appeals to both men and women. As you develop the marketing strategy, what differences might you consider in the product based on whether

a man or woman is buying? What about the marketing communications (message, choice of media)?

3. Disneyland has traditionally marketed to families; recently, however, new household life cycle patterns have led to changes in the marketing strategy. Identify three household life cycle stages that Disney may want to consider in the future.

MARKETING PLAN EXERCISE

ACTIVITY 5.1: Define Consumer Markets

For those marketing products to consumers (or through a channel that sells directly to consumers), understanding the purchase decision process of the target market is an essential element of the marketing plan. This exercise includes the following activities:

1. Develop a demographic profile of the customer to include
   a. Age
   b. Income
   c. Occupation
   d. Education
   e. Lifestyle (activities, interests, opinions)
2. Describe the motivation of the target consumer. Why is the consumer buying the product?
3. What external forces will influence the target consumer as he or she considers the purchase? For example, will the consumer's culture or subculture affect the purchase decision? How?
4. Describe the consumer's typical consumer purchase decision process? What is the likely process a consumer will go through in making the decision to purchase the product?

If you are using Marketing Plan Pro, a template for this assignment can be accessed at www.mhhe.com/marshalless1e.

CHAPTER 06

Understanding Customers: Business-to-Business Markets

LEARNING OBJECTIVES

- Recognize the importance of B2B marketing.

- Understand the differences between B2C and B2B markets.

- Understand the critical role of the buying center and each participant in the B2B process.

- Learn the B2B purchase decision process and different buying situations.

- Comprehend the role of technology in business markets.

ORGANIZATIONAL BUYING: MARKETING TO A BUSINESS

Many people believe marketing is focused primarily on consumers—the ultimate users of the product. This is due, at least in part, to the fact that most people experience marketing as a consumer. The reality, however, is that large consumer products companies purchase hundreds of billions of dollars of products and services every year. Everyone knows Hewlett-Packard (HP) and General Electric (GE) because of the products they sell to consumers, but these companies derive most of their revenue from selling to other businesses. Many companies that are primarily consumer oriented, such as Samsung Electronics Corp., sell in the business-to-business (B2B) market as well. Exhibit 6.1 shows the largest national business-to-business markets.

Samsung Electronics Co. operates in both the consumer and business markets and has historically sought to balance strategies and operations among many divisions. However, when the idea of consolidating operations into two main divisions was proposed, Samsung's executives were faced with a dilemma. They were concerned that the new, more efficient operating structure would make it easier to inadvertently better serve their business customers that also happened to be their consumer market competitors.[1]

In many cases, companies are selling products that end up as components in a finished product. General Electric is a world manufacturing leader in commercial

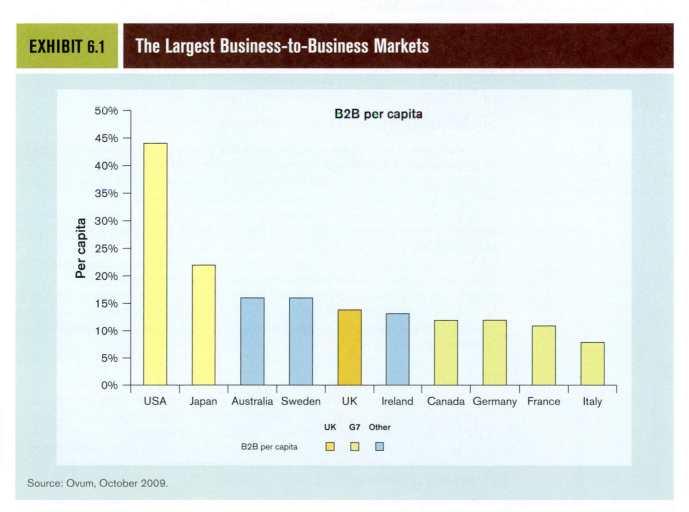

EXHIBIT 6.1 — **The Largest Business-to-Business Markets**

Source: Ovum, October 2009.

POWER YOUR GROWTH
with HP Color LaserJet MFP.
SAVE UP to 50%
on ENERGY and PAPER.

You have the ideas, we give you the right tools. With HP ColorLaserJet MFPs you can plan your growth with reduced spending. To find out about Instant-on Technology, automatic two-sided printing capability and other innovative ideas to cut printing costs, visit hp.com/colorlaserjet

HIT **PRINT** INTELLIGENTLY

HP derives most of its revenue selling business to business. Here HP highlights energy and cost-savings as a way in which a company can "Power [its] growth."

jet engines that power half of the jets flying today. Also, companies must purchase products to help them maintain their business. HP is a global company providing IT solutions to companies worldwide. Its products are not a component of another product but, rather, help a business run better. While many companies serve business-to-consumer markets, all companies operate in a business-to-business market as we will see in this chapter. From General Electric to Walmart, companies must understand and work with other companies as part of their business operations.[2]

In this chapter, we explore **B2B markets.** The first part of the chapter defines business-to-business markets and delineates the differences between B2B markets and consumer markets. Next, we discuss the business market purchase decision process, which is different from the process consumers use in making a purchase decision. Finally, the significant role of technology in business-to-business markets relationships will be presented.

DIFFERENCES BETWEEN BUSINESS AND CONSUMER MARKETS

Business markets and consumer markets are not the same. Five distinct differences dramatically affect marketing strategy and tactics (see Exhibit 6.2). These differences create unique opportunities and challenges for marketing managers because success in consumer marketing does not translate directly to business markets and vice versa.

Relationship with Customers

As we discussed in Chapter 3, many consumer product companies now focus on building strong relationships with their customers. However, even when a relationship is cultivated with the customer, it is impersonal and exists primarily through electronic communication or direct mail.

The opposite is true in business markets. The nature of business markets requires a more personal relationship between buyer and seller. Every relationship takes on additional significance as the sales potential of each customer increases. A strong personal relationship is critical because business customers demand fast answers, good service, and, in general, want a close relationship with suppliers.[3] As a result, companies selling in a B2B market invest more resources to foster and maintain personal contact with their customers than in a consumer market. In some cases, companies even invest in their suppliers to strengthen the relationship.

Walmart's rapid growth throughout the 1990s created an ideal situation for many of its suppliers, which were happy to make concessions in exchange for access to Walmart's vast retail network. But that growth stage could not last forever, and Walmart has been forced to focus on streamlining its stores' inventories. Suddenly, Walmart is ordering fewer products and is much pickier in the selection of suppliers. In many cases, even supplier/retailer relationships are ultimately controlled by the consumer market.[4]

	EXHIBIT 6.2	Differences between Business and Consumer Markets

	B2B Market (Business)	B2C Market (Consumer)
Relationship with customers	Invest more in maintaining personal relationships	Impersonal; exist through electronic communication
Number and size of customers	Fewer but larger customers	More customers but buy in smaller, less frequent quantities
Geographic concentration	Suppliers located strategically by the buyers	Could be anywhere in the world
Complexity of buying process	Complex process that can take a long time (years in some cases) and involve more people	Fewer people, often just one, directly involved in the purchase decision and the purchase decision is often based on personal and psychological benefits
Complexity of supply chain	Direct from supplier to manufacturer	Complex with products moving through the channel to reach the consumer
Demand for products	Derived from consumer demand, fluctuates with changes to consumer demand, and more inelastic (less price sensitive)	Consumer perceptions about their own needs mitigated by environmental factors and marketing stimuli

A more personal relationship most often connotes a greater emphasis on personal selling and, increasingly, technology. Customers want direct communication with company representatives and prefer someone they know and trust. The individual most responsible for maintaining a relationship is the salesperson. Personal selling also offers companies the most effective method for direct communication with the customer. Technology has greatly improved the quality and quantity of communications between buyer and seller. However, one-on-one personal communication is still the most important tool in developing and maintaining a strong customer relationship in business markets.

At the same time, technology plays a critical role in connecting buyer and seller. Integrating IT systems that enhance sales response times, provide better customer service, and increase information flow is now an accepted element in a successful B2B customer relationship. Customers demand not only a personal relationship with their vendors but also an efficient one. Most companies now require vendor Internet connectivity to increase efficiency.

Number and Size of Customers

Business markets are characterized by fewer but larger customers. Goodyear, for example, may sell one set of tires to a consumer over the course of three years, but every year the company sells millions of tires to Toyota Motor Corporation. Add up all the major automobile companies, and there are fewer than 25 business customers for Goodyear. Not surprisingly, the company maintains a dedicated sales force just for the automobile manufacturers.

The large size and small number of customers places a higher value on each customer. Although consumer products companies value customer relationships, it is not possible to satisfy every customer every time nor is it economically

EXHIBIT 6.3	The 5 Most "Wired" Cities in the United States

1. Seattle, Washington	4. Orlando, Florida
2. Atlanta, Georgia	5. Boston, Massachusetts
3. Washington, D. C.	

Source: *Forbes*, "Most 'Wired' Cities," www.forbes.com, October 18, 2009.

feasible. However, in a business market setting, losing even one large customer has striking implications for a company.[5] Walmart is Procter & Gamble's single biggest customer accounting for 15 percent of company sales (roughly equivalent to $12.5 billion). At its Arkansas office, P&G has a 300-member staff dedicated to one customer—Walmart.

Geographic Concentration

Business markets tend to concentrate in certain locations.[6] Historically, the automobile industry concentrated in the Midwest, particularly Detroit, and technology firms dominated Silicon Valley in California. As a result, their suppliers congregated nearby. A software developer, for example, that wants to be close to its primary customers should set up an office in San Jose, California. While the Internet allows people to live anywhere, the nature of business relationships means companies want to have a strong presence near their best customers. Exhibit 6.3 highlights the Internet connectivity of cities around the United States measuring broadband adoption, number of companies providing broadband access, and public access wi-fi hotspots per capita to determine the "most wired" cities.

Complexity of the Buying Process

The B2B customer buying process, discussed later in the chapter, is more complex than the consumer purchase decision process. It takes longer and involves more people, making the seller's job more challenging. In addition, as companies connect with customers, the number of relationships increases and it is difficult for one individual, the salesperson, to keep up with the complexity of the relationships.[7] Companies also face competing forces in critical decisions about their products (See Ethical Dimension 6).

Complexity of the Supply Chain

The movement of goods through a channel to the ultimate consumer requires a high level of coordination among the participants. A **supply chain** is the synchronized movement of goods through the channel. It is far more integrated than ever before as companies seek to keep production costs low, provide maximum customer input and flexibility in the design of products, and create competitive advantage. At the same time, the supply chain in B2B markets is generally more direct with suppliers and manufacturers working closely together to ensure efficient movement of products and services.

ETHICAL DIMENSION 6

Implications of Biofuels

As the United States and many other industrialized countries wrestle with the high cost of energy, few energy options offer a dual win for consumers—environmentally sensitive and fuel efficient. Coal, for example, is prevalent in some parts of the world, including the United States, but is harmful to the environment. Solar and wind power generation are clean energy sources but are difficult to harness in sufficient quantities to make a significant impact on the use of fossil fuel. One source of energy that both reduces the dependence on oil and offers a cleaner burning, is ethanol. Produced from corn, ethanol lowers the use of fossil fuel and has been a critical piece of the federal government's plan to lessen U.S. dependence on foreign oil. Current plans call for renewable fuels such as ethanol to account for 15 percent of gasoline burned in the United States by 2017. The move to biofuels is also happening in other parts of the world. Europe is requiring that nearly 6 percent of its diesel fuel come from plants by 2010.

The benefits of biofuels do not come without a cost. Livestock farmers have experienced a dramatic increase in the price of corn, doubling from $2 a bushel to over $4 a bushel. This price increase is due primarily to huge increases in demand for corn to make ethanol. The 2006 crop of 10.5 billion bushels of corn was the third largest ever recorded; nearly 20 percent of the corn was used in the production of ethanol, and 24 percent of the 2008 crop went into ethanol.

This focus on greater energy independence and more environmentally friendly fuel is creating difficult choices for companies, government officials, and farmers. Ethanol is becoming more readily available, but higher feed corn prices have led to higher prices for meat and poultry at the grocery store. Chicken feed costs, for example, are increasing an estimated $1.5 billion per year. Ultimately, some predict competition for bio products as producers choose between using corn and other plants for fuel or food.

Around the world, difficult choices are being made. In Germany, increased demand for rapeseed, used as a biofuel in Europe, has led to steep price increases for other uses of the product, such as cooking oil and protein meal. Indonesia and Malaysia suffered significant air pollution recently as millions of acres of forests were cleared to plant oil palms used in biofuels in Asia.

The use of corn as a biofuel is not particularly efficient as it takes 7 gallons of fossil fuel to produce 10 gallons of ethanol. Additionally, while it does produce lower greenhouse gases, the comparison with fossil fuels is not dramatic. Researchers are looking for more efficient biofuels. Pine groves, prairie grass, and other plants have even greater potential than corn, producing cleaner fuel with less energy.

From consumers to energy companies and farmers, the increased use of biofuels means choosing, at least in some cases, between greater energy dependence and higher food prices as limited quantities of critical plants raise prices for a variety of products.[8]

Ethical Perspective

1. **Oil companies:** Should they invest in alternative fuel technologies such as ethanol to reduce fossil fuel consumption?

2. **Consumers:** Should they be willing to pay higher food prices to achieve greater energy independence and cleaner burning fuel?

3. **Farmers:** Should they be required to invest in greater production of critical biofuel plants such as corn?

Demand for Products and Services Is Different in a Business Market

Product demand in business markets is different from consumer demand on three critical dimensions: derived demand, fluctuating demand, and inelastic demand. All three offer unique challenges and opportunities for marketers. For example, two of the three differences (derived and fluctuating demand) deal with the relationship between B2B and B2C demand and suggest B2B marketing managers must first understand their customer's markets before they can sell to the customer. The final dimension (inelastic demand) is an opportunity for a seller but must be managed carefully to maintain a successful relationship.

XL Capital positions itself as one of the leading global insurance/reinsurance companies with the ability and resources to handle large industrial risks anywhere in the world.

Courtesy XL Capital Group.

Derived Demand

Demand for B2B products originates from the demand for consumer products, or, put another way, demand for B2B products is **derived demand.** If consumers are not buying Toyota cars and trucks, then there is no need for Toyota to purchase Goodyear tires. Therefore, it is important for Goodyear to understand the consumer market for automobiles for two reasons. First, knowing what consumers are looking for in a car is critical to designing tires for those cars. Second, knowing the consumer automobile market is essential to create a value proposition that speaks to Toyota's need to sell more cars and trucks to consumers.

In addition to the demand for specific Toyota products, such as the Corolla or 4Runner, Goodyear scans the environment for anything that might affect consumer demand. Environmental factors have long-term and short-term effects on consumer product choices. For example, long-term economic factors such as the rapid rise in the price of gasoline have had a significant negative effect on the sales of SUVs, and short-term factors like a hurricane in Florida or the Southeast can limit distribution and sale of products in those areas for a while. B2B sellers understand that business customer success frequently means finding ways to assist them in their consumer markets. This is a challenge for business marketers because, despite having a great product and providing great service at a competitive price, they may still not get the business because consumer demand for their business customer's product is weak.

Sony went to great lengths to create a sound value proposition for its primary customers—retailers and movie studios—to ensure they would adopt the Blu-ray format over Toshiba's HD DVD. In what seemed like a grand victory for Sony, large industry players including Walmart and Warner Bros. picked Blu-ray, forcing Toshiba to surrender the format war. However, with the rapidly growing prominence of online media and the high price tag of both the Blu-ray discs and their players, consumers have not, to this point, widely adopted the Blu-ray format.[9]

Fluctuating Demand

The relationship between consumer demand and demand for business products presents a real challenge for business-to-business marketers. Small changes in consumer demand can lead to considerable shifts in business product demand and is referred to as the **acceleration effect.** This makes forecasting the sale of consumer products important because making even a small mistake in estimating consumer demand can lead to significant errors in product production.

Inelastic Demand

Business products experience fairly **inelastic demand,** meaning changes in demand are not significantly affected by changes in price. Apple, for example, will not buy more processors from Intel if Intel lowers the price nor will it buy fewer chips if Intel raises the price until the price increase becomes so high that Apple considers alternative vendors. Apple designs some of its computers around Intel processors and to change vendors creates disruption and costs in other areas of the manufacturing process. Price increases, particularly incremental changes, are often accepted because manufacturers are hesitant to disrupt manufacturing processes, which, in turn, creates inelastic demand in the short run. Exhibit 6.4 has two demand curves, D_1 and D_2. As price rises from P_1 to P_2 the demand changes.

The more elastic demand curve is the one with the largest shaded area—B. Demand in business-to-business markets is generally more inelastic than consumer markets, which means changes in price have less effect on demand—the smaller shaded area A. This makes D_2 an example of inelastic demand.

BUYING SITUATIONS

People involved in making business **buying decisions** face many choices as they move through the purchase decision process. Business buying decisions vary widely based on the:

- Nature of the purchase (large capital outlay like that needed for a new manufacturing plant versus simply ordering office supplies).
- Number of people involved in the decision (one or many).
- Understanding of the product being purchased (new to the firm or a familiar product purchased many times before).
- Time frame for the decision (short time requiring an immediate purchase decision or a longer lead time).

Some decisions require little or no analysis before the purchase decision. Others require updating information or changing existing purchase orders before the purchase decision can be made. Finally, some decisions require an in-depth analysis of the product. These three scenarios are referred to as straight rebuys, modified rebuys, and new purchases (see Exhibit 6.5).

Straight Rebuy

Many products are purchased so often that it is not necessary to evaluate every purchase decision. Companies use a wide range of products on a consistent basis (office supplies, raw materials) and simply reorder when needed. This type of purchase is called a **straight rebuy.** Increasingly, this is done automatically via secure

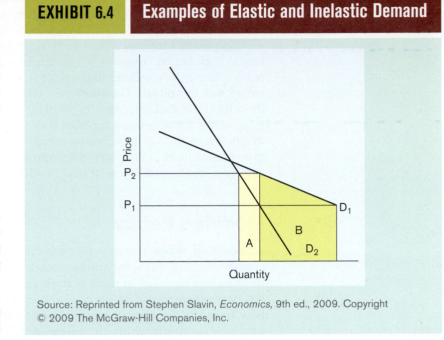

EXHIBIT 6.4 | **Examples of Elastic and Inelastic Demand**

Source: Reprinted from Stephen Slavin, *Economics*, 9th ed., 2009. Copyright © 2009 The McGraw-Hill Companies, Inc.

EXHIBIT 6.5	Types of Buying Situations
Straight rebuy	Reorder products that are used on a consistent basis
Modified rebuy	Familiar with product and supplier, but still seek additional information
New purchase	First-time purchase of product or service

Internet connections with approved or preferred suppliers. Far fewer people are involved with the purchase decision; often it is handled by one person in the purchasing department.

The goal of business sellers in straight rebuy situations is to become the preferred supplier. A company given approved status must be diligent and mindful of competitors seeking to displace it. Companies not on the approved list are called **out suppliers.** Their primary task is to obtain a small order, an opening, then leverage that opportunity to gain additional business. This is a challenge, however, if the approved supplier is doing a good job of meeting the customer's needs. From time to time, many companies order small quantities from nonapproved suppliers just to keep the approved supplier from becoming too complacent or to evaluate a potential new vendor.[10]

Modified Rebuy

A **modified rebuy** occurs when the customer is familiar with the product and supplier but is looking for additional information. Most often this need for change has resulted from one or more of three circumstances. First, the approved supplier has performed poorly or has not lived up to the customer's expectations. Second, new products have come into the market triggering a reappraisal of the current purchase protocols. Third, the customer believes it is time for a change and wants to consider other suppliers.

All three situations create opportunities for out suppliers to gain new business. When a purchase contract is opened up for a modified rebuy it represents the best opportunity for a new supplier. At the same time, however, the current approved supplier seeks to maintain the relationship. The approved supplier almost always has the advantage, particularly if it has a close relationship with the customer, because it knows the people involved and usually gets access to critical information first.

New Purchase

The most complex and difficult buying situation is the new purchase. A **new purchase** is the purchase of a product or service by a customer for the first time. The more expensive, higher risk, and greater the resource commitment, the more likely the company will engage in a full purchase decision process (outlined later in the chapter).

This process almost certainly involves a group throughout the entire decision process, even though the final decision may rest with a single individual. Because the company's purchasing personnel have had very little experience with the product, they seek information from a variety of sources. First and foremost, vendor salespeople are a key source of information about the product's capabilities. If they do their job well, they help the customer define its needs and how best to address them. Another avenue of information for companies is to hire consultants who, as unbiased experts, can assess and educate customers on their needs and possible solutions. Finally, the company must scan its own resources, including past purchase records, for relevant information.

Tropicana Pure Premium has become the most iconic brand of refrigerated, pasteurized orange juice. Started in Florida, Tropicana Products Inc., a division of PepsiCo, now distributes its product across the United States, but the company's success has come with a price. Although it is still the largest single purchaser of Florida citrus, Tropicana has been forced to supplement its orange supply with juice imported from Brazil to keep up with demand, a fact that it must include on the carton's back panel but not one it likes to promote.[11]

BUYING CENTERS

As we discussed, business purchases are seldom made by just one person, particularly in modified rebuy and new purchase situations. A number of individuals with a stake in the purchase decision come together to form a **buying center** that manages the purchase decision process and ultimately makes the decision. The individuals included in the buying center may have direct responsibility over the decision (purchasing department) or financial control of the company (senior management). In other cases, the individuals might have a specific expertise helpful to the decision (engineer, consultant).[12]

Buying centers usually are not permanent groups but are convened to make the decision and then disband. Also, individuals may participate in more than one buying center at any given time. Purchasing agents are apt to be members of several buying centers. In addition, while the vast majority of buying center participants work for the customer, others, such as outside consultants, are invited into the group because of their expertise. This happens, for example, in new purchases when a company believes it lacks sufficient internal knowledge and experience to make an informed decision. Most buying centers include a minimum of five people; however, they can be much larger. In larger multinational corporations, buying centers for companywide purchase decisions, such as a new corporate CRM system, can include dozens of people from all over the world.

Members of the Buying Center

Every participant in a buying center plays a certain role and some may play multiple roles (see Exhibit 6.6). In addition, an individual's role may change. As people move up in an organization, they can move from user to influencer and finally a

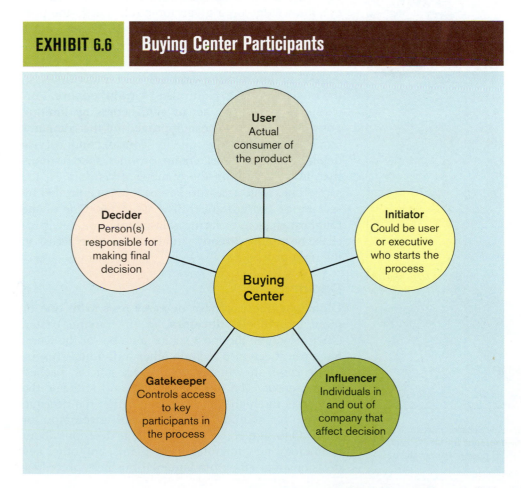

EXHIBIT 6.6 **Buying Center Participants**

- **User** Actual consumer of the product
- **Initiator** Could be user or executive who starts the process
- **Buying Center**
- **Influencer** Individuals in and out of company that affect decision
- **Gatekeeper** Controls access to key participants in the process
- **Decider** Person(s) responsible for making final decision

decider. These functions can be defined formally by the company or informally as a result of an individual's expertise or influence. Let's examine each of the five major roles.

User

Users are the actual consumer of the product and play a critical role. While typically not the decision makers, they do have a lot of input at various stages of the process. They are the first to recognize the problem based on a need, and they help define the product specifications. Finally, they provide critical feedback after the product purchase. As a result, their responsibility is enhanced in new purchase and modified rebuy situations when product specifications are being set for the purchase decision.

Initiators

The **initiator** starts the buying decision process usually in one of two ways. In one scenario the initiator is also the user of the product as in the secretary who reorders when office supplies run low. A second scenario occurs when senior executives make decisions that require new resources (manufacturing sites, product development, and information technology). In these situations the executives act as initiators to the purchase decision process.

Influencers

Individuals, both inside and outside the organization, with relevant expertise in a particular area act as **influencers,** providing information that is used by the buying center in making the final decision. Engineers are frequently called on to detail product requirements and specifications. Purchasing agents, based on their experience, are helpful in evaluating sales proposals. Marketing personnel can provide customer feedback. In all of these cases, the influencer's knowledge on a given topic relevant to the purchase decision can affect the purchase decision.

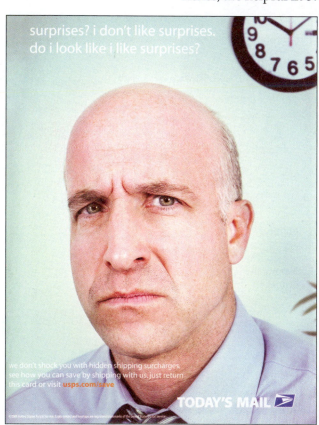

The USPS targets a concern among many decision makers: hidden fees that arise after a purchase. In this message the USPS seeks to minimize that issue suggesting the USPS does not apply charges after the package delivery.

Gatekeepers

Access to information and relevant individuals in the buying center is controlled by **gatekeepers.** Purchasing departments act as gatekeepers by limiting possible vendors to those approved by the company. Similarly, engineering, quality control, and service department personnel create product specifications that, in essence, limit the number of vendors. At the same time, basic access to key people is controlled by secretaries and administrative assistants. One of the toughest challenges facing salespeople in a new purchase or modified rebuy situation is getting access to the right people.

Deciders

Ultimately, the purchase decision rests with one or more individuals, **deciders,** in the buying center. Often it will be the most senior member of the team; however, it can also include other individuals (users, influencers), in which case the decision is reached by consensus. The more expensive and strategic the purchase, the higher in the organization the decision must go for final authority.[13] It is not uncommon for the CEO to sign off on major strategic decisions about technology, new manufacturing plants, and other key decisions that affect fundamental business processes.

EXHIBIT 6.7 | **Marketing Challenges in Buying Centers**

Who is part of the buying center? → Who are the most significant influencers? → What are the decision criteria for evaluating the various product options? → **Buying Center Target Market**

Costly capital equipment purchases often include the chief financial officer (CFO) who will most likely be a key decider. CFOs will employ a wide range of financial tools, including discounted cash flow analysis of the proposed investment, as they determine the most appropriate purchase decision.

Pursuing the Buying Center

Buying centers present marketers with three distinct challenges as presented in Exhibit 6.7. First, who is part of the buying center? Simply identifying the members of a buying center can be difficult and is made more challenging by gatekeepers whose role, in part, is to act as a buffer between buying center members and outside vendor representatives. The job of identifying membership in the buying center is made even more complex as participants come and go over time. Second, who are the most significant influencers in the buying center? This is critical in both preparing a sales presentation and following up. Targeting influencers is important in persuading the buying center to purchase the salesperson's product. Finally, what are the decision criteria for evaluating the various product options? A very real concern for salespeople is making sure their products perform well on critical evaluation criteria; however, without a good understanding of evaluation criteria it is not possible to assess the probability of the product's success.

THE PLAYERS IN BUSINESS-TO-BUSINESS MARKETS

B2B markets are not homogenous. The complexity of business markets rivals that of consumer markets with more than 20 million small businesses in the United States alone. The number grows dramatically when you include large corporations, nonprofit institutions, and government entities. The diversity of businesses coupled with the unique characteristics of business-to-business markets means companies selling in B2B markets need to know their markets very well. Let's explore each of the major categories of business markets to better understand their similarities and differences.

The North American Industrial Classification System (NAICS)

Historically, the basic tool for defining and segmenting business markets was a classification system known as the Standard Industrial Classification (SIC) codes developed by the U.S. government in the 1930s. The SIC system organized businesses into 10 groups that further broke down business categories based on their output (what they produced or their primary business activity). For many years, it was the foundation for business segmentation in the United States.

The SIC codes were updated in the 1990s and are now called the **North American Industrial Classification System (NAICS).** The system has been expanded to include businesses in Mexico and Canada. NAICS defines 20 major

EXHIBIT 6.8 | **NAICS Example**

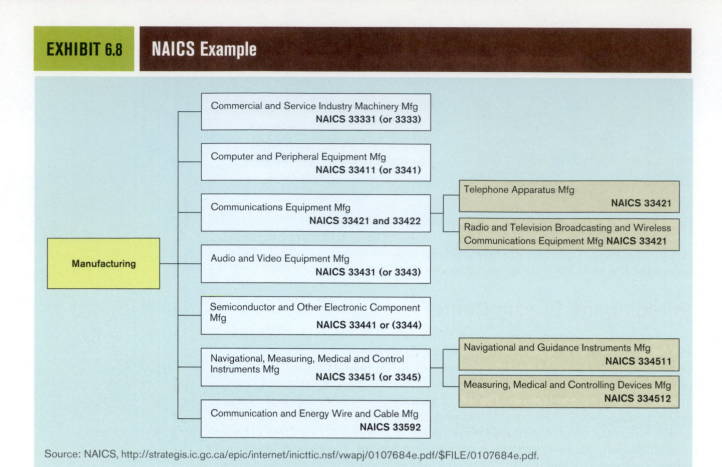

Source: NAICS, http://strategis.ic.gc.ca/epic/internet/inicttic.nsf/vwapj/0107684e.pdf/$FILE/0107684e.pdf.

business sectors based on a six-digit hierarchical code. The first five digits are standardized across Mexico, Canada, and the United States while the sixth digit enables countries to adjust the code to fit the country's own unique economic structure.[14]

The NAICS is not perfect; companies are classified on the basis of their primary output, which means that large companies with multiple businesses across different sectors are not accurately represented as they receive only one NAICS code. However, the system does offer a great starting point for researching a particular business market. It is possible to purchase detailed information on each of the codes in the system. This information includes data on companies listed in each code, number of employees, sales revenue, their location, and contact information. Exhibit 6.8 provides an example.

Manufacturers

One of the largest groups of business customers are manufacturers, which consume two types of products. First, components used in the manufacturing process are called **original equipment manufacturer (OEM)** purchases. Companies selling OEM products work to convince the OEM customer their products offer the best value (price and quality) to the OEM's customers. Intel's reputation for overall value among consumers has enabled the company to build a strong business with OEM computer manufacturers such as HP to the point that HP, and others, promote "Intel Inside."

OEM customers purchase in large quantities to support their own product demand. Two important outcomes result from this purchase power. First, OEM customers seek the very "best" prices from sellers. *Best* does not always mean lowest; other factors play an important role.[15] The assurance of product quality, ability to meet demand, just-in-time product delivery schedules, and other factors frequently figure into the final selection of product and vendor. The second result of large purchase quantities is the ability to dictate specific product specifications. OEM customers often compel suppliers to modify existing products and even develop new products. Sellers work closely with the OEM engineers and technicians to develop products that will fit the need of the OEM customer. The benefit is a high volume of product sales and the opportunity to develop a long-term strategic relationship.[16]

A second category of products purchased by manufacturers are called **end user purchases** and represent the equipment, supplies, and services needed to keep the business operational. There are two major types of end user purchases: **capital equipment** and **materials, repairs, and operational (MRO)** supplies and services. Capital equipment purchases involve significant investments and include major technology decisions (mainframe computers, ERP and CRM software packages) or critical equipment need in the manufacturing process (large drill presses, robotic assembly systems). Since these purchases are considered a long-term investment, customers evaluate not only the purchase price but also other factors such as cost of ownership, reliability, and ease of upgrading. The cost and long-term commitment of these purchases mean senior management is often involved in the final decision. Frequently a buying center will evaluate options and make a recommendation to senior management.

Demonstrating the value of a major purchase is critical to the final purchase decision. Cirrus Aircraft indicates its airplanes should be considered a member of the "staff" and will make executives more productive.

MRO supplies, on the other hand, are products used in everyday business operations and are typically not considered a significant expense. Purchasing agents or individuals close to the purchase decision, such as an office manager, are responsible for MRO purchases. Many of these purchases are straight rebuys; the individuals involved do not want to spend a lot of time making the purchase. Vendors in these industries are well aware that once they have a customer, the business is assured until the company does not perform up to customer expectations. Put another way, the business is theirs to lose.

Robert Bosch is one of the major suppliers of diesel engine technology in the world; in fact, it is quite difficult these days to manufacture a diesel vehicle without having to buy something from Bosch. As consumers around the world have become more conscious of their vehicle's fuel economy, many automakers have promoted the benefits of clean diesel vehicles as a viable alternative to the typically more expensive price tag and lower performance specs of their hybrid counterparts. Important components such as clean exhaust management systems must be supplied by Bosch to any automaker that manufactures a clean diesel car or truck.[17]

Resellers

Companies that buy products and then resell them to other businesses or consumers are called **resellers.** Home Depot, for example, buys home products and then resells them to consumers, building contractors, and other professionals in the construction industry. Chapter 12 provides an in-depth discussion of consumer resellers, but it is important to note that resellers have unique needs when it comes to purchase decisions. Just as manufacturers need end user products, resellers also need equipment and supplies to run their businesses. Retailers need technology such as computers and checkout counters to keep track of sales and inventory. Distributors need stocking and inventory management systems to maintain their distributions centers and also have the same MRO needs.

Government

The single largest buyer of goods and services in the world is the U.S. government. Combined with state and local governments, the value of purchases is over $2 trillion. Local, state, and particularly federal **government** entities have unique and frequently challenging purchase practices. Detailed product specifications must be followed precisely, and the purchase process is often long. The purchase decision by the Department of Defense on the F-22A Raptor fighter took four and a half years and involved thousands of product specifications.[18] While the government is theoretically open to all vendors, the reality is that experience with the government purchase process is usually a prerequisite to success.

Federal and state governments make a number of resources available to potential vendors; it is possible to obtain guidelines from the federal government. Furthermore, some private companies exist to offer assistance in learning about the process. The National Association of State Purchasing Officials publishes information on selling products and services to each of the 50 states. In addition, small-business organizations, such as the Small Business Administration, provide information on federal government contracts and contact personnel at government agencies.

Institutions

Institutions such as nonprofits, hospitals, and other nongovernment organizations (NGOs) represent a large and important market that has some unique characteristics. First, profitability does not play as significant a role in many of these organizations; rather, the delivery of service to the targeted constituency is the primary objective. Profit, or surplus as it is often called in the nonprofit community, is important but is not the fundamental driver in decision making. For example, Adventist Health System, which owns and operates health care facilities in 12 states, is a large nonprofit health care provider that considers a range of priorities in making important strategic decisions.[19] A second unique characteristic is a limited number of resources. Even the largest NGOs, including the Red Cross, do not have access to the capital and resources of most large for-profit organizations.

THE BUSINESS MARKET PURCHASE DECISION PROCESS

In some respects business market purchase decisions follow the same basic process as consumer decisions. As presented in Exhibit 6.9, a problem is recognized, information is collected and evaluated, a decision is made, and the product experience is then evaluated for future decisions. However, there are also significant differences between business market purchase decisions and consumer purchase

EXHIBIT 6.9 **Model of Business Market Decision Process**

Problem Recognition → Define the Need and Product Specifications → Search for Suppliers → Seek Sales Proposals—Response to RFP → Make the Purchase Decision → Post-Purchase Evaluation of Product and Vendor

decisions. These differences make the process more complex and require the involvement of more people. One key difference is that, while consumer decisions often include an emotional component, business goals and performance specifications drive organizations toward a more rational decision process.

As we discussed, the process is not used for every purchase decision. In straight rebuy situations, the problem is recognized and the order is made. Defining product specifications, searching for suppliers, and other steps in the process were probably done at one time but, once a supplier is selected, the purchase decision process becomes more or less automatic. A selected or approved list of suppliers shortens the decision process dramatically. Buyers go to the targeted vendor or choose from a list of suppliers and make the purchase. This process is consistent across organizations. Modified rebuys, on the other hand, are much more organization and situation specific. In some situations, the process may be more like a straight rebuy with some changes to product specifications or contract terms. In other situations, it may resemble a new purchase with an evaluation of new suppliers and proposals. New purchases will include all the steps in the process. As a rule, a new purchase takes longer because going through each of the steps takes time. In some cases, the process may take years as in the building of a new oil refinery or automobile assembly plant.

Problem Recognition

The business market purchase decision process is triggered when someone inside or outside the company identifies a need. In many cases, the need is a problem that requires a solution. The paper supply is running low and the office manager reorders more. A company's manufacturing facilities are at full capacity and it must consider options to increase production. In other situations, the need may be an opportunity that requires a new purchase. New technology can increase order efficiency or a new design of a critical component can improve the effectiveness of a company's own products, giving it an edge with consumers. As companies struggle to deal with higher energy prices, new alternative solutions, sometimes using older technologies, are being adopted for use in interesting ways.

Employees frequently activate the purchase process as part of their job. The office manager is responsible for keeping the office stocked with enough supplies. The vice president of strategic planning is tasked with planning for future manufacturing needs. However, salespeople from either the buying or selling company's sales force or channel partners also initiate the purchase process by helping identify a need or presenting an opportunity to increase efficiency or effectiveness. This is most likely to happen when the salesperson has established a trusted relationship with the company. Trade shows are also a source of new ideas; attendees often go to see what is new in the marketplace. Traditional marketing communications such as advertising and direct mail are less effective in business markets but are important in supporting the more personal communication efforts of salespeople.

Define the Need and Product Specifications

Once a problem has been identified, the next step is to clearly define the need. Individuals from across the organization clarify the problem and develop solutions. Not all problems lead to a new purchase. A vice president of information technology may notice an increase in call waiting times, but the issue could be a lack of training or a shortage of employees. The solution might include a new, expanded phone and call management system, but it will be up to management, working with other employees, to determine what is needed.

As part of describing the need, product specifications should be defined so that everyone inside and outside of the company knows exactly what is needed to solve the problem. This serves two important purposes. First, individuals inside the organization can plan for the future. Purchasing agents identify possible vendors while managers estimate costs and build budgets based on the specifications.

Users plan how to assimilate the new purchase into existing work processes. The buying center will use the product specifications to help evaluate vendor proposals. Putting product specifications into a document for distribution is known as a **request for proposal (RFP).** The second purpose of outlining product specifications is to guide potential suppliers. Product specifications as contained in the RFP become the starting point from which vendors put together their product solution. In the best-case scenario, there is a good fit between what the customer is asking for and the supplier's existing products.[20] Much more often, however, there are some specifications in which the potential products compare favorably and others where competitors excel. Exhibit 6.10 identifies the key sections of a request for proposal. RFPs generally require a great deal of information, and it takes a significant amount of time for a company to prepare a successful sales proposal.

The challenge for salespeople is to get involved in the purchase decision process as early as possible. If the salesperson, for example, has a strategic relationship with the customer, it may be possible to help define the product specifications. This is a real advantage because the vendor's salespeople can work to create specifications that present their products in the most favorable way. Product specifications are

---

EXHIBIT 6.10	Sections of a Request for Proposal

1. **Statement of Purpose:** Describe the extent of products and services your organization is looking for, as well as the overall objectives of the contract.

2. **Background Information:** Present a brief overview of your organization and its operations, using statistics, customer demographics, and psychographics. State your strengths and weaknesses honestly. Don't forget to include comprehensive information on the people who will handle future correspondence.

3. **Scope of Work:** Enumerate the specific duties to be performed by the provider and the expected outcomes. Include a detailed listing of responsibilities, particularly when subcontractors are involved.

4. **Outcome and Performance Standards:** Specify the outcome targets, minimal performance standards expected from the contractor, and methods for monitoring performance and process for implementing corrective actions.

5. **Deliverables:** Provide a list of all products, reports, and plans that will be delivered to your organization and propose a delivery schedule.

6. **Term of Contract:** Specify length, start and end dates of the contract, and the options for renewal.

7. **Payments, Incentives, and Penalties:** List all the terms of payment for adequate performance. Highlight the basis for incentives for superior performance and penalties for inadequate performance or lack of compliance.

8. **Contractual Terms and Conditions:** Attach standard contracting forms, certifications, and assurances. You may include requirements specific to this particular contract.

9. **Requirements for Proposal Preparation:** A consistent structure in terms of content, information, and document types simplifies things for the people evaluating the proposals. Therefore, you should request a particular structure for the proposal and provide an exhaustive list of documents you want to receive.

10. **Evaluation and Award Process:** Lay down the procedures and criteria used for evaluating proposals and for making the final contract award.

11. **Process Schedule:** Clearly and concisely present the time line for the steps leading to the final decision, such as the dates for submitting the letter of intent, sending questions, attending the preproposal conference, submitting the proposal.

12. **Contacts:** Include a complete list of people to contact for information on the RFP, or with any other questions. Incorporate their name, title, responsibilities, and the various ways of contacting them into this list.

Source: *RFP Evaluation Centers,* www.rfp-templates.com.

often written in such a way as to limit the number of vendors. Companies realize that not knowing the product specifications puts them at a disadvantage over other vendors. It is still possible to win the order, but the job becomes more difficult.

Search for Suppliers

Once the company's needs have been identified and production specifications have been outlined, business customers can identify potential suppliers. Two methods are commonly used to determine the list of vendors. First, companies create a list of preferred or approved suppliers and go to that list whenever a new purchase is being considered. The list can result from the company's cumulative experience. In this situation it is important to keep the list current with respect to existing vendors and also any new vendors.

A second, more complex method is to search for and identify potential suppliers. The Internet has become a valuable tool for companies in identifying potential suppliers. General search engines and even dedicated supplier search Web sites, such as Thomas Global Register, are easy to use and enable customers to identify specific potential vendors. Of course, companies still need to perform due diligence by checking vendor customer references, and in critical purchases it is advisable to research the vendor's financial stability and management capabilities.

Potential suppliers employ sophisticated SEO (search engine optimization) tools to get listed on the critical "first page"—the most desired location on any search results page. SEO has become an advantage for the highest bidder in the United States, which has made it more difficult for smaller suppliers to compete in this arena due to their comparative marketing budget restrictions. However, some smaller U.S. suppliers have exploited the advances in SEO technology by leveraging search engines as a way to promote their product and services to emerging foreign markets that have not yet been saturated by their larger competitors.[21]

Seek Sales Proposals in Response to RFP

Companies frequently solicit proposals from a number of vendors for two reasons. First, even if there is a preferred vendor, getting more information about available options from other suppliers is a good idea. If it is an open vendor search, then the proposal becomes a valuable source of information as well as the primary evaluation tool. Second, getting additional proposals helps in negotiating with the preferred vendor. When a vendor is aware that other proposals are under consideration, that vendor works harder to meet the expectations of the customer.

Sales proposals, particularly those submitted in response to an RFP, are written so they can be studied and sent to various individuals inside the company. At this stage, vendors may or may not be invited to make a presentation. If they are, a copy of the presentation will usually be submitted as part of the proposal. Numerous software packages can help create sophisticated sales proposal packages. Oracle, for example, includes a sales proposal module in its CRM solutions software. In addition, many companies have created their own proprietary software to aid salespeople in creating a sales proposal. Putting together a template that is used throughout the company helps unify the content and look of a sales proposal.

However, this step is usually characterized by limited vendor contact. Again, many companies are asked to submit proposals from which a smaller set of potential

Communicating with business customers usually involves salespeople working directly with the individuals in the buying center to develop best solution.

vendors will be selected. As a result, the sales proposal plays a critical role in marketing to businesses. Most of the time it is the first and best chance to impress the customer. In general, proposals accomplish two objectives. First, the proposal clearly specifies how the company's products will meet the product specifications detailed in the RFP. Second, the proposal makes the case for selecting the company by presenting any additional information such as unique product features, service programs, or competitive pricing to help persuade the customer.

Make the Purchase Decision

Once the proposals are submitted, the next step is the purchase decision. Given the time and analysis companies put into the decision process one might think the decision is straightforward. The reality, however, is more complex, as detailed in Exhibit 6.11. Often the final decision involves trade-offs between equally important evaluation criteria and equally qualified vendors.

Product Selection

The first purchase decision is the **product choice.** In many cases the product decision is based on a single criterion, for example product cost (the office manager purchasing printer paper at the lowest price). Single-criterion decisions usually fall into a straight rebuy or very limited modified rebuy situation and do not require a buying center to assist in the new purchase decision. Much of the time, however, no one product fits all the product specifications exactly. As a result, the final decision assesses the product against the product evaluation criteria and determines the optimal solution.[22] Consider a company purchasing a new office copier. The first response might be, "pick the best copier" but what is the definition of "best"? One person might define best as most copies per minute, another as lowest cost per copy, a third may consider the lowest maintenance costs to be the best. As a result, it is important to define the evaluation criteria and then follow a consistent and fair methodology in evaluating the sales proposals. Three primary criteria are used to evaluate the product choice.

Financial Criteria Financial criteria are a set of analyses and metrics grouped together to assess the cost of ownership. The actual purchase price is just one consideration in determining the real cost of a purchase. Maintenance and operating costs, repair charges, and supplies are all costs associated with ownership that can vary across product choices. These costs are then evaluated against the stated life of the product. This is important as some products with a higher initial price actually cost less over time because of the product's longer life. Financial analysis also evaluates the time it takes to break even on the investment. A company considering new equipment designed to lower manufacturing costs will want to know how long it will take to recoup the investment given the projected savings.

Business-to-business marketers understand that presenting a strong financial case for their products is an essential part of selling the product. As a result, many of these financial analyses are performed by the supplier and included in the sales proposal. Buyers then compare, and verify, the analyses across vendors.

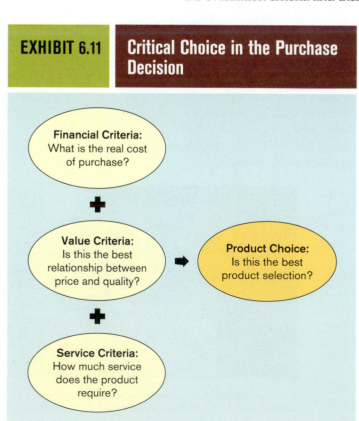

EXHIBIT 6.11 **Critical Choice in the Purchase Decision**

Financial Criteria:
What is the real cost of purchase?

+

Value Criteria:
Is this the best relationship between price and quality?

Product Choice:
Is this the best product selection?

+

Service Criteria:
How much service does the product require?

With sales of automobiles in Japan at their lowest level in more than two decades, it seems an odd time for Toyota to hold off on shifting production to overseas plants outside of its home country. In fact, with the Prius gas/electric hybrid model still proving to be the top-selling model in Japan, Toyota has had to bring in workers from other, less busy Toyota plants from around the world to help at the Tsutsumi plant in Japan. Although the United States is still the largest market for automobiles in the world, Toyota is not yet convinced that a U.S.-based plant will be the best home for production of its next-generation hybrid model.[23]

Value Criteria Value is the relationship between price and quality and it is a significant facet of the purchase decision. B2B buyers are aware that the lowest-cost product may not be the right product, especially in critical OEM equipment where failure can mean customer dissatisfaction or in strategic purchases such as a new IT system where failure can cause serious business disruption. On the other hand, it is costly to overengineer a product and purchase more than is needed for the situation. A computer network that must work 100 percent of the time is much more costly when considering the backup systems and redundant hardware and software needed to maintain it than a system with 95 percent run time. It is up to the buying center to determine the specifications needed to do the job.[24]

Buyers do not always need the highest-quality product, which is why most businesses carry multiple lines with different quality and price levels. Offering customers a choice increases the likelihood of success and minimizes the opportunity for competitors to target gaps in a company's overall product line.[25]

Service Criteria Buyers are concerned with the service requirements of a product because servicing equipment costs a company in two ways. First, there is the direct cost of service, including labor and supplies. Second, there is the indirect cost of downtime when a system is out of service, which means the equipment is not being used for its intended purpose.[26] Southwest flies only Boeing 737s in part because maintenance crews need to know only one plane, which makes it easier to maintain and service the 737.

Products are designed, in part, to minimize service costs. There are trade-offs, however, as companies seek the best compromise between product performance and lower service costs. Knowing the buyer's specific priorities with regard to performance, service, and other critical criteria is essential to designing and building the product that best fits the product specifications.

Supplier Choice

Businesses buy not just a product; they also make a **supplier choice.** Often, multiple sellers will be offering the same product or very similar product configurations. As a result, supplier qualifications become part of the purchase decision. Decision makers know a purchase decision can turn out badly if the wrong vendor is selected, even if the product choice is correct.[27]

The most fundamental criterion in vendor selection is **reliability,** which is the vendor's ability to meet contractual obligations including delivery times and service schedules. Strategic business-to-business relationships are based, in part, on a high level of trust between organizations. In those situations, the supplier's reliability becomes an essential factor in the final selection. Furthermore, a judgment is often made about the seller's willingness to go above and beyond what is specified in the contract. All things being equal, the seller with the best reliability and intangibles, like a willingness to do a little more than required, usually gets the order.[28]

Personal and Organizational Factors

Several additional factors affect product and supplier choices. Suppliers often find it difficult to understand the role these factors play in the final decision, but

Companies like IBM work with industries like the chemical and petroleum industry to develop comprehensive "one stop" solutions.

Reprinted courtesy of International Business Machines Corporation, Copyright 2008 © International Machines Corporation.

their influence can be profound. The first, **personal factors,** refers to the needs, desires, and objectives of those involved in the purchase decision. Everyone in the buying center comes with their own needs and goals. Someone might see this as an opportunity for promotion, another believes he or she will receive a raise if he or she can be successful, a third may want to impress management. It is not possible to separate the individual agendas people bring to the buying center from the purchase decision. In addition, individuals in the buying center come to the group with their own perspective of the decision. Engineers, for example, tend to focus on product performance and specifications. Accountants often concentrate on the cost and other financial considerations. Purchasing agents give attention to vendor quality and ease of ordering. One reason buying centers are effective is their ability to bring individuals with different perspectives together to evaluate possible product options.

Another influence on the product and supplier choice is organizational factors. The primary **organizational factor** is risk tolerance. Individuals and companies all have a certain tolerance for risk. Their product decisions will be influenced by their aversion to or acceptance of risk.[29] Consider the IT manager looking to purchase a new network for his company. Two suppliers have submitted proposals that meet the product specification. One is a local vendor with an excellent reputation. This vendor has quoted a lower price and guaranteed better service. The other is Cisco Systems, the world leader in network equipment and software. The manager for the company with a low risk tolerance will probably choose Cisco Systems. It represents the "safe" choice. His superiors would never question purchasing from the market leader. If the same individual works for a risk-tolerant organization, the decision might be to go with the vendor offering better price and service. The cost of a mistake is high. If the network goes down and the company suffers a business disruption because the supplier has performed poorly, questions about the supplier selection arise. Risk tolerance does play a role as the buying center moves closer to a final decision.

Post-Purchase Evaluation of Product and Supplier

Once the purchase decision is made, buyers begin the process of evaluation (see Exhibit 6.12). Initially, they assess product performance and the seller's response to any problems or issues. A key for business marketers is to make sure the customer understands the proper operation and maintenance of the product. At the same time, buyers consider the level of support provided by the seller and expect follow-up after the sale to be sure there are no problems. Dealing with complaints, resolving customer problems, and making sure the company is meeting customer expectations are critical to ensuring customer satisfaction.

The evaluation process is designed, in part, to help customers make better purchase decisions in the future. Being the current seller is a distinct advantage because, if the customer evaluates the purchase decision positively, there is no need to change the decision next time. In essence, the evaluation process, if handled properly, can be the best sales tool for the seller when it comes time for the next purchase decision.

Naturally, the opposite is also true. If the product performs poorly or the seller does not meet customer expectations, competitors can use those mistakes to trigger a modified rebuy or even a new purchase decision process that increases their probability of success. Losing a customer is disappointing; however, it also represents an opportunity. By using well-developed service recovery strategies, companies can reacquire customers.

Navteq is a market leader in creating maps used in navigation systems originally found only in luxury car models such as Cadillac and BMW. More recently they have become optional equipment in all sorts of makes and models. However, many drivers find Garmin devices more enticing due to their portability and standardized user interface, even if they have to deal with wires running from their dashboard. Suzuki noted the trade-off and decided to have its SX4 model feature an integrated navigation system made by Garmin that would be mounted inside the vehicle but also be removable for the driver's adventures on foot.[30]

THE ROLE OF TECHNOLOGY IN BUSINESS MARKETS

Technology has transformed the business purchase decision process. From the Internet to portable handheld optical scanning devices, technology has made the purchase decision process more efficient and effective. Technology has also pushed the purchase decision process closer to the product user because front-line managers can now make purchases directly.[31]

Sophisticated programs manage inventories and automatically replenish supplies. By linking directly with **electronic data interchange (EDI),** customer computers communicate directly with supplier computers to reorder as needed. Late deliveries, defective products, and other issues related to supplier performance can be identified and dealt with before they become a major problem. Collaboration between business buyers and sellers has increased significantly as a result of technology linkages.[32]

E-Procurement

B2B transactions have been growing at a phenomenal rate with online B2B commerce worldwide in excess of $1 trillion, a much larger amount than that generated by B2C online sales. The process of business purchasing online is referred to as **e-procurement.**[33] Let's examine the various e-procurement methods:

Industry purchasing sites: Industries have formed Web sites to streamline and standardize the e-procurement process. Steel, chemicals, paper, and automobile manufacturers have created integrated Web sites to assist their own purchasing departments in online purchasing and supplier selection.

Business function sites: Certain business functions have Web sites to standardize purchasing. For example, individual utilities formerly negotiated by phone to buy and sell electricity with each other; however, today the purchase of electricity by utility companies is done over a Web site dedicated to energy management.

Extranet to major suppliers: Many companies have set up direct links to approved suppliers to make the purchase easier and move it closer to front-line decision makers.[34] Office Depot, for example, has a number of direct relationships using EDI with thousands of companies.

Company buying sites: Many large companies have created their own Web sites to assist vendors. RFPs and other relevant supplier information as well as some contact information are accessible for review.

SUMMARY

Several significant characteristics differentiate business and consumer markets including the concentration and number of customers found in business markets. In addition, the buying process itself is often longer and more complex. The demand for products in B2B markets is also different, creating both a challenge and an opportunity for business sellers.

Different types of selling situations lead to very different types of customer decision processes. Business customers interact with their suppliers in very different situations from a straight rebuy to new purchases. The greatest opportunity for a business seller to win new business comes in modified rebuy and new purchase situations.

The buying center is a team of individuals, from inside and outside the organization, that engages in the purchase decision process and either makes or recommends to the decision maker the final product selection. It is essential for business sellers to identify and become familiar with the buying center involved in any purchase decision.

The purchase decision process includes six steps from problem identification through to purchase decision and post-purchase evaluation of the product and supplier. In a new purchase decision, the process can take months or even years and may involve dozens of individual customers inside the organization. The actual purchase decision involves two distinct decisions. Initially, based on an evaluation of product options against product specifications the product choice decision is made. Often a second decision about the supplier is also required.

Technology is playing a major role in business-to-business marketing. The growth of online purchasing, also known as e-procurement, has transformed B2B alliances and made the process faster and more accurate.

APPLICATION QUESTIONS

1. You are the marketing manager for HP laptop computers. Identify and briefly discuss the differences between the consumer market for laptops and the business market. Then give an example of each difference using college students as the consumer market and defense-related companies as the business market.

2. You work for Siemens Power Generations Systems and are responsible for the sale of large, expensive ($2 million to $5 million) turbine generators to power utility companies. You have been contacted by the Ever-sure Utility Corporation in Anytown, USA. Identify the buying center you are likely to find inside the company and how you would market the generators to the buying center group.

3. You are vice president for information technology at your university. Recently you have been authorized to upgrade the network servers on campus. Draft an RFP that will be given to prospective vendors to help guide them in their sales process.

MARKETING PLAN EXERCISE

ACTIVITY 6.1: Determine Business Market Relationships

This exercise has four primary activities:

1. Conduct an analysis of your key market opportunities to assess the fundamental nature of these markets. This analysis should include a description of:

   a. Who are the key companies in this market? How much business do you do with the industry leaders? What share of their total business do you have?

   b. Where are these companies located?

2. Identify the probable company structure and business center participants you would encounter in selling to your key business-to-business customer.

3. Put together a probable buying decision process for key B2B customers and discuss your internal process in selling to these customers in this process.

4. Develop a list of second-tier customers in key B2B markets that represent future potential customers.

If you are using Marketing Plan Pro, a template for this assignment can be accessed at www.mhhe.com/marshalless1e.

part THREE

Developing the Value Offering

CHAPTER 07

Segmentation, Target Marketing, and Positioning

LEARNING OBJECTIVES

- Explain the criteria for effective segmentation.

- Identify the various approaches to market segmentation.

- Describe the steps in target marketing.

- Understand the continuum of approaches to target marketing strategy.

- Define positioning and link it to the use of the marketing mix.

- Use and interpret perceptual maps.

- Identify sources of differentiation.

- Avoid potential positioning errors.

FULFILLING CONSUMER NEEDS AND WANTS

In one of the band's most famous anthems, Rolling Stones front man Mick Jagger proclaims:

> You can't always get what you want.
> But if you try sometimes you just might find
> You get what you need.

Now, it's a safe bet that Mick Jagger wasn't thinking about needs and wants in the context of marketing and consumers when he and Keith Richards wrote that song in 1968, but the message resonates for marketing managers nonetheless. In fact, the triad of activities illustrated in Exhibit 7.1—market segmentation, targeting, and positioning—get at the heart of marketing's ability to successfully create, communicate, and deliver value to customers and thus successfully fulfill their needs and wants.

In Chapter 1, you read about the evolution of marketing through a series of stages including pre-industrial revolution, focus on production and products, focus on selling, marketing concept, and post-marketing concept approaches. The last stage, which is really a more sophisticated extension of the original marketing concept, includes attention to multiple sources of differentiation, customer orientation, relationships, and mass customization and one-to-one marketing by which firms (enabled by modern technology such as CRM systems) are capable of adding unique value to meet individual customer needs. What distinguishes much of marketing today from that of the past is this capability to more precisely home in on specific customers and customer groups and offer products or services that have a clear and compelling value proposition for those specific customers.[1]

Accomplishing this first requires the use of **market segmentation** to divide a market into meaningful smaller markets or submarkets based on common characteristics. Once a segmentation approach is developed, marketing managers engage in **target marketing,** which involves evaluating the segments and deciding which shows the most promise for development. In most ways, selecting target markets (also called market targets) is truly an *investment* decision. That is, a company must decide where to best invest its limited resources in developing markets for future growth. Everything else being equal, it should invest in the target markets that promise the best overall return on that investment over the long run.[2]

Dutch beer company Heineken NV is utilizing a marketing technique that Disney, Apple, and Nike use to engage their target markets. Heineken opened a store in Amsterdam selling Heineken beer and clothing, music, and concert tickets. Heineken marketers designed the store as an investment primarily for promotional purposes and to build brand awareness rather than to make a profit. The company opened the store to appeal to their target audience: 18 to 22-year-old men.[3]

Finally, the way the firm ultimately connects its value proposition to a target market is through its positioning. **Positioning** relies on the communication of one or more sources of value to customers in a way that the customer can easily make the connection between his or her needs and wants and what the product has

EXHIBIT 7.1 — Market Segmentation, Target Marketing, and Positioning

Market Segmentation
Dividing a market into meaningful smaller markets or submarkets based on common characteristics.

Target Marketing
Evaluating the market segments, then making decisions about which among them is most worthy of investment for development.

Positioning
Communicating one or more sources of value to customers in ways that connect needs and wants to what the product has to offer. Positioning strategies are executed through the development of unique combinations of the marketing mix variables.

to offer. Positioning strategies are executed through the development of unique combinations of the marketing mix variables, introduced in Chapter 1 as the 4Ps: product (or more broadly—the offering), price, place (distribution/supply chain), and promotion.[4]

The process of effective market segmentation, target marketing, and positioning is one of the most complex and strategically important aspects of marketing management. It bridges the overall process of creating, communicating, and delivering value to customers in that if the segmentation is flawed, target selection is incorrect, or positioning is unclear, there is no *value* because the customer doesn't connect with the product. Having a product whose value proposition is a well-kept secret is not a good thing in marketing—marketing managers want the right customers to clearly recognize their products' value-adding capabilities.[5]

Let's first take a closer look at segmentation. Then we will go on to gain an understanding of target marketing. Finally, we will introduce positioning as a lead-in to the marketing mix chapters that follow. These three concepts are equally relevant in both the consumer and business marketplaces. The criteria used for developing segments are somewhat different between the two markets, but the general concepts and importance of the process are similar.

WHAT IS SEGMENTATION?

From a marketing manager's perspective, one way to think about markets is on a continuum that ranges from *undifferentiated,* where everybody essentially needs and wants the same thing, to *singular,* where each person has unique needs and wants. The territory between these two extremes is where segmentation approaches come into play.

Segmentation seeks to find one or more factors about members of a heterogeneous market that allow for dividing the market into smaller, more homogeneous subgroups for the purposes of developing different marketing strategies to best meet the segments' distinct needs and wants.[6] The operative word is *different,* as in **differentiation,** which means communicating and delivering value in different ways to different customer groups.[7] It is important to note that the basic logic and principles behind segmentation are sound, regardless of the basis on which a market is segmented:

- Not all customers are alike.
- Subgroups of customers can be identified on some basis of similarity.
- The subgroups will be smaller and more homogeneous than the overall market.
- Needs and wants of a subgroup are more efficiently and effectively addressed than would be possible within the heterogeneous full market.

Criteria for Effective Segmentation

Before developing and executing a segmentation approach, the marketing manager must be assured that several criteria for successful segmentation are met, as listed in Exhibit 7.2. The manager must satisfactorily answer these questions:

1. *Is the segment of sufficient size to warrant investing in a unique value-creating strategy for that segment as a target market?* Ultimately, there is no point doing market segmentation unless a positive return on investment is expected. Size of a segment doesn't necessarily mean number of customers—when Bombardier markets its small Learjets, it knows the number of potential buyers is limited. Yet, segmentation is still a valid approach because of differences in needs and wants among customers and the financial size of the transaction.

EXHIBIT 7.2 | **Criteria for Effective Segmentation**

1. Segment is of sufficient size to warrant investing in a unique value-creating strategy for that segment as a target market.
2. Segment is readily identifiable and can be measured.
3. Segment is clearly differentiated on one or more important dimensions when communicating the value of the product.
4. Segment can be reached (both in terms of communication and physical product) to deliver the value of the product, and subsequently can be effectively and efficiently managed.

2. *Is the segment readily identifiable and can it be measured?* Effective segmentation relies on the marketing manager's ability to isolate members of a submarket to create a unique appeal. Segmentation most often requires data and if secondary data on the markets of interest aren't available or if primary data can't be easily collected, it may not be possible to do segmentation.

3. *Is the segment clearly differentiated on one or more important dimensions when communicating the value of the product?* For segmentation to work properly, it must allow for the creation and execution of different marketing strategies to the different submarkets identified. Segments should be expected to respond differently to different marketing strategies and programs. Otherwise, there is no reason to differentiate.

4. *Can the segment be reached (both in terms of communication and physical product) in order to deliver the value of the product, and subsequently can it be effectively and efficiently managed?* Barriers to reaching a segment might include language, physical distance, or as in the case of some developing markets, transportation, technology, and infrastructure challenges. Firms have to be able to sustain their management of a target segment over time—if this activity becomes problematic it can be a drain on resources and result in poor ROI.

Even venerable brands like Walmart have to constantly be looking for new target markets and rejuvenated positioning strategies—in this case through fresh new looks in young fashion.

When considering segmentation, it is important to remember that an essential part of Marketing (Big M)—strategic marketing—is not just *identifying* existing segments but also *creating* new ones through product development strategies. The introduction of Apple's iPhone stimulated needs and wants on the part of consumers in uncharted areas in terms of a single product's capabilities to fulfill, thus creating a new market by opening up new avenues of value-enhancing possibilities.[8]

SEGMENTING CONSUMER MARKETS

In the consumer marketplace, the categories of variables used by marketing managers to develop segments can be conveniently grouped into four broad categories as illustrated by Exhibit 7.3: geographic, demographic, psychographic, and behavioral. Let's consider each of these segmentation approaches in turn.

Geographic Segmentation

One of the most straightforward approaches to segmentation is when evidence exists that consumers respond differently to marketing strategies and programs based on where they live. Thus, **geographic segmentation** divides consumer groups based

EXHIBIT 7.3 — Consumer Market Segmentation Approaches

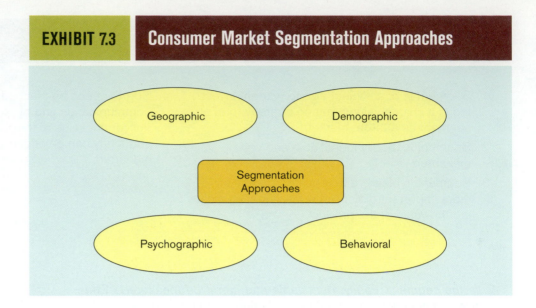

on physical location. The key question is, do consumption patterns vary among the geographic submarkets identified? If so, firms can make tailored adjustments in their products to satisfy those regional differences in needs and wants.[9]

Within the United States, some of the more popular approaches to geographic segmentation include:

- *By region*—Northeast, Southeast, Midwest, and West, for example.
- *By density of population*—urban, suburban, exurban, and rural, for example.
- *By size of population*—Exhibit 7.4 shows the top 20 standard metropolitan statistical areas (SMSAs) in the United States.

EXHIBIT 7.4 — Top 20 U.S. SMSAs

Rank	SMSA	Pop. (Millions)	Rank	SMSA	Pop. (Millions)
1.	New York	19.0	11.	Detroit	4.4
2.	Los Angeles	12.9	12.	Phoenix	4.3
3.	Chicago	9.6	13.	San Francisco	4.3
4.	Dallas	6.3	14.	Riverside, CA	4.1
5.	Philadelphia	5.8	15.	Seattle	3.3
6.	Houston	5.7	16.	Minneapolis	3.2
7.	Miami	5.4	17.	San Diego	3.0
8.	Atlanta	5.4	18.	St. Louis	2.8
9.	Washington, D.C.	5.4	19.	Tampa	2.7
10.	Boston	4.5	20.	Baltimore	2.7

Source: U.S. Census Bureau, 2008 census statistics posted July 1, 2008. Largest city in each SMSA is listed.

- *By growth in population*—Exhibit 7.5 highlights the top 10 fastest-growing markets from 2006 to 2007, by number of people and percentage growth.
- *By climate*—colder Northern states versus warmer Southern states.

Again, the key questions are whether segmenting by one or more of these geographic qualities means satisfying the criteria for effective segmentation and will it ultimately facilitate better communication and delivery of value to the submarkets

EXHIBIT 7.5	Growth in U.S. Cities

10 U.S. Metro Areas with Highest Numerical Growth (July 1, 2006–July 1, 2007)	
Metro Area	**Population Growth**
Dallas-Fort Worth-Arlington, Texas	162,250
Atlanta-Sandy Springs-Marietta, Ga.	151,063
Pheonix-Mesa-Scottsdale, Ariz.	132,513
Houston, Sugar Land-Baytown, Texas	120,544
Riverside-San Bernardino-Ontario, Calif.	86,660
Charlotte, Gastonia-Concord, N.C.-S.C.	66,724
Chicago-Naperville-Joliet, Ill.-Ind.-Wis.	66,231
Austin-Round Rock, Texas	65,880
Las Vegas-Paradise, Nev.	59,165
San Antonio, Texas	53,925

10 Fastest-Growing U.S. Metro Areas (July 1, 2006–July 1, 2007)	
Metro Area	**Percentage Growth**
Palm Coast, Fla.	7.2%
St. George, Utah	5.1
Raleigh-Cary, N.C.	4.7
Gainesville, Ga.	4.5
Austin-Round Rock, Texas	4.3
Myrtle Beach-Conway-North Myrtle Beach S.C.	4.2
Charlotte-Gastonia-Concord, N.C.-S.C.	4.2
New Orleans-Metairie-Kenner, La.	4.0
Grand Junction, Colo.	3.7
Clarksville, Tenn.-Ky.	3.7

Source: U.S. Census Bureau, released March 27, 2008.

than could be accomplished within the aggregate market? JCPenney, for example, segments its target market by geographic climate. Starting in early September, JCPenney begins marketing winter coats in its Chicago-area stores, an activity that won't begin until much later in Dallas, where customers are still expecting several more months of 80 to 90 degrees. The chain's Miami stores might never even stock traditional cold-weather apparel except in small quantities for travelers. JCPenney wisely recognizes different customer needs across different climates and builds its marketing plans accordingly.

Geographic segmentation is useful but, in most instances, is an insufficient segmentation criterion in and of itself. Because people in the United States are extremely mobile and because the demand for many products is not determined by where a person lives, additional types of segmentation are needed to successfully target customers.

Demographic Segmentation

Another straightforward approach to segmentation is via demographic variables. In Chapter 5, you learned that demographics are the statistical characteristics of human populations such as age or income that are used to identify markets. **Demographic segmentation** divides consumer groups based on a variety of readily measurable descriptive factors about the group. Many different demographic variables are available for measurement including age, generational group, gender, family, race and ethnicity, income, occupation, education, social class, and geodemographic group. Demographic segmentation is one of the most popular segmentation approaches because customer needs and wants tend to vary with some degree of regularity based on demographic differences and because of the relative ease of measurement of the variables.[10] Let's look at the major demographic variables more closely (see Exhibit 7.6).

EXHIBIT 7.6	Demographic Segmentation Variables

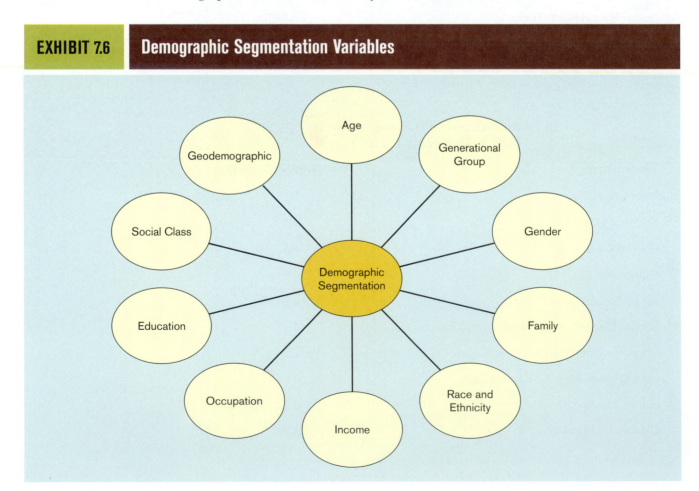

Age

Age segmentation presumes some regularity of consumer needs and wants by chronological age.[11] It is important to make the distinction between chronological age, actual age in years, and psychological or attitudinal age, which reflects how people see themselves.

McDonald's employs age segmentation to execute different marketing strategies to attract young children for a Happy Meal and older consumers for an early morning Egg McMuffin and coffee with friends. But marketers must take care to understand that age alone often is not sufficient for successful segmentation. Older consumers exhibit great differences from person to person on such things as income, mobility, and work status. In fact, marketing managers in companies ranging from travel to insurance to health care have come to realize that lumping older consumers into one group is not an effective segmentation approach because of the vast differences in other important variables.

Companies such as Dunkin' Donuts®, Coca-Cola, Eight O'Clock Coffee, and Bumble Bee Foods have turned to nostalgic marketing campaigns to remind consumers of the "good ol' days." Even though nostalgic ads run the risk of making a product look outdated, consumers of diverse ages enjoy the ads. Dave Melbourne, senior vice president of consumer marketing at Bumble Bee, states, "The trick is to evoke a brand's heritage in a contemporary way." The 110-year-old brand has since had success in reviving its jingle "Yum, Yum, Bumble Bee Bumble Bee Tuna" by poking fun at its own campaign.[12]

Some very relevant issues related to age segmentation in home gaming are addressed in Ethical Dimension 7.

Generational Group

One approach to age segmentation that helps get at the heart of differences in needs and wants is *generational segmentation*. Much research has been done on understanding differences in groups of people by generation. What defines a generational group and how does one know when a new generational group is emerging? Sociologists look for defining events such as wars, major economic upheaval, or sociocultural revolution as triggers for generational change. As with other segmentation approaches, the notion that different marketing strategies and programs can be developed and executed for different generational groups assumes some degree of homogeneity among the generational cohort.[13] The most recent generational groups, from oldest to youngest, along with their birth years are: the GI Generation (1901–1924), Silent Generation (1925–1945), baby boomers (1946–1964), Generation X (1965–1977), Generation Y (1978–1994), and Millennials (1994 to present). Exhibit 7.7 describes each of these generational cohorts including the core representative values of each.

The recession in 2009 forced a lot of baby boomers to rethink their employment plans (decode: they were laid off). For Robert Half International, one of the largest temporary staffing agencies, this has been a boom to business. Many companies would rather hire more experienced workers as "temps," especially for professional positions. According to CEO Harold "Max" Messmer Jr., "There are so many good people on the market, so we can say (to a client): Here is an outstanding candidate who, no offense, you might not have been able to attract before."[14]

The generational group that has traditionally been the apple of the marketing manager's eye is the baby boomers. This is because there are so many of them and because they personify conspicuous consumption—acquiring products for

Game On

Ask someone who is the typical video gamer and most people would describe a teenage boy locked in his room for hours with his eyes glued to a monitor that depicts him chasing, and being chased by, bad guys causing all kinds of mayhem. Although millions of young men fit this description, video gaming has also brought in new players creating unique and vastly different market segments. The hard-core gamers are still predominantly men, but research suggests that more than 75 percent of *casual* gamers worldwide are women. Gamers still tend to be younger; nearly a third of the gamers in the United States are under 18 and three-quarters of all gamers are under 50 years old.

The most popular video game genres are action (30 percent) and sports (17 percent). Popular video games include "Madden Football" and online, first-person shooter games such as "Halo." PC games are dominated by strategy and have titles like "World of Warcraft" and "The Sims" (in several versions). The largest titles, like the annual "Madden Football," are billion-dollar brands and generate unit sales in the hundreds of thousands.

As the market continues to expand, video and online gaming companies are seeking new business opportunities. With the broader demographic appeal, advertisers now consider video games a legitimate advertising channel, spending more than $500 million annually. Most of that money goes to put advertisers into the games. However, advertisers will spend $200 million to create "advergames," games designed specifically to promote a brand. Coca-Cola and other companies have created games to get young people connected to the brand. In addition, many of these companies have created virtual stores as part of Second Life and other virtual worlds.

Several key questions remain for the video gaming companies. Critics of violent video games suggest a harmful net effect on teenagers, primarily boys, acting out the violence. They reference the highly interactive, participative nature of the games that draws players into the violence. In addition, critics suggest the games reward the violent behaviors that players repeat over and over as they continue to play the game. Psychologists report that all these activities: (1) thwart interactivity, (2) reward violent behavior, and (3) through repetition, lead to learned acceptance of violence as appropriate behavior. An example of this violence/reward mentality in gaming is the "Grand Theft Auto" game franchise. In 2008, "Grand Theft Auto 4" broke the Guinness world record for the highest revenue generated in the first 24 hours of release of any form of entertainment media, *ever!*[15]

A second issue for video game critics is the length of time children play the games. In a recent study, researchers reported teenage boys play video games on average 13 hours per week. When this much exposure is coupled with the dominance of violent games among this age group, psychologists and many parents get more and more concerned about the long-term effects.[16]

Ethical Perspective

1. **Video game developers:** They are meeting the needs of a target market by developing video games that appeal to that market. Is that a problem? What responsibility do they bear for the potential negative effects on young people?

2. **Parents:** If parents are aware of the violence, how should they handle the purchase and use of video games by their children?

---

the pure enjoyment of the purchase. An interesting aspect of boomers is that the oldest among the group have just entered their early 60s, and the majority of them will soon be facing decisions about retirement and beyond. Much of the research on baby boomers indicates that—at least in their minds—they don't age.[17] Recall that a marketer must be cognizant of the difference between chronological age and attitudinal age. It is anticipated that this forever-young generation will enter the segment we would traditionally label as "older consumer" without an old outlook on life and the future. This has profound implications for marketers in that it turns on end the stereotypical approaches to what products are marketed to them and how they are marketed.[18] Many boomers will become more active, spend more money, and want to experience more new things after retirement than they ever did while they were employed—that is, if you can get them to retire. Many smart marketers who happen to be of Generation X or Y would do well to rethink the potential impact of successful strategies aimed at these ageless boomers.

Generation X is often thought of as a transitional generation. Its members are comfortable with much of the new-age technology but, unlike Gen Y, they didn't grow up with it, they had to learn it. Gen X is pegged as being a very

EXHIBIT 7.7 | **Generational Groups and Representative Values**

GI (16 million born 1901–1924)

- Financial security and conservative spending (shaped by hard times and the economic depression of the 1930s)
- No such thing as problems—only challenges and opportunities
- Civic minded
- Duty to family, community, and country
- Unified and team oriented

Silent (35 million born 1925–1945)

- Strength in human relation skills
- Respectful of others' opinions
- Trusting conformists
- Health, stability, and wisdom
- Civic life and extended families

Baby boomer (78 million born 1946–1964)

- Forever young
- Individualistic
- Conspicuous consumption—great acquirers of goods and services
- Idealistic: value- and cause-driven despite indulgences and hedonism
- The end justifies the means

Generation X (57 million born 1965–1977)

- Lack of trust in society
- Cynical and media-savvy
- Entrepreneurial
- Accept diversity
- Environmentally conscious
- Work to live, not live to work

Generation Y (60 million born 1978–1994)

- Pragmatic
- Optimistic
- Team players
- Savvy consumers
- Edgy
- Focused on urban style
- More idealistic than Gen X
- Technology comes naturally

Millennial (42+ million born 1994 to present)

- Multicultural
- Highly tech-savvy
- Educated
- Grown up in affluence
- Big spending power

entrepreneurial group, partly because many advancement opportunities in traditional firms have been thwarted by the overabundance of boomers who occupy those positions. It has been estimated that Gen X entrepreneurs are responsible for more than 70 percent of the new business start-ups in the United States. Gen X is not as consumption-crazed as the boomers, preferring more of a work-family life balance. For the marketing manager, this knowledge about the Gen X segment offers the opportunity to develop appeals to their independent spirit and practical nature.

Gen X is often referred to as the "baby bust" because it represents a natural cyclical downturn in birthrate. Because Gen X is such a small segment of the consumer market, many marketers have their eye squarely on the Gen Y and Millennial cohorts as the next great consumer frontier. Both of these groups are highly technology-savvy and don't balk at using any and every sort of communication medium to enhance their lives.[19]

Gender

Target Corporation claims that about 80 percent of the dollar sales in its stores are made to women. Many firms note that men account for the majority of online purchases. Such knowledge provides evidence of the power of *gender segmentation,* which recognizes differences in needs and wants of men versus women.

"I can eat most men under the table."

The sweetener for the real world.

Gen Xers appreciate products like Sweet'n Low that allow them to eat more of what they like.

Certainly, a wide variety of products are clearly marketed for the primary consumption of either men or women, but not both—think Rogaine, cigars, and athletic supporters versus pregnancy tests, lipstick, and bras, for example. In such cases, marketers can concentrate on linking the product's value-adding properties to its corresponding gender segment. What about cases in which a product appeals to both men and women, but on the basis of satisfying different— maybe subtly different—needs and wants?[20]

Take for example razors. Gillette learned some years ago that generally, women don't like to use a man's razor, which they had to do for decades because no thought was given to differences in gender usage preference. Research in the 1980s revealed that most women viewed men's razors as too bulky, with too many bells and whistles, and not feminine in color or design. Suddenly, Gillette found an underserved new submarket for segmenting its razor line: the female shaver! The result was a completely new brand and product line called Gillette Venus, whose tagline is "Reveal the Goddess in You." Venus comes in six models: Original Venus; Venus Embrace, which "embraces a whole new level of smoothness"; Venus Breeze, the only razor with built-in shave gel bars; Venus Vibrance, which gently exfoliates to reveal more radiant skin; Venus Divine, which contains "Intensive Moisture Strips" enriched with oils; and Venus Disposable, for the "Goddess on the Go."[21]

Family and Household

In years past, the concepts of family and household were fairly easy for marketers to define—a married man and woman, likely with children, and sometimes with other relatives such as a grandparent who had moved back in. Now, *family and household segmentation* can be more complex. Marketing managers are cognizant of all kinds of different family arrangements including singles, unmarried cohabiting couples, gay and lesbian couples, parents with 30-something offspring who boomeranged back home, very large extended families living in one household, and so forth. Many of these changes in the concept of family have evolved based on changing economic realities, social norms, and cultural/subcultural mores.

Marketers who want to use family and household in segmentation need to understand the overall picture. One way to portray this variable is through the **family life cycle,** which was introduced in Chapter 5 and represents a series of life stages defined by age, marital status, number of children, and other factors.[22]

When Amana introduced the microwave oven in the 1960s, it started out as a product that was marketed to the busy homemaker as a way to supplement her food preparation and make her day at home more efficient. Now, most new microwaves are sold to singles, both men and women, who, in many instances, don't use or even own a traditional oven.

Race and Ethnicity

Race and ethnicity segmentation has become of prime importance in the United States as the number of natural-born citizens of ethnic minorities grows and the number of immigrants has increased.[23] Exhibit 7.8 summarizes the U.S. minority population.

EXHIBIT 7.8

U.S. Minority Populations (Actual Population and Percentage of Total U.S. Population)

	1980	1990	2000	2008
Hispanic	14.6 million (6.4%)	22.4 million (9.0%)	35.3 million (12.5%)	45.5 million (15.1%)
African-American	26.5 million (11.7%)	30.0 million (12.3%)	34.7 million (12.3%)	38.8 million (12.8%)
Asian	3.50 million (1.5%)	7.2 million (2.9%)	10.2 million (3.6%)	13.4 million (4.4%)

Source: U.S. Census Bureau, 1980, 1990, 2000, and 2008 Census Statistics.

In recent years, most firms have jumped on the bandwagon of segmenting by race and ethnicity, partly because many of these submarkets are growing quite rapidly in terms of both size and buying power and partly because they have historically been ignored by mainstream marketers.[24] African-Americans account for slightly more than 12 percent of the U.S. population, a figure that has not been growing. In years past, very few products were marketed specifically to the African-American segment other than by firms specializing only in that segment. Hair and beauty product pioneer Johnson Products, founded in 1954, was an early believer in the power of developing products such as Ultra Sheen, Afro Sheen, Classy Curl, and others that brought the company consistently double-digit sales increases throughout the 1970s and 1980s. Ultimately, the product line became so attractive that it was acquired by mainstream beauty care manufacturer L'Oreal and eventually by Wella Corporation, another broad-line marketer of beauty care products. Today, almost all major cosmetic and beauty aid firms, from Avon to Procter & Gamble, market products specifically designed to appeal to this vital market segment.

In contrast to the stability of the African-American segment, the Hispanic and Asian-American segments are both growing at a rapid rate. As Exhibit 7.8 demonstrates, Hispanics have overtaken African-Americans as a percentage of the U.S. population. An obvious challenge with the Hispanic segment, at least from the perspective of recent immigrants, has been the language barrier.[25] In the past, marketers' use of the Spanish language and symbolism in communicating with customers has mostly been through attempts at humor. Consider Taco Bell's "Yo quiero Taco Bell"-uttering Chihuahua dog or the Frito Bandito, for example. But today, marketers are taking Spanish-speaking Americans very seriously.[26] Compared to other groups, these segments are younger, more oriented toward developing long-term relationships with people and brands, have more people per family and household, and have experienced a tantalizingly strong increase in disposable income.

Income

Income segmentation is based on a very quantifiable demographic variable, and it is usually analyzed in incremental ranges. The average income of U.S. families has been rising recently, but at a declining rate of increase compared to prior decades.[27] Marketers use income as a segmenting approach very frequently. Examples on the lower-income side include deep-discount retailers and dollar menus at fast-food restaurants. Examples at the higher end include luxury automobiles, gourmet restaurants, and exotic travel experiences. Interestingly though, there is not necessarily a direct correlation between income and price preferences. Southwest Airlines, for example, is a low-priced carrier yet maintains a certain cachet with many high-income customers largely because of its fun style and spirit.[28]

Using income alone as a segmentation approach has some problems. First, many people either purposely misstate or refuse to reveal their income on questionnaires and in interviews used in collecting data for identifying segments. Second, with the credit that is available in the U.S. consumer marketplace, actual income may not necessarily drive one's ability to purchase products that in prior days were reserved for those with more income.[29] Cars costing tens of thousands of dollars can be had by nearly anyone nowadays by extending payments out six or more years. Even the old standby of income segmentation, home ownership, has fallen victim to wild mortgage schemes during many years of low initial interest, no-interest, and 40- and 50-year terms to entice buyers to go ahead and sign their financial lives away (which we now know had the unintended consequence of facilitating a meltdown of the mortgage banking industry).

According to McKinsey & Company, 80 percent of the wealthiest consumers in China are under age 45, compared with 30 percent in the United States and 19 percent in Japan. Lancome, the largest luxury cosmetics and skin care brand in China, has tailored its anti-aging products to these young affluent consumers by convincing they that they need to take preventative action *now*.[30]

Occupation

Occupational segmentation recognizes that there may be a number of consistent needs and wants demonstrated by consumers based on what type of job they have. The U.S. Bureau of Census lists numerous standardized categories of occupations including Professional/Managerial, Technical, Government, Trades, Agricultural, Educator, Student, and Unemployed.[31] In the United States, the workplace and our peer group of fellow workers is one of the strongest reference groups, and as you learned in Chapter 5, reference groups can be very powerful influencers on consumer behavior. All sorts of product lines are directly affected by occupation, including the clothing, equipment, and other personal support materials needed to fit in with the occupational peer group. Sometimes the employer influences purchase choice by offering tuition reimbursement, health care preferred provider networks, or discounts on products and services for employees. As a segmentation variable, occupation is very closely related to income although the two are not perfectly correlated.[32] That is, many traditionally blue-collar jobs may pay higher wages than white-collar positions depending in part on the strength of the union within the firm and industry. Obviously, occupation is also related to education in that the latter usually enables the former.

Education

In U.S. society, research consistently shows that education is one of the strongest predictors of success in terms of type of occupation, upward mobility, and long-term income potential. Everything else being equal, *educational segmentation* might lead a firm to offer its products based on some anticipated future payoff from the consumer. Take credit cards, for example. Why are credit-card providers so eager to market themselves to college-bound high school seniors? Because they know that, even with low beginning credit limits, gaining usage early increases the chances of loyalty to the card over the long run—after the student finishes college, gains professional employment, and starts making a bigger salary. Unfortunately, educational segmentation works the other direction as well, which is a potential dark side of segmentation in general. Unscrupulous marketers have been accused of using educational segmentation (often combined with a language barrier) to intentionally take advantage of uneducated consumers in a host of ways including pushing unhealthy or untested products, encouraging bad financial investments, and promoting various illegal sales approaches such as taking the money for household or automobile repairs up front and employing illegal pyramid schemes.[33]

Social Class

Social class segmentation involves grouping consumers by a standardized set of social strata around the familiar lower class, middle class, and upper class, and each of these contains several substrata. Exhibit 7.9 shows a traditional approach to segmentation by social class in the United States.

The composition of social classes takes into account several important demographic variables including income, occupation, and education.[34] However, nowadays many mitigating factors might affect one's inclusion in one or the other of the class strata. Readily available credit has flattened the classes and made many luxury products affordable to a broad spectrum of consumers who in the past would not have been able to purchase them. And who doesn't know someone who is quite wealthy that also shops at Target for staple goods? Although the very upper and very lower strata are still potentially useful for segmentation, it has become increasingly difficult to segment among the groups within the big middle stratum. Because of this, most marketing managers today prefer to either defer to other demographic variables for segmentation or, more likely, to look at psychographics and behavioral segmentation approaches that capture much of what used to be evidenced by social class.[35]

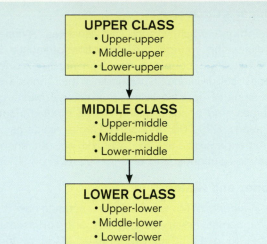

EXHIBIT 7.9 Traditional Social Class Strata in the United States

UPPER CLASS
• Upper-upper
• Middle-upper
• Lower-upper

MIDDLE CLASS
• Upper-middle
• Middle-middle
• Lower-middle

LOWER CLASS
• Upper-lower
• Middle-lower
• Lower-lower

Geodemographics

A hybrid form of segmentation that considers both geographic and demographic factors is called *geodemographic segmentation*. Typically, marketers turn to firms that specialize in collecting such data on an ongoing basis to purchase data relevant to their geographic area of focus.[36] Let's say for example that you are interested in coming into the Orlando metropolitan area with a new upscale type of convenience store and gas station to compete for customers, especially females, who don't like the ambience at a typical convenience store. Your research shows that it will be important to place your stores in neighborhoods trafficked by consumers who are more likely to be attracted to your upscale merchandise and more pleasant surroundings. Where do you turn for data on segments that might be a good match for your product?

One source is Nielsen's Claritas, which continually updates a large database called PRIZM-NE that is zip-code driven. PRIZM profiles every zip code in the United States by both demographic and lifestyle (psychographic) variables. Over time, PRIZM has discovered 66 "neighborhood types" into which all zip codes fall. Exhibit 7.10 describes several PRIZM clusters that might be potential customers for your new upscale convenience and gas store.

Judging from the description of the product, these PRIZM clusters seem to be likely segments of interest: Winner's Circle, Money and Brains, and Executive Suites. Certainly, other clusters not shown in Exhibit 7.10 might also fit your profile of assumed consumer needs and wants. The next step would be to seek zip codes whose location involves traffic patterns that will feed these consumer clusters into your convenience stores. These locations might involve being either close to housing additions or on key routes that members of these clusters take between home and work.

| EXHIBIT 7.10 | Sample PRIZM Clusters |

Winner's Circle

Among the wealthy suburban lifestyles, Winner's Circle is the youngest, a collection of mostly 25- to 34-year-old couples with large families in new-money subdivisions. Surrounding their homes are the signs of upscale living: recreational parks, golf courses, and upscale malls. With a median income of nearly $90,000, Winner's Circle residents are big spenders who like to travel, ski, eat out, shop at clothing boutiques, and take in a show.

Money and Brains

The residents of Money and Brains seem to have it all: high incomes, advanced degrees, and sophisticated tastes to match their credentials. Many of these city dwellers, who are predominantly white with a high concentration of Asian-Americans, are married couples with few children who live in fashionable homes on small, manicured lots.

Source: www.claritas.com.

Executive Suites

Executive Suites consists of upper-middle-class singles and couples typically living just beyond the nation's beltways. Filled with significant numbers of Asian-Americans and college graduates—both groups are represented at more than twice the national average—this segment is a haven for white-collar professionals drawn to comfortable homes and apartments within a manageable commute to downtown jobs, restaurants, and entertainment.

Psychographic Segmentation

Another approach to segmenting consumer markets is through **psychographic segmentation,** which relies on consumer variables such as personality and *AIOs* (activities, interests, and opinions) to segment a market. Psychographic segmentation is sometimes also referred to as segmentation by lifestyle or values. Psychographic segmentation builds on a purely demographic approach in that it helps flesh out the profile of the consumer as a human being and not just a location or demographic descriptor.[37] Psychographic segmentation brings individual differences into the profile along with the more readily measurable descriptive variables we have discussed so far.

An important challenge of using psychographic segmentation involves the reliability and validity of its measurement. Unlike geographic and demographic measures, which are relatively objective in nature, psychographic measures attempt to "get into the head" of the consumer. One way to better assure that such measures are reliable and valid is through the use of standardized questionnaires that reflect the experiences of a large number of users over an extended period. One popular psychographic instrument is **VALS™** (formerly known as **Values and Lifestyles),** a product of Strategic Business Insights (SBI), a spin out of SRI International. Want to know your own VALS™ type? Just go to www.strategicbusinessinsights.com/VALS, click on "VALS™ Survey," and complete a questionnaire.

In its marketing efforts during the 2009 recession, Denny's caught the attention of consumers that are motivated by value and price. As promised in its 2009 Super Bowl ad, Denny's offered its Grand Slam breakfast (valued at $5.99) free to consumers between 6 a.m. and 2 p.m. on February 3 at its restaurants around the country. Visitors were reacquainted with Denny's and reminded of their good food and value—hopefully resulting in a return visit at full price.[38]

VALS™ divides U.S. adults into eight groups that are determined both by primary motivation and by resources. Exhibit 7.11 portrays the basic VALS™

EXHIBIT 7.11   VALS™ Framework

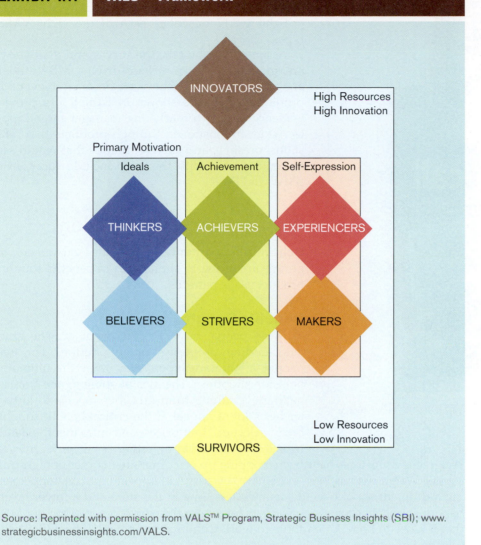

Source: Reprinted with permission from VALS™ Program, Strategic Business Insights (SBI); www. strategicbusinessinsights.com/VALS.

framework. Note that the key drivers in the system are the person's level of resources (high/low), innovation (high/low), and primary motivation (ideals, achievement, and self-expression). According to SBI, "Each of us is an individual. Yet each of us also has personality traits, attitudes, or needs that are similar to those of other people. VALS™ measures the underlying psychological motivations and resources that groups of consumers share that predict each group's typical choices as consumers." VALS™ has shown consistently strong evidence of reliability and validity.[39]

Again quoting SBI, "Consumers who are motivated primarily by ideals are guided by knowledge and principles. Consumers who are motivated primarily by achievement look for products and services that demonstrate success to their peers. And consumers who are motivated primarily by self-expression desire social or physical activity, variety, and risk." Notice the psychographics—the strong grounding of content in individual lifestyles and values. VALS™, or any similar psychographic instrument, works to help marketing managers successfully match people to products and helps focus the communication of value in ways that a particular VALS™ group is most likely to connect with. Product ownership, preferred media, hobbies, and so on are determined by integrating the VALS™ questionnaire into larger surveys such as MediaMark Research,

make the call

Music and fashion complete each other—just try to imagine one without the other. Together they give you the power to shed inhibitions, assume a new identity, express yourself. Supermodel Niki Taylor calls up the many sides of her personality with help from Nokia, the world's largest manufacturer of wireless phones.

NOKIA
Connecting People

www.NokiaUSA.com

Nokia is clearly messaging about a lifestyle in this ad—connecting a hip fashion image around their phones.

Intelligence, LLC. (MRI) or client private studies. Geographic concentrations of the VALS™ types are found using GeoVALS™.

Exhibit 7.12 describes each of the eight VALS™ types.

Assume that you take the survey and discover you are an Achiever. Lots of hard-driving MBA students and undergraduate business majors are Achievers. The profile of Achievers shown in Exhibit 7.12 provides evidence of how a marketing manager might appeal to Achiever consumers through products that reflect status, prestige, and success. Brands that would seem to connect well with this type include Ritz-Carlton, BMW, and Bose.

Behavioral Segmentation

Behavioral segmentation divides customers into groups according to similarities in benefits sought or product usage patterns.

Benefits Sought

Why do people buy? That is, what are the crucial value-adding properties of an offering? For many people, a Walmart Supercenter offers the ultimate in one-stop shopping. The idea of going to one store and getting everything from groceries to CDs to kitty litter has a lot of appeal, if the critical benefit sought is broad selection, low prices, and infrequent, extended trips to the store. On the other hand, in recent years Walgreens drugstores have been cropping up on corner after corner of high-traffic streets. Walgreens has been extremely successful in appealing to a shopper seeking a different set of benefits, namely less time in the store and a lower level of hassle. The chain caters to consumers for whom the convenience of having a store that is close to home or en route to work trumps other potential benefits such as selection and price.[40]

For many marketing managers, segmentation by benefits sought is the best place to start the process of market segmentation. You might begin by identifying groups interested in the specific bundle of benefits afforded by your offering and then move toward utilizing the other segmentation variables to further hone the profile of the core group that is attracted to your product's benefits.

Google uses behavioral targeting that tailors ads to people's interests and online behavior. The company uses stored browsing histories to trigger ads aimed at selling specific products for which a Google user has shown potential interest. Google expects to continue to increase its ad revenues significantly as it delivers a product's benefits to the right consumers.[41]

Usage Patterns

Segmentation by usage patterns includes usage occasions, usage rate, and user status. Occasions means specifically when the product is used. Why do you buy greeting cards? What causes you to take your significant other out for that special dinner? What makes you break down and rent that tux or buy that formal? Each of these purchases is driven by an occasion, and marketers are very savvy at playing to consumers' desires to use occasions as a reason to buy.[42]

EXHIBIT 7.12   **Description of the VALS™ Types**

Innovators

Innovators are successful, sophisticated, take-charge people with high self-esteem. Because they have such abundant resources, they exhibit all three primary motivations (ideals, achievement, and self-expression) in varying degrees. They are change leaders and are the most receptive to new ideas and technologies. Their purchases reflect cultivated tastes for upscale, niche products and services.

Thinkers

Thinkers are mature, satisfied, comfortable, and reflective. They tend to be well-educated and actively seek out information in the decision-making process. They favor durability, functionality, and value in products.

Believers

Believers are strongly traditional and respect rules and authority. Because they are fundamentally conservative, they are slow to change and technology-averse. They choose familiar products and established brands.

Achievers

Achievers have goal-oriented lifestyles that center on family and career. They avoid situations that encourage a high degree of stimulation or change. They prefer premium products that demonstrate success to their peers.

Strivers

Strivers are trendy and fun loving. They have little discretionary income and tend to have narrow interests. They favor stylish products that emulate the purchases of people with greater material wealth.

Experiencers

Experiencers appreciate the unconventional. They are active and impulsive, seeking stimulation from the new, offbeat, and risky. They spend a comparatively high proportion of their income on fashion, socializing, and entertainment.

Makers

Makers value practicality and self-sufficiency. They choose hands-on constructive activities and spend leisure time with family and close friends. Because they prefer value to luxury, they buy basic products.

Survivors

Survivors lead narrowly focused lives. Because they have the fewest resources, they do not exhibit a primary motivation and often feel powerless. They are primarily concerned about safety and security, so they tend to be brand loyal and buy discounted merchandise.

Source: Reprinted with permission from VALS™ Program. Strategic Business Insights (SBI), www.strategicbusinessinsights.com/VALS.

Listerine in an example of usage-based segmentation. Back when Listerine was marketed as just a mouthwash, it tended to be used sporadically or in the morning as part of the day's hygiene routine. But now that the product also addresses such oral concerns as gingivitis and gum disease, the usage rate is way up with many people developing a regular, twice-a-day regimen. This greatly enhanced the usage rate for the product.[43] Marketers often segment based on whether a consumer is a light, medium, or heavy user. Many firms subscribe to the concept of the *80/20 rule*—that 80 percent of the business is done by 20 percent of the users.

Degree of customer loyalty is another important focus for segmentation. In Chapter 3 we commented on the capability of CRM to aid marketing managers in identifying, tracking, and communicating with especially loyal patrons so marketers can implement strategies to keep those patrons loyal and reduce temptation to switch. In practice, loyalty programs for airlines and hotels, as well as frequent shopper cards for supermarkets and other retailers, all play on the notion of keeping the segment of heaviest users satisfied and using the product and of building a relationship between the customer and the brand and company.[44]

Segmenting users into groups such as former users, current users, potential users, first-time users, and regular users can be very advantageous. Often, firms will come up with extra incentives for former users to retry a product or for potential users to make that initial purchase. It is critical to influence the segment of first-time users to take the plunge and purchase. CRM programs enable marketing managers to customize the value offering, thus maximizing the appeal to each of these user status segments.

Firms Use Multiple Segmentation Approaches Simultaneously

We have seen that geographic, demographic, psychographic, and behavioral approaches to segmenting consumer markets all have strong potential. In practice, these approaches are not applied one at a time. Firms develop a profile of a segment that might include aspects of any or all of the segmentation approaches we have discussed. Exhibit 7.13 provides visual examples of a range of segmentation approaches, including combinations of several types of segmentation.

Developing the right segmentation strategy is one of the most important aspects of the marketing manager's role. Expertise in market segmentation is highly valued by companies across many industries because of the process's complexity and the potential for effective segmentation to have a major impact on a firm's success in the marketplace.[46]

EXHIBIT 7.13	Examples of Segmentation Approaches

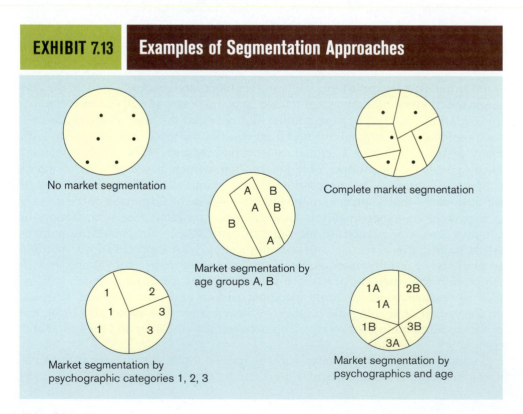

No market segmentation

Complete market segmentation

Market segmentation by age groups A, B

Market segmentation by psychographic categories 1, 2, 3

Market segmentation by psychographics and age

EXHIBIT 7.14　Business Market Segmentation Variables

- Demographic
  - Industry
  - Company size
  - Location
- Operating Variables
  - Technology
  - User status
  - Customer capabilities
- Purchasing Approaches
  - Purchasing function organization
  - Power structure

- Nature of existing relationship
- General purchasing policies
- Purchasing criteria
- Situational Factors
  - Urgency
  - Specific application
  - Size of the order
- Personal Characteristics
  - Buyer-seller similarity
  - Attitudes toward risk
  - Loyalty

Source: This listing is derived from an influential early book on business markets—Thomas V. Bonoma and Benson P. Shapiro, *Segmenting the Industrial Market* (Lexington, MA: Lexington Books, 1983).

Segmenting Business Markets

Chapter 6 provided an extensive treatment of the many important properties unique to business markets. The variables relevant to segmentation of business markets share some overlap with those in consumer markets, but it is worth highlighting several unique segmentation approaches here as well. Exhibit 7.14 summarizes several key approaches to business market segmentation.

In some ways, business market segmentation is more straightforward than that of consumer markets. This is partly because there is often a more defined universe of potential customers.[47] For example, using one variable from each set in Exhibit 7.14, a firm might create a profile segment for focus that includes one industry, current nonusers, price-focused, large quantity, and strong loyalty. In any given industry in the business-to-business market, this segmentation profile would probably narrow the segment to include just a few firms. This would allow for a focused approach to communicating and delivering value to this profile of firms. Of course, as with consumer markets, segments must meet the criteria for effective segmentation and if the profile above appears too narrow, one or more of the variables can be removed.

TARGET MARKETING

Target marketing is the process of evaluating market segments and deciding which among them shows the most promise for development. The decision to invest in developing a segment into a target market represents an important turning point in the marketing planning process because, from this point forward, the direction of a firm's marketing strategies and related programs are set.[48] The three steps in target marketing are:

1. Analyze market segments.
2. Develop profiles of each potential target market.
3. Select a target marketing approach.

Analyze Market Segments

A number of strategic factors come into play when analyzing whether a segment is a good candidate for investment as a target market. Many different factors should be considered in the analysis. The goal is to determine the relative attractiveness of the various segments using an ROI (return on investment) approach. Everything else being equal, it is prudent to assign a high level of attractiveness to segments that provide the quickest, highest-level, and longest-sustaining anticipated ROI.[49]

Several factors should be considered when analyzing segment attractiveness. The following are among the most important: segment size and growth potential, competitive forces related to the segment, and overall *strategic fit* of the segment to the company's goals and value-adding capabilities.

> Nokia, the world's largest mobile phone maker, has stepped up its targeting of the U.S. market for smartphones. It built a partnership with AT&T to carry its super-thin e71x smartphone for $100. Nokia decided that the U.S. market has the most promise for development after evaluating numerous other global markets, many of which are actually much more saturated with product than the United States.[50]

Segment Size and Growth Potential

When Procter & Gamble was considering acquiring Gillette in 2005, one strong attraction was entry into the lucrative shaving market, which would place P&G solidly into the men's toiletries market—a market space in which the company had little product representation. Later in the decade, the U.S. men's toiletries market was expected to hit $1 billion in sales, with an annual growth rate of 4 to 5 percent per year. The opportunity for P&G to gain a substantial chunk of those sales by acquiring Gillette (which has about 70 percent of the razor and blade business) was too tempting to pass up—even at the price of $57 billion. P&G sees its strategic investment in this new target market as an opening to developing more new products for men.

Segment Competitive Forces

In Chapter 2 we identified Michael Porter's six competitive forces that firms must be cognizant of when considering investment in new target markets. For P&G's Gillette razor and blade business, several of these predominate. First, rivalry among existing firms is fierce. Schick, a distant No. 2 to Gillette in market share, is nonetheless a scrappy competitor willing to match Gillette's penchant for grandiose innovation (think six-bladed Fusion) with some product bravado of its own (Quattro Chrome, Midnight, and Power versions). Second, a strong threat of substitute products is present in the form of convenient, heavily promoted electric shavers as well as an emerging product category of depilatories for men. Finally, bargaining power of suppliers has become more of an issue in the razor and blade industry primarily due to the rising cost of the metals required for production of today's finely honed blades. If the base price of steel and its transportation were to take a major spike upward, more consumers might become disenchanted with the constant replacement routine for blades and switch to electric shavers. Still, even with these competitive forces at play, P&G's analysis indicated a highly positive ROI for its entry into the market.

Strategic Fit of the Segment

Strategic fit means there is a good match of a target market to the firm's internal structure, culture, goals, and resource capabilities. In the case of the P&G acquisition of Gillette, P&G executives have been widely quoted as saying that one of the primary areas of attractiveness of entering the razor and blade segment was its natural fit within P&G's sophisticated supply chain system, especially in international markets. P&G has already dramatically increased the level of distribution of Gillette products in many countries, simply by plugging the existing products into P&G's vast network of customer relationships. The nature of Gillette's products was a great strategic fit for much of what P&G already does in the market.

Develop Profiles of Each Potential Target Market

Once the market segments have been analyzed, marketing managers need to develop profiles of each segment under consideration for investment as a target market. Especially within the context of marketing planning, specifying the attributes of each segment and describing the characteristics of a "typical" consumer within that segment—from a geographic, demographic, psychographic, and behavioral perspective—are invaluable to gaining a better understanding of the degree to which each segment meets the criteria set out by a firm for segment attractiveness and target market ROI. Subsequently, a decision can now be made on prioritizing the segments for investment to develop them as target markets.[51]

Usually, this analysis results in segments that fall within four basic levels of priority for development:

1. **Primary target markets–**those segments that clearly have the best chance of meeting ROI goals and the other attractiveness factors.
2. **Secondary target markets–**those segments that have reasonable potential but for one reason or another are not best suited for development immediately.
3. **Tertiary target markets–**those segments that may develop emerging attractiveness for investment in the future but that do not appear attractive at present.
4. Target markets to abandon for future development.

Select a Target Marketing Approach

The final step in target marketing is to select the approach. Exhibit 7.15 portrays a continuum of approaches to target marketing from very broad to very narrow. Four basic options in target marketing strategy are undifferentiated, differentiated, concentrated (also called focus or niche), and customized (or one-to-one).

Undifferentiated Target Marketing

The broadest possible approach is **undifferentiated target marketing**—which is essentially a one-market strategy, sometimes referred to as an unsegmented *mass market*. Firms whose market approach is grounded in Porter's competitive strategy of low cost may use a relatively undifferentiated target marketing strategy based primarily on the resulting price advantage.[52] Southwest Airlines and Walmart are two firms that have built their businesses on their inherent internal cost advantages, passing along a price advantage to the mass market. But most

EXHIBIT 7.15	Continuum of Target Marketing Approaches

Very Broad			Very Narrow
Undifferentiated target marketing	Differentiated target marketing	Concentrated target marketing	Customized target marketing

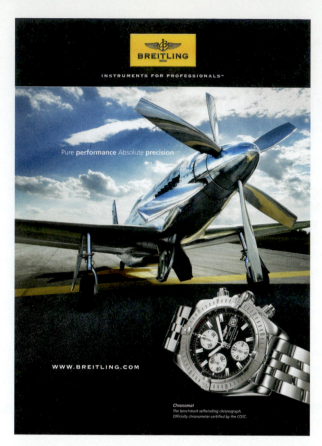

Breitling markets its Chronomat—"The benchmark selfwinding chronograph"—to a higher income target market.

firms don't have the kind of cost efficiencies it takes to operate such a target marketing approach and instead have to rely on developing sources of differentiation other than price.

Differentiated Target Marketing

Differentiated target marketing, often referred to as simply *differentiation,* means developing different value offerings for different targeted segments. Possible sources of differentiation are many and include innovation/R&D, product quality, service leadership, employees, convenience, brand image, technology, corporate social responsibility, and many others. A significant challenge with differentiation as a core market strategy is that competitors are constantly coming to market with new differentiators that trump the efficacy of the current ones. Overnight a new technological innovation or other strategic shift by a competitor can doom a firm's current source of differentiation to the junk heap.[53]

FedEx famously differentiates based on speed of delivery and dependability of overall service to appeal to a target market willing to pay a price premium for these attributes. When UPS moved full force into the overnight package segment, its differentiating message was about full integration of services for the user through a smorgasbord of services including ground, overnight, and integrated supply chain solutions even for small-to-medium size businesses. About the same time, FedEx entered UPS's lucrative over-the-road transport space with FedEx Ground. Initially, because of UPS's domination FedEx had a difficult time differentiating itself in a meaningful way and only recently has FedEx Ground begun to gain widespread usage at a level that would even come close to affecting UPS's domination of that market.

Concentrated Target Marketing

A **concentrated target marketing** approach, which Michael Porter refers to as a *focus strategy* and is also popularly called a *niche strategy,* involves targeting a large portion of a small market. Many start-up firms enter a marketplace as a focus player. Because they are not saddled with keeping up with competitive demands in the broader market, firms using concentrated target marketing can realize cost and operational efficiencies and better margins than many first positioned as differentiators.[54] The danger of being a focus player is that sometimes these firms get too successful and are no longer able to fly under the radar of the differentiators, especially if the niche they occupy is a growing niche within the larger market.

Customized (One-to-One) Marketing

With the proliferation of CRM, firms are able to develop more customized approaches to target marketing. In Chapter 1 we said that **customized (one-to-one) marketing,** as conceived by leading proponents Don Peppers and Martha Rogers, advocates that firms should direct energy and resources into establishing a learning relationship with each customer and then connect that knowledge with the firm's production and service capabilities to fulfill that customer's needs in as custom a manner as possible.[55] The related approach of mass customization allows flexible manufacturing, augmented by highly efficient ordering and supply chain systems, to drive the capability for a consumer to build a product from the ground up as is the case when you order a computer from Dell. In the context of target marketing, customization represents a target of one individual for whom a unique value offering is developed.

POSITIONING

Once market segments have been defined and analyzed and target markets have been selected for development, the firm must turn its attention to creating, communicating, and delivering the value offering to the target markets—that is, positioning the product so that consumers understand its ability to fulfill their needs and wants. The marketing mix of product, supply chain, price, and promotion is at the heart of positioning, and positioning strategies for a target market are executed through the development of unique combinations of these marketing mix variables.[56] Effective positioning is so important that the remaining chapters in this book are devoted to the various marketing mix elements.

IKEA, the Swedish home products retailer, positions itself as having a commitment to product design, consumer value, and clever solutions. IKEA is so confident in its model that it lists its marketing strategy, marketing positioning strategy, and marketing mix openly on its Web site. IKEA combines low price, function, the appropriate quality, and appealing design. The company keeps its customers hooked by offering discounts and other benefits through its "IKEA Family" loyalty program.[57]

Positioning doesn't occur in a vacuum; firms must position their offerings against competitors' offerings. Although McDonald's might love to think that for the hamburger lover "it's all about McDonald's," the truth is that consumers of fast-food burgers are constantly bombarded with the output of positioning strategies not just by McDonald's but by Burger King and Wendy's as well.

In practice, much of the consumer research described in Chapter 4 is designed to facilitate successful positioning. Many positioning studies start with focus groups that allow participants to talk about aspects of their experiences with a product. From the focus groups, a set of attributes is developed for further analysis. Attributes of a product represent salient issues that consumers consider when evaluating the product. For fast-food restaurants like McDonald's, the set of relevant attributes includes items such as cleanliness of the restaurant, speed of service, breadth of menu offerings, healthy food options, prices, employee courtesy, and numerous others.

Typically, after a series of focus groups to develop or confirm the relevant attributes, the positioning research moves to a survey methodology in which respondents rate the importance of each attribute, as well as the degree to which each of several competitors' products exhibit the attributes of interest.[58] For example, McDonald's might survey consumers about how important cleanliness of the restaurant, speed of service, breadth of menu offerings, healthy food options, prices, and employee courtesy are, and then ask them to provide their perceptions of how well McDonald's, Burger King, and Wendy's stack up in actually delivering these desired attributes.

The results of such a survey can be analyzed through a gap analysis that shows not only gaps by attribute in importance versus delivery, but also gaps among the competitors in delivery. Perhaps the analysis would reveal that McDonald's excels at healthy food options and cleanliness of the restaurant, but Burger King excels at breadth of menu offerings and prices. If that's the case, each firm has to decide if it is comfortable continuing to invest in these elements of positioning or if investment in other elements is warranted. Recently, Burger King has deliberately invested in positioning itself as the "non-healthy menu" choice, blatantly

EXHIBIT 7.16	Examples of Perceptual Maps Used in Positioning Decisions

Generic Price-Quality Perceptual Map

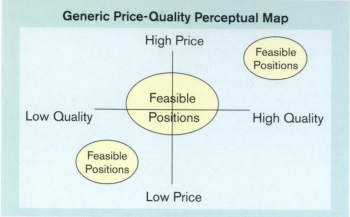

Perceptual Map for Hotel

Positioning involves trade-offs among relevant attributes, not just price and quality.

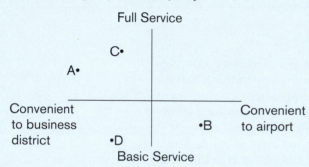

Perceptual Map for Automobile

Another example set of attributes.

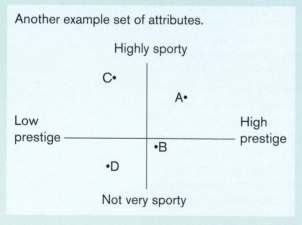

featuring in ads its bigger and much more decadent food items in terms of fat and calorie content than either McDonald's or Wendy's advertises (although each certainly offers a fair share of unhealthy items).[59]

Perceptual Maps

The data generated from the above analysis can be used to develop a useful visual tool for positioning called a **perceptual map,** which displays paired attributes in order to compare consumer perceptions of each competitor's delivery against those attributes.[60] Today this is usually accomplished by computer statistical software applications that plot each competitor's relative positioning on the attributes.

Exhibit 7.16 provides three different examples of paired attributes on a perceptual map. The first map shows a generic pairing of price and quality and identifies several quadrants of feasible positions based on price-quality pairings that result in positive perceived value by the customer. The logic is compelling as to why the other two quadrants are not feasible positioning. In the upper-left quadrant, marketing an inferior offering at a high price is the antithesis of good marketing management. It may seem that in the short run an opportunity exists to make a quick buck, but the approach runs counter to everything we've learned so far about value and building customer relationships as the core of successful marketing over the long run. The bottom-right quadrant's positioning of high quality at a low price seems attractive, but only firms that can legitimately sustain Porter's notion of low-cost strategy can reasonably consider such positioning. And even for those players, the idea of nurturing cost and efficiency savings in operations is not that you will take the entire savings to price; rather, Porter advocates that a low-cost strategy should afford the opportunity to take much of the savings to improved margins and increased reinvestment in product development, only reflecting perhaps a small price differential. Chapter 10 reveals the inherent dangers in positioning primarily based on low price.

The other two perceptual maps in Exhibit 7.16 show where existing competitors are in the market based on the attributes reported. Such perceptual maps can be very useful in helping visualize where to make strategic changes to either move your product closer to the main market (clusters of competition) or further differentiate your product away from the competitive cluster and into more unique market space. In this way, perceptual maps aid in **repositioning** a product, which involves understanding the marketing mix approach necessary to change present consumer perceptions of the product. McDonald's has recently been engaged in a repositioning strategy into more healthy food options to appeal to a primary target market of health-conscious baby boomers.

In actual practice, pairing just two attributes for consideration in making positioning decisions is overly simplistic. Data such as we described above are actually analyzed through a technique called multidimensional scaling that allows for interpretation of multiple attribute perceptions at the same time.

Sources of Differential Competitive Advantage

Effective differentiation is absolutely central to successful positioning strategies. Michael Porter, in his classic book *Competitive Advantage,* explains differentiation as follows:

> When employing a differentiation strategy, the organization competes on the basis of providing unique goods or services with features that customers value, perceive as different, and for which they are willing to pay a premium.[61]

Marketing managers can seek to create differentiation for their offerings in a variety of ways. The following are some of the most often used sources of differentiation.

Price leadership: efficiencies in cost of labor, materials, supply chain, or other operational elements enabling the price leader to charge less. Example: Walmart.

Innovative leadership: constantly developing the "next new thing." Example: Apple.

Service leadership: having an unusual and notable commitment to providing service to customers. Example: Ritz-Carlton, BMW.

Product leadership: performance, features, durability, reliability, style, and so on. Example: BMW.

Personnel leadership: hiring employees who are competent, reliable, courteous, credible, responsive, and able to communicate clearly. Example: Southwest Airlines.

Convenience leadership: making the product or service significantly easier to obtain. Example: Amazon.com.

Image leadership: symbols, atmosphere, and creative media. Example: BMW.

It is important to note that firms and brands often rely on multiple sources of differentiation simultaneously. Note above that BMW stakes a claim to differentiation by leadership in product, service, and image—a great position to be in.

Vittel+Energy strongly differentiates itself with the message that it "helps keep you hydrated and energised throughout the day, no matter what you're doing."

Positioning Errors

Sometimes, positioning strategies don't work out as planned. The following positioning errors can undermine a firm's overall marketing strategy:[62]

- *Underpositioning:* when consumers have only a vague idea about the company and its products, and do not perceive any real differentiation. Until recently, both Audi and Volkswagen suffered from underpositioning as many consumers struggled to identify salient points of differentiation between those brands and their competitors. However, both brands have beefed up their marketing communication to better clarify exactly what each stands for in the marketplace.

- *Overpositioning:* when consumers have too narrow an understanding of the company, product, or brand. Dell became so entrenched as a brand of PCs that it has been a bit of a struggle to extend the brand into other lucrative product lines. Neither HP nor Apple suffers from overpositioning; both have engaged in great positioning strategies over the long run.

- *Confused positioning:* when frequent changes and contradictory messages confuse consumers regarding the positioning of the brand. McDonald's found itself the victim of confused positioning as it moved out of the 1990s. It had tried (and failed) at so many diverse new product launches in the restaurants that many customers lost track of what the core of the brand was. Since then, under new top leadership, McDonald's has embraced its core differentiators of consistency of products and dependability of service, while growing new products at a much more conservative rate.

- *Doubtful positioning:* when the claims made for the product or brand are not regarded as credible by consumers. Sadly, firms that engage in unethical business practices often do not realize the magnitude of damage being done to their brand. Also, you will learn in the chapters on products and branding that trial is only the initial goal of marketing communication. After initial trial, firms need to ensure that the offering consistently meets or exceeds customer expectations so that repurchase—and loyalty—will occur, which is a process of customer expectations management. When FedEx promises 8 a.m. next-day delivery, it has to be sure its systems can actually produce such a level of performance all the time.

SUMMARY

Effective segmentation, target marketing, and positioning are central to marketing management because these decisions set the direction for the execution of the marketing plan. First, potential appropriate segmentation approaches must be identified. Second, the segments must be evaluated and decisions made about which to invest in for the most favorable ROI—these become your target markets. Finally, sources of differentiation must be identified that will result in customers perceiving fulfillment of needs and wants based on the value proposition of the offering.

APPLICATION QUESTIONS

1. Go to the Nielsen/Claritas Web site (www.mybestsegments.com) and click on "ZIP Code Look-Up". There you will find a demo that allows you to type in a zip code of your choice and find out what PRIZM clusters predominate in that geographic area.

   a. What do the findings tell you about the overall composition of potential customers within that zip code?

   b. Based on the array of clusters represented, what kinds of start-up businesses might flourish within the geographic area? Why do you believe those businesses in particular would be successful?

2. Go to the Strategic Business Insights (SBI) Web site (www.strategicbusiness insights.com/VALS) and click through to the section on VALS™. Find the VALS™ survey and complete the questionnaire to find your own VALS™ type.

a. Are the results surprising? Why or why not? Do you see yourself as part of the identified VALS™ segment?

b. If you are comfortable doing so, share your results with a few other people in the class and ask if they mind sharing their results with you. What is the consensus among the group about whether the survey actually captured a relevant profile about yourself and your classmates?

c. How might each of these brands benefit from the use of VALS™ as a psychographic segmentation tool:

   i. Outback Steak House.

   ii. Walt Disney World Theme Park.

   iii. Target Stores.

   iv. Samsung.

   v. Porsche.

3. Consider each of the brands below. Review the list of potential sources of differential competitive advantage (differentiation) highlighted in the chapter. For each: (*a*) indicate which one differentiation source you believe is most important to them currently and (*b*) indicate which other differentiation sources you believe might hold promise for development for them in the near future and *why*.

a. Carnival Cruise Lines.

b. Sears Craftsman Tools.

c. Avon.

d. Lowe's Home Improvement Stores.

e. The Salvation Army.

MARKETING PLAN EXERCISE

ACTIVITY 7.1: Identifying Target Markets

In this chapter you learned that effective segmentation, target marketing, and positioning favorably impact marketing management. For purposes of your marketing plan, we'll leave the specifics of developing your overall positioning strategies to the upcoming chapters on the marketing mix. At this point, the following steps are needed.

1. Consider the various approaches to segmenting your market(s). What segmentation approaches do you recommend? Why do you recommend those approaches over other available approaches?

2. Evaluate your proposed segments against the criteria for effective segmentation. What does this evaluation lead you to conclude about the best way to proceed?

3. Systematically analyze each potential segment on your list using the three steps you learned in the chapter: (1) assess each in terms of segment size and growth potential, segment competitive forces, and strategic fit of the segment; (2) for the short set that emerges, develop profiles of each potential target market, then identify each of your final set as primary, secondary, tertiary, or abandoned; (3) select the target marketing approach for each of your primary targets.

4. Identify the likely sources of differential advantage on which you will focus later in developing your positioning strategies.

If you are using Marketing Plan Pro, a template for this assignment can be accessed at www.mhhe.com/marshalless1e.

CHAPTER 08

The Product Experience: Product Strategy and Building the Brand

---

LEARNING OBJECTIVES

- Understand the essential role of the product experience in marketing.

- Define the characteristics of a product.

- Recognize how product strategies evolve from one product to many products.

- Understand the life of a product and how product strategies change over time.

- Recognize the essential elements in a brand.

- Learn the importance of brand equity in product strategy.

- Explain the role of packaging and labeling as critical brand elements.

- Define the responsibility of warranties and service agreements in building consumer confidence.

PRODUCT: THE HEART OF MARKETING

As we discussed in Chapter 1, the primary function of marketing and, more broadly speaking, the entire organization is to deliver value to the customer. The essential component in delivering value is the product experience, which is why it is considered the heart of marketing. When the product is wrong, no amount of marketing communications, no degree of logistical expertise or pricing sophistication will make it successful. Apple is widely regarded as a product innovator with the iPod, iPhone, iMac, and other products. However, the company has also experienced product missteps. One of the most notable was Newton, the first PDA, introduced in the early 1990s but discontinued after Palm brought out its line of smaller, more user-friendly products. While technically superior to Palm, Apple did not understand the key value drivers in the product. People wanted PDAs with connectivity to other computers, a reasonable combination of features, and a realistic price (early Newtons cost over $1,000).[1] Newton's failure highlights an interesting fact: the best product technically is not always the most successful product. People look for the product that delivers the best overall product experience.

Product Characteristics

Define the Product

What does the term *product* mean? Most people define a product as a tangible object; however, that is not accurate. The product experience encompasses a great deal more as we will learn over the next several chapters. Consider the customer walking into Starbucks; is he or she just buying a cup of coffee? Did the owner of a new Toyota Prius buy just a new car? The answer is that, while customers are buying a cup of coffee and a new car, they are also buying a product experience. It is important for the marketer to understand exactly what the customer includes in that experience. This is a particularly difficult challenge because different target markets will view the same product in completely different ways. Parents buying their daughter a pair of jeans would probably consider Aeropostale jeans to be just another pair of jeans; however, to the teenager, the same purchase makes an important statement about her and her choice of clothes.[2]

Product can be defined as anything that delivers value to satisfy a need or want and includes physical merchandise, services, events, people, places, organizations, information, even ideas. Most people have no problem considering a computer or car a product, but would these same individuals consider a get-away weekend at the Amelia Island Ritz Carlton in Florida a product? The Ritz-Carlton does and it develops a specific marketing strategy around the resort.

It is important to differentiate between a product and a product item. A product is a brand such as Post-it Notes or Tide detergent. Within each product a company may develop a number of product items, each of which represents a unique size, feature, or price. Tide powder detergent offers five "scents," including fragrance free, in a variety of sizes designed to reach a variety of target markets.[3] Each combination of scent and size represents a unique product item in the Tide product line and is known by a **stock keeping unit (SKU).** An SKU is a unique identification number used to track a product through a distribution system, inventory management, and pricing.

Essential Benefit

Why does someone purchase a plane ticket? The answer quite obviously is to get from one place to another. Simply stated, the essential benefit of purchasing a plane ticket is getting

The Apple Newton, while technically better than similar PDAs, failed in the marketplace because it did not deliver a better product experience than competitors such as Palm.

189

somewhere else; therefore, the essence of the airline product experience is transporting people. Successful airlines, indeed all companies, understand that before anything else they must deliver on the essential benefit.

The **essential benefit** is the fundamental need met by the product. No matter what other value-added product experiences are provided to the customer, the essential benefit must be part of the encounter. For example, an airline can offer low fares, an easy-to-navigate Web site, or in-seat video entertainment, but unless the customer receives the essential benefit (getting from Point A to Point B) the other items have very little meaning to the customer. Without the essential benefit, other benefits may actually increase the customer's dissatisfaction with the experience. What good are low fares if the customer doesn't arrive at the destination?

Core Product

Aircraft, pilots, flight attendants, baggage handlers, reservation agents, managers, and an IT system are a few of the elements needed to get people and their luggage from one place to another. An airline brings all those pieces together to create a product that efficiently and effectively delivers the essential benefit, transporting someone from Point A to Point B.

Companies translate the essential benefit into physical, tangible elements known as the **core product.** Some companies do it better than others, making this critical challenge an important differentiator separating successful companies from their competitors.[4] Southwest Airlines, for example, has done a very good job of translating the essential benefits of air travel. By using one kind of airplane, identifying efficiencies in everything from reservations to flight routes, and taking care of employees, the company is the industry leader in low-cost air travel and, in the process, revolutionized the entire airline industry.

As a company creates the core product experience, it is vital to clearly understand customer expectations. Every aspect of the product experience is evaluated by the customer and then considered against a set of expectations. When an airline creates a flight there is an expectation that the flight will arrive at its stated time. If the flight does not arrive on time, the passenger assesses the reasons. Was it the airline's fault, the weather, or something else? Airlines are sensitive about their on-time arrival percentage and where they rank relative to the competition because they know customers believe this is an important characteristic of the core product experience. The customer's evaluation of a product experience against a set of defined expectations is a critical element contributing to overall satisfaction or dissatisfaction with the product.[5]

Enhanced Product

The core product is the starting point for the product experience. All cell phones deliver on the essential benefit of mobile communication, but there is a vast difference between the introductory "free" phone offered by many service providers and the latest Treo or BlackBerry. Features, cutting-edge designs and colors, connectivity to other digital devices, and new functionality (such as digital media capability) differentiate one product from another. As consumers around the world become more sophisticated, companies are required to look beyond delivering great core products to creating products that enhance, extend, and encourage the customer.

Following the successful release of the iPhone, Apple's closest competitor in the smart phone arena, Research In Motion, decided to integrate touch-screen technology into its new BlackBerry Storm wireless handset. The new model offered BlackBerry's seamless business functionality as well as a sleek new touch-screen interface, but it was not received by consumers as well as RIM had hoped. The Storm's interface was not as elegant as that of the iPhone and its lack of a physical keyboard and iconic trackball made it unappealing to longtime BlackBerry users.[6]

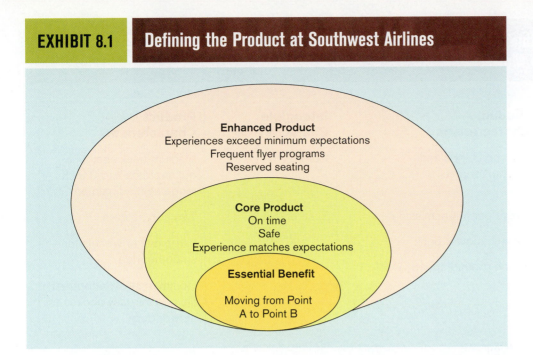

EXHIBIT 8.1 **Defining the Product at Southwest Airlines**

Enhanced Product
Experiences exceed minimum expectations
Frequent flyer programs
Reserved seating

Core Product
On time
Safe
Experience matches expectations

Essential Benefit

Moving from Point
A to Point B

The **enhanced product** extends the core product to include additional features, designs, and innovation that exceed customer expectations. In this way, companies build on the core product, creating opportunities to strengthen the brand. Consider Southwest Airlines once again, which has done a good job of delivering people on time and meeting customer expectations regarding low-cost air travel. Southwest added features such as frequent flyer opportunities and reserved seating to further augment the customer's air travel experience. Exhibit 8.1 shows how the essential benefit, core product, and enhanced product are created for Southwest Airlines.

Product Classifications

Products can be classified in four ways. Two of the four classifications define the nature of the product: tangibility and durability. The other two classification criteria deal with who uses the product: consumers or businesses. It is important to understand the nature and use of a product because marketing strategies differ among the various product classifications.

Tangibility: Physical Aspects of the Product Experience

Products, as opposed to services, have a physical aspect referred to as **tangibility.** Tangible products present opportunities (customers can see, touch, and experience the product) and also some challenges (customers may find the product does not match their personal tastes and preferences). Services are intangible. A significant challenge for marketers today is that many tangible products have intangible characteristics.[7] For example a significant element in an individual's satisfaction with a new car is the customer service before and after the purchase. Intangible products, on the other hand, such as services have tangible characteristics. For example, airlines introduce new airline seats to create a competitive advantage. Exhibit 8.2 identifies the tangible and intangible characteristics of a John Deere riding lawn mower.

Durability: Product Usage

Durability references the length of product usage. **Nondurable products** are usually consumed in a few uses and, in general, cost less than durable products. Examples of consumer nondurables include personal grooming products such as

Tangible Characteristic	Product Characteristic	Intangible Characteristic	Product Characteristic
Power	18.5 hp Briggs and Stratton engine	Comfort	Medium-back seat without armrests and 3-inch range seat adjustment
Performance	Hydro-gear transmission 42-inch mower deck 7 mph ground speed	Ease of use	Two cup holders Large caster wheels for smoother ride Commercial style footrest flips up for easy access to mower deck

Sources: http://shopproducts.howstuffworks.com/26HP-54-Garden-Tractor/SF-I/PID-38869959; and http://www.deere.com/en_US/ProductCatalog/HO/servlet/ProdCatProduct?pNbr=SKU21896&tM=HO.

toothpaste, soap, and shampoo, while business nondurables include office supplies such as printer ink, paper, and other less expensive, frequently purchased items. Because these products are purchased frequently and are not expensive, companies seek a wide distribution to make them as readily available as possible, create attractive price points to motivate purchase, and heavily advertise these products. **Durable products** have a longer product life and are often more expensive. Consumer durables include microwave ovens, washers/dryers, and certain electronics such as televisions. Business durables include products that may be used in the manufacturing process such as machine presses or IT networks, as well as equipment such as office furniture and computers to facilitate the running of the business.[8]

Consumer Goods

Consumers purchase thousands of products from an assortment of millions of choices. On the surface it may seem difficult to develop a classification system for the variety of products consumers purchase, but the reality is that consumer purchase habits fall into four broad categories: convenience, shopping, specialty, and unsought.

Frequently purchased, relatively low-cost products for which customers have little interest in seeking new information or considering other options and rely heavily on prior brand experience and purchase behavior are called **convenience goods.** These products include most items people buy regularly such as toiletries, gasoline, and paper products and fall into four categories. Staples are usually food products people buy weekly or at least once a month such as Folgers coffee or Dannon yogurt. Impulse products, as the name implies, are purchased without planning. If you think about the products available in vending machines, you will have a good idea of an impulse product. Finally, there are a host of products people purchase only in times of emergency. For example, as hurricanes approach communities, people rush out to purchase extra supplies of food, gas, batteries, and other products. It is not uncommon to see occasional shortages of some products as distribution systems are strained to meet unplanned spikes in demands for these everyday products.

Products that require consumers to do more research and compare across product dimensions such as color, size, features, and price are called **shopping goods.** Consumer products that fall into this category include clothes, furniture, and major appliances such as refrigerators and dishwashers. These products are purchased less frequently and are more costly than convenience goods. Price concerns, a variety of choices at various price levels, many different features, and a fear of making the wrong decision are among the factors that drive consumers to research these purchases. As a result, companies often develop product strategies that target product price points with particular features to appeal to the broadest range of consumers.

Specialty goods are a unique purchase made based on a defining characteristic for the consumer. The characteristic might be a real or perceived product feature such as Apple iPod's easy user interface or brand identification like Porsche's reputation for building sports cars. Whatever the attribute(s), consumers apply decision rules that frequently minimize the number of different product choices and focus less on price. They are also more willing to seek out the product; however, expectations about product service, salesperson expertise, and customer service are higher. Bang and Olufsen's line of high-end electronic equipment is not available in regular retail outlets. Rather the company has a limited number of retail stores in major cities. Consumers wanting to purchase Bang & Olufsen equipment must seek out those stores.

The final categories of goods, **unsought goods,** are products that consumers do not seek out and, indeed, often would rather not purchase at all. Insurance, particularly life insurance, is not a product people want to purchase. In general, customers do not want to purchase products or services related to sickness, death, or emergencies because, in part, the circumstances surrounding the purchase are not pleasant. As a result, companies have well-trained salespeople skilled in helping customers through the purchase process. These salespeople often must be supported by extensive marketing communications.

Business Goods

Businesses buy a vast array of products that can be classified into three broad areas based on two dimensions: (1) whether or not they are used in the manufacturing process and (2) cost. Goods incorporated into the company's finished product as a result of the manufacturing process are either materials or parts. **Materials** are natural (lumber, minerals such as copper) or farm products (corn, soybeans) that become part of the final product. **Parts** consist of equipment either fully assembled or in smaller pieces that will be assembled into larger components and, again, used in the production process.

In addition to the products that are used directly in the production process, companies purchase a number of products and services to support business operations. These can generally be placed on a continuum from low-cost/frequent purchases to very high-cost/infrequent purchases. **MRO** (maintenance, repair, operating) **supplies** are the everyday items that a company needs to keep running. While per unit cost is low, their total cost over a year can be high.

At the other end of the cost/purchase frequency continuum are **capital goods,** which are major purchases in support of a significant business function. Building a new plant or a new IT network can require large equipment purchases that cost millions of dollars and require significant customization. These purchases are negotiated over a period of months, sometimes years. Companies selling capital goods to businesses focus on personal selling and a high level of customer service with significant product customization.

Product Discrimination: Create a Point of Differentiation

A fundamental question in the product purchase decision-making process is what makes this product different? As a result, marketing managers must identify important characteristics that successfully differentiate their product from others in the customer's mind. Then they must produce those elements in the product itself, balancing a number of factors including customer preferences, costs, and company resources. Exhibit 8.3 identifies product discriminators and gives an example.

Form

The most elemental method of differentiating a product is to change its **form**—size, shape, color, and other physical elements. Many products considered very similar in functionality can be differentiated by variations in packaging or product delivery. Among the reasons cited for the growth in milk consumption over the past several years has been new packaging that delivers the product in smaller, more portable plastic containers that preserve freshness so the milk tastes better longer and is easier to use in more situations (see Exhibit 8.4). Additionally, dairies have developed methods to extend shelf life, improving freshness and accessibility.

Features

When asked what makes a product different, many people will respond by talking about features. A **feature** is any product attribute or performance characteristic and is often added or subtracted from a product to differentiate it from competitors. However, while delivering consumer value is the primary driver in making product decisions, a company must balance the features customers want with what they will pay at a given quality level.[10]

Interestingly, based on their research, competitors often create products with very different feature configurations. Cell phone manufacturers, for example, are constantly assessing the feature mix across their product line. When comparing similar Samsung versus Nokia models, a number of feature differences will be easily identified. One of the great challenges for marketers is determining the feature mix that best satisfies the needs and wants of the target audience and at what price? No competitors ever arrive at the same feature mix, which means decisions about which features to include and exclude are critical to a product's success.

Performance Quality

Should a company always build the highest-quality product? Some people would say the answer is yes. However, the answer is more complex than that. Essentially, companies should build products to the performance quality level that their target audience is willing to pay for. Often

Bombardier builds a wide range of railcars and locomotives to meet transportation needs around the world. This train was designed for a transportation system in Nottingham, England.

EXHIBIT 8.3 | **Product Discriminators**

Form		With 54-nozzle spray heads, WaterTile Ambient Rain overhead showering panels provide luxurious water delivery.
Features		The wealth of improvements and refinements in a TX4 sets it apart from any other taxi. New features include a Euro IV compliant engine, greener, cleaner, and delivering big torque at low speed and an improved in-car entertainment system, with superior sound and MP3 compatibility.
Performance Quality		Oil companies produce several grades of gasoline to meet the demands of consumers.
Conformance Quality		Crest Whitestrips are a good low-priced teeth whitener. The system also comes with a standard 60-day money back guarantee, should you not care for the results.
Durability		Timberland has a reputation for building high quality, durable products like these boots that come with a commitment to customer satisfaction.

(continued)

EXHIBIT 8.3 | Product Discriminators [continued]

Reliability		Carrier promotes the fact that its air conditioners are reliable. In addition, it provides different quality levels with varying warranties.
Repairability		Many bicycle manufacturers highlight the easy repair of the bikes. A key point is that anyone can fix most of the problems that may occur.
Style		*Vogue* magazine is all about keeping people up to date with the latest styles and trends.

this means a company will build products at multiple performance levels to meet demand at various price points. Keep in mind that the key is to deliver value to the customer.

EXHIBIT 8.4 | Form Variations for T.G. Lee Milk Products

The market's perception of the company's performance quality is critical in defining its market space. Companies generally try to match product performance quality with the market's perception of the brand. Timex will not develop a $25,000 watch because the market would not expect, and may not accept, a watch with production quality at that level from Timex, although they do expect it from Rolex.[11] At the same time, companies need to be careful not to lower performance quality too dramatically in an effort to cut costs or reach new markets. Losing control of a quality image can do significant harm to a brand's image. For example, product safety remains a critical concern for consumers.

ETHICAL DIMENSION 8.1

That Strawberry Came from Where?

Americans like fruits and vegetables; unfortunately, it is difficult to grow enough produce in the United States to meet the demand. This is particularly true for food manufacturers such as Kellogg, General Mills, and Kraft, which rely on imported produce from around the world to meet the demand. In addition, large retailers like Walmart are looking to stock fresh fruits and vegetables 365 days a year instead of having only a limited availability of the fresh produce that happens to be in season.

A small but rapidly growing source of fresh produce for American consumers is China. While total exports are a fraction of the total U.S. produce market, growth has been exponential. For example, in 2000, Chinese exports of fresh garlic amounted to 1 million pounds or less than 1 percent of U.S. demand; however, in 2005 China exported 73 percent of U.S. market demand and 83 percent in 2007. Strawberries are another example, with Chinese exports increasing from 1.5 million pounds in 2000 to 33 million pounds in 2007. Overall, Chinese exports of fresh produce are more than doubling every year.

As a consumer it is great to enjoy a strawberry in January, especially since prices have not gone up dramatically despite the need to transport the produce long distances. Food experts, however, are becoming increasingly concerned about the quality of the produce coming out of China. The FDA recently reported that 107 food imports from China were detained in one month because the products were preserved with harmful chemicals and pesticides. This comes after the tainted pet food scandal in 2007 where pet food from China was laced with a harmful chemical that killed a number of cats and dogs as well as milk with the dangerous chemical melamine in 2008.

Another issue driving the import of food products from China is the growth of organic foods. Dean Foods, Kellogg, and Walmart are importing organic strawberries, soybeans, mushrooms, and broccoli from China, and the same concerns about product quality exist, particularly since China didn't institute any organic food standards until 2005.

China is becoming a major exporter of food products worldwide, producing nearly half of the world's vegetables and 16 percent of the world's fruits. In addition, the nation is expanding the amount of land dedicated to vegetable and fruit farming. Currently, however, the quality-control standards established in the United States and other parts of the world to ensure product safety are not enforced. At the same time, consumers benefit from easy access to low-priced fruits and vegetables, and companies benefit from having product available for sale year-round. Yet the question still remains, is the strawberry safe?[12]

Ethical Perspective

1. **American companies importing Chinese produce:** Should they stop importing fresh produce from China until product quality and safety standards match those in the United States? If consumers want fresh produce year-round, shouldn't companies seek out the lowest-cost provider?

2. **U.S. federal government:** Should it ban fresh produce from China until product quality and safety is assured? What responsibility does the government have in ensuring the quality and safety of Chinese produce?

3. **Consumers:** What role do consumers have in making sure the food products they consume are safe?

Products that fail to meet quality standards can lead to a loss of consumer confidence. Ethical Dimension 8.1 discusses a growing concern about products shipped from China.

Conformance Quality

An important issue for consumers is **conformance,** which is the product's ability to deliver on features and performance characteristics promised in marketing communications. The challenge for marketers and manufacturing is that every product must deliver on those promises. A product is said to have high conformance quality when a high percentage of the manufactured products fulfill the stated performance criteria.[13] If someone opened a Coke and there was no "fizz" it wouldn't be a Coke. The challenge for Coca-Cola and its bottlers is to ensure that every Coke has just the right carbonation when the consumer opens the can or bottle anywhere in the world.

Durability

Consumer research and purchase patterns affirm that people find **durability,** the projected lifetime of the product under specific operating conditions, an important discriminating product characteristic and are willing to pay a premium for products that can demonstrate greater durability.[14] KitchenAid appliances have a reputation for durability that has translated into a price premium.

Reliability

A similar discriminator references the dependability of a product. **Reliability** is the percentage of time the product works without failure or stoppage. Businesses and consumers consistently report this is an important discriminator in their purchase decision; however, a product can be too reliable. While it is possible to build computers that will last for years and cost a premium, most computer manufacturers do not build them because computer technology changes so quickly and product improvements happen so fast that people will not pay the premium for a computer that will last for many years.[15] They know that better, cheaper technology will be available before the computer actually malfunctions.

Repairability

Increasingly, consumers and businesses evaluate the **repairability,** ease of fixing a problem with the product, as part of the product evaluation process. As a result, companies have built better diagnostics into their products to help isolate, identify, and repair products without the need for the costly repairs of a professional service.[16] Luxury cars such as the Lexus SC 430 are available with tires that enable the driver to continue driving even after the tire has been damaged. At the same time and where appropriate, products are designed to "call in" to repair services online or on the phone. Cell phone manufacturers and service providers work together to build self-diagnostic phones that can be accessed in the field by service technicians. The technician can look at the phone's functionality and actually do minor software upgrades or repairs during a phone call.

YOUR FIRST COURSE JUST CAME TRICKLING DOWN THE ALPS.

THE NEW EVIAN PALACE BOTTLE.

evian

In creating the "Palace bottle" Evian is taking a bottle of water and adding an element of style.

Style

One of the most difficult discriminators to accurately assess and build into a product is the look and feel of the product, or **style.** It is easy for someone to say a particular product has style, but designing it into a product can be a challenge. More than any other discriminator, style offers the advantage of being difficult to copy. While many companies from Sony to Samsung have tried to copy the iPod, no one has created a product that combines the functionality and elegance of Apple's product. Apple has a history of creating stylish products.

The real challenge is that style can be difficult to create consistently. Consumer tastes change over time, and what is considered stylish can quickly lose its appeal. Companies invest in information systems that help them spot trends. Once a trend is identified, product development teams must be able to translate it into design elements that can be incorporated into the product.[17] In some industries this is critical; for example, clothing manufacturers anticipate future trends, then use efficient production processes to design, build, and distribute their clothes while a particular style is still popular.

Product Plan: Moving from One Product to Many Products

Our discussion thus far has focused on a single product; however, companies generally create a range of products. These products can be variations or extensions of one basic product or completely different products. Most people would consider Post-it Notes, 3M's iconic brand of self-adhesive notes, a single product but over 600 Post-it products are sold in more than 100 countries.[18] When you couple the extensive range of Post-it products with the thousands of products offered by 3M across more than 40 core product lines, it becomes apparent why management must understand how a product fits into the company's product strategy. Developing a plan sets strategy not only for a single product, but also for all the products in the company's catalog.

Product Line

A **product line** is group of products linked through usage, customer profile, price points, and distribution channels or needs satisfaction. Within a product line, strategies are developed for a single product, but also for all the products in the line. For example, 3M develops a strategy for each Post-it product, such as Post-it cards, that identifies possible product uses, different target markets, and marketing messages. At the same time, the company combines individual products for specific markets to create consumer-based solution catalogs. Students can find Post-it products targeted for them and teachers can find a separate listing of products.

Even with success in the office computer market, Dell Inc. wanted to expand its product line from the "garden variety" line of PCs and gain a foothold in the high-performance gaming PC market by releasing the XPS line of high-performance PCs. However, Dell found that the XPS line, branded with the Dell name, was so successful that it was eating into sales of Dell's recently acquired Alienware line of PCs. As a result, Dell decided to phase out the XPS product line to make way for the already well-established Alienware brand in the high-end gaming PC market.[19]

Companies must balance the number of items in a product line. Too many items and customers find it difficult to differentiate between individual products. In addition, cost inefficiencies involved in producing multiple products lower margins for the entire product line. Too few products and the company runs the risk of missing important market opportunities.

Product Mix

Combining all the products offered by a company is called the **product mix.** Small, start-up companies frequently have a relatively limited product mix but, as companies grow, their list of products grows as well. Developing strategies for the entire product mix is done at the highest levels of the organization.[20] Large companies, like 3M or GE, have widely disparate product lines that encompass hundreds of products and thousands of product items. For example, 3M's product mix consists of more than 55,000 products that range from Post-it Notes to communication technology systems and a host of industrial applications.

Product Decisions Affect Other Marketing Mix Elements

Decisions about the product affect other elements of the marketing mix. Let's look at how two key marketing mix elements, pricing and marketing communications, are influenced by product decisions.

Pricing

Pricing is one of the key marketing mix components and will be covered in detail in Chapter 10; however, several key issues related to product line pricing are appropriately covered here. Individual product pricing within the context of a broader product line requires a clear understanding of the price points for all the products in the line. Often multiple price points are targeted at specific markets with unique features following a "good, better, best" product line strategy. This strategy develops multiple product lines that include products with distinct features at each particular price point to attract multiple target markets. When new products are introduced, marketers carefully consider customer perceptions of the product's feature mix and price point to avoid customer confusion.

Technology companies, for many years, have faced the challenge of pricing new products that are less expensive but with more features than previous models. Dell and HP are sensitive to pricing new products because as new, more powerful, less-expensive products come into the product mix, demand often drops for existing products. Dell prices new computer models to minimize disrupting demand for its existing products while, at the same time, lowering prices of existing products to create greater separation between the new product and current products.

Marketing Communications

A key strategic decision for marketers is the degree to which marketing communications focuses on a single product item versus a product brand. Usually, companies do both, but the emphasis on one approach versus the other makes a big difference in the communications strategy. For example, 3M focuses much of its Post-it marketing communications on the Post-it product line, emphasizing the brand. Contrast that with Haagen-Dazs, which focuses on specific products (ice cream, sorbet, and yogurt) and specific product items within each product (chocolate, almond hazelnut swirl, pineapple coconut).

A second communications issue is the allocation of communications budget dollars across product items in a product line. Haagen-Dazs has more than 30 specific kinds of ice cream and dozens of other products across its entire product line. The company must make decisions about the allocation of budget dollars to each product then each specific product item. This raises several challenges for marketing managers. Do they allocate dollars based on the most popular flavors like chocolate and vanilla? Or do they focus on new items such as Mayan chocolate to build a competitive edge with products that are not offered by the competition? New products almost always have additional communication budgets to support the product's introduction. The assumption is that, once the product is established, it will be possible to cut back on the heavy expenditure of a new product communications campaign (see Exhibit 8.5).

EXHIBIT 8.5 **Haagen-Dazs Promotes One Product Item**

even more de lechable

Eager to surpass perfection, we took our original Latin-inspired blend of caramel and sweet cream and added a touch of the world's finest cinnamon. Surely your sweet tooth will dance the rumba with delight.
New Häagen-Dazs® Cinnamon Dulce de Leche Ice Cream

Haagen-Dazs has been successful building a product line that features old favorites but also frequently introduces new product flavors.

Courtesy of Dreyer's Grand Ice Cream, Inc.

THE LIFE OF THE PRODUCT: BUILDING THE PRODUCT EXPERIENCE

Companies create, launch, and transform products as market conditions change over time. This product evolution is referred to as the **product life cycle (PLC)** and defines the life of a product in four basic stages: introduction, growth, maturity, and decline (see Exhibit 8.6).[21]

The PLC generally refers to a product category (touring bicycles) rather than a product item (Giant Sedona bicycles) although companies often track their own product items against an industry PLC. The PLC is a useful tool because it: (1) provides a strategic framework for market analysis, (2) tracks historical trends, and (3) identifies future market conditions. Giant Bicycles, for example, can evaluate the current touring bike market and then consider growth opportunities for the Sedona brand based on that product's position in the PLC.

Product Life Cycle Sales Revenue and Profitability

Notice there are two lines on the PLC graph. The top line charts the industry sales revenue for the product over time. The sales revenue line increases dramatically in introduction and growth stages as the product moves through the consumer adoption process. At some point, sales begin to decline. However, a sales decline does not necessarily mean the death of the product. Companies may create new products or market conditions may change, which can reinvigorate the product and start a new growth phase. Bottled water was long considered a product in decline until Evian, Dasani, Zephyrhills, and others developed new packaging, added new flavors, and emphasized the healthy aspects of water. Now the product category is experiencing a period of significant growth around the world.

The second line on the PLC graph is the total profits from the companies that compete in that industry. When the product is introduced, the category pioneer, the company introducing the product, has incurred product development costs.

EXHIBIT 8.6	The Product Life Cycle

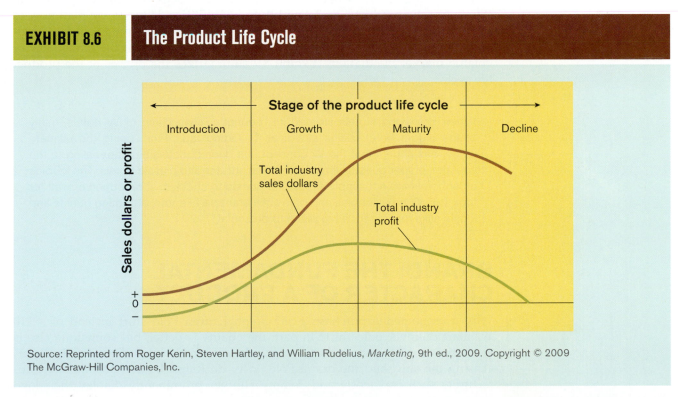

Source: Reprinted from Roger Kerin, Steven Hartley, and William Rudelius, *Marketing*, 9th ed., 2009. Copyright © 2009 The McGraw-Hill Companies, Inc.

At the same time, new companies entering the market also sustain product development and initial marketing costs associated with the product launch. As a result, the industry starts the PLC "in the red" (no profits). As the product category grows, successful companies recoup their initial costs and begin to realize a return on their investments.

Product Life Cycle Timeline

The speed at which products within a category move through the PLC is not consistent, and there is a great deal of variability across product categories. In some cases, a product moves through an entire cycle in a period of months and is replaced with the next product design. **Fads** come and go quickly, often reaching only a limited number of individuals but creating a lot of buzz in the marketplace.[22] Often, women's fashion is seasonal with a product line being introduced in the spring, moving through its growth cycle in the summer and fall, then finally into decline by winter. The cycle takes one selling season, in this case, one year. With other products such as men's suits, it may take decades from introduction to decline. Men's classic two-piece suits experience incremental changes every season, but the same basic design has been around for many years. The functionality of the product has made it an enduring style for men.

Product Life Cycle Caveats

It is important to note several caveats about the product life cycle. The PLC is a helpful conceptual tool that works best when viewed as a framework for studying a product category. It can be difficult to know with certainty what stage a product is in, particularly at transition points in the PLC. Rather, the PLC enables marketing managers to assess historical trends in the category and track how the product has behaved over time. Naturally, there may be different interpretations of the same data as marketing managers in one company look at the numbers and arrive at one conclusion while managers in another company arrive at a different conclusion.

The PLC works best when marketing managers focus on historical precedent. Where has the product been? And future possibilities. How do we plan now to be successful in the next stage? By using the PLC as a planning tool for developing new products, it is possible to avoid getting caught in the immediacy of volatile market fluctuations. Exhibit 8.7 summarizes the phases of the product life cycle.

When Starwood Hotels created its "boutique"-style chain of W hotels, many of the bigger hotel chains saw it as "a fading fad." Time, being the ultimate judge, has shown that the W concept has been successful in appealing to the younger, hipper guests who are now less attracted to classic hotels. The lobbies at W hotels are not simply a place for guests to check in at reception or wait for their taxi. W hotel lobbies and bars are vibrant party spots, attracting guests and locals alike looking for a hip place to be social.[23]

BRAND: THE FUNDAMENTAL CHARACTER OF A PRODUCT

Why does someone purchase a $65 Ralph Lauren Polo shirt instead of a $10 Walmart pullover polo shirt? In part, the quality is better, but something else is also driving the purchase—a complex relationship between the individual purchasing the shirt and the brand Polo. Why do Ralph Lauren and other manufacturers such as Lacoste and Tommy Hilfiger prominently display their logo

EXHIBIT 8.7 | Product Life Cycle

	Introduction Phase	Growth Phase	Maturity Phase	Decline Stage
Objective	Build market awareness for the product leading to trial purchase.	Differentiate product from those of new competitors, promoting rapid expansion.	Transition product from high growth to sales stability.	Determine the future of the product.
Profitability	Sales are low, typically high failure rate.	Sales grow at increasing rate.	Sales continue to increase but at a decreasing rate.	Long-run drop in sales.
	High marketing and product costs.	Profits become healthier as operations are streamlined.	Costs minimization has reached full extent.	Profit margins dramatically reduced.

Market Conditions

	Introduction Phase	Growth Phase	Maturity Phase	Decline Stage
Market Segment	Nonexistent.	New market segment now established.	Market is approaching saturation.	Changing consumer tastes and substitute products eat away at market segment.
Targeted Consumers	Innovators and Early Adopters	Early Adopters to Majority Adopters	Majority Adopters	Laggards
Competitive Environment	Little competition.	Many competitors enter market.	Marginal competitors dropping out.	Falling demand forces many out of market.
Competitor Reaction	Market followers will release product similar to that of the pioneer.	Large companies may acquire small pioneering firms.	Typified by models of products with an emphasis on style over function.	Firms that remain focus on specialty products.

Strategies

	Introduction Phase	Growth Phase	Maturity Phase	Decline Stage
Product	High-quality, innovative design providing new benefit to consumers.	More features and better design, learning from issues from first generation.	Product lines are widened or extended.	Consider product expenses in terms of return on investment.
	Features well-received and understood by target consumers.	Diversification of product and release of complementary products/services.	Work to further differentiate product from those of competitors.	Decide whether to invest further in product or allocate funding to new project(s).

(continued)

EXHIBIT 8.7   **Product Life Cycle [continued]**

	Introduction Phase	Growth Phase	Maturity Phase	Decline Stage
Price	Market penetration: Attractive price point to gain market share and discourage competitors.	New and improved models sold at high price points.	Target high-end market with differentiated product and higher price point.	Offer product at low price point to try to stimulate any remaining demand.
	Market skimming: High initial price point targeting less price-sensitive consumers to recoup R&D costs before competitors enter market.	Existing models or earlier generations move down in price.	Established competition makes price pressures more pronounced, forcing lower price strategy if product not well-differentiated.	Significant price pressures from both competitors and more price-sensitive consumers.
Marketing Communications	Inform and educate target audience about the product's features and benefits.	Link the brand with key product features and highlight differentiation between competitors.	Challenge of deciding between short-term sales promotions or investing more in the brand.	Cost of continued investment in marketing communications not justified by market conditions.
	Promotion focused on product awareness and to stimulate primary demand.	Promotion emphasizes brand advertising and comparative ads.		
Distribution	Wide distribution network with limited product Availability: Create anticipation by promoting excitement and sense of scarcity.	Broaden distribution networks to keep up with expanding market demand.	Product has reached its maximum distribution.	Reduced distribution channels.
	Limit distribution but increase product availability: Release to limited number of target markets with high availability. Intensive personal selling to retailers and wholesalers.	Maintain high levels of product quality and boost customer service efforts to keep up with product.	Channel members identify weak products and begin dropping out if necessary.	Channel members cease to support the product.

on merchandise? Because people who buy those products want others to know who manufactured the shirt, jacket, or pants. Equally important, the manufacturers want everyone to see the logo. Both customers and manufacturers realize the importance of the brand.

If asked, you could probably identify the logo for Ralph Lauren Polo but how would you define the Polo brand?[24] A **brand,** as defined by the American Marketing Association, is "a name, term, sign, symbol, or design, or a combination of them, intended to identify the goods or services of one seller or groups of sellers and to differentiate them from those of competitors." While the "Polo Pony" is a recognizable symbol of Polo products, customers and noncustomers assign a much deeper meaning to the brand. Let's focus on branding and critical elements in the branding process to learn more about this essential product building block. First we will discuss the many roles of a brand, including those assigned by customer, company, and competition as well as potential problems for a brand. Next, we'll examine an important concept—brand equity—which is used to frame the relationship of the brand to the customer. In addition, we examine four branding strategies. Finally, two other key elements of a customers' overall perception of a brand are examined: packaging and labeling as well as warranties and service agreements.

The importance of branding is not limited to consumer products. Business-to-business customers also consider brands when making purchase decisions. Brands are important for customers and companies, which is why marketing managers are vitally interested in learning as much as possible about their customers' brand perceptions then developing effective branding strategies.

Brands Play Many Roles

Brands take on different roles for customers, manufacturers, even competitors. No other single product element conveys more information about the company. **Brand strategy** is an integral part of the product development process because companies know that successful new products result from a well-conceived branding strategy. At the same time, established products are defined, in large measure, by their brand, and companies work very hard to protect this critical asset. Let's examine brand roles.

Customer Brand Roles

Whether the customer is a consumer or another business, brands have three primary roles. First, the brand conveys information about the product. Without any additional data, customers construct expectations about quality, service, even features based on the brand. Years after ending the marketing communications campaign, many customers see the FedEx logo and still think, "Absolutely, positively, overnight." The logo itself creates an expectation of service though FedEx now offers many delivery options and products.

Scent-Air Technology is one of the leading companies in the world that design custom fragrances to help consumers connect with a brand. For example, Lexus dealers pump a green tea and lemongrass aroma into showrooms, while Mandalay Bay uses a ventilation system to distribute a subtle coconut spice scent that complements the resort and casino's tropical theme. General Dynamics even incorporates scents into its military simulators and training environments to add an extra level of realism.[25]

Brands also educate the customer about the product. People assign meaning to their product experiences by brand and, over time, make judgments about which brands are best at meeting their needs and which are not. As a result, product evaluations and purchase decisions become less formidable as the customer relies on the cumulative brand experience to simplify the purchase process.[26] The thought process works something like this, "I have had great product experiences with Brand X in the past. I will purchase Brand X again making this purchase decision easier and faster." In essence the customer's "brand education" helps make the purchase decision with less effort. For many, home repair is daunting so hardware retailers such as Lowe's provide as much information as possible to reduce anxiety about the process. Indeed, Lowe's has worked hard to develop a reputation for making the home repair process easy for everyone.

A third brand role is to help reassure the customer in the purchase decision.[27] For many years there was a phrase in IT, "No one ever got fired for buying IBM." IBM's reputation and market dominance in the large computer and network server market meant that even if the product did not meet performance expectations, the customer felt more secure and less anxious about choosing IBM equipment. Older, established brands like Lysol provide a sense of security and reduce concerns about product quality.

Company Brand Roles

Brands also perform important roles for the brand's sponsor (manufacturer, distributor, or retailer). They offer legal protection for the product through a trademark. By protecting the brand, the company is able to defend essential product elements such as its features, patentable ideas in manufacturing or product design, and packaging.[28] A second critical role is that brands offer an effective and efficient methodology for categorizing products.[29] Sony has thousands of products across many product categories and branding helps keep track of those products.

Competitor Brand Roles

Market-leading brands provide competitors with a benchmark against which to compete. In industries with strong market-leading brands, competitors design and build products targeted specifically at the market leader. In these situations, the competitor leverages its product strength against the market-leading brand's perceived weakness. For years, pleasure motorboat manufacturers would frame their sales message with, "we are just as good as Sea Ray (the market leader) but less expensive." Sea Ray enjoyed a price premium in the market and competitors such as Regal, Chaparral, Rinker, and others would target their price points and feature mix against Sea Ray boats.

The Boundaries of Branding

While branding can have a strong effect on the product experience, it is not all-powerful. A good branding strategy will not overcome a poorly designed product that fails to deliver on the value proposition.[30] Too frequently companies put a good brand on a bad product, which often leads to erosion of the brand's value.

A brand must also be protected. Counterfeit products or illegal activities conducted under the name of another company's brand can do significant damage to the brand.[31] This is why companies aggressively protect their brands around the world. Read Ethical Dimension 8.2 to find out more about the challenge Diageo, a leading spirits manufacturer, confronts in using digital marketing strategies while it protects the company's brands by maintaining ethical guidelines on product usage and access to confidential company data.

Finally, there must be identifiable and meaningful differences among products. If all products are perceived to be equal then it is more difficult to create a **brand identity,** which is a summary of unique qualities attributed to the brand.[32] Commodities are difficult to brand because customers often fail to perceive a difference among products. Major oil companies such as Exxon, Shell, and BP want to differentiate their gasoline from competitors but find it difficult because most people do not perceive a difference.

Baileys' and the Digital Bar

While you may not be familiar with the company Diageo, you are almost certainly familiar with its brands, which hold dominant positions in their respective markets—Smirnoff (the No. 1 vodka in the world), Johnnie Walker (the No. 1 Scotch whisky in the world), Guinness (the No. 1 stout in the world), Captain Morgan (the No. 2 rum), Bailey's (the top liqueur), Jose Cuervo (the No. 1 tequila in the world), and Tanqueray (the No. 1 imported gin in the United States). The company's impressive list of brands is sold in more than 180 countries and dominates the premium spirit market with sales in excess of $15 billion.

Diageo, like many consumer product companies, is moving dramatically into digital marketing as it targets younger customers (Generations X and Y). However, unlike Procter & Gamble or Lever Brothers, Diageo and other alcohol companies must adhere to ethical standards on product usage. More specifically, the company is responsible for making sure it targets young people of legal drinking age. This creates a particular challenge in digital marketing as it is difficult, if not impossible, to know with certainty who is receiving the message. For example, a visit to a Diageo brand Web site will ask for the individual's birthday and location. If the visitor is from the United States, the individual must be over 21 to access the site; however, it is possible for someone to type in any date.

In an effort to more effectively target its younger customers, Diageo opened a virtual bar in Second Life virtual world. The company's marketing research suggests that it is one of the methods for reaching what it calls "digital natives," which are people who are most comfortable online and receive most of their information over the Internet. The company believes that more traditional marketing communications such as TV or print will not work with this group. However, the virtual bar has raised some significant concerns about corporate governance and reputation. Diageo is particularly concerned about underage avatars coming into the bar and uses employees to act as bouncers checking virtual identification.

Managers at Diageo are watching the virtual bar very carefully. While they acknowledge that reaching out to young people requires embracing new digital technologies, they are concerned about underage access to adult content and violating the ethical codes of conduct.[33]

Ethical Perspective

1. **Diageo:** The company faces a challenge—to find effective digital technologies that connect with younger customers while maintaining ethical standards regarding underage drinking. How should the company deal with this challenge? If you were CEO at Diageo would you sponsor a virtual bar in Second Life? Why or why not?

2. **Customers:** Do younger customers have a responsibility to voluntarily not participate in adult activities in virtual communities like Second Life?

3. **Government:** Given the growth of virtual communities, should the government create stricter guidelines for underage access to adult content?

BRAND EQUITY—OWNING A BRAND

Equity is about ownership and value. Equity is the difference between the price of an asset and the liability. The larger the difference between the asset and the liability, the more equity.

In a very real sense the same is true of brand equity. Every brand has positives—for example, Mercedes-Benz has a reputation for high-quality cars—and negatives—Mercedes also has a reputation for being expensive. The greater the perceived difference between the positives and negatives, the more a customer will develop equity in the brand. When customers take "ownership" of a brand, they make an "investment" that often extends beyond a financial obligation and includes emotional and psychological attachment. Then the company can realize a number of benefits, which we discuss in the next section; however, if the company does a poor job of managing the brand, such as lowering the product quality, those same customers may become negative. As a marketing manager, you want to learn about the brand equity of your products to better understand the relationship of your product to target markets and create more effective marketing strategies.[34]

Defining Brand Equity

Brand equity can be defined as "a set of assets (and liabilities) linked to a brand's name and symbol that adds to (or subtracts from) the value provided by a product or service to a firm or that firm's customers." This definition, developed by David Aaker, can be broken into five dimensions:[35]

- **Brand awareness:** The most basic form of brand equity is simply being aware of the brand. Awareness is the foundation of all other brand relationships. It signals a familiarity and *potential* commitment to the brand.

- **Brand loyalty:** This is the strongest form of brand equity and reflects a commitment to repeat purchases. Loyal customers are reassured by the brand and are often ambassadors to new customers. Loyal customers enable a company to reduce marketing costs, leverage trade relationships, and speak to competitive threats with greater success.

- **Perceived quality:** Brands convey a perception of quality that is either positive or negative. Companies use a positive perceived quality to differentiate the product and create higher price points. Rolex watches have been able to sustain a price premium long into their life cycle because of the perceived quality in design and performance of the product.

- **Brand association:** Customers develop a number of emotional, psychological, and performance associations with a brand. In many cases, these associations become a primary purchase driver, particularly with brand loyal users. Dell has a reputation as a mass-market computer company with reasonably good-quality products but poor customer service. As a result, competitors, such as Hewlett-Packard, have been able to create market opportunities by associating their brand with higher levels of product support and customer service.

- **Brand assets:** Brands possess other assets such as trademarks and patents that represent a significant competitive advantage. Google is very protective of its search algorithm intellectual property, which, in the view of the company, gives the company a significant advantage over other search engines.

Let's consider the implications of these dimensions for marketing managers. First, moving customers from brand awareness to loyalty requires a thorough understanding of the target market and a successful marketing strategy. This is accomplished by developing a strong value offering and then communicating that to the target market. This is an essential element of the marketing manager's job.[36] Second, as we discussed in Chapters 5 and 6, customers develop perceptions about a product and associate it with attitudes and even emotion that are encompassed in a product's brand equity. By learning how customers view competitors' as well as their own brand, managers seek to affect people's perceptions and attitudes about their product.[37] Finally, managers protect their brands because they represent a vital asset for the company. They are vigilant about how they are portrayed in the marketplace, particularly by competitors.

Both the customers and the company have a stake in the brand's success. People do not want to purchase a brand if there is a question about quality, performance, or some other dimension of the product experience. They seek to maximize the benefits of the purchase and minimize the disadvantages. At the same time, companies understand every brand has liabilities that must be overcome to enhance the customer's perceived equity in the product. As a result, marketing managers constantly battle to

Coca-Cola has created one of the most powerful global brands and its logo, displayed on a Coke truck in India, is recognized around the world.

EXHIBIT 8.8 | **The Most Valuable Brands in the World**

2009 Rank	2008 Rank	Name	Country	2008 Value ($ mil)	2009 Value ($ mil)	Change in Value (%)
1	1	Coca-Cola	U.S.	66,667	68,734	3%
2	2	IBM	U.S.	59,031	60,211	2
3	3	Microsoft	U.S.	59,007	56,647	−4
4	4	GE	U.S.	53,086	47,777	−10
5	5	Nokia	Finland	35,942	34,864	−3
6	8	McDonald's	U.S.	31,049	32,275	4
7	10	Google	U.S.	25,590	31,980	25
8	6	Toyota	Japan	34,050	31,330	−8
9	7	Intel	U.S.	31,261	30,636	−2
10	9	Disney	U.S.	29,251	28,447	−3

Source: *BusinessWeek*, September 28, 2009, p. 50.

increase brand equity or the customer's perception that the product's positive elements are greater than the negative elements. Brands do have real value and represent a significant company asset.[38] Exhibit 8.8 lists the most valuable brands in the world as measured by *BusinessWeek.* Note the value of these brands runs into the billions of dollars and changes are based on a number of things including changes in company strategy, brand success or failure, competitive pressures, and consumer acceptance.

Toyota Motor Corp. has created three overall brands of automobiles—each targeted at gaining the brand loyalty of specific consumer groups. The company goes to great lengths to ensure that the three main auto brands are separate, distinct, and loosely associated with each other in the minds of consumers. Lexus caters to the higher-end luxury car market, Scion appeals to a younger market hungry for freedom of expression, while the namesake brand promises value, quality, and dependability for any motorist. However, with the booming success of the Prius hybrid model, Toyota discovered that one of its car models had garnered a higher level of overall brand equity than one of the actual main brands, Scion.[39]

Benefits of Brand Equity

Building brand equity takes time and money. Given the necessary commitment of resources required to build brand equity, it is reasonable to question whether it is worth the investment. High brand equity delivers a number of benefits to the customers and manufacturers, retailers, and distributors or brand sponsors who control the brand. Three benefits are perceived quality, brand connections, and brand loyalty. Exhibit 8.9 considers each of these benefits from two perspectives, the customer and the company managing the brand or the brand sponsor, and the strategy. Many of these benefits are difficult to quantify but dramatically affect the success or failure of the brand.

EXHIBIT 8.9 **Benefits of Brand Equity**

Benefit	Customers	Brand Sponsor	Strategy Link
Perceived Quality	Gives customers a reason to buy. Infer level of quality that facilitates purchase decision.	Enables extension of product range. Price premium opportunity. Excellent differentiator.	Builds quality into entire customer experience. Quality can create price premium. Constantly validates the value proposition for the customer.
Brand Connections	Customers more likely to connect with a brand they know and understand. Generates a positive attitude toward the product.	Creates additional barrier to entry for competitors. Customer familiarity with the brand can be more important than familiarity with the product itself.	Opportunity to extend the brand to new products. Reinforces market presence.
Brand Loyalty	Expedites consumer purchase decision process. Prevents consumers from exploring other brand options.	Reduces long-term marketing costs. Gives sponsors additional channel leverage. Brand-loyal customers tell others about their experiences. Increases customers' willingness to forgive brand for negative experiences.	Greater flexibility with marketing budgets. Loyal customers become advocates for the brand and promote it through many means of communication (i.e., blogs, online communities, word of mouth).

BRANDING DECISIONS

Branding is a complex concept that brings together all the elements of a product into a single, focused customer idea. As a result, the branding decision is among the most important in marketing. Four basic strategic decisions in defining a brand are (1) stand-alone or family branding, (2) national or store branding, (3) licensing, and (4) co-branding.

Stand-Alone or Family Branding

Does the brand stand alone or exist as part of a brand family? Each choice has advantages and disadvantages. **Stand-alone brands** separate the company from the brand, which insulates the company if there is a problem with the brand. But stand-alone brands are expensive to create and maintain as there is little or no synergy between company brands. **Family branding** advantages and disadvantages are just the opposite. There is synergy among members of a brand family, but a negative event with one product often leads to negative publicity for the entire brand family.[40]

Unilever, a worldwide leader in consumer products, follows a stand-alone brand strategy in its personal care division with nine brands that operate independently of each other (AXE, Dove, Lifebuoy, Lux, Ponds, Rexona, Sunsilk, Signal, and Vaseline). Heinz, on the other hand, uses a family branding strategy with all products introduced under the Heinz brand (ketchup and other condiments).

Companies also use branding to extend a line. For example, White Wave Foods, manufacturer of International Delight coffee creamers, frequently adds new flavors to the line. Each new product extends the line of International Delight creamers. Increasingly, as companies seek new, creative ways to connect with customers, they are including them in the brand building process.[41] Also, a company can use its brand to expand into new product categories, known as a **category extension.**[42] Dell used its brand to expand into new product categories such as printers.

> There is undoubtedly a great deal of brand loyalty around Harley-Davidson motorcycles, which the bike manufacturer has not been afraid to capitalize on with accessories and merchandising. However, when the Harley-Davidson Cake Decorating Kit was released, even some of the company's most devout followers questioned whether the new brand extension was going too far.[43]

Yet another option is combining family brands with a more distinct individual product brand. Many companies follow a variation of this strategy. American Express recently introduced the One card that incorporates the American Express brand as well as its own stand-alone brand One. Sony, for years, has followed a strategy of linking individual brands (Bean, Discman, Trinitron) with the corporate logo and brand.

National or Store Branding

Another decision is whether the product should adopt a national or store brand strategy. Large consumer products companies such as Procter & Gamble create **national brands** that are sold around the country under the same brand. Gillette Fusion, Crest toothpaste, and many others are national brands that can be found anywhere. National brands enable manufacturers to leverage marketing resources by creating efficiencies in marketing communications, and distribution.[44] In addition, national brands generally have a higher perceived quality and, as a result, enjoy a price premium. However, developing a national brand is costly and lower-priced store brands are strong competitors in many product categories.[45]

An alternative to creating a national brand is a **store brand.** Many large retailers create a store brand to market their own products. For example, Walmart has a number of store brands such as Equate, which includes a broad range of personal care product categories (skin care, hair care, toothpaste, and others), and Ol' Roy dog food. Often contracting with the large manufacturers such as Procter & Gamble, retailers are able to compete directly with national brands by offering lower prices.

Licensing

Companies can also choose to extend their brand by **licensing**—offering other manufacturers the right to use the brand in exchange for a set fee or percentage of sales. There is very little risk to the brand sponsor, and licensing can generate incremental revenue. In addition, it can extend the brand and build more brand associations among new users creating additional benefits.[46] The brand sponsor does need to monitor the licensees to assure product quality and proper use of the brand. Finally, license partners should fit the company's overall marketing strategy for the brand.[47] Among the best followers of the license strategy are movies, which license their brand (the movie) to a wide range of companies (restaurants, toy manufacturers, and others). The movie *Star Trek* grossed more than

$300 million in worldwide box office sales within the first month of its release; but more importantly, the film successfully reinvigorated the Star Trek Franchise. With sequels in the works and a renewed public interest in the adventures of the starship Enterprise's clew, the creators of the movie will be able to add several hundred millions of dollars in revenue through agreements with a long list of licensees.

Co-Branding

Frequently a company discovers advantages to linking its products with other products inside the company or externally with products from other companies, called **co-branding.** Co-branding joins two or more well-known brands in a common product or takes two brands and markets them in partnership. One advantage of co-branding is the opportunity to leverage the strengths of each brand to increase sales beyond what they could do independently. In addition, it may open each product up to new markets as well as lower costs by sharing marketing communications expenses.[48]

There are also several potential disadvantages. First, companies that co-brand externally give up some measure of control over their brand; by joining brands each company sacrifices some control to market the co-branded product. If one of the brands encounters a problem, for example a quality issue, it can have a negative effect on the co-branded product. Another potential disadvantage is overexposure; a successful product does not want too many co-branded relationships because it can dilute the brand's image.[49]

Successful co-branding relationships work best when both brands come together as equals that make sense in the marketplace. Costco and American Express joined together to offer a Costco-American Express card that allows users to get rebates on their purchases at Costco while expanding the reach of American Express to Costco members. Critical decisions in the process revolve around resource commitments, which company is spending what, and what other resources are asked of each company. In addition, it is important for each company in the relationship to understand the performance objectives and expected benefits of each partner.

PACKAGING AND LABELING: ESSENTIAL BRAND ELEMENTS

The product package and label must perform several critical roles in support of the brand. As a result, marketers, product developers, and package design specialists are involved in package design early in product development. Then, as product updates occur, the package is reconfigured to accommodate product modifications.

Package Objectives

Protect

Above all, the package must protect the product. The challenge is defining how much protection is necessary and cost-effective. In some cases, as in a can of Coke, the package is a significant component of the product's overall cost so there is concern about any increases in package cost. However, the can of Coke must be strong enough to hold the carbonated beverage under variations in temperature and other use conditions. Additionally, Coca-Cola must consider a variety of package materials (plastic, metal), sizes, and shapes (regular can, Coke's classic "contour" design), and it must design each to operate more or less the same under a variety of situations. Protecting customers from unauthorized access to the product is also part of package design.

When David Butler was hired by Coca-Cola in 2005, he was charged with determining the future of the beverage giant's packaging design strategy. After looking at the company's recent track record of overexposing its logo in a mix of graphical elements and seasonal and/or sponsorship imagery, Butler concluded the Coca-Cola brand had been lost in the mix. He decided that the most effective way to implement a new packaging design strategy for Coke was to avoid the word *design* whenever possible and focus on the company's well-established core brand elements.[50]

Communicate

Packages communicate a great deal of information about the product. Some of that information is designed as marketing communications. At the point of sale, the package is the last marketing communication the customer will see before the purchase. Consequently, packaging plays a critical role in the company's overall marketing communications strategy, particularly for consumer products. Coke's distinctive contour bottle design is so unique the package can be identified in the dark. Additionally, packaging offers the brand sponsor the opportunity to present the trademark, logo, and other relevant information in an appealing and persuasive manner. As the customer stands in front of a shelf full of products in a store, the marketer wants the brand to be clearly visible to the buyer. This means packaging must be designed to easily communicate critical brand messages quickly through color or design cues.[51] The familiar Coke swirl logo is among the most recognized brand symbols in the world and is easily identified on a store shelf or in a vending machine.

Unique package design can create a distinctive competitive advantage. Coke's contour bottle and L'eggs' egg-shape package for hosiery are important components of the overall brand image for those products. Their distinctive package design increases brand awareness at the point of sale where the customer makes the final purchase decision. Exhibit 8.10 shows innovative examples of packaging.

Promote Usage

Package design also encourages product use. It does this in several ways. First, packages frequently show the product being used by a happy customer (Kashi Good Friends shows a couple enjoying a box of cereal), which supports the overall marketing message. This connects the product to the target customer. Second, in many cases, packages visually demonstrate a product. Avery Paper shows each product clearly on the box; for example, a box of clear white mailing labels shows the label and how it can be used. Third, marketers and package designers make extensive use of blister packs (products encased in clear plastic) and other package designs to visibly present and protect the product. When buying a SanDisk Cruzer flash drive it is much easier to visualize using it when you can see the product and have key features highlighted on the package.

Effective Packaging

Effective packaging accomplishes the objectives noted above in a persuasive, interesting, and visually appealing manner consistent with the target market's expectations. Materials, shape, colors, graphics, indeed all the design elements are used to create an aesthetically appealing package for the customer.

Aesthetics

Color plays a significant role in package design, indeed, in the entire branding strategy.[52] It is no accident that Coke's packaging has red as the dominant color

EXHIBIT 8.10 **Innovative Package Designs**

Chewy Chips Ahoy bag
Goal: Improve freshness and convenience
Backstory: After months of in-home research, Kraft discovered that its customers often transferred Chips Ahoy cookies to jars for easy access and to avoid staleness. The company solved both problems by creating a patented resealable opening on the top of the bag.
Bottom line: Since launching in July 2005, sales have doubled from the older packaging.

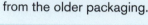

Crest Vivid White toothpaste package
Goal: Stand out on store shelves
Backstory: When Procter & Gamble's Crest set out to develop a premium whitening product in 2003, designers avoided creating yet another horizontal, graphics-heavy toothpaste box. Instead, they turned to the beauty aisle for inspiration. "We drew upon the vertical packaging and the deep metallic blue used to convey 'premium,'" says design manager Greg Zimmer.
Bottom line: Crest toothpaste sales have risen while competitor Colgate's sales have fallen, according to IRI.

Domino Sugar four-pound canister
Goal: Create a more user-friendly package
Backstory: To boost flat sales, Domino replaced the ubiquitous paper packaging for sugar. The easy-to-store plastic canister enables the Yonkers, New York, company to charge a premium for a package that actually contains less sugar.
Bottom line: The canister has become one of Domino's best-selling retail items.

(red connotes active and energetic) while Pepsi uses blue (fresh and relaxed). The colors reflect the brand and are carried through in the package design. Exhibit 8.11 relates the aesthetics of color to package design.

A visually appealing package, however, is not enough. It must be directed at the target audience to be successful. In most retail environments, a package has very little time to connect with the customer at the point of purchase. As a result, designs that are appropriate, interesting, and persuasive to the target market are critical.

Harmonizes with All Marketing Mix Elements

A successful product package coordinates with all other marketing mix elements and is an extension of the product's marketing strategy. At the point of purchase, the package reinforces marketing communications by connecting advertising images (logo, pictures on the package) to the customer. As a result, package designers frequently work closely with advertising and other marketing communications specialists to orchestrate an integrated message and look throughout the marketing communications process. Canon digital cameras are packaged in a small box dominated by a picture of the camera. The boxes stand alone as a promotional tool that includes the logo, camera model number, and picture. In addition, the package design and logo are coordinated with other collateral marketing literature as well as the Web site.

Labeling

The package label is an important and valuable location. Often there is not enough space to accommodate all the information relevant parties would like to include on the label. Consider, for example, that government agencies require certain information on almost every label while company attorneys want disclaimers to limit product liability. Also, marketing managers want promotional messages and brand information, while product managers would like product use instructions.

Legal Requirements

Labels must meet federal, state, even local rules and regulations. The Food and Drug Administration (FDA) requires all processed-food companies to provide detailed nutritional information clearly identifying calories, fats, carbohydrates, and other information. Other products must have warnings of a certain size that are easily read and understood by the customer.[53] Hazardous materials such as cleaning products, pesticides, and many other items require 14 different pieces of information be included on the label. It is easy to understand why space on the label is at such a premium.

EXHIBIT 8.11 **The Meaning of Color in Package Design**

Color plays an important role in package design. Each color conveys a different mood.

Source: Portions reproduced from Capital Books, *Colors for Your Every Mood*, with the permission of author and publisher, October 2009.

Consumer advocacy groups and government agencies evaluate labels to identify misleading or mislabeled products and there is a long history of legal prosecution for inappropriate, unethical, even illegal product labeling. In 1914, the federal government, through the Federal Trade Commission, first ruled misleading or blatantly phony labels were illegal and represented unfair competition. Since then, additional legislation has been passed by the federal government such as the Fair Packaging and Labeling Act (1967). States have also passed legislation, which, in most cases, supports federal legislation but also extends specific rules and policies (for example, the Michigan Food Label Law of 2000).

Consumer Requirements

Consumers want to use products out of the box, and package labeling is the most convenient place for initial use instructions. Additionally, product precautions, simple assembly information, and appropriate age for product use may also be

EXHIBIT 8.12   **Bounce Fabric Softener Packaging**

included on the package. Essentially, any information the consumer needs to make a product choice, particularly at the point of purchase, needs to be on the package.

Marketing Requirements

Since package labeling represents the last marketing opportunity before the purchase decision, as much label space as possible is allocated to marketing communications. Brand, logo, product image, and other relevant marketing messages take up the dominant space on the label. On a box of Procter & Gamble's Bounce fabric softener sheets, the brand name "Bounce" is approximately 50 percent of the space on the front panel and the rest of the space is a bright color (orange) with clean fresh images of a sun rising and a green field. P&G uses the entire front panel of the box to support the marketing efforts of the brand (see Exhibit 8.12).

WARRANTIES AND SERVICE AGREEMENTS: BUILDING CUSTOMER CONFIDENCE

Part of the customer's overall perception of a brand is the seller's commitment to the product. This commitment is most clearly articulated in the product's warranties and service agreements.[54] As part of the purchase contract with the customer, manufacturers are required by law to state the reasonable expectations for product performance. If the product does not meet those reasonable performance expectations, the customer has the legal right to return the product to the appropriate location for repair, replacement, or refund.

The two kinds of warranties are general and specific. **General warranties** make broad promises about product performance and customer satisfaction. These warranties are generally open to customers returning the product for a broad range of reasons beyond specific product performance problems. Many companies have adopted lenient policies that allow a product return without even asking the customer for a reason. Others require a reason, although there is often a great deal of latitude in what is an acceptable justification. **Specific warranties,** on the other hand, offer explicit product performance promises related to components of the product. Automobile warranties are specific warranties covering various components of the product with different warranties. The warranty for tires is by the tire manufacturer while warranties for the power train (engine, drive system) are generally different from the rest of the automobile.

Warranties Help Define the Brand

The manufacturer's promise of performance helps define the brand for the customer. Victorinox, maker of the famous Swiss Army knife, states its warranty as follows: "Swiss Army Brands, Inc., warrants its Victorinox Original Swiss Army Knives to be free from defects in material and workmanship for the entire life of the knife." Swiss Army Knives have the reputation of being among the best knives in the world, and the company's warranty supports that perception. A company willing to stand behind its product for life provides a lot of reassurance to the customer. In addition, there is an implied quality perception about a product warranted for life.

Cost versus Benefit

Honoring a warranty incurs costs. At one level, the company must be competitive and offer warranties consistent with the industry. However, companies constantly evaluate their warranties (length of time, return/replacement/refund policies, nature of product performance) to consider whether the benefits of the warranty exceed the costs.[55] This is particularly true when companies offer warranties above the industry average. For years, luxury carmakers such as Lexus, Mercedes-Benz, BMW, Audi, and others offered warranties (four years or 50,000 miles bumper to bumper) beyond that provided by other manufacturers (GM, Ford, Chrysler, which offered three years or 36,000 miles). Offering longer warranties helped validate the perception of a luxury, quality automobile manufacturer. Recently, however, Mercedes-Benz has quietly reduced its warranty coverage by eliminating some free scheduled maintenance because the costs were too high. At the same time, Hyundai and others have expanded their warranties to build consumer confidence in their cars. They realize that extending the period of warranty coverage demonstrates they are making better cars in a very tangible way.

Convey a Message to the Customer

Warranties convey a powerful message to the customer about perceived product quality and manufacturer commitment to customer satisfaction. Particularly with expensive products or purchase decisions in which the customer has anxiety, the warranty can play a significant role in the final product choice. As a result, companies focus a lot of time not only creating the warranty but also considering how best to communicate it to the customer. In some cases, as in FedEx's classic tag line "absolutely, positively overnight," the warranty becomes part of the advertising campaign. With most products, however, companies take a lower profile and build warranty statements into the overall marketing communications strategy and product information.[56]

SUMMARY

The product experience is the essential element in delivering value to the customer. Organizations understand that, no matter what else happens in the customer experience, the product must deliver on its value proposition to the customer. Products have a detailed set of characteristics that include defined customer benefits as well as core and enhanced product attributes. Companies develop individual product strategies consistent with broader product line and category strategies that, in turn, achieve corporate goals and objectives.

An essential element in any product is its brand. The brand conveys a great deal of information about the product and the customer experience. Packaging and labeling are also critical brand elements that convey a lot about the product to the customer. Customers attach great importance to the sellers' commitment to the products as conveyed in the product's warranties and service agreements.

APPLICATION QUESTIONS

1. You are a marketing manager for Starbucks. Describe the following as it relates to the product experience at Starbucks: essential benefit, core product, and enhanced product. Now imagine you are the marketing manager for Aquafresh Extreme toothpaste. Describe the product experience in terms of essential benefit, core product, and enhanced product.

2. Choose two comparable phones from Motorola and Nokia and examine each product. How does the product form differ between the two products? How are they the same? Now consider the features of the two products. What features are unique to each phone? Which phone, overall, appeals to you most and why?

3. You are the marketing manager for Coca-Cola products in the United States. Describe the product line for Coke branded products and briefly describe how each product differs from the other products in the Coke brand product line.

MARKETING PLAN EXERCISES

ACTIVITY 8.1: Define the Product Strategy

In this chapter we looked at the essential element in the marketing mix—the product. Developing an effective marketing plan begins with an understanding of your product, its role in the company's overall business strategy, and, more specifically, where it fits in the company's product mix. Additionally, it is important to establish a new-product development process that ensures a pipeline of potentially successful new products. Your assignment in this chapter includes the following activities:

1. Define the product to include:
    a. Value proposition.
    b. Characteristics.
    c. Nature of product (consumer versus business product, and what type of product it represents).

2. Identify the product's position in the product line (if offered with other similar products) and, more broadly, the company's overall product mix. Address the following:
    a. How would this product differ from other products in the product line (if appropriate)?
    b. What price point would this product target and is there any conflict with existing products?
    c. How does the marketing message differ for this product from other products in the product line?

3. Define a new-product development process for next-generation products. While the product may be new, it is important to have a plan in process for next-generation models.

If you are using Marketing Plan Pro, a template for this assignment can be accessed at www.mhhe.com/marshalless1e.

ACTIVITY 8.2: Define the Branding Strategy

As we have learned in this chapter, building a strong brand is critical to a product's long-term success. At the same time, it is important to understand how a product's position in its life cycle influences marketing mix decisions.
Specific activities include:

1. Create a package design for the product. Specifically, the design should include necessary legal statements, marketing communications, and other information considered important for the package.

2. Develop a warranty for the product. What elements are specifically covered in the warranty? Does the warranty meet, equal, or fail to meet market expectations and competitor warranties?

3. Create a branding strategy to include

   a. National/store.

   b. Stand-alone/family branding.

   c. Possible licensing considerations.

   d. Co-branding opportunities.

If you are using Marketing Plan Pro, a template for this assignment can be accessed at www.mhhe.com/marshalless1e.

CHAPTER 09

The Product Experience: New-Product Development and Service

LEARNING OBJECTIVES

- Recognize the importance of new-product development to long-term success.

- Understand the new-product development process.

- Comprehend the process consumers use in adopting a new product.

- Identify how new products become diffused in a market.

- Understand why service is a key source of potential differentiation.

- Explain the characteristics that set services apart from physical goods.

- Explain the service-profit chain and how it guides marketing management decisions about service.

NEW PRODUCTS–CREATING LONG-TERM SUCCESS

No matter how good a company's current products are, long-term growth depends on new products. This can be done in one of two basic ways: external or internal development. Both approaches have their advantages and disadvantages.

"New" Defined

What does the term *new* mean? Everyday, consumers see or hear marketing communications that talk about "new and improved." At the same time, people speak about buying a new car (which may in fact be a used car) as well as a new TV (which may be last year's model). Let's look at how the term is defined by the product's manufacturer and customers.

Company Perspective

Most people would define *new* as a product that has not been available before or bears little resemblance to an existing product, and one type of new product is actually referred to as a **new-to-the-world product,** because it has not been available before. Sometimes new-to-the-world products are so innovative they create a fundamental change in the marketplace and are known as *disruptive innovation.* They are called disruptive because they shift people's perspective and frequently alter their behavior by offering dramatically simpler, more convenient, and usually less-expensive products than currently exist. In the process they frequently make existing products less desirable. Desktop computers, cell phones, and PDAs are examples of new-to-the-world products considered disruptive innovations.[1]

A second type of new-to-the-world product, *sustaining innovations,* are newer, better, faster versions of existing products that target, for the most part, existing customers. Sustaining innovations can be revolutionary by taking the market in a new direction. They can also be **modifications to existing products** and represent incremental enhancements to current products.[2]

In the spring of 2009, General Electric announced a new optical disc technology that enables storing 500 GB of data (the equivalent of 100 DVDs) onto a single compact disc. But, after witnessing the negative effect the "next generation DVD" battle between Toshiba's HD-DVD and Sony's Blu-ray had on consumer confidence in next-generation disc technology, GE has decided to be careful with marketing its new product. The company is selling the new disc technology to the archive industry where physical storage devices will always be needed.[3]

Once a product has been developed and on the market, the company can extend the product by creating **additions to existing product lines.** For years, Coca-Cola has added new products to the Coke line, first with Diet Coke in the early 1980s and now many different Coke branded products including Coke Zero. These products are also available in various sizes and packaging, giving Coke many different product items. Exhibit 9.1 is another example of an addition to an existing product line.

Another "new" product approach is to **reposition existing products** to target new markets. The cell phone market used this strategy successfully to introduce cell phones in the mid-1990s. Originally cell phone service providers positioned the phones as a safety tool targeting individuals such as working women and moms. As the product became more widely adopted, the positioning of the product changed to become an important work tool. As the market for cell phones expands, the positioning has evolved to include younger users. Cell phones are

EXHIBIT 9.1

New Products Can Take the Form of Additions to an Existing Product Line

the dominant communication device for teenagers, and phones have been created for kids as young as seven.

Cost reduction, as the name implies, is a specific method for introducing lower-cost products that frequently focus on value-oriented product price points in the product mix. Generally this approach involves eliminating or reducing features, using less-expensive materials, or altering the service or warranty to offer the product at a lower price point to the market.[4]

Customer's Perspective

While the company follows a specific strategy in creating a new product, the customer is unaware and, in reality, often does not really care about how the product arrived in the marketplace. The customer's perspective is much more narrow and self-directed. The customer is most interested in an answer to the fundamental question—is this product new to me? From the company's perspective it is important to realize that every customer approaches a new product a little differently. For example, an individual going in to buy his or her first cell phone from a service provider can find the process intimidating. As a result, cellular providers handle those customers carefully to reduce anxiety, concentrating on things like ease of use and simple service packages. Experienced cell phone users are interested in talking about the latest phone capabilities, packages, and technology. One challenge companies face is dealing with historical customer perceptions. Ford, for example, is looking to maximize a one world, one car, and one name approach while dealing with negative perceptions about a product more than 30 years old—the Fiesta.[5]

Reasons for New-Product Success or Failure

Since new-product development is such a critical factor in the long-term success of an organization, you might think companies are good at the development process. Unfortunately, this is not the case; 70 to 80 percent of all new products worldwide fail. While it is true that many of those products are developed by small entrepreneurs, no company is immune to product failure. Have you ever heard of Levi's business wear or Mr. Coffee coffee or Dunkin' Donuts cereal? Probably not, because each of these new products failed despite the fact they were introduced by companies with a track record of marketing success. The reasons vary, but it is possible to identify the role of the company, customers, and competitors in the success or failure of a new product.[6]

Company

Success or failure of a new product is determined primarily by the actions of the company. Making bad decisions by not identifying the value proposition, designing and building a product that fails to meet customer expectations, poor marketing communications, inadequate distribution of the product, or incorrectly pricing the product are all factors that increase the likelihood of new-product failure.[7]

Other factors also contribute to a lack of success. Design and development of new products is expensive, and companies sometimes fail to adequately capitalize the process. This occurs in two ways. If new-product development does not follow a timeline, development costs will, all too frequently, exceed established budgets. Inadequate resource allocation forces companies to slow the development, redirect resources for one project to another, or even eliminate projects before product development has been completed. Companies with a strong commitment to new-product research and development have the flexibility to adjust; however, for many companies, the additional development costs mean difficult choices such as slowing the development process, reducing features, or even canceling a project. Start-up companies face another problem—lack of capital.[8] Access to capital markets is essential because many companies find it difficult to sustain new-product development using only the funds from ongoing operations. Large companies find it easier to access capital markets; however, small companies, particularly start-up organizations, find it difficult and expensive to generate outside funding.

Finally, competitive pressure, changes in target markets, and environmental conditions mandate shorter product development time. The Japanese auto manufacturers for years have enjoyed an advantage in product development, pushing U.S. automakers to develop cars at a much faster pace. U.S. manufacturers have reduced new-car development from nearly five years (in the 1980s) to 36 months; however, Toyota and Honda continued to shorten their time to market and now develop a new model in less than 30 months, which means cars more accurately reflect current consumer tastes and lower costs.[9]

Customers

Customers want products designed to meet their own specific needs, which connotes smaller, more focused target markets. One way companies manage specific customer needs is to create more specialized products that address the demands of smaller groups.

Consumers also change their purchase priorities abruptly, making product life cycles shorter. This is a particular problem for new products that lack a large base of brand-loyal customers. The product life cycle of a laptop computer in the 1990s was 12 months, now it is 9 months and it is expected to go even lower.

Competitors

Companies react to competitor products in different ways. Some companies have a reputation for being aggressive in the marketplace and attack a new competitor quickly while others take a less-aggressive approach. Frito-Lay, the world's largest seller of snack foods, controls the snack aisle in grocery stores around the world and fights hard to maintain that dominance. When new competitors try to gain shelf space, Frito-Lay will introduce coupons and retailer incentives to keep its position on the shelf.[10]

For new products it is particularly important to consider how market leaders will react to an introduction. Frito-Lay, for example, has a great deal of leverage with retailers, which makes it difficult to get critical shelf space. Moreover, a loyal customer base is less likely to try new products.

Environment

Environmental concerns are among the biggest challenges facing the new-product development process today. Government regulations and new legislation, for example, can dramatically alter the development of a new product. As the government raises the corporate average fuel economy (CAFE) standards, gas mileage requirements for automakers, the auto companies are directed to develop and build smaller, more fuel-efficient cars. Despite looking a lot like a car, the PT Cruiser was designated,

Kimberly-Clark's Huggies brand of disposable diapers has developed dozens of different diaper products for newborns, older babies, and toddlers, as well as specialized products for extra comfort, overnight, and swimming diapers. K-C even manufactures six kinds of baby wipes.

in terms of federal fleet mileage regulations, as a light truck to help Chrysler meet its CAFE federal requirements.[11]

Companies also must respond to societal demands. In many categories, new products today are more environmentally sensitive. Computer manufacturers now design their laptop batteries to be recyclable and encourage customers to dispose of batteries in an environmentally friendly manner. The challenge is to balance environmental concerns with product development costs. Research suggests that consumers prefer environmentally sensitive products, but are not willing to pay a significant price premium. If research development costs are too high, companies may price their product too high, increasing the probability of failure.

NEW-PRODUCT DEVELOPMENT PROCESS

The new-product development process consists of three main activities and eight specific tasks. Failure at any step significantly lowers the probability of long-term success. The three major activities in new-product development are: (1) identify product opportunities, (2) define the product opportunity, and (3) develop the product opportunity.

There is a great deal of variability in the new-product development time-line. Products that are truly new to the world can take months or even years to develop. For example, Eclipse Aviation, makers of the first very-light jet, the Eclipse 500, took more than eight years to develop and test the product. Marketers must balance the product development process with the ever-changing demands of the marketplace. Take too long in product development and the market may have changed, rush the process and the product may be poorly designed or lack quality.[12]

Identify Product Opportunities

The first step in the new-product development process, identify potential product opportunities, has two specific tasks. First, companies must generate sufficient new-product ideas. Very few product ideas make it through the entire process and, as we have seen already, far fewer products actually become successful. As a result, it is important to have a steady flow of new ideas into the development process. Second, ideas need to be evaluated before resources are committed to development.

Generate New Ideas

Product ideas are generated in one of two ways: internal or external to the firm. While companies develop a preference for one approach over the other, the reality is both internal and external sources produce good new-product ideas. A number of factors, including the company's commitment to innovation, the reputation of competitors for new-product development, and customer expectations affect which approach a company prefers.[13]

Internal Sources include employees from R&D, marketing, and manufacturing. Key employees know both the capabilities of the company and the needs of the market. Therefore, it is not surprising that internal sources are the single best source for new-product ideas. Funding product research is expensive; companies spend billions of dollars every year to generate product ideas.

People who work directly with customers are another source of ideas. As salespeople, customer service representatives, and others interact directly with customers, it is possible to identify new-product ideas. Often these ideas are incremental changes to existing products that solve a particular problem; however, occasionally the customer challenge requires a truly innovative solution.

External An excellent source of ideas comes from individuals and organizations not directly connected with the company. In some industries, such as Internet applications, small entrepreneurs drive innovation. Myspace.com is a unique Internet destination owned by News Corp., one of the largest media companies in the world. Started in 2003 by two entrepreneurs who wanted a "place to hang out," the social networking Web site has more than 117 million unique users globally and continues to add over 200,000 new accounts per day. Its purchase by News Corp. in 2006 exemplifies how larger companies continue to grow by acquisition of smaller companies with innovative new products.[14] Google, Yahoo, and Microsoft all maintain dedicated staff whose job it is to identify and acquire new start-up organizations with great product ideas.

Customers Customers are also an excellent source of product ideas. Solving their problems can lead to innovative solutions that have market potential beyond the immediate customer. Many companies encourage customer input directly online through e-mail and online discussion groups. Ford, BMW, Mercedes-Benz, and others sponsor user group bulletin boards that discuss improvements to existing products. While this will not likely lead to "new-to-the-world" products, it can lead to incremental or even substantial enhancements to existing products.

Over 20,000 companies are on Facebook, which speaks to the business potential of social media. One of the primary business uses of social media like Facebook is market research on a variety of topics like new product ideas.

By comparing the strategies of Apple and Motorola between 1999 and 2002, it is evident that decisions regarding whether or not to invest in R&D during tough times can have serious long-term implications. Apple boosted its R&D spending by 42 percentage even though revenues were falling, but Motorola decided to cut R&D spending by 13 percentage. After the successful release of its super-thin RAZR cell phone, Motorola had nothing "on deck" for any follow-up products. Meanwhile, Apple scored big with its iPod line of digital music players and iTunes software—spawning the digital music phenomenon.[15]

Distributors Distributors are a good source for new-product ideas particularly when they are the primary link between the customer and the company. Small organizations generally do not have the resources for a national sales force and use distributors in many markets. Odyssey Software is a developer of wireless business applications for the Windows platform that uses a network of global distributors to market its products.[16] The distributor network is a key partner in the development of new products for the company. In actuality, almost anyone outside the organization can generate a new-product idea.

Companies understand that even though the majority of ideas from external sources will not pass the screening process they still want to encourage people to submit their product concepts. HP gets thousands of product ideas from a variety of individuals every year; however, very few are actually developed.

Just What the Doctor Ordered

Anyone who has ever sat in a pediatric doctor's waiting room will appreciate the challenge of keeping sick kids happy while waiting for an average of 26.5 minutes. From the doctor's staff, to the parents and kids, the minutes spent in a waiting room can be difficult. KidCare TV, based in Tampa, has developed a service using a broadband Internet connection to deliver three- to five-minute segments over 32-inch flat-screen TVs placed in pediatrician waiting rooms. The potential market for KidCare TV is big with over 60,000 pediatricians in the United States, and the company already has over 1,000 TVs installed.

The charge to the pediatrician—zero, which certainly has appeal to the doctor by making the waiting room a quieter, less-stressful environment for parents and kids. The segments feature content directed toward kids, such as cartoons and fun, interactive exercises, and child care tips directed to the parents. KidCare introduces several 30-second commercials in each segment from companies such as Capri Sun juice and Gerber Life Insurance. The company has also produced a "take home" DVD that doctors can send home with new parents offering a wide range of tips and suggestions on how to take care of a newborn. Seventeen segments have been produced on topics like "Early to Bed—Establishing a Daily Routine," "Parents 9-1-1—Finding a Babysitter," and "Which Came First—Introducing Your Pet to the New Baby." KidCare

TV notes that all video segments are produced in strict accordance with AAP (American Academy of Pediatrics) guidelines. The segments are available in English or Spanish.

Doctors who have KidCare TV currently installed in their offices generally support the service. They note the segments support medical concepts and good parenting concepts, and because the content is delivered digitally, any complaints about a specific ad or segment can cause it to be deleted quickly with no disruption of service.

However, critics argue that the service simply reinforces the already negative practice of kids spending too much time watching television. For example, the spokesperson for the American Academy of Pediatrics suggests that advertisers, not the kids, are the real beneficiaries of the service. Pediatricians have argued for a long time that kids need to spend more time exercising and less time watching TV, and critics question whether a TV in the waiting room conflicts with that message.[17]

Ethical Perspective

1. **Parents:** As a parent, how would you react to seeing a TV in your pediatrician's waiting room?

2. **Pediatrician:** Is there any inconsistency between arguing that children should spend more time exercising and having a TV in the waiting room?

3. **KidCare TV:** How would you respond to critics who argue that having children watching TV in a doctor's waiting room reinforces negative behavior to a child?

Screen and Evaluate Ideas

Ideas need to be screened and evaluated as quickly as possible. The screening process has two primary objectives. First, eliminate product ideas judged unworthy of further consideration. New-product development is expensive and resources are scarce, so ideas are evaluated early to assess their viability. An idea is rejected for several reasons. Perhaps the proposal is just not very good or it may be reasonable but inconsistent with the company's overall business strategy. Evaluating ideas can sometimes create difficult choices for managers as they wrestle with broader societal issues.[18] Consider Ethical Dimension 9 regarding KidCare TV and what issues are raised by putting TVs in pediatric waiting rooms.

Two types of mistakes are associated with rejecting or moving forward with a new-product design, and both are potentially expensive for the company. The first is the **go-to-market mistake** made when a company fails to stop a bad product idea from moving into product development. This mistake runs on a continuum from very costly (the new product is not accepted and the company loses its initial investment) to not meeting targeted ROI projections (the product does not hit established benchmarks for profitability, or unit sales). Expensive mistakes often initiate a review of the screening process to figure out how the product made it through the development process. When the product fails to hit targeted benchmarks for success, the review may focus on errors in marketing strategy, target market adjustments, or competitive response to the product launch.

A **stop-to-market mistake** happens when a good idea is prematurely eliminated during the screening process. Almost every CEO can relate a story of the product success that got away. Most often companies are reluctant to talk about stop-to-market mistakes because it makes management uncomfortable and provides additional information about product development to competitors. For example, we have talked a lot about Apple, pointing out its wildly successful iPhone and iPod. But in addition to its failed Newton, which we discussed earlier, the company has also developed a number of other products that never made it to market. For example, the Macintosh PowerBook Duo Tablet was, arguably, the first tablet PC and was created in the early 1990s during the same period as Newton. Apple stopped development of the product, code-named PenLite, to avoid confusion with Newton. Among PenLite's many features was a wireless, full-function computer that connected with all PowerBook accessories.[19]

While revolutionary in design and function only 20 Concorde jets were manufactured. The high development costs and changing economic factors (rising energy prices) made the jet too expensive to buy and use. Only two airlines ever flew the Concorde—British Airways and Air France.

A second objective of the screening process is to help prioritize ideas that pass the initial screening and evaluation. All new-product concepts are not equal, and it is important to focus resources on those that best match the success criteria. The criteria used to prioritize the ideas vary by company but often include:

- Time to market (how long will it take to develop and get the product to market).
- ROI (what is the expected return for the dollars invested in the project).
- New product fit with overall company product portfolio.

This analysis includes an internal assessment by a team from specific areas across the company (finance, marketing, R&D, manufacturing, logistics).[20] Often these people are directly involved in new-product development and have a thorough understanding of the success criteria and the company's overall product portfolio. Additionally, a relevant member of senior management provides continuity with long-term strategic goals and leadership in the screening process. Members of the team are rotated to ensure fresh ideas as there is often a significant time commitment required and members of the assessment team have other responsibilities in the company.[21]

Define the Product Opportunity

Ideas that pass through the screening process move into a development phase to define the product potential and market opportunity. Three specific tasks in this stage are: (1) define and test the product idea, (2) create a marketing strategy for the product, and (3) analyze the product's business case.

Define and Test Product Concept

The product idea now needs to be clearly defined and tested. Ideas at this stage are frequently not fully developed or operational. At this point, depending on the concept, people and resources are allocated to move the product development forward and a budget is created to develop the product.

Product definition has three objectives. First, it defines the product's value proposition; what customer needs are being addressed and, in broad terms, at what price. Second, the definition briefly identifies the target market(s) and what is the purchase frequency. Third, the definition delineates the product's characteristics (look, feel, physical elements, and features of the product). As the product moves through development, the physical characteristics become more defined and particular features, often at different price points, are included in the prototypes.[22]

Target customers are useful in defining the product concept. Companies present models, limited prototypes, and verbal or written descriptions of the product concept to customers, individually or in focus groups. Computer graphics are also used to depict elements of the product and even functionality. For example, in the development of new jet airliners, Boeing and Airbus will develop sophisticated simulations that allow passengers to *virtually* sit in the airplane. In this way, customers get a more realistic perspective at a fraction of the cost to develop a full-scale working prototype.

During this phase, companies start getting market input to refine and develop the concept. Customers are asked about their attitudes toward the product idea and if they perceive the idea as different from other products on the market. Product developers want to know, Would you buy this product and how much are you willing to pay? The company needs to know if the product is appealing to the target audience. A second question is also essential in this testing, What would you like to change about the product concept? If customers suggest changes that are not feasible (too costly to implement, not technically possible), it dramatically reduces the viability of the project. Whenever possible, however, customer feedback is incorporated into the product's development. By making adjustments during this phase rather than waiting until after the launch, companies can increase the probability of success. Since the information is so critical, researchers use large samples of target customers to ensure confidence in the findings.

Toshiba relied heavily on customer feedback in the development of its award-winning Aquilion ONE medical CT scanner. When it developed the breakthrough helical scanning technology in the early 1990s, Toshiba engineers knew they were on to something but were not sure how to move forward. By consulting with customers in the medical field, Toshiba developed the scanner system from the ground up based on feedback from those who would be using it. This strategic development decision enabled Toshiba to lead the way to the future of medical imaging technology.[23]

Create Marketing Strategy

The product development process leads to a distinct set of physical characteristics and a detailed feature mix. As the product becomes better defined, marketing specialists develop a tentative, but detailed, marketing strategy. Even though the product is still under development, there are several reasons for preparing a marketing strategy now. First, defining the target market is helpful to the product developers. In addition to the basic market information (size, geography, and demographics), product developers appreciate knowing how the product will be used (context, environment) and psychographics of the market (the market's activities, interests, and opinions). Marketers also assess the market share potential at critical points in time (how much market share can the new product get after one year). At this point, tentative pricing, distribution, and marketing communications strategies are created that will be adapted as the product gets closer to rollout.[24] Often, as part of the initial marketing communications, appropriate publications will include articles about a new product. Finally, marketing managers begin to develop budgets for the product launch and estimates of the marketing communications budget, manufacturing capacity, and logistical needs.

In creating an effective new-product marketing strategy it is important to clearly identify the product benefits to the target audience. Here the MINI is identifying a benefit: buy a MINI and you won't be bored. For someone in the MINI's target market, this benefit is attractive.

Conduct Business Case Analysis

As the product definition is developed and a tentative marketing strategy created, a critical "go-no go" decision is made before the next product development stage. At this point, the costs have been small relative to the cost of moving to full product development, market testing, and launch. There is a lot of pressure to get the decision right because a mistake is expensive. The **business case analysis** is an overall evaluation of a product and usually assesses the product's probability of success. It is often done when there are changes to an existing marketing plan, such as an increase in the marketing communications budget. The business case would assess the feasibility of increasing the communications budget.[25] In new-product development, the business case focuses on two key issues. First, the total demand for the product over a specified period of time, usually five years, is determined. Second, a cash flow statement is developed that specifies cash flow, profitability, and investment requirements.

Total Demand Sales are defined in two ways: revenue (unit sales × price) and unit sales. Each provides important information. Revenue is the top line number in a profitability analysis and is affected by price variations common to global products with substantial price differences around the world. Because currencies fluctuate, which can lead to wide variations in revenue, and price increases can also dramatically affect total revenue, unit sales is often considered a more realistic picture of product growth and represents the number of units sold, in various product configurations, around the world.

Estimating total demand is a function of three separate purchase situations.

- **New purchases**—first-time sales. With new products, these sales are called trial purchases. This is also calculated as the trial rate (how many individuals in a particular target market have tried the product).
- **Repeat purchases**—the number of products purchased by the same customer. This can be important with frequently purchased products such as convenience goods that rely on frequent repeat purchases for success.
- **Replacement purchases**—the number of products purchased to replace existing products that have become obsolete or have malfunctioned. Estimates are made on the number of product failures in any given year based on the expected product life. As more products are sold into a market through first-time and repeat purchases, the number of replacement sales will increase.

Profitability Analysis To this point, costs have been primarily in R&D and market research. However, at the next step, the company will incur manufacturing, marketing, accounting, and the logistical costs of bringing the product to market. As a result, a thorough analysis is conducted of the short- and long-term product profitability.

Develop the Product Opportunity

If the result of the previous analysis is a "go" decision, then the number of people and the resources allocated to the product's development increases substantially. For much of the 20th century, companies would move a substantial number of new-product concepts through to this stage and use product development and market testing to screen and eliminate ideas. That changed in the 1990s as the cost of taking products to market increased dramatically while failure rates remained high. Companies now screen product ideas much earlier in the development process. As a result, far fewer product ideas make it to this stage, and those products targeted for further development and market testing have a much higher probability of actually being launched in the marketplace.[26]

Develop the Product

So far the product exists primarily as a concept, or at most, a working prototype, but if the product idea is to go forward it must move from viable product concept to a working product that meets customer needs profitably. The challenge for the development team is to design and build a product the customer wants to buy while hitting the company's success metrics—sales price, revenue, profit margins, unit sales, and cost to build.[27]

Previous research during concept testing provides substantial information about what customers are looking for in the product. Coupled with input from engineers, designers, and marketing specialists, the product definition developed earlier is operationalized. This process moves from a strategic understanding of the customer's basic needs to a specific operational definition of product's characteristics. Following this process, the product's physical characteristics are defined by targeting the essential benefits delivered to the customer.[28]

There are two product development models. The first incorporates more planning and follows a sequential timeline with key process metrics being met at each stage before moving on through the process. In this scenario, product development spends a lot of time creating a product that is considered close to the final product that will be rolled out to customers. Consequently, product testing is used primarily to affirm the extensive development done earlier in the process.

The next approach encourages more prototypes that incrementally move the product through the development process. Here the product does not need to be "perfect" before testing; rather, the idea is to continuously test the product and use the testing process to enhance the product and solicit customer feedback. Through this process, the market becomes aware of the product, and if properly managed, interest in the product is increased during development.

In this second method, the goal is to shorten the time spent in development, moving from development to testing as quickly as possible to minimize cost and get the product in the hands of potential users. The longer a company takes at this stage, the greater the likelihood that competitors learn of the product, customer preferences change, or external environment conditions dictate further product adjustments.

Product Testing Generally a product undergoes two types of testing. As the product's characteristics are being finalized, most of the testing is done internally by engineers, product specialists, and other employees. This type of testing, called alpha testing, helps clarify the basic operationalization of the product such as the physical characteristics and features.

At some point, the company will want potential customers to begin testing the product. Beta testing encourages customers to evaluate and provide feedback on the prototype. The product may be close to the final configuration but Beta tests allow for further product testing and refinement.[29]

Web-based radio stations and streaming digital music sites all attempt to analyze their users' musical tastes so that they can make recommendations for other artists or albums. But, as many users of these sites will agree, most of the recommendations are off the mark. The BBC is developing a revolutionary new system that will greatly improve on this process. The international media giant has relied heavily on the process of beta testing to be sure it gets it right. The BBC intends to use a two-tiered beta testing plan in which it first employs a small group of isolated testers to tweak the software in a controlled environment before releasing a beta test version to the public.[30]

Test the Market

Once the product has reached the point where the product development team is satisfied with its performance, physical characteristics, and features, it is ready to be tested in the marketplace. To maintain security, minimize product information leaks, and disrupt competitor intelligence, products are often given code names. Once the product moves to the marketplace testing stage, a marketing strategy is created for the test using the product's market name. Some elements of the strategy such as brand name and packaging will have been tested with consumers during product development.[31] For example, engineers work with package design professionals to ensure that first, the product is protected, and second, the packaging maximizes marketing communications opportunities.

The amount of market testing is a function of several critical factors that are in conflict with one another. First, a company must evaluate the cost of being wrong. While a great deal of money has been spent to this point, the cost of launching a product failure is much higher. The greater the risk of failure, the more market testing a company will want to do before a full product launch.

At the same time, market testing takes time, and competitors can take advantage to enhance their product mix or develop marketing strategies to counter a successful product launch. In addition, depending on the product, the selling season may dictate faster product rollout because waiting too long may cost the company significant sales. Ultimately, management must balance these factors and choose the optimum market testing strategy.[32]

Trader Joe's conducts a great deal of analysis before it introduces a new product in its stores. The company considers hundreds of new products every year but only a few make it onto store shelves.

Consumer Product Market Tests In creating the market test, management must make four key decisions:

- *Where:* The location of the market test is based on how well it reflects the potential target markets. Most market tests involve somewhere between two and five cities to mitigate regional differences in purchase patterns (if there are any).

- *How long:* Most test markets run less than a year. The test should be long enough to include several purchase cycles. With many consumer products, purchase cycles are relatively short (days or weeks) so there is less need for a long market test.

- *Data:* Critical information needed to make necessary decisions must be identified. Management frequently wants to know how long it takes for the product to move through the distribution system, tracking the product from manufacturing plant through to the point of sale (matching inventory as it leaves the plant with store sales). In addition, buyers are interviewed on their product experience.

- *Decision criteria:* Metrics for further action must be identified. At this stage it is difficult to pull a product, but if the product fails in the market test, management is faced with a difficult decision—drop the product or send it back for major redesign. If the product is a success, then the product launch decision is much easier. Exhibit 9.2 summarizes the decision criteria used in market tests.

Consumer product market testing has two goals. First, provide specific numbers to the business case estimates including new (trial purchases), repeat, and, if appropriate, initial replacement purchases. Additionally, information about buyer demographics is evaluated against earlier target market scenarios and is compared against company business case models and historical data. The company takes data from the market test and projects the future.

The second objective of market testing is to get feedback on the tactics that can be used to adjust the marketing plan before product launch. While a company will often hold back implementing the entire marketing plan for security reasons, input from customers, distributors, and retailers is helpful in adjusting the final marketing plan.

EXHIBIT 9.2

Summary of Decision Criteria in Market Tests

Category	Criteria
Financial	Gross margin Profit per unit shelf space Opportunity cost of capital needed to obtain the new item
Competition	Number of firms in the trading area Number of competing brands
Marketing strategy	Product uniqueness Vendor effort Marketing support Terms of trade: slotting allowances, off-invoice allowances, free cases, bill-back provisions Price
Other	Category growth Synergy with existing items

Source: www.emeraldinsight.com.

Business Product Market Test Products designed for business markets are tested differently than their consumer product counterparts. Essentially, the tests are smaller in scope and involve fewer individuals and companies; however, they are no less important in the new-product development process. Because business markets are smaller, beta testing often includes only a few key customers with a long-standing company relationship. If, on the other hand, the company has independent distributors, it identifies a limited number for the market test and provides additional support to them as the product is being tested.[33]

Often in parallel with beta testing, companies will use trade shows to solicit customer feedback. Trade shows are a cost-effective way to get customer input because they are an efficient and convenient location to introduce new products or test new-product ideas.

Product Launch

At this point in the new-product process, it is time to implement the marketing plan. By now, considerable time, money, and human capital have been expended in the development of the product. Management has decided to launch the product. Now it is time to define the product's objectives (sales, target markets, success metrics), specify the value proposition, plan the marketing tactics, and implement the marketing plan. As we mentioned earlier, all of this will already have been done, but any necessary adjustments are made after the market test.

The product launch is critical to the long-term success of the product. Products seldom recover from a poor launch. The pressure to create excitement, particularly for consumer products, leading to consumer trial purchase is a primary reason companies spend millions of dollars on a product launch.[34] Microsoft spent in excess of $500 million to introduce Vista in early 2007 and that does not include the hundreds of millions spent by Microsoft partners (Intel, Dell, and others) in support of Vista. However, the product met with mixed success, particularly among business users and was replaced with Windows 7.[35]

Many marketing communication dollars are front-loaded at the product launch with the goal of creating sufficient product interest that will turn into repeat and replacement purchases later. If the product is not successful early, management is often unwilling to spend additional dollars as the product becomes widely distributed. The end result can be a downward spiral with low product interest generating fewer sales, which leads to more cutbacks in marketing support.[36]

CONSUMER ADOPTION AND DIFFUSION PROCESS

A target market consists of many people with different predispositions to purchase a product. Some will want to adopt a product early; others will wait until much later. The rate at which products become accepted is known as the adoption process. Marketers are interested in knowing the rate at which a product will be adopted into a market as well as the timeline (how long will it take for the product to move through the process). Of particular interest in a new-product launch are the groups at the beginning of the process, innovators and early adopters.[37]

Consumer Product Adoption Process

As we have discussed, new products come in various forms, from new-to-the-world products to incremental changes to existing products, but the consumer adoption process is less concerned with the product definition and more concerned with the individual consumer's perception of the product. A product can be in the market for a long time and still be considered an innovation to an individual consumer. The **innovation diffusion process** is how long it takes a product to move from first purchase to last purchase (the last set of users to adopt the product). An individual moves through five stages before adopting a product:

1. *Awareness*–know of the product, but insufficient information to move forward through the adoption process.
2. *Interest*–receive additional information (advertising, word of mouth) and motivated to seek out added information for further evaluation.
3. *Evaluation*–combine all information (word of mouth, reviews, advertising) and evaluate the product for trial purchase.
4. *Trial*–purchase the product for the purpose of making a value decision.
5. *Adoption*–purchase the product with the intent of becoming a dependable user.

Marketers, particularly those involved in a new-product launch, want to move consumers through the process as quickly as possible. One reason to spend heavily at the product launch phase is to move people through awareness, interest, and evaluation, getting them to try the product quickly. Sales promotion tools (coupons, product sampling), endorsements, third-party reviews, and other marketing communications methods are all part of a strategy to move people toward trial purchase. Trial purchase is the focus of a product launch marketing plan, because if you can get consumers to try the product, you can win them over with superior product design, features, and value.[38]

The Diffusion of Innovations

Everyone in a target market falls into one of five groups based on their willingness to try the innovation (see Exhibit 9.3). A person can be an innovator or early adopter in one product category and a laggard in another. However, marketers want to identify where individuals fall on the innovation curve for a particular

EXHIBIT 9.3 | Consumer Product Adoption Chart

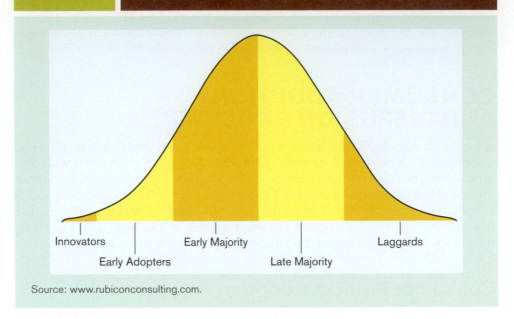

Innovators

Early Adopters

Early Majority

Late Majority

Laggards

Source: www.rubiconconsulting.com.

product or product class. Interestingly, the process by which products become diffused in a market remains remarkably constant. Research into the adoption of the Internet in the United States found it very similar to the adoption of color television in the United States in the 1960s.

The process begins with a very small group who adopt the product perhaps through targeted marketing (they are given the product to try, for example) or high involvement with the product. From there, larger numbers in the different groups move through the adoption process. Two-thirds of all adopters for a given product fall in the early and late majority. The final group, laggards, may not move into the adoption process until late in the product's life cycle.[39]

- **Innovators** (2.5 percent)—Product enthusiasts enjoy being the first to try to master a new product. Individuals in this group are prime candidates for beta testing and represent a good source of feedback late in the product development process or early in the product launch phase.

- **Early Adopters** (13.5 percent)—Product opinion leaders seek out new products consistent with the personal self-image. This group is not price-sensitive and is willing to pay the price premium for a product. At the same time, early adopters demand a high level of personalized service and product features.

- **Early Majority** (34 percent)—Product watchers want to be convinced of the product's claims and value proposition before making a commitment. This group is considered critical to long-term success as they take the product into the main stream.

- **Late Majority** (34 percent)—Product followers are price-sensitive and risk-averse. They purchase older generation or discontinued models with lower prices and fewer product features.

- **Laggards** (16 percent)—Product avoiders want to evade adoption as long as possible. Resistant to change, they will put off the purchase until there is no other option.

Today, microwave ovens come in all sizes and at least one is found in a high percentage of all homes. However, the product followed the diffusion process. At first, the product was slow to be accepted because of health concerns and the fact that many people simply did not know how to use it properly.

WHY SERVICE IS IMPORTANT

These last two chapters have focused on the essential element in delivering value to the customer—the product experience. Much of that discussion was based on a physical product but there is another critical component of a successful product experience— service. In fact, in today's economy for many firms service *is* the core offering.

There's no debate that today we operate in an economy that is increasingly focused on intangible offerings—services—instead of just physical goods. A **service** is a product in the sense that it represents a bundle of benefits that can satisfy customer wants and needs, yet it does so without physical form. As such, the value a customer realizes from purchasing a service is not based on its physical attributes, but rather on some other effect the service has on him or her in fulfilling needs and wants. And differences in the quality of a service can be profound; just think for a moment about the best and worst experiences you've had with a server in a restaurant. Even if the food itself is good, it is the service aspect of a meal out that everyone remembers most. All the data suggest that we now live in a predominantly **service economy.** More than 80 percent of jobs in the United States are service-related. Compare that to 55 percent of jobs in 1970. The Bureau of Labor Statistics expects service jobs to account for *all* new domestic job growth for the foreseeable future, partly because the number of jobs outside the service sector is actually declining. Jobs represented in the **service sector** of the economy include such important categories as intellectual property, consulting, hospitality, travel, law, health care, education, technology, telecommunications, and entertainment—all high-growth job categories. In terms of U.S. gross domestic product, in 2008 services accounted for more than 70 percent. Impressively, services account for about 84 percent of all nonfarming-related jobs in the United States. The long-term shift from goods-producing to service-producing employment is expected to continue. Service-providing industries are expected to account for about 15.2 million new wage and salary jobs generated from 2008 to 2016, while goods-producing industries will see overall job loss. In today's workplace everyone is involved in service in some way; everyone has customers either outside or inside the firm, or both.

Changing U.S. demographics represent a major driver for why the service sector is thriving. For example, as baby boomers begin to retire and spend their discretionary income on travel and entertainment, firms in those industries will prosper. As the baby boomers continue to age, health services will begin to predominate their spending. In the meantime, the fixation of Generation Y and Millennials toward all things technological will continue to drive impressive growth in gaming, music, computing, cellular phone, and other technological industries.

Service as a Differentiator

In Chapter 7, we mentioned that service leadership and personnel leadership are two important sources of differentiation for a company. Recall that differentiation means communicating and delivering value in different ways to different customer groups. Presumably these groups are segments that show the most promise for return on marketing investment. As a marketing manager, a significant challenge with using differentiation as a core market strategy is that competitors are constantly coming to market with new differentiators that trump the efficacy of the current ones.

In his book *On Great Service,* Leonard Berry, a leading expert in the field of services marketing, advocates that a focus on service and on enabling employees to effectively deliver service can be one differentiator that is hard for the competition to replicate. Many firms are reluctant to invest in great service, largely because it takes time and patience before a return on the investment may be noticeable. But Berry's point is that although the payback might take time, once a firm is able to deliver great service as a core differentiator it is much more likely to provide a sustainable competitive advantage than are most other sources of differentiation.[41]

A New Dominant Logic for Marketing

That service is central to marketing management today is embodied in an important article that appeared in one of the field's leading journals, the *Journal of Marketing,* titled "Evolving to a New Dominant Logic for Marketing." The **new dominant logic for marketing** implies a shift in worldview from the traditional goods versus services dichotomy to recognition of the following:

> Customers do not buy goods or services: [T]hey buy *offerings* which render services which create value. . . . The traditional division between goods and services is long outdated. The shift in focus to services is a shift from the means and the producer perspective to the utilization and the customer perspective.

In a service-centered view, tangible goods serve as "appliances" for service provision rather than ends in themselves such that in some ways the product becomes secondary or incidental to the service it propagates. This perspective has profound implications for how marketing managers approach their business in a world of increasingly commoditized physical goods. The most fundamental question is "Just *what is it* that we are marketing?" Or, put another way: What is the product and where does its value come from? A service-centered perspective is very consistent with a customer-centric approach in which people, processes, systems, and other resources are to be aligned to best serve customers. It disposes of the limitations of thinking about marketing in terms of goods taken to the marketplace and instead leads to opportunities for expanding the market by assisting the customer in the process of specialization and value creation.[42]

An overall service-centered view is fundamental to successful marketing management today. The remainder of this chapter is devoted to providing insights for effectively capitalizing on the service opportunities associated with an offering. First, unique characteristics of services are described that set services apart from physical goods for marketing managers. Second, the concept of the service-profit chain is introduced. Third, service attributes are discussed along with a continuum of products from pure goods to pure services. Fourth, the concept of service quality is introduced along with its measurement and uses by management. Finally, service blueprinting is introduced as a way for a marketing manager to map out the overall service delivery system for a business.

CHARACTERISTICS OF SERVICES

Services possess several distinct characteristics different from physical goods. As illustrated in Exhibit 9.4, these are intangibility, inseparability, variability, and perishability.

Korean Air shows the sumptuous nature of its 180-degree reclining seats to differentiate its premium class service from competitors.

Intangibility

A service cannot be experienced through the physical senses. It cannot be seen, heard, tasted, felt, or smelled by a customer. This property represents the **intangibility** of services versus goods; goods can easily be experienced through the senses.

How do customers draw conclusions about a brand if they can't actually try the product before purchase? This is one of the challenges of intangibles. Strong branding can be an important way to make a service seem more tangible. Service firms use strong imagery to send out signals about their products, increase trust, and ease customer uncertainty about what is being purchased. Marketing communications provide cues about the dependability of the service, replacing to an extent the ability customers have to try physical products in advance of purchase. When it comes to making purchase decisions about services, customers draw conclusions from what tangibles they can experience—things like the company's people, Web site, marketing communications, office ambience, and pricing. In a service setting, the importance and impact of marketing is heightened considerably because in many cases there's little else tangible for the customer to experience before purchase.[43]

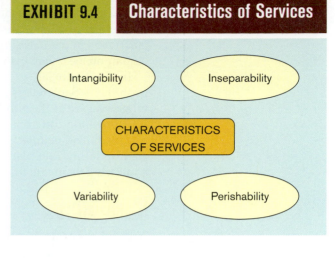

EXHIBIT 9.4 | **Characteristics of Services**

Intangibility

Inseparability

CHARACTERISTICS OF SERVICES

Variability

Perishability

For many small businesses, having to purchase and maintain a computer server is simply out of the question. Instead, they can pay a provider such as Microsoft to take care of their server-related needs, such as data storage and processing, and replace all of that hardware and staff with a simple Internet connection. It may sound appealing, but providers have discovered that it is challenging to market "cloud" computing services due to their intangibility. The reality is that many companies are uncomfortable with the idea of not having their own physical servers or in-house IT support staff.[44]

Sometimes it is possible to enhance tangibility of a service through a bit of customer trial. For example, MBA programs often encourage prospective students to come to open houses or visit classes to gain a sense of how the school they are considering approaches teaching and learning. Vacation rentals such as Hilton Grand Vacation Club and Marriott Vacation Club actively solicit guests for tours of their facilities while prospects are visiting the area to allow them to experience a taste of what the location is like as a regular vacation destination. And advertising agencies make portfolios of past work available to prospective clients as a sampling of the firm's creative capabilities.[45]

Inseparability

Even with the best efforts at enhancing a service's tangibility, a customer still can't really experience it until it is actually consumed. This characteristic represents the **inseparability** of a service—it is produced and consumed at the same time and cannot be separated from its provider. With physical goods, the familiar process is production, storage, sale, and then consumption. But with services, first the service is sold and then it is produced and consumed at the same time. Perhaps it is more accurate to think of a service as being *performed* rather than produced.[46] In a theatrical play or an orchestral concert, many individuals have a part in the performance. Similarly, the quality of a service encounter is determined in part by the interaction of the players. Most elegant restaurants structure their customer encounters as elaborate productions involving servers, the wine steward, the maître d', the chef, and of course the table of diners. Benihana restaurants take the concept of service as drama to truly new heights of customer involvement and excitement—the company's tagline is "an experience at every table."

The inseparability of performance and consumption of services heightens the role of the human service providers in the customer's experience. It also leads to opportunities for considerable customization in delivering the service. Finicky customers in the hair stylist's chair can coax just the right cut. Want two scoops of cinnamon ice cream instead of one on that apple torte? Just ask the server.

In the financial services industry, for example, customization of services is prominent. Bank tellers are empowered to take a quick look at your account record when you are at the window to make a deposit and might very likely suggest you do something different with your money if you're not currently optimizing your returns.[47] And cellular service providers know that if they don't proactively suggest updating rate plans, customers will be more likely to walk away once their contracted years are fulfilled.

Variability

An offshoot of the inseparability issue, **variability** of a service means that because it can't be separated from the provider, a service's quality can only be as good as that of the provider him-/herself.[48] Ritz Carlton, Nordstrom, Disney, and Southwest Airlines have become iconic firms in their industries largely by focusing on their people—hiring, training, keeping, and promoting the very best people they can get. Legendary Southwest Chairman Herb Kelleher built a business in part around ensuring that his people were *different* from typical airline employees— more engaged, fun, and fiercely loyal to the company.[49] The same can be said for the other firms above. Focusing on employees as a source of differentiation in marketing is usually a smart move, mainly because so many firms just can't seem to pull it off very well. The point is to remove much of the variability of customers' experiences with your service and instead provide a more dependable level of quality. Go into any Nordstrom and work with any of Nordstrom's sales associates and you will very likely experience the same high level of satisfaction with the service. The same is true for Ritz Carlton and any of the great service organizations.[50]

Goods, in general, tend to be much more standardized than services because, once a firm has invested in continuous process improvement and quality control in its manufacturing operations, products flow off the line with very little variation. With services, continual investment in training, retraining, and good management of people are required if variability is to be consistently low. It is in this area where the disciplines of marketing, operations, leadership, and human resource management probably have their closest intersection. What makes Ritz-Carlton great? A quick answer is: its people. But what makes its people great? World-class operations, leadership, and HR practices. And the net effect for Ritz-Carlton is that its branding and market positioning are largely defined by its wonderful people and the way they handle each customer as a valued guest. For service firms, great marketing cannot take place without a strong overarching culture that values employees.

Perishability

If you schedule an appointment for a routine physical with your physician and then simply don't show up, the doctor loses the revenue from that time slot. That's **perishability**—the fact that a service can't be stored or saved up for future use.[51] Perishability is a major potential problem for service providers, and explains why, under the circumstances above, many physicians have a policy of charging the patient for the missed appointment. Ever wonder why an airline won't issue a refund or let you change your super-low-fare ticket after the door closes and the plane leaves without you? It's because the value of that empty seat—its ability to generate incremental revenue for the airline—dropped to zero when the door closed and the plane backed away from the gate.

Fluctuating demand is related to perishability of services.[52] Consider rental car firms such as Hertz, Avis, and the like in a city such as Orlando, which brings in both tourists and conventions. If demand were relatively constant, the rental car companies could keep the same basic inventory on the lot at all times. However, in the case of both individual vacationers and conventioneers, demand for cars varies considerably by season, and for the latter is driven by the size of the convention. The worst scenario is for the city to attract a huge convention and for the rental firms not to have sufficient cars available. No cars, no revenue for Hertz and Avis. Not to mention, the convention organizers would likely think twice before scheduling their event in Orlando again.

Because demand for most goods tends to be more stable and because they can generally be stored for use after purchase, this critical issue of synchronizing supply and demand is easier to deal with for goods than for services. Hertz and Avis don't want to maintain huge extra inventories of vehicles on off-peak periods; hence they might use price incentives to promote more rentals during those times. Or, they might literally move cars around—pulling in massive numbers of extra vehicles from other nearby markets such as Miami or Tampa to take care of high demand periods. One thing they know for sure is that if there are no cars on the lot, any opportunity for revenue perishes.

THE SERVICE-PROFIT CHAIN

In a now-famous *Harvard Business Review* article published in 1994, followed up by a book several years later, James Heskett and his colleagues proposed a formalization of linkages between employee and customer aspects of service delivery called the **service-profit chain.** Because of the inseparability and variability of services, employees play a critical role in their level of success. The service-profit chain, which is portrayed in Exhibit 9.5, is designed to help managers better understand the key linkages in a service delivery system that drive customer loyalty, revenue growth, and higher profits.

EXHIBIT 9.5	The Service-Profit Chain

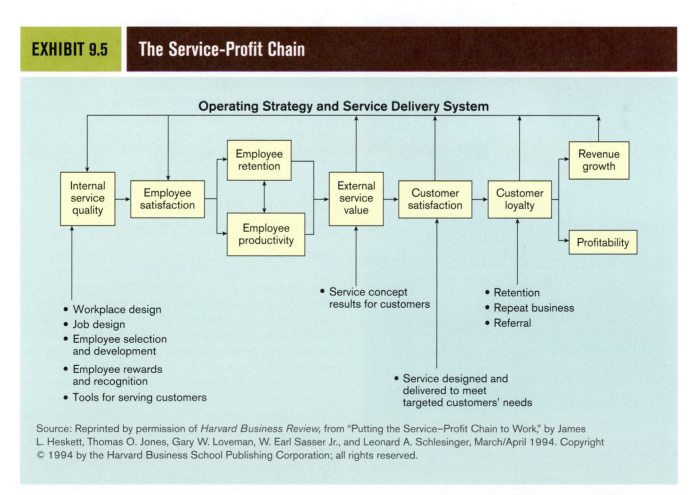

Source: Reprinted by permission of *Harvard Business Review*, from "Putting the Service–Profit Chain to Work," by James L. Heskett, Thomas O. Jones, Gary W. Loveman, W. Earl Sasser Jr., and Leonard A. Schlesinger, March/April 1994. Copyright © 1994 by the Harvard Business School Publishing Corporation; all rights reserved.

Internal Service Quality

This aspect of the service-profit chain includes elements of workplace design, job design, employee selection and development processes, employee rewards and recognition approaches, and availability of effective tools for use by employees in serving customers. Considerable evidence exists that **internal marketing,** treating employees as customers and developing systems and benefits that satisfy their needs, is an essential element of internal service quality. Firms practicing internal service quality are **customer-centric**—they place the customer at the center of everything that takes place both inside and outside the firm. Firms that are customer-centric exhibit a high degree of customer orientation, which means they do the following:

1. Instill an organization-wide focus on understanding customers' requirements.
2. Generate an understanding of the marketplace and disseminate that knowledge to everyone in the firm.
3. Align system capabilities internally so that the organization can respond effectively with innovative, competitively differentiated, satisfaction-generating goods and services.

No matter how many times a corporation claims it is "customer-centric," the truth is that most consumers think companies are inherently bad. In the past, it required a substantial investment of time and money for a company to reach out to its customers to build stronger relationships with them. Today, with the existence of wikis, blogs, online communities, and social networking sites, any company can use the Web as a powerful medium in which to connect with customers. The drawback is that companies can't hide from the Web community or let themselves become misrepresented due to their absence.[53]

In the context of internal service quality, it is assumed that a firm's culture, business philosophy, strategy, structure, and processes will be aligned in order to create, communicate, and deliver value to customers. Finally, a focus on internal service quality implies that employees hold a **customer mind-set,** meaning that employees believe that understanding and satisfying customers, whether internal or external to the firm, is central to doing their job well.[54]

Satisfied, Productive, and Loyal Employees

Great service doesn't happen without great people. A big part of making the service-profit chain work is creating an environment in which all employees can be successful. Internal marketing is an integral element of this, and Harrah's Entertainment is a great example of a firm that almost obsessively focuses on facilitating the success of its people, regardless of their position, and especially if they are in direct contact with customers. It's not surprising Harrah's has such a zest for internal marketing and enablement of employee success. Leonard Schlesinger, one of the original authors of the service-profit chain concept, went on to become Harrah's CEO. During his tenure, the company became the most successful hotelier/casino in Las Vegas and continues to expand elsewhere as well. Harrah's stable

Management consulting services provider Accenture learned the hard way that having celebrities as spokespeople sometimes can be risky. The firm announced in late 2009 that they were discontinuing their association with Tiger Woods.

of brands includes Caesars, Bally's, Paris, Rio, Flamingo, World Series of Poker, and others.[55]

To be executed effectively, internal marketing must include the following critical elements: competing for talent, offering an overall vision, training and developing people, stressing teamwork, modeling desired behaviors by managers, enabling employees to make their own decisions, measuring and rewarding great service performance, and knowing and reacting to employees' needs. Perhaps most important of all, employees must have a deep understanding of the brand and must be able to consistently articulate a clear, concise message to customers that reflects the firm's service strategy and branding.[56] At Harrah's, Schlesinger points with pride to the fact that everyone in the firm understands and can articulate its branding and values.

In 2008, JCPenney started its CustomerFIRST program, in which the retailer examined the management tactics of businesses that were considered to be "legendary" for their customer service. JCPenney concluded that the best way to invest in customers' satisfaction was to invest in employees. The company retrained all 150,000 store employees to be more autonomous, empowering them to use their judgment rather than getting the manager on duty any time they faced a customer service situation. This sense of ownership, coupled with a newly instated employee recognition program, made JCPenney employees more satisfied with their jobs and boosted the retailer's overall level of customer service.[57]

Greater Service Value for External Customers

There is strong evidence that attention to internal service quality and to employee satisfaction, productivity, and retention result in stronger value to external customers of a service. Remember that when the concept of value was introduced in Chapter 1 we discussed it as a ratio of what a customer gives versus what he or she gets in return from a purchase. Importantly, the customer inputs are not just financial—customers give up time, convenience, and other opportunities in making a purchase choice. Customers set their expectations for the value they hope to derive from a service based largely on the evidence provided by the marketer before the purchase. A fundamental rule in marketing is to not set customer expectations so high that they cannot be effectively met on a consistent basis.[58] This is because it is always better to underpromise and overdeliver than the reverse scenario. This concept is often called **customer expectations management.**

What does Southwest Airlines promise the flyer? The airline doesn't have traditional assigned seating, a first-class cabin, or even "real food" on flights. But it doesn't promise any of these things. In fact, it's built a business out of snubbing the other big airlines' approaches (and made a lot of money doing so). What Southwest *does* promise is a fun, on-time flight. So long as it can continue to deliver against that message, customers will likely continue to see Southwest as a great travel value.

Customer Satisfaction and Loyalty

In the service-profit chain, meeting or exceeding customer expectations leads to customer satisfaction, since the service was designed and delivered in a manner that added value. A strong correlation exists between satisfied and loyal customers. Loyalty sparks high **customer retention**—low propensity to consider switching to other providers—as well as repeat business, referrals, and **customer advocacy,** a willingness and ability on the part of a customer to participate in communicating the brand message to others within his or her sphere of influence.[59]

EXHIBIT 9.6 Causes of Switching Behavior

Pricing

- High price
- Price increases
- Unfair pricing
- Deceptive pricing

Inconvenience

- Location/hours
- Wait for appointment
- Wait for service

Core Service Failure

- Service mistakes
- Billing errors
- Service catastrophe

Service Encounter Failures

- Uncaring
- Impolite

- Unresponsive
- Unknowledgeable

Response to Service Failure

- Negative response
- No response
- Reluctant response

Competition

- Found better service

Ethical Problems

- Cheat
- Hard sell
- Unsafe
- Conflict of interest

Involuntary switching

- Customer moved
- Provider closed

Source: Susan M. Keaveney, "Customer Switching Behavior in Service Industries: An Exploratory Study," *Journal of Marketing*, April 1995, pp. 71–82. Reprinted with permission of the American Marketing Association.

Why do customers consider switching from one service provider to another? Reasons run the gamut from low utility to various forms of service failure to concerns about a firm's practices. A summary of causes of switching behavior is presented in Exhibit 9.6.

Harrah's Entertainment understands the strong linkage between high customer satisfaction and loyalty and invests heavily in its most highly satisfied customers to ensure their loyalty and advocacy. Exhibit 9.7 portrays this relationship.

CRM and database marketing are key tools that allow Harrah's Entertainment, as well as any firm interested in increasing satisfaction and loyalty and improving retention, to use the concepts in Exhibit 9.7 to focus on serving the most profitable customers. For Harrah's, this approach manifests itself through the Total Rewards loyalty program. Harrah's has found that its ROI for customers in the "Zone of Affection" is considerably higher than in the other zones ("Indifference" and "Defection"). Very satisfied customer "apostles" are the ones that Harrah's wants to develop to the fullest extent to keep them coming back and spending money in its hotels and casinos. Research indicates that, although investing in indifferent customers to improve their satisfaction may yield some returns, only when customers reach the "Zone of Affection" do they truly maximize their profitability to the brand.

Nikon Corporation, the Japanese technology firm best known for its line of high-resolution cameras, uses sophisticated CRM software provided by Microsoft Dynamics. Nikon discovered that its global retail distribution network had become so overwhelming that the information needed for customer service was scattered among various systems, databases, and locations. By implementing the new CRM software, Nikon was able to create a centralized data pool of consumer and retailer information—enabling the company to better connect with its customers and have a closer working relationship with its retailers.[60]

EXHIBIT 9.7 | Focus on the Most Satisfied Customers

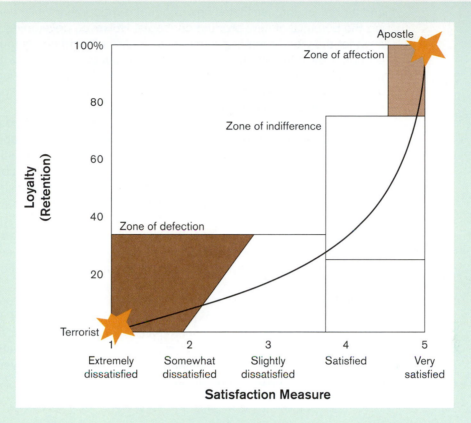

Revenue and Profit Growth

In the context of Exhibit 9.7, customers that are "satisfied" and "very satisfied" are identified through Harrah's Total Rewards loyalty program cards, which they use at hotel check-in, in slot machines, and at all gaming tables. They truly are the apple of the eye of Harrah's employees while they are on the property, and more broadly they represent the total focus of Harrah's marketing efforts—largely through direct marketing approaches with customized offers. Like slots? You'll get an invitation to a slot tournament. Poker's your thing? Look for an invitation to a poker tournament. It's not that Harrah's is disinterested in or doesn't want the money of the other customers, but it has learned from its research that customers in the "Zone of Affection" spend considerably more money and provide a substantially greater return on customer investment than others.[61]

Harrah's embraces customer satisfaction measurement; and it segments markets based on satisfaction score groups. The ultimate Harrah's customer is the "apostle"—highly satisfied, fiercely loyal, a frequent Harrah's guest who serves as a strong advocate for the Harrah's experience to friends and acquaintances. For the service-profit chain to provide insight for marketing managers into how to best develop and execute service strategies, a variety of metrics must be in place with measures taken continually. In fact, all aspects of the chain—from internal service quality to employee issues to value to satisfaction and loyalty to financial performance—must be quantified and used for marketing management decision making.

SUMMARY

Critical to a company's long-term success is the development of new products and a process that facilitates new-product development while carefully assessing the potential of new-product concepts. However, developing a new product, even for the world's leading companies, is difficult, and nearly four out of five products fail in the first three years. A new product can be "new to the world," a product that has not been introduced before; however, it may also include products that have been upgraded or even existing products that have been repositioned to appeal to a new market.

The new-product development process involves marketing research and product development research. As the product is under development, companies assess the market potential and develop preliminary marketing strategies and plans to be executed once the product receives authorization for rollout from management. The cost of new-product development is rising and can reach into the billions of dollars for products such as automobiles, pharmaceuticals, and technology.

Companies want to know how their products will be accepted in the marketplace in a process called the diffusion of innovation. This process identifies five customer groups and demonstrates how products are adopted by different user groups over time.

In today's competitive marketplace, service is an important source of differentiation. But services have unique characteristics that must be understood as well as attributes that make services quite different from goods. An important concept for marketing managers to master is the service-profit chain, which provides a framework for linking elements of the service delivery system that drive customer loyalty, revenue growth, and higher profits.

APPLICATION QUESTIONS

1. You are the marketing manager for McGraw-Hill responsible for new-product development. Recently, your technology development department created a new software application that enables students to learn marketing management more effectively. Take the product through the new-product development process. What would you need to know to make a launch decision for the product?

2. As a product manager for Nokia you are responsible for the introduction of a new line of mobile devices targeted at business users. The company's R&D team has presented you with a list of possible new features that can be added to the product in the next 18 months. When and how would these new features be added to the existing line of cell phones?

3. The service-profit chain guides managers toward understanding and facilitating successful linkages in the service delivery system to drive loyalty, revenue growth, and higher profits.

   a. What functional areas of a firm must a marketing manager effectively interface with to implement a service-profit chain approach?

   b. What potential impediments do you foresee in implementing the service-profit chain in an organization? How might these impediments best be overcome?

   c. What do you believe are the key advantages in implementing a service-profit chain approach?

MARKETING PLAN EXERCISES

ACTIVITY 9-1: New-Product Development

In this chapter we looked at the essential element in the marketing mix—the product. Developing an effective marketing plan begins with an understanding of your product, its role in the company's overall business strategy, and, more specifically, where it fits in the company's product mix. Additionally, it is important to establish a new-product development process that ensures a new product pipeline of potentially successful new products. Marketing plan activities in this chapter include the following:

1. Define a new-product development process for next-generation products. While the product may be new, it is important to have a plan in place for next-generation models.

   a. Do you want to expand existing products into new markets?

   b. Define expected features that will likely be added over the next 36 months and a timeline for introduction.

2. Does the company want to be known as innovative with regards to new-product development?

3. Chart the diffusion of the company's product into the market. Define each of the groups in the diffusion process.

If you are using Marketing Plan Pro, a template for this assignment can be accessed at www.mhhe.com/marshalless1e.

ACTIVITY 9-2: Differentiating via Service Quality

In the marketing plan, consider how you might effectively use service as a source of differentiation for your offering(s). As you learned in this chapter, to successfully accomplish this, you must be sensitive to nuances of services versus goods and also be able to ensure that the people and processes in your firm are able to properly support the service.

1. Evaluate the opportunity to utilize service as an important differentiator.

2. Employ a service-profit chain approach to identify people and operational aspects of tour plan to support service differentiation.

3. Develop specific action plans and metrics in support of your service differentiation approach.

If you are using Marketing Plan Pro, a template for this assignment can be accessed at www.mhhe.com/marshalless1e.

CHAPTER 10

Managing Pricing Decisions

LEARNING OBJECTIVES

- Understand the integral role of price as a core component of value.

- Explore different pricing objectives and related strategies.

- Identify pricing tactics.

- Describe approaches to setting the exact price.

- Determine discounts and allowances to offer to channel members.

- Understand how to execute price changes.

- Examine legal considerations in pricing.

PRICE IS A CORE COMPONENT OF VALUE

You have learned that *value* is a ratio of the bundle of benefits a customer receives from an offering compared to the costs incurred by the customer in acquiring that bundle of benefits. From the customer's perspective, many but not all of those costs are reflected within the price paid for the offering. There are other types of costs, such as time invested in the purchase process or the opportunity costs of choosing one offering over another. But for most purchasers, regardless of whether the setting is B2C or B2B, the vast majority of costs are associated with the purchase price. As such, price—or more specifically the customer's *perception* of the offering's pricing—is a key determinant of perceived value. When customers exhibit strongly held beliefs that a firm's offerings provide high value, they are much more likely to remain loyal to the firm and its brands as well as actively tell others about their favorable experiences. Thus, marketing managers must take pricing decisions very seriously.[1]

From a marketing planning and strategy perspective, Michael Porter has consistently advocated that firms that are able to compete based on some extraordinary efficiency in one or more internal processes bring to the market a competitive advantage based on **cost leadership.** And although firms competing on cost leadership will likely also engage in one of Porter's other competitive strategies (differentiation or focus/niche), their core cost advantages translate directly to an edge over their competitors based on much more flexibility in their pricing strategies as well as their ability to translate some of the cost savings to the bottom line.[2]

For example, Southwest Airlines is widely regarded as a cost leader in its industry, which has become a critical factor in this era of high fuel costs. Southwest's internal process efficiencies stem from several important sources. First, it flies mostly the same type of plane—various series of the Boeing 737. This makes the maintenance process much more efficient than carriers whose fleet includes multiple types of aircraft. Second, Southwest has a very simple process of booking passengers and, until recently, had never even tested the idea of assigned seats. Finally, it avoids the delay-prone hub-and-spoke route system used by most of its competitors, instead often opting for smaller airports in major metropolitan areas (Midway in Chicago instead of O'Hare, for example). These and other internal efficiencies translate into a cost structure second to none in the industry.

But what does such cost leadership mean for Southwest's pricing decision making? A knee-jerk response might be to simply lower fares to match the level of cost advantage. That might increase sales volume, but it also might start a price war with other airlines that have cost advantages (AirTran and JetBlue, for instance). A more strategic approach—and the approach Southwest actually uses—is to translate part of its cost advantage into a more transparent, mileage-driven pricing structure for customers but at the same time take a portion of the cost advantage to increase the firm's profit margins, partly to reward shareholders and partly to reinvest for the firm's growth.

Most importantly, Southwest's pricing model contributes not only to its financial performance but also is an integral part of its overall value proposition and provides a valuable lesson for the way a marketing manager should approach pricing decisions—that is, pricing decisions cannot be made in a vacuum but rather must consider the whole of the firm's offering, especially the concurrent decisions the firm is making about branding and products, service approaches, supply chain, and marketing communication. For the marketing manager, pricing is much more than an economic break-even point or a cost-plus accounting calculation. Price is a critical component that plays into a customer's assessment of the value afforded by a firm and its offerings. As such, managerial decisions about pricing should be undertaken methodically and always with a focus on how price

Is Goodwill Good or Just Good Business?

A small school 90 minutes from Mexico City is so poorly funded that it cannot afford toilet paper for the lavatories, but, thanks to Intel, an eighth-grade class is searching the Internet on new laptops. Intel, one of the largest technology companies in the world, is testing a program called "Classmate" that offers laptop computers for educational systems in poorer countries for around $300 each. While still expensive for the poorest nations, the company has pledged to lower costs even further and plans call for a $200 model.

At the same time, Dr. Nicholas Negroponte, professor at the Massachusetts Institute of Technology and co-founder of the MIT media lab, has been working on the XO computer through his One Laptop per Child (OLPC) foundation whose mission is to deliver computers to kids around the world for $100. OLPC has enlisted the help of Google, eBay, and Advanced Micro Devices (AMD)—AMD just happens to be Intel's major competitor in the chip market.

Although both organizations seek a similar goal—getting inexpensive laptops into the hands of poorer students—their approaches are very different. Negroponte is creating a new device with a specially designed interface that represents a dramatic departure from the world standard Microsoft Windows/Intel operating environment. Intel, on the other hand, is using its substantial leverage with suppliers to drive costs out of a standard laptop, preferring to work within existing hardware including its own chips and software products. Intel is testing its product in more than 35 countries while OLPC is still working on finalizing the product design.

Critics of Intel's approach suggest that, rather than goodwill, the company's focus on delivering low-cost computers to schoolchildren is designed to create a new market for its own products. As the world moves from desktop computers to laptops and, of more concern to Intel, mobile devices such as cell phones, the company has experienced slower growth and greater competition from AMD. Intel does not dominate the market for mobile-device computer chips in the same manner it does the computer market. Some experts believe that although the margins are low the market for very low-cost computers is huge and represents a growth opportunity for Intel.

Negroponte and OLPC have accused Intel of trying to drive the XO computer project out of business and suggest this is because OLPC buys it chips from AMD. Negroponte also argues that, although Intel's computers are inexpensive, the company views low-end computers as a market and not a human right.[3]

Ethical Perspective

1. **Intel:** Is it unethical for Intel to pursue the Classmate project if its primary purpose is to target a new market? Should the company be encouraged to develop the Classmate computer without a profit incentive; that is, should it offer the project only at cost?

2. **Governments:** Should governments support the OLPC project with its nonprofit perspective and low-cost computer over Intel's for-profit Classmate project?

---

impacts the all-important cost-versus-bundle-of-benefits assessment that equates to customer perceived value.[4] Ethical Dimension 10 evaluates some of these pricing concepts in terms of social responsibility.

Wealthy consumers in China are considerably younger than those in the United States and Japan. As a result, premium-priced brands such as Louis Vuitton and Gucci are modifying their strategies to appeal to affluent 20- and 30-somethings in China. These brands have been promoting 500 yuan ($73) to 1,000 yuan ($146) bags to this segment to tap into its high disposable income.[5]

The rest of this chapter details the important pricing decision-making process from a marketing manager's perspective: establish pricing objectives and related strategies; select pricing tactics; set the exact price; determine channel discounts and allowances; execute price changes; and understand legal considerations in pricing. Exhibit 10.1 portrays these elements of managing pricing decisions.

EXHIBIT 10.1 | Elements of Managing Pricing Decisions

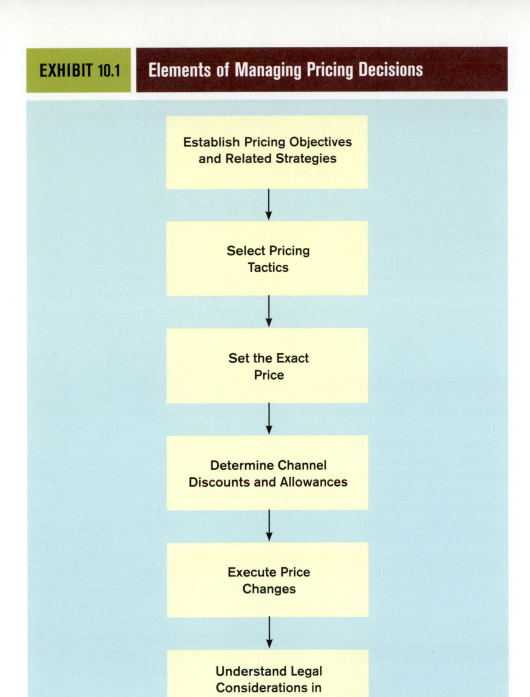

Establish Pricing Objectives
and Related Strategies

↓

Select Pricing
Tactics

↓

Set the Exact
Price

↓

Determine Channel
Discounts and Allowances

↓

Execute Price
Changes

↓

Understand Legal
Considerations in
Pricing

ESTABLISH PRICING OBJECTIVES AND RELATED STRATEGIES

As illustrated in the Southwest Airlines example, pricing objectives are but one component leading to an overall value proposition. However, a product's price tends to be so visible and definitive that customers often have trouble moving past price to consider other critical benefits the product affords. This characteristic puts pressure on marketing managers to establish pricing objectives that best reflect and enhance the value proposition, while at the same time achieving the firm's financial objectives. Striking a balance between these two forces sometimes makes pricing an especially challenging part of marketing.[6]

Pricing objectives are the desired or expected result associated with a pricing strategy. Pricing objectives must be consistent with other marketing-related objectives (positioning, branding, etc.) as well as with the firm's overall objectives (including financial objectives) for doing business.[7] Exhibit 10.2 portrays several of the most common pricing objectives, along with their related strategies.

> Fast-food chains all have an objective to drive traffic through attractive pricing. Subway fired the first salvo with its $5 foot-long sub, which quickly became the yardstick for fast-food deals. Subway, the nation's largest restaurant chain, has made the $5 promotion permanent for a variety of subs and occasionally offers it on all of its subs. The chain uses penetration pricing to get ahead of competitors Quiznos, Domino's, and Pizza Hut.[8]

The decision of which pricing objective or objectives to establish is driven by many interrelated factors. As you learn about each of the approaches, keep in mind that most firms attempt to balance a range of issues through their pricing objectives, including internal organization-level goals, internal capabilities, and a host of external market and competitive factors.

Penetration Pricing

Market share is the percentage of total category sales accounted for by a firm. When a firm's objective is to gain as much market share as possible, a likely pricing strategy is **penetration pricing,** sometimes also referred to as pricing for maximum marketing share. In markets where customers are sensitive to price and where internal efficiencies lead to cost advantages allowing for acceptable margins even with aggressive pricing, a penetration objective can create a powerful barrier to market entry for other firms, thus protecting market share.

Sometimes penetration pricing is used as part of a new-product introduction. In both the B2C and B2B markets, it is common for prices to be set low initially to ward off competition and then for prices to creep up over time.[9] Such pricing is built into the product's budget over the life cycle of the item. Recall from Chapter 8 that as a product progresses through the product life cycle, margins tend to be at their highest during the maturity stage. This is partly because weaker competitors tend to drop out due to penetration pricing earlier in the cycle (introduction and growth stages), which creates the potential for remaining firms to decrease spending and raise prices during the maturity stage.

Be careful with a penetration pricing strategy. Because price is a cue for developing customer perceptions of product quality, the value proposition may be reduced if a low price belies the product's actual quality attributes.[10] An axiom in marketing is that customers always find it more palatable when a firm reduces a price than when it raises a price, and a corollary to the axiom is that once a price has been changed (one way or the other), changing it back creates confusion about positioning and brand image.

Price Skimming

A strategy of **price skimming** addresses the objective of entering a market at a relatively high price point. In proposing price skimming, the marketing manager usually is convinced that a

EXHIBIT 10.2	Pricing Objectives and Related Strategies

Objective: Market share maximization

Strategy: Penetration pricing

Objective: Market entry at the highest possible initial price

Strategy: Price skimming

Objective: Profit maximization

Strategy: Target ROI

Objective: Benchmark the competition

Strategy: Competitor-based pricing

Objective: Communicate positioning through price

Strategy: Value pricing

strong price-quality relationship exists for the product. This might be done to lend prestige to a brand, or skimming is sometimes used in a new-product introduction by a firm with a first-mover advantage to skim early sales while the product has a high level of panache and exclusivity in the marketplace.[11]

Major developers of gaming consoles, including Nintendo, Microsoft, and Sony, always introduce a new platform with the objective of price skimming. Plasma televisions all started with very high price points and have gradually inched pricing downward as more and more customers began to purchase. Pharmaceutical companies justify very high introductory prices for new medications based on a necessity to recoup exorbitant R&D costs associated with their industry. Those same drugs steadily decline in price as more advanced competitive drugs come along, and, when patent protection runs out, the price drops precipitously as generic versions of the drug flood the market.

> Xerox launched a new high-priced product, the ColorQube multifunction printer series, aimed at businesses. The pitch was the product's ability to save money in the long run thanks to its capability to save users over 60 percent on color printouts. The result: Xerox makes better margins now and customers' costs are reduced over time.[12]

Regardless of the motivation for a price skimming strategy, as with penetration pricing, when multiple-year budgets are developed, marketing managers must consider the likelihood of competitive entry and adjust pricing projections accordingly. An initial pricing objective of skimming will require modification over time based in part on the rate of adoption and diffusion by consumers.

In general, skimming can be an appropriate pricing objective within the context of a focus (niche) strategy. By definition, such an approach positions a product for appeal to a limited (narrow) customer group or submarket of a larger market. Because niche market players typically attract fewer and less-aggressive competitors than those employing differentiation strategies within the larger market, a focus strategy can usually support higher prices and the potential for skimming can be extended. The ability to use price skimming declines precipitously, however, if the product migrates from a niche positioning to that of a differentiated product within the larger market.[13]

Profit Maximization and Target ROI

Pricing objectives very frequently are designed for profit maximization, which necessitates a **target return on investment (ROI)** pricing strategy. Here, a bottom-line profit is established first and then pricing is set to achieve the target. Although this approach sounds straightforward, it actually brings up an important reason pricing is best cast within the purview of marketing instead of under the sole control of accountants or financial managers in a firm. When pricing decisions on a given product are made strictly to bolster gross margins, bottom-line profits, or ROI without regard to the short- and long-term impact of the pricing strategy on other important market- and customer-related elements of success, the product becomes strategically vulnerable. Marketing managers are in the best position to take into account the competitor, customer, and brand image impact of pricing approaches.[14]

Still, in preparing product budgets and forecasts, marketing managers are expected to pay close attention to their organization's financial objectives. During the research that leads to a decision to introduce a new product or modify an existing one, one key variable of interest is whether the market will bear a price point that enhances the firm's overall financial performance. Often, **price elasticity of demand**—the measure of customers' price sensitivity estimated by dividing relative changes in quantity sold by relative changes in price—becomes central to whether a product can even be viably introduced within the context of a firm's financial objectives.[15] The basic price elasticity (e) equation is portrayed below:

$$e = \frac{\% \text{ change in quantity demanded}}{\% \text{ change in price}}$$

Unfortunately, price sensitivity is notoriously one of the most difficult issues to determine through market research. Sometimes, historical records or secondary data can provide evidence of pricing's impact on sales volume. When primary research methods are used to ask customers about pricing—whether through survey, focus group, experiments, or other methodology—they most often place the respondent into a hypothetical "what if" mode of thinking in which they are asked to predict how one price or the other might impact their decision to buy. This is a very difficult assertion for a person to make and can lead to bad data and ultimately poor pricing decisions. Importantly, in many instances, much of a customer's reaction to pricing is more psychological or emotional in nature than rational and logical.[16]

Finally, the idea of pricing based on purely economic models and solely for profit maximization raises important ethical concerns, especially in cases where essential products are in short supply. The latest wonder drugs, building materials after a major disaster, and new technologies needed for emerging markets are but three examples in which pricing for pure profit motive can damage both a firm's image and ultimately its relationships with customers. And as oil prices have soared over recent years, more and more consumer groups have been actively calling for investigation of the pricing practices of the big oil companies, and Congress has periodically called in the CEOs to testify about their profits. At the same time, independent distributors, gasoline retailers, and end-user consumers of gasoline have all struggled because of the high prices.[17]

Competitor-Based Pricing

Gaining a thorough understanding of competitors' marketing practices is a key element of successful marketing planning and execution. A competitor's price is one of the most visible elements of its marketing strategy, and you can often infer the pricing objective by carefully analyzing historical and current pricing patterns. Based on such analysis, a firm may develop **competitor-based pricing** strategies. This approach might lead the marketing manager to decide to price at some market average price, or perhaps above or below it in the context of penetration or skimming objectives.

> To compete with Subway's $5 foot-long meal deal, competitors Quiznos, Domino's, Pizza Hut, and Kraft have developed competitor-based pricing strategies. Domino's launched a $5 toasted sub, Quiznos has a $4 torpedo sandwich, and Kraft has introduced frozen sandwiches under its DiGiorno and California Pizza Kitchen brands for under $4. The price competition got so nasty that Subway sent Domino's a cease-and-desist letter in response to an ad stating that Domino's beat Subway in a national taste test by a 2-to-1 margin.[18]

The logic of competitor-based pricing is quite rational unless (a) it is the *only* approach considered when making the ultimate pricing decisions or (b) it leads to exaggerated extremes in pricing such that on the high end a firm's products do not project customer value or on the low end price wars ensue. A **price war** occurs when a company purposefully makes pricing decisions to undercut one or more competitors and gain sales and net market share.[19] Such was the case in the early 1990s when Sears embarked on a short-lived "low-price" strategy to compete with Walmart on certain high-profile goods, sparking a major price war. Sears management, concerned at the time about losing the Gen X market to Walmart and other discounters, fired the first salvo by publicly announcing a list of items on which it would not be undersold. One of these items, branded disposable diapers such as Pampers and Luvs, led the way in Sears' ads nationwide at prices well below cost.

Unfortunately for Sears, management grossly underestimated the power of Walmart to thwart such competitive threats. First, Walmart's chairman went public in the press by reiterating that Walmart was the true low-price king in retailing (the company's tagline at the time was "Low Prices . . . Always") and assuring customers Walmart would match any advertised Sears price. Then, within days and in market after market, Walmart took to the newspapers with full-page ads discounting diapers to ridiculous levels never before seen, thus negating Sears' approach. This price war was short-lived and forced Sears to immediately rethink its pricing strategy.

Stability Pricing

A potentially more productive strategy related to competitor-based pricing is **stability pricing,** in which a firm attempts to find a neutral *set point* for price that is neither low enough to raise the ire of competition nor high enough to put the value proposition at risk with customers. Many factors go into selecting a specific product's stability price point. In markets where customers typically witness rapidly changing prices, stability pricing can provide a source of competitive advantage.[20] Southwest Airlines employs a stability pricing strategy by displaying only five or six fares to a particular destination, with price points based on when the ticket is purchased and the days of the week the customer will be traveling. Unlike most other domestic carriers, Southwest actually prices based on the distance of the trip and is less tied to load-maximization formulas in which a fare can change minute by minute depending on ticket sales. The airline's stability pricing approach has proved highly popular with customers, and it's been successful for the firm as its seat occupancy rate continues to be among the highest in the industry.

Value Pricing

Firms that have an objective of utilizing pricing to communicate positioning use a **value pricing** strategy. Value pricing overtly attempts to consider the role of price as it reflects the bundle of benefits sought by the customer. Because value is in the eyes of the beholder, affected by his or her perceptions of the offering coupled with the operative needs and wants, pricing decisions are strongly driven by the sources of differential advantage a product can realistically deliver. Effectively communicating a product's differential advantages is at the heart of positioning strategy, and exposure to these elements spurs the customer to develop perceptions of value and a subsequent understanding of the value proposition.[21]

Value pricing is complex and overarches the other pricing objectives discussed so far. Through value pricing, a marketing manager seeks to ensure that the offering meets or exceeds the customer's expectations—that is, the customer does the mental arithmetic that calculates whether the investment in the offering is likely to provide sufficient benefits to justify the cost. Put another way, value pricing considers the whole deliverable and its possible sources of differential

The Butlins Hotel in the United Kingdom sends a strong value pricing signal by showing all the great extra activities you can engage in if you stay at the property.

EXHIBIT 10.3 **Generic Price-Quality Positioning Map**

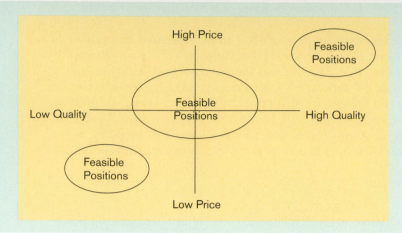

advantage—image, service, product quality, personnel, innovation, and many others—the whole gamut of elements that create customer benefit. For instance, Toyotas and Hondas cost more to purchase initially than other comparable vehicles, but they last longer, require fewer repairs, are more fuel-efficient, and hold their resale value much better; overall, they have a lower lifetime cost of ownership.

From this assessment, the marketing manager makes a pricing decision that best reflects that product's capacity to be perceived as a good customer value. This high-impact decision helps frame customers' reactions and their relationship with the product and the company. Not surprisingly, Toyota and Honda drivers tend to be very brand loyal, with a very high repeat purchase rate, and many multiple-car families of one or the other.

Would a firm ever benefit from pricing without regard to value? This is an intriguing question that can best be illustrated through the example of a positioning map like the one in Chapter 7. Exhibit 10.3 provides a positioning map with price on one axis and quality on the other. In this instance, we're using the term *quality* rather generically to simply connote a range of differential advantages that might comprise the perceived bundle of benefits for the offering.

Notice in Exhibit 10.3 that a diagonal range of feasible positioning options exists based on matching price to the benefits achieved. For most products, as long as the customer perceives the ratio of price and benefit to be at least at equilibrium, perceptions of value will likely be favorable. Thus, a poorer-quality product offset by a super-low price can be perceived as a good value just as a higher-quality product at a high price can be.

A key lesson marketing managers should draw about value pricing highlights an important point about managing customer expectations: Overpromising and underdelivering is one of the quickest ways to create poor value perceptions and thus alienate customers. Marketers will do well to not overpromise benefits, but rather should communicate and deliver a realistic level of benefits for a price.[22]

Coca-Cola has adopted a "value-based" compensation system for the creative agencies that do work for its numerous brands. Coca-Cola will now pay agencies for *results achieved* rather than *hours worked*, creating a need for change in the agencies' pricing model. This approach is becoming common in accounting, consulting, legal, and other professional service firms that are eliminating traditional pricing by billable hours. Ron Baker, author of *Pricing on Purpose*, believes that more firms need to price based on the value of their *ideas*, not their time.[23]

But what happens when one strays off the favorable diagonal of price/benefit harmony? In the lower-right quadrant—high quality/low price—a penetration strategy might be in play. Or perhaps a firm is taking advantage of its cost leadership by offering a somewhat reduced price. However, over the long run, reducing price too much based on either of these pricing strategies can unnecessarily damage both margins and brand image. Penetration is usually intended to be a temporary strategy, giving the product a chance to gain a strong foothold in market share while warding off competition for a time. Michael Porter has long advocated that cost leadership based on value chain efficiencies should not be

Like many off-airport parking facilities, TheParkingSpot features much lower prices than on-airport parking but hopefully (because of the shuttles) without a concurrent loss of convenience.

wholesale translated to low prices—the reason the approach is called *cost* leadership, not *price* leadership. Successful cost leaders tend to offer a somewhat lower price in the marketplace, but they also translate a substantial portion of their efficiencies to margin, thus enhancing the long-term growth and performance of the firm. Bottom line, it may be all right to play in the bottom-right quadrant temporarily in the case of penetration or to creep slightly into that quadrant over the long haul with a properly executed cost leadership approach.

Clearly, operating in the upper-left (high price/low benefits) quadrant can be problematic. Some firms utilize price skimming strategies, especially on product introductions, even when all the bugs have yet to be worked out of the product. New technology products are notorious for having surprises in quality, functionality, and reliability crop up soon after introduction. When this happens, it can be extremely damaging to the value proposition and to the brand. In such cases, from an ethical perspective, one could question the firm's intent. Did the company rush a product to market to beat an impending entry by competition, pricing it high due to first-mover advantage, all the while knowing that serious quality problems existed? Firms and brands that continually attempt to operate in the high-price/low-benefits quadrant do not survive over the long run as customer trust is damaged. Unfortunately, some highly unscrupulous companies perpetuate their operations in this quadrant by constantly changing company name, location, and brand names. Stories of customer rip-offs are particularly prolific in the service sector (from construction to financial services to health care) because in this sector the offering is inextricably linked to the provider and it's difficult to assess quality until after the service is rendered.

SELECT PRICING TACTICS

Once management establishes the overall pricing objectives and strategies, it's time to develop and execute the pricing tactics in the marketplace that will operationalize the strategies. Exhibit 10.4 summarizes tactical pricing approaches.

As with establishing pricing strategies, for a variety of reasons firms frequently rely on combinations of pricing tactics in the marketplace rather than putting all their eggs in one basket. As you read about each approach, don't think of it as a stand-alone strategy but instead consider how it might work in tandem with other approaches that a marketing manager might decide to employ.

EXHIBIT 10.4 | Tactical Pricing Approaches

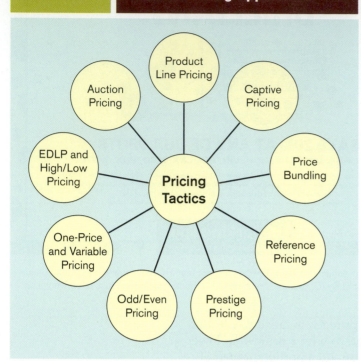

EXHIBIT 10.4 — Tactical Pricing Approaches

Pricing Tactics:
- Product Line Pricing
- Captive Pricing
- Price Bundling
- Reference Pricing
- Prestige Pricing
- Odd/Even Pricing
- One-Price and Variable Pricing
- EDLP and High/Low Pricing
- Auction Pricing

Product Line Pricing

As you have learned, firms rarely market single products. Most products are part of an overall product line of related offerings; and this is true whether the product is in the B2C or B2B marketplace, or in the realm of goods or service. **Product line pricing** (or **price lining**) affords the marketing manager an opportunity to develop a rational pricing strategy across a complete line of related items. As a customer is evaluating the choices available within a firm's product line, the **price points** established for the various items in the line need to make sense and reflect the differences in benefits offered as the customer moves up and down the product line.

Consider the different types of rooms offered by a resort hotel on Maui. At top properties such as the Fairmont Kea Lani in Wailea, even a room on a lower floor with a limited view might easily run well over $400 per night during peak season. Exhibit 10.5 shows the array of room types and prices across the product line—the different grades of guest room.

In price lining, the escalation of product prices up the product line has to consider factors such as real cost differences among the various features offered, customer assessments of the value added by the increasing level of benefits, and prices competitors are charging for similar products. Price lining can greatly simplify a customer's purchase decision making by clearly defining a smorgasbord of offerings based on different bundles of benefits at different prices. Regardless of the product category, customers often approach a purchase with some preconceived range of price acceptability in mind, and product line pricing helps guide them toward the best purchase match to their needs while facilitating easy comparison among offerings.[24]

Price lining can occur at a level much broader in scope than individual products. For example, Marriott has branded its entire family of accommodations based on different value propositions, supported by clearly delineated pricing

EXHIBIT 10.5 | Product Line Pricing by Room Type at the Fairmont Kea Lani on Maui

Room Type	Description	Price
Moderate Suite	Limited view—parking facility or side street	$485
Fairmont Suite	Tropical garden or mountain view	$499
Partial Ocean View	Angled ocean view from lanai	$559
Ocean View	Partial ocean view	$725
Poolside	Direct walkout to upper lagoon pool	$725
Deluxe Ocean View	Spectacular full ocean view	$775
Signature Kilohana	Popular corner suite, panoramic ocean view, wrap-around lanai	$1,100

strategies. Its offerings include Ritz-Carlton and JW Marriott for the most discriminating patron, Marriott and Renaissance at the next level of full service, and an array of differentially positioned brands such as Courtyard, Residence Inn, Spring Hill Suites, Fairfield Inn, and TownPlace Suites. Marriott clearly communicates the differences and value in each of these brands, partly by how each is priced in relation to the others. By now you should have a strong sense of how strategically important price is within the marketing mix as a cue for customer's perceptions of value.[25]

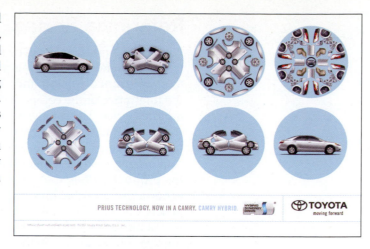

PRIUS TECHNOLOGY. NOW IN A CAMRY. CAMRY HYBRID. HYBRID SYNERGY DRIVE. TOYOTA moving forward

Toyota's Prius and Camry Hybrid appeal to customers interested in similar core features but at different price points (Camry is larger and has more features). Portraying a morphing process allows Prius' strong positive image to communicate that Camry Hybrid's Synergy Drive is the same as the one found in the popular (and well known) Prius.

Captive Pricing

Captive pricing, sometimes called **complementary pricing,** entails gaining a commitment from a customer to a basic product or system that requires continual purchase of peripherals to operate.[26] What is the most *profitable* part of Hewlett-Packard's office products business: printers or ink cartridges? It's the cartridges. And although other sources for replacement cartridges exist for HP machines, the company does a great job of convincing users that only genuine HP cartridges can be depended on for high-quality performance.

Like HP in printers, Gillette built its business in razors by hooking customers on the latest and greatest new multi-blade system through every type of promotion possible from Super Bowl ads to free samples. Gillette counts on the fact that we will go back time and again to repurchase the replacement blades that carry the real margins the company is after.

Captive pricing is just as common in the service sector, where it is sometimes called two-part pricing. Any firm that charges a monthly access fee, membership, retainer fee, or service charge and then bills by the specific service provided is using this pricing approach.

Price Bundling

When customers are given the opportunity to purchase a package deal at a reduced price compared to what the individual components of the package would cost separately, the firm is using a **price bundling** strategy.[27] Cable television providers want you to buy the full gamut of entertainment products from them, and the more you add to your bundle—digital television, premium channels, downloadable movies, local and long-distance phone service, cellular service, gaming, high-speed Internet—the better the deal becomes compared to the total of the individual prices of each piece of the bundle.

A potential dark side to price bundling is that, in some industries, it can become unclear just what the regular, or unbundled, price is for a given component of a package. The cable/telecommunications industry is regulated to the point that this is less an issue, but in unregulated industries, unscrupulous firms sometimes set artificially high prices for the sake of pushing customers into buying a package. Later in the chapter we will review several of the most important legal considerations related to pricing.

Beyond legalities, ethical issues sometimes arise with regard to price bundling. For example, car shoppers often find every car on the lot within a given model has many of the same features automatically bundled as add-ons. How many of those features would you buy if you had a choice? The extra features being bundled typically carry much larger margins than the margin on the core vehicle itself. If you special order a car without the bundle, chances are you will be waiting months for it to be delivered to the lot—*if* the dealer will even order it for you.

Reference Pricing

As in price bundling, it can be useful for customers to have some type of comparative price when considering a product purchase. Such a comparison is referred to as **reference pricing** and, in the case of price bundling, the reference price is the total price of the components of the bundle if purchased separately versus the bundled price. The savings would be expected to stimulate purchase of the bundle so long as the perceived value realized is sufficient.

Reference pricing is implemented in a number of ways. Sometimes a product catalog might show a manufacturer's suggested list price next to the actual price the product is offered for in the catalog. In retail stores, in any given product category a private-label product (say, the Walgreens brand for instance) is often purposely displayed on a shelf right next to its national brand equivalent. The retailer hopes the savings realized by the direct price comparison of a bottle of Walgreens' mint mouthwash versus the bottle of Scope next to it will be enough to stimulate purchase. Reference pricing is very heavily used in B2B price lists, often reflecting price level differences depending on how many items are purchased or reflecting the amount saved by a firm's special "contract rate" with a vendor versus what a noncontract rate would be.

Clearly, reference pricing can create a powerful psychological impact on a customer by virtue of the savings (real or imagined) demonstrated by the comparison. Ever have a salesperson tell you that a price increase is imminent, and if you don't purchase today, you'll pay more tomorrow? Customer hedging behaviors against pricing uncertainty are driven by referencing projected prices in the future. And, of course, a sale or promotional price provides a strong reference point and, if the comparative difference is great enough, shoppers flock to the store as if going into battle to take advantage of temporary price reductions while they are in effect.[28]

Prestige Pricing

As mentioned earlier, one rationale for establishing a price skimming objective is **prestige pricing**—lending prestige to a product or brand by virtue of a price relatively higher than the competition. With prestige pricing, some of the traditional price/demand curves cannot properly predict sales or market response because it violates the common assumption that increasing price decreases volume. From the perspective of financial returns, prestige pricing is a phenomenal approach because, everything else being equal, commanding a premium price reflects directly on margins and bottom line.[29]

Prestige pricing plays on psychological principles that attach quality attributions to higher-priced goods—a typical response to some higher-priced products is that they must be better than their competitors otherwise the price would be lower. When the Norwegian glacier water Voss entered the U.S. market in 2002, it entered with a prestige pricing strategy that helped create a whole new category of ultra-premium bottled waters. Order Voss in a chic restaurant and you can expect to pay $12 to $15 per bottle. What's the value proposition that would support such a high price? The exclusivity of distribution, unique cylinder shape of the bottle, and exotic glacial imagery all combine so that a premium price actually enhances the customer's feelings of experiencing something really special (yes, water can be an experiential purchase). Promotion of Voss water has included numerous product placements showing celebrities and others among the rich and famous partaking of the brand. Had Voss entered the market without such a prestige pricing strategy it is highly unlikely it would have achieved the buzz and early cult status it did.

Odd/Even Pricing

Odd pricing simply means that the price is not expressed in whole dollars, while **even pricing** is a whole dollar amount ($1.99 versus $2.00, for example). Odd pricing originally came about before the advent of sales taxes and widespread credit card use to bolster cash register security and reduce theft. That is, if a customer brings a $5.00 item to a clerk and presents a $5.00 bill for payment, it was believed that the temptation would be greater for the clerk to simply pocket the bill and not record the sale. It was reasoned that if the clerk had to make change—say a nickel if the item were priced at $4.95—the likelihood was higher that the sale would actually be rung into the cash register.[30]

Now, the rationale for odd pricing is very different and it is often regarded as a key element of **psychological pricing,** or creating a perception about price merely from the image the numbers provide the customer. Studies indicate that at certain important price breaks—$9.99 versus $10.00, $99.95 versus $100.00, and so on—customers mentally process the price as significantly lower because of the reduced digit count in the price point.[31] However, odd pricing can backfire if misapplied. For example, it seems acceptable for a bottle of Voss to be prestige priced at $12.95 instead of $13.00, but a physician, management consultant, or CPA wouldn't want to charge a client $195 instead of simply $200 for services rendered.

> Nokia introduced its e71x phone, at the time the thinnest smartphone in the United States, at a price point of an even $100. The company is convinced the device has just the right features at the right price point at the right time. Its attractive price is posing a challenge to the higher-priced iPhone and BlackBerry.[32]

One-Price Strategy and Variable Pricing

An ethnocentric aspect of the U.S. marketplace is the nearly total reliance by marketers on a **one-price strategy** with end-user consumers. That is, except for temporary price reductions for promotional or clearance purposes, the price marked on a good is what it typically sells for. The Snicker bar at the convenience store is 99 cents regardless of whether you are a schoolchild or corporate CEO, and the clerk doesn't want to bargain with you about the price. A one-price strategy makes planning and forecasting infinitely easier than the alternative approach, **variable pricing,** which is found in many other countries and cultures but is relatively rare in the United States. With variable pricing, customers are allowed—even encouraged—to haggle about prices. Ultimately, *the* price is whatever the buyer and seller agree to—a marked price is nothing more than a starting point for negotiation. Variable pricing is traditional in the United States with a few consumer goods—cars, boats, houses, and the like. But it is the pervasive way of doing business with all sorts of products across large parts of the globe.

In the U.S. service sector, variable pricing is much more common. It is also more common in B2B in general versus B2C. When variable pricing is used in the United States, in some cases it carries legal limitations. Many pricing laws have been enacted specifically to protect both channel purchasers and end-user consumers from a variety of unfair pricing practices.

Target and Walmart have historically used different pricing tactics—Target relies on high/low pricing with heavy promotion while Walmart relies more heavily on everyday low pricing (EDLP).

Logo reprinted Courtesy of Target Brands, Inc. and Walmart Stores, Inc.

Everyday Low Pricing (EDLP) and High/Low Pricing

The rise of Walmart as the world's largest corporation has brought the concept of **everyday low pricing (EDLP)** to the forefront of global consumer consciousness. EDLP is not an option just for retailers; it's an important strategic choice for nearly any firm. The fundamental philosophy behind EDLP is to reduce investment in promotion and transfer part of the savings to lower price. Thus, firms practicing an EDLP strategy typically report substantially reduced promotional expenditures on their financial statements. They instead rely much more on generating buzz in the market about the EDLP to create and maintain customer traffic and sales volume. EDLP, when successfully implemented, has a strong advantage of reducing ups and downs in customer traffic, thus making forecasting more accurate.

The antithesis to EDLP is a **high/low pricing** strategy, in which firms rely on periodic heavy *promotional pricing*, primarily communicated through advertising and sales promotion, to build traffic and sales volume. The promotional investment is offset by somewhat higher everyday prices. Why would a firm elect high/low pricing instead of EDLP? Usually, the firm has little choice because of what competitors are doing. It takes a long time for any product or service provider to convince the market that it has EDLP. Most often, firms use various elements of promotion to build sales of new products, shore up sales of declining products, or combat competitors' promotional activity in the same marketplace. Some industries truly are over the top in employing high/low pricing strategies—airlines, auto dealerships, and personal computers are a few that run so many price promotions that customers are conditioned to wait and rarely purchase a product at full price. When high/low pricing reaches this fevered pitch in an industry, it almost always hurts the bottom line of all firms.[34]

Auction Pricing

Auctions have been around for centuries. In an auction, in which individuals competitively bid against each other and the purchase goes to the high bidder, the market truly sets the price (although some minimum bid amount is often established by the seller). As a strategy, **auction pricing** has gained in prominence as Internet commerce has come of age. The most famous example of auction pricing is eBay. Whereas in the past prices at auction were wholly dependent on the level of demand represented by a fairly small number of people either physically gathered at the auction location or connected through traditional telecommunication, today the Internet provides a vast electronic playing field for customers to participate in the auction on a real-time basis.

This phenomenon has resulted in a marketplace in which auction prices can be considerably more reflective of the real value of an offering versus other static price purchase environments. Besides standard auction approaches (buyers bid for a seller's offering), online **reverse auctions** are now very common in which sellers bid prices to capture a buyer's business. Priceline.com is a prominent example of a reverse auction firm that serves as a clearinghouse for extra capacity from airlines, hotels, and cruise lines.[36]

SET THE EXACT PRICE

To set an exact price for an offering, be it a good or service, marketing managers should consider several calculations to arrive at the optimal price. We will discuss four methods here that are frequently used: cost-plus pricing/markup on cost, markup on sales price, average-cost pricing, and target return pricing.

Cost-Plus Pricing/Markup on Cost

Cost-plus pricing is really just a general heuristic that builds a price by adding a standardized markup on top of costs for an offering, hence the term **markup on cost**.[37] First an estimate of costs involved must be developed. In accounting courses, you learn that determining costs is no easy task. For example, many different types of costs can be considered, including fixed and variable costs, direct costs and indirect costs, and shared or overhead costs, which might be allocated to the offering on some prorated basis. Nevertheless, once a cost has been established, cost-plus pricing requires the predetermination of some standardized markup percentage that is to be applied based on company guidelines. Often, managers will receive a list of standard markup amounts by product line. Easy pricing decision making is the advantage of cost-plus pricing, but for most firms it is too simplistic.

Consider the following example. Assume the firm desires a standard markup of 50 percent over cost. Thus:

$$\begin{aligned} \text{Cost} &= \$\ 7.00 \\ \text{Markup on cost } (.50 \times \$7.00) &= +\$\ 3.50 \\ \text{Price} &= \$10.50 \end{aligned}$$

Markup on Sales Price

In determining markup, one approach is to use the sales price as a basis. Consider the following example:

$$\begin{aligned} \text{Sales price} &= \$12.00 \\ \text{Cost} &= \$\ 7.00 \\ \text{Markup} &= \$\ 5.00 \end{aligned}$$

The markup percentage is $\$5.00 \div \$12.00 = 41.7$ percent. That is, the $5.00 markup is 41.7 percent of the sales price. In most applications, when a marketing manager simply refers to "markup," he or she is referring to this calculation—**markup on sales price,** which uses the sales price as a basis of calculating the markup percentage. This is because most important items on financial reports (gross sales, revenue, etc.) are sales, not cost, figures.[38]

All else being equal, calculating a markup on cost makes the markup appear higher than a markup on price even though the dollar figures are identical. For the above example, the markup on cost is $\$5.00 \div \$7.00 = 71.4$ percent, which seems more attractive than the 41.7 percent we calculated above. Sometimes marketers will refer to "100 percent markup," usually meaning they are simply doubling the cost to establish a price.

Average-Cost Pricing

Often pricing decisions are made by identifying all costs associated with an offering to come up with what the average cost of a single unit might be.[39] The basic formula for **average-cost pricing** is:

All costs ÷ Total number of units = Average cost of a single unit

To make this calculation requires predicting how much of the offering will be demanded. Assuming total costs of $100,000 and forecasted total number of units of 250, the average cost of a single unit is:

$$\$100,000 \div 250 = \$400$$

One can then add a profit margin to the total cost figures to calculate a likely price for a unit of the offering:

$$\$100,000 \text{ total cost} + \$25,000 \text{ profit margin} = \$125,000$$

Thus, the average price of a single unit based on the above profit margin is:

$$\$125,000 \div 250 \text{ unit} = \$500$$

Caution is warranted in employing average-cost pricing, as it is always possible that the quantity demanded will not match the marketing manager's forecast. Let's assume that instead of 250, the actual number of units in the above example turns out to be only 200. Revenue would drop to $100,000 but total costs would not drop proportionately because many of the costs are incurred regardless of sales volume. This example vividly illustrates the point made earlier in the chapter that it is unwise to base pricing decisions on costs alone. Market and customer factors must also be carefully considered in establishing a price.

Target Return Pricing

To better take into account the differential impact of fixed and variable costs, marketing managers can use **target return pricing.** First, a few definitions are in order. Fixed costs are incurred over time, regardless of volume. Variable costs fluctuate with volume. And total costs are simply a sum of the fixed and variable costs.[40] To use target return pricing, one must first calculate total fixed costs. Second, a target return must be established. Let's assume that total fixed costs are $250,000 and the target return is set at $50,000 for a total of $300,000.

Next, a demand forecast must be made. If demand is forecast at 1,500 units:

$$(\text{Fixed costs} + \text{Target return}) \div \text{Units} = (\$250,000 + \$50,000) \div 1,500$$
$$= \$200 \text{ per unit.}$$

Suppose the variable costs per unit are $50. This results in a price per unit of:

$$\$200 + \$50 = \$250$$

As with average-cost pricing, the effectiveness of target return pricing is highly dependent on the accuracy of the forecast. In the example above, if customer demand comes in at 1,000 units instead of 1,500, at a price of $250 the marketing manager will experience a $50 per unit loss!

DETERMINE CHANNEL DISCOUNTS AND ALLOWANCES

Discounts are direct, immediate reductions in price provided to purchasers. **Allowances** remit monies to purchasers after the fact. In general, in B2B transactions marketing managers must be cognizant of several types of discount and allowance approaches that essentially amount to price adjustments for channel buyers. While the pricing discounts and purchasing allowances mentioned in this section primarily pertain to B2B, in some instances, end-user consumers may be offered some of the same price adjustments.

Sellers offer discounts and allowances for a variety of reasons. Paying a bill early, purchasing a certain quantity, purchasing seasonal products during the off-season, or experiencing an overstock on certain products are common rationale for offering various

discounts and allowances. At its essence, the approach hopes to impact purchaser behavior in directions that benefit the selling firm by sweetening the buying organization's terms of sale.

Cash Discounts

Sellers offer **cash discounts** to elicit quicker payment of invoices. The rational purchaser weighs the discount offered for early payment versus the value of keeping the money until it is due. Ideally the cash discount results in financial advantage for both parties. Cash discounts are stated in a typical format such as 2%/10, Net/40, which translates to the buyer receiving 2 percent off the total bill if payment is received within 10 days of invoice date, but after that point there is no discount and the whole invoice is due within 40 days of the invoice date.

Trade Discounts

Trade discounts, also sometimes called functional discounts, provide an incentive to a channel member for performing some function in the channel that benefits the seller. Examples include stocking a seller's product or performing a service related to that product, such as installation or repair, within the channel. Trade discounts are normally expressed as a percentage off the invoice price.

Quantity Discounts

Quantity discounts are taken off an invoice price based on different levels of product purchased. Quantity discounts may be offered on an order-by-order basis, in which case they are noncumulative, or they may be offered on a cumulative basis over time as an incentive to promote customer loyalty. From a legal standpoint, it is essential that quantity discounts are offered to all customers on an equally proportionate basis so that small buyers as well as large buyers follow the same rules for qualification. The later section on legal considerations in pricing extends the discussion about fairness in pricing practices.[41]

Seasonal Discounts

Firms often purchase seasonal products many months before the season begins. For example, a retailer might purchase a winter apparel line at a trade show a year before its season, accept delivery in August, begin displaying it in September, yet cold weather may not hit until November or December. To accommodate such lengthy sales processes, firms offer **seasonal discounts,** which reward the purchaser for shifting part of the inventory storage function away from the manufacturer.[42] Seasonal discounts are often expressed as greatly extended invoice due dates. In the winter clothes line example, terms of 2%/120, Net/145 would not be unusual.

Promotional Allowances

Within a given channel, sellers often want purchasers to help execute their promotional strategies. A consumer products marketer like P&G, for example, depends heavily on wholesalers, distributors, and retailers to promote its brands. When a retailer runs an ad for a P&G brand such as Crest toothpaste, it is nearly always in response to **promotional allowances** provided by the manufacturer. Ordinarily, upon proof of performance of the promotion, the retailer will receive a check back from the manufacturer to compensate for part of the promotional costs. The allowance might be calculated as a percentage of the invoice for Crest purchased from P&G or it might be a fixed dollar figure per dozen or per case.[43]

Geographic Aspects of Pricing

A variety of geographically driven pricing options are common within a channel. Among those most used are FOB pricing, uniform delivered pricing, and zone pricing.

FOB Pricing

FOB stands for free on board, meaning that title transfer and freight paid on the goods being shipped are based on the FOB location. For example, FOB-origin or FOB-factory pricing indicates that the purchaser pays freight charges and takes title the moment the goods are placed on the truck or other transportation vehicle. The greater the distance between shipper and customer, the higher the freight charges to the customer. In contrast, FOB-destination indicates that until the goods arrive at the purchaser's location, title doesn't change hands and freight charges are the responsibility of the seller.[44]

Uniform Delivered Pricing

Many direct-to-consumer marketers such as Amazon, Dell, and Lands' End practice **uniform delivered pricing,** in which the same delivery fee is charged to customers regardless of geographic location within the 48 contiguous states.[45] Pricing rates are quoted for other locations, and expedited delivery is generally available for a higher fee.

Zone Pricing

In a **zone pricing** approach, shippers set up geographic pricing zones based on the distance from the shipping location. The parcel post system of the U.S. Postal Service is set up this way.[46] Rates are calculated for the various combinations of sending and receiving zones.

EXECUTE PRICE CHANGES

Over time, price changes are inevitable. A marketing manager may want to raise or lower a price for competitive or other reasons, or competitors may make price changes that require a considered pricing response from your own firm. Among the marketing mix variables, price is the easiest and quickest to alter, so sometimes firms overrely on price changes to stimulate additional sales or gain market share. You've already seen that establishing pricing objectives and strategies and implementing pricing tactics is complex and entails important managerial decisions. It is important to also recall that in the overall scope of marketing planning and strategy, pricing does not take place in a vacuum. That is, a change in an offering's price—either up or down—can dramatically impact the effectiveness of the overall marketing mix variables in reflecting your offering's positioning in the eyes of customers.

> To hedge against the need for price increases, the giant retailer Costco took the unusual step of commissioning its own pumpkin patches. For years, Costco has offered customers a pumpkin pie for $5.99, selling more than a million of the store-baked pies in the three days before Thanksgiving. Despite margins getting whacked by higher prices on canned pumpkin, Costco has opted to maintain its price. Jeffrey Lyons, head of fresh food buying, began testing a way to get around the food-processors' high prices, asking some of the farms that grow its melons to cultivate pumpkins.[47]

It is important for marketing managers to conduct appropriate market research in advance of major price changes to try to determine the likely impact of a price change on customer perceptions of the offering and likelihood to purchase. Both qualitative research approaches, such as focus groups, and quantitative approaches, such as surveys and experiments, can be designed to determine the degree to which an anticipated price change might influence customer response. Ideally, price changes upward will reflect the **just noticeable difference (JND)** in a price, which is the amount of price increase that can be taken without affecting customer demand.

If a potential upward price change is being driven by pressure on margins, creative marketers often look for ways to save margin without increasing price. Over the years, candy manufacturers have been severely affected by swings in the price of sugar. As the sugar price has gone up, a good portion of the profit margin of a candy bar has been preserved by simply reducing the size of the bar. Today's chocolate lovers would be amazed at seeing how much larger a Snickers bar was in 1970 versus today; the basic bar has shrunk by more than one-third during that time. While the price of a bar has also risen dramatically during that period (an average of four times the 1970 price), the price increase would have been even more dramatic without the reduction in ounces.

In addition to reducing the offering in terms of size or quantity, other nonprice approaches to mitigating the pressure to maintain margins include altering or reducing discounts and allowances, unbundling some services or features from the original offering, increasing minimum order quantities, or simply reducing product quality. However, marketing managers should be cautious when they begin to consider altering the product itself to retain margins; customer response to such tinkering might be negative.

A worst-case scenario occurs when a firm takes a price decrease on an offering to stimulate volume and grow share, only to have one or more competitors immediately and aggressively jump in to meet or beat the price decrease, resulting in a price war. Price wars are the quickest way to destroy margins and bottom-line profit. The old marketing adage "We'll price our product lower but make it up on volume" doesn't work when competitive price pressure forces prices below cost!

Assume that you, as a marketing manager, just found out that a competitor has taken a price increase or decrease. You must evaluate the change and select the appropriate response for your product line. The basic principles and cautions about competing on price are the same, regardless of whether your firm or a competitor fires the first shot. If your firm is the market leader, you may find that competitors tend to create similar but somewhat inferior offerings at attractive prices in an attempt to knock you off as leader.

When formulating a response to a competitor's price reduction, remember to consider your offering from the perspective of its overall value proposition to customers and not be too quick to react in kind with a price decrease. In the case of a competitor's price increase, perhaps based on escalating costs or margin pressure, analysis may reveal the increase is an opportunity to both gain a price advantage and perhaps increase your volume and share, especially if you are a cost leader and can maintain desired margins at your current price. Or you may simply wish to take a concurrent price increase and enjoy the related margin enhancement. Remember, a cost leadership strategy does not necessarily imply price leadership; rather, the best cost leader firms take a portion of their cost leadership to margin and perhaps a portion to price advantage.

UNDERSTAND LEGAL CONSIDERATIONS IN PRICING

In the process of setting pricing objectives and developing and implementing pricing strategies and tactics, marketing managers must be aware that some aspects of pricing decision making can be very sensitive legally. Laws at the national, state, and local level are in place that impact a

The trend in consumer products is toward bigger packs with more product inside—per piece, gum is cheaper in a 17-piece pack than in the 5-piece packs of yesteryear.

firm's pricing practices. Federal legislation includes the Sherman Antitrust Act (1890), Clayton Act (1914), Robinson-Patman Act (1936), and Consumer Goods Pricing Act (1975). The Federal Trade Commission (FTC) actively monitors and enforces federal pricing laws. Several of the more important legal considerations in pricing and their associated regulatory bases are discussed below.

Price Fixing

Companies that collude to set prices at a mutually beneficial high level are engaged in **price fixing.** When competitors are involved in the collusion, horizontal price fixing occurs.[48] The Sherman Act forbids horizontal price fixing, which could result in overall higher prices for consumers since various competitors are all pricing the same to maximize their profits.

When independent members of a channel (for example, manufacturers, distributors, and retailers) collude to establish a minimum retail price, referred to as retail price maintenance, vertical price fixing occurs. Vertical price fixing is illegal under the Consumer Goods Pricing Act, and for good reason. Vertical price fixing assures everybody in the channel is satisfied with their "cut" of the profits, but the profit boost is achieved by increased prices to consumers.

Price Discrimination

Price discrimination occurs when a seller offers different prices to different customers without a substantive basis, such that competition is reduced. The Robinson-Patman Act explicitly prohibits giving, inducing, or receiving discriminatory prices except under certain specific conditions such as situations where proof exists that the costs of selling to one customer are higher than to another (such as making distribution to remote locations) or when temporary, defensive price reductions are necessary to meet competition in a specific local area.[49]

Deceptive Pricing

Knowingly stating prices in a manner that gives a false impression to customers is **deceptive pricing.** Deceptive pricing practices are monitored and enforced by the FTC. Deceptive pricing may take several forms. Sometimes, firms will set artificially high reference prices for merchandise just before a promotion so that an advertised sale price will look much more attractive to customers.[50] Or a seller may advertise an item at an unbelievably low price to lure customers into a store, and once the customer arrives refuse to sell the advertised item and instead push a similar item with a much higher price and higher margin. When this occurs and it can be demonstrated that a seller had no true intent to actually make the lower-priced item available for sale, the practice is called **bait and switch** and is illegal. Finally, the ubiquitous reliance of retailers on scanner-based pricing has opened a plethora of stealth pricing fraud schemes, perpetrated by dishonest retailers who label an item on the shelf sign at a lower price than it is actually priced within the scanner database. For certain, some of the scanner errors result from mistakes and not fraud, but the nontransparent nature of scanner pricing puts a burden on the customer to return to the days of "buyer beware."

Predatory Pricing

A strategy to intentionally sell below cost to push a competitor out of a market, then raise prices to new highs, is called predatory pricing. Predatory pricing is illegal but prosecuting it can be very tricky because intent must be proved. Other plausible explanations exist for drastic price reductions including inventory overstocks, so proving that predatory pricing has occurred is difficult.

Fair Trade and Minimum Markup Laws

Fair trade laws were popular in the past because they allowed manufacturers to establish artificially high prices by limiting the ability of wholesalers and retailers to offer reduced or discounted prices. Fair trade laws varied greatly from state to state, depending largely on how strong the independent retailer and wholesaler lobby was in a particular locale. These laws protected mom-and-pop operators from the price discounting by chain stores.[51]

Closely associated with fair trade laws are **minimum markup laws,** which require a certain percentage markup be applied to products. In one extreme case in the early 1970s, the State of Oklahoma took legal action against Target Corporation to force the discounter to obey Oklahoma's minimum markup law that prohibited advertising a wide variety of merchandise for less than a 6 percent profit. This effectively shut down Target's ability to advertise **loss leader products,** items (typically paper towels, toilet paper, toothpaste, and the like) sacrificed at prices below cost to attract shoppers to the store.[52] Target fought back by creating special versions of its famous full-color Sunday advertising inserts for Oklahoma shoppers that showed in very large type the nationally advertised sales price accompanied by a disclaimer clearly showing a much higher "in Oklahoma" price. In effect, the ads told Oklahomans they couldn't get the same prices as the rest of the country, and it didn't take long for Oklahoma consumers to come to their senses and realize that the state's fair pricing law might protect small retailers but it hurt everyday shoppers. In 1975, the federal Consumer Goods Pricing Act repealed all state fair trade laws and minimum markup laws.

SUMMARY

Clearly, price is a critical element in an offering's perceived value. Marketing managers must establish clear pricing objectives and related strategies, supported by well-executed pricing tactics. In setting the exact price, it is best to compare several approaches before making a decision. Several channel discounts and allowances are available that can impact purchaser behavior in ways that benefit the selling firm. Price changes are inevitable, and marketing managers must anticipate customer and competitor responses. Finally, marketing managers must be sensitive to legal ramifications of certain pricing practices.

APPLICATION QUESTIONS

1. Why might penetration pricing potentially hurt brand image and product positioning in the long run? Given this risk, why would a marketing manager use penetration pricing? Identify a brand (other than the examples in the chapter) that you believe is engaged in penetration pricing.

2. Pricing against competitors is common. Yet, the approach carries some significant problems.

   a. What are the advantages of competitor-based pricing?

   b. What are the risks of using competitor-based pricing exclusive of other approaches?

   c. Identify a few industries in which taking competitor-based pricing into account might be especially beneficial when developing an overall pricing strategy. What caused you to select the industries you did?

3. Select any three of the pricing tactics identified in the chapter. For *each* tactic:
    a. Identify a brand (other than the examples in the chapter) that you believe is currently employing that tactic.
    b. Provide evidence to support the use of that tactic.
    c. Is the use of the tactic effective? Why or why not?
    d. What factors might cause a need to abandon this tactic in favor of another?

MARKETING PLAN EXERCISE

ACTIVITY 10-1: Pricing Your Offering

As you learned in this chapter, your approach to pricing is an integral aspect of positioning your offering. Price sends a signal to customers about the offering's quality and other characteristics. At the same time, effective pricing ensures margins and profits needed for continued success.

1. Review the options for pricing objectives and strategies and establish an appropriate set for your offering.
2. Review the various available pricing tactics and select a mix of tactics that you believe is most appropriate for your offering.
3. Consider the methods of establishing an exact price presented in the chapter. Use these approaches to develop a comparative set for review. Select a final price for the offering.
4. What channel discounts and allowances will you provide on your offering?

If you are using Marketing Plan Pro, a template for this assignment can be accessed at www.mhhe.com/marshalless1e.

part FOUR

Communicating and Delivering the Value Offering

CHAPTER 11

Managing Marketing Channels and the Supply Chain

LEARNING OBJECTIVES

- Define a value network and how organizations operate within this approach.

- Identify various types of intermediaries and distribution channels.

- Understand the impact of intermediary contributions via physical distribution functions, transaction and communication functions, and facilitating functions.

- Explain the different types of vertical marketing systems.

- Utilize suitable criteria to select appropriate channel approaches.

- Identify the logistics aspects of supply chain management.

THE VALUE CHAIN AND VALUE NETWORKS

The concept of the value chain, which was introduced in Chapter 2, is worth revisiting at this point. The value chain portrays a synthesis of primary and support activities utilized by an organization to design, produce, market, deliver, and support its products (see Exhibit 11.1).

EXHIBIT 11.1	Porter's Generic Value Chain

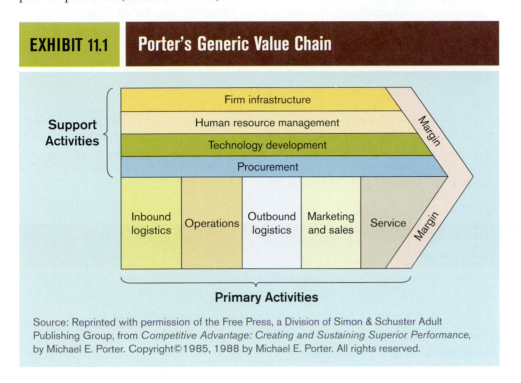

Source: Reprinted with permission of the Free Press, a Division of Simon & Schuster Adult Publishing Group, from *Competitive Advantage: Creating and Sustaining Superior Performance*, by Michael E. Porter. Copyright©1985, 1988 by Michael E. Porter. All rights reserved.

Several of the value chain activities are directly relevant to what you will read about in this chapter, including inbound and outbound logistics, operations issues, and procurement. In fact, emblematic of the central role that channel and supply chain issues play in forming the value proposition of modern firms, it is telling that today more and more marketing managers are turning to elements of the "place P" within the 4Ps of the marketing mix for sources of differential competitive advantage.[1] How value is added by successfully managing a firm's channels and supply chain is the central topic of this chapter.

At the broadest level, a firm might view itself as an integral part of a **value network,** which may be thought of as an overarching system of formal and informal relationships within which the firm participates to procure, transform and enhance, and ultimately supply its offerings in final form within a market space. Value networks are fluid and complex. They are composed of potentially numerous firms with which a company interacts vertically within its channel of distribution and horizontally across other firms whose contributions are essential to getting the right offering to the right customers. A value network perspective is a macro-level strategic approach that is being adopted by many firms in part because of the intense competition to cut costs and maximize process efficiencies every step of the way to market. The approach

Thinnovation.

The world's thinnest notebook. 13.3" widescreen display. Full-sized keyboard. ● MacBook Air

Apple adds value for customers in many ways through innovation, technology, and great marketing, service, and logistics.

suggests opportunities for breaking outside of traditional thinking that marketing is encapsulated *within* an organization, and instead suggests looking for such opportunities as alliances, strategic partnerships, nontraditional channel approaches, and outsourcing opportunities to provide unique sources of competitive edge.[2]

Green Mountain Coffee distributes its coffee to supermarkets and offices, sells its single-cup brewers at retailers such as Walmart, and has partnered with or acquired brands including Newman's Own Organics and Tully's. Green Mountain understands that having the lowest price is not the only factor that draws customers. Marketing Vice President T.J. Whalen states, "It is often the best value and a value that allows a consumer to feel that they're making the right choice for their circumstance."[3]

At its core, a value network exists to co-create value. The aim is **value co-creation** by the participating suppliers, customers, and other stakeholders in which the members of the network combine capabilities according to their expertise and the competencies required from the situation.[4] The key elements of a value network are portrayed in Exhibit 11.2.

EXHIBIT 11.2	Elements of a Value Network

- The overarching process focus is on value co-creation.
- A shared vision exists within the network with a common aim of fostering value co-creation.
- Value co-creation is viewed as emanating from the expertise and competencies of all parties within the network.

- Network and team *relationships* are key elements in the co-creation of the value.
- This value is viewed as *network value*.
- Relationship conflicts are viewed as potential barriers to the creation of network value and a process for conflict co-management is essential.

Source: Derived from Stephen L. Vargo and Robert F. Lusch, "Evolving to a New Dominant Logic for Marketing," *Journal of Marketing* 68 (January 2004), pp. 1–17.

Based on the concept of value networks, a whole new breed of organization is arising called a **network organization,** or **virtual organization,** because it eliminates many in-house business functions and activities in favor of focusing only on those aspects for which it is best equipped to add value.[5] Such approaches are often pursued to provide quicker market response and to free resources to focus on the firm's core deliverables. Network firms usually formalize contracts with suppliers, distributors, and other important partners to contribute the aspects of the value chain those entities do best, then draw on their own internal capabilities to focus on core internal sources of value. Some network organizations operate much like a shell in which most or all of the actual manufacturing, distribution, operations, and maybe even R&D and marketing execution are outsourced to efficient experts.[6] Ethical Dimension 11 provides an interesting look at global outsourcing at Apple.

In the future, more firms, and especially start-ups, entrepreneurial organizations, and those whose core products are in the critical introduction and growth phases, will opt for a network organization approach to take advantage of the value network concept. This prediction is based on a competitive need for firms to be **nimble** in all aspects of their operation—that is, to be in a position to be maximally flexible, adaptable, and speedy in response to the many key change drivers affecting business today such as rapidly shifting technology, discontinuous

ETHICAL DIMENSION 11

Outsourcing "Cool"

The Apple iPhone and iPhone 3G are an undeniable success. A "game changer," the iPhone has taken cell phones to a new level by offering a wide range of features (digital music player, Internet surfing, cell phone, PDA, e-mail) in an elegant touch-screen device with a huge display. The product incorporates a number of innovative designs that require sophisticated products from companies all over the world including Samsung chips and flash memory, Balda touch-screen, and Philips power management.

Of course, the unstoppable iPod dominates the digital music download market with a 70 percent market share. Over 100 million have been sold since its introduction in 2001 supported by an entire community of accessories from speakers to cases. As with iPhone, Apple did not invent the digital music player (i.e., MP3) but improved the product by creating innovative features in the iPod and changing the market perception. However, Apple does not assemble either iPod or iPhone because the challenges of handling the thousands of sensors, chips, and other parts is labor-intensive as well as technologically challenging. The company uses foreign manufacturers mostly in Asia because of their ability to handle complex technology manufacturing and their lower labor costs.

Apple chose Hon Hai Precision Industry in Taiwan to manufacture all iPod Nanos worldwide. Operating under the trade name Foxconn, the company is No. 4 on *BusinessWeek*'s IT 100 with sales exceeding $40 billion. The manufacture of Nanos is less than 5 percent of the company's total revenue. Hon Hai Precision Industry has been criticized for using sweatshop labor conditions in China to increase productivity. Hon Hai sued two Chinese reporters who had filed negative reports about the company's labor practices. Apple sent a team to China to investigate the allegations and reported that, while there were some abuses, overall the company was a good employer. Hon Hai has not experienced significant problems as a result of questions about its labor policies; however, the company has kept a very low profile and that is the way Apple prefers it. Negative publicity about events such as the working conditions in China can potentially damage Apple's carefully developed brand image.

Apple's brand image as a maker of cool, innovative products appeals to a broad range of people. Part of that image is based on the perception that Apple is a responsible corporation that is environmentally concerned and labor friendly.[7]

Ethical Perspective

1. **Apple:** How aggressive should Apple be in making sure its suppliers follow strict labor rules and policies? Should the company enforce U.S. labor standards or simply the standards of the local country?

2. **Consumers:** If you were aware that Apple was using a supplier that violated established labor practices, would you buy an Apple product? Do you research a company's policies about supplier labor practices or environmental policies before buying a product? If you don't, should you?

---

innovation, fickle consumer markets, and relentless market globalization.[8] Taking a value network approach frees up internal resources so a firm can be more nimble in addressing external uncontrollable opportunities and threats, thus yielding a potential competitive advantage over firms that have high costs associated with performing many of the value chain functions themselves. A network organization facilitates concentration on one's own distinctive competencies while efficiently gathering value from outside firms that are concentrating their efforts in their own areas of expertise within your value network.

Many organizations are beginning to consider their customers—both end users and within a channel—as important members of a value network. Firms cultivate customer involvement in various aspects of product and market development to enable customer advocacy, which is a willingness and ability on the part of a customer to participate in communicating the brand message to others within his or her sphere of influence. There are several potential value-adding ways to involve customers, both in B2B and B2C settings, including participation in ongoing research, customer advisory panels, and providing recognition, rewards, and delightful surprises for customers that participate in the relationship at a high level.

Overall, managing marketing channels and the supply chain is a fruitful area of concentration for marketing managers because of its potential to enhance the value of the firm's goods and services in a variety of ways. As you read further about the various specific components of the "place P" in the marketing mix, keep in mind that in today's business environments the boundaries of just *how* these value-adding activities are delivered and *by whom* within the value network is a very open opportunity. As we have learned, these decisions are made with the knowledge that intelligent investment in the primary and support activities within the value chain should positively enhance profit margin through more efficient and effective firm performance.

CHANNELS AND INTERMEDIARIES

A **channel of distribution** consists of interdependent entities that are aligned for the purpose of transferring possession of a product from producer to consumer or business user. Put another way, a channel is a system of interdependent relationships among a set of organizations that facilitates the exchange process.[10] Most channels are not direct from producer to consumer. Instead, they contain a variety of **intermediaries,** formerly called middlemen, that play a role in the exchange process between producer and consumer.[11] Many types of intermediaries exist, and they usually fall within two principal categories: **merchant intermediaries,** who take title to the product, and **agent intermediaries,** who do not take title to the product.[12] Agent intermediaries perform a variety of physical distribution, transaction and communication, and facilitating functions that make exchange possible. Exhibit 11.3 provides further insight about major types of intermediaries.

On the surface, intermediaries seem unnecessary. Wouldn't it be much more efficient for all channels to be direct from producer to consumer like Dell or Avon? The answer goes back to what we learned in Chapter 2 about the different types of utilities—form, time, place, and ownership. Sometimes you might hear a phrase such as, "We save you money by cutting out the middleman!" But in reality, cutting out intermediaries is not a guarantee of saving consumers' money. In the long run, channel intermediaries tend to continue to

Frito-Lay uses a direct channel of distribution to retailers through which products are delivered by their own trucks, usually several times per week.

EXHIBIT 11.3 | Major Types of Intermediaries

MIDDLEMAN: Independent business entity that links producers and end-user consumers or organizational buyers.

MERCHANT MIDDLEMAN: Middleman that buys goods outright, taking title to them.

AGENT: Business entity that negotiates purchases, sales, or both but does not take title to the goods involved.

MANUFACTURERS' AGENT: Agent that usually operates on an extended contract, often sells within an exclusive territory, handles noncompeting but related lines of goods, and has limited authority to price and create terms of sale.

DISTRIBUTOR: Wholesale middleman, found especially when selective or exclusive distribution is common and strong promotional support is needed. Sometimes used synonymously for a wholesaler.

WHOLESALER: Entity primarily engaged in buying, taking title to, storing (usually), and physically handling goods in large quantities. Wholesalers resell the goods (usually in smaller quantities) to retailers or to organizational buyers.

JOBBER: Middleman that buys from manufacturers and sells to retailers. This intermediary is sometimes called a "rack jobber" to connote the service of stocking racks or shelves with merchandise.

FACILITATING AGENT: Entity that assists in the performance of distribution tasks other than buying, selling, and transferring title (examples include trucking companies, warehouses, importers, etc.).

RETAILER: Entity primarily engaged in selling to end-user consumers.

Source: *Dictionary of Marketing Terms*, 2nd ed., Peter D. Bennett, ed. (Chicago: American Marketing Association, 1995).

participate in a channel only as long as their value added to the channel supports their inclusion. If an intermediary of any of the types shown in Exhibit 11.3 doesn't carry its weight, the channel structure eventually will change accordingly to maximize efficiencies across the utilities. Thus, channel members add their value by bridging gaps in form, time, place, and ownership that naturally exist between producers and consumers.

Exhibits 11.4 and 11.5 illustrate examples within two distinct channel situations: one with end-user consumers as the final element in the channel and one ending with an organizational buyer in which the product is used within the business. The exhibits call attention to the fact that channels are distinguishable

EXHIBIT 11.4 | End-User Consumer Channels

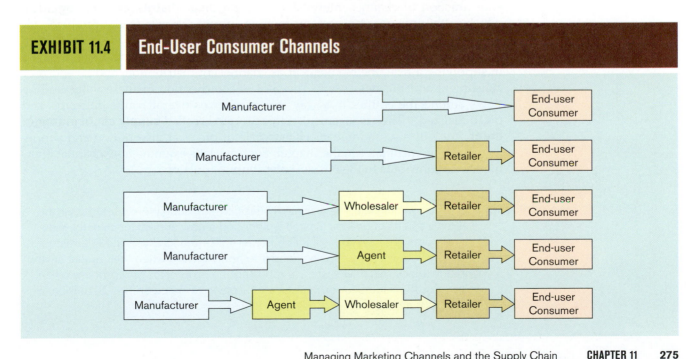

EXHIBIT 11.5 **Organizational Channels**

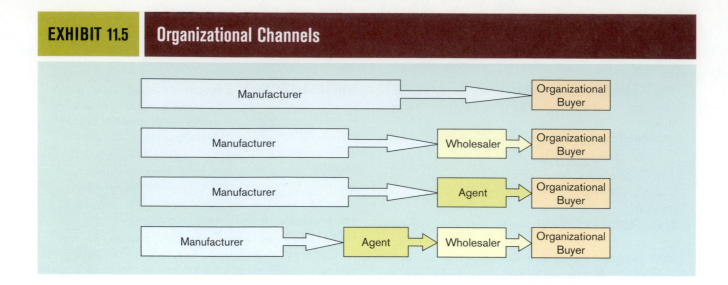

based on the number of intermediaries they contain—the more intermediaries that are involved, the longer the channel. A **direct channel,** portrayed as the first example in each exhibit, has no intermediaries and operates strictly from producer to end-user consumer or business user. An **indirect channel** contains one or more intermediary levels, as represented by all the other examples within each exhibit[13].

FUNCTIONS OF CHANNEL INTERMEDIARIES

Channel intermediaries enhance utilities by providing a wide array of specific functions. Their contributions can be classified into physical distribution functions, transaction and communication functions, and facilitating functions.

Physical Distribution Functions

One function of channel intermediaries is **physical distribution,** or **logistics,** which is the integrated process of moving input materials to the producer, in-process inventory through the firm, and finished goods out of the firm through the channel of distribution. A **supply chain** represents all organizations involved in supplying a firm, the members of its channels of distribution, and its end-user consumers and business users. The goal is coordination of these value-adding flows among the entities in a way that maximizes overall value delivered and profit realized.[14] The management of this process is called **supply chain management.** We will discuss more specific aspects of physical distribution and supply chain management later in the chapter. For now, let's examine how channel intermediaries contribute to the physical distribution function.

For Costco Wholesale, even minor tweaks to the supply chain can save the company millions of dollars. Costco is adopting a new system for all of its warehouse depots. The system will utilize buzzers (like the kind you get in a restaurant to tell you when your table's ready) to notify drivers when their trucks have been unloaded. This new system is reducing the drop/unloading process by an average of 25 minutes for each truck and is saving Costco around $7 million in annual labor costs.[15]

Breaking Bulk

In many industries, such as consumer health products, when finished goods come off a firm's production line, the manufacturer packages the individual pieces into large cartons for shipping into the channel of distribution. This is a convenient way for manufacturers to ship out the product. However, consumers shopping in a drugstore, whether a national chain such as Walgreens or an independent pharmacy in your hometown, don't need to see 144 units of a shampoo or deodorant on a store shelf. The function of **breaking bulk** occurs within a channel to better match quantities needed to space constraints and inventory turnover requirements.[16] Importantly, like most channel functions, breaking bulk could be performed by different types of intermediaries, in the case of Walgreens by the retailer's own warehouse and in the case of the local pharmacy by a drug wholesaler such as McKesson.

Accumulating Bulk and Sorting

In some industries, rather than breaking bulk, the intermediaries perform a process of **accumulating bulk**—that is, they take in product from multiple sources and transform it, often through **sorting** it into different classifications for sales through the channel.[17] Eggs, for example, might come into a processing house from individual farm operators for sorting by grade and size, then to be packaged and sent on their way to retailers.

Creating Assortments

Intermediaries engage in **creating assortments** when they accumulate products from several sources and then make those products available down the channel as a convenient assortment for consumers.[18] Assume for a moment you are looking for a new high-definition television (HDTV). With no channel intermediaries you would have to review the entire line of HDTVs from each manufacturer to truly understand the different product features offered across product lines. But walk into Best Buy or go to the retailer's Web site and an assortment across those manufacturers is already waiting for your review, selected by Best Buy's expert buying staff based on features and value. Most consumers appreciate the convenience associated with having an assortment of choices available for review.

Reducing Transactions

We've already seen how the introduction of even one intermediary into a channel can contribute to greatly **reducing transactions** necessary to complete an exchange. While it might seem counterintuitive to those who are not studying marketing management, channels with intermediaries actually tend to save end-user consumers money over what most direct producer to consumer distribution approaches would cost, given the same product.[19] Manufacturers' costs would skyrocket if they held the responsibility for interfacing with and delivering products to every one of their end users. Consider that conveniently located retailers save consumers a lot of money by reducing travel costs versus buying directly from a manufacturer. As mentioned earlier, in the long run, channel intermediaries remain in the channel only as long as they are adding efficiencies, reducing costs, and adding value within that channel.

Transportation and Storage

Relatively few producers operate their own transportation networks or provide warehousing facilities. Producers make money by pushing finished goods out the door and into the channel of distribution. As such, **transportation and storage** functions are among the most commonly provided channel intermediary activities. In the publishing industry, Amazon.com and other online booksellers play an invaluable role to both publishers and consumers by ensuring that sufficient inventories of the right books are available for shipping across a variety of transportation choices, from UPS ground to next-day air depending on the urgency of the order.

Transaction and Communication Functions

Another category of intermediary contribution within a channel is the performance of transaction and communication functions. These functions include:

- *Selling.* Often, intermediaries provide a sales force to represent a manufacturer's product line. This could take the form of manufacturers' representatives, or brokers, that represent a product line down the channel. Alternatively, the salespeople might work for a wholesaler or retailer.[20]

- *Buying.* Both wholesalers and retailers perform an important function by evaluating products and ultimately simplifying purchase decisions by creating assortments.[21]

- *Marketing communications.* Intermediaries frequently receive incentives from manufacturers to participate in helping promote products in the channel.[22] When a Target ad features Tide laundry detergent, it's a safe bet that Target has received a promotional allowance from P&G to feature the brand. Likewise, that shelf tag in your neighborhood pharmacy featuring a special price on Rolaids very likely was placed there by the pharmacy's wholesaler as part of a promotion by Pfizer.

Facilitating Functions

In a channel, **facilitating functions** performed by intermediaries include a variety of activities that help fulfill completed transactions and also maintain the viability of the channel relationships. These include:

- *Financing.* Without readily available credit at various stages in the distribution process, many channels could not operate. In any given channel, when credit is required by one channel member it may be facilitated by another channel member such as a producer, wholesaler, or retailer, depending on the situation. Alternatively, credit may be facilitated by outside sources such as banks and credit card providers.[23]

- *Market research.* Because intermediaries are closer to end-user consumers and business users than manufacturers, they are in an ideal position to gather information about the market and consumer trends. Collecting and sharing market and competitive information helps members of the channel continue to offer the right product mix at the right prices.[24]

Intermediaries can assist companies by understanding customers' changing attitudes and behaviors, especially in response to price inflation. For example, PepsiCo may need to reverse-engineer products and packaging to meet a price-conscious customer's desired price point. A customer may go for a 99 cent soda rather than the $1.29 container even if the latter has 50 percent more volume—purely because it has a lower price point.[25]

- *Risk-taking.* A big part of how an intermediary can add value is by reducing the risk of others in the channel. Any of the major physical distribution functions described above that are assumed by a channel member comes with potential risks and liabilities.[26] For example, accumulating bulk in perishable goods comes with a risk of spoilage if customer demand estimates are inaccurately high. Also, when product liability lawsuits are filed, the defendants named are nearly always anyone within the distribution channel that played a part in getting the product to market.

- *Other services.* Services performed by intermediaries run a gamut of activities such as training others in the channel on how to display or sell the products, repair and maintenance of products after a sale, and providing customized software for inventory management, accounting and billing, and other operational processes.

DISINTERMEDIATION AND E-CHANNELS

Driven largely by the advent of electronic commerce and online marketing, **disintermediation,** or the shortening or collapsing of marketing channels due to the elimination of one or more intermediaries, is common in the electronic channel. In the early days of e-commerce, many entrepreneurs rushed to market with a Web site to sell their favorite products. This dot-com boom quickly turned to a bust, however, in part because many of these new-age marketers didn't understand the basics of distribution channels. Simply opening a Web site that features a product is one thing, but it's another thing entirely to invest in the infrastructure and capabilities needed to consistently fulfill orders in a timely and accurate manner. Most postmortems on the cause of the dot-com bust point to poor channel and supply chain practices as the No. 1 reason so many of those initial e-marketers failed. That is, customer expectations were peaked by the novelty and convenience of buying online only to be dashed by delays and errors in product fulfillment after the sale.[27]

Today, electronic commerce has settled into a more rational position as one of several approaches within marketing management for distributing and promoting goods and services. E-marketers are much more savvy about how they set up and manage their channels and realize that disintermediation may not improve aggregate channel performance. The trend toward more stability in online shopping was facilitated in large measure by the entry of firms such as UPS and FedEx into the market of providing a broad range of integrated supply chain solutions.

Recently, many e-commerce (and other) firms are finding that handing over one or more of their core internal functions, such as most or all of their supply chain activities, to other (third-party) companies that are experts in those areas allows the firm to better focus on its core business. This approach, which is referred to as **insourcing** or **third-party logistics,** is attractive for many firms whose core competencies do not include elements of supply chain management. The trend has opened up opportunities for firms such as UPS and FedEx, as well as a host of other smaller firms, to change their business focus from mere shippers into broad-based logistics consultancies that handle all aspects of clients' supply chain functions.[28]

Hulu, an online video service that offers free hit TV shows, movies, and clips, has become the sixth most visited Web site for online viewing. Hulu made a critical decision not to outsource its site design and the underlying computer code. This decision was made primarily so that the firm could maintain better branding control—protecting the integrity of its image and the customer experience.[29]

VERTICAL MARKETING SYSTEMS

Whereas standard marketing channels are comprised of independent entities, a **vertical marketing system (VMS)** consists of vertically aligned networks behaving and performing as a unified system.[30] A VMS can be set up in three different ways: corporate systems, contractual systems, and administered systems. At its essence, in a VMS a channel member *(a)* owns the others, *(b)* has contracts with them, or *(c)* simply forces cooperation through sheer clout within the channel.

Corporate Systems

In **corporate VMS,** a channel member has invested in backward or forward **vertical integration** by buying a controlling interest in other intermediaries. In the Midwest, what is now the Braum's Ice Cream and Dairy Store chain started in the 1930s as a family dairy farm in Kansas. Over time the Braum family acquired almost every aspect of its distribution channel—milk processing, other product manufacturing, transportation, warehousing, and the Braum's stores. An owned, or corporate, VMS such as that practiced by Braum's creates a powerful competitive advantage in the marketplace due to cost and process efficiencies realized when a channel is strictly controlled by one entity.

Contractual Systems

A **contractual VMS** consists of otherwise independent entities that are bound together legally through contractual agreement. The most famous example of this arrangement is a **franchise organization,** which is designed to create a contractual relationship between a franchisor that grants the franchise and the franchisee, or the independent entity entering into an agreement to perform at the standards required by the franchisor.[31] *Entrepreneur* magazine reports that franchising remains the highest-potential start-up and growth mechanism for small-business owners, and it's an effective way to expand a distribution channel quickly and efficiently. Subway, the world's largest franchise system, has over 27,000 outlets in 85 countries.

Another common contractual VMS is the **retailer cooperative,** or co-op. In this era of chain stores, independent retailers across a variety of product categories have banded together to gain cost and operating economies of scale in the channel. Associated Grocers is a retailer-owned co-op of more than 200 stores that, through enhanced buying and distribution power, can better compete with supermarket chains than if the stores were buying separately.[32] A variation on this concept is the **wholesaler cooperative,** such as Ace Hardware or Rexall Pharmacies, in which retailers contract for varying degrees of exclusive dealings with a particular wholesaler.[33]

Administered Systems

In an **administered VMS,** the sheer size and power of one of the channel members places it in a position of channel control. The lead player in such situations may be referred to as the **channel captain** or **channel leader,** signifying its ability to control many aspects of that channel's operations.[34] For years, P&G was the channel captain in every channel in which it was a member based on the clout of its extensive stable of No. 1 brands. It became notorious for dictating terms of sale, limiting quantities of promotional goods to intermediaries, and steamrolling uncooperative wholesalers and retailers into submission. But the rise of giant retailers—Walmart, in particular—shifted the power in the channel and forced P&G to become more customer-compliant.

It is possible that an administered VMS can be more formally structured through strategic alliances and partnership agreements among channel members that agree to work in mutual cooperation. Today, P&G and Walmart have developed a strategic alliance that includes connectivity of inventory, billing systems, and market research. The result is improved inventory management, more efficient invoice processing, and product development that better serves the consumer marketplace. Approaches such as this are often referred to as **partner relationship management (PRM) strategies.** The goal of PRM is to share resources, especially knowledge-based resources, to effect optimally profitable relationships between two channel members.[35]

CHANNEL BEHAVIOR: CONFLICT AND POWER

The very nature of channels, especially traditional channels composed of independent entities, fosters differences in channel power among members. **Channel power** is the degree to which any member of a marketing channel can exercise influence over the other members of the channel. As we saw with the administered VMS, power can directly influence the relationships within the channel. Ultimately, **channel conflict** can occur in which channel members experience disagreements and their relationship can become strained or fall apart. Unresolved channel conflict can result not only in an uncooperative and inefficient channel, but it can also ultimately impact end-user consumers through inferior products, spotty inventory, and higher prices.

Amazon CEO Jeff Bezos is using the Internet to sell electronic books on Amazon's Kindle e-reader, which aims to transform the book business to a digital model. As Kindle is becoming more and more a major distributor of news, Amazon will have to be careful of potential channel conflicts with major newspapers. But in the end, the customer is the real focus as Bezos believes, "There is a genuine opportunity to make the cost structure of printing and distribution much more attractive."[36]

French and Raven have identified five important sources of power that are relevant in a channel setting. Those power sources are illustrated in Exhibit 11.6 and explained below.

- *Coercive power.* **Coercive power** involves an explicit or implicit threat that a channel captain will invoke negative consequences on a channel member if it does not comply with the leader's request or expectations. Walmart has

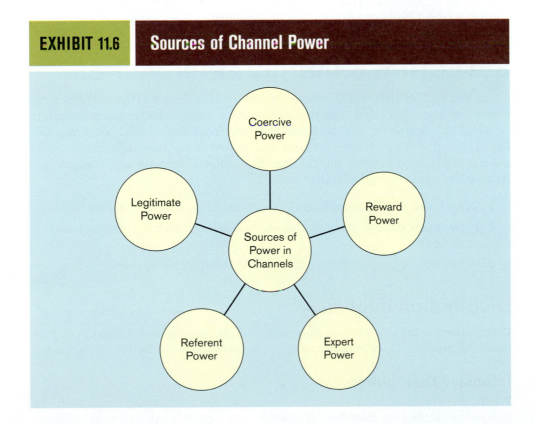

EXHIBIT 11.6 Sources of Channel Power

exceedingly tight standards for how shippers must schedule delivery appointments at a Walmart distribution center. If the truck misses the appointment by even a few minutes, the error results in punitive financial consequences for the vendor. If the problem becomes repetitive, a vendor will be placed on probation as an approved source.

- *Reward power.* Despite Walmart's ability to coerce, few vendors will turn up their nose at potential business from the retailing giant just because they can be difficult to work with. Naturally, the motivating force is Walmart's huge **reward power** in the form of writing big orders.

- *Expert power.* Often, channel members adopt an approach of utilizing their unique competencies to influence others in the channel. **Expert power** might take the form of sharing important product knowledge, such as a representative from Clinique setting up a demonstration for cosmetic consultants in a Nordstrom store to stimulate sales expertise. Or, it might involve sharing of information such as Kroger Supermarkets providing consumer preference data to Frito-Lay to get it to produce a special flavor of chips for a specific geographic area that Kroger serves.

- *Referent power.* When a channel member is respected, admired, or revered based on one or more attributes, that member enjoys **referent power** within the channel. Only the best of the best brands can rely on this power source. In frozen foods, Stouffer's (a unit of Nestlé) commands a level of respect well above the competition because of its outstanding quality standards, successful marketing and branding strategies, and cooperativeness with retailers. When frozen-food sections of supermarkets are reset to accommodate new-product entries and remove discontinued items, Stouffer reps are often trusted to help store clerks reset the shelves and in many instances Stouffer's is given prime display space in the freezer case.

- *Legitimate power.* **Legitimate power** results from contracts such as franchise agreements or other formal agreements. When McDonald's requires franchisees that want to participate in the latest scratch-off game to sign an agreement as to how the game will be promoted and administered in the store, it is exercising legitimate power to control misuse of the promotional activity.[37]

SELECTING CHANNEL APPROACHES

Given the plethora of choices of channel intermediaries and channel structures that we've reviewed, marketing managers have a lot to consider when designing or selecting the channel approach that will best meet their needs. When marketing planning, a good channel decision can be one of the most important within the entire planning process and can lead to market advantage over competitors. Among the issues for consideration are:

1. What is the level of distribution intensity sought within the channel?
2. How much control and adaptability is required over the channel and its activities?
3. What are the priority channel functions that require investment?

Distribution Intensity

Distribution intensity refers to the number of intermediaries involved in distributing the product. Distribution strategies can be intensive, selective, or exclusive.

Intensive Distribution

When the objective is to obtain maximum product exposure throughout the channel, an **intensive distribution** strategy is designed to saturate every possible intermediary and especially retailers. Intensive distribution is typically associated with low-cost **convenience goods. Impulse goods** are also appropriate for intensive distribution, as their sales rely on the consumer seeing the product, feeling an immediate want, and being able to purchase now.

Selective Distribution

Shopping goods, goods for which a consumer may engage in a limited search, are candidates for **selective distribution.** Examples of goods that fit this approach include most appliances, midrange fashion apparel, and home furnishings. A selective distribution strategy may require that intermediaries provide a modicum of customer service during the sale and, depending on the type of good, follow-up service after the sale. Intermediary reputation, especially of the retailers, can be an asset in selective distribution. For example, selecting a retailer whose brand connection enhances and is compatible with the product is essential. Distributing a Kenneth Cole watch or accessory at either Kmart or Tiffany & Company is not a good fit, but gaining distribution in Dillard's and Macy's makes a lot of sense.

Exclusive Distribution

When a manufacture opts for **exclusive distribution** in a channel, it is often part of an overall positioning strategy built on prestige, scarcity, and premium pricing. In Chapter 10 you read about Voss Water's highly successful entry into the ultra-premium bottled water market. Voss's prestige was greatly enhanced by a distribution strategy that involved only one wholesale distributor per state, which had to be a liquor, wine, and spirits wholesaler with relationships already built among the exclusive restaurants and hotels that Voss was targeting. Exclusive distribution also often arises because a significant personal selling effort is required with the consumer before product purchase. Products that possess complex or unique properties that only a one-to-one in-person interaction with a customer can explain are often best served by intermediaries with specialized sales capabilities.[38]

Avis selectively stocks varying quantities of Hummer H3s at its rental locations depending on the profile of rental customers in the different locales.

Channel Control and Adaptability

Review of the types of intermediaries in Exhibit 11.3 and channel examples in Exhibits 11.4 and 11.5 reveals a variety of options that can lead to more or less control and adaptability over the channel. Hiring an in-house sales force, investing in a fleet of trucks, building a warehouse facility, pursuing a corporate VMS through vertical integration, and engaging in a contractual VMS with other intermediaries each would increase a firm's control of the channel but at the same time limit its flexibility to change if the competition and other external forces require it. Other options, such as brokers, manufacturer's agents, and common carriers have the opposite effect in that a firm's influence and control in the channel is minimized but great flexibility is attained to dramatically and quickly alter aspects of the channel if needed.

In deciding on the right balance between control and flexibility in a channel, marketing managers must consider the type of products involved, cost issues among the various options, strength of belief in the accuracy of the sales forecast, and likelihood that major changes will occur in the customer or competitive marketplace that would necessitate restructuring the channel. Often, customers drive the ultimate choice a marketing manager makes about a channel, as flexibility or control differentially impact the value proposition from one customer to the next.

Prioritization of Channel Functions—Push versus Pull Strategy

The third aspect of channel decisions by marketing managers relates to what channel functions are most important to the success of the particular products. In large measure, this decision is framed by whether the general approach is a push strategy or a pull strategy. A **push strategy** means that much of the intensive promotional activities take place from the manufacturer downward through the channel of distribution. Think of this approach as an investment by the manufacturer in intermediaries so that they will have a maximal incentive to stock, promote, sell, and ship the firm's products. Push strategies usually are supported by heavy allowance payments to intermediaries for helping accomplish the manufacturer's goals. Examples include funding an extra incentive to a wholesale drug salesperson for pushing a particular medication to an independent pharmacy, or paying a **slotting allowance** or **shelf fee** to secure distribution in an intermediary's inventory listing and warehouse or onto a retail shelf.[39]

In contrast, a manufacturer employing a **pull strategy** focuses much of its promotional investment on the end-user consumer. In this case, heavy advertising in mass media, direct marketing, couponing, and other direct-to-consumer promotion are expected to create demand from intermediaries from the bottom of the channel upward. A pull strategy doesn't mean a manufacturer wouldn't engage in any channel incentives, but rather that the incentives would likely be greatly reduced versus a push strategy.[40]

Obviously, a number of important marketing management decisions about channel structure and types of intermediaries to best utilize are influenced by the degree to which the channel intermediaries are relied on to help create and support demand. The degree of push versus pull used is fundamental in framing the channel structure and relationships that are likely to optimize a product's success.

LOGISTICS ASPECTS OF SUPPLY CHAIN MANAGEMENT

Physical distribution, or logistics, is the integrated process of moving input materials to the producer, in-process inventory through the firm, and finished goods out of the firm through the channel of distribution. Traditionally, logistics was thought of as an internal flow going one direction—**outbound logistics.** That is, it was thought that logistics started with production and ended with receipt of finished good by the end-user consumer or business user. From a supply chain perspective, logistics professionals today tend to take a more holistic view of physical distribution. Thus, along with outbound logistics, it is important to consider **inbound logistics**—sourcing materials and knowledge inputs from external suppliers to the point at which production begins.

Today, the concept of reverse logistics must also be taken into account. **Reverse logistics** deals with how to get goods back to a manufacturer or intermediary after purchase. Product returns result for many reasons including spoilage and breakage, excess inventory, customer dissatisfaction, and overstocks.[41] In particular, online sellers in both the B2C and B2B space recognize that an inherent aspect of electronic commerce is the increased likelihood of product return. Returns are higher in this channel in large part because of the inability to physically examine the merchandise before purchase. Smart online sellers build return allowances—either free, with shipping charges, or with a restocking fee—into their pricing model. To do this, the seller must work out an efficient and customer-friendly procedure for how merchandise is to be returned. In many cases, the selling firm partners with one logistics company to handle the reverse logistics, in Dell's case UPS.

Several logistics aspects of supply chain management require close attention by marketing managers. These are order processing, warehousing and materials handling, inventory management, and transportation.

Order Processing

Receiving and properly processing customer orders is a critical step in getting a product moving through the supply chain. It is also a point at which mistakes can easily occur, and when a mistake occurs in the order it usually carries through the whole fulfillment system. If the item ordered is in stock, outbound processing from inventory occurs. If the item is not in stock, referred to as a **stock-out,** then inbound replenishment processes are triggered.

Fortunately, in many modern organizations, order processing has become highly mechanized. Sophisticated and integrated **enterprise resource planning (ERP) systems** now manage much of the logistics process for many firms. ERP is a software application designed to integrate information related to logistics processes throughout the organization. Once data are entered, they are automatically linked through internal systems and become available for use with all relevant decisions that rely on the ERP information. ERP enables employees throughout the system, whether in sales, billing, customer service, or some other group, to take ownership of their piece of the supply chain and to accurately communicate order status both to the customer and among themselves.[42]

Food distributor Sysco operates very complex supply chain logistics. Customized technology tools are used to execute a unique logistical plan daily to supply goods to U.S. restaurants, cafeterias, sports stadiums, and other places that serve food. Sysco uses Roadnet, a software program developed by UPS, to determine the most efficient routes for its trucks. Sysco has been very successful; in 2009 it was ranked 62nd in revenue ($37.5 billion) among Fortune 500 firms.[43]

Warehousing and Materials Handling

In an ideal supply chain, materials of all kinds are handled as few times as possible. Any warehouse needs to be designed so that after goods are received and checked in, they move directly to their designated storage locations. Efficient, orderly, clean, and well-marked warehouses enhance the flow of goods.

Decisions must be made about the optimal size for a warehouse, how many warehouses to have, and where they should be located to minimize transportation costs. The last point is especially important if the warehouse serves as a distribution center in which functions such as breaking and accumulating bulk occur for ultimate reshipping to customers.

Inventory Management

To ensure that inventories of both raw materials and finished goods are sufficient to meet customer demand without undue delay, firms utilize sophisticated **just-in-time (JIT) inventory control systems.** A JIT system's goal is to balance the double-edge sword of potentially having too many goods on hand and creating unnecessary warehousing costs, with the chance of having so little inventory in

Logistics issues are obviously critical in shipping food products such as chocolates. Exposure to too much heat or cold can ruin the inventory in transit.

stock that stock-outs occur requiring expensive rush production and express delivery situations.[44]

PRM arrangements often open up their collective IT systems for data sharing toward more reliable JIT inventory management. Walmart's legendary capability of real-time analysis and data transmission to vendors about inventories at any store or distribution center location has created a substantial competitive advantage over many other retailers. In any industry, customers expect product to be in stock and available, and when it's not they quickly become prone to switching to competitors. One component of ERP systems is usually **materials requirement planning (MRP).** MRP guides overall management of the inbound materials from suppliers to facilitate minimal production delays.[45]

Transportation

With the cost of fuel today, it is not unusual for transportation costs to run as much as 10 percent of cost of goods sold. Effective transportation management is one way that many firms keep a lid on costs while also optimizing delivery options for customers. Exhibit 11.7 provides a comparison of several transportation options on a variety of criteria such as dependability, cost, speed, and suitable products. The decision about which one or what mix of these transportation options to choose will have a major impact on a firm's bottom line.

Sysco has embarked on a national supply chain initiative to drive inefficiencies out of all aspects of its system. One area of opportunity is how much product it can load onto a truck—the "truck fill rate." The firm is using a transportation management system (TMS) software application that has contributed to increased fill rates and concurrent reductions in the number of inbound freight miles traveled by increasing its truck fill rates.[46]

EXHIBIT 11.7	Comparative Attributes across Different Transportation Modes

Low Cost	Speed	Reliability of Delivery	Ability to Deliver to Many Geographical Areas	Reputation for Delivering Undamaged Goods
1. Pipeline	1. Air	1. Pipeline	1. Motor	1. Pipeline
2. Water	2. Motor	2. Air	2. Rail	2. Water
3. Rail	3. Rail	3. Motor	3. Air	3. Air
4. Motor	4. Pipeline	4. Rail	4. Water	4. Motor
5. Air	5. Water	5. Water	5. Pipeline	5. Rail

Note: Numbers indicate relative ranking based on general trade-offs of cost versus other attributes of each mode.

LEGAL ISSUES IN SUPPLY CHAIN MANAGEMENT

As with pricing practices, a variety of laws impact the decision making about channels and logistics. Among others, the Sherman Antitrust Act (1890), Clayton Act (1914), and Federal Trade Commission Act (1914) provide much of the basis for legislation impacting supply chains. Three key legal issues related to distribution are exclusive dealing, exclusive territories, and tying agreements.

Exclusive Dealing

When a supplier creates a restrictive agreement that prohibits intermediaries that handle its product from selling competing firms' products, **exclusive dealing** has occurred. Whether a particular arrangement is legal depends on whether it interferes with the intermediary's right to act independently or the rights of competitors to succeed—that is, is competition lessened by the arrangement? Exclusive dealing lessens competition if it (1) accounts for substantial market share, (2) involves a substantial dollar amount, and (3) involves a big supplier and smaller intermediary, which sets up a case for coercion.

Exclusive dealing may be legal if the parties show exclusivity is essential for strategic reasons, such as to maintain product image. High-fashion brands often engage in exclusive dealing with retailers so that their image is not sullied by being merchandised in the store next to step-down labels. Also, if limited production capacity on the part of the supplier legitimately restricts its sales capabilities, exclusive dealing may also be legal. In this case, the point of the exclusive deal is to try to ensure the limited quantities of product have the best possible chance of being "sold through" to end users.[47]

Exclusive Territories

An **exclusive territory** protects an intermediary from having to compete with others selling a producer's goods. Can a producer always grant an intermediary an exclusive territory for sales purposes? Not necessarily. For this practice to be legal, it would have to be demonstrated that the exclusivity doesn't violate any statutes on restriction of competition. This issue often manifests itself in the context of suppliers limiting the number of retail outlets within a certain geographic area. One possible defense of exclusive territories might be that the costs of a new store (restaurant, retailer, dealer, etc.) entering the market are so great that the nature of the market and risks involved demand an opportunity for exclusivity.[48]

Tying Contracts

If a seller requires an intermediary to purchase a supplementary product to qualify to purchase the primary product the intermediary wishes to buy, a **tying contract** is in place. Example: "You can buy my printer, but to do so you *must* sign a contract to buy my ink"—thus, the products are "tied together" as terms of sale. Tying contracts are illegal, but historically it has often been difficult to prove whether an agreement is or isn't a tying contract in a court of law.[49]

SUMMARY

Channel and supply chain decisions are central to creating a firm's value proposition. Competitive advantage can be gained through effective and efficient channel management, physical distribution, and logistics. Vertical marketing systems and partner relationship management strategies add attractive levels of integration among channel members. The aim of such value networks is value co-creation by the participating suppliers, customers, and other stakeholders in which the members of the network combine capabilities according to their expertise and the competencies required from the situation.

APPLICATION QUESTIONS

1. Consider the concept of value co-creation.

   a. In your own words, explain the concept of value co-creation.

   b. What are some specific ways value can be co-created?

   c. Provide an example of a specific value network you believe results in a high level of value co-creation.

   d. Provide an example of a specific firm or firms that could benefit by establishing a value network and engaging in value co-creation. In what ways would this approach be an improvement over their existing business approach?

2. Consider the issue of disintermediation in electronic channels.

   a. Do you believe that *all* channels will disintermediate down to simple direct channels over time? Why or why not?

   b. Does your opinion change if the question is asked only about B2C channels? Only for B2B channels? Why?

3. Consider this statement: "It's important in business today for all firms to work to cut out the middleman. Intermediaries represent costs that can be saved by finding ways to cut them out of the system. Down-channel buyers always benefit when this happens." Do you agree with this statement? Why or why not? Be specific in arguing your point based on what you learned in the chapter.

MARKETING PLAN EXERCISE

ACTIVITY 11: Establishing Distribution Channels for Your Offering

Selecting the most appropriate channels of distribution for your offering and then working out the overall best approach to establishing and operating your supply chain is a critical element of your marketing plan.

1. Define and describe the value network within which you will operate. Develop an approach to ensure that your supply chain operation is as nimble as possible.

2. Decide what type of channel configuration is optimal for you and what intermediaries should be part of the channel.

3. Select what physical distribution functions you will accomplish in-house and how these will be set up. Then, select what physical distribution functions you will outsource and to whom.

4. Identify what aspects of e-channels you must address.

5. Decide:

   a. What level of distribution intensity you seek within each channel.

   b. How much control and adaptability is required over the channel and its activities.

   c. The priority channel functions that require investment.

6. Develop your plans for the following logistics functions:

    a. Order processing.

    b. Warehousing and materials handling.

    c. Inventory management.

    d. Transportation.

If you are using Marketing Plan Pro, a template for this assignment can be accessed at www.mhhe.com/marshalless1e.

CHAPTER 12

Points of Customer Interface: Bricks and Clicks

LEARNING OBJECTIVES

- Learn the significant drivers changing the customer interface.

- Understand the role of retailing in delivering customer value.

- Recognize the characteristics of retailing in order to differentiate among retailers.

- Assess the strengths and weaknesses of each of the major retail formats.

- Identify the evolving role of e-commerce in retail strategy.

- Create a retail strategy based on an understanding of key retail decisions.

THE CHANGING RULES OF CUSTOMER INTERFACE

The way companies approach the customer interface has changed dramatically as better technology, increased knowledge and growing sophistication of customers, and fierce competition have raised the stakes in relating to customers. The customer-company interface is a critical element in creating customer value. Companies seek better and more frequent interaction with their customers. At the same time, customers are more attached to their products. The result has been a concerted effort by both companies and their customers to redefine the customer interface.[1]

Customer Touchpoints

The Chapter 3 discussion about customer touchpoints focused on collecting information from and, where possible, providing information back to the customer. Certainly, that is a critical component of touchpoints, particularly as it relates to customer relationship management. Here, however, we are going to address the importance of the touchpoint in creating and reinforcing the company-customer connection.

Customer touchpoints occur in many ways—retail store, direct-mail piece, e-mail, company Web site, and even advertising. In some cases, there is two-way interaction (retail store visit, Web site bulletin board) while in other cases the interaction is one way as in advertising or direct mail. However, no matter the nature of the touchpoint, the customer is connecting with the company as part of a specific strategy to contact that person a certain number of times over a given period.[2]

Retail banks are constantly trying to find ways to better connect with customers, both current and potential. While their most loyal customers tend to be older, they realize that members of Gen X and Gen Y represent the future. Younger consumers perceive customer touchpoints in a different way. For instance, generational research has shown that younger people can be more impatient and harder to please than baby boomers. They are also more sensitive to fees and prefer to avoid visiting the local branch. Retail banks, such as WaMu (now a part of Chase), have recognized these generational differences by improving the online banking experience and reducing fees.[3]

Go to the Customer

Customers are no longer satisfied interacting with a company or product based primarily on visiting a retail store. They want access to the company (information, customer service) immediately, whatever their location. As a result, customer service has revolutionized service delivery by improving telephone support, pushing more information through mobile communications, and, of course, creating effective, customer-oriented Web sites that address a wide range of customer requests from product information, purchase, and customer support.[4]

Customer Interface 24/7

Higher service expectations have created a demand for 24/7 service, support, and information. Customers want access to the company when it is convenient for them, and this means extending customer service and support beyond normal business hours. Increasingly, customers connect in the early morning, evening, or weekends and consider convenience and access to customer service in the decision-making process. In addition, the global nature of company operations coupled

EXHIBIT 12.1 | **Five Popular Offshore Call Center Destinations**

The Philippines
- Good English-language skills.
- Mushrooming call centers are putting pressure on labor supply.
- Call centers located primarily in Manila and nearby Makati.
- High infrastructure costs.
- People are in tune with U.S. culture.

India
- India has a huge reservoir of educated workforce comfortable with the English language.
- It has a 12-hour time difference with the United States and 6 to 7 hours with Europe.
- Low labor cost but high attrition rate.
- Low infrastructure cost.

South Africa
- It is in the same time zone as the European region.
- Shares cultural and historical affinity with Europe.
- People proficient in European and African languages.

Ireland
- Shares the same time zone as EU countries.
- Highly developed infrastructure.
- Well-educated workforce.
- Language advantage.

Singapore
- Has a free trade agreement with the United States.
- *Global Information Technology Report 2005–2006* ranks Singapore second in IT readiness after the United States.
- The country has a good and efficient regulatory environment.
- Politically stable.

Source: Sourcingmag.com, www.sourcingmag.com/content/c060619a.asp.

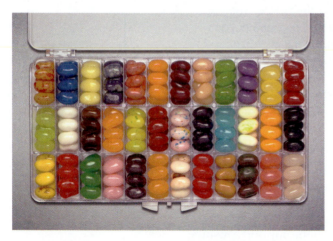

Jelly Bellys reaches out to consumers in a variety of ways beyond its product. The company's Web site offers visitors fun activities and lists of company-sponsored events.

with worldwide access to the Internet means at least minimal customer support must go on 24/7/365 days a year. Specifically, Web sites generate customer contact all the time, and responding to the customer quickly, accurately, and persuasively increases the pressure to improve customer service and response infrastructure. Companies create call centers around the world to handle regional customer traffic over the course of a 24-hour business cycle. Additionally, companies create global call center strategies that enable 24-hour response despite the problems of multiple time zones.[5] For example, companies including Dell maintain call centers in India to handle calls in the evening and later time zones (West Coast) (see Exhibit 12.1).

RETAILING

Retailing is any business activity that creates value in the delivery of goods and services to consumers for their personal, nonbusiness consumption and is an essential component of the supply chain. As we discussed in Chapter 11, an efficient, effective supply chain moves materials from manufacturer to consumer. Retailing, in whatever form, is the point of contact in the supply chain with the consumer of the product.

The retail sector plays a fundamental role in terms of employment and economic activity for any economy. In the United States, for example, retailing accounts for nearly 22 percent of all employment and generates 10 percent of the gross domestic product. More importantly, it provides a vital connection between companies and customers. Retailing plays a critical role in economies around the world and is growing in a number of emerging countries (see Exhibit 12.2).

The Role of Retailing

In an increasingly interconnected world where consumers communicate directly with manufacturers, some question the long-term viability of retailing. They suggest that retailing, at least traditional store-based retailing, will give way to Internet-based shopping experiences such as Amazon. However, despite predictions about the demise of traditional retailing in the late 1990s, the retail sector continues to grow.[6] While the Internet has definitely altered the retail landscape, retailers still perform four critical functions that add value for companies and consumers. Let's examine each of these functions.

Most people know Walmart is the world's largest retailer, and the world's second largest retailer, Carrefour based in France, is a powerful retailer with thousands of different retail formats around the world.

Offer Variety for Consumers

Retailers create an assortment of products that fit the consumer's needs. Some retailers define their assortment of products very broadly and offer a wide variety of products to consumers. Walmart and Target carry everything from food,

| EXHIBIT 12.2 | Top 10 Global Retail Market Opportunities |

2009 rank	Country	Region	Country risk	Market attractiveness	Market saturation	Time pressure	Global Retail Development Index score
		Weight	25%	25%	30%	20%	
1	India	Asia	54	34	86	97	68
2	Russia	Eastern Europe	31	58	51	100	60
3	China	Asia	62	42	47	74	56
4	United Arab Emirates	MENA	89	66	50	21	56
5	Saudi Arabia	MENA	70	46	68	39	56
6	Vietnam	Asia	34	16	74	97	55
7	Chile	Latin America	77	58	51	33	55
8	Brazil	Latin America	52	60	68	31	53
9	Slovenia	Eastern Europe	100	64	12	33	52
10	Malaysia	Asia	65	47	48	45	51

| Legend | 0 = high risk
100 = low risk | 0 = low attractiveness
100 = high attractiveness | 0 = saturated
100 = not saturated | 0 = no time pressure
100 = urgency to enter |

Source: http://www.atkearney.com/index.php/Publications/at-kearneys-global-retail-development-index.html, A.T. Kearney analysis.

clothing, hardware, garden, to automotive products. Grocery chains like Wegmans and Albertsons want to become "one-stop shops" offering consumers so many options they will consider it their first choice when shopping.[7] Around the world, new retail concepts are developed that appeal to particular consumers needs.

A typical supermarket carries between 20,000 and 30,000 product items. While that may seem like a large number, it is only a small fraction of all the products available. As a result, it is critical to select the right variety of products based on the demographics of the store's shoppers. The single college student shopping at a supermarket close to campus does not likely require the large economy box of detergent that the homemaker across town needs. Keep in mind that manufacturers make dozens of sizes and formats of each product. Procter & Gamble makes over 45 different Tide products, not including the various box sizes. An individual store will likely carry three to five different Tide products in a couple of box sizes.[8]

Separate Large Product Volume into Consumer Purchase Quantities

Supply chains work most efficiently and effectively when producing large volumes of products and moving them through the distribution system in bulk. However, consumers don't need or want the quantities produced by manufacturers. Retailers play a vital role assimilating the large quantities produced by manufacturers and offering smaller, more consumer-friendly quantities for the consumer.[9] Samsung, for example, produces hundreds of 42-inch flat-panel LCD TVs each day, but an individual consumer needs only one at any given time. Retailers such as Best Buy as well as online retailers like Amazon enable Samsung to manufacture in efficient product volume then transport the televisions from plants in Asia to any retailer in the United States where it is possible to purchase a single TV at a competitive price.

Maintain Inventory Levels

One of the most important retailer functions is holding inventory in advance of a consumer purchase. Consumers around the world want to purchase when they are ready and expect the product to be available on demand. However, there is a cost of keeping products close to the customer. Products move through the supply chain in large quantities and are stored in warehouses that can be owned by manufacturers, distributors, or the retailer. It is from these warehouses that online retailers often ship directly to the consumer.

Many consumers, however, want to see the product in person before purchasing it. Additionally, in many cases, they want to take the product home for immediate consumption. As a result, retailers provide a valuable service to the consumer by keeping the product in inventory ready for purchase. At the same time, the retailers' inventory helps manufacturers because it stores the product close to consumers and makes it easier for them to purchase.[10]

Effective inventory management is not just for large retailers. Regardless of the company's size, consumers expect to get what they want when they want it. Third-party service providers, such as Fidelitone Logistics, that have historically worked with large retailers like Best Buy are now doing more to cater to small and medium-sized businesses. These providers offer channel distribution logistics services and e-commerce software solutions that integrate supply chain functions and link inventory management with sales.[11]

Make Additional Services Available to Consumers

Retailers offer additional services that facilitate the purchase for the consumer. Financing and purchase options (cash, credit card, checks) are important financial services consumers expect, but these services require a significant investment by the retailer. In many retail environments, consumers want advice in evaluating product options, which means having trained personnel available to answer questions and provide customer service. The opportunity to test a product before purchase enhances the purchase experience but requires retailers to plan for the service and allocate resources.[12] Clothing stores, for example, allocate space for dressing rooms to allow people to try on the product before purchase.

These critical functions add value to the purchase for the consumer and provide an effective customer interface for the supply chain. As a result, retailing, despite profound changes, remains critical to the supply chain and consumer marketing.

Characteristics of Retailers

With more than 1.5 million store-based retailers in the United States it may seem impossible to identify a classification system that would be useful for all retailers. While there is certainly great variety in the number and type of retailers, four specific characteristics define retailers. Understanding these characteristics is essential because they define the retail environment, and marketing managers know that creating an effective retail strategy begins with knowledge of merchandise assortment, level of service, and the retail value proposition. Let's consider each element.

Type of Merchandise

One of the most fundamental characteristics used to classify retailers is by type of merchandise. Several years ago the United States, Canada, and Mexico created a unified classification system for all business activity that was based on a system from the 1920s developed by the U.S. Census Bureau. As discussed in Chapter 6, the North American Industry Classification System (NAICS) assigns a hierarchical six-digit code based on the company's products and services. The first two digits of the code identify the business sector while the last four categorize a specific business subdivision. Most merchandise retailers fall into the 44 and 45 sectors while services are in 71 (arts, entertainment, and recreation) and 72 (accommodation and food services).[13]

Assortment

Even within a particular product category, the variety and assortment of products carried by retailers can be very different. **Variety** is the number of product categories offered by a retailer and is referred to as **product breadth. Assortment** is the number of different product items within a product category and is referred to as the **product depth.**[14]

It is possible, for example, to purchase a briefcase from a department store, warehouse club or superstore, or luggage store. Wilson's Leather Stores is a specialty clothing and accessories retailer specializing in leather products. Its primary product lines include women and men's clothing as well as travel and business-related leather merchandise. The company carries an extensive line of leather briefcases. Costco, the successful warehouse club, also carries briefcases. However, Wilson's Leather has less variety across product lines but more assortment within a few product lines focused on leather products than Costco, which has a large variety of product categories but very little assortment within each product category. Despite the fact they both carry briefcases, target market differences as well as distinct variations in the products offered suggest the two companies do not compete directly (see Exhibit 12.3).

Services Imparted to Consumers

Consumers expect a minimum level of services from all retailers that generally includes flexible payment options, proper merchandise display, convenient store hours, and easy access. However, beyond the basic services, retailers have a wide range of options based on their market strategy and consumer needs.[15] Most pharmacies, for example, do not deliver prescriptions to the home. A few local pharmacies in many markets, however, do provide home delivery, and consumers in those markets find the service helpful. While the average grocery store carries thousands of products, some differentiate themselves by providing a little extra service. When a

EXHIBIT 12.3	Comparison of Wilson's Leather Stores Briefcase Selection versus Costco		

	Number of Styles Offered	Price Range
Wilson's Leather Stores	32	$ 79–$199
Costco	2	$68.98–$159.98

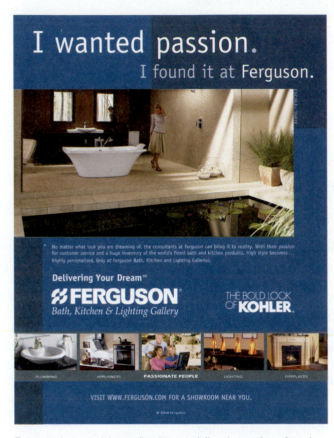

Ferguson is a specialty retailer that specializes in a variety of products for the bath and kitchen. The company has trained salespeople that work with builders, contractors, and consumers.

customer does not find a product he wants, chains such as Publix will order and store the product for a customer even if it is not part of their normal inventory.

Differences in the Value Equation

The **value equation,** as we have discussed, defines value in terms of price and delivered benefits to the customer. Retailers make critical decisions about each of these elements in the value equation. A general rule in retailing is that broader, deeper product assortments and expanded service options require a higher price to cover increased costs. In other words, carrying more inventories or providing additional services has a cost that ultimately must be covered by the consumer. At the same time, the growth of warehouse clubs (Costco, Sam's Warehouse) and discount stores (Walmart, Target) reflects a strong consumer focus on lower prices, which means fewer services and limited assortments and variety. Essentially, those retailers are making the decision to focus on price as the driver in the value equation.

Specialty retailers, on the other hand, focus on value-added benefits such as greater product selection, more experienced service personnel, and other services. For those retailers, the focus is on the delivered benefits and, as a result, prices are higher. The trade-off between delivered benefits and price is a critical decision for retailers, and they are constantly evaluating their mix of product/service benefits and pricing strategy based on internal company objectives and comparison shopping against the competition.[16]

STORE RETAILERS

Two broad categories define traditional store retailing in industrialized countries, particularly the United States: food and general merchandise retailers.

Food Retailers

As recently as 20 years ago virtually all food sales in the United States were at conventional supermarkets; today that figure is only 61 percent. General merchandise retailers have become **food retailers** and conventional supermarkets carry more general merchandise. Indeed, the largest food retailer in the world is Walmart with over $100 billion in food and related sales. Exhibit 12.4 lists the world's largest food retailers.

EXHIBIT 12.4   **World's Five Largest Food Retailers**

Retail Sales Rank (FY 08)	Name of Company	Country of Origin	2008 Group Sales* (US$mil)	2008 Retail Sales (US$mil)	2008 Group Income (loss)* (US$mil)	Formats	Countries of Operation
1	Walmart Stores, Inc.	USA	$378,799	$374,526	$12,731	Cash & carry/warehouse club, discount department store, hypermarket/supercenter/superstore, supermarket	Argentina, Brazil, Canada, China, Costa Rica, El Salvador, Guatemala, Honduras, Japan, Mexico, Nicaragua, Puerto Rico, United Kingdom, United States
2	Carrefour S.A.	France	125,966	121,361	1,775	Cash & carry/warehouse club, convenience/forecourt store, discount store, hypermarket/supercenter/superstore, supermarket	Algeria, Argentina, Belgium, Brazil, China, Colombia, Dominican Republic, Egypt, France, French Polynesia, Greece, Guadeloupe, Indonesia, Italy, Malaysia, Martinique, Oman, Poland, Portugal, Qatar, Reunion, Romania, Saudi Arabia, Singapore, Spain, Switzerland, Taiwan, Thailand, Turkey, Tunisia, United Arab Emirates
3	Tesco plc	UK	73,499	67,147	3,015	Convenience/forecourt store, department store, discount department store, hypermarket/supercenter/superstore, supermarket	China, Czech Republic, Hungary, Japan, Republic of Ireland, Malaysia, Poland, Slovakia, South Korea, Thailand, Turkey, United Kingdom
4	Metro AG	Germany	94,831	93,899	781	Apparel/footwear specialty, cash & carry/warehouse club, department store, electronics specialty, hypermarket/supercenter/superstore, other specialty, supermarket	Austria, Belgium, Bulgaria, China, Croatia, Czech Republic, Denmark, France, Germany, Greece, Hungary, India, Italy, Japan, Luxembourg, Moldova, Morocco, Netherlands, Poland, Portugal, Romania, Russia, Serbia and Montenegro, Slovakia, Spain, Sweden, Switzerland, Turkey, Ukraine, United Kingdom, Vietnam
5	The Kroger Co.	USA	76,000	76,000	1,181	Convenience/forecourt store, hypermarket/supercenter/superstore, other specialty, supermarket	United States

Sources: http//www.freshplaza.com/news_detail.asp?id=36583; 2008 Walmart Annual Report, http//walmartstores.com/investors/; 2008 Carrefour Group Annual Report, http://www.carrefour.com/cdc/finance/publications-and-presentations/annual-reports/; 2008 Tesco plc Annual Report, http://www.investorcentre.tescopic.com/; 2008 Metro AG Annual Report, http://www.metrogroup.de/servlet/PB/menu/1198800_12/index.html; 2008 The Kroger Co. Annual Report, http://www.thekrogerco.com/finance/financialinfo_reportsandstatements.htm

Food retailers occupy a unique retail space and face a number of specific challenges. Much of the food retailer's product mix is perishable (dairy, meat, fruits, vegetables) so companies develop sophisticated supply chains that keep products moving into the store while carefully balancing inventory levels to reduce spoilage. Another unique challenge for food retails is that profit margins are low relative to other retailing concepts with net margins averaging 1 percent of sales.[17]

The growth of low-cost alternatives to conventional supermarkets has created a dramatic shift in the food retail market space. Conventional supermarkets are responding to new competitors with

- Greater emphasis on freshness—using just-in-time delivery and maximizing the advantage of their established supply chain.
- Targeting new markets such as health-conscious consumers—incorporating more organic, low-fat, high-quality food into their product mix.
- Creating a neighborhood atmosphere and upgrading facilities—maximizing the location advantage (being close to the consumer) they have in many communities.[18]

General Merchandise Retailers

There is a great deal of variance in the nature of general merchandise retailers, especially since many have moved aggressively into non-store retailing, particularly e-retailing.

Advantages of Store Retailing

Personal Contact with Product Test-driving a car, trying on a sweater or dress, or watching a TV in the showroom are all examples of the single greatest benefit of store retailing, the ability to see, touch, and test the product. Sophisticated graphics software programs can take someone inside the car, show the sweater, or simulate the TV picture, but that is not the same as experiencing the product firsthand.

Personal Service In-store retailing offers the option of choosing the service level. For example, consumers don't expect great service when they visit a discount store or warehouse club but still respond favorably when asked about service if the basic minimums (shelves stocked, quick checkout, trained helpful customer service counter employees) are met. Consumers wanting a high level of service in purchasing clothes, for example, can visit boutiques or department store clothing departments and get a much higher level of personal service.

Although its original business model was focused on direct online retailing, Dell Computer, Inc., realized how important store retailing is in making a connection with consumers. By creating Dell Direct Store retail locations, the computer company gave consumers the opportunity to experience the technology and features Dell has to offer in a much more personal environment than the Web browser. Also, consumers could now speak with a Dell sales associate who could provide them with personalized assistance in customizing the perfect computer for their individual wants and needs. Store retailing enabled Dell to add a necessary level of personal touch to the buying experience, all while still maintaining their direct shipping method.[19]

Payment Options In industrialized countries, credit/debit cards are the preferred payment method; however, people appreciate options and the opportunity to choose other payment methods including cash. In-store retailing offers consumers the most payment options and is the only retailing format that easily accommodates cash payment.

Social Experience Of all the retail channels, stores offer the greatest social interaction and entertainment experience. One of the reasons cited for the continued growth of store retailing is the social environment created in a store. Chat rooms, bulletin boards, and other forms of online interaction do not match the experience of interacting with other people in person.[20] Book retailers Barnes & Noble and Borders allocate significant space in their stores to social interaction including coffee shops created specifically to encourage social contact.

Immediate Need Fulfillment Even with overnight delivery offered by catalog and online retailers, there is still a delay between purchase and product acquisition. Store retailing enables the consumer to begin using the product immediately.

Reduced Risk to the Consumer Being able to see the product and knowing there is a physical location where they can go for customer service greatly reduces the risk of the purchase to consumers. Many consumers will do lengthy research on electronic products, searching product reviews and user feedback online; however, retailers such as Best Buy continue to grow because once a decision about the product has been made the consumer wants to purchase the product in a store. They make this decision even though online retailers often offer lower prices.[21]

NON-STORE RETAILING

Marketing managers understand that customers can and will connect with a company in a variety of situations, and while in-store retailing is a very successful and powerful customer interface, an effective retail strategy must consider a wide range of other retail environments. **Non-store retailing** uses alternative methods to reach the customer that do not require a physical location. This allows consumers to purchase from their homes or some other convenient location and includes catalogs, direct selling, television home shopping, vending machines, and electronic retailing.[22]

Catalog Retailers

While consumers visit a store to view merchandise, **catalog retailers** offer their merchandise in the comfort of a consumer's home using a printed or online catalog. One of the oldest forms of retailing, catalog retailing has become extremely popular as two-income households often lack the time for an in-store retail experience and appreciate the convenience of shopping when they choose from home.[23] These households often have sufficient income to purchase a variety of products and services. Exhibit 12.5 lists the world's largest catalog retailers. Two of the largest catalog retailers (Dell and IBM) sell technology-related products around the world, which suggests people are comfortable ordering technology without necessarily seeing it. As home delivery companies UPS, DHL, and FedEx expand their networks, it becomes easier to purchase products from anywhere.

Catalog retailers face three challenges. First, *getting the catalog in the hands of the right target audience is costly.* Creating, printing, and mailing catalogs is an expensive and time-consuming process taking months and costing $5 to $10 per catalog. Second, *breaking through the clutter to reach the consumer is difficult.* Catalog retailers mail 17 billion catalogs a year. When combined with other direct-mail solicitations and junk mail, the consumer often doesn't

A critical element in any direct-selling organization's strategy is connecting customers to sales representatives. Avon, one of the largest direct-selling organizations in the world, uses advertisements to encourage customers to contact their Avon representative.

EXHIBIT 12.5 | **World's Largest Catalog Retailers**

Rank	Company	2008 Direct Sales (in $ millions)	2007 Direct Sales (in $ millions)	Market Segment
1	Dell	$61,133.0	57,420.0	Computers
2	Thermo Fisher Scientific	10,498.0	9,746.4	Laboratory research supplies
3	Staples	8,929.9	6,614.2	Office supplies
4	IBM	8,679.2	9,592.7	Computer hardware, software and services
5	CDW	8,071.0	8,145.0	Computers
6	Henry Schien	6,395.0	5,904.0	Dental, medical, and veterinary supplies
7	Wesco International	6,110.8	6,003.5	Electrical and maintenance supplies
8	United Stationers	4,986.9	4,646.4	Office and facility supplies
9	OfficeMax	4,310.0	4,816.1	Office supplies
10	Office Depot	4,142.1	4,518.4	Office supplies

Sources: 2008 Dell, Inc., Annual Report, http://content.dell.com/us/en/corp/d/corp-comm/ir-FY08-in-Review.aspx?c=us&l=en&s=corp&redirect=1; 2008 IBM Annual Report, http://www.ibm.com/annualreport/2008/; 2008 Office Depot Annual Report, http://investor.officedepot.com/phoenix.zhtml?c=94746&p=irol-reportsAnnual; http://www.sribd.com/doc/12937197/OFFICEMAX-INC-10K-Annual-Reports-20090225; United Stationers 2008 Annual Report – Form 10-k, http://www.sec.gov/Archives/edgar/data/355999/000104746909001918/a2190940z10-k.htm; 2008 Wesco International Annual Report, http://phx.corporate-ir.net/External.File?item=UGFyZW50SUQ9MzUzMxxDaGIsZEIEPS0xfFR5cGU9Mw==&t=1; 2008 Henry Schien Annual Report, http://investor.hentryschein.com/phoenix.zhtml?c=74322&p=irol-reportsannual; 2008 CDW Annual Report, http://www.cdw.com/content/about/investor-relations.asp; 2008 Staples Annual Report, http://investor.staples.com/phoenix.zhtml?c=96244&p=irol-reportsAnnual; 2008 Thermo Fisher Scientific Annual Report, http://phx.corporate-ir.net/phoenix.zhtml?c=89145&p=irol-reportsannual.

take the time to read the catalog. Finally, *building and maintaining the order fulfillment and CRM systems used by catalog retailers is expensive.* Most of the $125 billion in catalog sales is generated by large, sophisticated retailers; many small catalog companies do not have the resources to be competitive.[24]

Direct Selling

Avon, Mary Kay, and Tupperware are familiar brands around the world and important companies in a significant non-store retail channel—direct selling. **Direct selling** involves independent businesspeople contacting consumers directly to demonstrate and sell products or services in a convenient location, often the consumer's home or workplace. The order is placed and fulfilled by the salesperson, who usually delivers the product directly to the consumer.[25]

While popular in the United States ($31 billion in sales), the real success of direct selling lies in markets outside of North America ($82 billion). Direct selling appeals to many people because it allows them to become independent agents and set their own work schedules. Of the 62 million salespeople in direct selling worldwide, more than 80 percent work part-time.

Television Home Shopping

Often overlooked as a major retail concept, **television home shopping** generates over $10 billion in sales each year. Two networks, QVC and HSN, dominate the market. While the potential market includes almost everyone with cable television in the United States, the actual number of viewers is small. As a result, both networks have allocated resources to their online operations seeking to expand beyond the market of television viewers. The primary advantage of this retail format is the ability to show and demonstrate the product. Unlike catalogs, however, shoppers must wait for the product to show up on the screen, which limits sales. To deal with this limitation, the networks have gone to scheduling products for certain times so consumers know when to plan their viewing.[27]

Vending Machines

Perhaps you haven't thought of vending machines as a retail concept, but sales from vending machines in the United States exceed $16 billion annually. **Vending machine retailing** sells merchandise or services that are stored in a machine then dispensed to the consumer when the payment has been made. An extremely popular form of retailing, vending machines can be found throughout the world. Japan boasts one vending machine for every 23 people.

While popular with consumers, vending machines are not particularly profitable. Rising costs in labor, gasoline, and maintenance, coupled with a very competitive environment that limits price increases, keeps margins low.[28]

Advantages of Non-Store Retailing

Ease of Use Non-store retail channels offer the shopper an easy shopping experience. Consumers may review the product when it is convenient for them at a location of their choosing and make the purchase when it fits their schedule. This experience contrasts sharply with the in-store experience and is a major reason non-store retailing is growing in popularity.

Safe Shopping Environment Higher crime rates for theft and assault in many areas have increased concerns about the safety of in-store shopping. It isn't that people are afraid of crime in the store; rather, the concerns generally involve other activities connected to the in-store shopping experience such as traveling to the store or walking alone in a parking lot. This makes non-store shopping a safer choice for consumers concerned about security and safety issues such as senior citizens, who report safety concerns are a major factor in choosing non-store retailing options.[29]

Quality of Visual Presentation While not as good as seeing the product live, non-store retailing does a good job of presenting products in a positive visual format through well-designed catalogs, direct-mail materials, and online content.[30]

ONLINE–ELECTRONIC COMMERCE

Electronic commerce refers to any action using electronic media to communicate with customers; facilitate the inventory, exchange, and distribution of goods and services; or make payment. It is the fastest-growing customer interface and has fundamentally changed the way companies and customers interact. Electronic commerce has created new business opportunities and enabled existing business models to be more efficient. The two critical forms of electronic commerce are business-to-consumer and business-to-business.

Business to Consumer—E-Retailing

Electronic retailing is the communication and sale of products or services to consumers over the Internet. E-retailing is the fastest-growing retail format, although it has not eliminated more traditional retailing concepts such as store or catalog retailing as suggested in the late 1990s.[31] Electronic retailing has been growing at double-digit rates and now accounts for a relatively small but rapidly increasing percentage of all retail sales in the United States (see Exhibit 12.6).

E-retailing offers even the smallest entrepreneur the opportunity to open a shop on the Internet. However, although many small companies utilize e-retailing, the vast majority of e-retail sales and Internet traffic is dominated by large traditional retailers. Companies such as Walmart, Best Buy, American Express, and many others offer products and services as well as extensive customer support online. Today, most of these companies coordinate a sophisticated brick (store, physical location) and click (online) strategy that links the retail formats. Williams-Sonoma, for example, allows shoppers to purchase online but return products to the store, offering a seamless shopping experience for its consumers.

The greatest success in electronic retailing has been in products where convenience and price are key drivers in the purchase decision. People do enjoy shopping at Barnes & Noble or Borders, but they also appreciate the convenience of shopping online for books. Companies such as e-Trade and traditional financial organizations such as Morgan Stanley are successful offering low-cost trading options and other services online. As consumers become more comfortable evaluating products and making purchase decisions online, they expand their electronic shopping experience. Apple's iTunes redefined the retail music industry with online music downloads accounting for 10 percent of all music purchased and is the second-largest music retailer behind only Walmart.[32] This change has been relatively fast and dramatic as music companies develop new business models to accommodate the changes in the marketplace.

Click-only retailers produce a lot of their revenue from non-retail operations. Amazon, for example, actually generates a significant portion of its revenue acting as the "back office" e-commerce fulfillment and Web site development for large retailers such as Target and Borders. Another high-profile online-only consumer Web site is eBay, which is not really a retailer; rather, it brings buyers and sellers together in a sort of shopping bazaar.[33]

Advantages of Electronic Retailing

Extensive Selection No other channel offers the breadth and depth of selection. From information search to purchase, the Internet gives consumers greater access to more choices and different product options. In less time than it takes someone to drive to Barnes & Noble and find a book, it is possible to visit the Barnes & Noble Web site, order the book (probably at a lower price), and have it shipped for next-day delivery.[34]

EXHIBIT 12.6 Growth of Electronic Retailing

		Retail Sales ($ millions)		E-commerce as a Percent of Total	Percent Change from Prior Quarter		Percent Change from Same Quarter a Year Ago	
		Total	E-commerce		Total	E-commerce	Total	E-commerce
2006	Q1	$966,276	$25,012	2.6%	3.1%	7.6%	7.5%	24.5%
	Q2	971,912	25,824	2.7	0.6	3.2	6.0	21.5
	Q3	976,919	26,989	2.8	0.5	4.5	4.8	19.5
	Q4	977,869	28,311	2.9	0.1	4.9	4.3	21.8
2007	Q1	996,673	29,758	3.0	1.9	5.1	3.1	19.0
	Q2	1,009,371	31,586	3.1	1.3	6.1	3.9	22.3
	Q3	1,013,290	32,359	3.2	0.4	2.4	3.7	19.9
	Q4	1,023,501	33,531	3.3	1.0	3.6	4.7	18.4
2008	Q1	1,024,224	33,795	3.3	0.1	0.8	2.8	13.6
	Q2	1,033,794	34,237	3.3	0.8	1.8	2.4	8.3
	Q3	1,018,818	34,356	3.4	−1.4	0.3	0.3	5.7

Source: www.marketingcharts.com/direct/retail-e-commerce-sales-growth-slows-up-just-1-4644/commerce-dept-4q99-to-1q08-total-retail-and-online-salesjpg/.

Considerable Information Available for Product Research and Evaluation The Internet has dramatically expanded consumers' knowledge, offering an almost unlimited number of Web sites that research, evaluate, and recommend products and services. From retailers (Best Buy in electronics) to independent testing organizations (CNet in technology) consumers can find information on anything.[35] For example, if a consumer wants to find out more about a 1958 John Deere 420T tractor, all he or she has to do is visit www.antiquetractors.com. If a consumer wants a 1935 Whittall Bird of Paradise rug, he or she can simply check out eBay. Additionally, many sites offer additional tools such as side-by-side product comparisons, video product reviews, or three-dimensional interactive product displays that educate consumers in an entertaining and visually informative manner.

Web sites that feature customer reviews continue to grow in popularity. Increasingly, people believe that customer reviews are one of the best ways to get an unbiased take on a product. Although it is common for companies to include customer reviews on their Web sites, many consumers are suspicious of "customer" reviews that are not published by third-party sites. As a result of this perception, popular Web sites such as CNET.com offer company-sponsored links that direct users to the company's Web site from a customer review they read at CNET.com.[36]

Build Product Communities The Internet brings together groups of individuals with a shared interest to create virtual communities. These communities share information, ideas, and product information. Babycenter.com offers parents a one-stop source for information about babies, children, and parenting. These sites are an excellent communication channel for companies marketing products

Thrifty Rent-A-Car combines an online strategy (clicks) with its retail stores (bricks) to create better service for its business customers.

Courtesy Thrifty Car Rental

to relevant target markets. Johnson & Johnson is a primary sponsor of Babycenter.com and refers to the site as a "trusted partner" on its own baby products Web site.[37]

Individualized Customer Experience The Internet allows a great deal of personalization for both the consumer and the company. Consumers can get one-on-one interaction from a customer service representative and create their own Web content based on personal preferences. At the same time, companies can tailor messages and Web content by analyzing consumer Web history. The end result is a more customized, personal experience for the consumer.

Disadvantage of Electronic Retailing

Electronic retailing has a number of advantages; however, there are several drawbacks.

Easier for Customers to Walk Away The customer is in total control of the Web experience and has the opportunity to walk away at any time. In sharp contrast to a personal-selling situation or even a retail store, the customer can simply click to another site. This puts additional pressure on the Web site to attract and then hold on to visitors. In evaluating a Web site, one of the key measures is its "stickiness," which refers to the amount of time visitors remain at the site. A good Web site not only attracts a lot of visitors, but it also gets them to remain and explore the site.

Reduced Ability to Sell Features and Benefits Web sites now incorporate sophisticated tools to display and highlight critical features and benefits. However, unless the customer initiates additional contact via Web live chat, phone, or e-mail, it is not possible to engage the customer to answer questions or deal with objections.

Security of Personal Data While companies work hard to make their Web sites secure and keep personal data such as credit-card numbers private, many consumers still have concerns about the security of their data. These concerns lead some consumers to limit their electronic purchases.[38]

Business-to-Business Electronic Commerce

While the Internet has reshaped the way businesses and consumers interact, it has had a much more significant role in the business-to-business customer interface. B2B electronic commerce now accounts for nearly 30 percent of all business transactions and is growing at 17 percent per year. Exhibit 12.7 highlights the importance of B2B activity.

Many companies now require their vendors to do business online. Disney suppliers become part of Disney's EDI (electronic data interchange) network and process orders via the Internet. This requires an initial investment of thousands of dollars to get the infrastructure (hardware and software) to connect with Disney. Walmart, a pioneer in the application of technology into business processes, directly connects its large suppliers such as Procter & Gamble with its IT network so orders for individual stores are received at P&G and shipped directly to each store.

EXHIBIT 12.7

Ad Spending Growth Rates for B2B Internet Activity

US B2B Media Spending, 2005–2010 (in $ millions)						
	2005	**2006**	**2007**	**2008**	**2009**	**2010**
Total spending*	$22,285	$23,688	$25,131	$26,740	$28,358	$30,172
Online ad spending	$ 1,537	$ 1,951	$ 2,431	$ 2,912	$ 3,410	$ 3,939
Online ad spending growth	24.9%	26.9%	23.7%	20.7%	17.1%	15.5%
Online ad spending % of total	6.9%	8.2%	9.6%	10.9%	12.0%	13.1%

*Includes B2B magazines, trade shows and exhibitions, online advertising, and online content and communities.

Source: Veronis Suhler Stevenson, PQ Media, AdScope, Agricom, American Business Media, BPA International, Center for Exhibition Research, IMS/TheAuditor, PERQ, SRDS, TNS Media Intelligence/CMR, Tradeshow Week, eMarketer calculations.

Source: www.emarketer.com, accessed November 2008.

Sophisticated enterprise resource planning (ERP) and customer relationship management (CRM) software packages can improve the productivity of any organization willing to pay the cost of purchasing and maintaining the software to market leaders SAP and Oracle. For many nonprofit organizations, however, the fees are too high. Fortunately, other vendors provide similar, though less sophisticated, services for a fraction of the price. Service providers such as Net-Suite, Inc., offer more integrated and simplified e-commerce software options that are less expensive and tailored to the needs and capabilities of many nonprofit organizations.[39]

The Internet has also increased the efficiency of B2B relationships through dedicated B2B sites that facilitate the exchange of products and services. This has made many markets, such as the wholesale distribution of electricity, more efficient as buyers and sellers get together quickly. Known as **market makers,** these sites (such as Lendingtree.com for mortgage and other loans) bring buyers and sellers together.[40]

Customer communities are, as the name suggests, sites where customers come and share stories about their vendor experiences. These sites enable customers to evaluate vendors and then make better product decisions. Nortel sponsors a customer community program to encourage customer dialogue and deliver the most current information and education on its portfolio of products, solutions, and enabling technologies. The company's goal is to offer customers insight into Nortel while providing a forum for feedback and commentary.[41]

RETAIL STRATEGY

Developing an effective retail strategy involves making a series of decisions on six key factors. In essence, working through these six areas will enable the marketing manager to consider critical questions, such as which markets to target, and then

For years Dunkin' Donuts focused on selling a limited line of products (donuts). Recently the company has expanded its products to include breakfast sandwiches, gourmet coffee, even coffee equipment. It is expanding its product assortment to take on the retail coffee market leader, Starbucks.

develop specific tactics, such as the store environment, to develop the best retail strategy. Let's examine these six keys to a successful retail strategy.

Retail Target Market

Retail strategy begins with a clear understanding of the **retail target market,** the group of consumers targeted by a retailer. Often multiple retailers will target the same group. For instance Sak's Fifth Avenue and Nieman Marcus both target upscale, fashion-conscious consumers. Retailers identify retail target markets using a variety of characteristics such as geographic location, demographics, lifestyle, product benefits, or buying situation.[42]

Ultimately a retailer's goal is to build a loyal group of customers. The best defense against a strong competitor is a loyal group of customers who want to shop at a particular retailer. **Retail positioning** in the consumer's mind is created through the use of a variety of tools that build a retail brand image. The Gap's image offers reasonably priced clothing with good service. T.J. Maxx is known as being a fashion-oriented clothing store with less service and a lower price. By using perceptual mapping techniques, retailers can see where they stand relative to competitors on key characteristics such as service, price, and product selection.

Retailers also use **loyalty programs** that reinforce benefits of purchasing at the retailer and reward consumers for being loyal. As part of a broader customer relationship management strategy, loyalty programs offer discounts and other benefits to customers that strengthen the relationship. Sophisticated data mining programs allow retailers to develop individual loyalty incentives that address specific customer purchase patterns.[43]

A strong component of Men's Wearhouse's overall success is the company's effective use of customer loyalty programs. Historically, the retailer focused on adult males ranging from young professionals to retirees. Recently, however, Men's Wearhouse entered the teen market offering prom-related services such as tuxedo rentals. When the company designed a customer loyalty program targeted at teens, Men's Wearhouse knew it had to integrate social media somehow. The Web site www.virtualprom.com, uses a viral customer loyalty program that awards customers a 10 percent discount for every referral made through a social networking site.[44]

Location

The single most critical decision in store retailing is the physical location of the store for two important reasons. First, research strongly suggests that location is a vital consumer choice factor in selecting a store. Small differences in site location can have a big effect on the success of a given store.[45] For example, it may appear that being on any corner of a busy street intersection would be sufficient for a new Shell gas station. However, choosing the wrong corner (cars don't have access, traffic flow favors another corner) can be more costly than not being there at all.

Second, store retailing requires a complex logistics network to make it work effectively, and a good location strategy is essential in that process. Food Lion grocery stores recently pulled out of several markets in Florida because it was not able to create an efficient network of retail stores in key markets. In central Florida, the company did not have enough stores to support the necessary warehousing and transportation infrastructure. Retailers must be thinking not only of a single store location but also the location strategy for future stores and how that will fit into a logistics network. At the same time, retailers need to be sensitive about cannibalization of existing store sales and do not want to overpopulate a given area with too many stores. That approach effectively takes sales from one location and gives it to another. Over time, retailers must be sensitive to the proper density of stores in an area.

Types of Locations

There are many types of locations for store retailers. Each location has advantages and disadvantages. Retail managers make the location decision after considering a number of trade-offs. For example, large malls bring a lot of people into a location but leasing space is more expensive. In addition, for retailers of large products, such as TVs, the mall may prevent direct store access so customers find it difficult to get the product home.

Site Location Criteria

Three primary criteria for considering a particular location are: (1) characteristics of the specific site, (2) characteristics of the trading area surrounding the site, and (3) estimated sales from a store at a specific location. The first criteria, characteristics of the specific site, are used to assess the viability of the site if developed as proposed. The most fundamental factor is customer access—do a sufficient number of customers (traffic flow) have relatively easy access to the site (accessibility)? Companies seek a balance of sufficient car traffic to bring people to the site but not so much to create congestion and limit access. Other factors such as parking and current (as well as projected) tenants are also evaluated. Finally, it is important to identify any building, tenant, or other code restrictions that must be dealt with before building the store.

The second criterion is an analysis of the trading area, or the geographic area from which customers will be drawn. Retailers are particularly interested in the demographic and lifestyle characteristics of the trading area to assess how well the characteristics of the trading area match the retailer's characteristics. Obviously, the closer the match the greater the likelihood that site is a good fit.

Finally, once information about the trading area is collected it is possible to estimate the potential sales for the store site. Several models are available, and many companies use their own proprietary models to estimate sales. Retailers want to be reasonably confident that potential sales opportunity exists before investing in a particular site.

Product Mix Assortment

As we discussed earlier, a retailer's product assortment is an essential characteristic that defines the retailer in the marketplace. As a result, choosing the right product mix that aligns the retailer's corporate objectives with the target market's needs is a critical element in the retail strategy. Initially, the focus is on defining the product breadth (how many different product items) and product depth (how many variations of a particular product) of the product assortment.

Defining the product assortment, however, is only the first component in developing a product mix assortment. Management must make decisions about specific product items. The analysis begins with an assessment of **merchandise categories,** an assortment of items considered substitutes for each other. A mother, for example, looking to purchase pants for her son might consider a number of options (jeans or corduroys, dress or play). Those options represent a merchandise category. Retailers do not define merchandise categories in the same way but, rather, create categories that fit their sales and strategy.[46] Walmart might break out toothpaste and mouthwash into separate categories while a grocery store chain such as Wegmans combines the two into a category called dental care. When a particular brand accounts for sizable sales, the retailer may even create a category based on the brand such as Macy's does with Ralph Lauren/Polo.

National versus Private-Label Brands

In putting the product assortment together, retailers must decide the mix of national versus private-label brands. **National brands** are products created, manufactured, and marketed by a company and sold to retailers around the country and the world. The manufacturing company is responsible for all aspects of product creation, production, distribution, and marketing. The retailer, in turn, sells the product, making a percentage markup and, in most cases, supporting the marketing efforts of the manufacturer with additional marketing communications.

There are a variety of national brand strategies. In some cases, companies create a family brand (Sony) as well as subbrands (XSeries Walkman MP3 Players) for specific product categories. In other cases, the manufacturer develops distinct brands that do not share names or any identifiable connection. Most people are not aware that AXE men's grooming products, Country Crock spreads, Ben & Jerry's, and Bertolli are all part of Unilever, a global consumer products company (see Exhibit 12.8).

Private-label brands, also known as store or house brands, are products managed and marketed by retailers. Generally, private-label brands offer a lower price point product relative to the national brand. Retailers set design and product characteristics then contract with outside manufacturers. Manufacturers are not identified, and the retailer accepts full responsibility for distribution and marketing of the product. Private-label brands are proprietary to the retailer with some, such as Craftsman, becoming major brands in their own right. Historically, private-label brands were viewed as lower quality but that is changing. Increasingly, consumers see little difference between national and private-label branded products in many product categories such as raisin bran cereal and chocolate chip cookies.

Private-label and national brands both have advantages and disadvantages. National brands tend to be supported with excellent product design, support, and marketing communications by their manufacturers. They enhance the image of the retailer and help generate additional store traffic. As a result, retailers spend relatively less on marketing with national brands than their own private-label brands.[47]

EXHIBIT 12.8	Selected Global Brands for Unilever
Axe	Austria, Belgium, Canada, Central and South America, Chile, Czech Republic, Europe, France, Germany, Hungary, Mexico, Netherlands, Poland, Portugal, Slovakia, United Kingdom
Becel, Flora	Australia, Austria, Belgium, Brazil, Canada, Chile, Czech Republic, Denmark, Europe, Finland, Germany, Greece, Hungary, Italy, South Africa, Spain, Sweden, Switzerland, United Kingdom, United States
Ben & Jerry's	France, Hong Kong, Ireland, Korea, Netherlands, Sweden, United States
Bertolli	Austria, Belgium, Canada, Czech Republic, Finland, France, Germany, Global, Hungary, Italy, Netherlands, United Kingdom, United States
Blue Band, Rama, Country Crock, Doriana	Austria, Belgium, Brazil, Chile, Czech Republic, Europe, Germany, Hungary, Netherlands, Slovakia, Sweden, Switzerland, Turkey, United States
Close Up	Brazil, India

At the same time, however, national brand manufacturers charge higher prices to the retailer and exert greater control over final sales prices, which translates into lower gross margins than private-label brands. Since national brands are sold at different retailers, there is always price pressure, and retailers, as a rule, make less money on national brands. Finally, because national brands are not associated with the particular retailer, there is not as much retailer loyalty as brand loyalty.

Private-label brands, when successful, offset many negative issues associated with national brands. Margins tend to be higher and the retailer has greater flexibility in pricing and product design. However, marketing costs are higher as the retailer must spend additional resources to support the private-label brand.

Pricing

There are two basic retail pricing strategies: high/low and everyday low pricing (EDLP). Retailers must choose the strategy that best fits their overall corporate strategy. **High/low pricing** offers frequent discounts primarily through sales promotions to stated regular prices. Historically, sales occurred at certain times of the year (after the holidays); however, retail price competition has become relentless, driving many retailers to offer constant sales and promotions. The mix of high and low prices allows retailers to differentiate their pricing to different target markets by charging a higher price to less price-sensitive consumers and lower prices to more price-sensitive shoppers. Another benefit of high/low pricing is that sales and sales promotional activities generate excitement and draw people into the store. Finally, it is much easier to move slow merchandise with significant sales promotions. Pricing has become a significant issue as many retailers compete for the same customers.[48] The Ethical Dimension looks at this issue in the context of the popular Harry Potter books and movies.

Everyday low pricing (EDLP) is the approach used by stores that maintain a price point somewhere between high and deeply discounted sales prices. Supermarkets, home improvement stores, and discount stores have been the primary adopters of this strategy. This approach does not preclude sales promotions that offer lower prices, and many retailers using EDLP pricing also offer a **low price guarantee policy** that guarantees consumers the lowest price for any given product by matching the sales price of competitors. EDLP can help build customer loyalty because customers know they can rely on consistently low prices. Once an EDLP strategy is in place, the retailer spends less on marketing communications and advertising because sales promotions are not a big part of the strategy and, as a result, do not need to be advertised. Finally, because inventory tends to fluctuate less, it is easier to manage inventory levels.[49]

In-Store Experience

A key aspect of the customer's overall satisfaction with a retailer is the in-store experience, which begins before the customer enters the store. The retailer's advertising and Web site create expectations for the customer that will be evaluated during the shopping experience. The in-store experience is based on two factors: services and environment.

As we discussed earlier, the service mix offered by the retailer is a key differentiator in the overall retail experience. Three levels of services must be considered:

- Services that enhance the **shopping experience:** services that make shopping more enjoyable, such as fitting rooms, knowledgeable and helpful sales staff, convenient store hours, store displays.

IKEA has built a global reputation offering high-quality products at low prices in a unique in-store experience. Its retail stores are large, in excess of 100,000 square feet, and many products must be assembled by the customer.

ETHICAL DIMENSION 12

The Dark Side of Harry Potter's Magic

The numbers are magical; more than 400 million books sold worldwide, $4 billion plus in box office receipts, a $50 million attraction at Universal Orlando, and an author who is now one of the wealthiest women in the world. The world of Harry Potter has certainly been good to J. K. Rowling; it has generated billions of dollars for publishers and moviemakers; and it has been very entertaining for millions of fans.

Given the worldwide phenomenon that is Harry Potter, one would expect the companies most associated with the wizard to be riding a wave of success. However, in most cases, the opposite is true. Scholastic, Harry's publisher in the United States, has seen its stock fall below pre-Harry levels. Bloomsbury, the publisher of Harry Potter outside the United States, has reported a significant drop in earnings and its stock is down 40 percent in 18 months. Big booksellers including Tesco, Amazon, Walmart, Barnes & Noble, and Borders introduced the books at significant discounts (more than 50 percent). Amazon concedes that it did not make any money selling Harry Potter books. The company sold more than 1 million copies of *Harry Potter and the Deathly Hallows* and believes many of those buyers continue to shop at Amazon. With the series now complete, at least for the moment, the Harry Potter phenomenon lives on primarily in movies.

The pricing policies of the big booksellers created problems for smaller, independent booksellers that were forced to reduce prices and create more interesting ways to bring people into their stores. Historically, retailers sold new books at full price using the profits from the new titles to offset discounted older books. The success of Harry Potter, however, created an interesting problem as retailers offered each new Harry Potter title at discounted prices just to drive traffic into the stores. This new retail pricing model has created challenges for the book industry and a shakeout of the market.

Independent bookstores have tried to find ways to offset the price advantage offered by Amazon, Walmart, and other large booksellers by offering special events and other incentives to get customers into their stores. Unfortunately, there are many opportunities for fans of books like the Potter series to connect including chat rooms, dedicated Potter Web sites, and fan clubs.

No doubt Harry Potter aficionados appreciated buying the books at a discount; however, this new pricing model created challenging dynamics in the book business. Independent bookstores find it difficult to survive in the crowded marketplace dominated by brick retailers like Walmart, click retailers like Amazon, and the mega booksellers like Barnes & Noble and Borders, which offer a coffee shop experience inside their stores.[50]

Ethical Perspective

1. **Large bookstore chains:** Should they continue to offer new books at significant discounts to increase foot traffic despite losing money on the books?

2. **Independent bookstores:** How should they respond to new book prices that are lower than their purchase costs?

3. **Consumers:** Should customers encourage market forces to keep prices lower, or should they encourage smaller, independent bookstores?

- Services that enhance the **sales experience:** services that make the sales experience easier, such as policies that make it easy to return merchandise for credit or refund, multiple payment methods, easy shipping and delivery options.

  - Services that enhance the **retailer experience:** services that strengthen the customer's perception of the retailer, such as loyalty programs, easy store access, additional facilities like restaurants, support services for young children and infants.

Customers bundle their product purchase with other experiences to develop an overall impression of the retailer. Retailers understand that when the products are similar, as is the case with national branded products, the in-store experience differentiates one retailer from another. Bass Pro Shops offers shoppers the opportunity to try fishing gear in a large tank and test rifles on a shooting range. Bookstores such as Barnes & Noble have

Victoria's Secret offers a pleasant shopping experience with fitting rooms and trained staff to facilitate the purchase.

created special children's sections complete with small tables and chairs to encourage children and their parents to read together. Some stores even have stages that bring children into the store for special events.

The environment is fundamental in setting the tone for the shopping experience. Store layout and displays, interior colors, even the music in the store all work together to create an atmosphere that it is hoped will make the customer feel comfortable. A cluttered or poorly designed store layout, inappropriate interior lighting and colors, music that is not consistent with the product or the target market all dampen the customer's shopping experience. Indeed, research suggests that the tempo of music played in the store affects the amount of time spent shopping and, consequently, the average sale.

> Apple's decision to open its own retail stores has been a good one for several reasons, not the least of which is the effective extension of the Apple brand. To consumers, Apple Stores symbolize a level of exclusivity while offering a physical location where people can experience Apple's products first-hand. Microsoft couldn't help but notice the positive effect Apple Stores had on consumer perceptions about Apple; so, Microsoft decided to follow suit and open its own retail locations. The company believes that having its own line of retail stores will help differentiate the Microsoft brand, which has been a challenge for the company due to the ubiquitous nature of its products in the marketplace.[51]

Marketing Communications

Retailers use a wide range of marketing communications to reach their target markets. As we will explore in Chapters 13 and 14, an effective marketing communications strategy requires careful planning, great execution, and coordination. Generally, retailers focus on two key objectives in their marketing communications. First, marketing communications generate customer traffic. Historically, that meant encouraging people to physically visit the store but, increasingly, that also means sending people to the retailer's Web site. Advertising directed at new products or store specials is designed to stimulate retail traffic. Second, marketing communications drive customer purchases. Coupons, sales promotions, in-store sampling are examples of communications that motivate product purchase. Retailers must make sure their marketing communications are consistent with their store image as well as appropriate for the target market. Walmart, for example, would likely not advertise in *Vanity Fair* or *Esquire*.

SUMMARY

The company customer interface is an essential element in the overall customer value experience. Technology has dramatically changed how, where, and when customers choose to interact with a company. These changes have created a number of opportunities, and companies have had to develop new, innovative tools to enhance their customer service and support.

Despite the growth of electronic retailing, traditional retailing continues to flourish for a number of reasons. Non-store retailing also continues to grow. E-retailing, while still a small percentage of all retail sales, is growing faster than any other form of retailing. Although the growth of business-to-consumer e-retailing has been rapid, business-to-business e-commerce has grown even faster and now accounts for over 30 percent of all business transactions. Developing an effective retail strategy involves assessing six critical areas that consider strategic questions as well as specific tactics to best address those strategic questions.

APPLICATION QUESTIONS

1. You are the merchandise manager for Best Buy electronics and have been asked to expand the assortment of music products. Industry trends suggest more people are downloading their music online. How would you assess whether or not to allocate another 200 square feet in each store to CD sales? Do you think it is a good idea? Why or why not?

2. You are the director of site location strategy for Burger King. Develop a location strategy for expanding the number of stores in your town. How would you choose a location for the next store?

3. From a student's perspective, what functions are available on your campus Web site (for example, class registration, payment, delivery of course materials)? How would you assess the ease of use for the Web site? What functions does the campus Web site perform well and which does it perform poorly?

MARKETING PLAN EXERCISE

ACTIVITY 2.1: The Customer Interface

No matter your product experience, it is essential to consider the process by which customers will interface with the product. If, for example, the product is to be marketed through retail channels, identifying possible retailers and channels is essential. Furthermore, no matter what the Web objectives, developing an effective Web strategy is also essential. Specifically, develop a strategy for interfacing with your customer:

1. Define the characteristics of the channel and, more specifically, determine what is the best approach for reaching the customer (retail, online, in-company sales force, distributors).

2. If you are using a retail channel, define your retail strategy:
   a. Who is your target market?
   b. Which retailers best fit your strategy and where are they located?
   c. What is your retail pricing strategy?
   d. What kind of in-store experience do you want for your customer?
   e. What is your marketing communications with retailers?

3. Define the Web strategy for the product:
   a. Functionality of Web site (online purchasing, streaming product demo videos, retail locator or showing the customer where and how the product can be purchased).
   b. Look and feel of the Web site.

If you are using Marketing Plan Pro, a template for this assignment can be accessed at www.mhhe.com/marshalless1e.

CHAPTER 13

Integrated Marketing Communications: Promotional Strategy, Advertising, Sales Promotion, and Public Relations

LEARNING OBJECTIVES

- Appreciate the significance of the concept of integrated marketing communications (IMC) and its impact on marketing management.

- Identify the elements of the promotion mix and the pros and cons of each element.

- Connect the concept of the AIDA model to important issues in promotional strategy.

- Describe the components of the marketing manager's role in promotional strategy.

- Understand key concepts of advertising, sales promotion, and public relations as they pertain to marketing management.

INTRODUCTION TO PROMOTION AND INTEGRATED MARKETING COMMUNICATIONS (IMC)

Marketing managers usually communicate with customers through **promotion,** which involves various forms of communication to inform, persuade, or remind. This communication is accomplished through elements of the **promotion mix–advertising, sales promotion, public relations (PR), personal selling, direct marketing,** and **interactive marketing.** These elements, sometimes also called the marketing communications mix, are defined in Exhibit 13.1 The first three tend to be relatively less personal in nature than the last three. That is, advertising, sales promotion, and PR often are developed for receipt by a mass audience, while personal selling, direct marketing, and interactive marketing by their nature are more one-to-one marketing.

The promotion mix is very important in marketing planning. The development of **promotion mix strategies,** or simply *promotional strategies,* involves decisions about which combination of elements in the promotion mix is likely to best communicate the offering to the marketplace and achieve an acceptable ROI for the marketer, given the product and target markets involved. The effectiveness and efficiency of promotional strategies are often tracked on the basis of a **promotional campaign,** which attributes promotional expenditures to a particular creative execution aimed at a particular product or product line during a specified time period. In fact, much of marketing has operated on a campaign-to-campaign basis for ongoing planning purposes.

EXHIBIT 13.1	Definitions of Elements of the Promotion Mix
Advertising	Paid form of relatively less personal marketing communications often through a mass medium to one or more target markets. Example media include television, radio, magazines, newspapers, and outdoor.
Sales Promotion	Provides an inducement for an end-user consumer to buy your product or for a salesperson or someone else in the channel to sell it. Designed to augment other forms of promotion; rarely used alone. Examples of consumer inducements are coupons, rebates, and sweepstakes. Inducements for channel members often involve special monies or prizes for pushing a particular offering.
Public Relations (PR)	Systematic approach to influencing attitudes, opinions, and behaviors of customers and others. Often executed through publicity, which is an unpaid and relatively less personal form of marketing communications usually through news stories and mentions at public events.
Personal Selling	One-to-one personal communication with a customer by a salesperson, either in person or electronically in some way that provides two-way dialogue.
Direct Marketing	An interactive marketing system that uses one or more advertising media to affect a measurable response and/or transaction at any location. Personal communication with a customer by means other than a salesperson.
Interactive Marketing	An Internet-driven relationship between companies, their brands, and customers. Interactive marketing enables customers to control information flow and encourages customer-company interaction as well as a higher level of customer service.

The Rise of Integrated Marketing Communications (IMC)

Within the last decade, the inclusion of electronic marketing channels, more sophisticated research, customer database management, and integrated CRM systems began to enable the management of customer relationships and communication with customers on a more one-on-one basis, creating less dependency on traditional promotion through mass media. At the same time, various traditional media outlets began to become very fragmented; we now have literally thousands of cable and satellite dish television channels, hundreds of specialty magazines, micro-specialty genres in radio programming, and ready access to news, information, and entertainment online. These trends have caused the marketing field to rethink how to do promotion. Don Schultz and his colleagues are widely credited with introducing the concept of integrated marketing communications in the mid-1990s as a new paradigm for communicating offerings to a target market. **Integrated marketing communications (IMC)** is a strategic approach to communicating the brand and company message to targeted customers in ways that are clear, concise, and consistent and yet are customizable as needed to maximize the impact on a particular audience.[1]

Think of the difference in IMC versus more traditional promotion mix strategies along the lines of the illustrations in Exhibits 13.2 and 13.3. Exhibit 13.2 portrays the concept of a traditional promotion mix decision—separate assessment of whether to invest in promoting the offering through one or more of the promotion mix elements. In contrast, Exhibit 13.3 captures the different nature of IMC decision making—a holistic and interrelated decision process, integrative, connected to the overall brand message, yet still fully customizable to different customer groups.

An IMC approach lends itself to better integration of the communication elements, hence the term *integrated* marketing communications. Exhibit 13.3 connotes that marketing managers' consideration of the elements takes place in a holistic decision process. That is, each element impacts the others and the whole is likely more than the sum of the parts. A strong focus on a unified branding message

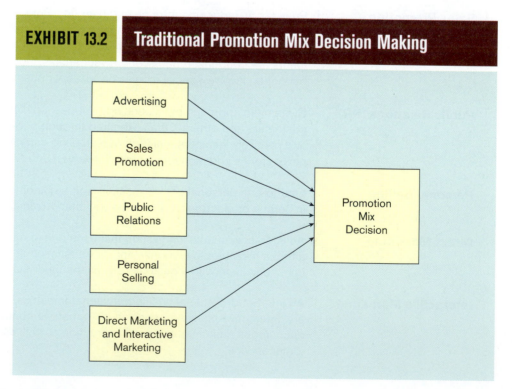

EXHIBIT 13.2 Traditional Promotion Mix Decision Making

EXHIBIT 13.3	IMC Decision Making

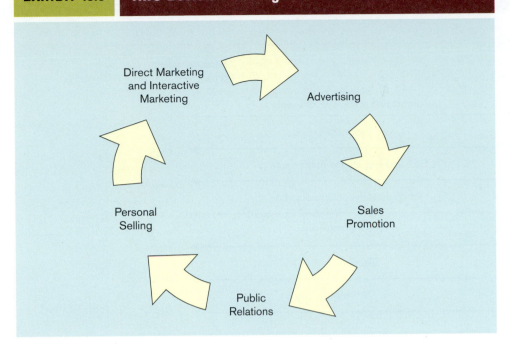

and theme occurs throughout the process. In contrast, Exhibit 13.2 implies that the elements are developed separately and, while they do combine later to provide a promotional mix strategy, they are not necessarily viewed holistically as central to the brand. Because an IMC approach is an inherently more strategic approach to communicating with customers, managers employing it are much more likely to consistently communicate the right brand messages to the right customers at the right time via the right media.

IMC and the Promotion Mix

What kinds of decisions are involved in developing and executing IMC strategy? Consider Exhibit 13.4, which assesses the impact of a variety of marketing management factors on the decision of whether to pursue an advertising/sales promotion-driven IMC strategy versus a personal selling-driven approach. As you can see, a gamut of critical issues from buyer information needs to purchase size to the configuration of the marketing mix elements all influence the decision about where to invest promotional budget dollars. In fact, in many marketing planning situations, among all the elements of the marketing mix, promotional budgeting decisions involve the lion's share of the overall marketing budget—often surpassing packaging, distribution, and other marketing elements by a wide margin.

The allocation of promotional marketing budget monies across the various elements of the promotion mix is a complex decision. Each promotional form has its own individual pros and cons, and Exhibit 13.5 on page 319 provides a selection of some of these. Within the IMC

Entertainers use strong IMC, including stylish marquee ads such as these for Cirque du Soleil's *Zumanity* and comedienne Rita Rudner to create buzz about their performances.

EXHIBIT 13.4   **Illustrative Factors Influencing IMC Strategy**

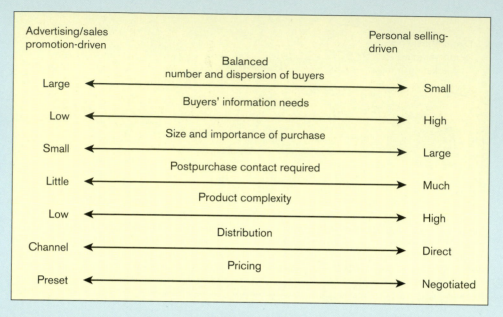

Advertising/sales promotion-driven		Personal selling-driven
	Balanced number and dispersion of buyers	
Large	←————————————→	Small
	Buyers' information needs	
Low	←————————————→	High
	Size and importance of purchase	
Small	←————————————→	Large
	Postpurchase contact required	
Little	←————————————→	Much
	Product complexity	
Low	←————————————→	High
	Distribution	
Channel	←————————————→	Direct
	Pricing	
Preset	←————————————→	Negotiated

Source: Reprinted from David W. Cravens and Nigel F. Piercy, *Strategic Marketing*, 8th ed., 2006. Copyright © 2006 The McGraw-Hill Companies, Inc.

approach, it is the *integration* of the elements—not just each individual element—and the resulting *synergies* of the branding message that make the strongest sustainable impact on customers.

Push and Pull Strategies

Two fundamental approaches to promotional strategy are *push* and *pull* strategies. These are depicted in Exhibit 13.6 on page 320. The specific promotion mix elements selected for investment will vary depending on the relative degree of push or pull desired.

In a **push strategy,** the focus is on the channel of distribution and in getting the offering into the channel. Members of the channel are targeted for promotion and are depended on to then push the offering into the hands of end users. A push strategy typically relies on a combination of personal selling and sales promotion directed toward channel members.[2] In a **pull strategy,** the focus shifts to stimulating demand for an offering directly from the end user. Advertising, consumer-directed sales promotion, PR, or direct and interactive marketing can be combined in various ways to target end users, creating demand that results in the channel making an offering available for purchase. In practice, push and pull strategies are rarely used mutually exclusively.[3] Rather, a promotional strategy is developed that strikes the best balance of investment of promotional funds in both push and pull strategies that make sense for the product and market involved.

Internal Marketing and IMC

A final critical aspect of IMC that bears mentioning at this point is internal marketing. **Internal marketing** is the application of marketing concepts and strategies inside an organization. Much research has shown that if members

EXHIBIT 13.5 | Selected Pros and Cons of Individual Promotion Mix Elements

Promotion Mix Element	Pros	Cons
Advertising	• Many media choices • Efficiently reaches large numbers of customers • Great creative flexibility	• Shotgun approach reaches many outside the target • Oversaturation of ads lessens impact • High production costs
Sales Promotion	• Stimulates purchase directly through incentive to buy • Serves as an effective accompaniment to other promotion forms	• Can lead customers to continually wait for the next coupon, rebate, etc. • Brand may be impacted by price-cutting image
Public Relations	• Unpaid communication seen as more credible than paid forms • Association of offering with quality media outlet enhances brand	• Low control of how the message turns out • Highly labor intensive cost of mounting PR campaigns
Personal Selling	• Strong two-way communication of ideas • Directly eases customer confusion and persuades purchase	• Very expensive cost per customer contact • Salesperson may go "off message" from brand to secure the sale
Direct Marketing and Interactive Marketing	• Message customization without high costs of personal selling • Strong relationship building especially when customer can control the interaction	• Spam and other unwanted correspondence when targeting is poorly executed • Reliance on CRM and database marketing requires constant updating

of an organization aren't knowledgeable about its offerings, don't understand who the customers are, and can't effectively articulate the branding message, successful marketing management is very difficult. Employees of a firm are potentially its best and most trusted brand and message ambassadors. Properly armed, they can articulate what the firm and its offerings stand for in ways that nobody else can.[4]

Great brand marketers today pay a lot of attention to ensuring that *everybody* in the firm has pride of ownership in its brand, products, and services. From Southwest Airlines to Caterpillar to Apple, great marketing companies are placing a high priority on enabling each and every employee to communicate the marketing message. Most firms successful in internal marketing enlist the help of the human resources department to include indoctrination of all employees in the brand messages beginning with employee orientation programs and continuing when new products are introduced or new markets are entered.

EXHIBIT 13.6 | Push and Pull Promotional Strategies

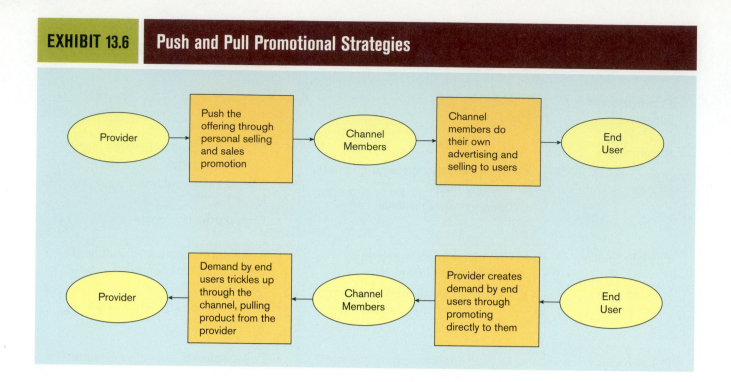

Southwest Airlines uses internal marketing to differentiate itself from its competition. Its employees are known to provide excellent service, which is enabled by its internal marketing that begins at new employee orientation. Leadership Development Director Cheryl Hughey states, "We have always had a philosophy that we will treat our employees the same way that we treat our external customers." Southwest's culture encourages employee celebration—daily and also through companywide events, banquets, Halloween, and Spirit Parties (biannual gatherings of all Southwest Employees). It's easy to see why Southwest employees have pride in the brand and reflect that pride to flyers through great service.[5]

Looking Ahead

This chapter and the next provide a managerially relevant overview of issues involved in promotion mix decision making. In the remainder of this chapter, you will learn about a hierarchy of effects model in promotional strategy development and the marketing manager's role in promotional strategy. Then, we've divided the chapter coverage of the promotion mix elements by relatively less personal approaches (this chapter includes an introduction to advertising, sales promotion, and PR) and relatively more personal promotional approaches (Chapter 14 covers personal selling, direct marketing, and interactive marketing).

Perhaps more than any other areas of marketing management covered in this book, promotion and IMC as a topic is incredibly broad and specialized. Consider that each element of the promotion mix is often a separate course of study in college, and sometimes even more than one course. Your task as a student of marketing management is to gain an understanding of the process of promotional strategy decision making and especially the basic promotional tools and decision options available for marketing planning. An appropriate place to begin is by introducing the hierarchy of effects model.

HIERARCHY OF EFFECTS MODEL

Buyers often pass through purchase decision processes in three steps: cognitive (learn), affective (feel), and behavioral (do). These stages are portrayed in various models to illustrate this hierarchy of effects in the context of customer response to marketing communications. Here we will illustrate one popular version of such models, the **AIDA model,** so-named because the effects build in this order: Attention (or Awareness), Interest, Desire, and Action. The attention stage correlates to the cognitive step of buyer decision making, the interest and desire stages to the affective step, and the action stage to the behavioral step.[6] Exhibit 13.7 portrays the AIDA model.

Where the target customers fit on the model is critically important to effective selection and execution of the promotion mix. Below are tips for maximizing success in promoting across the various stages of the AIDA model. Exhibit 13.8 rates the general appropriateness of applying each of the promotion mix elements depending on the stage of the hierarchy of effects of the targets.

EXHIBIT 13.7	AIDA Model

Attention	**Cognitive Step**
Interest	**Affective Step**
Desire	
Action	**Behavioral Step**

Attention

If target customers are essentially unaware of an offering, most of the investment in communication must be in raising awareness and gaining their attention. Depending on the situation, this may involve developing awareness for a whole new set of customer needs and wants as well as revealing that your product exists to address those needs and wants. In the initial introduction of the Prius, Toyota put much effort into building awareness of the emerging need for hybrid cars and also into educating potential customers about what a hybrid car actually is.

EXHIBIT 13.8	Appropriateness of Promotion Mix Elements at AIDA Stages

Promotion Mix Element	Attention Stage	Interest Stage	Desire Stage	Action Stage
Advertising	▲ ▲ ▲	▲ ▲ ▲	▲ ▲	▲ ▲
Sales Promotion	▲ ▲	▲ ▲	▲ ▲ ▲	▲ ▲ ▲
Public Relations	▲ ▲ ▲	▲ ▲ ▲	▲ ▲	▲
Personal Selling	▲	▲	▲ ▲ ▲	▲ ▲ ▲
Direct Marketing and Interactive Marketing	▲	▲ ▲	▲ ▲ ▲	▲ ▲

▲ = Generally least appropriate for use
▲ ▲ ▲ = Generally most appropriate for use

This ad for Aleve gains readers' attention quickly. Notice that the letters are people who are able to move around flexibly, presumably because Aleve has quelled their joint pain.

Essentially, the automaker created a product category from scratch, and for a while there was little return on the promotional investment. However, when gas prices began to soar and environmental issues became more prominent, Prius was in a prime position to become the leader in its product category, gaining a first-mover advantage and making it difficult for competitors to catch up. Now, every major car manufacturer is jumping into the category.

Gaining attention and building initial awareness can be a daunting task for marketers. Tremendous expenditures may be required to establish a foothold with customers, especially when a brand is relatively unknown or a product category is in its infancy. Chapter 5 covered different categories of adopters depending on how willing a potential customer is to try and buy a new product. At the attention stage of the AIDA model, marketing managers hope to use promotions to gain awareness of their offering with the innovators and early adopters. If marketers can influence these groups to purchase, innovators and early adopters can get others to jump on the bandwagon.

In many cases, gaining attention requires investment in mass appeal forms of promotion, especially advertising and PR. When ultra-premium Voss water was introduced in the United States, marketers relied heavily on PR to create awareness, connecting the water to celebrities and gaining product placements in movies and in magazines sold in outlets frequented by the target customers.

Interest

To translate customer attention into interest requires persuasive communication. For more technical or complicated products, this means beginning to inform customers more specifically about what a product offering can do for *them*—how it helps fulfill needs and wants. To stimulate interest, the promotion must begin to touch a customer's "hot buttons."

For example, generating awareness about the original iPhone was not a problem for Apple; the buildup in the media was gargantuan for months before the initial product introduction. But what would stimulate a person to move beyond just awareness that the product exists to interest in possibly pursuing purchase? Apple masterfully used its early promotion to point out the elegance of the form and integrated functionality of the iPhone to begin to convince customers that any ordinary Smartphone simply would not do. Interest was piqued by the communication of product features and benefits, and also by the imagery suggesting that the iPhone was something really different.

Desire

Moving from interest to desire means that a customer has to move past a *need* and begin to really *want* the product. Promotion feeds desire through strong persuasive communication. At this stage, salespeople and customized direct and interactive marketing often enter the promotion mix. Messages are altered to influence customers to feel that they simply can't do without the item. Some of the innovators and early adopters are showing off their purchases to holdouts.

Such was certainly the case with the iPhone. Many people undoubtedly let their friends and co-workers see and touch their prized possession—sharing the experience of its functionality and form. Apple wisely fueled the momentum through targeted direct mailings and e-mailings, inviting potential customers into Apple stores so that salespeople could fully demonstrate the broad spectrum of product virtues. The interest stage of the hierarchy is generally where the emotional part of buyer decision making peaks, and much of the promotional message is centered on creating positive feelings for the brand and product.

Action

The action stage is the purchase itself. To stimulate ultimate purchase, marketers often rely on salespeople, accompanied by some form of sales promotion, to close the sale. Sales promotion, by its nature, stimulates purchase. For the customer, it can be a coupon, rebate, or other special "extra" that pushes them over the edge to buy. Also, the reason sales organizations put so much emphasis on training salespeople in closing techniques is that they are often the final stimulant to purchase.

Growing evidence suggests that Gen Y and Millennials may respond differently from prior generations to promotional strategies. These differences may be attributable to the hierarchy of effects they go through in making purchase decisions. Previous generations, which have been the focus of marketing for years (i.e., Gen X and older), did not grow up with the same level of information availability and access as these younger groups. As a result, marketers have traditionally been placed in the pivotal role of outbound information providers for these customers, largely through promotion. This is true not only in the B2C marketplace, but also in B2B markets where organizational buyers traditionally relied on their salespeople for information about products and markets. Gen Y and Millennials have experienced a very different set of circumstances related to information. Because of the Internet and related communication technology, they are accustomed to doing their own research on products, developing their own opinions, and then taking action with less influence from traditional promotional approaches (including salespeople).

This is not to say that the role of the marketing manager in developing promotional strategy is less important when it comes to the younger generation. Rather, the caution is that the response of younger generations to different promotional approaches is not the same as that of previous generations. They are much less likely to want to be "sold to," are generally disinterested in mass advertising, and tend to place high value on objective information for decision making, likely from sources outside of traditional promotion. For example, communication going on in MySpace, blogs, message boards, chat rooms, and other forms of virtual communities carries much more weight than other communication forms. Although many of these qualities make marketing to the younger generations more difficult, their unique attitudes toward marketing also create important opportunities for marketers. For example, they are generally very tuned in to brands, thus affording an opportunity for marketing managers to smartly integrate branding into promotional themes. Ethical Dimension 13 explores important issues related to the teenage market.

In doing marketing planning in the 21st century, the marketing manager who addresses these preferences among the important Gen Y and Millennial markets will gain a competitive edge over marketers that attempt to capture this business through more traditional promotion forms.

Today's supermarkets are getting out of the way of shoppers to stimulate purchase. More stores are utilizing smart shopping carts, mobile coupons, and self-checkout lanes to let customers help themselves. The retailers are finding people are actually willing to pay more when they feel more in control of the purchase process.[7]

The Resourceful Teen and Promotional Ethics

Today's teenagers are more plugged in than any other generation in history. Facebook, MySpace, SMS text messaging, and many more technology tools enable teens to connect with each other and the world in unprecedented ways. More than any other generation, teens have made social networking and, more broadly, an online lifestyle a significant part of their lives. Their online experiences coupled with the new media's ability to track and store user information offers innovative opportunities to connect, communicate, and market to this important demographic. Marketers are empowered as never before by the ability to track individual activities, analyze large amounts of information, and develop unique, individually targeted messaging and products to teens. For example, Facebook now allows advertisers to create display ads using information from individual users posted in their profiles.

However, two critical questions for teen marketers are: How much information should we collect? And what is the most appropriate online marketing strategy from an ethical and business strategy perspective? While the Children's Online Privacy Protection Act (COPPA) requires marketers to get parental consent to collect personal information on anyone younger than 13, no law regulates advertising or direct marketing to teenagers over the age of 13. Marketing managers face difficult ethical and strategic questions as they learn to operate in the online social networking world of teenagers.

A key issue for both marketers and teenagers is the degree to which information presented in the social networking environment should be used by companies. Private details about an individual are available for analysis, but how much and to what degree should marketers use the information to create individual specific messaging? In addition, much of the individual data is self-generated, and there are few checks and balances to validate information. Companies have the ability to connect a sophisticated understanding of teenagers with an individual's personal data to develop targeted communications. However, people on the Internet often make themselves a few years younger (or older in the case of teenagers) or several inches taller. Today's resourceful teenagers create identities that allow them access to age-restricted Web sites such as eBay, which requires a buyer or seller to be 18. Marketers can present messaging to students that may not be appropriate for the individual. For example, someone under 21 may indicate a different age online and receive liquor or beer advertising.

Teenagers do appreciate effective branding and marketing at the same time marketers seek greater access to the teen market. On the surface, it would appear easier than ever to find and speak to the teen market, but things are not always as they seem.[8]

Ethical Perspective

1. **Marketers:** Should a marketer be allowed to use information from an individual's social networking profile? Is targeted messaging based on analysis of personal information ethical?

2. **Teenagers:** Should teenagers be able to provide false information to gain access to Web sites restricted by age or some other characteristic?

THE MARKETING MANAGER'S ROLE IN PROMOTIONAL STRATEGY

As mentioned at the beginning of the chapter, the field of promotion is very broad and requires much specialization to effectively execute. As a part of the marketing field, the area of promotion more than any other tends to be heavily outsourced. Creative companies such as advertising and PR agencies have the focus and expertise to add substantial value to the execution of a marketer's promotional planning. And because of the unique nature of personal selling, most firms set up the sales organization as virtually a separate entity from marketing or outsource it in the form of external distributors or brokers that represent a company's offerings to customers within the channel. But the proliferation of outsourcing of marketing communications and separation of sales from marketing does not absolve the marketing manager from the need to understand the basics of promotion so that the agency's contributions, as well as those of the sales force, can be properly integrated into the marketing planning process.

The seven major elements of the marketing manager's role in managing promotion are identified in Exhibit 13.9 as follows: identify targets for promotion, establish goals for promotion, select the promotion mix, develop the message, select media for use in promotion, prepare promotion budget, and establish measures of results.

Identify Targets for Promotion

You learned in Chapter 7 that target marketing is a process of evaluating market segments and deciding which are most attractive for investment in development. We also discussed that positioning involves communicating one or more sources of value to customers in ways that the customer can easily make the connection between his or her needs and wants and what the product has to offer. The promotional mix strategy is a crucial element in positioning a firm's offerings effectively. It is not possible for the marketing manager to make sense of developing a promotional strategy until the targets are selected.[9]

Establish Goals for Promotion

Before moving forward to develop a promotion mix, the marketing manager must establish goals for promotion. Having a great product but being a best-kept secret is not a favorable position. Earlier we defined promotion as the means by which various forms of communication are used to inform, persuade, or remind potential customers. Exhibit 13.10 summarizes these essential goals of promotion and how each might be achieved.

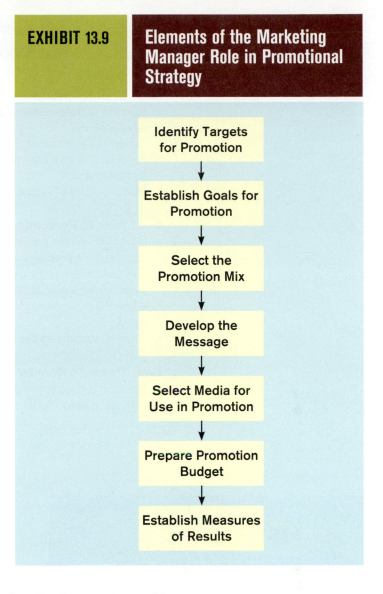

EXHIBIT 13.9 | **Elements of the Marketing Manager Role in Promotional Strategy**

Identify Targets for Promotion

↓

Establish Goals for Promotion

↓

Select the Promotion Mix

↓

Develop the Message

↓

Select Media for Use in Promotion

↓

Prepare Promotion Budget

↓

Establish Measures of Results

Goal One: To Inform

How does a customer know that Hilton is running a temporary special on room rates in its Orlando hotels? Or what the store hours are for Macy's annual white sale? Or that a $100 rebate is available on that Canon digital camera you've had your eye on? Or that the next-generation iPhone is about to be released? One important goal of promotion is providing information—about a firm and its offerings. Unless you are fortunate enough to be in the position of Steve Jobs at Apple, where the media start clamoring months in advance for a glimpse of the next new product and are willing to devote prime publication real estate to extolling its virtues (and possibly foibles), chances are you will have to resort to paid forms of promotion to get your information across to potential customers.

Goal Two: To Persuade

Rarely is the communication of facts sufficient for marketers to effectively make their case to potential customers, who are faced with many competing brands and product options. Promotion provides the opportunity to state your offering's advantages and to give the customer a reason to select you over the competition. Why should a construction project lease Caterpillar equipment instead of Kamatsu?

EXHIBIT 13.10 | **Goals for Promotion**

Goal One: To Inform
- Indicate features when introducing new products or making product modifications.
- Explain product functionality.
- Articulate what a company and its brands stand for in order to develop a clear image.
- Discuss various uses and applications for the product.

Goal Two: To Persuade
- Impact customer perceptions of a product, especially in comparison to competitor's products.
- Get customers to try a product, hopefully resulting in a more permanent switch from a competitor.
- Influence customers to purchase right now due to some strong benefit or need.
- Drive customers to seek more information online or through a salesperson.

Goal Three: To Remind
- Maintain a customer relationship with a brand.
- Provide impetus for purchase based on some impending event.

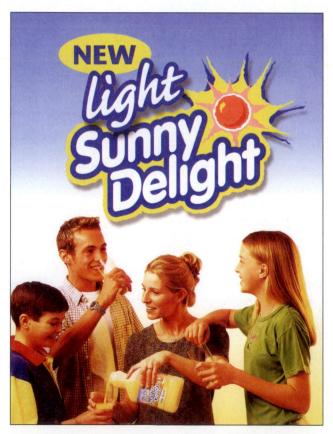

This ad for Sunny Delight is designed in part to remind readers that they have other choices for a tasty beverage besides soda.

What are the advantages of the Toyota Camry over the Honda Accord, and vice versa? Can a person *really* get a healthy meal at McDonald's? Persuasive communication is at the core of marketing and affords companies the chance to put their best foot forward for customers. Of course, persuasion can be taken to extremes, and the potential for crossing an ethical or legal line in promotion is a constant problem for marketers.

The downsides of crossing that line can be severe. In the 1970s, Listerine, playing on its "kills germs" theme, advertised that regular use could "reduce the number and severity of colds," a product claim that was blatantly untrue. The federal government forced the manufacturer to run high-profile retraction ads for several months, severely damaging the public trust and costing substantial revenue and market share to archrival Scope. In promotion, a certain degree of **puffery,** or relatively minor embellishments of product claims to bolster the persuasive message, generally is legal. However, in today's litigious environment, determining the fine line between puffery and making a false claim is best left to attorneys not marketers.

Goal Three: To Remind

For brands that are already top-of-mind for many customers, a primary goal of promotion is to keep the brand and its imagery at the forefront. Essentially, Coca-Cola has 100 percent brand awareness among U.S. consumers (as well as in many other parts of the globe). So why does Coke need to invest in promotion? Marketers must constantly communicate with customers to maintain brand loyalty and reduce the tendency to switch to other brands. For example, the income tax preparation firm Jackson Hewitt starts reminding Americans through a fall promotion that income tax season is right around the corner. Jackson Hewitt wants to plant the seed early so that after the first of the year you will pull together your papers and make an appointment to have your tax return prepared. Reminding customers is a key goal of promotion and often stimulates direct purchase.

Select the Promotion Mix

Promotion mix decisions are dependent on several factors. These include the nature of the offering, stage of the offering in the product life cycle, nature of the market, and available budget.

Nature of the Offering

Some key questions must be answered about the product itself. You learned in Chapters 5 and 6 that B2C products and markets differ in important ways from B2B products and markets. Often, goods and services offered in the B2B marketplace tend to be more complex than those sold to end-user consumers. Also, you learned in Chapter 9 that services possess several distinct characteristics different from physical goods. Whether in the B2B or B2C space, the more complex, intangible, unique, and new an offering, the more challenging the communication about it will be and the more likely that relatively more personal forms of promotion will have to be relied on. In such cases, personal selling and direct or interactive marketing afford a greater opportunity for potential customers to become educated about the offering.[10]

Another related issue to consider is the strength of the brand. Promotion of brands that are already well-known and that carry high positive brand equity allow for more reliance on relatively less personal forms of promotion such as advertising, sales promotion, and PR. The brand itself often carries the day in such communication; for example, when Apple introduced iPhone the equity built up among loyal Apple users made purchase nearly a fait accompli.

Stage of the Offering in the Product Life Cycle

Chapter 8 introduced you to the concept of the product life cycle (PLC). Now it is important to make a connection between the PLC and promotion mix decision making. Exhibit 13.11 portrays the PLC and associated promotion mix considerations.[11]

Walt Disney World has many diverse target markets, thus Disney provides a wide array of promotions for Florida residents and out-of-state travelers. For example, during one promotion, Florida residents got a free ticket to any Disney park on their birthday. Disney has also offered travelers staying five nights at a Disney hotel a limited-time free Disney dining plan—a savings of $40 per day per adult.[12]

Nature of the Market

Whether in the B2B or B2C space, the nature of the market served affects promotion mix decisions. Among the important factors:

- *Level of heterogeneity of target customers.* The more target groups and the more diverse the targets, the wider array of promotion mix applications to be developed.[13]

- *Level of geographic dispersion of target customers.* Obviously, online interactive approaches permeate geographic borders much more efficiently than traditional advertising. Geographic constraints are especially challenging for using face-to-face personal selling, since buyers and sellers have to physically get together.

EXHIBIT 13.11 | **Promotion Mix Decisions across the PLC**

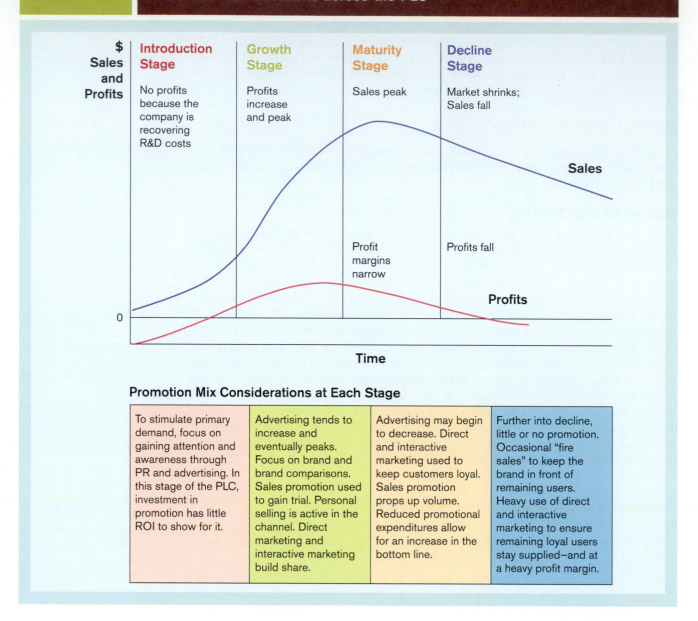

$ Sales and Profits

Introduction Stage
No profits because the company is recovering R&D costs

Growth Stage
Profits increase and peak

Maturity Stage
Sales peak

Decline Stage
Market shrinks; Sales fall

Profit margins narrow

Profits fall

Sales

Profits

0

Time

Promotion Mix Considerations at Each Stage

To stimulate primary demand, focus on gaining attention and awareness through PR and advertising. In this stage of the PLC, investment in promotion has little ROI to show for it.	Advertising tends to increase and eventually peaks. Focus on brand and brand comparisons. Sales promotion used to gain trial. Personal selling is active in the channel. Direct marketing and interactive marketing build share.	Advertising may begin to decrease. Direct and interactive marketing used to keep customers loyal. Sales promotion props up volume. Reduced promotional expenditures allow for an increase in the bottom line.	Further into decline, little or no promotion. Occasional "fire sales" to keep the brand in front of remaining users. Heavy use of direct and interactive marketing to ensure remaining loyal users stay supplied—and at a heavy profit margin.

- *Type of purchase decision to be made.* Is the purchase typically a routine, low customer involvement purchase or is it a specialized purchase with higher customer involvement?[14]

- *Level and type of competition.* If there are many competitors in the same market space, and especially if they are also actively engaged in promoting their offerings, consideration must be given to ensuring your promotion stands out from those of the competition. This may entail going with a promotion mix that seems unusual for the situation but assures notoriety. For example, CUTCO promotes its cutlery only through direct personal selling to consumers. All of its major competitors use more traditional forms of promotion, such as advertising and sales promotion through retail channels.[15] On many occasions CUTCO's management has been asked why it doesn't adopt more traditional promotional forms for household products. The simple answer is that it is the most profitable company in the industry and it wants neither to increase promotional expenditures by turning to advertising nor to risk getting lost among a sea of other brands in department stores.

Available Budget

Ultimately, the budget can constrain decisions about the elements of the promotion mix in which to invest. Costs of different media vary widely. At the high end, making a single face-to-face sales call can easily cost $500 to several thousand dollars depending on the industry. Prime 30-second ads on the Super Bowl go for more than $2 million. It is very common for firms, and especially start-up firms, to find they are undercapitalized and to begin to cut their promotion budget during the critical introductory and growth phases of the PLC. This action tends to direct their promotional activities in ways that minimize the cost per customer contact, not necessarily toward the most effective or appropriate promotional approaches for their target customers.

Personal selling, some types of sales promotion (big rebates and product sampling for example), and labor-intensive PR initiatives carry very high costs per contact. Advertising, on the other hand, generally has much lower cost per contact. Unfortunately, low cost per contact is not the whole story, and marketing is littered with failed promotion plans that tried to squeeze an underfunded promotion budget by chasing low-cost-per-contact options.[16] A central aspect of the marketing manager's role when developing a promotion mix is consideration of trade-offs among the available budget, the nature of the market, the stage in the PLC, and the nature of the offering.

Promotion in general should be viewed as an *investment*, not a cost. From an accounting statement perspective, promotional expenses will show up as costs. But the budget for promotion dollars should be developed as an investment to grow a brand rather than as an afterthought of last year's revenues.

Develop the Message

This task is a very common one for outsourcing by a marketing manager, especially in larger organizations. Much of the message design process requires strong creative energy to come up with a **promotional appeal** that is appropriate for the offering and market, connects well with the brand, and has a high likelihood of ultimately taking the target through the AIDA steps toward purchase.[17] Three broad categories of promotional appeals are rational appeals, emotional appeals, and moral appeals.

Rational Appeals

A **rational appeal** centers on benefits an offering can provide to a customer. Quality of the product, associated service, low price, good value, dependability, and performance are potential benefits that can be communicated.[18] Ads featuring the Maytag repairman, who never has anything to do because a Maytag simply doesn't break down, is a rational appeal (tempered with a good dose of humor) pointing out that nobody likes having to pay to fix an appliance.

Emotional Appeals

In contrast, an **emotional appeal** plays on human nature using humor, drama, joy, adventure, sorrow, love, surprise, guilt, shame, fear—the whole gamut of human emotions and aspirations—in developing promotional messages. Effectively crafted, such message approaches can have a high impact on target customers

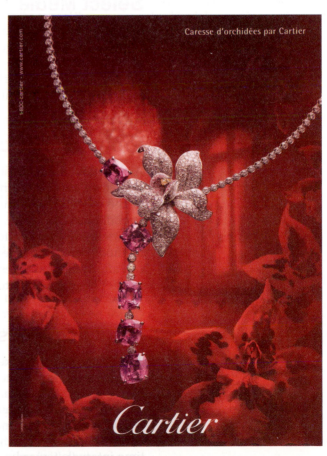

The brand *Cartier* itself evokes emotion, and focusing a fairly simple ad on the product itself serves to augment feelings of prestige and success associated with the brand.

EXHIBIT 13.12

Top 20 U.S. Advertisers

Rank	Advertiser	Total U.S. Ad Spending in 2006 (billions)	Average Daily Ad Spending in 2006 (millions)
1	Procter & Gamble	$4.9	$13.4
2	AT&T	3.3	9.0
3	General Motors	3.3	9.0
4	Time Warner	3.1	8.5
5	Verizon Wireless	2.8	7.7
6	Ford Motor	2.6	7.1
7	GlaxoSmithKline	2.4	6.6
8	Walt Disney	2.3	6.3
9	Johnson & Johnson	2.3	6.3
10	Unilever	2.1	5.8
11	Toyota Motor	2.0	5.5
12	Sony	2.0	5.5
13	DaimlerChrysler	2.0	5.5
14	General Electric	1.9	5.2
15	Sprint Nextel	1.8	4.9
16	McDonald's	1.7	4.7
17	Sears	1.7	4.7
18	L'Oreal	1.5	4.1
19	Kraft Foods	1.4	3.8
20	Macy's	1.4	3.8
Total		$46.5	$127.7

Source: *Ad Age 2007 Marketing Profiles Yearbook*, June 25, 2007, p. 10.

Despite these challenges, advertising is not only a potentially highly effective promotional vehicle (when applied properly) but it is also a part of the very fabric of the U.S. culture and, increasingly, of the global culture. The craze associated with the annual Super Bowl advertisements is a testament to the power of advertising to excite the masses.

Types of Advertising

There are two major types of advertising: institutional advertising and product advertising. The choice of which approach to use depends on the promotional goals and the situation.

Institutional Advertising

The goal of **institutional advertising** is to promote an industry, company, family of brands, or some other issues broader than a specific product. Institutional advertising is often used to inform or remind, but to a lesser degree to persuade. Earlier you read about the concept of corporate identity in the context of the sender of communication.[24] Many customers pay a great deal of attention to the organization behind an advertising message, how socially responsible the company is, and what values it stands for. Institutional advertising can help build and enhance a corporate brand or family brand. For instance, P&G runs institutional ads about a charitable cause it supports—the Special Olympics. Certain families of P&G brands (Crest, Pampers, etc.) generally are featured as well. Such an approach helps build the corporate identity of P&G and can enhance its brands through positive association.

Sometimes entire industries will run institutional advertising. You may recall ads the California Dairy Council runs on national television. The ads feature "happy cows" and carry the tagline "Great cheese comes from happy cows. Happy cows come from California." The council developed a logo that is prominently displayed in the ads, and presumably the expectation is that a consumer would look for that logo on a wedge of cheese in the dairy case, selecting it over cheese from elsewhere, a bit like the famous "Intel Inside" branding on computers. Consider these additional examples of industry-sponsored institutional advertising, manifest through catchy taglines:

- Cotton, the fabric of our lives.
- The incredible edible egg.
- Pork, the other white meat.
- Beef, it's what's for dinner.

Institutional advertising is a particularly smart strategy during the early phases of the PLC and AIDA model in that it can enhance feelings of trust in potential customers with a message that is broader than just "buy me." Institutional advertising is also often employed when a company or industry needs to dig out from a PR problem.

Product Advertising

The vast majority of advertising is **product advertising,** designed to increase purchase of a specific offering (good or service). Three principal types of product advertising are available: pioneering advertising, competitive advertising, and comparative advertising. The decision on which to employ often depends on the stage of the PLC.

Pioneering advertising stimulates primary demand. Hence, it tends to be used during the introductory and early growth stages of the PLC when it is important to gain purchase by innovators and early adopters. From an AIDA model perspective, pioneering advertising seeks to gain awareness and initial interest. Marketing managers introducing new products almost always focus advertising on this form, letting potential customers know what the product is and how it is used. The appeal is usually more rational than emotional.[25]

Marketing managers employ **competitive advertising** to build sales of a specific brand. Here, the appeal often shifts to more emotion and the goal is persuasion

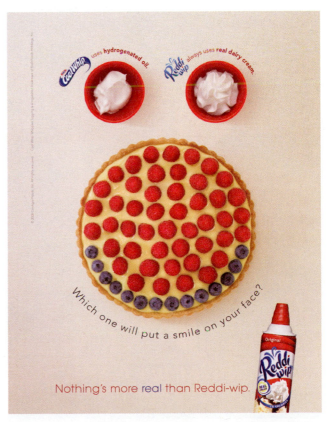

This comparative ad by Reddi-wip takes on rival CoolWhip by pointing out that Reddi-wip always uses real dairy cream, not hydrogenated oil.

as well as providing information. Building a positive customer attitude toward the brand is a key component of competitive advertising, and this approach is heavily used during the growth and early maturity stages of the PLC. Triggering the desire and action stages of the AIDA model is a focus of the message.[26]

In **comparative advertising,** two or more brands are directly compared against each other on certain attributes.[27] Comparative advertising is common during the maturity stage of the PLC, as attempts at shaking out weaker competitors are generally part of a marketing strategy. Obviously, a key to successfully employing this approach is having one or more legitimate claims about your brand that put it in a favorable position against the competition. Apple has run a series of humorous comparative ads on television in which two guys stand side by side and sling barbs back and forth about features of the Mac versus the PC. Through IMC, the images of the two actors appear everywhere Apple has messages about itself—online, stores, print ads, and so on.

Comparative advertising works especially well when you are not No. 1 in a product category because you can put the market leader on the defensive. Examples of comparative advertising by a No. 2 brand include Pepsi versus Coke, Avis versus Hertz, and Burger King versus McDonald's. However, it is a very risky advertising approach when you *are* the top brand. Customers may perceive that you are on the defensive, when in reality you are not. The psychology of a top brand stooping to comparisons with a lower brand usually does not make sense. Most experts recommend avoiding comparative advertising if your brand is the leader.

Advertising Execution and Media Types

In selecting which types of advertising media to employ, the marketing manager must consider reach and frequency. **Reach** measures the percentage of individuals in a defined target market that are exposed to an ad during a specified time period. **Frequency** measures the average number of times a person in the target market is exposed to the message. Obviously, the greater the reach and higher the frequency, the more expensive the overall advertising campaign will be. As you might imagine, because advertising budgets are not unlimited, trade-offs are usually required in balancing reach and frequency within budgetary constraints. Goals are generally set and budgeted based on a desired level of reach and frequency. During the course of a campaign, the marketing manager may intentionally vary the reach and frequency. For example, the intensity of the campaign might start heavily to gain initial exposure then be reduced to stave off advertising wearout.

Advertising execution is the way an advertisement communicates the information and image. A variety of different types of advertising execution are available. Earlier in the chapter you learned about three general types of promotional appeals: rational, emotional, and moral. Think of the different approaches to advertising execution as the creative operationalization of these different types of appeal. Exhibit 13.13 presents several of the more common advertising execution approaches.

Seven broad categories of advertising media are available: television, radio, newspapers, magazines, outdoor (billboard, bus and train signs, etc.), direct

Perfect home baked pastry every time

The Pillsbury Doughboy is a long-standing animated spokesperson for the company's dinner rolls.

EXHIBIT 13.13 | **Common Approaches to Advertising Execution**

Slice of Life	Portrays regular people in everyday settings. A college student doing laundry with Tide in the laundromat.
Humor	Gains attention and interest through humorous portrayal. Budweiser's famous frogs are not soon forgotten.
Mood/Affect	Sets a positive tone around the offering. Sandals Resorts provides visual images to back the theme of "Luxury Included."
Research Based	Often used in comparative ads, a brand provides scientific evidence of its superiority. Listerine Whitening Strips dissolve faster than Crest Whitestrips.
Demonstration	Physically shows how the product works. Efferdent tablets dropped into a glass of water to clean dentures.
Musical	Uses music or a specific song to connect directly to a brand or product. Mazda's famous "Zoom, zoom, zoom" jingle became an integral part of its advertising.
Endorser	Connects a celebrity, actor posing as an authority figure (with appropriate disclaimer), company officer, or everyday consumer with the product to sanction and support its use. Sally Field endorsing Boniva, the anti-osteoporosis drug.
Lifestyle	Portrays ways a product will connect with a target customer's lifestyle. Ford F150 pickup trucks navigating through the back roads of America.
Fantasy Creation	Offers a fantasy look at how it might be if a customer purchases the product. Lamisil for toenail fungus portrays an idyllic social life for users once they stamp out that pesky fungus.
Animation and Animal	An animated character or an animal is featured in the ads, sometimes as a spokesperson. The GEICO Gecko.

mail, and the Internet. Each of these media types has a variety of pros and cons that must be considered by marketing managers in deciding how to allocate advertising dollars. Exhibit 13.14 summarizes some of the more important issues when making media choices.

In reviewing the pros and cons of each of the major media choices, it becomes apparent that decisions on media selection always involve trade-offs. One issue inherent to most media forms is some degree of **clutter**—the level of competing messages on that medium. Clutter is sometimes described in the context of the overall din of advertising, meaning that consumers are bombarded by so many messages that they become confused or have difficulty distinguishing what ad goes with what brand. Rising above the din is an overarching goal in media selection and creative execution of the message.

The Role of the Creative Agency

Advertising and PR are among the most outsourced functions in marketing, and with good reason. Most organizations naturally focus on their own product or service expertise; thus, developing sufficient internal expertise in the creative side of promotion would be extremely costly and could reduce their focus on their

EXHIBIT 13.14 **Pros and Cons of Key Advertising Media**

Type of Media	Pros	Cons
Television	• Combines multimedia • Appeals to multiple senses • Works for both mass coverage or selected markets • Infomercial option	• Impressions are fleeting • Short shelf life • Din (clutter) of competing ads • TiVo effect—cutting out ads • High cost
Radio	• Quick placement and high message immediacy • Easy selectivity by market and station programming • Low cost • Geographic flexibility	• Audio only • Short shelf life • Din of competing ads
Newspapers	• Flexible • Timely • Highly credible medium	• Short shelf life • Big city and national papers can be very costly • Poor reproduction quality, especially in color • Low pass-along rate
Magazines	• Many titles; high geographic, demographic, and lifestyle selectivity • Good reproduction quality and color • High pass-along rate	• Long lead time for ad placement due to production • Final location of ad within the publication often cannot be guaranteed
Outdoor	• Repeat exposure in heavy traffic areas • Relatively low cost • Fewer competing ads • Easy geographic targeting	• Space and structure limits creative execution • Sometimes requires longer than desired commitments to a location • Public discontent over environmental clutter
Direct Mail	• High audience selectivity • Creates feel of one-to-one marketing • Flexible	• Overuse and "junk mail" image • Too many competing ads • Relatively high cost
Internet	• Interactive capabilities • Flexible • Timely • Low cost per exposure	• Reader in control of exposure (click-through) • Spam • Variations in connectivity speed and computers

core business. For many marketing managers, the relationship with their firm's creative agency is an important part of the job. Agencies vary from specialized firms that focus on an industry or on a particular area of promotion, such as print media or product placement. Others are full-service shops that manage all aspects of their clients' IMC strategy. Because of the proliferation of an IMC approach in many firms today, the trend is toward more full-service creative agencies and even toward integration of marketing planning and branding services with traditional agency tasks. Almost always a client is billed an hourly rate, plus the costs of media purchases.

Large fast-food restaurant chains usually outsource their advertising and PR to creative agencies. Fast-food company Wendy's/Arby's Group, Inc., has been reevaluating its advertising and marketing strategy for the Wendy's brand. Some of the prior ads (remember the red-haired boy?) brought awareness but didn't lead to actual sales. Such strategy reassessments often lead firms to change creative agencies for a fresh approach.[28]

Over the past several years, another major trend has been the development of strategic partnerships between creative agencies and full-service Web builders. For many marketers, the Web site is the core of their marketing communications strategy. Often a new-product introduction or rebranding initiative focuses largely on the Web site, with print and other media types used primarily to drive customers to the Web. Some of the very largest agencies have even established their own comprehensive Web operations and perform a full gamut of Web services for clients including Web site building and maintenance, hosting, management of direct e-mail correspondence with customers, and management of the client's overall CRM system.

It is likely that the importance of the outsourced full-service marketing agency will continue to grow into the next decade. As marketing itself becomes more strategic within organizations, more and more of the tactical or programmatic aspects of marketing that were formerly handled in-house will be outsourced. In such a scenario, the importance of the marketing manager role is heightened, as that individual will be the frontline person in a firm that is charged with managing all aspects of the outsourced agency relationship.

SALES PROMOTION

Sales promotion was defined earlier as a promotion mix element that provides an inducement for an end-user consumer to buy a product or for a salesperson or someone else in the channel to sell it. Sales promotion is designed to augment other forms of promotion and is rarely used alone. This is because sales promotion initiatives rely on other media forms such as advertising and direct or interactive marketing as a communication vehicle. Think of sales promotion as prompting a "buy now" response; that is, it is squarely aimed at the action (behavior) stage of the AIDA model.

Sales promotion can be aimed directly at end-user consumers, or it can be targeted to members of a channel on which a firm relies to sell product. In the latter case, sales promotion is an important element of a push strategy. One additional potential target for sales promotion is a firm's own sales force. Bonus payments, prizes, trips, and other incentives to induce a salesperson to push one product over another are forms of internal sales promotion. Salesperson incentives will be discussed further in Chapter 14. For now, let's look at sales promotion to consumers and to channel members.

Sometimes a sales promotion can backfire, sending consumers mixed signals and tarnishing a company's image. KFC's grilled chicken launch was to be the biggest in the chain's history. Oprah Winfrey promoted it by referring to a coupon for free chicken on her Web site for a limited time. The power of Oprah resulted in KFC giving away considerably more chicken than anticipated. KFC independent franchise operators stopped giving away the free chicken, thus angering customers who claimed false advertising. Ultimately, Yum! Brands (KFC's corporate parent) resolved the issue by giving customers who were unable to get the deal a rain check for a free grilled chicken meal and an added drink.[29]

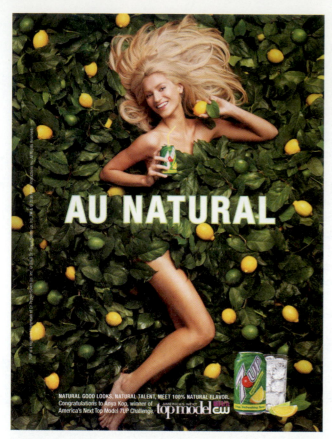

This ad ties into a 7Up sales promotion by featuring the winner of the contest "America's Next Top Model 7UP Challenge."

7UP is a registered trademark of Dr. Pepper/Seven Up, Inc. © 2008 Dr. Pepper/Seven Up, Inc. Used with permission. All rights reserved.

Sales Promotion to Consumers

When a firm is looking to gain product trial, spike distribution, shore up sagging quarterly sales, or rekindle interest in a waning brand, sales promotion can be an appropriate choice for investment of promotion dollars. Exhibit 13.15 summarizes nine popular consumer sales promotion approaches.

As with most promotional elements, marketing managers rarely select only one form of consumer sales promotion for execution. Many of the sales promotion options complement each other and all are potentially complementary of the overall promotion mix. One potential downside to sales promotion is a tendency by some firms and industries to overrely on sales promotion to bring in sales on a regular basis. This occurs because of sales promotion's power to elicit an actual purchase. Consider the proliferation of rebates on new-car purchases. Car manufacturers essentially "train" car shoppers not to look for a new vehicle unless a rebate is being offered. Ultimately, if sales promotion becomes institutionalized in such a manner, firms simply build a hefty cushion into the "everyday" price of the product, thus negating any real benefit to the customer of the promotion. Overuse of sales promotion is not a good promotional strategy and can lead to a general cheapening of brand image and distrust by customers.

Sales Promotion to Channel Members

Several sales promotion approaches are available for use with members of a firm's channel of distribution. Typically, these channel members would be distributors, brokers, agents, and other forms of middlemen. The purpose is to stimulate them to push your product, resulting in more sales in the channel and ultimately to end users.

Trade shows can be a very fruitful form of sales promotion. A **trade show** is an industry- or company-sponsored event in which booths are set up for the dissemination of information about offerings to members of a channel. Sometimes actual sales occur at a trade show, but often the primary purpose is promotion to attendees. Sales leads are obtained and passed along to the firm's sales organization for follow-up after the trade show.[30]

Another form of sales promotion to a channel is **cooperative advertising and promotion.** In cooperative advertising, a manufacturer provides special incentive money to channel members for certain performances such as running advertisements for one of the manufacturer's brands or doing product demonstrations with potential customers. The idea of cooperative advertising and promotion is that the manufacturer shares promotional expenses with channel members in the process of marketing to end-user consumers.[31]

Sometimes money is made available for a channel member in the form of a special payment for selling certain products, making a large order, or other specific performance. This form of channel-focused sales promotion is called an **allowance.** In addition, as with the consumer market, contests and displays with point-of-purchase materials are also frequently used as sales promotion approaches in the channel.[32]

EXHIBIT 13.15 **Consumer Sales Promotion Options**

Sales Promotion Approach	Description	Comments	Example
Product sampling	A physical sample of the product is given to consumers.	Excellent for inducing trial. Sample can be received by mail or in a store.	Gillette sends out a free razor to induce switching from an older model.
Coupons	An instant price reduction at point of sale, available in print media, online, or in-store.	Coupon usage is generally down among consumers. Still a good inducement to "buy now."	Inside the free razor from Gillette is a coupon for $1.00 off the purchase of a pack of blades.
Rebates	A price reduction for purchase of a specific product during a specific time period.	Possibly instant at point of sale, but more frequently requires submission and delay in processing.	Sharp offers a $100 rebate through Best Buy for purchase of a flat-screen television during February.
Contests and sweepstakes	Appeal to consumers' sense of fun and luck. May suggest a purchase but legally must be offered without a purchase requirement.	Contests require some element of skill beyond mere chance. Sweepstakes are pure chance.	McDonald's famous Monopoly game—the more you eat, the more you play (and vice versa!).
Premiums	Another product offered free for purchasing the brand targeted in the promotion.	Gives the customer a bonus for purchase. Products may be complementary or unrelated.	Burger King offers the latest Spider-Man toy with purchase of a meal.
Multiple-purchase offers	Incentive to buy more of the brand at a special price.	Typically "buy 2, get 1 free" or similar.	Centrum Vitamin offer—buy a bottle of 100, get an extra mini-bottle of 20.
Point-of-purchase materials	Displays set up in a retail store to support advertising and remind customers to purchase.	Especially good at driving purchase toward a featured brand in a product category at the store aisle.	Stand-up display and front window poster in Blockbuster of the latest DVD release.
Product placements	Having product images appear in movies, on television, or in photographs in print media.	Strong connections with the show or story, as well as to any associated celebrities.	Coca-Cola cups always on the desks of the American Idol judges.
Loyalty programs	Accumulate points for doing business with a company. Designed to strengthen long-term customer relationships and reduce switching.	Especially popular among the airline and hospitality industry. Credit card providers often facilitate.	American Airlines AAdvantage program, facilitated by CitiCard, MasterCard, and American Express cards.

PUBLIC RELATIONS (PR)

Earlier in the chapter we defined public relations (PR) as a systematic approach to influencing attitudes, opinions, and behaviors of customers and others. PR is often executed through **publicity,** which is an unpaid and relatively less personal form of marketing communications usually through news stories and mentions at public events.[33]

PR is a specialized field. Usually, undergraduate and graduate marketing programs do not include training in PR. Many PR professionals receive specialized training in communication, and outstanding PR people are highly sought after. Some firms have in-house PR departments, while others outsource much or all of the PR function to external agencies. Major responsibilities of a PR department might include any of the following activities:

- Gaining product publicity and buzz.
- Securing event sponsorships (for the company and its brands).
- Managing a crisis.
- Managing and writing news stories.
- Facilitating community affairs.
- Managing relationships with members of the local, national, and global media (media relations).
- Serving as organizational spokesperson.
- Educating consumers.
- Lobbying and governmental affairs.
- Handling investor relations.

However, few PR departments perform all of these functions; some of the above functions are often spread across other areas of a firm, such as investor relations to the finance department and lobbying and governmental affairs to the legal department.

We'll focus on the three core functions of PR that are most closely aligned with the role of the marketing manager: gaining product publicity and buzz, securing event sponsorships, and crisis management.

Gaining Product Publicity and Buzz

Especially when it comes to new product offerings, gaining publicity in news outlets and other public forums can provide a major boost to sales. During the introductory phase of the PLC, communication of information is a central promotional goal. The most credible and trusted information sources for potential customers are those that write or tell about a product for free. Newspaper and magazine articles, Web postings and blogs, social marketing Web sites, news stories on television and radio—all of these forms of communication can be cultivated through an active PR program. Many new products have benefited from the initial awareness generated by a well-placed story in a publication or on a Web site frequented by targeted customers.

Although the media employed are free, by no means is the process of securing the story placements free. In fact, PR can account for a great deal of money in a promotion budget due to the work hours required to constantly be writing stories and cultivating media outlets. But the payoff on that investment can be substantial due to the buzz generated among everyday consumers about a brand. **Buzz,** or word-of-mouth communication, is the communication generated about a brand in the marketplace. Buzz is not limited to current customers or even potential customers; when buzz about a brand hits the marketplace, it can even permeate pop culture.

One company that does a great job of generating buzz is Patagonia. The clothing and gear company promotes a lifestyle of adventure, and employees are encouraged to live what the company promotes. Patagonia allows flex time for employees to leave the office any time to hike, surf, run, and walk. Founder Yvon Couinard encourages outdoor activities with employees to renew and focus on protecting the environment and creating sustainable business practices. Couinard is convinced this is a wise investment in buzz-generating publicity, and thus a sound promotional strategy. For Patagonia it has paid off as customers strongly associate the brand with quality, adventure, and sustainability.[34]

Securing Event Sponsorships

Event sponsorships, having your brand and company associated with events in the sports, music, arts, and other entertainment communities, can add tremendous brand equity and also provide substantial exposure with the right target customers. Event sponsorships have become a mainstay of promotional strategy. A huge success story for marketers in event sponsorship is NASCAR, which appeals to millions of loyal and passionate racing fans. Consumers transfer their loyalty and passion about NASCAR directly to the brands represented by the sponsorships. No wonder NASCAR cars are referred to as "speeding billboards."[35]

Closely related to event sponsorship is issue sponsorship, in which a firm and its brands connect with a cause or issue that is especially important to its customers. McDonald's achieved a huge PR coup several years ago when it discarded its styrofoam sandwich containers for more environmentally friendly cardboard boxes. This action was well-received by members of the green movement and generated a great deal of positive buzz for McDonald's. Like publicity, the right sponsorships can generate positive buzz in the marketplace that enhances brand image.

After Danica Patrick became the first woman to win an IndyCar race, NASCAR sponsors hoped she would switch and join NASCAR. Marketers believe that Ms. Patrick would provide new sponsorship opportunities for the NASCAR brand, especially with female-oriented products. Speculation is that marketers would spend $50 million or more to have their brands associated with her. Danica has already endorsed P&G's Secret deodorant and currently has agreements with GoDaddy.com and Boost Mobile.[36]

Crisis Management

Crisis management is a planned, coordinated approach for disseminating information during times of emergency and for handling the effects of unfavorable publicity.[37] When Hurricane Charley hit Orlando, Florida, a few years ago, the Orlando Utility Commission (OUC), Orlando's main electric provider, mobilized its crisis management team immediately, putting into action a plan team members had practiced many times. Although power was out for some residents for more than a week, customer feedback on how OUC handled the crisis was far superior to that of other utilities and governmental entities in the region. Roseanne Harrington, vice president for marketing communications and community relations at OUC, attributes the positive customer attitude to constant updates provided to patrons, being truthful and realistic in setting expectations for return of service (not overpromising), and diligent attention to getting customers back in service as quickly as possible. All firms should have a crisis management plan in place for contingencies that are relevant to their industry and customers.

SUMMARY

Developing promotional strategies is an integral part of marketing management and marketing planning. A firm's investment in promotion often involves a substantial amount of money. Fostering an integrated marketing communications (IMC) approach in an organization ensures consistency in communication of the brand and promotional messages across all internal and external communication channels. Although marketing managers are rarely experts in all areas of promotion, they must be well-versed in the process of IMC and how it connects to the overall marketing plan.

APPLICATION QUESTIONS

1. Consider a major purchase you have made recently. Review the AIDA model (Exhibit 13.7) and accompanying discussion.

   a. Think back on the process that led up to your purchase and reconstruct the types of promotion that you experienced during each stage of the AIDA model. Which of the promotional forms was most effective in your situation, and why?

   b. As you reconstruct this purchase experience and the promotional messages you received during it, what other promotion mix elements that you did *not* experience at the time might have been effective in convincing you to make the purchase? At what stage of the AIDA model would they have been helpful, and in what ways do you believe they might have impacted your decision process?

2. The chapter discusses the role of the marketing manager in promotional strategy (Exhibit 13.9 and accompanying discussion). The trend today in both large and small firms is for much of the promotion function to be outsourced.

   a. Comment on this outsourcing trend. What are the major reasons for the trend? What are the pros and cons? What is your personal view about outsourcing all or part of promotion?

   b. Assume you are a marketing manager for a firm that outsources promotion to a creative agency. In what ways does this arrangement impact your job? In particular, concentrate on how it impacts your marketing planning (being mindful that promotion planning is a key element). How would you interact with the agency as a manager representing your firm (assume you have responsibility for the agency relationship with your company)? That is, what are the key things you should do to ensure a productive relationship?

3. Review the Common Approaches to Advertising Execution (Exhibit 13.13) and Pros and Cons of Key Advertising Media (Exhibit 13.14). Review some ads in any three of the seven different types of media identified, watching for examples of the different execution approaches.

   a. Make notes about the ads you reviewed and the different types of media execution you witnessed. Which ads do you think were the most effective? Why?

   b. For the same ads, based on the chapter's list of pros and cons for each, identify specific examples of ads for which one or more of the pros and cons apply.

   c. Share your findings with another student or with the class.

MARKETING PLAN EXERCISE

ACTIVITY 13.1 Promoting Your Offering

The promotion plan is an integral part of any marketing plan, and often carries a significant portion of the marketing budget. Develop the following elements for promoting your offering:

1. Review the promotion mix elements and begin to develop goals for promotion and a promotional strategy utilizing the elements of the mix that are most appropriate for your offering.

2. Link the promotional strategy to PLC stages as well as the stages your customers will go through on the AIDA model.

3. Decide how you intend to manage promotion for the offering. Decide on outsourced elements versus elements that will be handled in-house. Establish a structure and process for promotion management.

If you are using Marketing Plan Pro, a template for this assignment can be accessed at www.mhhe.com/marshalless1e.

CHAPTER 14

Integrated Marketing Communications: Personal Selling, Direct Marketing, and Interactive Marketing

---

LEARNING OBJECTIVES

- Learn the process of relationship selling.

- Understand the major job responsibilities of sales management.

- Recognize the most significant challenges facing personal communication.

- Identify the major tools in direct marketing.

- Value the use of direct marketing communications in an integrated communications strategy.

- Understand the limitations of direct marketing.

- Learn how to create an effective Internet marketing campaign.

TOWARD A MORE PERSONAL COMMUNICATION WITH THE CUSTOMER

Advertising, sales promotion, and public relations are essential tools in an integrated marketing communications strategy. However, they are all, for the most part, unidirectional. In other words, the company communicates with the customer but the customer has limited ability to provide feedback. Companies know that it is important to communicate directly with the customer and, in turn, enable the customer to communicate directly with the company. As a result, effective integrated marketing communications incorporates interactive, personal communication elements.

The three personal communication methods most widely adopted are personal selling, direct marketing, and interactive marketing. They have the potential to connect the company with the customer as well as encourage the customer to interact with the company in a way that significantly strengthens the relationship. However, if managed poorly, they can profoundly harm the relationship with the customer. Companies know that interactive communication is critical to long-term success and dedicate resources to ensure the quality of the relationship between the company and customer.

Richardson, a prominent sales performance improvement firm, offers an online sales call planning software solution aptly called SalesCaliPlanner. The real-time application provides salespeople with information about the potential client, as well as step-by-step coaching and reinforcement to help drive the dialogue. Although SalesCaliPlanner is primarily designed to help salespeople close more deals over the phone, the application also has features that provide sales managers with information about their organization's sales call performance. This information has helped sales managers at Dell Computer, Campbell's Foods, and DuPont Chemicals provide more constructive feedback to their salespeople.[1]

PERSONAL SELLING–THE MOST PERSONAL FORM OF COMMUNICATION

With the average cost of a sales call exceeding $300 and the Internet's interactive capabilities, some people have predicted the decline of personal selling as an effective marketing communications tool. However, this has not been the case; indeed, IBM, Pfizer, and other companies are expanding their sales forces. While there is no question that selling is among the most expensive forms of marketing communication, personal selling offers three distinct advantages over other marketing communications methods:

- *Immediate feedback to the customer.* Customers don't want to wait for information. Increasingly, they demand accurate information quickly, putting pressure on companies for immediate, personal communication with a salesperson or customer service representative.[2]
- *Ability to tailor the message to the customer.* No other marketing communication method does a better job of creating personal, unique customer messages in real time. Salespeople generate distinctive sales messages that directly address customer problems and concerns.[3]
- *Enhance the personal relationship between company and customer.* Salespeople and the personal selling function are the single most effective approach for establishing and enhancing the personal relationship between company and customer. In particular, business-to-business (B2B) customers appreciate the efficiency of the Internet and other communication tools but

Personal selling offers three distinct advantages: immediate customer feedback, ability to create unique customer messages, and enhancing the customer relationship. The selling function can be a strategic advantage for the company.

expect a personal relationship with their suppliers. There is no substitute for a salesperson working with the customer one-on-one to solve problems.[4]

Activities in Personal Selling

Personal selling is a two-way communication process between salesperson and buyer with the goal of securing, building, and maintaining long-term relationships with profitable customers. To be successful in this process, salespeople need a variety of skills that change all the time. Research suggests salespeople today are expected to be more skilled, available, as well as better communicators than ever before. Four basic selling activities composed of dozens of individual tasks define the salesperson's job: communicate, sell, build customer relationships, and manage information. The challenge for many companies is defining the correct mix of activities and then adapting the activities as the selling environment changes.[5] Exhibit 14.1 identifies the four major selling activities and specific tasks associated with each activity.

EXHIBIT 14.1	Matrix of Selling Activities

	Communicate	Sell	Build Customer Relationships	Manage Information
Technology	1. E-mail 2. Make telephone calls/leave voice-mail messages	1. Script sales pitch 2. Create customer-specific content 3. Provide relevant technology to customer	1. Create useful company Web page content 2. Develop good team skills inside the company	Develop database management skills to manage customer database
Non-technology	1. Enhance language and overall communication skills 2. Develop effective presentation skills	1. Learn relationship selling skills 2. Conduct research of customer's business 3. Define and sell value-added services to customer 4. Follow up after customer contact 5. Identify and target key customer accounts 6. Listen effectively	1. Develop strong supplier alliances 2. Build rapport with all members of the customer's buying center 3. Network inside the company and throughout the customer's business 4. Build trust 5. Coordinate customer relationships inside the company	1. Develop time management skills 2. Organize information flow to maximize the effectiveness and reduce irrelevant data

Communicate

Effective communication is an essential selling activity. As the point of contact between customer and company, a salesperson must communicate effectively with both. With the customer, the salesperson needs good verbal communication skills to present the sales message. Equally important are good presentation skills that incorporate technology (PowerPoint, wireless access) into the sales presentation. Finally, customers expect near constant access to the company so the salesperson must also have mobile communications skills.[6]

Communication with the company is also important. As discussed in Chapter 4, salespeople represent an excellent source of market information; they are familiar with customers and their needs. Customer feedback is also an excellent source of new-product ideas. Finally, field salespeople frequently find out about competitor or marketplace changes before anyone else in the company. All this information needs to be collected, analyzed, and disseminated to appropriate marketing managers.

Sell

Everyone agrees that the basic activity of a salesperson is selling, but what exactly does that mean? Selling requires a complex set of tasks to reach the point where the customer agrees to purchase the product. From customer research early in the process through the sales presentation and customer support after purchase, the sales process is difficult.[7] We will explore the sales process a little later in the chapter.

Build Customer Relationships

Customers demand a close, strategic relationship with suppliers, and, as the primary point of contact with the company, salespeople are expected to build and support the customer relationship. This means spending time with the customer, developing excellent customer relationship management skills, and ultimately building trust with a customer.[8]

Information Management

Salespeople today must be excellent information managers, collecting information from a variety of sources (their own company, customers, competitors, and independent information sources), determining what is relevant, and then presenting it to the customer. For example, managing the flow of customer information inside the company to ensure the right people get the right information at the right time takes time and follow-up. Often, information is collected from customers and other external sources such as transportation companies to facilitate an order inside the company. Customers will have preferred shipping times that need to be coordinated with transportation companies to ensure on-time arrival. At the same time, being sensitive to customer security concerns means controlling access to information.[9]

Key Success Factors

Because selling involves such a diverse set of activities, it is considered one of the most difficult careers in business. While the variety of sales jobs makes it impossible to generalize to every situation, research has identified the following critical success factors:[10]

- *Listening.* Many people have the impression that salespeople are great talkers. While it is important to be a good communicator, the reality is that great salespeople are skillful listeners. They know that to really learn the customer's needs and then create a value-based solution it is essential to listen.

- *Follow-up.* When a salesperson commits to doing something, the customer expects it to be done. Follow-up and addressing customer concerns is a critical skill.

- *Ability to adapt sales style from situation to situation.* Being able to adjust the sales style from one sales situation to another in real time based on customer feedback, called **adaptive selling,** is critical to long-term success. The "one size fits all" approach does not work with customers expecting personalized service.

- *Persistence.* Building customer relationships takes time and effort. Long-term success is not based on a single sale but, rather, a relationship, which makes the salesperson (and company) a critical partner with the customer in the customer's success.

- *Good verbal communication skills.* Effective communication skills have never been more important. Customers expect a salesperson to be good at verbal communications and incorporate appropriate technologies into the presentation.

- *Effective personal planning and time management.* Customers demand it and good salespeople recognize the importance of effective time management. As salespeople take on more activities and customer expectations increase, managing time becomes essential in relationship building.

- *Ability to interact with individuals at every level of the organization.* Salespeople interact with a wide range of people inside their customer organizations. As a result, they must be just as comfortable in front of C level executives (CEOs) as well as lower-level managers.

Sales in B2C versus B2B Markets

In terms of sheer numbers, most salespeople are employed in various kinds of retail selling, or B2C. These jobs involve selling products to end users for their personal use. Examples of these types of sales positions are direct sellers such as Mary Kay and Tupperware, residential real estate agents, and retail store salespeople. However, much more relationship selling is done by salespeople in B2B markets.

Some personal characteristics and sales activities are similar across both B2C and B2B markets. Good interpersonal and communication skills, excellent knowledge of the products being sold, an ability to discover customer needs and solve their problems are common characteristics to both sales environments. Similarly, managers must recruit and train appropriate people no matter what the sales job, provide them with objectives that match the firm's overall marketing program, then supervise, motivate, and finally evaluate their performance.[11]

But B2C and B2B selling also differ in some important ways. Many of the goods and services sold by B2B salespeople are more expensive and technically complex than those in B2C. In addition, B2B customers tend to be larger and engage in extensive decision-making processes involving many people.

Classifying Sales Positions

While retail selling employs more people, personal selling plays a more important and strategic purpose in business-to-business markets. Because of the important strategic function of personal selling in business-to-business markets, our discussion of sales positions will focus on different sales positions in the B2B market. There are many different types of sales jobs that require a variety of specific and unique skills. However, no matter what the job title, the salesperson's primary responsibility is to increase business from current and potential customers by providing a good value proposition to customers and effectively dealing with their concerns. The four major types of sales positions are trade servicer, missionary seller, technical seller, and solutions seller.

Trade Servicer

Trade servicers are the group of resellers such as retailers or distributors with whom the sales force does business. Their primary responsibility is to increase business from current or potential customers by providing them with merchandising and promotional assistance. For example, the Procter & Gamble salesperson selling soap products to individual store managers at a large grocery is an example of a trade servicer.

Missionary Seller

Missionary salespeople often do not take orders from customers directly but persuade customers to buy their firm's product from distributors or other suppliers. Anheuser-Bush does missionary selling when its salespeople call on bar owners and encourage them to order a particular brand of beer from the local distributor. Although the sales model is changing, pharmaceutical reps, or detailers, historically called on doctors as representatives of the pharmaceutical manufacturers. When Pfizer introduced Zyrtec, a top-selling allergy drug, its salespeople communicated with physicians to alert them to the efficacy of the product, explain its advantages over other allergy medication such as Allegra and Clarinex, and to influence them to prescribe it to their patients. Keep in mind that the Pfizer salesperson does not "sell" any product directly to the patient.[12]

Technical Seller

An example of **technical selling** is the sales engineer from General Electric who calls on Boeing to sell the GE90 jet engine to be used in Boeing aircraft. The trend is for most technical selling to be done in cross-functional teams. The complexity of many of the products and associated services involved in technical selling makes it difficult for any one salesperson to master all aspects of the sale. Cross-functional teams often include someone who is technically competent in the product (engineer), a customer service specialist, a financial analyst, and an account manager responsible for maintaining the customer-company relationship.

Solutions Seller

More and more customers look for strategic partners who provide comprehensive solutions to their business problems. **Key account salespeople,** those responsible for managing large accounts, are skilled in developing complex solutions to a particular customer problem.[13] In addition, in industries such as information technology, customers look to suppliers for wide-ranging solutions from IT infrastructure design to defining product specifications, to purchase and installation of equipment or software, and support after the sale. A Hewlett-Packard or IBM salesperson, for example, needs to know not only a great deal about hardware and software but also the customer's business in order to develop a solution to the customer's IT problems.

The Personal Selling Process

Because personal selling is so important in establishing and maintaining customer relationships, particularly in B2B markets, many companies create a separate personal selling function that operates independently from the rest of marketing. As a result, marketing managers often do not have salespeople reporting directly to them. However, marketing managers need to understand the personal selling process for two reasons. First, in companies where salespeople play an important role, personal selling is the single most critical connection to the customer. From selling to customer service, salespeople are often the customer's primary contact point with the company. Marketing

Technical selling often involves trained specialists available to address customer concerns in the field.

EXHIBIT 14.2	The Personal Selling Process

Prospecting for Customers

↓

Opening the Relationship

↓

Qualifying the Prospect

↓

Making the Sales Presentation

↓

Handling Customer Objections

↓

Closing the Sale

↓

Following up with Customers

managers need a clear understanding of the selling process because it has such a profound effect on the customer relationship. Second, a number of marketing activities such as customer service and marketing communications will be affected by the personal selling function. Understanding the selling process helps marketing managers better plan a marketing communications strategy and coordinate other marketing activities such as customer service.

Exhibit 14.2 shows the stages in the personal selling process. Although the selling process involves only a few steps, the specific activities involved at each step vary greatly depending on the type of sales position and the firm's overall customer relationship strategy. Consequently, marketing managers must ensure that a firm's sales program incorporates sufficient policies to guide each salesperson while at the same time coordinating the selling effort with the firm's marketing and relationship strategy. The same selling process is used by B2C and B2B salespeople, although how the process works varies greatly between the two environments. For example, B2C salespeople generally do not actively prospect for customers, since the customer is visiting the store, or follow up with the customer after the sale.

Prospecting for Customers

Prospecting is critical because recruiting new customers is an essential element in a company's growth strategy. Marketing managers encourage salespeople to use a variety of sources to identify relevant prospects including trade association and industry directories, other customers and suppliers, and referrals from company marketing efforts.

Telemarketing and other direct marketing efforts, which we will discuss in the next section, are also used to generate prospective customers. **Outbound telemarketing** involves calling potential customers at their home or office, either to make a sales call via telephone or to set up an appointment for a field salesperson. **Inbound telemarketing,** where prospective customers call a toll-free number for more information, is also used to identify and qualify prospects. When prospects call for more information, a telemarketing representative determines the extent of interest and assesses the prospect qualifications, then passes the contact information on to the appropriate salesperson. The Internet also generates potential new customer leads. Many companies, particularly those selling complex products, use the Internet to provide technical product information to customers. Then salespeople follow up on legitimate inquiries with a traditional sales call.

In coordinating the marketing effort, marketing managers must understand how much emphasis salespeople give to prospecting for new customers versus calling on existing customers. The appropriate policy depends on the selling and customer relationship strategy of the company, the nature of the product, and the firm's customers. Working with sales managers, the marketing manager considers the right mix of activities for the salesperson. For example, firms that have established customer relationships or products that require substantial service after the sale generally encourage salespeople to devote most of their effort to servicing existing customers.[14]

Consumer awareness about the company as well as brand perception affect the process of generating new sales leads. Not surprisingly, the company's Internet presence plays a significant role in attracting potential clients. Today, however, just having a Web site is not enough; it needs to reflect the company's personality and exceed customer expectations. Studies have indicated that a typical Web site visitor stays on the home page for only seven seconds before deciding to stay or leave. In a way, the Web site is similar to a sales representative who has just a few seconds to make a good first impression with a potential client.[15]

Opening the Relationship

In the initial approach to the prospective customer, the sales representative should try to determine who has the greatest influence or authority in the purchase. For example, when the firm's product is inexpensive and purchased routinely, salespeople are frequently instructed to deal with the purchasing department. At the other end of the continuum, complex, technical products generally require an extensive sales effort calling on influencers and decision makers in various departments and different managerial levels. When the purchase involves people across the customer's organization, the salesperson often works with a team.

Qualifying the Prospect

Before salespeople spend much time trying to establish a relationship with the prospective account, it is important to qualify the prospect to determine if the company is a legitimate potential customer. The process involves answering five questions:

- Does the prospect have a need for the company's products?
- Can the prospect derive added value from the product in ways that the company can deliver?
- Can the salesperson effectively contact, communicate, and work with the prospect over an extended time period (the time it takes to complete the sale and follow up after the sale)?
- Does the prospect have the financial ability and authority to make the sale?
- Will the sale be profitable for the company?

Sales Presentation

Communicating the Sales Message The **sales presentation** is the delivery of information relevant to meet the customer's needs and is the heart of the selling process. It is the process salespeople use to transition customers from interest in the product to purchase of the product. The stereotype of a sales presentation is a salesperson talking in front of a customer or group of customers. In reality, sales presentations are carefully choreographed interactions in which the salesperson tries to discern the customer's real needs while at the same time providing critical information in a persuasive way so the customer appreciates the benefits and advantages of the product. Remember, the goal of the sales process is not simply to make the sale but to create a strong value proposition that will lead to a mutually beneficial long-term relationship.[16]

Setting Goals and Objectives Ultimately, the goal of the presentation is to secure a purchase commitment from the customer. However, the salesperson does not just walk in asking for the purchase order. Successful salespeople understand that the purchase order does not come until customers believe the company's products offer the best solution to their needs. In defining the goal, salespeople consider where the customer is in the buying process and have a clear understanding of the customer relationship.[17] New customers, for example, generally need more information about company products, policies, and procedures than existing customers. Based on an analysis of these factors, salespeople identify at least one of five principal goals for the presentation. At some point, however, the goal of the presentation will be to obtain customer action.

- Educate the customer by providing enough knowledge about the company's products.
- Get the customer's attention.
- Build interest for the company's products.
- Nurture the customer's desire and conviction to purchase.
- Obtain a customer commitment to action (purchase).

Steps in a Sales Presentation

Much of the work for the presentation is done before meeting the customer. However, invariably the customer offers new information, presents a different problem, disagrees with the value proposition, or presents the salesperson with any one of a hundred other challenges. This means that while salespeople need to be well-prepared, they must also have the flexibility to adjust the presentation in real time. An effective sales presentation consists of three steps:

1. *Identify the customer needs.* Research suggests that being able to correctly identify customer needs is one of the key characteristics that distinguish high-performing salespeople. Selling is based, in large part, on the salesperson's ability to identify those needs and develop win-win solutions that benefit both the company and customer.

2. *Apply knowledge to customer needs.* This step, providing solutions that solve customer problems, is the essence of a salesperson's role in the relationship-selling process and is a critical link between what the company has to offer and the customer's needs. Good salespeople can explain product performance characteristics, service turnaround times, and many other important features. Those facts are important, but customers, whether they are consumers or other businesses, do not buy features. They buy solutions to problems. So it is fundamental that salespeople link knowledge of the company's products to customer need solutions. This process is often referred to as **FAB (Features, Advantages, and Benefits).**

   The FAB approach is designed to make the company's products more relevant for customers. A **feature** is any material characteristic or specification of a product. Antilock brakes on a Cadillac Escalade are an example of a feature. An **advantage** is the particular product/service characteristic that helps meet the customer's needs. The Escalade's antilock brakes help the SUV stop faster than normal brake systems. A **benefit** is the advantageous outcome from the advantage found in the product feature. The SUV will provide greater security for the driver and passengers.

3. *Satisfy customer needs.* No matter how much negotiating is involved before the final purchase decision or how tough it is to close the sale, customer satisfaction is the desired objective of every sales presentation. The nature of the sales presentation creates stress for the customer. The salesperson is asking the customer to choose change by selecting the company's product. As a result, salespeople understand the importance of minimizing **change conflict** for the customer. The best way to manage customer change conflict is to manage the customer's expectations.[18] Salespeople learn to clearly define the value proposition and deliver on all promises made during the presentation.

Handling Objections–Negotiating Win-Win Solutions

Casual observation may suggest there are many different customer concerns; however, when you look closely, customer anxieties fall into four areas. Customers often mask true concerns with general problems, but successful salespeople know how to identify and clarify true objections.[19]

Product Need The customer may not be convinced there is a need for the product. The customer's perspective can be summarized as, "We've always done it one way; why should we start something new now?" Key to the answer is a well-conceived value proposition that explains clearly how the product will benefit the customer and how it will be better than the existing solution.[20] It is important to remember that customers are generally not risk takers.

A much more common concern is whether the customer views the salesperson's product as a better solution than existing options. The customer is already familiar with the current products and change means learning a new product. Careful preparation is critical in dealing with questions about competitors, which is why salespeople spend a great deal of time learning about competitor products.

Company Trust Personal selling is based, in part, on mutual trust between the buyer and seller. As we discussed, most customers already have a supplier, and while they may not be totally satisfied, they are familiar with them. For example, they know the process for resolving a problem (who to call, expected wait times, costs, etc.). If the customer is unaware of the company, a common concern is the company's ability to deliver what is needed, when it's needed, and where it's needed.[21] This is a legitimate concern as the customer puts the company at risk by choosing the salesperson's company as the supplier. In other situations, customers may not object to the salesperson's company but are happy with their existing supplier.

Cisco has developed an excellent reputation with its customers. It is leveraging that reputation with a sophisticated line of teleconferencing products. Business customers have confidence in Cisco, which translates into business opportunities.

More Time One of the most common customer objections is, "I need more time to consider the proposal." Certainly, concern about making a purchase decision too quickly is legitimate; however, the most likely scenario is that the value proposition has not been sufficiently developed.

Price Salespeople consistently report that price is the most common customer apprehension. In many cases, the customer has legitimate objections about the price of a product. Nevertheless, the price objection usually means the customer has not accepted the value proposition. In essence, if the customer does not perceive that the product benefits exceed the price, there will be no sale. The salesperson is left with two options. Lower the price until it is below the product's perceived benefits, or raise the perceived benefits until they exceed the price.[22]

Closing the Sale

Closing the sale is obtaining commitment from the customer to make the purchase. The close is not a discrete event but rather a nonlinear process that begins with the approach to the customer. Research suggests salespeople make four critical mistakes in closing. First, a negative attitude about the customer or situation can affect the sales presentation and customer relationship. Second, the failure to conduct an effective pre-approach shows a lack of preparation that turns off customers. Third, too much talking and not enough listening demonstrates a lack of interest in finding out the customer's real needs. Fourth, using a "one size fits all" approach indicates the salesperson lacks creativity and is unwilling to focus on the customer's unique situation.[23]

Follow-up after the Sale

One of the most critical aspects in the selling process is not what happens before the purchase decision but what happens after, the **follow-up.** Salespeople often rely on support people inside the company to help in post-sales service. Customer service personnel, product service call centers, technicians, and others are part of the follow-up process. But no matter who else has contact with the customer, the customer will hold the primary salesperson most responsible for the level and quality of service and support after the sale.

Customers expect three activities after the purchase decision: (1) delivery, installation, and initial service of the product, (2) any training needed to operate the equipment correctly, and (3) the effective and efficient disposition of appropriate customer problems that arise from the product purchase. Not meeting those expectations is a primary reason for customer complaints.[24] The next purchase decision is based to a large extent on the customer's experience with the product and the company.

T-Mobile, a brand of Deutsche Telekom, has made substantial investments in upgrading its customer support system. Wireless customers can manage virtually all aspects of their account via the T-Mobile Web site, reducing the need to either visit a T-Mobile store or call customer service. In fact, the knowledge management system even provides real-time "Instant Messaging" support to customers with questions about service, phone, or billing problems. Customers appreciate having the option to chat with a customer service representative via instant messaging because, increasingly, people use their cell phone as their primary phone.[25]

Organizing the Sales Force

Since salespeople work closely with many departments inside the company, marketing managers have a real interest in working with sales managers to organize the sales force to maximize the efficiency and effectiveness of not only the sales force but also everyone in the company that interacts with the customer. The best sales structures are based on the company's objectives and strategies. In addition, as the firm's environment, objectives, or marketing strategy changes, its sales force must be flexible enough to change as well.[26]

Company Sales Force or Independent Agents

Maintaining a sales force is expensive, and companies are constantly assessing the most practical method to reach customers. One option is to use independent agents instead of company salespeople. It is not unusual for a company, such as IBM, to use both company salespeople and independent agents. Using independent sales agents is referred to as **outsourcing the sales force.**

The decision to use independent agents or a company sales force involves four factors.

- *Economic:* Basic analysis of the costs and expected revenue associated with maintaining a sales force is weighed against outsourcing to independent agents.
- *Control:* A critical factor is the amount of control senior management believes is necessary for the sales function. A company sales force offers complete control in key areas such as recruiting, training, and compensation. On the other hand, independent agents operate without direct company management supervision.

- *Transaction costs:* Finding a good replacement for a poor-performing independent sales agent can be difficult, and once one is found, it is often months before the new agent learns enough about the product and its applications to be effective in the sales job. **Transaction cost analysis (TCA)** states that when substantial transaction-specific assets are necessary to sell a manufacturer's product, the cost of using and administering independent agents is likely higher than the cost of hiring and managing a company's sales force.[27]
- *Strategic flexibility:* In general, a vertically integrated distribution system incorporating a company sales force is less flexible than outsourcing. Independent agents can be added or dismissed at short notice, especially if no specialized assets are needed to sell the product. Furthermore, it is not necessary to sign a long-term contract with independent agents. Firms facing uncertain and rapidly changing competitive or market environments and industries characterized by shifting technology or short product life cycles often use independent agents to preserve flexibility in the distribution channel.

Geographic Orientation

The simplest and most common method of organizing a company sales force is geographic orientation. Individual salespeople are assigned to separate geographic territories. In this type of organization, each salesperson is responsible for performing all the sales activities in a given territory. The geographic sales organization has several advantages. First, and most importantly, it tends to have the lowest cost because (1) there is only one salesperson in each territory, (2) territories tend to be smaller than other organizational structures so travel time and expenses are minimized, and (3) fewer managerial levels are required for coordination so sales administration and overhead expenses are lower. Second, the simplicity of the geographical structure minimizes customer confusion because each customer is called on by one salesperson. The major disadvantage is that it does not encourage or support any division or specialization of labor. Each salesperson is expected to be good at many things (various customer needs, product applications and specifications).

Product Organization

Some companies have a separate sales force for each product or product category. The primary advantage of a product organization is that individual salespeople can develop familiarity with the technical attributes, applications, and most effective selling methods associated with a single product. Also, there tends to be a closer relationship between sales and engineering, product development, and manufacturing when salespeople focus on one product or product category. Finally, this structure enables greater control in the allocation of selling effort across various products. Management can then adjust sales assets based on the needs of individual products. The major disadvantage is the duplication of effort with salespeople across different products assigned to the same geographic territory. This generally leads to higher sales costs.

Customer Type or Market Organization

It has become increasingly popular for organizations to structure their sales force by customer type as IBM did when it created separate sales teams to call on small and large business customers. Organizing by customer type is a natural extension of creating value for the customer and reflects a market segmentation strategy. When salespeople specialize in calling on a particular type of customer, they gain a better understanding of those customers' needs and requirements. They can be trained to use different selling approaches for different markets and to implement specialized marketing and promotional programs.[28]

A related advantage is that as salespeople become familiar with the customers' specific needs, they are more likely to discover ideas for new products and marketing approaches that will appeal to those customers. The disadvantage, as with product organization, is that sales costs are higher as a result of having multiple salespeople operating in the same geographic area. In addition, when customers have different departments operating in different industries, two or more salespeople from the same company may be calling on the same customer.

Sales Force Size

Companies want to be sure that every salesperson is needed to achieve the company's long-term goals. At the same time, having too few salespeople means sales are almost certainly being lost. Consequently, both sales and marketing managers have a significant interest in determining the proper sales force size. Several methods can be used to determine the correct sales force size. The most common is called the **workload method** based on the premise that all salespeople should undertake an equal amount of work. The method has advantages and disadvantages. First, it is easy to understand and recognizes that different types of accounts should be called on with different frequencies. Second, the data to estimate the sales force are readily available. But the method does not allow for differences in sales response among customers that receive the same sales effort. Also, it assumes all salespeople use their time with equal efficiency, which is not the case.

The method involves six steps.

- *Classify all the company's customers into categories.* Often the classification is based on the sales to each customer and to prioritize accounts as A, B, C based on sales volume

- *Determine the frequency with which each type of account should be called on and the desired length of each sales call.* This analysis is based on management insights or a more formal analysis of historical data.

- *Calculate the workload involved in covering the entire market.* This calculation should include the total amount of work involved in covering each class of account.

- *Determine the time available for each salesperson.* Estimate the number of hours a typical salesperson works per week, and then multiply that by the number of weeks the salesperson works during the year.

- *Apportion the salesperson's time by task performed.* Not all the salesperson's time is involved in direct selling to the customer. A great deal of time is spent on nonselling activities such as making reports, meetings, and service calls.

- *Calculate the number of salespeople needed.* The number of salespeople the company will need is determined by dividing the total number of hours required to service the entire market by the number of hours available per salesperson for direct selling activities.

Managing the Sales Force

Sales and marketing work together to deliver value to the customer and achieve company objectives. While primary responsibility for managing a sales force generally falls to sales managers, integrating the marketing and sales function requires a coordinated effort with marketing managers. Understanding how salespeople are managed helps marketing managers better understand the selling function and coordinate sales with the rest of the marketing department. The sales function is unique in the organization and requires talented management to maximize its efficiency and effectiveness. Managing a sales force involves five primary responsibilities: salesperson performance, recruitment and selection, training, compensation and rewards, and performance evaluation.

Salesperson Performance: Motivating the Sales Force

Understanding salesperson performance is important to sales managers because almost everything they do influences sales performance one way or another. For example, how the manager selects salespeople and the kind of training they receive affects their aptitude and skills. The compensation program and the way it is administered influences motivation and overall sales performance.

> The entrance of Generation Y into the workforce has rewritten some of the rules of managing sales force motivation. Unlike their baby boomer parents, Gen Yers are more distrustful of organizations and imposed corporate ideologies. To motivate these individuals, sales managers must focus on tactics that promote earning their trust and need to take an interest in their careers. Sales managers at companies such as Google and Intuit understand they must communicate with Gen Y salespeople face-to-face and avoid micromanagement tactics to more effectively motivate their staff. They also recognize that Gen Yers place a greater emphasis on balancing life and work.[29]

As presented in Exhibit 14.3, salesperson performance is a function of five factors: (1) role perceptions, (2) aptitude, (3) skill level, (4) motivation, and (5) personal, organizational, and environment factors.

Role Perceptions The role of a salesperson is the set of activities or behaviors to be performed by the salesperson. This role is largely defined through the expectations, demands, and pressure communicated to the salesperson by role partners. These partners include people inside as well as outside the company with a vested interest in how a salesperson performs the job—top management, the salesperson's sales manager, customers, and family members. How salespeople perceive their roles has significant consequences that affect job satisfaction and

EXHIBIT 14.3 Model of Salesperson Performance

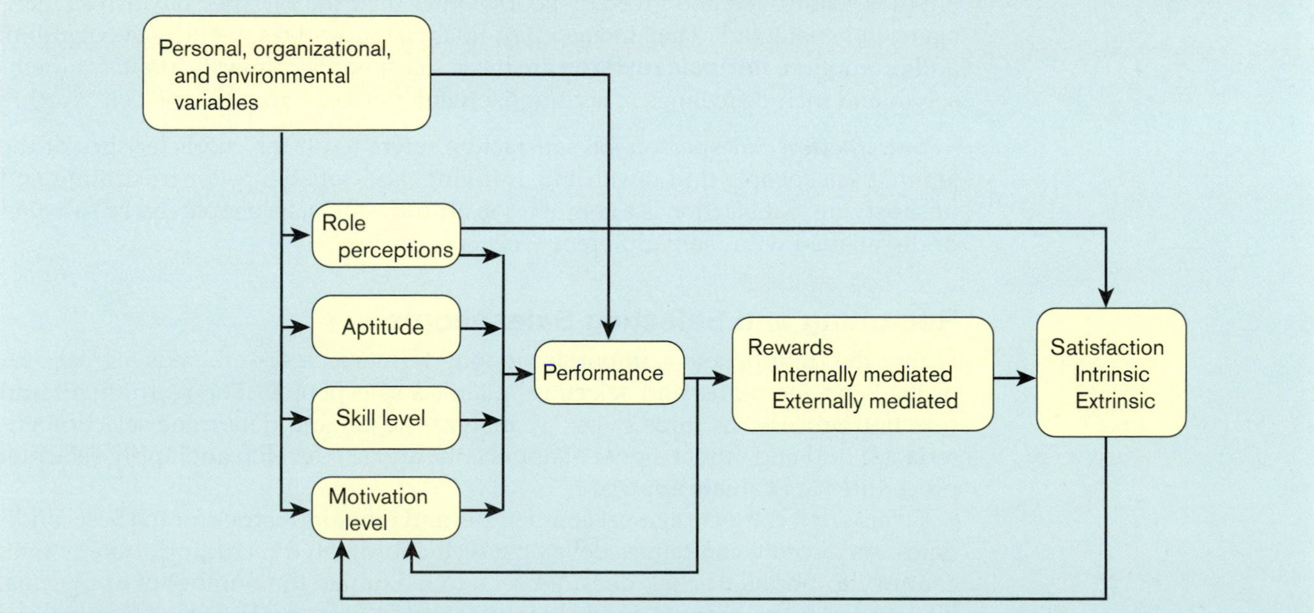

Source: Adapted from Mark W. Johnston and Greg W. Marshall, *Sales Force Management*, 9th ed, 2009. Copyright © 2009 The McGraw-Hill Companies, Inc.

motivation, which, in turn, have the potential to increase sales force turnover and hurt performance.[30]

Sales Aptitude: Are Good Salespeople Born or Made? Sales ability has historically been considered a function of (1) physical factors such as age and physical attractiveness, (2) aptitude factors such as verbal skills and sales expertise, and (3) personality characteristics such as empathy. However, there is no proof these measures, by themselves, affect sales performance. As a result, most managers believe the things a company does to train and develop its salespeople are the most important determinants of success.

Sales skill levels **Sales skill levels** are the individual's learned proficiency at performing necessary sales tasks. They include such learned abilities as interpersonal skills, leadership, technical knowledge, and presentation skills. The relative importance of each of these skills and the need for other skills depends on the selling situation.[31]

Motivation **Motivation** is how much the salesperson wants to expend effort on each activity or task associated with the sales job. Sales managers constantly try to find the right mix of motivation elements that direct salespeople to perform sales activities. Unfortunately, motivational factors that work well with one person may not motivate another. For example, an autocratic managerial style may work with a midcareer salesperson but have a profound negative effect on a senior salesperson. In addition, a number of motivational factors are not directly under the sales manager's control such as personal family issues or general economic conditions.[32]

Organizational, Environmental, and Personal Factors Organizational factors include company marketing budget, current market share for the company's products, and the degree of sales management supervision. Personal and organizational variables such as job experience, the manager's interaction style, and performance feedback all affect the amount of role conflict and ambiguity salespeople perceive.[33] In addition, the desire for job-related rewards (such as higher pay or promotion) differs with age, education, family size, career stage, and organizational climate.

Rewards A company bestows a variety of rewards on any given level of performance. There are two types of rewards—extrinsic and intrinsic. **Extrinsic rewards** are those controlled and given by people other than the salesperson such as managers and customers. They include pay, financial incentives, security, recognition, and promotion. **Intrinsic rewards** are those salespeople primarily attain for themselves and include feelings of accomplishment, personal growth, and self-worth.[34]

Satisfaction Salesperson job satisfaction refers to all the characteristics of the job that salespeople find rewarding, fulfilling, and satisfying—or frustrating and unsatisfying. Satisfaction is a complex job attitude and salespeople can be satisfied or dissatisfied with many different aspects of the job.[35]

Recruiting and Selecting Salespeople

Hiring the right people is important to long-term success, so there is a great deal of focus on recruiting and selecting qualified salespeople. The recruitment and selection process has three steps: (1) analyze the job and determine selection criteria, (2) find and attract a pool of applicants, and (3) develop and apply selection procedures to evaluate applicants.

Firms often compete against competitors and other industries for the best candidates. As a result, companies develop a well-coordinated recruiting strategy that, contrary to popular belief, does not seek to maximize the number of applicants. Having too many recruits overloads the selection process. The true objective of a successful recruiting strategy is to identify a few exceptionally qualified recruits.[36]

EXHIBIT 14.4   Sales Training Topics

Source: Adapted from Mark W. Johnston and Greg W. Marshall, *Relationship Selling*, 3rd ed, 2010. Copyright © 2010 The McGraw-Hill Companies, Inc.

Training

Sales managers often work with marketing managers to identify training objectives that integrate the needs of the salesperson with corporate marketing objectives and include: (1) improved customer relationships, (2) increased productivity, (3) improved morale, (4) lower turnover, and (5) improved selling skills. The challenge for sales managers is measuring the effectiveness of sales training.[37]

Sales training most often involves one or more of the seven topics listed in Exhibit 14.4 ranging from product knowledge to very specialized topics such as communication and customer relationship building. The key for sales managers is fitting the sales training content to the needs of the individual salespeople.

The UK-based training firm Sales 101 specializes in the creation of games and activities that serve as effective sales force training tools. One product, called SalesMaster, is a training mechanism that has been designed around people's natural capacity to learn new concepts and skills through play. Multinational companies, including thermal analysis instrument manufacturer TA Instruments and risk consulting firm Marsh, Inc., claim that the training tool has been effective in a range of situations such as training new staff and developing the technical skills of existing staff. SalesMaster carries out all of these functions while providing an enjoyable and completely flexible game-based interface.[38]

Compensation and Rewards

The total financial compensation paid to salespeople has several components designed to achieve different objectives. A **salary** is a fixed sum of money paid at regular intervals. Most firms that pay a salary also offer **incentive pay** to encourage better performance. Incentives are generally commissions tied to sales volume or profitability, or bonuses for meeting or exceeding specific performance targets (for example, meeting quotas for a particular product). Such incentives direct salespeople's efforts toward specific strategic objectives during the year, as well as offer additional rewards for top performers. A **commission** is payment based on short-term results, usually a salesperson's dollar or unit sales volume. Since there is a direct link between sales volume and the amount of commission received, commission payments are useful for increasing salespeople's sales efforts.[39] Exhibit 14.5 summarizes the components and objectives of financial compensation plans.

In addition to financial compensation, sales managers (and management across the company) also incorporate a range of **nonfinancial incentives.** Most sales managers consider promotional opportunities second only to financial incentives as effective sales force motivators. This is particularly true for young,

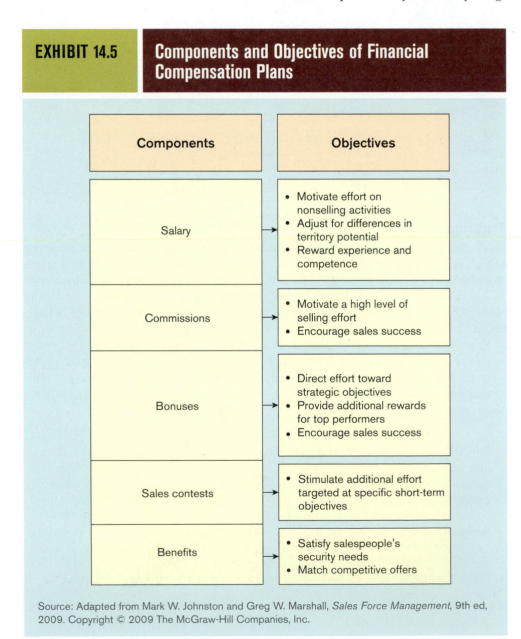

EXHIBIT 14.5 — **Components and Objectives of Financial Compensation Plans**

Components	Objectives
Salary	• Motivate effort on nonselling activities • Adjust for differences in territory potential • Reward experience and competence
Commissions	• Motivate a high level of selling effort • Encourage sales success
Bonuses	• Direct effort toward strategic objectives • Provide additional rewards for top performers • Encourage sales success
Sales contests	• Stimulate additional effort targeted at specific short-term objectives
Benefits	• Satisfy salespeople's security needs • Match competitive offers

Source: Adapted from Mark W. Johnston and Greg W. Marshall, *Sales Force Management*, 9th ed, 2009. Copyright © 2009 The McGraw-Hill Companies, Inc.

well-educated salespeople who tend to view their sales position as a stepping-stone to a senior management position.

Evaluating Salesperson Performance

A fundamental issue is monitoring sales activity and evaluating salesperson performance. Salespeople should be evaluated solely on those elements of the sales process they control. To do this a company develops objective and subjective measures that distinguish between controllable and noncontrollable factors.

When someone updates their profile on Facebook or Twitter, they can't wait to get feedback from their friends. But when it comes to performance reviews at work, that same person often isn't as enthusiastic. Companies, such as Accenture, are familiar with this phenomenon and are exploring ways to make performance evaluations more popular. Software providers like Rypple have developed interorganizational performance evaluation software that borrows heavily from popular social networking Web sites such as Twitter. For instance, the software enables salespeople to post questions about their performance in the hopes that they will get anonymous feedback. A wide range of companies, including Great Harvest Bread Co. and Mozilla, are among Rypple's clients.[40]

The end result is that many activities critical to long-term success such as building customer satisfaction go unmeasured. These other measures fall into two broad categories: (1) objective measures and (2) subjective measures. **Objective measures** reflect statistics the sales manager gathers from the firm's internal data. **Subjective measures** rely on personal evaluations by someone connected to the salesperson's sales process, usually the immediate sales manager or a customer. Objective measures fall into two major categories: (1) output measures and (2) input measures. **Output measures** show the results of the efforts expended by the salesperson while **input measures** focus on the efforts of salespeople during the sales process (see Exhibit 14.6).

DIRECT MARKETING

Chapter 12 discussed direct marketing in terms of its role in the distribution network; here the focus is on direct marketing as a promotional tool. Direct marketing is among the fastest-growing marketing communication methods. As defined by the Direct Marketing Association, **direct marketing** is an interactive marketing system that uses one or more advertising media to affect a measurable response and/or transaction at any location. The term *direct marketing* includes a number of communication channels: direct mail, catalogs, telemarketing, and Internet marketing. Historically, direct mail was the most widely used method; however, that has been replaced by the Internet.[41]

Creating a Direct Marketing Campaign

A direct marketing campaign encompasses a series of specific steps.

Set Strategy for Campaign

As one element of a marketing communications strategy, the direct marketing campaign is incorporated into a broader promotional strategy. As part of that strategy, the direct marketing campaign should specify two criteria. First, what are the specific, quantifiable objectives? Direct marketing, unlike other marketing communications tools, can be measured, and it is important that marketing managers state objectives in specific, quantifiable terms. Second, marketing

EXHIBIT 14.6 — Examples of Output and Input Measures

Output Measures

- Orders
  - Number of orders
  - Average size of orders
  - Number of canceled orders
- Accounts
  - Number of active accounts
  - Number of new accounts
  - Number of lost accounts
  - Number of overdue accounts
  - Number of prospective accounts

Input Measures

- Calls
  - Total number of calls
  - Number of planned calls
  - Number of unplanned calls
- Time and time utilization
  - Days worked
  - Calls per day (call rate)
  - Selling time versus non-selling time
- Expenses
  - Total
  - By type
  - As a percentage of sales
  - As a percentage of quota
- Nonselling activities
  - Letters to prospects
  - Phone calls to prospects
  - Number of formal proposals developed
  - Advertising displays set up
  - Number of meetings held with distributors/dealers
  - Number of training sessions held with distributor/dealer personnel
  - Number of calls on distributor/dealer customers
  - Number of service calls made
  - Number of overdue accounts collected

Source: Adapted from Mark W. Johnston and Greg W. Marshall, *Sales Force Management*, 9th ed., 2009. Copyright © 2009 The McGraw-Hill Companies, Inc.

---

managers should identify the target market for the campaign and include demographic characteristics, lifestyle, and reasons direct marketing is an appropriate communications methodology for the market. At all times it is essential that the direct marketing campaign is consistent with and supports the overall marketing communications strategy.

Specify Direct Marketing Channels

A number of direct marketing channels are available to marketers. As a result, a key task for marketing managers is aligning the direct marketing strategy with the most effective direct marketing media based on the unique advantages and disadvantages of each one.

Identify Qualified Target Customers

Direct marketing, by nature, is more focused on specific customers than other nonpersonal communication media such as advertising or public relations. As a result, a critical step is to identify, qualify, and target a group of customers for the direct marketing campaign. There are primarily two sources of customers. The first is internally generated prospects that consist of prior customers or inquiries (through direct-mail campaigns or the company Web site). It is important to consider internal contacts first for two reasons. Internal names have demonstrated an interest in the company either through a purchase or inquiry. In addition, internally generated prospects are less expensive than the second customer source—external lists from outside vendors. List companies such as InfoUSA and Dun & Bradstreet specialize in developing and selling lists to direct marketers. In addition, companies sometimes make their customer lists available for purchase for a fee. Recently, however, Yahoo and others have been criticized for this practice.

Develop and Test the Offer for the Campaign

This is the basic element of a direct marketing campaign. Sophisticated database management programs enable companies to create specific offers for individual customers by matching customer information with the offer. One advantage of direct marketing is the ability to easily test alternative offer options. By targeting different individuals with unique offers, it is possible to quickly and accurately understand what messages are working well.

Analyze Results of Offer

Once the campaign is under way it is important to analyze the results. Analysis of the data can discover the revenue, cost, and overall profitability of each individual included in the campaign. No other marketing communications channel has that level of data for analysis.

Direct Marketing Channels

Direct marketing media accessible to marketing managers include direct mail, telemarketing, and e-mail. Other direct media do not allow for individual targeted communication but do enable the prospect to respond immediately; an example of this is television infomercials.

Direct Mail

Direct mail is one of the least expensive direct marketing channels with costs of $.75 to $2.00 per message, and despite frequent complaints about the amount of junk mail (totaling billions each year), it is still an effective channel for reaching targeted customers. Direct mail is much more effective in B2C than B2B markets because reaching the appropriate individual inside an organization is difficult.

University students, alumni, faculty, and staff are able to show their support every time they swipe their credit card through the use of "affinity" cards. Co-branding credit cards with nonprofit organizations such as colleges and universities is nothing new for many financial institutions. Some, like the University of Michigan and University of Minnesota, have multimillion-dollar arrangements with credit-card companies. However, due to the pressures associated with wanting to maintain a good relationship with the card issuers, schools rarely negotiate favorable terms for their students and are quick to divulge their personal information.[42]

One drawback to direct mail is the low response rate. Since it is easily discarded or, if read, not acted upon, the average direct-mail response rate as reported by the Direct Marketing Association is only 2.77 percent. Put another way, a little more than 97 percent of the direct mail is not acted on, making it relatively inefficient.

Components in a Direct-Mail Offer The contents or elements in a direct-mail offer include:

- Outside envelope: The offer comes in an envelope that must get the prospect's attention. Colorful illustrations, a more "personal" address, and a unique envelope feature (size, color, shape) all contribute to the prospect opening the envelope.
- Sales collateral: The offer is conveyed in the sales material inside the envelope. Most often this includes a letter detailing the offer and a brochure that presents a more graphic presentation of the material.
- Contact information: The offer gives contact information in several places. It is also important to provide multiple contact opportunities—toll-free number, response card, and Web site. Companies have found mentioning discounts such as coupons in the direct mail and then posting them on the Web site increases response rates as prospects are moved to additional action. If a response card is included, then a postage-paid return envelope is also included in the packet of material.

Telemarketing

Telemarketing has come under a lot of criticism in recent years. As noted in Chapter 12, the National Do Not Call Registry, as well as state restrictions, severely limits "cold call" telemarketing calls. However, despite its negative reputation and high cost per contact ($1 to $3), research conducted by the Direct Marketing Association suggests telemarketing works; indeed, it had one of the highest response rates of any direct marketing channel—8.55 percent. The challenge for the telemarketer is to break through the negative initial reaction and make a personal connection with the customer. Creating a tailored sales presentation that adjusts to customer feedback is a significant advantage for telemarketers after they have established a relationship.

Successful telemarketing campaigns contain three essential elements. First, access to an accurate list of qualified prospects is very important. Research suggests a good list of prospects boosts the success rate by 60 percent. Second, the offer must persuade the prospect to act immediately. Enhancing the offer to encourage immediate action includes a lower price, discounts on shipping, added product features and benefits. In addition, the offer must convey a sense of exclusivity demonstrating that the product cannot be purchased anywhere else. Finally, the telemarketer must engage the prospect with the highest ethical standards. Given the negative perception of telemarketing and the frequent abuses of unwanted telephone solicitations, most people perceive a high degree of risk in purchasing over the phone. As a result, the telemarketer must offer, and stand behind, money-back guarantees as well as, when possible, nationally recognized brand names.

Catalogs

Catalog marketers use a variety of different types of catalogs including full-line catalogs, specialty catalogs designed for small customer groups, as well as B2B catalogs to target potential buyers. The average consumer catalog purchase is $150, and more than 70 percent of Americans use catalogs. Keys to success include useful lists of customers and prospects to target, precise inventory control to monitor costs and enhance customer satisfaction, and careful brand management to maintain the company's integrity and reputation.

Seamless integration with the company's Web site is indispensable as consumers interact with the company through many channels. For example, the process may begin when a consumer looks at a catalog then orders online, or they may see something online and then call the company.[43] Catalog marketers have expanded globally, taking advantage of the Internet to target customers in Asia and Europe. U.S. catalog companies L.L. Bean and Lands' End have found success, particularly in Japan.

INTERACTIVE MARKETING

The Internet has redefined the relationship between companies and customers. In less than 15 years, it has established a powerful new communication channel. **Interactive marketing** is an Internet-driven relationship between companies, their brands, and customers. It enables customers to control information flow and encourages customer-company interaction as well as a higher level of customer service.[44] Even though it represents less than 20 percent of U.S. commerce and less than 10 percent of global business, the Internet and, more broadly, interactive electronic marketing are the future. In both B2C and B2B markets, electronic interactive channels are considered essential elements in an overall marketing communications strategy. Indeed, many companies including Procter & Gamble and General Motors are shifting communication budgets to Internet marketing and away from traditional communication channels, particularly network television.

Customers drive interactive marketing, controlling when, where, and how they interact. While companies expand access to information and explore new methods to facilitate the exchange process, customers define the relationship on their terms. The speed of this transformation has caught many companies by surprise. Finding what works, and equally important what doesn't work, on the Internet presents a number of challenges. For example, as customers become more connected to a

ETHICAL DIMENSION 14

Whose Review Is It Anyway?

Product sites such as CNET.com and Edmunds.com as well as Web logs (blogs) have become popular information sources for consumers about a variety of products and services. One popular element of these sites is the comments/reviews offered by product users. In most cases, individuals rate the product then write a review of their product experience. Sponsoring Web sites are clear that the product reviews are offered by individuals not affiliated with the site. Essentially, readers are told to be very careful in assigning too much validity to any one review or comment since the veracity of the post is not known. Having said that, product reviews are important and consumers consistently regard other people's product experiences as a critical factor in helping them make a product purchase decision.

Until a few years ago the assumption was that reviews were written by product users with no connection to the company or the Web site. However, that is not always the case. A number of companies have been caught paying bloggers to post positive reviews and other information. Indeed, the practice has become so widespread that several companies are now in the business of linking advertisers with bloggers willing to post information about a company's products. One of those companies, PayPerPost, reports over 8,700 advertisers and 50,000 bloggers. Bloggers earn between $5 and $100 per post depending on the length of the post and popularity of the blog. Advertisers with PayPerPost include large

companies such as Hewlett-Packard and *Sports Illustrated;* however, smaller companies also use the service. Wallhogs.com, a small manufacturer of life-size wall cutouts and prints, believes the positive feedback created by bloggers hired through PayPerPost had a significant effect on the company's initial success.

Critics charge the process is deceptive by giving the impression that a posting is from a legitimate blogger instead of a paid endorsement. In addition, they argue that the paid blog postings artificially inflate advertiser rankings, a key metric used by Google to list sites in the search engine. In an effort to counter claims that the postings are deceiving, PayPerPost changed its policies and now requires bloggers to include a "disclosure badge," which identifies the post as being company-sponsored.[45]

The ability of individuals to share product experiences is an important and evolving part of the Internet. Does the use of bloggers paid by advertisers damage the credibility of product experience posts?

Ethical Perspective

1. **Advertisers:** Should advertisers hire bloggers to post positive product experiences? Should they require bloggers to indicate whether or not they have been paid to post their review?

2. **Consumers:** Should bloggers post whether or not they are paid by an advertiser? Does it make any difference whether bloggers are being paid to post reviews to "neutral" product Web sites and blogs?

---

company, their expectations about service and the customer–company relationship also increase. In addition, combining traditional marketing communications channels with online, interactive media has proven to be a challenge. Communicating with customers is faster using e-marketing media, which often creates a challenge coordinating online and traditional marketing messages. Ethical Dimension 14 discusses one interactive communication tool, the use of company-sponsored Web bloggers to present information about a product, which has come under criticism for misrepresenting the nature of the relationship between company and blogger.

The Online Customer Interface

The company's Web site is the primary point of connection with the online customer. Customers visit a Web site to get information, ask questions, register complaints, develop a sense of community with other users, and purchase the product. As a result, it must do a number of things well. Performing the traditional role of retail storefront, the Web site conveys the company's value proposition to anyone that visits the site. Effective sites are able to draw new potential customers "inside" to check out the company's products and services.

At the same time, the Web site must service existing customers by providing access to customer service and information in an efficient and effective manner. Several researchers define the Web site interface on seven dimensions (see Exhibit 14.7).

EXHIBIT 14.7   **Summary of Seven Design Elements of the Customer Interface**

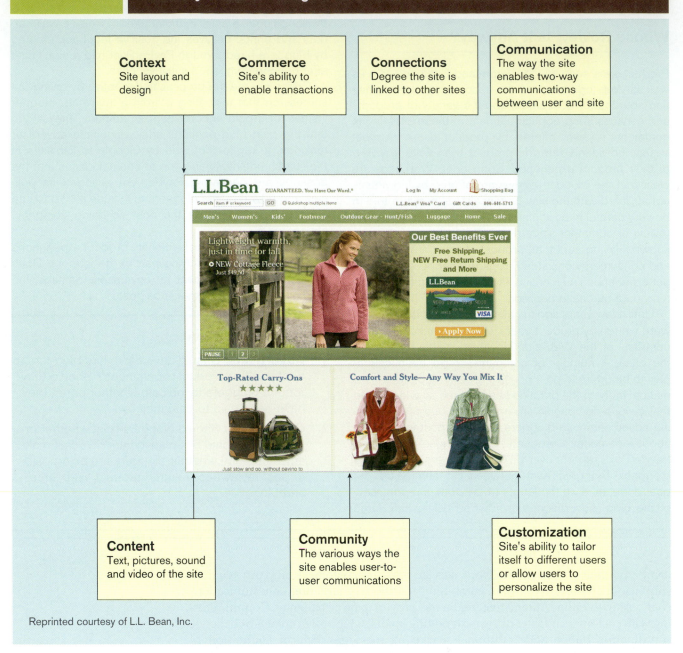

Reprinted courtesy of L.L. Bean, Inc.

Context

Context refers to the overall layout, design, and aesthetic appeal of the site. More and more, broadband and high-speed Internet has led to more graphics, video, and interesting design features that make the Web site more appealing. The challenge for the Web designer is balancing the aesthetic appeal of high graphic content with the download time for graphics and other complex visual elements. The "look and feel" of the site must be consistent with the company or product's overall brand image. For example, visit the L.L. Bean Web site and then go to Lucky Brand jeans to see how different companies approach the layout and design of a Web site.

Content

In the 1990s companies put their existing print materials (catalogs, for example) on the Web site and there was little in the way of original Web content.

Today, company Web sites incorporate a great deal of Web-specific content. Volkswagen created ads that ran only on its Web site, while Costco and Best Buy have a specific Web strategy that displays products not available in stores. Text, photos, charts, and graphics are all part of Web content.

Community

A key advantage of interactive electronic marketing is the opportunity to create a community of users or visitors to the site. Blogs and company bulletin boards encourage a sense of community that enhances the customer's company and product experience. Companies are still learning how to effectively harness the power of community for their products. In many cases, the most powerful online communities have been established by third parties such as Kelly Blue Book, an auto industry site.

Customization

The ability to create a unique individual experience with a company Web site adds great value to the customer interface. Customers appreciate and expect customization of their Web site experience. Simple customization includes turning off the sound to the site and reducing the graphic interface (html versus flash sites). More customized sites enable customers to choose content and context. Yahoo, for example, allows users to create their own Yahoo experience defining the look and content of their Yahoo Web page.

Communication

The interactive electronic channel allows companies to communicate with customers in three ways. First, companies communicate to customers and visitors to the Web site one-on-one through e-mail. Second, customers and interested visitors communicate directly with the company via e-mail through customer service requests. Finally, companies use instant messaging for customer service requests and sales inquiries. Symantec software, for example, has representatives available online to walk customers through questions about service or products.

Connection

The Internet allows for communication among many sources. Information sites such as Edmunds.com (automobiles) and cnet.com (electronics) offer a lot of information at the site but also allow users to access company and retailer Web sites when they need more information or wish to make a purchase. This kind of connectivity greatly expands the usefulness of the site for the user.

One technology that has become relatively common enables companies to connect with their customer wherever the customer is located. GPS technology has migrated from purpose-built navigation devices to mobile phones, giving marketers the ability to target customers more directly. For instance, adding GPS technology to the Apple iPhone and BlackBerry Storm created all kinds of new ways to connect with consumers including real-time, location-specific sales promotions.[46]

Commerce

The number of products purchased on the Internet has grown dramatically over the last five years. Some products, such as music, are now purchased primarily over the Internet either through retail sites such as Amazon or music download sites like iTunes. Web designers know that creating a simple, easy to understand, and secure purchase experience is essential for success in online commerce. Customers are still concerned with online purchase security; however, the convenience, pricing, and selection of the online purchase experience have led to significant growth in consumer online purchasing.

Online Advertising Decisions

The Internet offers companies a wide range of advertising options. Companies create sophisticated analysis programs that review an individual's Web traffic, how long people remain on the page, their Web browsing history, and many other characteristics to target specific ads. As a result, companies are changing their advertising strategies to include more interactive electronic media.

Banner ads are small boxes containing graphics and text and have a hyperlink embedded in them. Clicking on a banner ad will take you to the company's Web site. In a response similar to the reaction to telemarketing, there is a growing negative perception toward banner ads. While still prevalent throughout the Internet, the click-through rate is very low and companies have expanded to other forms of Internet advertising.

Search-related ads have shown the greatest growth in the last several years because 35 percent of all Internet searches are for products and services. Companies pay to be included on the page as the results of the search inquiry come up. Complex algorithms developed by Google, Yahoo, and others place ads based on an analysis of keywords. Advertisers pay based on the position of the ad on the search results page as well as the number of click-throughs. While the response rate is low, around 2 percent, the cost is also low (less than $.50 per click-through) compared to more than $1 per lead from an ad in the telephone directory.

Interstitials are more graphic, visually interesting ads that move across the Web page. As with banner ads, people find these ads distracting, and antivirus software from Norton, McAfee, as well as Windows enables users to block them.

High-traffic Web sites sell **sponsorships** that enable companies to subsidize some section of Web page on the site. Edmunds.com offers a number of sponsorship opportunities. For example, as customers evaluate vehicles, they are made aware of a "premier dealer" in their area that is helping to sponsor the site.

Internet advertising is growing and there is no indication the demand is slowing. Costs are still low relative to other advertising channels such as television, and, since it is much more targeted and measured, advertisers appreciate the ability to know exactly how well their dollars are working on the Internet.

VIRAL MARKETING

More than a year before the release of *Batman: The Dark Knight*, Warner Bros. created a Web site featuring the fictional character, Harvey Dent, and his political campaign. As the campaign continued, other Web sites such as www.whysoserious.com were created to build interest, although visitors to the sites did not know, at first, the purpose of the sites. The Web sites generated a lot of traffic and over time, visitors realized it was part of the new Batman movie and, more specifically, "The Joker" character, played by deceased actor Heath Ledger, was revealed. With the death of Ledger, Warner Bros. adapted its campaign to offer fans the opportunity to mourn the death of the young star with a Web site to post comments and memorials.[47]

Interest in the movie was created not by spending money on traditional advertising tools such as print or television advertising. Rather, Warner Bros. used a technique called **viral marketing** to create buzz about a product using word of mouth or Internet social networks. The American Marketing Association defines viral marketing as a "marketing phenomenon that facilitates and encourages people to pass along a marketing message. Nicknamed viral because the number of people exposed to a message mimics the process of passing a virus or disease from one person to another."

Marketing managers have known how valuable strong word of mouth can be in a product's success. However, with the growth of social networking on the

Internet and the ability of marketers to target individuals more carefully, it is now possible to create marketing communication campaigns that incorporate a word-of-mouth, one-on-one methodology.

Viral Marketing Guidelines

In many respects, successful viral marketing requires a very different approach to marketing communications than, for example, advertising or personal selling. When it works, it can be possible to connect the success of the viral marketing with sales success. One successful viral marketing effort was the Mentos-Diet Coke "geyser" ad, which showed the effect of dropping several Mentos in a bottle of Diet Coke. The Mentos ad generated 5 million views in three months. People viewing the ad were encouraged to participate in "Make your own Mentos geyser" competitions and the company distributed thousands of product samples. The result was a 20 percent sales increase, which it attributes to the ad. However, the link between a viral marketing campaign and sales is often not that easy to establish. Let's consider some guidelines.

Measuring Success

One of the biggest challenges marketing managers face in viral marketing is measurement. While it is certainly easy to know how many hits there are to a particular Web site, translating that into marketing metrics, such as higher unit sales, is more difficult. As a result, marketers often define broad goals for a viral campaign. Another viral campaign started by Mentos, the Mentos-intern, encourages Web site visitors to assign tasks to a 19-year-old student intern named Trevor. Success for the campaign was not defined in terms of sales but "how well the campaign can integrate the idea of Mentos into pop culture." This more broadly defined goal may be appropriate since more defined metrics such as unit sales are difficult to identify.

Connect People to the Experience

One key to a successful campaign is enabling participants to be part of the experience. When Microsoft and Bungie Interactive were leading up to the release of the sequel to their wildly popular *Halo* video game, they created a unique way to get gamers involved in the experience well before the title's release. At the end of the first official trailer for *Halo* 2, they flashed a Web site URL—www.ilovebees.com. It started out as a seemingly innocent site about a Napa, California, honey company, but became increasingly garbled in what appeared to be the result of some sort of hacker attack. The strange occurrences on the Web site began to refer to alien races in the *Halo* galaxy and eventually provided GPS coordinates to pay-phone locations around the country. Those who went to the phones at the times dictated by posts on the Web site received calls from an automated female voice that would give them further clues regarding what was happening to the Web site and how it affected the *Halo* universe. This marketing campaign enabled Microsoft and Bungie to create a mythology around *Halo* 2, thus further heightening gamers' level of anticipation for its release.[48]

Target a Younger Demographic

Viral marketing works well with a younger demographic and enables marketers to reach out to a different market segment. For example, Folgers's "Happy Morning" viral video campaign was a creative stretch for the company that has focused primarily on an older market segment. The video, a funny send-up on happy morning commercials, was widely distributed to video Web sites and represented Folgers' first significant attempt to reach younger audiences using a viral marketing strategy. The ability to target younger audiences without offending existing target markets that are not likely to be part of the same social networks gives companies the freedom to experiment.

SUMMARY

Companies understand that successful integrated marketing communications incorporates interactive, personal communication elements. The three personal communication methods most widely adopted are personal selling, direct marketing, and interactive marketing. Together these tools have the potential to connect the company with the customer as well as encourage the customer to interact with the company in ways that appreciably strengthen the relationship. Personal, interactive customer communication is important, and companies dedicate significant resources to ensure the quality of the company-customer communication relationship.

APPLICATION QUESTIONS

1. You are the vice president of sales for a $30 million manufacturer of home building materials. The company employs 50 salespeople around the country to market the company's products to hardware stores and major building contractors. The CEO believes the company needs to cut costs and wants to reduce the sales force by 50 percent. You have been asked to come in and explain why that is a bad long-term strategy for the company. Discuss why salespeople are critical to the success of the company.

2. Identify three important personal characteristics that a key account salesperson for a global manufacturer of networking hardware would need to be successful. The company sells multimillion-dollar product solutions to telecommunications companies and *Fortune* 100 global organizations.

3. You are the marketing director for the local Red Cross chapter. Create a direct marketing campaign to generate money that is needed for a new building. What should be included in the direct marketing campaign?

MARKETING PLAN EXERCISE

ACTIVITY 14.1: Building the Interpersonal Relationship

A critical component of your company's marketing communications is the interpersonal connection to the customer. Developing an effective interpersonal communications strategy is essential and can include: (1) sales force, (2) Web site, and (3) direct marketing. In this exercise, you will create an interpersonal communications strategy as part of the overall marketing communications plan. The following tasks are part of the strategy:

1. Review the overall marketing communications plan and determine the role of interpersonal marketing communications in communicating with target customers.

2. If personal selling is part of the marketing communications plan, create a sales strategy to include nature of sales force (company sales force or external sales team), sales structure, hiring/recruiting policies, and compensation program.

3. By this point in the marketing plan, you have already spent time considering an interactive Web strategy. Here you will develop the marketing communications element. Specific questions you should address include the following. What are the objectives of the interactive marketing communications program? How much and in what format will the company's products and services be presented

on the Web site? What action do you want someone visiting the Web site to take after viewing the marketing communications?

4. Determine the level of direct marketing for the company. Specifically, define the role of direct marketing in the overall marketing communications plan. Next, identify specific objectives for the direct marketing effort. Finally, create a direct marketing campaign and follow-up plan.

If you are using Marketing Plan Pro, a template for this assignment can be accessed at www.mhhe.com/marshalless1e.

GLOSSARY

A

acceleration effect When small changes in consumer demand lead to considerable shifts in business product demand.

accumulating bulk A function performed by intermediaries that involves taking product from multiple sources and sorting it into different classifications for sales through the channel.

adaptive selling Being able to adjust the sales style from one sales situation to another in real time based on customer feedback.

additions to existing product lines An extension to an existing product that has already been developed and introduced to the market.

administered vertical marketing system (VMS) When the channel control of a vertical marketing system is determined by the size and power of one of its channel members.

advantages The particular product/service characteristic that helps meet the customer's needs.

advertising Paid form of relatively less personal marketing communications often through a mass medium to one or more target markets.

advertising execution The way an advertisement communicates the information and image.

advertising response function An effect in which, beyond a certain ad spending level, diminishing returns tend to set in.

advertising wearout When customers become bored with an existing advertising campaign.

agent intermediaries Intermediaries who do not take title to the product during the exchange process.

AIDA model A model designed to illustrate the hierarchy of effects in the context of customer response to marketing communications. It states that the effects build in this order: Attention (or Awareness), Interest, Desire, and Action.

allowances A remittance of monies to the consumer after the purchase of the product.

aspirational purchases Products bought outside the individual's social standing.

assortment The number of different product items within a product category.

attitude Learned predisposition to respond to an object or class of objects in a consistently favorable or unfavorable way.

attitude-based choice A product choice that relies on an individual's beliefs and values to direct his or her assessment.

attribute-based choice A product choice based on the premise that product choices are made by comparing brands across a defined set of attributes.

auction pricing A pricing tactic in which individuals competitively bid against each other and the purchase goes to the highest bidder.

average-cost pricing A pricing decision made by identifying all costs associated with an offering to come up with what the average cost of a single unit might be.

awareness set A reduced set of possible alternatives a consumer considers after eliminating available options based on gathered information and personal preference.

B

bait and switch When a seller advertises a low price but has no intent to actually make the lower priced item available for sale.

banner ads Internet advertisements that are small boxes containing graphics and text, and have a hyperlink embedded in them.

behavioral data Information about when, what, and how often customers purchase products and services as well as other customer "touches."

behavioral segmentation Dividing consumer groups based on similarities in benefits sought or product usage patterns.

benefits The advantageous outcome from the advantage found in a product feature.

Boston Consulting Group (BCG) Growth-Share Matrix A popular approach for in-firm portfolio analysis that categorizes business units' level of contribution to the overall firm based on two factors: market growth rate and competitive position.

brand A name, term, sign, symbol, or design, or a combination of these elements, intended to identify the goods or services of one seller or groups of sellers and to differentiate them from those of competitors.

brand assets Other assets brands possess such as trademarks and patents that represent a significant competitive advantage.

brand association When customers develop a number of emotional, psychological, and performance associations with a brand. These associations become a primary purchase driver, particularly with brand loyal users.

brand awareness The most basic form of brand equity is simply being aware of the brand. Awareness is the foundation of all other brand relationships.

brand equity A set of assets and liabilities linked to a brand's name and symbol that adds to or subtracts from the value provided by a product or service to a firm or that firm's customers.

brand identity A summary of unique qualities attributed to a brand.

brand loyalty The strongest form of brand equity and reflects a commitment to repeat purchases.

brand strategy The unique elements of a brand that define the products sold by a firm.

breaking bulk A shipping method used by manufacturers to better match quantities needed in terms of the space constraints and inventory turnover requirements of their buyers.

B-2-B (business-to-business) markets Markets in which a firm's customers are other firms, characterized by few but large customers, personal relationships, complex buying processes, less price sensitive demand.

business case analysis An overall evaluation of a product that usually assesses the product's probability of success.

buying center A number of individuals with a stake in a purchase decision who manage the purchase decision process and ultimately make the decision.

buying decision Decisions made throughout the purchase decision process that vary widely and are based on factors such as nature of the purchase, number of people involved in the decision, understanding of the product being purchased, and time frame for the decision.

buzz Word-of-mouth communication generated about a brand in the marketplace.

C

capital equipment A firm's significant, long-term investments in critical equipment or technology necessary for its manufacturing and production activities.

capital goods Major purchases in support of significant business functions.

captive pricing (complementary pricing) A pricing tactic of gaining a commitment from a customer to a basic product or system that requires continual purchase of peripherals to operate.

cash discounts A percentage discount off invoice to elicit quicker payment by the customer.

catalog retailer A retailer that offers merchandise in the form of a printed or online catalog.

category extensions When a firm uses its brand to expand into new product categories.

causal research Descriptive research designed to identify associations between variables.

census A comprehensive record of each individual in the population.

change conflict A customer's reluctance to choose change by selecting a company's product.

channel captain (channel leader) The lead player in an administered vertical marketing system (VMS).

channel conflict Disagreements among channel members that can result in their relationship becoming strained or even falling apart.

channel of distribution A system of interdependent relationships among a set of organizations that facilitates the exchange process.

channel power The degree to which any member of a marketing channel can exercise influence over the other members of the channel.

classical conditioning Learning that takes place by associating a stimulus (marketing information, brand experience) and response (attitude, feeling, behavior).

closed-ended questions Question format that encourages respondents to provide specific responses.

closing the sale Obtaining commitment from the customer to make the purchase.

clutter The level of competing messages on a particular medium.

co-branding Joins two or more brands in a common product or takes two brands and markets them in partnership.

coercive power An explicit or implicit threat that a channel captain will invoke negative consequences on a channel member if it does not comply with the leader's request or expectations.

cognitive learning Active learning that involves mental processes that acquire information to work through problems and manage life situations.

commission Incentive payment based on short-term results.

comparative advertising Advertising in which two or more brands are directly compared against each other on certain attributes.

competitive advertising Advertising intended to build sales of a specific brand through shifting emotional appeal, persuasion, and providing information.

competitive scenario analysis Analyzing competitors using various scenarios to predict competitor behavior.

competitive strategy An organization-wide strategy designed to increase a firm's performance within the marketplace in terms of its competitors.

competitor-based pricing A pricing strategy in which a firm decides to price at some market average price in context with prices of competitors.

complete set The very large set of possible alternatives a consumer considers during the initial search for information.

concentrated target marketing (focus or niche strategy) The target marketing approach that involves targeting a large portion of a small market.

conformance A product's ability to deliver on features and performance characteristics promised in marketing communications.

consideration (evoked) set A refined list that encompasses the strongest options an individual considers in a purchase decision once he or she has obtained additional information and carried out an evaluation.

consumer marketing The practice of marketing toward large groups of like-minded customers.

contractual VMS The binding of otherwise independent entities in the vertical marketing system legally through contractual agreements.

convenience goods Frequently purchased, relatively low-cost products for which customers have little interest in seeking new information about or considering other product options.

cooperative advertising and promotion When a manufacturer provides special incentive money to channel members for certain promotional performance.

core competencies The activities a firm can do exceedingly well.

core product The physical, tangible elements that make up a product's essential benefit.

corporate-level strategic plan An umbrella plan for the overall direction of the corporation developed above the strategic business unit (SBU) level.

corporate vertical marketing system (VMS) The investment of a channel member in backward or forward vertical integration by buying controlling interest in other intermediaries.

cost leadership A marketing strategy in which a firm utilizes its core cost advantages to gain an advantage over competitors due to flexibility in pricing strategies as well as its ability to translate cost savings to the bottom line.

cost reduction A specific method for introducing lower-cost products that frequently focuses on value-oriented product price points in the product mix.

cost-plus pricing Building a price by adding standardized markup on top of the costs associated with the offering.

creating assortments The process of accumulating products from several sources to then make those products available down the channel as a convenient assortment for consumers.

crisis management A planned, coordinated approach for disseminating information during times of emergency and for handling the effects of unfavorable publicity.

CRM (customer relationship management) A comprehensive business model for increasing revenues and profits by focusing on customers.

cultural values Principles shared by a society that assert positive ideals.

culture A system of values, beliefs, and morals shared by a particular group of people that permeates over time.

customer advocacy A willingness and ability on the part of a customer to participate in communicating the brand message to others within his or her sphere of influence.

customer communities Web sites where customers come and share stories about their vendor experiences.

customer expectations management The process of making sure the firm does not set customer expectations so high that they cannot be effectively met on a consistent basis.

customer loyalty A customer's commitment to a company and its products and brands for the long run.

customer marketing The practice of marketing that focuses on developing relationships with individuals.

customer mind-set An individual's belief that understanding and satisfying customers, whether internal or external to the organization, is central to the proper execution of his or her job.

customer orientation Placing the customer at the core of all aspects of the enterprise.

customer retention Low propensity among a firm's customer base to consider switching to other providers.

customer satisfaction The level of liking an individual harbors for an offering.

customer switching A customer changes from purchasing one product to purchasing another competing product.

customer touchpoints The company touches the customer in some way—retail store, direct mail piece, Web site—thus allowing information about him or her to be collected.

customer-centric Placing the customer at the core of the enterprise and focusing on investments in customers over the long term.

customized (one-to-one) marketing A marketing strategy that involves directing energy and resources into establishing a learning relationship with each customer to increase the firm's customer knowledge.

D

data collection The distribution of a survey to its respondents, recording of the respondents' responses, and making the data available for analysis.

data mining A sophisticated analytical approach to using the massive amounts of data accumulated through a firm's CRM system to develop segments and microsegments of customers either for purposes of market research or development of market segmentation strategies.

data warehouse A compilation of customer data generated through touchpoints that can be transformed into useful information for marketing management decision making and marketing planning.

database marketing Direct marketing involving the utilization of the data generated through CRM practices to create lists of customer prospects who are then contacted individually by various means of marketing communication.

deceptive pricing Knowingly stating prices in a manner that gives a false impression to customers.

decider An individual within the buying center who ultimately makes the purchase decision.

degree of affiliation The amount of interpersonal contact an individual has with the reference group.

demographic segmentation Dividing consumer groups based on a variety of readily measurable descriptive factors about the group.

demographics The characteristics of human populations and population segments, especially when used to identify consumer markets.

derived demand Demand that originates from the demand for consumer products in business-to-business (B-2-B) marketing.

descriptive research Research designed to explain or illustrate some phenomenon.

desirability The extent and direction of the emotional connection an individual wishes to have with a particular group.

differentiated target marketing The target marketing approach that involves developing different value offerings for different targeted segments.

differentiation Communicating and delivering value in different ways to different customer groups.

direct channel A channel that has no intermediaries and operates strictly from producer to end-user consumer or business user.

direct foreign marketing A company develops local distribution and service representation in a foreign market.

direct marketing An interactive marketing system that uses one or more advertising media to affect a measurable response and/or transaction at any location.

direct selling A form of non-store retailing that involves independent businesspeople contacting consumers directly to demonstrate and sell products or services in convenient locations.

discounts Direct, immediate reductions in price provided to purchasers.

disintermediation The shortening or collapsing of marketing channels due to the elimination of one or more intermediaries.

distinctive competencies A firm's core competencies that are superior to those of their competitors.

distribution intensity The number of intermediaries involved in distributing the product.

diversification strategies Strategies designed to seize on opportunities to serve new markets with new products.

durability The length of product usage.

durable product Products with a comparatively long product life that are often expensive.

E

early adopter A consumer who is a product opinion leader who seeks out new products consistent with his or her personal self-image.

early majority Consumers who are product watchers who want to be convinced of the product's claims and value proposition before making a commitment to it.

electronic commerce (e-commerce) Any action that uses electronic media to communicate with customers, facilitate the inventory, exchange, and distribution of goods and services, or facilitate payment.

electronic data interchange (EDI) Sophisticated programs that link a customer with its suppliers to manage inventories and automatically replenish supplies.

electronic retailing The communication and sale of products or services to consumers over the Internet.

emotional appeal Promotional appeal that plays on human nature using a variety of human emotions and aspirations in developing promotional messages.

emotional choice A product choice based more on emotional attitudes about a product rather than rational thought.

end-user purchase A category of products purchased by manufacturers that represents the equipment, supplies, and services needed to keep their business operational.

enhanced product Additional features, designs, or innovations that extend beyond the core product to exceed customer expectations.

enterprise resource planning (ERP) system A software application designed to integrate information related to logistics processes throughout the organization.

e-procurement The process of online business purchasing.

essential benefit The fundamental need met by a product.

even pricing A pricing tactic in which the price is expressed in whole dollar increments.

event sponsorship Having your brand and company associated with events in the sports, music, arts, and other entertainment communities.

everyday low pricing (EDLP) A pricing tactic that entails relatively low, constant prices and minimal spending on promotional efforts.

exchange The giving up of something of value for something desired.

exclusive dealing When a supplier creates a restrictive agreement that prohibits intermediaries that handle its product from selling competing firms' products.

exclusive distribution Distribution strategy built on prestige, scarcity, and premium pricing in which a producer distributes its products to only one or very few vendors.

exclusive territory The protection of an intermediary from having to compete with others selling a producer's goods.

expert power A channel member's utilization of its unique competencies and knowledge to influence others in the channel.

exploratory research Research geared toward discovery that can either answer the research question or identify other research variables for further study. It is generally the first step in the marketing research process.

extensive information search When a consumer makes a purchase decision based on a thorough process of investigation and research.

external information sources Sources of information outside the individual that include independent groups, personal associations (friends and family), marketer-created information (advertising), and experiences (product trial).

extrinsic rewards Rewards controlled or given by people other than the salesperson, such as managers and customers.

F

FAB A selling approach designed to make the company's products more relevant for customers by explaining the products features, advantages, and benefits.

facilitating functions Activities that help fulfill completed transactions and also maintain the viability of the channel relationships.

fads A product that moves through its life cycle quickly, often in months, and is then replaced.

fair trade laws Laws designed to allow manufacturers to establish artificially high prices by limiting the ability of wholesalers and retailers to offer reduced or discounted prices.

family A group of two or more people living together and related by birth, marriage, or adoption.

family branding The creation of brands that have synergy between them in terms of the overall company brand.

family life cycle The changes in life stage that transform an individual's buying habits.

features Any product attribute or performance characteristic.

firing a customer The shifting of investment of resources from a less attractive customer to more profitable ones.

first-mover advantage When a firm introduces a new market offering, thus defining the scope of the competitive marketplace.

fluctuating demand When the level of consumer demand is not constant, having serious implications related to the perishability of services.

FOB (free on board) Determination of title transfer and freight payment based on shipping location.

focus group A qualitative research method that consists of a meeting (either in person or increasingly online) of 6 to 10 people that is moderated by a professional who carefully moves the conversation through a defined agenda in an unstructured, open format.

follow-up A company's actions after the customer has decided to purchase the product.

food retailer Any retailer that includes food as a part of its breadth of merchandise.

form The physical elements of a product, such as size, shape, and color.

formalization The formal establishment of a firm's structure, processes and tools, and managerial knowledge and commitment to support its culture.

franchise organization A contractual relationship between a franchisor who is the grantor of the franchise, and the franchisee who is the independent entity entering into an agreement to perform at the standards required by the franchisor.

frequency The average number of times a person in the target market is exposed to the message.

functional-level plans Plans for each business function that makes up one of the firm's strategic business units (SBUs). These include core business functions within each SBU such as operations, marketing, finance, as well as other pertinent operational areas.

G

gatekeeper An individual who controls access to information and relevant individuals in the buying center.

GE Business Screen A popular approach for in-firm portfolio analysis that categorizes business units' level of contribution to the overall firm based on two factors: business position and market attractiveness.

gender roles Behaviors regarded as proper for men and women in a particular society.

general warranty Broad promises about product performance and customer satisfaction.

generic strategy An overall directional strategy at the business level.

geographic segmentation Dividing consumer groups based on physical location.

global experience learning curve An understanding of marketing beyond a company's home market that develops over time as the company gets more international business experience.

global marketing A firm treats all world markets (including the company's own domestic market) as a single market with many different segments.

goals General statements of what the firm wishes to accomplish in support of the mission and vision.

go-to-market mistake When a company fails to stop a bad product idea from moving into product development.

government Local, state, and federal entities that have unique and frequently challenging purchasing practices for manufacturing firms.

H

high-involvement learning The learning process in which an individual is stimulated to acquire new information.

high/low pricing A pricing strategy in which the retailer offers frequent discounts, primarily through sales promotions, to stated regular prices.

household life cycle (HLC) A structured set of chronological activities a particular household follows over time.

I

impulse goods Goods whose sales rely on the consumer seeing the product, feeling an immediate want, and being able to purchase now.

inbound logistics The process of sourcing materials and knowledge inputs from external suppliers to the point at which production begins.

inbound telemarketing When a prospective customer contacts a company for more information.

incentive pay Generally commissions tied to sales volume or profitability, or bonuses for meeting or exceeding specific performance targets.

in-depth interview A qualitative research method that consists of an unstructured (or loosely structured) interview with an individual who has been chosen based on some characteristic of interest, often a demographic attribute.

indirect channel A channel that contains one or more intermediary levels.

indirect foreign marketing Doing business with international customers through intermediaries or limited direct contact. The company has no formal channel relationships or global marketing strategy.

inelastic demand When changes in demand are not significantly affected by changes in price.

influencer An individual, either inside or outside the organization, with relevant expertise in a particular area who provides information used by the buying center in making a final buying decision.

initiator The individual who starts the buying decision process.

innovator A consumer who is a product enthusiast who is among the first to try to master a new product.

innovation diffusion process The length of time it takes a product to move from first purchase to last purchase.

input measures The efforts of salespeople during the sales process.

inseparability The characteristic of a service in which it is produced and consumed at the same time and cannot be separated from its provider.

insourcing (third-party logistics) Handing over one or more core functions to a third-party supplier with expertise in those areas so the firm can better focus on its core business.

institutional advertising Advertising that promotes industry, company, family of brands, or some other issues broader than a specific product.

institutions Nongovernmental organizations driven by the delivery of service to the target constituency, rather than by profits.

instrumental performance The actual performance features of the product in terms of what it was promised to do.

intangibility The characteristic of a service in which it cannot be experienced through the physical senses of the consumer.

integrated marketing communications (IMC) A strategic approach to communicating the brand and company message to targeted customers in ways that are clear, concise, and consistent and yet are customizable as needed to maximize the impact on a particular audience.

intensive distribution A distribution strategy designed to saturate every possible intermediary, especially retailers.

interactive marketing An Internet-driven relationship between companies, their brands, and customers. Interactive marketing enables customers to control information flow and encourages customer-company interaction as well as a higher level of customer service.

intermediaries Organizations that play a role in the exchange process between producers and consumers.

internal information search A search for information stored in memory and accessed by the individual.

internal marketing The treating of employees as customers and developing systems and benefits that satisfy their needs to promote internal service quality.

international marketing A company makes the commitment to produce products outside its domestic market.

interstitials Graphic, visually interesting Internet advertisements that move across the Web page.

intrinsic rewards Rewards that salespeople attain for themselves, such as feelings of accomplishment, personal growth, and self-worth.

involvement A significant outcome of an individual's motivation that mediates the product choice decision. It is activated by three elements: background and psychological profile, aspirational focus, and the environment at the time of purchase decision.

J

just-in-time (JIT) inventory control system An inventory management system designed to balance levels of overstock and stock-out in an effort to reduce warehousing costs.

just noticeable difference (JND) The amount of price increase that can be taken without impacting customer demand.

K

key account salespeople Salespeople responsible for the firm's largest customers.

L

laggard A consumer who is a product avoider who evades adoption until there is no other product choice.

language An established system of ideas and phonetics shared by members of a particular culture that serves as their primary communication tool.

late majority Consumers who are product followers who are price sensitive, risk averse, and generally prefer products with fewer features.

learning Any change in the content or organization of long-term memory or behavior.

legitimate power A channel member's ability to influence other members based on contracts or other formal agreements.

licensing When a firm offers other manufacturers the right to use its brand in exchange for a set fee or percentage of sales.

lifestyle An individual's perspective on life that manifests itself in activities, interests, and opinions.

lifetime value of a customer The measurement of important business success factors related to long-term relationships with customers.

limited information search When a consumer makes a purchase decision based on incomplete information and/or lack of personal knowledge.

long-term memory Enduring memory storage that can remain with an individual for years or even a lifetime.

loss leader products Products sacrificed at prices below costs in an effort to attract shoppers to the retail location.

low-involvement learning The learning process in which an individual is not prompted to value new information, characterized by little or no interest in learning about a new product offering.

low-price guarantee policy A pricing strategy used by retailers that guarantees consumers the lowest price for any given product by matching the sales price of competitors.

loyalty programs Programs that reinforce the customer's benefits of purchasing at the retailer.

M

macroeconomics The study of economic activity in terms of broad measures of output and input as well as the interaction among various sectors of an entire economy.

management research deliverable The definition of what management wants to do with marketing research.

market creation Approaches that drive the market toward fulfilling a whole new set of needs that customers did not realize was possible or feasible before.

market development strategies Strategies designed to allow for expansion of the firm's product line into heretofore untapped markets, often internationally.

market information system (MIS) A continuing process of identifying, collecting, analyzing, accumulating and dispensing critical information to marketing decision makers.

market makers Web sites that bring buyers and sellers together.

market mavens Individuals who have information about many kinds of products, places to shop, and other facets of markets, and initiate discussions with consumers and respond to requests from consumers for market information.

market orientation The implementation of the marketing concept, based on an understanding of customers and competitors.

market penetration strategies Strategies designed to involve investing against existing customers to gain additional usage of existing products.

market research The methodical identification, collection, analysis, and distribution of data related to discovering then solving marketing problems or opportunities and enhancing good decision making.

market segmentation Dividing a market into meaningful smaller markets or submarkets based on common characteristics.

market share The percentage of total category sales accounted for by a firm.

market-driven strategic planning The process at the corporate or strategic business unit (SBU) level of a firm that acts to marshal the various resource and functional areas toward a central purpose around the customer.

marketing The activity, set of institutions, and processes for creating, communicating, delivering, and exchanging offerings that have value for customers, clients, partners, and society at large.

Marketing (big M) The dimension of marketing that focuses on external forces that affect the organization and serves as the driver of business strategy.

marketing (little m) The dimension of marketing that focuses on the functional or operational level of the organization.

marketing concept Business philosophy that emphasizes an organization-wide customer orientation with the objective of achieving long-run profits.

marketing control The process of measuring marketing results and adjusting the firm's marketing plan as needed.

marketing dashboard A comprehensive system of metrics and information uniquely relevant to the role of the marketing manager in a particular organization. Dashboards provide managers with up-to-the-minute information necessary to run their operation.

marketing intelligence The collecting, analyzing, and storing of data from the macro environment on a continuous basis.

marketing management The leading and managing of the facets of marketing to improve individual, unit, and organizational performance.

marketing metrics Tools and processes designed to identify, track, evaluate, and provide key benchmarks for improvement of marketing activities.

marketing mix (4Ps of marketing) Product, price, place, and promotion—the fundamental elements that comprise the marketer's tool kit that can be developed in unique combinations to set the product or brand apart from the competition.

marketing plan The resulting document that records the marketing planning process in a useful framework.

marketing planning The ongoing process of developing and implementing market-driven strategies for an organization.

marketing's stakeholders Any person or entity inside or outside a firm with whom marketing interacts, impacts, and is impacted by.

markup on cost The addition to the price of an offering after costs have been considered.

markup on sales price Using the sales price as a basis for calculating the markup percentage.

mass customization Combining flexible manufacturing with flexible marketing to greatly enhance customer choice.

mass marketing The classic style of consumer marketing in which a firm views all consumers as equal reactors to a firm's marketing strategies.

materials Natural or farm products that become part of the final product.

materials requirement planning (MRP) The overall management of the inbound materials from suppliers to facilitate minimal production delays.

materials, repairs, and operational (MRO) Products used in everyday business operations that are not typically considered to be a significant expense for the firm.

mechanical observation A variation of observational data that uses a device to chronicle activity.

memory Where people store all past learning events.

merchandise category An assortment of items considered substitutes for each other.

merchant intermediaries Intermediaries who take title to the product during the exchange process.

microeconomics The study of individual economic activity.

minimal information search When a consumer makes a purchase decision based on very little information or investigation.

minimum markup laws Laws that require retailers to apply a certain percentage of markup to their products for sale.

mission statement The verbal articulation of an organization's purpose, or reason for existence.

missionary salespeople Salespeople who do not take orders from customers directly but persuade customers to buy their firm's product from distributors or other suppliers.

modifications to existing products Creating newer, better, faster versions of existing products that target, for the most part, existing customers.

modified re-buy A buying decision in which a customer is familiar with the product and supplier in a purchase decision, but is looking for additional information because of one or more of three circumstances: the supplier has performed poorly, new products have come into the market, or the customer believes it is time for a change.

moral appeal Promotional appeal that strikes a chord with a target customer's sense of right and wrong.

motivation The stimulating power that induces and then directs an individual's behavior.

multiattribute model A model that measures an individual's attitudes toward an object by evaluating it on several important attributes.

N

national brands Products created, manufactured, and marketed by a company and sold to retailers around the country and the world.

network organization (virtual organization) Organizations that eliminate many in-house business functions and activities in favor of focusing only on those aspects for which they are best equipped to add value.

new dominant logic for marketing A shift in worldview from the traditional goods versus services dichotomy to recognition of both goods and services as "offerings" that create value for consumers.

new purchase A buying decision in which the purchase of a product or service by a customer is for the first time.

new-to-the-world product A product that has not been available before or bears little resemblance to an existing product.

nimble To be in a position to be maximally flexible, adaptable, and speedy in response to the many key change drivers affecting business.

nondurable product Products that are usually consumed in a few uses and, in general, are of low cost to the consumer.

nonfinancial incentives Sales force motivators beyond financial compensation.

nonprobability sampling The selection of individuals for statistical research in which the probability of everyone in the population being included in the sample is not identified.

non-store retailer A retailer that uses alternative methods to reach the customer that do not require a physical location.

nonverbal communication The means of communicating through facial expressions, eye behavior, gestures, posture, and any other body language.

North American Industrial Classification System (NAICS) A system developed by the United States, Canada, and Mexico that classifies companies on the basis of their primary output to define and segment business markets.

objective measures Statistics the sales manager gathers from the firm's internal data.

objectives Specific, measurable, and potentially attainable milestones necessary for a firm to achieve its goals.

observational data The documentation of behavioral patterns among the population of interest.

odd pricing A pricing tactic in which the price is not expressed in whole dollar increments.

one-price strategy A pricing tactic in which the price marked on a good is what it typically sells for.

one-to-one marketing Directing energy and resources into establishing a learning relationship with each customer and connecting that knowledge with the firm's production and service capabilities to fulfill that customer's needs in as customary a manner as possible.

online database Data stored on a server that is accessed remotely over the Internet or some other telecommunications network.

open-ended questions Question format that encourages respondents to be expressive and offers them

the opportunity to provide more detailed, qualitative responses.

operant conditioning Learning that takes place by rewarding a desirable behavior, for example a product trial or purchase, with a positive outcome that reinforces that behavior.

opinion leaders Individuals with expertise in certain products or technologies who classify, explain, and then bestow information to a broader audience.

organizational factors Organization-wide beliefs and attitudes that factor into a purchase decision.

organizational learning The analysis and refinement phase of the CRM process that is based on customer response to the firm's implementation strategies and programs.

original equipment manufacturer (OEM) Manufacturing firms that sell products that are used as integral manufacturing components by their customer companies.

out supplier A company that is not on a firm's list of approved suppliers.

outbound logistics The process of a product's movement from production by the manufacturer to purchase by the end-user consumer.

outbound telemarketing Calling potential customers at their home or office, either to make a sales call via telephone or to set up an appointment for a field salesperson.

output measures The results of the efforts expended by the salesperson.

outsourcing the sales force Using independent sales agents to sell a company's products.

P

partner relationship management (PRM) strategies A strategic alliance that includes connectivity of inventory, billing systems, and market research among marketing channel members.

parts Equipment that is either fully assembled or in smaller pieces that will be assembled in larger components and then used in the production process.

penetration pricing A pricing strategy in which a firm's objective is to gain as much market share as possible.

perceived quality The conveyed perception of quality of a brand that is either positive or negative.

perception A system to select, organize, and interpret information to create a useful, informative picture of the world.

perceptual maps A visual tool used in positioning that allows for comparing attributes to gauge consumer perceptions of each competitor's delivery against those attributes.

perishability The characteristic of a product or service in which it cannot be stored or saved for future use.

personal factors The needs, desires, and objectives of those involved in a purchase decision.

personal selling A two-way communication process between salesperson and buyer with the goal of securing, building, and maintaining long-term relationships with profitable customers.

personality An individual's set of unique personal qualities that produce distinctive responses across similar situations.

physical distribution (logistics) The integrated process of moving input materials to the producer, in-process inventory through the firm, and finished goods out of the firm through the channel of distribution.

pioneering advertising Advertising intended to stimulate primary demand, typically during the introductory or early growth stages of an offering.

portfolio analysis A tool used in strategic planning for multibusiness corporations that views SBUs, and sometimes even product lines, as a series of investments from which it expects maximization of returns.

positioning The communication of sources of value to customers so they can easily make the connection between their needs and wants and what the product has to offer.

post-purchase dissonance A feeling of doubt or anxiety following a recent purchase, generally attributed with high-involvement, large purchases.

preferred state An individual's desires that reflect how he or she would like to feel or live in the present time.

prestige pricing A pricing tactic that lends prestige to a product or brand by virtue of a price relatively higher than the competition.

price bundling A pricing tactic in which customers are given the opportunity to purchase a package deal at a reduced price compared to what the individual components of the package would cost separately.

price discrimination Occurs when a seller offers different prices to different customers, without a substantive basis, such that competition is reduced.

price elasticity of demand The measure of customers' price sensitivity estimated by dividing relative changes in quantity sold by relative changes in price.

price fixing When companies collude to set prices at a mutually beneficial high level.

price points Prices established to convey the differences in benefits offered as the customer moves up and down the product line.

price skimming A pricing strategy in which a firm enters a market at a relatively high price point, usually in an effort to create a strong price-quality relationship for the product.

price war When a company purposefully makes pricing decisions to undercut one or more competitors and gain sales and net market share.

pricing objectives The desired or expected results associated with a pricing strategy that is consistent with other marketing-related objectives.

primary data Data collected specifically for a particular research question.

primary group A reference group an individual has frequent contact with.

primary target markets Market segments that clearly have the best chance of meeting ROI goals and the other attractiveness factors.

private-label brands Products managed and marketed by retailers, also known as store or house brands.

probability sampling The specific protocol used to identify and select individuals from the population in which each population element has a known non-zero chance of being selected.

product Anything that delivers value to satisfy a need or want and includes physical goods, services, events, people, places, organizations, information, and ideas.

product breadth The number of different product categories offered by a retailer.

product advertising Advertising designed to increase purchase of a specific offering.

product choice The end result of evaluating product alternatives in the purchase decision process.

product demand Demand within business markets affected by three critical dimensions: derived demand, fluctuating demand, and inelastic demand.

product depth: The number of different product items within a product category offered by a retailer.

product development strategies Strategies designed to recognize the opportunity to invest in new products that will increase usage from the current customer base.

product life cycle (PLC) The life of a product as identified in four stages: introduction, growth, maturity, and decline.

product line A group of products linked through usage, customer profile, price points, and distribution channels or needs satisfaction.

product line pricing (price lining) A pricing tactic in which a firm affords the marketing manager an opportunity to develop a rational pricing approach across a complete line of related items.

product mix The combination of all the products offered by a firm.

production orientation The maximization of production capacity through improvements in products and production activities without much regard for what is going on in the marketplace.

promotion Various forms of communication to inform, persuade, or remind.

promotion mix The elements of promotion, including advertising, sales promotion, public relations (PR), personal selling, direct marketing, and interactive marketing.

promotion mix strategies Decisions about which combination of elements in the promotion mix is likely to best communicate the offering to the marketplace and achieve an acceptable ROI for the marketer.

promotional allowances Sales promotions initiated by the manufacturer and carried out by the retailer, who is then compensated by the manufacturer.

promotional appeal The connection an offering establishes with customers; includes rational appeals, emotional appeals, and moral appeals.

promotional campaign Promotional expenditures to a particular creative execution aimed at a particular product or product line during a specified time period.

psychographic segmentation Dividing consumer groups based on variables such as personality and AIOs: activities, interests, and opinions.

psychological pricing Creating a perception about price merely from the image the numbers provide the customer.

public relations (PR) Systematic approach to influencing attitudes, opinions, and behaviors of customers and others.

publicity An unpaid and relatively less personal form of marketing communications, usually through news stories and mentions at public events.

puffery Relatively minor embellishments of product claims to bolster the persuasive message.

pull strategy Promotional and distribution strategy in which the focus is on stimulating demand for an offering directly from the end user.

push strategy Promotional and distribution strategy in which the focus is on stimulating demand within the channel of distribution.

Q

qualitative research Less structured research not meant to be used for statistical analysis that can employ methods such as surveys and interviews to collect data.

quantitative research Research used to develop a measured understanding using statistical analysis to assess and quantify the results.

quantity discounts Discounts taken off an invoice price based on different levels of product purchased.

R

rational appeal Promotional appeal that centers on the benefits an offering can provide to a customer.

reach The percentage of individuals in a defined target market that are exposed to an ad during a specific time period.

real state An individual's perceived reality of present time.

reducing transactions The process of lowering the number of purchasing transactions carried out by a firm by utilizing the services of intermediaries.

reference group A group of individuals whose beliefs, attitudes, and behavior influence (positively or negatively) the beliefs, attitudes, and behavior of an individual.

reference pricing A pricing strategy in which a firm gives customers comparative prices when considering purchase of a product so they are not viewing a price in isolation from prices of other choices.

referent power A channel member's ability to influence other members based on respect, admiration, or reverence.

relationship orientation Investing in keeping and cultivating profitable current customers instead of constantly having to invest in gaining new ones.

relationship-based enterprise A firm that strives to facilitate long-term, win-win relationships between buyers and sellers.

reliability The percentage of time a product works without failure or stoppage.

repairability The ease of fixing a problem with a product.

repeat purchase A function of total demand that considers the number of products purchased by the same customer.

replacement purchase A function of total demand that considers the number of products purchased to replace existing products that have either become obsolete or malfunctioned.

reposition existing products Identify for new markets for existing products.

repositioning Using the marketing mix approach to change present consumer perceptions of a firm's product or service.

request for proposal (RFP) The document distributed to potential vendors that outlines an organization's product or service needs. It serves as a starting point from which vendors put together their product solution.

research problem The definition of what information is needed to help management in a particular situation.

resellers Companies that buy products and then resell them to other businesses or consumers for a profit.

retail positioning The retailer's brand image in the consumer's mind.

retail target market The group of consumers targeted by a retailer.

retailer cooperative (co-op) The binding of retailers across a variety of product categories to gain cost and operating economies of scale in the channel.

retailer experience The overall experience a consumer has shopping at a retail location or online.

retailing Any business activity that creates value in the delivery of goods and services to consumers for their personal, nonbusiness consumption and is an essential component of the supply chain.

return on customer investment (ROCI) A calculation that estimates the projected financial returns from a customer. It is a useful strategic tool for deciding which customers deserve what levels of investment of various resources.

return on marketing investment (ROMI) What impact an investment in marketing has on a firm's success, especially financially.

reverse auctions When sellers bid prices to buyers and the purchase typically goes to the lowest bidder.

reverse logistics The process of moving goods back to the manufacturer or intermediary after purchase.

reward power A channel member's ability to coerce vendors by offering them incentives.

S

salary A fixed sum of money paid at regular intervals.

sales experience The level of ease a consumer experiences in purchasing and returning merchandise at a retailer.

sales orientation The increase of sales and consequently production capacity utilization by having salespeople "push" product into the hands of customers.

sales presentation The delivery of information relevant to meet the customer's needs.

sales promotion An inducement for an end-user consumer to buy a product or for a salesperson or someone else in the channel to sell it.

sales skill levels The individual's learned proficiency at performing necessary sales tasks.

sample A subgroup of the population selected for participation in research.

SBU-level strategic plan Planning that occurs within each of the firm's strategic business units (SBUs) designed to meet individual performance requirements and contribute satisfactorily to the overall corporate plan.

search-related ads Paid advertisements featured in Internet search engine results based on analysis of keywords entered in the search field.

seasonal discounts Discounts that reward the purchaser for shifting part of the inventory storage function away from the manufacturer.

secondary data Data collected for some other purpose than the problem currently being considered.

secondary group A reference group with which an individual has limited contact.

secondary target markets Market segments that have reasonable potential but for one reason or another are not best suited for development immediately.

selective awareness A psychological tool an individual uses to help focus on what is relevant and eliminate what is not relevant.

selective distortion The process in which an individual can misunderstand information or make it fit existing beliefs.

selective distribution A distribution strategy in which goods are distributed only to a limited number of intermediaries.

selective retention The process of placing in one's memory only those stimuli that support existing beliefs and attitudes about a product or brand

service A product that represents a bundle of benefits that can satisfy customer wants and needs without having physical form.

service economy An economy that is predominantly comprised of service-related jobs.

service sector The portion of an economy that is comprised of service-related jobs.

service-profit chain The formalization of linkages between employee and customer aspects of service delivery.

shopping experience The consumer's holistic experience while looking for and evaluating products during the purchase decision process.

shopping goods Products that require consumers to do research and compare across product dimensions like color, size, features, and price.

short-term memory The information an individual recalls at the present time. Sometimes referred to as working memory.

situation analysis An analysis of the macro- and micro-level environment within which a firm's marketing plan is being developed.

slotting allowance (shelf fee) Extra incentives paid to wholesalers or retailers by the manufacturer for placing a particular product into inventory.

social class A ranking of individuals into harmonized groups based on demographic characteristics such as age, education, income, and occupation.

societal marketing The concept that, at the broadest level, members of society at large can be viewed as a stakeholder for marketing.

specialty goods Unique products in which consumers' purchase decision is based on a defining characteristic.

specific warranty Explicit product performance promises related to components of the product.

sponsorships Spaces sold on high traffic Web sites that enable companies to subsidize some section of the Web page on the site.

stability pricing A pricing strategy in which a firm attempts to find a neutral set point for price that is neither low enough to raise the ire of competition nor high enough to put the value proposition at risk with customers.

stand-alone brands Brands created to be separate from a company brand that can insulate the company if there is a problem with the brand.

stock keeping unit (SKU) A unique identification number used to track a product through a distribution system, inventory management, and pricing.

stock-out When an item is not in stock.

stop-to-market mistake When a product that is a good idea is prematurely eliminated during the screening process and ultimately never introduced to the market.

store brands Brands created by retailers for sale only in their store locations.

straight rebuy A buying decision that requires little evaluation because the products are purchased on a consistent, regular basis.

strategic marketing The long-term, firm-level commitment to investing in marketing—supported at the highest organization level—for the purpose of enhancing organizational performance.

strategic type Firms of a particular strategic type have a common strategic orientation and a similar combination of structure, culture, and processes consistent with that strategy. Four strategic types are prospectors, analyzers, defenders, and reactors—depending on a firm's approach to the competitive marketplace.

strategic vision Often included within a firm's mission statement, it is a discussion of what the company would like to become in the future.

strategy A comprehensive plan stating how the organization will achieve its mission and objectives.

style The look and feel of a product.

subculture A group within a culture that shares similar cultural artifacts created by differences in ethnicity, religion, race, or geography.

subjective measures Personal evaluations by someone connected to the salesperson's sales process.

supplier choice Selecting between multiple suppliers offering similar product configurations by examining their qualifications.

supply chain A complex logistics network characterized by high levels of coordination and integration among its members.

supply chain management The process of managing the aspects of the supply chain.

survey A quantitative research method that employs structured questionnaires given to a sample group of individuals representing the population of interest and that are intended to solicit specific responses to explicit questions.

sustainability The practicing of business that meets humanity's needs without harming future generations.

sustainable competitive advantage The resulting advantage a firm has when it invests in distinctive competencies.

SWOT analysis A convenient framework used to summarize key findings from a firm's situational analysis into a matrix of strengths, weaknesses, opportunities, and threats.

symbolic performance The image-building aspects of the product in terms of how it makes the consumer feel after purchase.

T

tactical marketing Marketing activities that take place at the functional or operational level of a firm.

tangibility The physical aspects of a product.

target marketing Evaluating market segments and making a decision about which among them shows the most promise for development.

target return on investment (ROI) A pricing strategy in which a bottom-line profit is established first and then pricing is set to achieve that target.

target return pricing A pricing decision made by considering fixed and variable costs and then demand forecasting to determine the price per unit.

technical selling Selling that requires a salesperson to have technical understanding of the product or service.

television home shopping A form of non-store retailing that involves showcasing products on a television network that can be ordered by the consumer.

tertiary target markets Market segments that may develop emerging attractiveness for investment in the future but that do not appear attractive at present.

touchpoints The intersection of a selling firm with a customer via a media channel.

trade discounts An incentive to a channel member for performing some function in the channel that benefits the seller.

trade servicer Resellers such as retailers or distributors with whom the sales force does business.

trade show An industry- or company-sponsored event in which booths are set up for the dissemination of information about offerings to members of a channel.

transaction cost analysis (TCA) A tool that measures cost of using different types of selling agents.

transportation and storage Commonly provided intermediary functions for producers that do not perform these functions themselves.

tying contract A formal requirement by the seller of an intermediary to purchase a supplementary product to qualify to purchase the primary product the intermediary wishes to buy.

U

undifferentiated target marketing (mass market) The broadest approach to target marketing that involves offering a product or service that can be perceived as valuable to a very generalized group of consumers.

uniform delivered pricing When the same delivery fee is charged to customers regardless of geographic location within a set area.

unsought goods Products that consumers do not seek out and often would rather not purchase at all.

user Actual customers of a product or service who have a great deal of input at various stages of the buying decision process, but are typically not decision makers.

utility The want-satisfying power of a good or service. There are four types of utility: form utility, time utility, place utility, and ownership utility.

V

VALS™ (Values and Lifestyles) A psychographic instrument developed by SRI Consulting that divides U.S. adults into groups based on their primary motivation and resources.

value A ratio of the bundle of benefits a customer receives from an offering compared to the costs incurred by the customer in acquiring that bundle of benefits.

value chain The synthesis of activities within a firm involved in designing, producing, marketing, delivering, and supporting its products or services.

value co-creation The combining of capabilities among members of a value network to create value.

value equation Value in terms of price and delivered benefits to the customer.

value network An overarching system of formal and informal relationships within which the firm participates to procure, transform, and enhance, and ultimately supply its offerings in final form within a market space.

value pricing A pricing strategy in which a firm attempts to take into account the role of price as it reflects the bundle of benefits sought by the customer.

value proposition The whole bundle of benefits a company promises to deliver to the customer, not just the benefits of the product itself.

value-creating activities Activities within a firm's value chain that act to increase the value of its products and services for its customers. These can take the form of either primary activities or support activities.

variability The characteristic of a service in which its service quality can only be as good as that of its provider.

variable pricing A pricing tactic in which customers are allowed or encouraged to haggle about prices.

variety The number of different product categories offered by a retailer.

vending machine retailing The selling of merchandise or services that are stored in a machine then dispensed to the consumer when the payment has been made.

vertical marketing system (VMS) Vertically aligned networks behaving and performing as a unified system.

viral marketing Entertaining and informative messaging created by a firm intended to be passed among individuals and delivered through online and other media channels.

W

wholesaler cooperative When retailers contract for varying degrees of exclusive dealings with a particular wholesaler.

workload method A method for determining the correct size of a company's sales force based on the premise that all salespeople should undertake an equal amount of work.

Z

zone pricing When shippers set up geographic pricing zones based on the distance from the shipping location.

ENDNOTES

CHAPTER 1

1. www.marketingpower.com, accessed May 17, 2008.

2. Susan Berfield, "Getting the Most Out of Every Shopper," *BusinessWeek,* February 9, 2009, pp. 45–46.

3. Pola B. Gupta, Paula M. Saunders, and Jeremy Smith, "Traditional Master of Business Administration (MBA) versus the MBA With Specialization: A Disconnection Between What Business Schools Offer and What Employers Seek," *Journal of Education for Business* 82, no. 8 (2007), pp. 307–12.

4. David W. Stewart, "How Marketing Contributes to the Bottom Line*,"* *Journal of Advertising Research* 48, no. 1 (2008), p. 94.

5. Malcolm A. McNiven, "Plan for More Productive Advertising," *Harvard Business Review* 58, no. 2 (1980), p. 130.

6. Mitchell J. Lovett and Jason B. MacDonald, "How Does Financial Performance Affect Marketing? Studying the Marketing-Finance Relationship from a Dynamic Perspective," *Journal of the Academy of Marketing Science* 33, no. 4 (2005), pp. 476–85; and Ramesh K.S. Rao and Neeraj Bharadwaj, "Marketing Initiatives, Expected Cash Flows, and Shareholders' Wealth," *Journal of Marketing* 72, no. 1 (2008), pp. 16–26.

7. Judith Crown, "How Coach Defies the Odds," *BusinessWeek,* March 27, 2008, www.businessweek.com/magazine/content/08_14/b4078057208129.htm, accessed May 22, 2009.

8. Peter F. Drucker, *The Practice of Management* (New York: Harper and Row, 1954), pp. 37–38.

9. Peter F. Drucker, *Management: Tasks, Responsibilities, Practices* (New York: Harper and Row, 1973), p. 63.

10. Shaun Powell, "The Management and Consumption of Organisational Creativity," *Journal of Consumer Marketing* 25, no. 3 (2008), pp. 158–66.

11. Rosa Chun and Gary Davies, "The Influence of Corporate Character on Customers and Employees: Exploring Similarities and Differences," *Journal of the Academy of Marketing Science* 34, no. 2 (2006), pp. 138–47.

12. John Grant, "Green Marketing," *Strategic Direction* 24, no. 6 (2008), pp. 25–27.

13. Stanley Holmes, "Nike Goes Green," *BusinessWeek,* September 25, 2006, pp. 106–08.

14. Michael J. Barone, Kenneth C. Manning, and Paul W. Miniard, "Consumer Response to Retailers' Use of Partially Comparative Pricing," *Journal of Marketing* 68, no. 3 (2004), pp. 37–47; and Dhruv Grewal and Joan Lindsey-Mullikin, "The Moderating Role of the Price Frame on the Effects of Price Range and the Number of Competitors on Consumers' Search Intentions," *Journal of the Academy of Marketing Science* 34, no. 1 (2006), pp. 55–63.

15. Jyh-shen Chiou and Cornelia Droge, "Service Quality, Trust, Specific Asset Investment, and Expertise: Direct and Indirect Effects in a Satisfaction-Loyalty Framework," *Journal of the Academy of Marketing Science* 34, no. 4 (2006), pp. 613–28.

16. Mehul Srivastava, "What the Nano Means to India," *BusinessWeek,* May 11, 2009, pp. 60–61.

17. "Henry Ford Quotes," UBR Inc., www.people.ubr.com/historical-figures/by-first-name/h/henry-ford/henry-ford-quotes.aspx, accessed May 15, 2008.

18. Louis E. Boone and David L. Kurtz, *Contemporary Marketing* (Hinsdale, IL: The Dryden Press, 1974), p. 14.

19. General Electric Company, *1952 Annual Report* (New York: General Electric Company, 1952), p. 21.

20. Neil H. Borden, "The Concept of the Marketing Mix," *Journal of Advertising Research* 4 (June 1964), pp. 2–7; and E. Jerome McCarthy, *Basic Marketing: A Managerial Approach* (Homewood, IL: Irwin, 1960).

21. Bernard Cova and Robert Salle, "Marketing Solutions in Accordance with the S-D Logic: Co-creating Value with Customer Network Actors," *Industrial Marketing Management* 37, no. 3 (2008), pp. 270–77.

22. Evangelia D. Fassoula, "Transforming the Supply Chain," *Journal of Manufacturing Technology Management* 17, no. 6 (2006), pp. 848–60.

23. Stephen Baker, "The Next," *BusinessWeek,* March 9, 2009, pp. 42–46.

24. Mary Jo Bitner and Bernard H. Booms, "Marketing Strategies and Organizational Structures for Service Firms," in *Marketing of Services,* J. Donnelly and W. George, eds. (Chicago: American Marketing Association, 1981), pp. 47–51.

25. V. Kumar and J. Andrew Petersen, "Using a Customer-Level Marketing Strategy to Enhance Firm Performance: A Review of Theoretical and Empirical Evidence," *Journal of the Academy of Marketing Science* 33, no. 4 (2005), pp. 504–20; and Stephen L. Vargo and Robert F. Lusch, "Evolving to a New Dominant Logic for Marketing," *Journal of Marketing* 68, no. 1 (2004), pp. 1–17.

26. Sundar Bharadwaj, Terry Clark, and Songpol Kulviwat, "Marketing, Market Growth, and Endogenous Growth Theory: An Inquiry into the Causes of Market Growth," *Journal of the Academy of Marketing Science* 33, no. 3 (2005), pp. 347–60.

27. Jay Greene, "How Nike's Social Network Sells to Runners," *BusinessWeek,* November 6, 2008, www.businessweek.com/magazine/content/08_46/b4108074443945.htm, accessed May 22, 2009.

28. Vargo and Lusch, "Evolving to a New Dominant Logic for Marketing."

29. Mark W. Johnston and Greg W. Marshall, *Relationship Selling,* 2nd ed. (New York: McGraw-Hill/Irwin, 2008), p. 5.

30. George S. Day, "Managing Market Relationships," *Journal of the Academy of Marketing Science* 28, no. 1 (2000), pp. 24–31.

31. Jena McGregor, "When Service Means Survival," *BusinessWeek,* March 2, 2009, pp. 26–31.

32. Simon J. Bell, Seigyoung Auh, and Karen Smalley, "Customer Relationship Dynamics: Service Quality and Customer Loyalty in the Context of Varying Levels of Customer Expertise and Switching Costs," *Journal of the Academy of Marketing Science* 33, no. 2 (2005), pp. 169–84; and Girish Ramani and V. Kumar, "Interaction Orientation and Firm Performance," *Journal of Marketing* 72, no. 1 (2008), pp. 27–45.

33. Don Peppers and Martha Rogers, *The One-to-One Manager: Real World Lessons in Customer Relationship Management* (New York: Doubleday Business, 2002).

34. Jagdish N. Sheth, Rajendra S. Sisodia, and Arun Sharma, "The Antecedents and Consequences of

Customer-Centric Marketing," *Journal of the Academy of Marketing Science* 28, no. 1 (2000), pp. 55–67.

35. www.dell.com, accessed May 15, 2008.

36. Fred Wiersema, *The New Market Leaders: Who's Winning and How in the Battle for Customers* (New York: Free Press, 2001), pp. 48–58.

37. Heather Green, "How Amazon Aims to Keep You Clicking," *BusinessWeek,* March 2, 2009, pp. 34–40.

38. Efhymios Constantinides and Stefan J. Fountain, "Web 2.0: Conceptual Foundations and Marketing Issues," *Journal of Direct, Data and Digital Marketing Practice* 9, no. 3 (2008), pp. 231–45.

39. Anonymous, "Search and Seizure," *Marketing Health Services* 28, no. 1 (2008), p. 6.

40. Barton Goldenberg, "Conquering Your 2 Biggest CRM Challenges*," Sales & Marketing Management* 159, no. 3 (2007), p. 35.

41. Ruth Maria Stock and Wayne D. Hoyer, "An Attitude-Behavior Model of Salespeople's Customer Orientation," *Journal of the Academy of Marketing Science* 33, no. 4 (2005), pp. 536–53.

42. Marco Vriens, "Strategic Research Design," *Marketing Research* 15, no. 4 (2003), p. 20.

43. Lovett and MacDonald, "How Does Financial Performance Affect Marketing?"; and Steven H. Seggie, "Assessing Marketing Strategy Performance*," Journal of the Academy of Marketing Science* 34, no. 2 (2006), pp. 267–69.

44. www.msi.org, accessed May 17, 2008.

45. Frederick E. Webster, Jr., Alan J. Malter, and Shankar Ganesan, "Can Marketing Regain Its Seat at the Table?" *Marketing Science Institute Working Paper Series*, Report No. 03-113 (2004).

46. M. Theodosiou, and L.C. Leonidou, "International Marketing Policy: A Integrative Assessment of the Empirical Research," International Business Review, 2003, Vol. 12 (2), pp. 141–71.

47. "How P&G Plans to Clean Up," *BusinessWeek,* April 13, 2009, pp. 44–45.

48. Katrijn Gielens, Marnik G. Dekimpe, "The Entry Strategy of Retail Firms into Transition Economies," *Journal of Marketing*, 2007, Vol. 71 (2), pp. 196–210; and Jasmine E.M. Williams, "Export Marketing Information-gathering and Processing in Small and Medium-sized

Companies," *Marketing Intelligence and Planning*, 2006, Vol. 24 (5), pp. 477–92.

CHAPTER 2

1. Peter C. Verhoef, "Understanding the Effect of Customer Relationship Management Efforts on Customer Retention and Customer Share Development," *Journal of Marketing,* Vol. 67, Iss. 4, October 2003, pp. 30–45.

2. Stephanie Coyles and Timothy C. Gokey, "Customer Retention Is Not Enough*," Journal of Consumer Marketing,* Vol. 22, Iss. 2/3, 2005, pp. 101–06.

3. http://hyundaiassurance.walkawayusa.com/, accessed May 14, 2009.

4. Anders Gustafsson, Michael D. Johnson, and Inger Roos, "The Effects of Customer Satisfaction, Relationship Commitment Dimensions, and Triggers on Customer Retention," *Journal of Marketing,* Vol. 69, Iss. 4, October 2005, pp. 210–18.

5. Seongjae Yu, "The Growth Pattern of Samsung Electronics: A Strategy Perspective," *International Studies of Management & Organization,* Vol. 28, Iss. 4, Winter 1998/1999, pp. 57–73.

6. Michael D. Johnson, Andreas Herrman, and Frank Huber, "The Evolution of Loyalty Intentions," *Journal of Marketing,* Vol. 70, Iss. 2, April 2006, pp. 122–32.

7. Ronald Grover, "Selling by Storytelling," *BusinessWeek,* May 25, 2009, pp. 48–49.

8. Kusum L. Ailawadi and Bari Harlam, "An Empirical Analysis of the Determinants of Retail Margins: The Role of Store-Brand Share," *Journal of Marketing,* Vol. 68, Iss. 1, January 2004, pp. 147–65.

9. Frederick F. Reichheld, *Loyalty Rules! How Leaders Build Lasting Relationships in the Digital Age.* Cambridge, MA: Harvard Business School Press, 2001.

10. Michael E. Porter, *Competitive Advantage.* New York: Simon & Schuster, 1985.

11. J. David Hunger and Thomas H. Wheelen, *Essentials of Strategic Management* 4th edition. Upper Saddle River, NJ: Prentice Hall, 2007.

12. Eric M. Olson, Stanley F. Slater and G. Tomas M. Hult, "The Performance Implications of Fit among Business Strategy, Marketing Organization Structure, and Strategic Behavior,"

Journal of Marketing Vol. 69, Iss. 3, July 2005, pp. 49–65.

13. Thomas L. Friedman, *The World is Flat: A Brief History of the Twenty-First Century.* New York: Farrar, Stratus and Giroux, 2005.

14. Wayne McPhee and David Wheeler, "Making the Case for the Added-Value Chain," *Strategy and Leadership* Vol. 34, Iss. 4, 2006, pp. 39–48.

15. Roland T. Rust, Katherine N. Lemon, and Valarie A. Zeithaml, "Return on Marketing: Using Customer Equity to Focus Marketing Strategy," *Journal of Marketing,* Vol. 68, Iss. 1, January 2004, pp. 109–27.

16. Richard W. Mosley, "Customer Experience, Organisational Culture, and the Employer Brand," *Journal of Brand Management,* Vol. 15, Iss. 2, November 2007, pp. 123–35.

17. Kerry Capell, "Vodafone Announces App Store," *BusinessWeek,* www.businessweek.com/globalbiz/content/may2009/gb20090512_965232.htm, accessed May 18, 2009.

18. P. Rajan Varadarajan, Satish Jayachandran, and J. Chris White, "Strategic Interdependence in Organizations: Deconglomeration and Marketing Strategy," *Journal of Marketing,* Vol. 65, Iss. 1, January 2001, pp. 15–29.

19. Karen Norman Kennedy, Jerry R. Goolsby, and Eric. J. Arnold, "Implementing a Customer Orientation: Extension of Theory and Application," *Journal of Marketing* Vol. 67, Iss. 4, October 2003, pp. 67–81.

20. Garmine Gallo, "How to Sell More Than a Product," *BusinessWeek,* May 19, 2009, www.businessweek.com/smallbiz/content/may2009/sb20090519_058809.htm, accessed May 22, 2009.

21. Roland T. Rust, Katherine N. Lemon, and Valarie A. Zeithaml, "Return on Marketing: Using Customer Equity to Focus Marketing Strategy," *Journal of Marketing* Vol. 68, Iss. 1, January 2004, pp. 109–27.

22. Karen Dubinsky, "Brand is Dead," *Journal of Business Strategy,* Vol. 24, Iss. 2, March/April 2003, pp. 42–43.

23. "The Experience Curve–Reviewed: IV. The Growth Share Matrix or The Product Portfolio," *Boston Consulting Group* Online, www.bcg.com/impact_expertise/publications/files/Experience_Curve_IV_Growth_Share_Matrix_1973.pdf, accessed May 16, 2008.

24. Andrew E. Polcha, "A Complex Global Business' Dilemma: Long Range Planning vs. Flexibility," *Planning Review,* Vol. 18, Iss. 2, March/April 1990, pp. 34–40.

25. Robert Slater, *Jack Welch and the GE Way: Management Insights and Leadership Secrets of the Legendary CEO*. Boston: McGraw-Hill, 1998.

26. J. David Hunger and Thomas H. Wheelen, *Essentials of Strategic Management* 4th edition. Upper Saddle River, NJ: Prentice Hall, 2007.

27. Noel Tichy and Ram Charan, "Speed, Simplicity, Self-Confidence: An Interview with Jack Welch," *Harvard Business Re-view,* September-October 1989, p. 113.

28. Mohanbir Sawhney and Jeff Zabin, "Managing and Measuring Relational Equity in the Network Economy," *Journal of the Academy of Marketing Science,* Vol. 30, Iss. 4, Fall 2002, pp. 313–33.

29. Lorraine Woellert, "HP's Hun-saker Papers," *BusinessWeek* Online, October 4, 2006, www.businessweek.com/technology/content/oct2006/tc20061003_396787.htm, accessed May 22, 2008.

30. Bishnu Sharma, "Marketing Strategy, Contextual Factors, and Performance: An Investigation of their Relationship," *Marketing Intelligence & Planning,* Vol. 22, Iss. 2/3, 2004, pp. 128–44.

31. Mark B. Houston, Beth A. Walker, Michael D. Hutt, and Peter H. Reingen, "Cross-unit Competition for Market Charter: The Enduring Influence of Structure," *Journal of Marketing,* Vol. 65, Iss. 2, April 2001, pp. 19–35.

32. David Mercer, *Marketing Strategy: The Challenge of the External Environment.* Thousand Oaks, CA: Sage, 1998.

33. Robert L. Cardy, "Employees as Customers?," *Marketing Management,* Vol. 10, Iss. 3, September/October 2001, pp. 12–14.

34. Regina D. Woodall, Charles L. Colby, and A. Parasuraman, "Evolution" to Revolution," *Marketing Management,* Vol. 16, Iss. 2, March/April 2007, p. 29.

35. Ronald Grover, "The Payoff From Targeting Hispanics," *BusinessWeek,* April 20, 2009, p. 76.

36. Chaman L. Jain, "Benchmarking the Forecasting Process," *Journal of Business Forecasting Methods & Systems,* Vol. 21, Iss. 3, Fall 2002, pp. 12–16.

37. Rajdeep Grewal and Patriya Tansuhaj, "Building Organizational Capabilities for Managing Economic Crisis: The Role of Market Orientation and Strategic Flexibility," *Journal of Marketing,* Vol. 65, Iss. 2, April 2001, pp. 67–81.

38. Hunger and Wheelen, *Essentials of Strategic Management.*

39. Gary Chaison, "Airline Negotiations and the New Concessionary Bargaining," *Journal of Labor Research,* Vol. 28, Iss. 4, September 2007, pp. 642–57.

40. Kennedy, Goolsby and Arnold, "Implementing a Customer Orientation."

41. Ross Goodwin and Brad Ball, "What Marketing Wants the CEO to Know," *Marketing Management,* Vol. 12, Iss. 5, September/October 2003, pp. 18–23.

42. Robert Inglis and Robert Clift, "Market-oriented Accounting: Information for Product-level Decisions," *Managerial Auditing Journal,* Vol. 23, Iss. 3, 2008, pp. 225–39.

43. David Welch, "GM: Live Green or Die; The Lumbering, Money-Losing Giant Finally Sees That Gas Engines Are a Losing Bet. But Is It Too Late?," *BusinessWeek,* May 26, 2008, Issue 4085, pp. 36–41.

44. Heather Green and Robert D. Hof, "Six Million Users: Nothing to Twitter At," *BusinessWeek,* March 16, 2009, pp. 51–52.

45. Douglas W. Vorhies and Neil A. Morgan, "Benchmarking Marketing Capabilities for Sustainable Competitive Advantage," *Journal of Marketing,* 2005, Vol. 69 (1), pp. 80–96.

46. Janet Adamy, "McDonald's Seeks Way to Keep Sizzling," *The Wall Street Journal,* March 10, 2009, http://online.wsj.com/article_email/SB123664077802177333-lMyQjAxMDI5MzI2ODYyNDgwWj.html, accessed May 28, 2009.

47. Moon Ihlwan and David Kiley, "Hyundai Floors it in the U.S.," *BusinessWeek,* February 23, 2009, pp. 30–31.

48. Denis Smith, "Business (not) as Usual: Crisis Management, Service Recovery, and the Vulnerability of Organisations," *Journal of Services Marketing,* Vol. 19, Iss. 5, 2005, pp. 309–21.

49. Tobin Hensgen, Kevin C. Desouza, and Maryann Durland, "Initial Crisis Agent-Response Impact Syndrome (ICARIS)," *Journal of Contingencies and Crisis Management,* Vol. 14, Iss. 4, December 2006, pp. 190–98.

50. Dean Foust, "The BusinessWeek 50: The Best Performers," *BusinessWeek,* April 6, 2009, p. 57.

51. William B. Locander, "Staying Within the Flock," *Marketing Management,* Vol. 14, Iss. 2, March/April 2005, pp. 52–55.

52. Henry Mintzberg, *The Rise and Fall of Strategic Planning.* New York: Financial Times Prentice Hall, 2000.

53. Andrew E. Polcha, "A Complex Global Business Dilemma: Long Range Planning vs. Flexibility," *Planning Review,* Vol. 18, Iss. 2, March/April 1990, pp. 34–40.

CHAPTER 3

1. Bob Thompson, *What Is CRM?* http://www.customerthink.com, CRM Knowledge Item.

2. Adrian Payne and Pennie Frow, "A Strategic Framework for Customer Relationship Management," *Journal of Marketing,* Vol. 69, Iss. 4, October 2005, pp. 167–76.

3. George Day, "Capabilities for Forging Customer Relationships," *MSI Report* #00–118. Cambridge, MA, Marketing Science Institute, 2000.

4. Chuck Salter, "Chick-fil-A's Recipe for Customer Service," *Fast Company,* www.fastcompany.com/resources/customer/chickfila.html, accessed June 1, 2009.

5. Ronald S. Swift, *Accelerating Customer Relationships: Using CRM and Relationship Technologies.* Upper Saddle River, NJ: Prentice Hall PTR, 2001.

6. Don Peppers and Martha Rogers, *Managing Customer Relationships: A Strategic Framework.* Hoboken, NJ: John Wiley & Sons, Inc., 2004.

7. Payne and Frow, "A Strategic Framework."

8. Swift, *Accelerating Customer Relationships.*

9. Stephen F. King and Thomas F. Burgess, "Understanding Success and Failure in Customer Relationship Management," *Industrial Marketing Management,* Vol. 37, Iss. 4, June 2008, pp. 421–31.

10. Stanley A. Brown, ed., *Customer Relationship Management: A Strategic Imperative in the World of E-Business.* Toronto: John Wiley & Sons Canada, 2000, pp. 8–9.

11. Saleha Mohsin, "At 50, the Mini Is Going Strong," *BusinessWeek,* May 15, 2009, www.businessweek.com/globalbiz/content/may2009/gb20090515_054848.htm?campaign_id=msnbc, accessed May 22, 2009.

12. Anders Gustafsson, Michael D. Johnson, and Inger Roos, "The Effects of Customer Satisfaction, Relationship Commitment Dimensions, and Triggers on Customer Retention," *Journal of Marketing,* Vol. 69, Iss. 4, October 2005, pp. 210–18.

13. Mohanbir Sawhney and Jeff Zabin, "Managing and Measuring Relational Equity in the Network Economy," *Journal of the Academy of Marketing Science,* Vol. 30, Iss. 4, Fall 2002, pp. 313–33.

14. Frederick F. Reichheld, *Loyalty Rules! How Leaders Build Lasting Relationships in the Digital Age.*

Cambridge, MA: Harvard Business School Press, 2001.

15. Day, "Capabilities for Forging Customer Relationships."

16. Timothy R. Aurand, Linda Gorchels, and Terrence R. Bishop, "Human Resource Management's Role in Internal Branding: An Opportunity for Cross-functional Brand Messaging Synergy," *The Journal of Product and Brand Management,* Vol. 14, Iss. 2/3, 2005, pp. 163–70; and Scott Davis, "Marketers Challenged to Respond to Changing Nature of Brand Building," *Journal of Advertising Research,* Vol. 45, Iss. 2, June 2005, pp. 198–200.

17. Sawhney and Zabin, "Managing and Measuring Relational Equity."

18. Naveen Donthu and Boonghee Yoo, "Marketing Management Support Systems: Principles, Tools, and Implementation," *Journal of Marketing,* Vol. 65, Iss. 4, October 2001, pp. 122–25.

19. Werner Reinartz, Jacquelyn S. Thomas, and V. Kumar, "Balancing Acquisition and Retention Resources to Maximize Customer Profitability," *Journal of Marketing,* Vol. 69, Iss. 1, January 2005, pp. 63–79.

20. Nicole E. Coviello, Roderick J. Brodie, Peter J. Danaher, and Wesley J. Johnston, "How Firms Relate to their Markets: An Empirical Examination of Contemporary Marketing Practices," *Journal of Marketing,* Vol. 66, Iss. 3, July 2002, pp. 33–47.

21. Peter C. Verhoef, Understanding the Effect of Customer Relationship Management Efforts on Customer Retention and Customer Share Development," *Journal of Marketing,* Vol. 67, Iss. 4, October 2003, pp. 30–45.

22. Neil A. Morgan, Eugene W. Anderson, and Vikas Mittal, "Understanding Firm's Customer Satisfaction Information Usage," *Journal of Marketing,* Vol. 69, Iss. 3, July 2005, pp. 131–51.

23. Burt Helm, "Getting Inside the Customer's Mind," *BusinessWeek,* September 22, 2008, pp. 88.

24. James E. Richard, Peter C. Thirkell, and Sid L. Huff, "An Examination of Customer Relationship Management (CRM) Technology Adoption and Its Impact on Business-to-Business Customer Relationships," *Total Quality Management & Business Excellence,* Vol. 18, Iss. 8, October 2007, pp. 927–45.

25. Bob Lewis, "The Customer is Wrong," *InfoWorld,* Vol. 24, Iss. 2, January 14, 2002, pp. 40–41.

26. Dan Warmenhoven, "Protect Me, Protect My Data," *BusinessWeek* Online, June 8, 2006, www.businessweek.

com/technology/content/jun2006/tc20060608_894982.htm, accessed May 27, 2008.

27. Jena McGregor, "Customer Service Champs," *BusinessWeek,* March 5, 2007, pp. 52–64.

28. Leonard L. Berry, *On Great Service: A Framework for Action.* New York: The Free Press, 1995.

29. Coviello et al., "How Firms Relate to Their Markets."

30. Peppers and Rogers, *Managing Customer Relationships.*

31. Chuck Salter, "Chick-fil-A's Recipe for Customer Service," *Fast Company,* www.fastcompany.com/resources/customer/chickfila.html, accessed June 1, 2009.

32. Swift, *Accelerating Customer Relationships* p. 42.

33. Payne and Frow, "A Strategic Framework."

34. Day, "Capabilities for Forging Customer Relationships."

35. Patricia Kilgore, "Personalization Provides a Winning Hand for Borgata," *Printing News,* December 11, 2006, pp. 7–8.

36. Karen Norman Kennedy, Felicia G. Lassk, and Jerry R. Goolsby, "Customer Mind-Set of Employees throughout the Organization," *Journal of the Academy of Marketing Science,* 30, Spring 2002, pp. 159–71.

37. Jonathan Blum, "Happy Customers—and No Service Staff," *CNNMoney.com,* May 21, 2008, http://money.cnn.com/2008/05/19/smallbusiness/customer_service.fsb/index.htm, accessed May 31, 2009.

38. Kimberly Griffiths, "Got Satisfaction?" *Industrial Distribution,* October 1, 2006, p. 34.

39. Chuck Chakrapani, "The Relationship-Based Enterprise," *Marketing Research,* Vol. 13, Iss. 1, Spring 2001, pp. 39–40.

40. Kelly Shermach, "Cram for CRM Effectiveness," *Sales & Marketing Management,* May 2006, p. 20.

41. Ben Thompson, "Back on the Road Again," *Business Management.com,* Quarter 3, 2009, www.busmanagement.com/article/Back-on-the-Road-Again/, accessed June 1, 2009.

42. A number of concepts in this section are derived from the following outstanding book, which is the best single source for understanding marketing dashboards. It is highly recommended as a guidebook on the topic for marketing managers: Patrick LaPointe, *Marketing by the Dashboard Light: How to Get More Insight, Foresight, and Accountability from Your Marketing Investments,* New York: ANA, 2005.

43. Gail J. McGovern, David Court, John A. Quelch, and Blair Crawford, "Bringing Customers into the Boardroom," *Harvard Business Review,* Vol. 82, Iss. 11, November 2004, pp. 70–80.

44. Jeremy Whyte, "Turning Data into Profit: Using the Customer Experience to Drive Improvement and Growth at Oracle," January 13, 2009, www.customermanagementiq.com/Columnarticle.cfm?externalID=547&ColumnID=17, accessed May 31, 2009.

45. Thorsten Wiesel, Bernd Skiera, and Julián Villanueva, "Customer Equity: An Integral Part of Financial Reporting," *Journal of Marketing,* Vol. 72, Iss. 2, March 2008, pp. 1–14.

46. Leigh McAlister, Raji Srinivasan, and MinChung Kim, "Advertising, Research, and Development, and Systematic Risk of the Firm," *Journal of Marketing,* Vol. 71, Iss. 1, January 2007, pp. 35–49.

47. The single best source for understanding ROMI is the following book, which is highly recommended for marketing managers: Guy R. Powell, *Return on Marketing Investment,* Albuquerque, RBI Press, 2002. Many of the key concepts in this section emanate from this book. The ideas in this section are drawn from that source.

48. Claes Fornell, Sunil Mithas, Forrest V. Morgeson III, and M.S. Krishnan, "Customer Satisfaction and Stock Prices: High Returns, Low Risk," *Journal of Marketing,* Vol. 70, Iss. 1, January 2006, pp. 3–14; and Roland T. Rust, Katherine Lemon, and Valarie A. Zeithaml, "Return on Marketing: Using Customer Equity to Focus Marketing Strategy," *Journal of Marketing,* Vol. 68, Iss. 1, January 2004, pp. 109–27.

49. Behram Hansotia and Brad Rukstales, "Incremental Value Modeling," *Journal of Interactive Marketing,* Vol. 16, Iss. 3, Summer 2002, pp. 35–46.

50. Dominique M. Hanssens, Daniel Thorpe, and Carl Finkbeiner, "Marketing When Customer Equity Matters," *Harvard Business Review,* Vol. 86, Iss. 5, May 2008, p. 117; and Rick Ferguson, "Word of Mouth and Viral Marketing: Taking the Temperature of the Hottest Trends in Marketing," *Journal of Consumer Marketing* Vol. 25, Iss. 3, 2008, pp. 179–82.

51. Tim Ambler, "Don't Cave in to Cave Dwellers," *Marketing Management,* Vol. 15, Iss. 5, 2006, pp. 25–29.

52. Anne Field, "Strategies: Mission Possible," *BusinessWeek*

Online, December 14, 2007, www.businessweek.com/print/magazine/content/07_72/s0712038774148.htm, accessed June 11, 2008.

53. In this section, the example formulas and descriptions are selected from the following outstanding treatise on marketing metrics, which is a must-have book for marketing managers: Paul W. Farris, Neil T. Bendle, Phillip E. Pfeifer, and David J. Reibstein, *Marketing Metrics: 50 + Metrics Every Executive Should Master,* Upper Saddle River, NJ: Pearson/Wharton School Publishing, 2006.

54. William O. Bearden, R. Bruce Money, and Jennifer L. Nevins, "A Measure of Long-Term Orientation: Development and Validation," *Journal of the Academy of Marketing Science,* Vol. 34, Iss. 3, Summer 2006, pp. 456–67.

55. Kusum L. Ailawadi, Donald R. Lehmann, and Scott A. Neslin, "Marketing Response to a Major Policy Change in the Marketing Mix: Learning from Proctor & Gamble's Value Pricing Strategy," *Journal of Marketing,* Vol. 65, Iss. 1, January 2001, pp. 44–61.

56. Kusum L. Ailawadi, Karen Gedenk, Christian Lutzky, and Scott A. Neslin, "Decomposition of the Sales Impact of Promotion-Induced Stockpiling," *Journal of Marketing Research,* Vol. 44, Iss. 3, August 2007, pp. 450–67.

57. Thorsten Henning-Thurau, Victor Henning, and Henrik Sattler, "Consumer File Sharing of Motion Pictures," *Journal of Marketing,* Vol. 71, Iss. 4, October 2007, pp. 1–18; and Raghavan Srinivasan, Sreeram Ramakrishnan Sundara, and Scott E. Grasman, "Identifying the Effects of Cannibalization on the Product Portfolio," *Marketing Intelligence & Planning,* Vol. 23, Iss. 4/5, 2005, pp. 359–71.

58. Paul W. Farris, Neil T. Bendle, Phillip E. Pfeifer, and David J. Reibstein, *Marketing Metrics: 50 + Metrics Every Executive Should Master.* Upper Saddle River, NJ: Pearson/Wharton School Publishing, 2006, p. 317.

59. Lynette Ryals, "Making Customer Relationship Management Work: The Measurement and Profitable Management of Customer Relationships," *Journal of Marketing,* Vol. 69, Iss. 4, October 2005, pp. 252–61.

60. Gary K. Hunter and William D. Perreault, Jr., "Making Sales Technology Effective," *Journal of Marketing,* Vol. 71, Iss. 1, January 2007, pp. 16–34.

61. Cristina Gimenez and Eva Ventura, "Logistics-Production, Logistics-Marketing and their External Integration: Their Impact on Performance," *International Journal of Operations & Production Management,* Vol. 25, Iss. 1, 2005, pp. 20–38.

62. Robert C. Blattberg, Richard Briesch, and Edward J. Fox, "How Promotions Work," *Marketing Science,* Vol. 14, Iss. 3, Summer 1995, pp. 122–32.

63. Hsiao-Fan Wang and Wei-Kuo Hong, "Managing Customer Profitability in a Competitive Market by Continuous Data Mining," *Industrial Marketing Management* Vol. 35, Iss. 6, August 2006, pp. 715–23.

64. Vanitha Swaminathan, Richard J. Fox, and Srinivas K. Reddy, "The Impact of Brand Extension Introduction on Choice," *Journal of Marketing,* Vol. 65, Iss. 4, October 2001, pp. 1–15.

65. David W. Stewart and Paul A. Pavlou, "From Consumer Response to Active Consumer: Measuring the Effectiveness of Interactive Media," *Journal of the Academy of Marketing Science,* Vol. 30, Iss. 4, Fall 2002, pp. 376–96.

66. Jessica Mintz, "Bing It On: Microsoft Overhauls Search, Again," *BusinessWeek,* May 28, 2009, www.businessweek.com/ap/tech/D98FGLB01.htm http://www.businessweek.com/ap/tech/D98FGLB01.htm, accessed June 2, 2009.

CHAPTER 4

1. Anne L. Souchon, John W. Cadogan, David B. Procter, and Belinda Dewsnap, "Marketing Information Use and Organizational Performance: The Mediating role of Responsiveness," *Journal of Strategic Marketing,* 2004, Vol. 12 (4), pp. 231–42.

2. "J.D. Power and Associates Reports: Del Webb Ranks Highest in Satisfying Buyers of Homes in Active Adult Communities," *PR Newswire,* September 13, 2006.

3. Cliff Edwards and Bruce Einhorn, "So Maybe Apple was Onto Something," *BusinessWeek,* April 14, 2008, p. 51.

4. Roger Bennett, "Sources and Use of Marketing Information by Marketing Managers," *Journal of Documentation,* 2007, Vol. 63 (5), p. 702; and Hean Tat Keh, Thi Mai Nguyen, Hwei Ping Ng, "The Effects of Entrepreneurial Orientation and Marketing Information on the Performance of SME's," *Journal of Business Venturing,* 2007, Vol. 22 (4), pp. 592–611.

5. Paul Ingenbleek, "Value-Informed Pricing in Its Organizational Context: Literature Review, Conceptual Framework, and Directions for Future Research," *Journal of Product and Brand Management,* 2007, Vol. 16 (7), 441–58.

6. Stephen H. Wildstrom, "The Best New Bluetooth Headsets," *Business-Week* Online, May 13, 2009, www.business.com/mediacenter/podcasts/techmaven/techandu_05_13_09.htm

7. Gerrit H. Van Bruggen, Ale Smidts, Berend Wierenga, "The Powerful Triangle of Marketing Data, Managerial Judgment, and Marketing Management Support Systems," *European Journal of Marketing,* 2001, Vol. 35 (7), pp. 796–816.

8. Stephen F. King and Thomas F. Burgess, "Understanding Success and Failure in Customer Relationship Management," *Industrial Marketing Management,* 2008, Vol. 37 (4), pp. 421–39.

9. Joao F Proenca, Teresa M. Fernandez, P.K. Kannan, "The Relationship in Marketing: Contribution of a Historical Perspective," *Journal of Macromarketing,* 2008, Vol. 28 (1), pp. 90–106.

10. Becky Ebenkamp, "The Big Problem with MicroTrends," *Brandweek,* January 21, 2008, pp 10–11.

11. Peter Svensson, "iPhone Triggers A Touch-Screen Craze," *The SeattleTimes,* July 14, 2008.

12. Craig Stedman, "Failed ERP Gamble Haunts Hershey," *Computerworld,* Nov. 1, 1999, Vol. 33 (44), pp. 1–2.

13. Sajjad Matin, "Clicks Ahoy! Navigating Online Advertising in a Sea of Fraudulent Clicks," *Berkeley Technology Law Journal,* 2007, Vol. 22 (1), pp. 533–55; and Brian Grow and Ben Elgin, "Click Fraud," *BusinessWeek,* October 2, 2006, pp. 46–57.

14. Connie R. Bateman and JoAnn Schmidt, "Do Not Call Lists: A Cause for Telemarketing Extinction or Evolution," *Academy of Marketing Studies Journal,* 2007, Vol. 11 (1), pp. 83–107; and Herbert Jack Rotfeld, "Misplace Marketing: Do-not-Call as the U.S. Government's Improvement to Telemarketing Efficiency," *The Journal of Consumer Marketing,* 2004, vol. 21 (4/5), pp. 242–59.

15. Taylor Buley, "Social Media's Criminal Attraction," *Forbes,* May 4, 2009, www.forbes.com/2009/5/4/facebook-worm-security/technology-security-facebook.html

16. Thomas W. Miller, "At the Junction," *Marketing Research,* 2007, Vol. 19 (4), pp. 8–14.

17. Alan Tapp, "A Call to Arms for Applied Marketing Academics," *Marketing Intelligence and Planning,* 2004, Vol. 22 (5), pp. 579–96.

18. Dianne Altman Weaver, "The Right Questions," *Marketing Research,* 2006, Vol. 18 (1), pp. 17–18.

19. Janice Denegri-Knott, Detiev Zwick, Jonathan E. Schroeder, "Mapping Consumer Power: An Integrative Framework for Marketing and Consumer Research," *European Journal of Marketing,* 2006, Vol. 40 (9/10), pp. 950–71.

20. Erin Biba, "Virtual Events and Measuring ROI Keys," *BtoB* V. 93, Issue 1, Chicago, January 14, 2008, p. 13.

21. Gordon A. Wyner, "Redefining Data," *Marketing Research,* 2004, Vol. 16 (4), pp 6–7.

22. Naomi R. Henderson, "Twelve Steps to Better Research," *Marketing Research,* 2005, Vol. 17 (2), pp. 36–37.

23. David Stokes and Richard Bergin, "Methodology or "Methodolatry"? An Evaluation of Focus Groups and Depth Interviews?" *Qualitative Market Research,* 2006, Vol. 9 (1), pp. 26–38.

24. Clive Boddy, "A Rose by Any Other Name May Smell as Sweet but Group 'Group Discussion' is Not Another Name for a 'Focus Group' Nor Should It Be," *Qualitative Market Research,* 2005, Vol. 8 (3), pp. 248–56.

25. Jennifer Comiteau, "Why the Traditional Focus Group Is Dying," *Adweek,* October 31, 2005, pp. 24–27.

26. Gordon Wyner, "Survey Errors," *Marketing Research,* 2007, Vol. 19 (1), pp. 6–7.

27. Catherine A. Roter, Robert A. Rogers, George C. Hozier, Jr., Kenneth G. Baker, and Gerald Albaum, "Management of Marketing Research Projects: Does Delivery Method Matter Anymore in Survey Research," *Journal of Marketing Theory and Practice,* 2007, Vol. 15 (2), pp. 127–145; and Sharon Loane, Jim Bell, and Rob McNaughton, "Employing Information Communication Technologies to Enhance Qualitative International Marketing Enquiry," *International Marketing Review,* 2006, Vol. 23 (4), pp. 438–53.

28. Stephen Baker, "Data Mining Moves to Human Resources," *BusinessWeek,* March 12, 2009, www.businessweek .com/magazine/content/09_12/6412 406224092.htm=top+news_top+ news+index++temp_top+story.

29. Edward Blair, and George M. Zinkhan, "Nonresponse and Generalizability in Academic Research," *Academy of Marketing Science Journal,* 2006, Vol. 34 (1), pp. 4–8.

30. Peter Keliner, "Can Online Polls Produce Accurate Findings," *International Journal of Market Research,* 2004, Vol. 46, pp. 3–15; and Olivier Furrer and D. Sudharshan, "Internet Marketing Research: Opportunities and Problems," *Qualitative Market Research,* 2001, Vol. 4 (3), pp. 123–30.

31. N.L. Reynolds, A.C. Siminitiras, and A. Diamantopoulos, "Theoretical Justification of Sampling Choices in International Marketing Research: Key Issues and Guideliens for Researchers," 2003, Vol. 34 (1), pp. 80–90.

32. Bill Blyth, "Mixed Mode: The Only 'Fitness' Regime?" *International Journal of Marketing Research,* 2008, Vol. 50 (2), pp. 241–56.

33. Nick Sparrow, "Quality Issues in Online Research," *Journal of Advertising Research,* 2007, Vol. 47 (2), pp. 179–91; and Elisabeth Deutskens, Ad de Jong, Ko de Ruyter, and Martin Wetzels, "Comparing the Generalizability of Online and Mail Surveys in Cross National Service Quality Research," *Marketing Letters,* 2006, Vol. 17 (2), pp. 119–32.

34. Kai Wehmeyer, "Aligning IT and Marketing–The Impact of Database Marketing and CRM," *Journal of Database Marketing & Customer Strategy Management,* 2005, Vol. 12 (3), pp. 243–57; Joshua Weinberger, "Database Marketers Mine for Perfect Customer Segmentation," *Customer Relationship Management,* 2004, Vol. 8 (10), p. 19; and Hoda McClymont and Graham Jocumsen, "How to Implement Marketing Strategies using Database Approaches, "*Journal of Database Marketing and Customer Strategy Management,* 2003, Vol. 11 (2), pp. 135–49.

35. R. Dale Wilson, "Developing New Business Strategies in B2B Markets by Combining CRM Concepts and Online Databases," *Competitiveness Review,* 2006, Vol. 16 (1), pp. 38–44.

36. David Ward, "Master of All You Survey," *PRweek,* 2006, Vol. 9 (38), pp. 22.

37. Steve Ranger, "How Firms Use Business Intelligence," *BusinessWeek* Online, May 24, 2007, http://www. businessweek.com/globalbiz/ content/ may2007/gb20070524_006085. htm?chan=search, May 24, 2008 and Colin Beasty, "Minimizing Customer Guesswork," *Customer Relationship Management,* 2006, Vol. 10 (6), p. 45.

38. Emily Steel, "Start-Up's Algorithm for Success-Demand Media Bundles Niche Content in Bid to Amass A Huge Audience," *The Wall Street Journal* (Eastern Edition), May 8 2009, B4.

39. Krisztina Holly, "CERN's Collaborative Management Model," *BusinessWeek* Online, May 20, 2009, Accessed June 3, 2009, www.business-week.com/innovate/content/may2009/id20090520_115971.html

40. Anna Lund Jepsen, "Factors Affecting Consumer Use of the Internet for Information Search," *Journal of Interactive Marketing,* 2007, Vol. 21 (3), pp. 21–33.

CHAPTER 5

1. S. Mark Young, James J. Gong, and Wim A Van der Stede, "The Business of Selling Movies," *Strategic Finance,* 2008, Vol. 89 (9), pp. 35–42; and Jon Silver and John McDonnell, "Are Movie Theaters Doomed? Do Exhibitors See the Big Picture as Theaters Lose Their Competitive Advantage?" *Business Horizons,* 2007, Vol. 50 (6), pp. 491–501.

2. P. Sullivan and J. Heitmeyer, "Looking at Gen Y Shopping Preferences and Intentions: Exploring the Role of Experience and Apparel Involvement,*" International Journal of Consumer Studies,* 2008, Vol. 32 (3), pp. 285–99.

3. Mila Goodman, "Personas 2.0," *Target Marketing,* Vol. 31, Issue 7, July 2008, pp. 35–36

4. Christian Lindholm, "Designing the Next Facebook," *Forbes,* May 20, 2009, accessed June 3, 2009, http://www. forbes.com/2009/05/19/facebook-design-nokia-technology-intelligent-tectnology-design.html.

5. Paul G. Patterson, "Demographic Correlates of Loyalty in a Service Context," *Journal of Services Marketing,* 2007, Vol. 21 (2), pp. 112–21.

6. Lisa E. Bolton, Americus Reed II, Kevin G. Volpp, Katrina Armstrong, "How Does Drug and Supplement Marketing Affect a Healthy Lifestyle? *Journal of Consumer Research,* 2008, Vol. 34 (5), pp. 713–26.

7. Cara Peters, Christie H. Amato, and Candice R. Hollenbeck, "An Exploratory Investigation of Consumers' Perceptions of Wireless Advertising," *Journal of Advertising,* 2007, Vol. 36 (4), pp. 129–46; "A Pocketful of Marketing," *Inc.* 2008, p. 79; and Catherine Holahan, "The "Sell" Phone Revolution," *Business-Week,* April 23, 2007, pp. 94–97.

8. Maureen E. Hupfer and Brian Detior, "Beyond Gender Differences: Self-Concept Orientation and Relationship-Building Orientation on the Internet," *Journal of Business Research,* 2007, Vol. 60 (6), pp. 613–28; and J. Michael Pearson, Ann Pearson, and David Green, "Determining the Importance of Key Criteria in Web Usability," *Management Research News,* 2007, Vol. 30 (11), pp. 816–29.

9. Phil Johnson, "What Lobster Dunks Can Teach Us About Marketing To Emotions," *Advertising Age,* June 3, 2008, accessed June 3, 2009, http://adage.com/smallagency/ post?article_ID=127487

10. M. Fishbein and I. Ajzen, *Belief, Attitude, Intention, and Behavior: An Introduction to Theory and Research,* Reading MA: Addison–Wesley. 1975.

11. Maxwell Winchester and Jenni Romaniuk, "Positive and Negative Brand Beliefs and Brand Defection/Update," *European Journal of Marketing,* 2008, Vol. 42 (5/6), pp. 553–68.

12. Pamela Miles Horner, "Perceived Quality and Image: When All Is Not "Rosy", *Journal of Business Research,"* 2008, Vol. 61 (7), pp. 715–31.

13. Louise Story, "Anywhere the Eye Can See, It's Likely to See an Ad," *New York Times,* 2007, January 15, B1.

14. "The Caveman: Evolution of a Character," *Adweek,* 2007, Vol. 48 (11), p. 9.

15. Elizabeth Cowley, "How Enjoyable Was It? Remembering an Affective Reaction to a Previous Consumption Experience," *Journal of Consumer Research,* 2007, Vol. 34 (4), pp. 494–510, Moonhee Yang and David R. Roskos-Ewoldsen, "The Effectiveness of Brand Placements in the Movies: Levels of Placements, Explicit and Implicit Memory, and Brand Choice Behavior," *Journal of Communication,* 2007, Vol. 57 (3), pp. 469–82.

16. Elizabeth Howlett, Scot Burton, and John Kozup, "How Modification of the Nutrition Facts Panel Influences Consumers at Risk of Heart Disease". The Case of TransFats, *Journal of Public Policy and Marketing,* Vol. 27, Issue 1, pp. 83–97, Spring 2008.

17. Ming-tiem Tsai, Wen-ko Liang, and Mei-Ling Liu, "The Effects of Subliminal Advertising on Consumer Attitudes and Buying Intentions, *International Journal of Management,* 2007, Vol. 24 (1), pp. 3–15; and Sheri J. Broyles, "Subliminal Advertising and the Perpetual Popularity of Playing to People's Paranoia," *Journal of Consumer Affairs,* 2006, Vol. 40 (2), pp. 392–407.

18. Brian D. Till and Sarah M. Stanley, "Classical Conditioning and Celebrity Endorsers: An Examination of Belongingness and Resistance to Extinction," *Psychology and Marketing,* 2008, Vol. 25 (2), pp. 179–94.

19. Gordon R. Foxall, M. Mirella, and Yani de Soriano, "Situational Influences on Consumers' Attitudes and Behaviors," *Journal of Business Research,* 2005, Vol. 58 (4), pp. 518–33.

20. Marcus Cunha Jr., Chris Janiszewski, and Juliano Laran, "Protection of Prior Learning in Complex Consumer Learning Environments," *Journal of Consumer Research,* 2008, Vol. 34 (6), pp. 850–68.

21. Rebecca Reisner, "Keeping Pom Wonderful," *BusinessWeek,* January 6, 2009, p. 37.

22. Katja Magion-Muller and Malcolm Evans, "Culture, Communications, and Business: The Power of Advanced Semiotics," *International Journal of Marketing Research,* 2008, Vol. 50 (2), pp. 169–82.

23. David Pearson, "French Language Purists Put Brakes on Car Makers," *The Wall Street Journal,* April 4, 2007, p. B5b.

24. Jennifer Fishbein, "The World's Best Airports," *BusinessWeek,* February 27, 2008, http://www.BusinessWeek .com/globalbiz/content/feb2008/ gb20080227_985704.html

25. Alexandra Montgomery, "U.S. Families 2025: In Search of Future Families," *Futures,* 2008, Vol. 40 (4), pp. 377–89.

26. Julie Tinson, Clive Nancarrow, and Ian Brace, "Purchase Decision Making and the Increasing Significance of Family Types," *The Journal of Consumer Marketing,* Vol. 25 (1), pp. 45–56.

27. Rex Y. Du and Wagner A. Kamakura, "Household Life Cycles and Lifestyles in the United States," *Journal of Marketing Research* (2006), no. 43, 1, pp. 121–32.

28. Palaniappan Thiagarajan, Jason E. Lueg, Nicole Ponder, Sheri Lokken Worthy and Ronald D. Taylor, "The Effect of Role Strain on the Consumer Decision Process of Single Parent Households," *American Marketing Association, Conference Proceedings,* Summer 2006, Vol. 17, p. 124.

29. Caroline Goode and Robert East, "Testing the Marketing Maven Concept," *Journal of Marketing Management,* 2008, Vol. 24 (3/4), pp. 265–81; and Lawrence F. Feick and Linda L. Price, "The Market Maven: A Diffuser of Marketplace Information," *Journal of Marketing,* 1987, Vol. 51 (1), pp. 83–98.

30. Katherine White and Darren W. Dahl, "Are All Out-Groups Created Equal? Consumer Identity and Dissociative Influence," *Journal of Consumer Research,* 2007, Vol. 34 (4), pp. 525–40, Jennifer Edson Escalas and James R. Bettman, "Self-Construal, Reference Groups, and Brand Meaning," *Journal of Consumer Research,* 2005, Vol. 32 (3), pp. 378–90; and Terry L. Childers and Akshay R. Rao, "The Influrnce of Familiar and Peer-Based Reference Groups on Consumer Decisions," *Journal of Consumer Research,* 1992, Vol. 19 (2) pp. 198–212.

31. Daisuki Wakabayashi, "Windows 7 Aims to Simplify," *Reuters,* October 28, 2008.

32. Zafar U. Ahmed, James P. Johnson, Xiz Yang, and Chen Kehng Fatt, "Does Country of Origin Matter for Low Involvement Products? *International Marketing Review,* 2004, Vol. 21 (1), pp. 102–15; and Wayne D. Hoyer, "An Examination of Consumer Decision Making for Common Repeat Purchase Product," *Journal of Consumer Research,* 1984, Vol. 11 (3), pp. 822–30.

33. Todd Wasserman, "A Yellow Light Flashes for Green, Organic," *Brandweek,* December 9, 2008.

34. On Amir and Jonathan Levan, "Choice Construction versus Preference Construction" The Instability of Preferences Learned in Context," *Journal of Marketing Research,* 2008, Vol. 45 (2), pp. 145–61.

35. Mohammed M. Nadeem, "Post Purchase Dissonance: The Wisdom of 'Repeat' Purchase," *Journal of Global Business Issues,* 2007, Vol. 1 (2), pp. 183–94.

CHAPTER 6

1. Evan Ramstad, "Corporate News: Samsung Overhaul will Form 2 Divisions," *The Wall Street Journal* (Eastern Edition), January 16, 2009, A3.

2. Thomas L. Powers and Jay U. Sterling, "Segmenting Business-to-Business Markets: A Micro-Macro Linking Methodology," *The Journal of Business and Industrial Marketing,* 2008, Vol. 23 (3), pp. 170–86.

3. Brian N. Rutherford, James S. Boles Hiram C. Barksdale, Jr. and Julie T. Johnson, "Buyer's Relational Desire and Numbers of Suppliers Used: The Relationship between Perceived Commitment and Continuance," *Journal of Marketing Theory and Practice,* 2008, Vol. 16 (3), pp. 247–58.

4. Mike Troy, "Partnership Under Pressure," *Retailing Today,* April/May 2009, p. 5.

5. Ruben Chumpitaz Caceres and Nicholas G. Paparoidamis, "Service Quality, Relationship Satisfaction, Trust, Commitment and Business-to-Business Loyalty," *European Journal of Marketing,* 2007, Vol. 41 (7/8), pp. 836–48; and Papassapa Rauyruen and Kenneth E. Miller, "Relationship Quality as Predictor of B2B Customer Loyalty," *Journal of Business Research,* 2007, Vol. 60 (1), pp. 21–35.

6. Srilata Zaheer and Shalini Manrakhan, "Concentration and Dispersion in Global Industries: Remote Electronic Access and Location of Economic Activities," *Journal of International Business Studies,* 2001, Vol. 32 (4), pp. 667–87.

7. Tao Gao, M. Joseph Sirgy, and Monroe M. Bird, "Reducing Buyer Decision Making Uncertainty in Organizational Purchasing: Can Supplier Trust, Commitment, and Dependency Help?" *Journal of Business Research,* 2005, Vol. 58 (4). pp. 397–409.

8. Rachel Smolker, "Go Ahead, Blame Biofuels," *BusinessWeek,* May 20, 2008, p. 24; and John Carey and Adrienne Carter with Assif Shammen, "Food vs. Fuel," *BusinessWeek,* February 5, 2007, pp. 58–61.

9. "Toshiba Climbs on 'HD DVD' Exit," *BBC News*, February 18, 2008.

10. Leonidas C. Leonidou, "Industrial Manufacturer-Customer Relationships" the Discriminating role of the Buying Situation, *Industrial Marketing Management,* 2004, Vol. 33 (8), pp. 731–45.

11. Sara Kennedy, "Growers, Tropicana at odds over Citrus 'dumping'", *McClatchy-Tribune News,* March 9, 2008, Washington.

12. G. Tomas M. Hult, David J. Ketchen, Jr. and Brian R. Chabowski, "Leadership, the Buying Center, and Supply Chain Performance: A Study of Linked Users, Buyers, and Suppliers," *Industrial Marketing Management,* 2007, vol. 36 (3), pp. 393–408.

13. Marcel Paulssen and Matthias M. Birk, "Satisfaction and Repurchase Behavior in a Business to Business Setting: Investigating the Moderating Effect of Manufacturer, Company and Demographic characteristics," *Industrial Marketing Management,* 2007, Vol. 36 (7), pp. 983–95.

14. Marydee Ojala, "SIC Those NAICS on Me: Industry Classification Codes for Business Research," *Online,* 2005, Vol. 29 (1), pp. 42–45; and Robert P. Parker, "More U.S. Economic Data Series Incorporate the North American Industry Classification System," *Business Economics,* 2003, vol. 38 (2), pp. 57–60.

15. Kun Liao and Paul Hong, "Building Global Supplier Networks: A Supplier Portfolio Entry Model," *Journal of Enterprise Information Management,* 2007, Vol. 20 (5), pp. 511–23; and Chiaho Chang, "Procurement Policy and Supplier Behavior-OEM vs. ODM," *Journal of Business and Management,* 2002, Vol. 8 (2), pp. 181–98.

16. Masaaki Kotabe, Michael J. Mol and Janet Y. Murray, "Outsourcing, Performance, and the Role of E-Commerce: A Dynamic Perspective," *Industrial Marketing Management,* 2008, Vol. 37 (1), pp. 37–48 and Bruno Schilli and Fan Dai, "Collaborative Life Cycle Management Between Suppliers and OEM," *Computers in Industry,* 2006, Vol. 57 (8/9), pp. 725–29.

17. David Kiley, "Paging Doctor Diesel." *BusinessWeek,* July 22, 2008, p. 14.

18. Robert S. Dudney, "Beyond the F-22 Problem" *Air Force Magazine,* 2008, Vol. 91 (3), p. 2.

19. Diane Sears, "Joining Forces," *Florida Trend,* 2008, Vol. 50 (13), p. 66.

20. Jesus Cerquides, Maite Lopex-Sanchez, Antonio Reyes-Moro, and Juan A. Rodruguez-Aguilar, "Enabling Assisted Strategy Negotiations in Actual World Procurement Scenarios," *Electronic Commerce Research,* 2007, Vol. 7 (3/4), pp. 189–221; and Mike Brewster, "Perfecting the RFP," *Inc.,* 2005, p. 38.

21. Christopher Hosford, "Thinking Global May Help U.S. Marketers," *BtoB,* Volume 94, Issue. 4, Chicago, April 6, 2009.

22. S.Y. Chou, C.Y. Shen and Y.H. Chang, "Vendor Selection in a Modified Re-Buy Situation Using a Strategy Aligned Fuzzy Approach," *International Journal of Production Research,* 2007, Vol. 45 (14), pp. 3113–24.

23. "Toyota Plant on a Roll with Hit Prius," *Associated Press,* June 5, 2009.

24. S. Sen, H. Basligil, C.G. Sen, and H. Baracli, "A Framework for Defining both Qualitative and Quantitative Supplier Selection Criteria Considering the Buyer-Supplier Integration Strategies*," International Journal of Production Research,* 3008, Vol. 46 (7), pp. 1825–39.

25. Felix T.S. Chan and Niraj Kumar, "Global Supplier Development Considering Risk Factors Using Fuzzy Extended AHP-based Approach," *Omega,* 2007, Vol. 35 (4), pp. 417–31; and Donna Gill and B. (Ram) Ramaseshan, "Influences on Supplier Repurchase Selection of UK Importers," *Marketing Intelligence and Planning,* 2007, Vol. 25 (6), pp. 597–611.

26. Ruth N. Bolton, Katherine N. Lemon, and Peter C. Verhoef, "Expanding Business to Business Customer Relationships: Modeling the Customer's Upgrade Decision," *Journal of Marketing,* 2008, Vol. 72 (1), pp. 46–60; and James M. Barry, Paul Dion, and William Johnson, "A Cross Cultural Examinations of Relationship Strength in B2B Services," *Journal of Services Marketing,* 2008, Vol. 22 (2), pp. 114–31.

27. Maria Holmlund, "A Definition, Model and Empirical Analysis of Business to Business Relationship Quality," *International Journal of Service Industry Management,* 2008, Vol. 19 (1), pp. 32–46.

28. Havard Hansen, Bendik M. Samuelsen, and Pal R. Siseth, "Customer Perceived Value in B-to-b Service Relationships: Investigating the Importance of Corporate Reputation," *Industrial Marketing Management,* 2008, Vol. 37 (2), pp. 206–20; and Jeffrey E. Lewin and Wesley J. Johnston, "The Impact of Supplier Downsizing on Performance, Satisfaction over Time, and Repurchase Decisions," *Journal of Business and Industrial Marketing,* 2008, Vol. 23 (4), pp. 249–63.

29. Wayne A. Neu and Stephen W. Brown, "Manufactuers Forming Successful Complex Business Services: Designing an Organization to Fit the Market," *International Journal of Service Industry Management,* 2008, Vol. 19 (2), pp. 232–39.

30. Anonymous, "Garmin Navigation to Be Standard Equipment in Suzuki SX4," *PR Newswire*, New York, April 28, 2008.

31. Blanca Hernandez Ortega, Julio Jimenez Martinez, and Ja Jose Martin De Hoyos, "The Role of Information Technology Knowledge, in B2B Development," *International Journal of E-Business Research,* 2008, Vol. 4 (1), pp. 40–55.

32. Christian Tanner, Ralf Wolffle, Petra Schubert, and Michael Quade, "Current Trends and Challenges in Electronic Procurement: An Empirical Study," *Electronic Markets,* 2008, Vol. 18 (1), pp. 8–19.

33. Juha Mikka Nurmilaakso, "Adoption of e-Business Functions Migration from EDI Based on XML Based e-Business Frameworks in Supply Chain Integration," *International Journal of Production Economics,* 2008, Vol. 113 (2), pp. 721–41.

34. T. Ravichandran, S. Pant, and D. Chatterjee, "Impact of Industry Structure and Product Characteristics on the Structure of Be2 Vertical Hubs," *IEEE Transactions on Engineering Management,* 2007, Vol. 54 (3), p. 506.

CHAPTER 7

1. Nicole E. Coviello, Roderick J. Brodie, Peter J. Danaher, and Wesley J. Johnston, "How Firms Relate to their Markets: An Empirical Examination of Contemporary Marketing Practices," *Journal of Marketing,* Vol. 66, Iss. 3, pp. 33–57.

2. Jacquelyn S. Thomas and Ursula Y. Sullivan, "Managing Marketing Communications with Multichannel Customers," *Journal of Marketing* Vol. 69, Iss. 4, October 2005, pp. 239–51; and Stephen L. Vargo and Robert F. Lusch,

"Evolving to a New Dominant Logic for Marketing," *Journal of Marketing,* Vol. 68, Iss. 1, January 2004, pp. 1–17.

3. "Heineken Markets Brand to Young Men," *The Wall Street Journal,* July 7, 2008, p. B.5, accessed May 21, 2009, from ABI/INFORM Global Database.

4. Javier Rodriguez-Pinto, Ana Isabel Rodriguez-Escudero, and Jesus Gutierrez-Cilian, "Order, Positioning, Scope, and Outcomes of Market Entry," *Industrial Marketing Management,* Vol. 37, Iss. 2, April 2008, pp. 154–66.

5. Anders Gustafsson, Michael D. Johnson, and Inger Roos, "The Effects of Customer Satisfaction, Relationship Commitment Dimensions, and Triggers on Customer Retention," *Journal of Marketing,* Vol. 69, Iss. 4, October 2005, pp. 210–18; and Ajay Kalra and Ronald C. Goodstein, "The Impact of Advertising Positioning Strategies on Consumer Price Sensitivity," *Journal of Marketing Research,* Vol. 35, Iss. 2, May 1998, pp. 210–25.

6. Cenk Koca and Jonathan D. Bohlmann, "Segmented Switchers and Retailer Pricing Strategies," *Journal of Marketing,* Vol. 72, Iss. 3, May 2008, pp. 124–42.

7. Allan D. Shocker, Barry L. Bayus, and Namwoon Kim, "Product Complements and Substitutes in the Real World: The Relevance of "Other Products," *Journal of Marketing,* Vol. 68, Iss. 1, January 2004, pp. 28–40.

8. Arik Hesseldahl, "The iPhone Legacy: Pricier Smartphones?" *BusinessWeek* Online, November 1, 2007, www.businessweek.com/technology/content/oct2007/tc20071031_825744.htm?chan=search, accessed: May 22, 2008.

9. Leonard M. Lodish, "Another Reason Academics and Practitioners Should Communicate More," *Journal of Marketing Research,* Vol. 44, Iss. 1, February 2007, pp. 23–25.

10. Tat Y. Chan, V. Padmanabhan, and P. B. Seetharaman, "An Econometric Model of Location and Pricing in the Gasoline Market," *Journal of Marketing Research* Vol. 44, Iss. 4, November 2007, pp. 622–35; and Jeff Wang and Melanie Wallendorf, "Materialism, Status Signaling, and Product Satisfaction," *Journal of the Academy of Marketing Science,* Vol. 34, Iss. 4, Fall 2006, pp. 494–506.

11. Subim Im, Barry L. Bayus, and Charlotte H. Mason, "An Empirical Study of Innate Consumer Innovativeness, Personal Characteristics, and New-product Adoption Behavior," *Journal of the Academy of Marketing Science,* Vol. 31, Iss.

1, Winter 2003, pp. 61–74; and Sudhir N. Kale and Peter Klugsberger, "Reaping Rewards," *Marketing Management,* Vol. 16, Iss. 4, July/August 2007, p. 14.

12. Matthew Boyle, "Sweet Brand of Youth," *BusinessWeek,* April 13, 2009, p. 11.

13. Charles D. Schewe and Geoffrey Meredith, "Segmenting Global Markets by Generational Cohorts: Determining Motivations by Age," *Journal of Consumer Behaviour,* Vol. 4, Iss. 1, October 2004, pp. 51–64.

14. Aili McConnon, "For a Temp Giant, a Boom in Boomers," *BusinessWeek,* June, 2009, p. 54.

15. "Grand Theft Auto IV Breaks Guinness World Records with Biggest Entertainment Release of All Time," ING.com, May 13, 2008, http://ps3.ign.com/articles/873/873531p1.html, accessed May 29, 2008.

16. "2007 Essential Facts about the Computer and Video Game Industry," *Sales, Demographic, and Usage Data,* Entertainment Software Association. www.theesa.com/facts/pdfs/ESA_EF_2007.pdf, accessed May 27, 2008.

17. Anne L. Balazs, "Expenditures of Older Americans," *Journal of the Academy of Marketing Science,* Vol. 28, Iss. 4, Fall 2000, pp. 543–46; and Christopher D. Hopkins, Catherine A. Roster, and Charles M. Wood, "Making the Transition to Retirement: Appraisals, Post-transition Lifestyle, and Changes in Consumption Patterns," *Journal of Consumer Marketing,* Vol. 23, Iss. 2, 2006, pp. 89–101.

18. Stuart Van Auken, Thomas E. Barry, and Richard P. Bagozzi, "A Cross-Country Construct Validation of Cognitive Age," *Journal of the Academy of Marketing Science,* Vol. 34, Iss. 3, Summer 2006, pp. 439–56.

19. Mark Andrew Mitchell, Piper McLean, and Gregory B. Turner, "Understanding Generation X . . . Boom or Bust Introduction," *Business Forum,* Vol. 27, Iss. 1, 2005, pp. 26–31.

20. Qimei Chen, Shelly Rodgers, and William D. Wells, "Better than Sex," *Marketing Research,* Vol. 16, Iss. 4, Winter 2004, pp. 16–22.

21. www.gillettevenus.com/us/, accessed May 29, 2008.

22. Rex Y. Du and Wagner A Kamakura, "Household Life Cycles and Lifestyles in the United States," *Journal of Marketing Research,* Vol. 43, Iss. 1, February 2006 pp. 121–32.

23. Andrew Lindridge and Sally Dibb, "Is 'Culture' a Justifiable Variable for Market Segmentation? A Cross-cultural

Example," *Journal of Consumer Behaviour,* Vol. 2, Iss. 3, March 2003, pp. 269–87.

24. Frederick A. Palumbo and Ira Teich, "Market Segmentation Based on Level of Acculturation," *Marketing Intelligence & Planning,* Vol. 22, Iss. 4, 2004, pp. 472–84.

25. Frederick A. Palumbo and Ira Teich, "Segmenting the U.S. Hispanic Market Based on Level of Acculturation," *Journal of Promotion Management,* Vol. 12, Iss. 1, 2005, pp. 151–73.

26. Mark R. Forehand and Rohit Deshpande, "What We See Makes Us Who We Are: Priming Ethnic Self-awareness and Advertising Response," *Journal of Marketing Research,* Vol. 38, Iss. 3, August 2001, pp. 336–4.

27. Carmen DeNavas-Walt, Bernadette D. Proctor, and Jessica Smith, "Income, Poverty, and Health Insurance Coverage in the United States: 2006," *US Census Online,* August 2007, www.census.gov/prod/2007pubs/p60-233.pdf, accessed May 23, 2008.

28. C. B. Bhattacharya and Sankar Sen, "Consumer-Company Identification: A Framework for Understanding Consumers' Relationships with Companies," *Journal of Marketing,* Vol. 67, Iss. 2, April 2003, pp. 76–88.

29. Ben Levisohn and Brian Burnsed, "The Credit Rating in Your Shoe Box," *BusinessWeek* Online, April 10, 2008, www.businessweek.com/magazine/content/08_16/b4080052299512.htm?chan=search, accessed May 23, 2008.

30. Tina Wang, "China's Affluent Youth Boom," *Forbes,* April 14, 2009, www.forbes.com/2009/04/14/china-consumers-wealthy-markets-economy-luxury.html, accessed June 5, 2009.

31. http://www.census.gov.

32. Paul G. Patterson, "Demographic Correlates of Loyalty in a Service Context," *Journal of Services Marketing* Vol. 21, Iss. 2, 2007, pp. 112–21.

33. Madhubalan Viswanathan, Jose Antonio Rosa, and James Edwin Harris, "Decision Making and Coping of Functionally Illiterate Consumers and Some Implications for Marketing Management," *Journal of Marketing,* Vol. 69, Iss. 1, January 2005, pp. 15–31.

34. Charles M. Schaninger and Sanjay Putrevu, "Dual Spousal Work Involvement: An Alternative Method to Classify Households/Families," *Academy of Marketing Science Review,* Vol. 2006, 2006, pp. 1–21.

35. Rob Lawson and Sarah Todd, "Consumer Lifestyles: A Social Stratification

Perspective," *Marketing Theory* Vol. 2, Iss. 3, September 2002, pp. 295–308.

36. David J. Faulds and Stephan F. Gohmann, "Adapting Geodemographic Information to Army Recruiting: The Case of Identifying and Enlisting Private Ryan," *Journal of Services Marketing,* Vol. 15, Iss. 3, 2001, pp. 186–211.

37. Geraldine Fennell, Greg M. Allenby, Sha Yang, and Yancy Edwards, "The Effectiveness of Demographic and Psychographic Variables for Explaining Brand and Product Category Use," *Quantitative Marketing and Economics,* Vol. 1, Iss. 2, June 2003, pp. 223–44.

38. Beth Kowitt, "Denny's Free Breakfast Grand Slam," *CNN Money,* February 4, 2009, http://money.cnn.com/2009/02/03/news/companies/dennys_breakfast.fortune/, accessed June 5, 2009.

39. "VALS Survey," *SRI Consulting Business Intelligence* Online, www.sric-bi.com/VALS/, accessed May 25, 2008.

40. James Frederick, "Walgreens Leaders Reaffirm Strategy, Outlook," *Drug Store News,* February 16, 2004.

41. Robert Hof, "Behavioral Targeting: Google Pulls Out the Stops," *BusinessWeek,* March 11, 2009, www.businessweek.com/technology/content/mar2009/tc20090311_349208.htm, accessed June 5, 2009.

42. Florian V. Wangenheim and Tomas Bayon, "Behavioral Consequences of Overbooking Service Capacity," *Journal of Marketing,* Vol. 71, Iss. 4, October 2007, pp. 36–47; and Ruth N. Bolton, Katherine N. Lemon, and Peter C. Verhoef, "The Theoretical Underpinnings of Customer Asset Management: A Framework and Propositions for Future Research," *Journal of the Academy of Marketing Science,* Vol. 32, Iss. 3, Summer 2004, pp. 271–93.

43. Sarah Plaskitt, "Listerine Boosts Sales by 20%," *B&T Magazine* Online, May 22, 2003, www.bandt.com.au/news/49/0c016749.asp, accessed May 25, 2008.

44. Yuping Liu, "The Long-Term Impact of Loyalty Programs on Consumer Purchase Behavior and Loyalty," *Journal of Marketing,* Vol. 71, Iss. 4, October 2007, pp. 19–35.

45. Jeremy Quittner, "Turn On, Tune In, Tweet Out," *BusinessWeek SmallBiz,* April/May 2009, pp. 46–47.

46. V. Kumar and J. Andrew Petersen, "Using Customer-Level Marketing Strategy to Enhance Firm Performance: A Review of Theoretical and Empirical Evidence," *Journal of the Academy of Marketing Science,* Vol. 33, Iss. 4, Fall 2005, pp. 504–20; and David Feldman, "Segmentation Building Blocks," *Marketing Research,* Vol. 18, Iss. 2, Summer 2006, p. 23.

47. Thomas L. Powers and Jay U. Sterling, "Segmenting Business-to-Business Markets: A Micro-Macro Linking Methodology," *Journal of Business & Industrial Marketing* Vol. 23, Iss. 3, 2008, pp. 170–77.

48. Peter R. Dickson, Paul W. Farris, and Willem J. M. I. Verbeke, "Dynamic Strategic Thinking," *Journal of the Academy of Marketing Science,* Vol. 29, Iss. 3, Summer 2001, pp. 216–38.

49. Eric Almquist and Gordon Wyner, "Boost Your Marketing ROI with Experimental Design," *Harvard Business Review,* Vol. 79, Iss. 9, October 2001, pp. 135–47.

50. Olga Kharif and Jack Ewing, "Nokia Targets the U.S. Market," *BusinessWeek,* March 30, 2009, www.businessweek.com/technology/content/mar2009/tc20090329_098616.htm, accessed June 4, 2009.

51. Gary L. Frazier, "Organizing and Managing Channels of Distribution," *Journal of the Academy of Marketing Science,* Vol. 27, Iss. 2, Spring 1999, pp. 226–51; and Darren W. Dahl and Page Moreau, "The Influence and Value of Analogical Thinking during New Product Ideation," *Journal of Marketing Research,* Vol. 39, Iss. 1, February 2002, pp. 47–61.

52. J. David Hunger and Thomas H. Wheelen, *Essentials of Strategic Management,* 4th edition. Upper Saddle River, NJ: Prentice Hall, 2007.

53. Subin Im and John P. Workman Jr., "Market Orientation, Creativity, and New Product Performance in High-Technology Firms," *Journal of Marketing,* Vol. 68, Iss. 2, April 2004, pp. 114–32.

54. Bruce Buskirk, Stacy M. P. Schmidt, and David L. Ralph, "Patterns in High-Tech Firms Growth Strategies by Seeking Mass Mainstream Customer Adaptations," *The Business Review, Cambridge,* Vol. 8, Iss. 1, Summer 2007, pp. 34–40.

55. Don Peppers and Martha Rogers, *The One-to-One Manager: Real World Lessons in Customer Relationship Management.* New York: Doubleday Business, 2002.

56. David A. Schweidel, Eric T. Bradlow, and Patti Williams, "A Feature-Based Approach to Assessing Advertisement Similarity," *Journal of Marketing Research,* Vol. 43, Iss. 2, May 2006, pp. 237–43.

57. http://www.ikea.com/ms/en_GB/about_ikea/press_room/student_info.html, accessed May 14, 2009.

58. Andrew Curry, Gill Ringland, and Laurie Young, "Using Scenarios to Improve Marketing," *Strategy & Leadership,* Vol. 34, Iss. 6, 2006, pp. 30–39.

59. "Burger King's Monster 923 Calorie Burger," *Metro News* Online, November 6, 2006, www.metro.co.uk/news/article.html?in_article_id=23982&in_page_id=34, accessed May 25, 2008.

60. Detelina Marinova, "Actualizing Innovation Effort: The Impact of Market Knowledge Diffusion in a Dynamic System of Competition," *Journal of Marketing,* Vol. 68, Iss. 3, July 2004, pp. 1–20.

61. Michael E. Porter, *Competitive Advantage.* New York: Simon & Schuster, 1985.

62. David W. Cravens and Nigel F. Piercy, *Strategic Marketing,* 9/e. Boston: McGraw-Hill/Irwin, 2009.

CHAPTER 8

1. Albert M. Muniz Jr. and Hope Jensen Schau, "Religiosity in the Abandoned Apple Newton Brand Community," *Journal of Consumer Research,* 2005, Vol. 31 (4), pp. 737–48; and Hope Jensen Schau and Albert Muniz, "A Tale of Tales: The Apple Newton Narratives," *Journal of Strategic Marketing,* 2006, Vol. 14 (1), pp. 19–28.

2. Julee Kaplan, "Aeropostale Targets Teen Charities," *WWD,* 2008, Vol. 195 (13), p. 14.

3. Jack Neff, "Tide's Washday Miracle: Not Doing Laundry," *Advertising Age,* 2007, Vol. 78 (45), p. 12.

4. Andreas B. Eisingerich and Tobias Kretschmer, "In E-Commerce, More Is More," *Harvard Business Review,* 2008, Vol. 86 (3), pp. 20–35.

5. Lance A. Bettencourt and Anthony W. Ulwick, "The Customer-Centered Innovation Map," *Harvard Business Review,* 2008, Vol. 86 (5), p. 109.

6. Don Reisinger, "The BlackBerry Storm is No iPhone," *CNET News,* October 8, 2008, http://news.cnet.com/the-BlackBerry-storm-is-no-iphone/; Lance Whitney, "BlackBerry Outsells the iPhone 3G," *CNET News,* May 4, 2009, http://news.cnet.com/BlackBerry-outsells-the-iphone-3G.

7. Stephen L. Vargo and Robert F. Lusch, "From Goods Go Service(s): Divergences and Convergences of Logics," *Industrial Marketing Management,* 2008, Vol. 37 (3), pp. 254–68.

8. Preyas S. Desai, Oded Koenigsberg, and Devarat Purohit, "The Role of Production Lead Time and Demand Uncertainty in Marketing Durable Goods," *Management Science,* 2007 vol. 53 (1), pp. 150–59.

9. Bombardier Company, Bombardier 2008 Annual Report.

10. Marc Abrahams, "A Pointed Lesson about Product Features," *Harvard Business Review,* 2006, Vol. 84 (3), pp. 21–23.

11. Ben Levisohn, "Keep That Rolex Ticking," *BusinessWeek,* March 24, 2008, Issue 4076, p. 21; and Stacy Meichtry, "How Timex Plans to Upgrade Its Image," *Wall Street Journal,* June 21, 2007, p. B6.

12. Chuniai Chen, Jun Yang, Christopher Findlay, "Measuring the Effect of Food Standards on China's Agricultural Exports," *Review of World Economics,* 2008, Vol. 144 (1), 83–107; and David Kesmodel and Nicholas Zamiska, "China Curbs Garlic, Ginger Exports to U.S.," *Wall Street Journal,* September 18, 2007, p. D7.

13. Djoko Setijono, Jens J. Dahlgaard, "The Value of Quality Improvements," *The International Journal of Quality and Reliability Management,* 2008, Vol. 25, (3), pp. 292–306; and Gavriel Melirovich, "Quality of Design and Quality of Conformance: Contingency and Synergistic Approaches," *Total Quality Management and Business Excellence,* 2008, Vol. 17 (2), pp. 205–20.

14. Rajeev K. Goel, "Uncertain Innovation with Uncertain Product Durability," *Applied Economics Letters,* 2006, Vol. 13 (13), pp. 829–42.

15. Kamalini Ramdas and Taylor Randall, "Does Component Sharing Help or Hurt Reliability? An Empirical Study in the automotive Industry," *Management Science,* 2008, Vol. 54 (5), pp. 922–39; and Niranjan Pati and Dayr Reis, "The Quality Learning Curve: An Approach to Predicting Quality Improvement in Manufacturing and Services," *Journal of Global Business Issues,* Vol. 1 (2), pp. 129–41.

16. Bimai Nepal, Leslie Monplaisir, and Nanua Singh, "A Framework to Integrate Design for Reliability and Maintainability in Modular Product Design, *International Journal of Product Development,* 2007, Vol. 4 (5), pp. 459–674.

17. Ravinda Chitturi, Rajagopal Raghunathan and Vijar Mahajan, "Delight By Design: The Role of Hedonic Versus Utilitarian Benefits, *Journal of Marketing,* 2008, Vol. 72 (3), pp. 48–61.

18. Penelope Green, "While You Were Out, the Post-It Went Home," *New York Times,* June 28, 2007, p. F1.

19. Brooke Crothers, "Report: Dell Phasing Out XPS Gaming Systems," CNET News, May 12, 2008, http://news.cnet.com/8301-13924_3-9942497-64.html.

20. Muhammad A. Noor, Rick Rabiser, and Paul Grunbacher, "Agile Product Line Planning: A Collarborative Approach and a Case Study," *The Journal of Systems and Software,* 2008, Vol. 81 (6), pp. 868–81.

21. Peter N. Golder and Gerald J. Tellis, "Growing, Growing, Gone: Cascades, Diffusion, and Turning Points in the Product Life Cycle," *Marketing Science,* 2004, Vol. 23 (2), pp. 207–21.

22. Kate Niederhoffer, Rob Mooth, David Wiesenfeld, Jonathon Gordon, "The Origin and Impact of CPG New Product Buzz: Emerging Trends and Implications," *Journal of Advertising,* 2007, Vol. 47 (4), pp. 420–36.

23. Michael Adams, "W . . . A Decade of WOW," Hospitality Design, Vol. 31, Issue 3, New York, April 2009, pp. 116–121.

24. Jonathan Birchall, "Ralph Lauren Aims to Double Sales in Asia and Europe," *Financial Times,* May 29, 2008, p. 17; and John Brodie, "It's Ralph's World," *Fortune,* 2007, Vol. 156, (6), pp. 64–68.

25. Scent-Air Technology Company Web Site, "Scent Studies," Accessed November 8, 2009, www.scentair.com/scentstudies/index.php?subsectionD=DgssiD=9.

26. Arch G. Woodside, Suresh Sood, Kenneth E. Miller, "When Consumers and Brands Talk: Storytelling Theory and Research in Psychology and Marketing," *Psychology & Marketing,* 2008, Vol. 25 (2), pp. 97–111.

27. Franz Rudolf Esch, Tobia Langner, Bernd H. Schmitt, and Patrick Gaus, "Are Brands Forever? Brand Knowledge and Relationship Affect Current and Future Purchases," *The Journal of Product and Brand Management,* 2006, Vol. 15 (2), pp. 98–105.

28. William Kingston, "Trademark Registration Is Not a Right," Journal of Macromarketing, 2006, Vol. 26 (1), pp. 17–26.

29. Madhubalan Viswanathan and Terry L. Childers, "Understanding How Product Attributes Influence Product Categorization: Development and Validation of Fuzzy Set–based Measures of Gradedness in Product Categories," *Journal of Marketing Research,* 1999, Vol. 36, (1), pp. 75–95.

30. Pamela Miles Homer, "Perceived Quality and Image: When All Is Not "Rosy," *Journal of Business Research,* 2008, Vol. 61 (6), pp. 715–30.

31. Julie Manning Magid, Anthony D. Cox, and Dena S. Cox, "Quantifying Brand Image: Empirical Evidence of Trademark Dilution," *American Business Law Journal,* 2006, Vol. 43 (1), pp. 1–43.

32. Bing Jing, "Product Differentiation Under Imperfect Information: When Does Offering a Lower Quality Pay?" *Quantitative Marketing and Economics,* 2007, Vol. 5 (1), pp. 35–62.

33. Andy McCue, "Virtual Booze: Diageo Taps Second Life," *BusinessWeek* Online, June 11, 2007, http://www.businessweek.com/globalbiz/content/jun2007/gb20070611_608713.htm?chan=search; and Jenny Wiggins, "Emerging Markets Are Also Crucial Target Areas," *Financial Times,* February 15, 2008, p. 21.

34. William B. Locander and David L. Luechauer, "Building Equity," *Marketing Management,* 2005, Vol. 14 (3), pp. 45–48.

35. David Aaker, "*Managing Brand Equity,*" Free Press, 1991.

36. Saikat Banaerjee, "Strategic Brand-culture Fit: A Conceptual Framework for Brand Management," *Journal of Brand Management,* 2008, Vol. 15 (5), pp. 312–22.

37. "The New Brand Landscape," *Marketing Health Services,* 2008, Vol. 28 (1), p. 14; and Helen Stride and Stephen Lee, "No Logo? No Way, Branding in the Non-Profit Sector," *Journal of Marketing Management,* 2007, Vol. 23 (1/2), pp. 107–22.

38. Matthew Yeung and Bala Ramasamy, "Brand Value and Firm Performance Nexus: Further Empirical Evidence," *Journal of Brand Management,* 2008, Vol. 15 (5), pp. 322–36.

39. Todd Wasserman, "Scion Balances Edgy Image with 'Value'", *Brandweek,* Vol. 50, Issue 2, January 12, 2009, p. 10.

40. Jing Lei, Niraj Dawar, and Jos Lemmink, "Negative Spillover in Brand Portfolios: Exploring the Antecedents of Asymmetric Effects," *Journal of Marketing,* Vol. 72 (3), pp. 111–29.

41. Satish Nambisan and Priya Nambisan, "How to Profit from a Better "Virtual Customer Environment," *MIT Sloan Management Review,* 2008, Vol. 49 (3), pp. 53–70.

42. Ingrid M. Martin, David W. Stewart and Shashi Matta, "Branding Strategies, Marketing Communication, and Perceived Brand Meaning: the Transfer of

Purposive, Goal Oriented Brand Meaning to Brand Extensions," *Journal of the Academy of Marketing Science,* 2005, Vol. 33 (3), pp. 275–95.

43. Barry Silverstein, "Brand Extensions: Risks And Rewards," brandchannel.com, January 5, 2009, www.brandchannel.com/features_effect.ASP?pd_id=457

44. N. Amrouche, G. Martin-Herran, and G. Zaccour, "Pricing and Advertising of Private and National Brands in a Dynamic Marketing Channel," *Journal of Optimization Theory and Applications,* Vol. 137 (3), pp. 465–84.

45. Tsung-Chi Liu and Chung-Yu Want, "Factors Affecting Attitudes toward Private Labels and Promoted Brands," *Journal of Marketing Management,* 2008, Vol. 24 (3/4), pp. 283–99; and Kyong-Nan Kwon, Mi-Hee Lee and Yoo Jin Kin, "The Effect of Perceived Product Characteristics on Private Brand Purchases," *The Journal of Consumer Marketing,* 2008, Vol. 25 (2), pp. 105–22.

46. Najam Saqib, Rajesh V. Manchanda, "Consumers Evaluations of Co-Branded Products, the Licensing Effect," *The Journal of Product and Brand Management,* 2008, Vol. 17 (2), pp. 73–89.

47. Klaus-Peter Wiedmann and Dirk Ludewig, "How Risky Are Brand Licensing Strategies in View of Customer Perceptions and Reactions?" *Journal of General Management,* 2008, Vol. 33, (3), pp. 31–50.

48. Alokparna Basu, Monga, Loraine Lau-Gesk, "Blending Co Brand Personalities; An Examination of the Complex Self," *Journal of Marketing Research,* 2007, Vol. 44 (3), pp. 389–402.

49. Wei-Lun Chang, "A Typology of Co-branding Strategy: Position and Classification," *Journal of the American Academy of Business,* March 2008, Vol. 12 (2), pp. 220–27.

50. Jessie Scanlon, "Coke's New Design Direction," *BusinessWeek,* August 25, 2008, p. 17.

51. Ulrich R. Orth and Keven Malkewitz, "Holistic Package Design and Consumer Brand Impressions," *Journal of Marketing,* 2008, Vol. 72 (3), pp. 64–81.

52. Thomas J. Madden, Kelly Hewett, and Martin S. Roth, "Managing Images in Different Cultures: Across National Study of Color Meanings and Preferences," *Journal of International Marketing,* 2000, Vol. 8 (4), pp. 90–108.

53. Eric F. Shaver and Curt C. Braun, "Caution: How to Develop an Effective Product Warning," *Risk Management,* 2008, Vol. 55 (6), pp. 46–52.

54. Rebecca J. Slotegraaf and J. Jeffrey Inman, "Longitudinal Shifts in the Drivers of Satisfaction with Product Quality: The Role of Attribute Resolvability," *Journal of Marketing Research,* 2004, Vol. 41 (3), pp. 269–83.

55. D.N.P. Murthy, O. Solem, and T. Roren, "Product Warranty Logistics: Issues and Challenges," *European Journal of Operational Research,*" 2004, Vol. 156 (1), pp. 110–25.

56. Shallendra Pratap Jain, Rebecca J. Slotegraaf, and Charles D. Lindsey, "Towards Dimensionalizing Warranty Information: The Role of Consumer Costs of Warranty Information," *Journal of Consumer Psychology,* 2007, Vol. 17 (1), pp. 70–88.

CHAPTER 9

1. Glen M. Schmidt and Cheryl T. Druehl, "When Is a Disruptive Innovation Disruptive?", *Journal of Product Innovation Management,* 2008, 25 (4), pp. 347–62; and Lee G. Demuth III, "A Viewpoint on Disruptive Innovation," *Journal of American Academy of Business,* 2008, Vol. 13 (1), pp. 86–92.

2. Geoffrey A. Moore, "Darwin and the Demon: Innovating within Established Enterprises," *Harvard Business Review,* 2005, Issue 82 (7/8), pp. 86–98.

3. Darren Waters, "A New Format War?" BBC News_ dot.life, April 27, 2009.

4. Kenneth J. Petersen, Robert B. Handfield, and Gary L. Ragatz, "Supplier Integration into New Product Development: Coordinating Product, Process and Supply Chain Design," *Journal of Operations Management,* Vol. 23 (3/40), pp. 371–89.

5. Alex Taylor III, "Can This Care Save Ford?" *Fortune,* 2008, Vol. 157 (9), pp. 170–72; and David Kiley, One World, One Car," *BusinessWeek,* 2008, Issue 4076, p. 63.

6. Cornelia Droge, Roger Calantone, and Nukhet Harmancioglu, "New Product Success: Is It Really Controllable by Managers in Highly Turbulent Environments?" *Journal of Production Innovation Management,* 2008, Vol. 25 (3), pp. 272–90.

7. "Innovation Is More Than Just a Good Idea," *Strategic Direction,* 2008 Vol. 24 (8), p. 25.

8. Serkan Aydin, Ayse Tanbsel Cetin, and Gokhan Ozer, "The Relationship between Marketing and Product Development Process and Their Effects on Firm's Performance," *Journal of Academy of Marketing Studies,* 2007, Vol. 11 (10), pp. 53–69.

9. "Ford's European Arm Lends a Hand: Cars*," The Economist,* March 8, 2008, Vol. 385 (Issue 8570), p. 82.

10. Jennifer Ordonez, "Taking the Junk out of Junk Food," *Newsweek,* 2007, (Vol. 150 (15), pp. 46–47; and Russell Flannery, "China's Is a Big Prize," *Forbes,* 2004, (Issues 173 (10), pp. 163–64.

11. Peter Huber, "Toyota's MPG Game," *Forbes,* 2007, Vol. 180 (13), pp. 100.

12. "Eclipse 500 Wins Export Approvals," *Flight International,* 2008, Vol. 173 (5137), p. 12; and Bruce Nussbaum, "The Best Product Design of 2007*," BusinessWeek,* 2007, Issue 4044, pp. 52.

13. Rajesh Sethi and Zafar Iqbal, "State Gate Controls, Learning Failure, and Adverse Effect on Novel New Products," *Journal of Marketing,* 2008, Vol. 72 (1), pp. 118–32.

14. Maria Bartiromo, "Chris DeWolfe on MySpace's Widening Web of Users," *BusinessWeek,* 2008, (Issue 5086), p. 25.

15. Justin Scheck And Paul Glader, "R&D Spending Holds Steady in a slump," *The Wall Street Journal,* April 6, 2009.

16. "Odyssey Software's Athena Add-In for Microsoft's System Center Configuration Manager 2007 Names "Best of Tech Ed 2008 IT Professional Awards Finalist," *PR Newswire,* June 3, 2008.

17. "KidCare Medical Television Network Launches Digital Television Network," *Wireless News,* December 26, 2007, p. 1.

18. John Saunders, Veronica Wong, Chris Stagg, and Mariadel Mar Souza Fontana, "How Screening Criteria Change during Brand Management," *Journal of Product and Brand Management,* 2005, Vol. 14 (4/5), pp. 239–50.

19. "Apple Prototypes: 5 Product We Never Saw," Applegazette, June 20, 2008, www.applegazette.com/mac.

20. Raul O. Chao and Stylianon Kavadias, "A Theoretical Framework for Managing the New Product Development Portfolio: When and How to Use Strategic Buckets," Management Science, 2008, Vol. 54 (5), pp. 907–22.

21. Dean Richard Prebble, Gerritt Anton De Waal, and Cristiaan de Groot, "Applying Multiple Perspectives to the Design of a Commercialization Process," R&D Management, 2008, Vol. 38 (3), pp. 311–27.

22. Karan Girotra, Christian Terwiesch and Karl T. Ulrich, "Valuing R&D Projects in a Portfolio: Evidence from the Pharmaceutical Industry," *Management Science,* 2007, Vol. 53 (9), pp. 1452–66.

23. "Toshiba's Aquilion ONE Honored with Medical Design Excellence Award," *Business Wire*, New York, April 6, 2009.

24. Lenny H. Pattikawa, Ernst Verwaal and Harry R. Commandeur, "Understanding New Product Project Performance," *European Journal of Marketing*, 2006, Vol. 40 (11/12), pp. 1178–93.

25. Nukhel Armancioglu, Regina C. McNally, Roger J. Calantone, and Serdar S. Durmusoglu, "Your New Product Development (NPD) Is Only as Good as Your Process; an Exploratory Analysis of New NPD Process Design and Implementation," *R&D Management*, 2007, Vol. 37 (95), pp. 399–415.

26. Glen L. Urban and John R. Hauser, "Listening In to Find and Explore New Combinations of Customer Needs," *Journal of Marketing*, 2004, Vol. 68 (2), pp. 72–90.

27. B. Sorescu and Jelena Spanjol, "Innovation's Effect on Firm Value and Risk: Insights from Consumer Packaged Goods," *Journal of Marketing*, 2008, Vol. 72 (2), pp. 114–131.

28. J. Brock Smith and Mark Colgate, "Customer Value Creation: A Practical Framework," *Journal of Marketing Theory and Practice*, 2007, Vol. 15 (1), pp. 7–24.

29. Sanjiv Erat and Stylianos Kavadias, "Sequential Testing of Product Designs: Implications for Learning," *Management Science*, 2008, Vol. 54 (5) pp. 956–69.

30. Tim Ferguson, "BBC Tests Web 2.0 Technology for Music," *BusinessWeek* January 21, 2009

31. Wei-Lun Chang, "A Typology of Co-Branding Strategy: Position and Classification," *Journal of the Academy of Business*, 2008, Vol. 12 (92) pp. 220–27.

32. Sharan Jagpal, Kamel Jedidi, and M. Jamil, "A Multibrand Concept Testing Methodology for New Product Strategy," *Journal of Product Innovation Management*, 2007, Vol. 24 (1), pp. 34–51.

33. Destan Kandemir, Roger Calantone and Rosanna Garcia, "An Exploration of Organizational Factors in New Product Development Success," *Journal of Business and Industrial Marketing*," 2006, Vol. 21 (5), pp. 300–18.

34. Robert G. Cooper, "Perspective: The Stage Gate Idea to Launch Process–Update, What's New and NexGen systems," *Journal of Product Innovation Management*, 2008, vol. 25 (3), pp. 213–29; and Ming-hung Hsieh, Kuen-Hung, and Jun-Ren Wang, "The Moderating Effects of Market Orientation and Launch Proficiency on the Product Advantage Performance Relationship," *Industrial Marketing Management*, 2008, Vol. 37 (5), pp. 580–99; and Susan Jung Grant and Alice M. Tybout, "The Effect of Temporal Frame Information Considered in New Product Evaluation: The Role of Uncertainty," *Journal of Consumer Research*, 2008, Vol. 34 (6), pp. 897–912.

35. Aaron Ricadela, "Big Business Starts to Sour on Vista," *BusinessWeek*, 2008, Issue 4085, p. 48.

36. Henrik Sjodin, "Upsetting Brand Extensions: An Enquiry into Current Customer Inclination to Spread Negative Word of Mouth," *Journal of Brand Management*, 2008, Vol. 15 (4), pp. 258–62; and Kate Niederhoffer, Rob Mooth, David Wiesenfield, and Jonathan Gordon, "The Origin and Impact of CPG New Product Buzz: Emerging Trends and Implications," *Journal of Advertising Research*, 2007, Vol. 467 (4), pp. 420–38.

37. Christophe Van Den Butte and Yogesh V. Joshi, "New Product Diffusion with Influentials and Imitators," *Marketing Science*, 2007, Vol. 26 (3), pp. 400–24.

38. Kapil Bawa and Robert Shoemaker, "The Effects of Free Sample Promotions on Incremental Brand Sales," *Marketing Science*, 2004, Vol. 23 (3), pp. 345–64.

39. Morris Kalliny, Angela Hausman, "The Impact of Cultural and Religious Vaues on Consumer's Adoption of Innovation," *Journal of the Academy of Marketing Studies*, Vol. 11 (1), pp. 125–37; and Stacy L. Wood and C. Page Moreau, From Fear to Loathing? How Emotion Influences the Evaluation and Early Use of Innovations," *Journal of Marketing*, Vol. 70 (3), pp. 44–60.

40. "Crunchy Roll Implements Akamai to Enhance Its Dynamic Digital Content Experience for Customers," *Business Wire*, New York, June 9, 2009.

41. Leonard L. Berry, *On Great Service: A Framework for Action*, New York, The Free Press, 1995.

42. Stephen L. Vargo and Robert F. Lusch, "Evolving to a New Dominant Logic for Marketing," *Journal of Marketing*, Vol. 68, Iss. 1, January 2004, pp. 1–17.

43. Michael K. Brady, Brian L. Bourdeau, and Julia Heskel, "The Importance of Brand Cues in Intangible Service Industries: An Application to Investment Services," *Journal of Services Marketing*, Vol. 19, Iss. 6/7, 2005, pp. 401–11.

44. Mike Schaffner, "Analyzing the Cloud," *Forbes*, April 29, 2009; and Lindsay Clark, "Cloud Computing: Cloud is Good News for Small Business," ComputerWeekly.com, April 14, 2009.

45. Harvir S. Bansal, Shirley F. Taylor, and Yannik St. James, "Migrating' to New Service Providers: Toward a Unifying Framework of Customers' Switching Behaviors," *Journal of the Academy of Marketing Science*, Vol. 33, Iss. 1, Winter 2005, pp. 96–116.

46. Jeremy J. Sierra and Shaun McQuitty, "Service Providers and Customers: Social Exchange Theory and Service Loyalty," *Journal of Services Marketing*, Vol. 19, Iss. 6/7, 2005, pp. 392–401.

47. Don Kuehnast, "Customer Relationship Management Solution Energizes Bank Sales Environment," *Microsoft Business Solutions CRM Customer Case Study*, 2004.

48. Christian Homburg, Wayne D. Hoyer, and Martin Fassnacht, "Service Orientation of a Retailer's Business Strategy: Dimensions, Antecedents, and Performance Outcomes," *Journal of Marketing*, Vol. 66, Iss. 4, October 2002, pp. 86–102; and Medhi Mourali, Michael Laroche, and Frank Pons, "Individualistic Orientation and Customer Susceptibility to Interpersonal Influence," *Journal of Services Marketing*, Vol. 19, Iss. 3, 2005, pp. 164–74.

49. William J. Holstein, "At Southwest, the Culture Drives Success," *Business-Week* Online, February 21, 2008, www.businessweek.com/managing/content/feb2008/ca20080221_179423.htm?chan=search, accessed May 28, 2008.

50. Jena McGregor, "Customer Service Champs," *BusinessWeek*, March 3, 2008, pp. 37–50.

51. Rajshekhar G. Javalgi, Thomas W. Whipple, Amit K Ghosh, and Robert B. Young, "Market Orientation, Strategic Flexibility, and Performance: Implications for Services Providers," *Journal of Services Marketing*, Vol. 19, Iss. 4, 2005, pp. 212–22.

52. Kenneth J. Klassen and Thomas R. Rohleder, "Combining Operations and Marketing to Manage Capacity and Demand in Services," *Service Industries Journal*, Vol. 21, Iss. 2, April 2001, pp. 1–30.

53. G. Michael Maddock And Ralphael Louis Vitón, "Social Media Exposes Corporate Psychopath," *BusinessWeek* August 26, 2008.

54. D. Todd Donovan, Tom J. Brown, and John C. Mowen, "Internal Benefits of Service-Worker Customer Orientation: Job Satisfaction, Commitment, and Organizational Citizenship Behaviors," *Journal of Marketing*, Vol. 68, Iss. 1, January 2004, pp. 128–46.

55. Margaret Littman, "Playing for Keeps," *ABA Journal,* Vol. 91, June 2005, pp. 71–72.

56. Ceridwyn King and Debra Grace, "Exploring the Role of Employees in the Delivery of the Brand: A Case Study Approach," *Qualitative Market Research,* Vol. 8, Iss. 3, 2005, pp. 277–96.

57. Greg T. Spielberg, "Readers Weigh In On Customer Service," *BusinessWeek* February 19, 2009.

58. Deepak Sirdeshmukh, Jagdip Singh, and Barry Sabol, "Customer Trust, Value, and Loyalty in Relational Exchanges," *Journal of Marketing,* Vol. 66, Iss. 1, January 2002, pp. 15–38.

59. Lawrence A. Crosby and Brian Lunde, "Loyalty Linkage," *Marketing Management* Vol. 16, Iss. 3, May/June 2007, p. 12; and James H. McAlexander, John W. Schouten, and Harold F. Koening, "Building Brand Community," *Journal of Marketing,* Vol. 66, Iss. 1, January 2002, pp. 38–55.

60. Nikon Corporation: New CRM Software Gives Sales And Management More Flexibility," *Microsoft Dynamics-Case Studies*, August 6, 2008.

61. Sudhir N. Kale and Peter Klugsberger, "Reaping Rewards," *Marketing Management* Vol. 16, Iss. 4, July/August 2007, p. 14.

CHAPTER 10

1. Richard G. Netemeyer, Balaji Krishnan, Chris Pullig, and Guangping Wang, "Developing and Validating Measures of Facets of Customer-based Brand Equity," *Journal of Business Research,* Vol. 57, Iss. 2, February 2004, pp. 209–24.

2. Richard J. Speed, "Oh Mr. Porter! A Re-Appraisal of Competitive Strategy," *Marketing Intelligence & Planning,* Vol. 7, Iss. 5,6, 1989, pp. 8–11.

3. Bruce Einhorn, "Intel Inside the Third World," *BusinessWeek,* July 9 & 16, 2007, pp. 38–40; and Reena Jana, "Behind the Intel/OLPC Breakup," *BusinessWeek* Online, January, 8, 2008, www.businessweek.com/print/innovate/content/jan2008/id2008018_145303.htm, accessed June 2, 2008.

4. Roy W. Ralston, "The Effects of Customer Service, Branding, and Price on the Perceived Value of Local Telephone Service," *Journal of Business Research,* Vol. 56, Iss. 3, March 2003, pp. 201–13.

5. Tina Wang, "China's Affluent Youth Boom," *Forbes*, April 14, 2009, http://www.forbes.com/2009/04/14/china-consumers-wealthy-markets-economy-luxury.html, accessed June 5, 2009.

6. Kent B. Monroe, "Pricing Practices that Endanger Profits," *Marketing Management,* Vol. 10, Iss. 3, September/October 2001, pp. 42–46.

7. George J. Avlonitis and Kostis A. Indounas, "Pricing Objectives and Pricing Methods in the Services Sector," *Journal of Services Marketing,* Vol. 19, Iss. 1, 2005, pp. 47–57.

8. Emily Bryson York, "Subway's $5 Foot-long Becomes Yardstick for Fast-Food Meal Deals," *Advertising-Age*, June 8, 2009, http://adage.com/article?article_id=137119, accessed June 8, 2009.

9. Yikuan Lee and Gina Colarelli O'Connor, "New Product Launch Strategy for Network Effects Products," *Journal of the Academy of Marketing Science,* Vol. 31, Iss. 3, Summer 2003, pp. 241–55.

10. Angel F. Villarejo-Ramos and Manuel J. Sanchez-Franco, "The Impact of Marketing Communication and Price Promotion on Brand Equity," *Journal of Brand Management,* Vol. 12, Iss. 6, August 2005, pp. 431–44.

11. Ana Garrido-Rubio and Yolanda Polo-Redondo, "Tactical Launch Decisions: Influence on Innovation Success/Failure," *Journal of Product and Brand Management,* Vol. 14, Iss. 1, 2005, pp. 29–38.

12. Anna Kattan, "Xerox Bets on Pricey Printers," *CNN Money*, June 1, 2009, http://money.cnn.com/2009/06/01/technology/xerox_pricey_printers.fortune/index.htm, accessed June 4, 2009.

13. Ioana Popescu and Yaozhong Wu, "Dynamic Pricing Strategies with Reference Effects," *Operations Research,* Vol. 55, Iss. 3, May/June 2007, pp. 413–32.

14. Mark Burton and Steve Haggett, "Rocket PLAN," *Marketing Management,* Vol. 16, Iss. 5, September/October 2007, p. 32.

15. Tulin Erdem, Michael P. Keane, and Baohong Sun, "The Impact of Advertising on Consumer Price Sensitivity in Experience Goods Markets," *Quantitative Marketing and Economics,* Vol. 6, Iss. 2, June 2008, pp. 139–76.

16. Harun Ahmet Kuyumcu, "Emerging Trends in Scientific Pricing," *Journal of Revenue and Pricing Management,* Vol. 6, Iss. 4, December 2007, pp. 293–99.

17. Tina Seeley, "CFTC Targets Shipping, Storage in Oil Investigation (Update2)," *Bloomberg,* May 30, 2008.

18. Emily Bryson York, "Subway's $5 Foot-long Becomes Yardstick for Fast-Food Meal Deals," *AdvertisingAge*, June 8, 2009, http://adage.com/article?article_id=137119, accessed June 8, 2009.

19. Tridib Mazumdar, S. P. Raj, and Indrajit Sinha, "Reference Price Research: Review and Propositions," *Journal of Marketing,* Vol. 69, Iss. 4, October 2005, pp. 84–102; and Xueming Luo, Aric Rindfleisch, and David K. Tse, "Working with Rivals: The Impact of Competitor Alliances on Financial Performance," *Journal of Marketing Research,* Vol. 44, Iss. 1, February 2007, pp. 73–83.

20. Marc Vanhuele and Xavier Dreze, "Measuring the Price Knowledge Shoppers Bring to the Store," *Journal of Marketing,* Vol. 66, Iss. 4, October 2002, pp. 72–85.

21. Kusum Ailawadi, Donald R. Lehmann, and Scott A. Neslin, "Market Response to a Major Policy Change in the Marketing Mix: Learning from Procter & Gamble's Value Pricing Strategy," *Journal of Marketing* Vol. 65, Iss. 1, January 2001, pp. 44–61.

22. Stephan Zielke and Thomas Dobbelstein, "Customers' Willingness to Purchase New Store Brands," *Journal of Product and Brand Management,* Vol. 16, Iss. 2, 2007, pp. 112–21.

23. *The Economist*, "Advertising's New Model-Clock-watchers No More," May 14, 2009, http://www.economist.com/business/displaystory.cfm?story_id=13649160&CFID=59963071&CFTOKEN=43887680, accessed on June 4, 2009.

24. Michaela Draganska and Dipak C. Jain, "Consumer Preferences and Product-Line Pricing Strategies: An Empirical Analysis," *Marketing Science,* Vol. 25, Iss. 2, March/April 2006, pp. 164–75.

25. Baba Shiv, Ziv Carmon, and Dan Ariely, "Placebo Effects of Marketing Actions: Consumers May Get What They Pay For," *Journal of Marketing Research,* Vol. 42, Iss. 4, November 2005, pp. 383–93.

26. Michael Levy, Dhruv Grewal, Praveen K. Kopalle, and James D. Hess, "Emerging Trends in Retail Pricing Practice: Implications for Research," *Journal of Retailing,* Vol. 80, Iss. 3, 2004, pp. 13–21.

27. Chris Janiszewski and Marcus Cunha Jr., "The Influence of Price Discount Framing on the Evaluation of a Product Bundle," *Journal of Consumer Research* Vol. 30, Iss. 4, March 2004, pp. 534–46.

28. Daniel J. Howard and Roger A. Kerin, "Broadening the Scope of Reference Price Advertising Research: A Field Study of Consumer Shopping

Involvement," *Journal of Marketing,* Vol. 70, Iss. 4, October 2006, pp. 185–204.

29. James McClure and Erdogan Kumcu, "Promotions and Product Pricing: Parsimony versus Veblenesque Demand," *Journal of Economic Behavior & Organization* Vol. 65, Iss. 1, January 2008, pp. 105–17.

30. Robert M. Schindler and Alan R. Wiman, "Effects of Odd Pricing on Price Recall," *Journal of Business Research,* Vol. 19, Iss. 3, November 1989, pp. 165–77.

31. John Huston and Nipoli Kamdar, "$9.99: Can "Just-Below" Pricing Be Reconciled with Rationality?" *Eastern Economic Journal,* Vol. 22, Iss. 2, Spring 1996, pp. 137–45.

32. Olga Kharif and Jack Ewing, "Nokia Targets the U.S. Market," *Business-Week,* March 30, 2009, http://www. businessweek.com/technology/content/ mar2009/tc20090329_098616.htm, accessed June 4, 2009.

33. Victor Epstein, "New Low-Cost Airline Targets Smaller Markets," *BusinessWeek,* May 26, 2009, http://www. businessweek.com/ap/financialnews/ D98E3LPO0.htm, accessed June 5, 2009.

34. Kathleen Seiders and Glenn B. Voss, "From Price to Purchase," *Marketing Management,* Vol. 13, Iss. 6, November/ December 2004, pp. 38–43.

35. "Record-Setting Ferrari Price," *BusinessWeek,* May 27, 2008, http://www. businessweek.com/lifestyle/content/ may2008/bw20080523_079089.htm, accessed June 5, 2009.

36. Christian Terwiesch, Sergei Savin, and Il-Horn Hann, "Online Haggling at a Name-Your-Own-Price Retailer: Theory and Application," *Management Science* Vol. 51, Iss. 3, March 2005, pp. 339–52.

37. Chris Guilding, Colin Drury, and Mike Tayles, "An Empirical Investigation of the Importance of Cost-plus Pricing," *Managerial Auditing Journal,* Vol. 20, Iss. 2, 2005, pp. 125–37.

38. J. Isaac Brannon, "The Effects of Resale Price Maintenance Laws on Petrol Prices and Station Attrition: Empirical Evidence from Wisconsin," *Applied Economics,* Vol. 35, Iss. 3, February 2003, pp. 343–49.

39. Chuan He and Yuxin Chen, "Managing e-Marketplace: A Strategic Analysis of Nonprice Advertising," *Management Science,* Vol. 25, Iss. 2, March/April 2006, pp. 175–87.

40. Ben Vinod, "Retail Revenue Management and the New Paradigm of Merchandise Optimisation," *Journal*

of *Revenue and Pricing Management,* Vol. 3, Iss. 4, January 2005, pp. 358–68.

41. George J. Avlonitis and Kostis A. Indounas, "Pricing Practices of Service Organizations," *Journal of Services Marketing,* Vol. 20, Iss. 5, 2006, pp. 346–57.

42. Keith S. Coulter, "Decreasing Price Sensitivity Involving Physical Product Inventory: A Yield Management Application," *Journal of Product and Brand Management* Vol. 10, Iss. 4/5, 2001, pp. 301–17.

43. Kusum L. Ailawadi and Bari Harlam, "An Empirical Analysis of the Determinants of Retail Margins: The Role of Store-Brand Share," *Journal of Marketing,* Vol. 68, Iss. 1, January 2004, pp. 147–65.

44. Fred S. McChesney and William F. Shughart, II, "Delivered Pricing in Theory and Policy Practice," *The Antitrust Bulletin,* Vol. 52, Iss. 2, Summer 2007, pp. 205–28.

45. Hiroshi Ohta, Yan-Shu Lin, and Masa K. Naito, "Spatial Perfect Competition: A Uniform Delivered Pricing Model," *Pacific Economic Review,* Vol. 10, Iss. 4, December 2005, pp. 407–20.

46. Pradeep K. Chintagunta, Jean-Pierre Dube, and Vishal Singh, "Balancing Profitability and Customer Welfare in a Supermarket Chain," *Quantitative Marketing and Economics,* Vol. 1, Iss. 1, March 2003, pp. 111–46.

47. Jena McGregor, "Costco's Artful Discounts," *BusinessWeek*, October 9, 2008, http://www.businessweek. com/magazine/content/08_42/ b4104058856320.htm, accessed June 5, 2009.

48. John M. Connor, "Forensic Economics: An Introduction with Special Emphasis on Price Fixing," *Journal of Competition Law & Economics,* Vol. 4, Iss. 1, March 2008, pp. 21–59.

49. Siva Viswanathan, Jason Kuruzovich, Sanjay Gosain, and Ritu Agarwal, "Online Infomediaries and Price Discrimination: Evidence from the Automotive Retailing Sector," *Journal of Marketing,* Vol. 71, Iss. 3, July 2007, pp. 89–107.

50. Allan J. Kimmel, "Deception in Marketing Research and Practice: An Introduction," *Psychology & Marketing,* Vol. 18, Iss. 7, July 2001, pp. 657–61.

51. Jules Stuyck, Evelyne Terryn, and Tom van Dyck, "Confidence through Fairness? The New Directive on Unfair Business-to-Consumer Commercial Practices in the Internal Market," *Common Market Law Review,* Vol. 43, Iss. 1, February 2006, pp. 107–52.

52. Patrick DeGraba, "The Loss Leader Is a Turkey: Targeted Discounts from Multi-product Competitors," *International Journal of Industrial Organization,* Vol. 24, Iss. 3, May 2006, pp. 613–28.

CHAPTER 11

1. Sjoerd Schaafsma and Joerg Hofstetter, "Raising the Game to a New Level," *ECR Journal: International Commerce Review,* Vol. 5, Iss. 1, Summer 2005, pp. 66–69.

2. Lee G. Cooper, "Strategic Marketing Planning for Radically New Products," *Journal of Marketing,* Vol. 64, Iss. 1, January 2000, pp. 1–16.

3. Natalie Zmuda, "Green Mountain Takes on Coffee Giants Cup by Cup," *Advertising Age,* June 1, 2009, http:// adage.com/cmostrategy/article?article_ id=136977, accessed June 6, 2009.

4. Bernard Cova and Robert Salle, "Marketing Solutions in Accordance with the S-D Logic: Co-creating Value with Customer Network Actors," *Industrial Marketing Management* Vol. 37, Iss. 3, May 2008, pp. 270–77.

5. Jennifer Rowley, "Synergy and Strategy in E-business," *Marketing Intelligence & Planning,* Vol. 20, Iss. 4/5, 2002, pp. 215–22.

6. Ravi S. Achrol and Michael J. Etzel, "The Structure of Reseller Goals and Performance in Marketing Channels," *Journal of the Academy of Marketing Science,* Vol. 31, Iss. 2, Spring 2003, pp. 146–63.

7. Arik Hesseldahl, "The iPhone Eyes BlackBerry's Turf," *BusinessWeek* Online, June 11, 2008, www. businessweek.com/print/magazine/ content/08_25/b4089038650669.htm, accessed June 13, 2008; and Arik Hesseldahl, "Taking the IPhone Apart," *BusinessWeek* Online, July 3, 2007, www. businessweek.com/print/technology/ content/jul2007/tc2007072_957316. htm, accessed June 11, 2008.

8. "Tie Your Own Bow Tie; How to Make Smart Product Management Decisions," *Strategic Direction,* Vol. 23, Iss. 5, 2007, pp. 5–8.

9. Joe Fine "OfficeMax's Wacky Marketing Strategy," *BusinessWeek,* January 29, 2009, http://www.business-week.com/magazine/content/09_06/ b4118065841575.htm, accessed June 5, 2009.

10. Stephen Keysuk Kim, "Relational Behaviors in Marketing Channel Relationships: Transaction Cost Implications," *Journal of Business Research,* Vol. 60, Iss. 11, November 2007, pp. 1125–34.

11. Junhong Chu, Pradeep K. Chintagunta, and Naufel J. Vilcassim, "Assessing the Economic Value of Distribution Channels: An Application to the Personal Computer Industry," *Journal of Marketing Research,* Vol. 44, Iss. 1, February 2007, pp. 29–41.

12. Daniel C. Bello and Nicholas C. Williamson, "The American Export Trading Company: Designing a New International Marketing Institution," *Journal of Marketing* Vol. 49, Iss. 4, Fall 1985, pp. 60–69.

13. Alberto Sa Vinhas and Erin Anderson, "How Potential Conflict Drives Channel Structure (Direct and Indirect) Channels," *Journal of Marketing Research,* Vol. 42, Iss. 4, November 2005, pp. 507–15.

14. Aksel I. Rokkan, Jan B. Heide, and Kenneth H. Wathne, "Specific Investments in Marketing Relationships: Expropriation and Bonding Effects," *Journal of Marketing Research,* Vol. 40, Iss. 2, pp. 210–24.

15. Jena McGregor, "Costco's Artful Discounts," *BusinessWeek*, October 9, 2008, http://www.businessweek.com/magazine/content/08_42/b4104058856320.htm, accessed June 5, 2009.

16. Michael Ketzenberg, Richard Metters, and Vicente Vargas, "Quantifying the Benefits of Breaking Bulk in Retail Operations," *International Journal of Production Economics* Vol. 80, Iss. 3, December 2002, pp. 249–63.

17. E. Bashkansky, S. Dror, R. Ravid, and P. Grabov, "Effectiveness of Product Quality Classifier," *Quality Engineering,* Vol. 19, Iss. 3, July 2007, p. 235.

18. Jason M. Carpenter, "Demographics and Patronage Motives of Supercenter Shoppers in the United States," *International Journal of Retail & Distribution Management,* Vol. 36, Iss. 1, 2008, pp. 5–16.

19. Devon S. Johnson and Sundar Bharadwaj, "Digitization of Selling Activity and Sales Force Performance: An Empirical Investigation," *Journal of the Academy of Marketing Science* Vol. 33, Iss. 1, Winter 2005, pp. 3–18.; and Xueming Luo and Naveen Donthu, "The Role of Cyber-intermediaries: A Framework Based on Transaction Cost Analysis, Agency, Relationship Marketing, and Social Exchange Theories," *Journal of Business & Industrial Marketing,* Vol. 22, Iss. 7, 2007, pp. 452–58.

20. Joseph Pancras and K. Sudhir, "Optimal Marketing Strategies for a Customer Data Intermediary," *Journal of Marketing Research* Vol. 44, Iss. 4, November 2007, pp. 452–58.

21. Virpi Havila, Jan Johanson, and Peter Thilenius, "International Business-relationship Triads," *International Marketing Review,* Vol. 21, Iss. 2, 2004, pp. 172–86.

22. Kevin Lane Keller, "Building Customer-based Brand Equity," *Marketing Management* Vol. 10, Iss. 2, July/August 2001 pp. 14–19.

23. Phillip Bond, "Band and Nonbank Financial Intermediation," *Journal of Finance,* Vol. 59, Iss. 6, December 2004, pp. 2489–2530.

24. Joseph Pancras and K. Sudhir.

25. John Quelch, "How Marketers Can Manage Price Inflation," *BusinessWeek,* http://www.businessweek.com/managing/content/jun2008/ca2008065_742702.htm, accessed June 5, 2009.

26. Amal R. Karunaratna and Lester W. Johonson, "Initiating and Maintaining Export Channel Intermediary Relationships," *Journal of International Marketing* Vol. 5, Iss. 2, 1997, pp. 11–32.

27. Bert Rosenbloom, "The Wholesaler's Role in the Marketing Channel: Disintermediation vs. Reintermediation," *International Review of Retail, Distribution, and Consumer Research* Vol. 17, Iss. 4, September 2007, pp. 327–39.

28. Kenneth K. Boyer and G. Tomas M. Hult, "Extending the Supply Chain: Integrating Operations and Marketing in the Online Grocery Industry," *Journal of Operations Management,* Vol. 23, Iss. 6, September 2005, pp. 642–61; and Thomas L. Friedman, *The World Is Flat 3.0: A Brief History of the Twenty-First Century.* New York: Picador, 2007.

29. Evan Hessel, "Hulu's March to Dominance," *Forbes.com*, April 30, 2009, http://www.forbes.com/2009/04/30/hulu-abc-nbc-fox-business-media-hulu.html, accessed June 10, 2009.

30. Ravi S. Achrol and Michael J. Etzel.

31. Gilles Corriveau and Robert D. Tamilla, "Comparing Transactional Forms in Administered, Contractual, and Corporate Systems in Grocery Distribution," *Journal of Business Research,* Vol. 55, Iss. 9, September 2002, pp. 771–73.

32. L. Lynn Judd and Bobby C. Vaught, "Three Differential Variables and Their Relation to Retail Strategy and Profitability," *Journal of the Academy of Marketing Science,* Vol. 16, Iss. 3,4, Fall 1988, pp. 30–37.

33. Tim Burkink, "Cooperative and Voluntary Wholesale Groups: Channel Coordination and Interim Knowledge Transfer," *Supply Chain Management,* Vol. 7, Iss. 2, 2002, pp. 60–70.

34. Gilles Corriveau and Robert D. Tamilla.

35. Nancy Nix, Robert Lusch, Zach Zacharia, and Wesley Bridges, "Competent Collaborations," *Marketing Management,* Vol. 17, Iss. 2, March/April 2008, p. 18.

36. Jeffrey O'Brien, "Amazon's Next Revolution," *CNNMoney.com*, May 26, 2009, http://money.cnn.com/2009/05/26/technology/obrien_kindle.fortune/?postversion=2009052605, accessed June 10, 2009.

37. John R. P. French and Bertram Raven, *The Bases of Social Power.* Ann Arbor: University of Michigan Press, 1959.

38. Boonghee Yoo, Naveen Donthu, and Sungho Lee, "An Examination of Selected Marketing Mix Elements and Brand Equity," *Journal of the Academy of Marketing Science,* Vol. 28, Iss. 2, Spring 2000, pp. 195–211.

39. P. Rajan Varadarajan, Satish Jayachandran, and J. Chris White, "Strategic Interdependence in Organizations: Deconglomeration and Marketing Strategy," *Journal of Marketing,* Vol. 65, Iss. 1, January 2001, pp. 15–28.

40. Frederick E. Webster Jr., "Understanding the Relationships among Brands, Consumers, and Resellers," *Journal of the Academy of Marketing Science,* Vol. 28, Iss. 1, Winter 2000, pp. 17–23.

41. Vaidyanathan Jayaraman and Yadong Luo, "Creating Competitive Advantages through New Value Creation: A Reverse Logistics Perspective," *Academy of Management Perspectives,* Vol. 21, Iss. 2, May 2007, pp. 56–73.

42. Stanley C. Gardiner, Joe B. Hanna, and Michael S. LaTour, "ERP and the Reengineering of Industrial Marketing Processes: A Prescriptive Overview for the New-age Marketing Manager," *Industrial Marketing Management,* Vol. 31, Iss. 4, July 2002, pp. 357–65.

43. Jian Lynn Yang, "Veggie Tales," *CNNMoney.com*, May 27, 2009, http://money.cnn.com/2009/05/26/technology/yang_sysco.fortune/index.htm?postversion=2009052709, accessed June 10, 2009.

44. Dale G. Sauers, "Evaluating Just-in-time Projects from a More Focused Framework," *Quality Process,* Vol. 34, Iss. 1, January 2001, p. 160.

45. Alan D. Smith, "Effective Supplier Selection and Management Issues in Modern Manufacturing and Marketing

Service Environments," *Services Marketing Quarterly,* Vol. 29, Iss. 2, 2007, pp. 45–65.

46. Sysco Corporation 2008 Annual Report, "Letter to Shareholders," http://www.sysco.com/investor/OnlineAnnualReport/, accessed June 10, 2009.

47. Richard J. Gilbert, "Exclusive Dealing, Preferential Dealing, and Dynamic Efficiency," *Review of Industrial Organization,* Vol. 16, Iss. 2, 2000, pp. 167–84.

48. Howard P. Marvel and Stephen McCafferty, "Comparing Vertical Restraints*," Journal of Economics and Business,* Vol. 48, Iss. 5, December 1996, pp. 473–86.

49. Alan J. Meese, "Tying Meets the New Institutional Economics: Farewell to the Chimera of Forcing," *University of Pennsylvania Law Review,* Vol. 146, Iss. 1, November 1997, pp. 1–98.

CHAPTER 12

1. Jeffery F. Rayport and Bernard J. Jaworski, "Best Face Forward," *Harvard Business Review,* 2004, Vol. 82 (12), pp. 47–62.

2. Richard W. Mosley, "Customer Experience, Organizational Culture and Employer Brand," *Journal of Brand Management,* Vol. 15 (2), pp. 123–35.

3. "Younger Generation of Customers are Less Loyal to Banks; Banks Must Shift Gears to Attract and Retain Gen X and Gen Y," *PR Newswire.* New York. July 22, 2008.

4. Tin-Peng Liang, Hung-Jen Lai, Yi-Cheng Ku, "Personalized Content Recommendation and User Satisfaction Theoretical Synthesis and Empirical Findings," *Journal of Management Information Systems,* 2006–2007, Vol. 23 (3), pp. 45–61.

5. Jane W. Licata, Goutam Chakraborty and Balaji C. Krishnan, "The Consumer's Expectation Formation Process Over time," *The Journal of Services Marketing,*" 2008, Vol. 22 (3), pp. 176–91.

6. Stuart E. Jackson, "Making Growth Make Sense for Retail and Franchise Businesses," *Journal of Business Strategy,* 2008, Vol. 29 (3), pp. 48–64.

7. Kirthi Kalyanam, Sharad Borle, and Peter Boartwright, "Deconstructing Each Item's Category Contribution," *Marketing Science,* 2007, Vol. 26 (3), pp. 327–44.

8. Andrew Baxter, "Profile: Tide and Ariel Clean Up," *Financial Times,* April 21, 2008, p. 6; and Robert Berner, "How P&G Pampers New Thinking," *BusinessWeek,* 2008, Issue 4079, p. 73.

9. Chandra K. Jaggi, SK Goyal, SK Goel, "Retailer's Optimal Replenishment Decisions with Credit Linked Demand under Permissible Delay in Payments," *European Journal of Operational Research,* 2008, Vol. 190 (1), pp. 130–48; and R. Glenn Richey Jr., Mert Tokman, and Lauren R. Skinner, "Exploring Collaborative Technology Utilization in Retailer-Supplier Performance," *Journal of Business Research,* 2008, Vol. 61 (8), pp. 842–60.

10. Martin A. Koschat, "Store Inventory Can Affect Demand: Empirical Evidence form Retailing," *Journal of Retailing,* 2008, Vol. 84 (2), pp. 165–81.

11. Ericka Morphy, "Inventory Management on a Shoestring," *Ecommerce Times.* May 29, 2009.

12. James G. Maxham III, Richard G. Netemeyer, and Donald R. Lichtenstein, "The Retail Value Chain: Linking Employee Perceptions to Employee Performance, Customer Evaluations and Store Performance, *Marketing Science,* 2008, Vol. 27 (2), p. 147–69; and Aron O'Cass and Debra Grace, "Understanding the Role of Retail Service in Light of Self-image Store Image Congruence," *Psychology and Marketing,* 2008, Vol. 25 (6), pp. 521–39.

13. Christina ML Kelton, Margaret K Pasquale, and Robert P. Rebeliein, "Using the North American Industry Classification System (NAICS) to Identify National Industry Cluster Templates for Applied Regional Analysis," *Regional Studies,* 2008, Vol. 42 (3), pp. 305–20.

14. Jie Zhang and Aradhna Krishna, "Brand Level Effects of Stockkeeping Unit Reductions," *Journal of Marketing Research,* 2007, Vol. 44 (4), pp. 545–61 and Felipe Caro and Jeremie Gallien, "Dynamic Assortment with Demand Learning for Season Consumer Goods*," Management Science,* 2007, Vol. 63 (2), pp. 276–83.

15. Dan Padgett and Micahael S. Mulvey, "Differentiation Via Technology: Strategic Positioning of Services Following the Introduction of Disruptive Technology," *Journal of Retailing,* 2007, Vol. 83, (4), pp. 375–91.

16. G.H. Griffiths and A. Howard, "Balancing Clicks and Brands–Strategies for Multichannel Retailers," *Journal of Global Business Issues,* 2008, Vol. 2 (10) pp. 69–74.

17. Sameer Kumar, "A Study of the Supermarket Industry and Its Growing Logistics Capabilities," *International Journal of Retail & Distribution Management,* 2008, Vol. 36 (3), pp. 192–210.

18. Susan Reda, "Wegman of My Dreams," *Stores,* 2008, Vol. 90 (3), p. 10; and "Tesco's American Dream: Doing It Differently," *Strategic Direction,* 2008, Vol. 24 (2), p.11.

19. "Alienware Computers Now Offered at Dell Direct Stores Across Canada," *Business Wire.* New York, May 20, 2009.

20. Haiyan Hu and Cynthia R. Jasper, "Social Cues in the Store Environment and Their Impact on Store Image," *International Journal of Retail and Distribution Management,* 2006, Vol. 34 (1), pp. 25–49.

21. Peter J. McGoldrick and Matalie Collins, "Multichannel Retailing: Profiling the Multichannel Shopper," *The International Review of Retail, Distribution and Consumer Research,* 2007, Vol. 17 (2), pp. 139–52.

22. Asim Ansari, Carl F. Mela, and Scott A. Neslin, "Customer Channel Migration," *Journal of Marketing Research,* 2008, Vol. 45 (1), pp. 60–77.

23. Bill Merrilees and Tino Fenech, "From Catalog to Web: B2B Multichannel Marketing Strategy," *Industrial Marketing Management,* 2007, Vol. 36 (1), pp. 44–61.

24. Ruby Roy Dholakia, Miao Zhao, and Nikhilesh Dholakia, "Multichannel Retailing: A Case Study of Early Experiences," *Journal of Interactive Marketing,* 2005, Vol. 19 (2), pp. 63–75.

25. Dennis L. Duffy, "Direct Selling as the Next Channel," *Journal of Consumer Marketing,* 2005, Vol. 22 (1), pp. 43–46.

26. "Tupperware Applauds Best in Class of Chicago," *PRNewswire (Reuters).* Chicago. April 16, 2009.

27. Clyde A. Warden, Stephen Chi-Tsun Huang, Tsung Chi Liu, and Wann-Yih Wu, "Global Media, Local Metaphor: Television Shopping and Marketing as Relationship in America, Japan and Taiwan," *Journal of Retailing,* 2008, Vol. 84 (1), pp. 119–34; and Enrique Bigne Alcaniz, Silvia Sanz Blas, and Francisco Toran Torres, "Dependency in Consumer Media Relations: An Application to the Case of Teleshopping," *Journal of Consumer Behavior,* 2006, Vol. 5 (5), pp. 397–411.

28. Eliot Maras, "In the Face of Challenge, Opportunity Beckons," *Automatic Merchandiser,* May 2008, Vol. 50 (5), p. 6; and Eliot Maras, "Badly Needed Consumer Research Is Here, So Use It," *Automatic Merchandiser,* Jan. 2007, Vol. 49 (1), p. 4

29. David R. Bowes, "A Two-Stage Model of the Simultaneous Relationship

Between Retail Development and Crime," *Economic Development Quarterly,* 2007, Vol. 21 (1), pp. 79–92; and Richard Peiser and Jiaqui Xioong, "Crime and Town Centers: Are Downtowns More Dangerous than Suburban Shopping Nodes?" *Journal of Real Estate Research,* 2003, Vol. 25 (4), pp. 577–89.

30. Eric M. Olson, Stanley F. Slater and Christine SH Olson, "Dolls and Sense," *Marketing Management,* 2006, Vol. 15 (5) pp. 14–20; and Leigh Sparks, "A Catalogue of Success? Argos and Catalogue Showroom Retailing," *The Services Industry Journal,* 2003, Vol. 23 (2) pp. 79–89.

31. "Online Sales to Climb Despite Struggling Economy," *National Retail Federation,* April 8, 2008, www.nrf.com/modules.php?name=news&sp_id=499.

32. Jim Dalrymple, "Apple Is Number Two Music Retailer in the United States," *MacWorld,* 2008, Vol. 25 (5), p. 28.

33. "Business: The Three Survivors; Yahoo, eBay, and Amazon," *The Economist,* 2008, Vol. 387 Issue 8585, pp. 69–90.

34. Pearl Pu, Li Chen, Pratyush Kumar, "Evaluating Product Search and Recommender Systems for E-Commerce Environments," *Electronic Commerce Research,* 2008, Vol. 8 (1/2), pp. 1–28.

35. Andreas B. Eisingerich and Tobia Kretschmer, "In E-Commerce, More is More," *Harvard Business Review,* 2008, Vol. 86 (3), pp. 20–38; and Amanda Spink, Bernard J. Jansen, "Trends in Searching for Commerce Related Information on Web-Search Engines," *Journal of Electronic Commerce Research,* 2008, Vol. 9 (2), pp. 154–60.

36. Rick McRoskey, "Where Customers Go to Praise (or Bash) You," *BusinessWeek.* August 15, 2008.

37. Christy M.K. Cheung, Matthew K.O. Lee, and Neil Rabojohn, "The Impact of Electronic Work of Mouth: The Adoption of Online Opinions in Online Customer Communities," *Internet Research,* 2008, Vol. 18 (3), pp. 229–41; Dina Mayzlin, "Promotional Chat on the Internet," *Marketing Science,* 2006, Vol. 25 (2), pp. 155–65.

38. Kyosti Pennanen, Tarja Tiainen, and Harri T. Luomala, "A Qualitative Exploration of a Consumer's Value Based e-Trust Building Process: A Framework Development," *Qualitative Market Research,* 2007, Vol. 10 (1), pp. 28–42.

39. "Non-Profit Organizations Switch From Microsoft Great Plains to NetSuite for End-to-End Business Automation at a Fraction of the Cost; NetSuite Enables Non-profit Organizations to Focus on Core Social Goals While Lowering TCO and Improving the Bottom Line," *PR Newswire.* New York. November 19, 2008.

40. Myonung Soo Kim and Jae Hyeon Ahn, "Comparison of Trust Sources of an Online Market Maker in the E-Marketplace: Buyers and Seller's Perspectives," *Journal of Computer Information Systems,* 2006, Vol. 47 (1), pp. 84–95.

41. Rene Algesheimer and Paul M. Dholakia, "Do Customer Communities Pay Off?" *Harvard Business Review,* 2006, Vol. 84 (11), pp. 26–41.

42. Yasemin Boztu and Thomas Reutterer, "A Combined Approach for Segment Specific Market Basket Analysis," *European Journal of Operational Research,* 2008, Vol. 187 (1), pp. 294–310.

43. Lars Meyer Waarden, "The Influence of Loyalty Programme Members on Customer Purchase Behaviour," *European Journal of Marketing,* 2008, Vol. 42 (1/2), pp. 87–102; and Jennifer Rowley, "Reconceptualizing the Strategic Role of Loyalty Schemes," *Journal of Consumer Marketing,* 2007, Vol. 24 (6), pp. 366–80.

44. Christopher Heine, "Men's Wearhouse Brings Localized Social Media to Prom," *Brandweek.* April 29, 2009.

45. Dinesh K. Gauri, K. Sudhir, and Debabrata Talukdar, "The Temporal and Spatial Dimensions of Price Search: Insights from Matching Household Survey and Purchase data," *Journal of Marketing Research,* 2008, Vol. 45 (2), pp. 226–41.

46. Vishal Gaur and Dorothee Honhon, "Assortment Planning and Inventory Decisions under a Locational Choice Model," *Management Science,* 2006, Vol. 52 (10) pp. 1528–44.

47. Miguel I. Gomez, Vithala R. Rao, and Edward W. McLaughlin, "Empirical Analysis of Budget and Allocation of Trade Promotions in the U.S. Supermarket Industry," *Journal of Marketing Research,* 2007, Vol. 44 (3), pp. 410–27.

48. Ruiliang Yan, Pricing Strategy for Companies with Mixed Online and Traditional Retailing Distribution Markets," *Journal of Product and Brand Management,* 2008, Vol. 17 (1) pp. 48–62.

49. Joydeep Srivastava and Nicholas H. Lurie, "Price Matching Guarantees as Signals of Low Store Prices: Survey and experimental evidence," *Journal of Retailing,* 2004, Vol. 80 (2), pp. 117–31.

50. Sarah Arnott, "Potter Publisher Sees New Magic," *BusinessWeek Online,* April 2, 2008, http://www.businessweek.com/print/globalbiz/content/apr2008/gb2008042_889246.htm; and Diane Brady, "The Twisted Economics of Harry Potter," *BusinessWeek,* July 2, 2007, pp. 46–47.

51. Ina Fried, "Microsoft follows Apple into the retail business," *cnet News.* February 19, 2009.

CHAPTER 13

1. Don E. Schultz and Phillip J. Kitchen, "Integrated Marketing Communications in U.S. Advertising Agencies: An Exploratory Study," *Journal of Advertising Research,* Vol. 37, Iss. 5, September/October 1997, pp. 7–18.

2. P. Rajan Varadarajan, Satish Jayachandran, and J. Chris White, "Strategic Interdependence in Organizations: Deconglomeration and Marketing Strategy," *Journal of Marketing,* Vol. 65, Iss. 1, January 2001, pp. 15–28.

3. Frederick E. Webster Jr., "Understanding the Relationships among Brands, Consumers, and Resellers," *Journal of the Academy of Marketing Science,* Vol. 28, Iss. 1, Winter 2000, pp. 17–23.

4. Emim Babakus, Ugar Yavas, Osman M. Karatepe, and Turgay Avci, "The Effect of Management Commitment to Service Quality on Employees' Affective and Performance Outcomes," *Journal of the Academy of Marketing Science,* Vol. 31, Iss. 3, Summer 2003, pp. 272–86.

5. Southwest Airlines Web site, http://www.southwest.com/about_swa/about_swa.html, accessed June 15, 2009; William Atkinson, "Inside Job," *MeetingsNet,* November 1, 2005, http://meetingsnet.com/corporatemeetingsincentives/mag/meetings_inside_job/, accessed June 16, 2009.

6. Yu-Shan Lin and Jun-Ying Huang, "Internet Blogs as a Tourism Marketing Medium: A Case Study," *Journal of Business Research,* Vol. 59, Iss. 10/11, October 2006, pp. 1201–05.

7. Damian Joseph, "Supermarket Strategies: What's New at the Grocer," *BusinessWeek,* June 8, 2009, http://www.businessweek.com/innovate/content/jun2009/id2009068_540314.htm, accessed June 15, 2009.

8. Anastasia Goodstein, "Marketing to Teens Online," *BusinessWeek* Online, November 7, 2007, www.businessweek.com/print/technology/content/nov2007/tc2007117_522831.htm, accessed June 11, 2008.

9. Thomas Reutterer, Andreas Mild, Martin Natter, and Alfred Taudes, "A Dynamic Segmentation Approach for Targeting and Customizing Direct

Marketing Campaigns," *Journal of Interactive Marketing* Vol. 20, Iss. 3/4, Summer/Fall 2006, pp. 43–57.

10. Chatterjee, Subimal, Yong Soon Kang and Debi Prasad Mishra, "Market Signals and Relative Preference: The Moderating Effects of Conflicting Information, Decision Focus, and Need for Cognition," *Journal of Business Research,* Vol. 58, Iss. 10, October 2005, pp. 1362–70.

11. Mark Burton and Steve Haggett, "Rocket PLAN," *Marketing Management* Vol. 16, Iss. 5, September/October 2007, p. 32.

12. Walt Disney World Web site, http://disneyworld.disney.go.com/, accessed June 15, 2009.

13. Davod A. Schweidel, Peter S. Fader, and Eric T. Bradlow, "Understanding Service Retention within and across Cohorts Using Limited Information," *Journal of Marketing,* Vol. 72, Iss. 1, January 2008, pp. 82–94.

14. Brian Wansink, Robert J. Kent, and Stephen J. Hoch, "An Anchoring and Adjustment Model for Purchase Quantity Decisions," *Journal of Marketing Research,* Vol. 35, Iss. 1, February 1998, pp. 71–81.

15. "Illinois State Continues Sales Curriculum Incorporating Cutco, Vector Marketing Program," *PRWeb.com,* March 4, 2008, www.prweb.com/releases/cutco/vector/prweb741974.htm, accessed June 19, 2008.

16. John I. Coppett and Roy Dale Voorhees, "Telemarketing: Supplement to Field Sales," *Industrial Marketing Management,* Vol. 14, Iss. 3, August 1985, pp. 213–16.

17. Joo-Gim Heaney, Ronald E. Goldsmith, and Wan Jamaliah Wan, "Status Consumption among Malaysian Consumers: Exploring Its Relationships with Materialism and Attention-to-Social-Comparison-Information," *Journal of International Consumer Marketing,* Vol. 17, Iss. 4, 2005, pp. 83–98.

18. Hae-Kyong Bang, Mary Anne Raymond, Charles R. Taylor, and Young Sook Moon, "A Comparison of Service Quality Dimensions Conveyed in Advertisements for Service Providers in the USA and Korea: A Content Analysis," *International Marketing Review,* Vol. 22, Iss. 3, 2005, pp. 309–27.

19. Kathleen Mortimer, "Identifying the Components of Effective Service Advertisements," *Journal of Services Marketing,* Vol. 22, Iss. 2, 2008, pp. 104–13.

20. Olive Garden Web site, "Serving our Communities," http://www.olivegarden.com/company/community/, accessed June 15, 2009.

21. Ziad Swaidan, Mohammed Y. A. Rawwas, and Scott J. Vitell, "Culture and Moral Ideologies of African Americans," *Journal of Marketing Theory and Practice,* Vol. 16, Iss. 2, Spring 2008, pp. 127–37.

22. Margaret Henderson Blair, "An Empirical Investigation of Advertising Wearin and Wearout," *Journal of Advertising Research,* Vol. 40, Iss. 6, November/December 2000, pp. 95–100.

23. John R. Hauser and Steven M. Shugan, "Defensive Marketing Strategies," *Marketing Science,* Vol. 27, Iss. 1, January/February 2008, pp. 88–112.

24. Janas Sinclair and Tracy Irani, "Advocacy Advertising for Biotechnology," *Journal of Advertising,* Vol. 34, Iss. 3, Fall 2005, pp. 59–63.

25. Glen L. Urban, Theresa Carter, Steven Gaskin, and Zofia Mucha, "Market Share Rewards to Pioneering Brands: An Empirical Analysis and Strategic Implications," *Management Science,* Vol. 32, Iss. 6, June 1986, pp. 645–59.

26. Peter J. Danaher, André Bonfrer, and Sanjay Dhar, "The Effect of Competitive Advertising Interference on Sales for Packaged Goods," *Journal of Marketing Research,* Vol. 45, Iss. 2, April 2008, pp. 211–25.

27. Chingching Chang, "The Relative Effectiveness of Comparative and Noncomparative Advertising: Evidence for Gender Differences in Information-Processing Strategies," *Journal of Advertising,* Vol. 36, Iss. 1, Spring 2007, pp. 21–35.

28. "Wendy's May Pick New Lead Ad Agency," *BusinessWeek,* May 29, 2009, http://www.businessweek.com/ap/financialnews/D98FU8N00.htm, accessed June 15, 2009.

29. "KFC Grilled Chicken Also Has A Secret Recipe," *BusinessWeek,* May 25, 2009, http://www.businessweek.com/ap/financialnews/D98D1FTG0.htm, accessed June 16, 2009; Bruce Schreiner, "KFC: Grilled Chicken Frenzy Brought Good Publicity," *BusinessWeek,* May 25, 2009, http://www.businessweek.com/ap/financialnews/D98D1FTG3.htm, accessed June 16, 2009.

30. Li Ling-yee, "The Effects of Firm Resources on Trade Show Performance: How Do Trade Show Marketing Processes Matter?" *Journal of Business & Industrial Marketing,* Vol. 23, Iss. 1, 2008, pp. 35–47.

31. Salma Karray and Georges Zaccour, "Could Co-op Advertising Be a Manufacturer's Counterstrategy to Store Brands?" *Journal of Business Research,* Vol. 59, Iss. 9, September 2006, pp. 1008–15.

32. Sang Yong Kim and Richard Staelin, "Manufacturer Allowances and Retailer Pass-through Rates in a Competitive Environment," *Marketing Science,* Vol. 18, Iss. 1, 1999, pp. 59–77.

33. Hyun Seung Jin, Jaebeom Suh, and D. Todd Donavan, "Salient Effects of Publicity in Advertised Brand Recall and Recognition: The List-Strength Paradigm," *Journal of Advertising* Vol. 37, Iss. 1, Spring 2008, pp. 45–57.

34. Lois Kelly, *Beyond Buzz: The Next Generation of Word-of-Mouth Marketing*, New York: AMACOM, 2007, pp. 104–105.

35. "Win Sunday, Sell Monday," *LoganRacing.com,* www.loganracing.com/Marketing/NASCAR_General.html, accessed June 10, 2008.

36. Rich Thomaselli, "What Danica Patrick Could Do for NASCAR Sponsors" *Ad Age,* June 9, 2009, http://adage.com/article?article_id=137186, accessed June 10, 2009.

37. Joseph Eric Massey and John P. Larsen, "Qualitative Research–Case Studies–Crisis Management in Real Time: How to Successfully Plan for and Respond to a Crisis," *Journal of Promotion Management,* Vol. 12, Iss. 3/4, 2006, pp. 63–97.

CHAPTER 14

1. "Richardson Releases New CRM Sales Call Planning Module with Build-in Real-time Coaching . . .," *PR Newswire.* San Francisco. March 17, 2009.; "Client Results," Richardson Company Web site. Accessed June 20, 2009. http://www.richardson.com/Client-Results/Our-Clients.

2. David Mayer and Herbert M. Greenberg, "What Makes a Good Salesperson," *Harvard Business Review,"* 2006, Vol. 84 (7/8) pp. 164–79.

3. Mark C. Johlke, "Sales Presentation Skills and Salesperson Job Performance," *Journal of Business and Industrial Marketing,"* 2006, Vol. 21 (5), pp. 311–29.

4. Chia-Chi Chang, "What Service Fails: The Role of the Salesperson and the Customer," *Psychology & Marketing,* 2006, Vol. 23 (3), pp. 203–18; and Julia T. Johnson, Hiram C. Barksdale Jr., and James S. Boles, "The Strategic Role of the Salesperson in Reducing Customer Defection in Business Relationships," *Journal of Personal Selling and Sales Management,* 2001, vol. 21 (2), pp. 123–35.

5. Richard G. McFarland, Gautam N. Challagalla, Tasadduq A. Shervani, "Influence Tactics for Effective Adaptive Selling," *Journal of Marketing,* 2006, Vol. 70 (4), pp. 103–17.

6. David T. Norris, "Sales Communication in a Mobile World: Using the Latest Technology and Retaining the Personal Touch," *Business Communication Quarterly,* 2007, Vol. 70 (4), pp. 492–510.

7. Philippe Declos, Rodolfo Luzardo and Yasir H. Mirza, "Refocusing the Sales Force to Cross-Sell," *The McKinsey Quarterly,* 2008, (1), pp. 13–15; and Robert M. Peterson and George H. Lucas, "What Buyers Want Most from Salespeople: A View from the Senior Level," *Business Horizons,* 2001, Vol. 44 (5), 39–45.

8. Robert W. Palmatier, Lisa K. Scheer, and Jan-Benedict E.M. Steenkamp, "Customer Loyalty to Whom? Managing the Benefits and Risks of Salesperson-Owned Loyalty," *Journal of Marketing Research,* 2007, Vol. 44 (2), pp. 185–201.

9. Sandra S. Liu and Lucette B. Comer, "Salespeople as Information Gatherers: Associated Success Factors," *Industrial Marketing Management,* 2007, Vol. 36 (5), pp. 565–79; and Leroy Robinson Jr., Greg W. Marshall, and Miriam B. Stamps, "An Empirical Investigation of Technology Acceptance in a Field Sales Force Setting," *Industrial Marketing Management,* 2005, Vol. 34 (4), pp. 407–22.

10. David Mayer and Herbert M. Greenberg, "What Makes a Good Salesperson," *Harvard Business Review,*" 2006, Vol. 84 (7/8) pp. 164–79; Fernando Jaramillo and Greg. W. Marshall, "Critical Success Factors in the Personal Selling Process: An Empirical Investigation of Ecuadorian Salespeople in the Banking Industry," *International Journal of Bank Marketing,* 2004, Vol. 22 (1), pp. 9–21; and Sean Dwyer, John Hill, and Warren Martin, "An Empirical Investigation of Critical Success Factors in the Personal Selling for Homogenous Goods," *Journal of Personal Selling & Sales Management* 2000, Vol 20 (3), pp. 151–60.

11. Jagdish N. Sheth and Arun Sharma, "The Impact of the Product to Service Shift in Industrial Markets and the Evolution of the Sales Organization," *Industrial Marketing Management,* 2008, Vol. 37 (3), pp. 260–77; and Philip Kriendler and Goapl Rajguru, "What B2B Customers Really Expect," *Harvard Business Review,* 2006, vol. 84 (40), pp. 22–37.

12. "The Doctor Won't See You Now," *BusinessWeek,* 2007, issue 4020, p. 30.

13. Paolo Guenzi, Cahterine Pardo, Laurent Georges, "Relational Selling Strategy and Key Account Managers Relational Behaviors: An Exploratory Study," *Industrial Marketing Management,* 2007, Vol. 36 (1), pp. 121–38.

14. Dian Ledingham, Mark Kovac, Heidi Locke Smith, "The New Science of Sales Force Productivity," *Harvard Business Review,* 2006, Vol. 84 (9), pp. 124–40.

15. Maribeth Kuzmeski, "Your Brand Defines You," *National Underwriter.* Life & Health. March 3, 2008.

16. Lewis Hershey, "The Role of Sales Presentations in Developing Customer Relationships," *Services Marketing Quarterly,* 2005, Vol. 26 (3), pp. 41–59.

17. Joshua Rossman, "Value Selling at Cisco," *Marketing Management,* 2004, Vol. 13 (2), pp. 16–23.

18. Thomas N. Ingram, "Future Themes In Sales and Sales Management: Complexity, Collaboration, and Accountability," Jour*nal of Marketing Theory and Practice,* 2004, Vol. 12 (40), pp. 18–29.

19. Kim Sydow Campbell, Lenita Davis and Lauren Skinner, "Rapport Management During the Exploration Phase of the Salesperson Customer Relationship," *Journal of Personal Selling & Sales Management,* 2006, Vol. 26 (4), pp. 359–72.

20. Jim Braselton and Bruce Blair, "Cementing Relationships," *Marketing Management,* 2007, Vol. 16 (3), pp. 14–29.

21. John E. Swan, Michael R. Bowers, Lynne D. Richardson, "Customer Trust in the Salesperson: An Integrative Review of Meta Analysis of the Empirical Literature," *Journal of Business Research,* 1999, Vol. 44 (2), pp. 93–108; and Jackie L.M. Tam and Y.J. Wong," Interactive Selling: A Dynamic Framework for Services," *Journal of Services Marketing,* 2001, Vol. 15 (4/5), pp. 379–95.

22. Tom Nagle and John Hogan, "Is Your Sales Force a Barrier to More Profitable Pricing . . . or Is It You?" *Business Strategy Series,* 2007, Vol. 8 (5), pp. 365–79.

23. Joseph J. Belonax Jr. , Stephen J. Newell, and Richard E. Plank, "The Role of Purchase Importance on Buyer Perceptions of the Trust and Expertise Components of Supplier and Salesperson Credibility in Business to Business Relationships," *Journal of Personal Selling & Sales Management,* 2007, Vol. 27 (3), pp. 247–60; Thomas V. Bonoma, "Major Sales: Who Really Does the Buying," *Harvard Business Review,* 2006, Vol. 84 (7/8), pp. 172–90; and Edward C. Bursk, " Low Pressure Selling,"

Harvard Business Review, 2006, Vol. 84 (7/8), pp. 150–69.

24. Gordon A. Wyner, "The Customer," *Marketing Management,* 2005, Vol. 14 (1), pp. 8–10.

25. T-Mobile Company Web site. Accessed May 21, 2009. http://www .t-mobile.com.

26. Andris A. Zoltners, Prabhakant Sinha, and Sally E. Lorimer, "Match Your Sales Force Structure to Your Business Life Cycle," *Harvard Business Review,* 2006, Vol. 84 (7/8), pp. 80–97.

27. Erin Anderson, "The Salesperson as Ouside Agent or Employee: A Transaction Cost Analysis," *Marketing Science,* 2008, Vol. 27 (1), pp. 70–86.

28. Ernest Waaser, Marshall Dahneke, Michael Pekkarinen, and Micahel Weissel, "How You Slice It: Smarter Segmentation of Your Sales Force," *Harvard Business Review,* 2004, Vol. 82 (3), pp. 105–22.

29. Sean Carey, "Leadership Skills Training For Generation Y," *httools.* February 3, 2009.; Bea Fields, "How Do You Attract and Retain Generation Y? Learn From Google, Intuit and Disney," Fast Company. June 17, 2008.

30. C. Fred Miao and Ken R. Evans, "The Impact of Salesperson Motivation on Role Perceptions and Job Performance: A Cognitive and Affective Perspective, "*Journal of Personal Selling & Sales Management,* 2007, Vol. 27 (1), pp. 89–103.

31. Willem J. Verbeke, Frank D. Belschak, Arnold B. Bakker, and Bart Dietz, "When Intelligence Is (Dys) Functional Achieving Sales Performance," *Journal of Marketing,* 2008, Vol. 72 (4), pp. 44–57.

32. Fernando Jaramillo and Jay Prakas Mulki, "Sales Effort: The Intertwined Roles of the Leader, Customers, and the Salesperson," *Journal of Personal Selling & Sales Management,* 2008, Vol. 28 (1), pp 37–51; and C. Fred Miao, Kenneth R. Evans and Zou Shaoming, "The Role of Salesperson Motivation in Sales Control Systems–Intrinsic and Extrinsic Motivation Revisited,*" Journal of Business Research,* 2007, Vol. 60 (5), pp. 417–32.

33. Clive Muir, "Relationship Building and Sales Success: Are Climate and Leadership Key?" *The Academy of Management Perspectives,* 2007, Vol. 21 (1), pp. 71–89; and Ken LeMeunier-FitzHugh and Nigel F. Piercy, "Does Collaboration between Sales and Marketing Affect Business Performance,*" Journal of Personal Selling &*

Sales Management, 2007, Vol. 27 (3), pp. 207–20.

34. Dong Hwan Lee, "The Moderating Effect of Salesperson Reward Orientation on the Relative Effectiveness of Alternative Compensation Plans, "Journal of Business Research, 1998, vol. 43 (2), pp. 63–78.

35. George R. Franke, Jeong-Eun Park, "Salesperson Adapative Selling Behavior and Customer Orientation: A Meta-Analysis, Journal Of Marketing Research, 2006, Vol. 43 (4), pp. 34–50; and Charles E. Pettijohn, Linda S. Pettijohn, and A.J. Taylor, "Does Salesperson Perception of the Importance of Sales Skills Improve Sales Performance, Customer Orientation, Job Satisfaction, and Organizational Commitment, and Reduce Turnover," Journal of Personal Selling & Sales Management, 2007, Vol. 27 (1), p. 75.

36. Rene Y. Darmon, "Controlling Sales Force Turnover Costs Through Optimal Recruiting Training Policies," European Journal of Operational Research, 2004, Vol. 154 (10) pp. 291–308; and Phan Tej Adidam, "Causes and Consequences of High Turnover by Sales Professionals," Journal of American Academy of Business, 2006, Vol. 10 (1), pp. 137–42.

37. Joe M. Ricks, Jr., Jacqueline A. Williams, and William A. Weeks, "Sales Trainer Roles, Competencies, Skills, and Behaviors: A Case Study," Industrial Marketing Management, 2008, Vol. 37

(5), pp. 593–610; and Mark P. Leach and Annie H. Liu, "Investigating Interrelationships Among Sales Training Methods," Journal of Personal Selling & Sales Management, 2003, Vol. 23 (4), pp. 327–40.

38. "Sales 101: SalesMaster Processes and Methodology," Sales 101 Company Web site. Accessed June 20, 2009. www.sales-101.com/sales-master.htm.; "Testimonials," Sales 101 Company Web site. Accessed June 20, 2009. http://www.sales-101.co.uk/testimonials.htm.

39. Tará Burnthorne Lopez, Christopher D. Hopkins, and Mary Anne Raymond, "Reward Preferences of Salespeople: How Do Commissions Rate," Journal of Personal Selling & Sales Management, 2006, Vol. 26 (4), pp. 381–87; and Sridhar N. Ramaswami and Jagdip Singh, "Antecedents and Consequences of Merit Pay Fairness for Industrial Salespeople," Journal of Marketing, 2003, Vol. 67 (4), pp. 46–60.

40. Jena McGregor, "Performance Review Takes a Page from Facebook," BusinessWeek. March 12, 2009.

41. Raquel Ortega, "Impact of Direct to Consumers Marketing Strategies on Firm Market Value," International Journal of Consumer Studies, 2004, Vol. 28 (5), pp. 466–80; and Jacquelyn S. Thomas, Werner Reinartz, and V. Kumar, "Getting the Most Out of All Your Customers," Harvard Business Review, 2004, Vol. 82 (7/8), pp. 116–29.

42. Jessica Silver-Greenberg and Ben Elgin, "The College Credit-Card Hustle," BusinessWeek. July 28, 2008.

43. Asim Ansari, Carl F. Mela, and Scott A. Neslin, "Customer Channel Migration," Journal of Marketing Research, 2008, Vol. 45 (1), pp. 60–75.

44. George M. Zinkhan, "The Marketplace, Emerging Technology and Marketing Theory," Marketing Theory, 2005, Vol. 5 (1), pp. 105–16.

45. Dee Gill, "Blogging Ethics 101," Crain's Chicago Business, 2007, Vol. 30 (46), p. 33; and Jon Fine, "Polluting the Blogosphere," BusinessWeek Online, July 10, 2006, www.businessweek.com/magazine/content/06_28/b3992034.htm.

46. Damian Joseph, "The GPS Revolution: Location, Location, Location," BusinessWeek – Innovation. May 27, 2009.

47. Marshall Crook and Peter Sanders, "Will Marketing Change after Star's Death?" Wall Street Journal, Jan. 24 2008, B1.

48. John F. Tanner Jr., Christophe Fournier, Jorge A. Wise, Sandrine Hollet, and Juliet Poujoi, "Executives Perspectives of the Changing Role of the Sales Profession: Views from France, United States, and Mexico," Journal of Business & Industrial Marketing, 2008, Vol. 23 (3), pp. 193–207; and David Welch, "Death of the Car Salesman," BusinessWeek, November 27, 2006, p. 33.